Business Concentration and Price Policy

A CONFERENCE OF THE
UNIVERSITIES-NATIONAL BUREAU COMMITTEE
FOR ECONOMIC RESEARCH

ARNO PRESS
A New York Times Company
New York — 1975

Editorial Supervision: Eve Nelson
Reprint Edition 1975 by Arno Press Inc.

Copyright © 1955 by Princeton University Press
Reprinted by permission of the National
   Bureau of Economic Research, Inc.

NATIONAL BUREAU OF ECONOMIC RESEARCH
PUBLICATIONS IN REPRINT
ISBN for complete set: 0-405-07572-3
See last pages of this volume for titles.

Manufactured in the United States of America

————◆————

Library of Congress Cataloging in Publication Data

Universities-National Bureau Committee for Economic
   Research.
   Business concentration and price policy.

   (National Bureau of Economic Research publications
in reprint)
   Reprint of the ed. published by Princeton University
Press, Princeton, as v. 5 of the Special conference
series of the National Bureau of Economic Research.
   Includes bibliographical references.
   1. Big business. 2. Price policy. I. Title.
II. Series. III. Series: National Bureau of
Economic Research. Special conference series ; 5.
[HB221.U56 1975]   338.8   75-19699
ISBN 0-405-07579-0

BUSINESS CONCENTRATION
AND PRICE POLICY

NATIONAL BUREAU OF ECONOMIC RESEARCH

Special Conference Series

Business Concentration and Price Policy

A CONFERENCE OF THE
UNIVERSITIES-NATIONAL BUREAU COMMITTEE
FOR ECONOMIC RESEARCH

A REPORT OF THE
NATIONAL BUREAU OF ECONOMIC RESEARCH, NEW YORK

PUBLISHED BY
PRINCETON UNIVERSITY PRESS, PRINCETON

1955

CONTENTS

CONTENTS

INTRODUCTION

GEORGE J. STIGLER

THE Conference on Business Concentration and Price Policy was held at Princeton University, June 17-19, 1952. The conference was organized, under the sponsorship of the Universities–National Bureau Committee for Economic Research, by a steering committee consisting of Corwin Edwards, Carl Kaysen, Edward S. Mason, George J. Stigler, chairman, and Clair Wilcox; and Gideon Rosenbluth was the (I must gratefully say, highly efficient) secretary. The papers and discussions in this volume have been revised since they were delivered.

One task that economists have long taken seriously is that of explaining what determines the behavior of an industry. Under what conditions do prices fall (or rise) with expansion of output? How does the industry change its methods of production in response to changes in prices of inputs? When will customers be classified and each class asked to pay a different price? Will relatively large profits lead to an increase in the number of firms and, if so, how rapidly? Such questions—to which many economists would like to add less-studied questions such as: How does industry structure affect the rate of technological advance?—are at the center of modern economic analysis.

When one turns to the empirical investigation of such questions, he must at the outset determine what industries are. (Most empirical studies have dealt almost exclusively with manufacturing industries, and we shall follow this regrettable tradition here.) Almost invariably the empirical workers have accepted, perhaps with minor modifications such as Rosenbluth applies to the Canadian data, the practices of the census officials who compile the data. They cannot be blamed: the task of appraising the relevance of census classifications to questions of industrial organization is so vast that it would swallow up any more specific investigation the economist had in mind.

Moreover, it is not obvious that the census classification is inappropriate to our interests, which here center in questions of competition and monopoly. Conklin and Goldstein summarize the principles of the present classification. These principles rest fundamentally upon similarity of products or production processes of establishments (plants) which are to be combined into one industry. Particular

3

attention is paid to supply conditions, and "the industry generally represents a group of close competitors, producing close substitute commodities." Homogeneity is sought: most of the products attributed to the industry must be accounted for by the establishments in the industry, and most of the products of the establishments in the industry must fall into the industry defined by its major products. The fact that in the application of such rules to specific industries, census bureaus are influenced by opinions of businessmen, demands of other government agencies, etc., insures that the classifications are not insulated from business experience and public policy.

Yet the rules are intrinsically ambiguous. Economists have written acres on the problem of defining the closeness of substitute products, and no doubt problems of equal complexity are encountered in estimating the similarity of production processes. The influence of business attitudes and public policy is also not an unmixed blessing, for the classifications that are germane to taxation, labor problems, tariffs, and the like are not necessarily suitable to the analysis of problems of competition and monopoly.

Price theory has certain direct implications for this problem of defining industries that have not received adequate recognition in official practice, and they deserve at least brief comment here. An industry should embrace the maximum geographical area and the maximum variety of productive activities in which there is strong long-run substitution. If buyers can shift on a large scale from product or area B to A, then the two should be combined. If producers can shift on a large scale from B to A, again they should be combined.

Economists usually state this in an alternative form: All products or enterprises with large long-run cross-elasticities of either supply or demand should be combined into a single industry. In this form it is perhaps forbidding to the statistical worker, for generally cross-elasticities are calculated from empirical equations relating quantity supplied or demanded of one commodity to a host of prices, and we do not have—and cannot in the reasonable future expect to get—enough of these equations to base a general census upon them. But much more feasible methods of detecting substitution exist. If establishments making wooden office furniture in one year shift in considerable numbers within a year or two to making metal office furniture, this is conclusive evidence of high supply substitution—and can be measured with information now

4

collected but not published. If numerous buyers of cardboard shipping containers in one year are found to be buyers of wooden or burlap containers soon thereafter, this is conclusive evidence of high demand substitution—and can be measured with the type of information now collected.

One important application of the rule of high substitution is to international trade. If a commodity is on either an export or an import basis, its concentration' should usually be measured for a market larger than the domestic area. If the commodity is on an export basis, foreign buyers have alternative sources of supply, which must be included in the "industry"; if it is on an import basis, domestic buyers have alternative domestic supply sources, which again should be combined with the foreign supply. In either case it is necessary to take account of the industry structure abroad, but this extension of the area of work of the Bureau of the Census may not be objectionable to its staff.[1]

Once supplied with the frequency distribution of firms by size within properly defined industries, how shall we measure concentration? The large-scale statistical studies have so far employed measures that are directly formed by the disclosure rules of censuses. Despite Rosenbluth's welcome assurance that it does not seem to matter whether we take the proportion of the industry's output coming from the largest three, four, or other small number of firms or the number of firms required to account for, say, three-quarters of the industry's output, we can be certain of one defect in the calculation of these measures. It lies in the time period.

One of Marshall's greatest contributions to economics was to show that calendar time units are seldom a proper basis for measuring economic forces and to elaborate a schema of short- and long-run periods which were defined in terms of the forces which dominate them. The classification was especially relevant to competitive industries because long-run forces can usually be assumed to be negligible in the short run. Under monopoly, however, long-run forces may be decisive even in the short run because the monopolist reaps a large share or all of the future effects of his current policies. A good concentration measure (like a good industry concept) should relate to the long run. This has always been recognized

[1] The problem of the market area is greatly complicated if tariffs or quotas permit price discrimination between domestic and foreign markets, except in the extreme case when the two markets are completely independent and must be treated separately.

implicity; no one has ever said that concentration rises in late afternoon as eastern factories close down.

The long run is defined in terms of the period necessary for specified changes to take place, and two such changes or forces seem specially significant in studies of monopoly. One is on the demand side: How long a time is required for buyers to move along their long-run demand curves? If buyers can make fairly complete adjustments to prices only by such time-consuming procedures as moving their plants or radically modifying them, this period may be of several years' duration. The second force is on the supply side: How long a time is required for outsiders to detect large profits and to enter the industry? Normally I would expect this period to be at least as short as the demand period (although this conjecture has hardly any empirical basis) if no conventional barriers to entry, such as patents and raw material control, exist. Clearly calendar length of the long run may vary widely among industries.

Since the long-run forces may require a fairly long period of calendar time to work themselves out, one might infer that concentration measures should be calculated for periods of, say, five years. But against this must be put the consideration that the long run does not always completely dominate the short run: it may be sensible, for example, to behave monopolistically for a few years and then to lose one's monopolistic position. It is one of the tasks of empirical research to determine the relative roles of these arguments,[2] and I should think that we ought to have concentration measures calculated for three, five, and possibly even ten years, as well as for the inevitable one year.

The other question remains: Which parameters of the frequency distribution of firm sizes are relevant to the behavior of the industry? The relative output of a small number of firms, which is now used, is surely one relevant parameter, although most of the proof for this assertion still lies in the formal theory of oligopoly and not in empirical studies. Until we get the empirical studies, we are not likely to progress far in the refinement of concentration measures. It is easy enough to introduce additional parameters whose relevance to the behavior of the industry can be plausibly argued: for example, I would expect to find also that the absolute number of firms and the degree of instability in the shares of the

[2] From the viewpoint of social policy, short-run monopolies are of course much less important, and—with present durations of antitrust court actions—almost beyond control.

6

largest firms from year to year were important in influencing the industry's behavior. But plausibility is at least as much an effect of skillful argument as an evidence of probability of truth in an area as complicated and unexplored as oligopoly, and there is little point in multiplying such parameters at the present time.

Scitovsky properly emphasizes the fact that our interest in concentration is not restricted to its effects on the allocation of resources among firms—the traditional focus of the theory of monopoly. We are also interested in the effects of concentration on the distribution of income, the distribution of political power, the efficiency with which resources are used within the firm, etc. Wholly different measures of concentration may be called for in the empirical study of these other facets of the monopoly problem. The relationship of monopoly to the distribution of income, for example, surely involves the absolute sizes of firms and the distribution of ownership of monopolies. Important as these other problems are, however, one may still argue that the traditional focus on the power of the firm in the market is basic, for if this power is absent all the other problems vanish (as monopoly problems).

Miller examines an important deficiency in the traditional theory of monopoly, from which the concentration studies stem. The neoclassical theory of competition and monopoly was developed with two paramount objectives: to provide a clear and consistent theory of economic behavior, and to be analytically manageable. Both of these objectives were met fairly well by defining competition in terms of a stationary economy—one in which consumers' tastes, production techniques, and productive resources were stable through time. The resulting theory is immensely useful in a wide range of economic problems; but it is not directly applicable to problems raised by economic development—the rapid growth, and frequently unpredictable changes, in consumer demands and productive techniques and resources.

Schumpeter has sketched with great brilliance the possible paradoxes in applying the theory of stationary economies to historical developments.[3] The argument is weighty and clearly poses the problem of constructing a definition of competition which is suited to firms in a changing economy. Schumpeter's "solution," which was to label as monopoly all departures from perfect competition in a stationary society, is not useful. Real progress in this area seems also

[3] Joseph A. Schumpeter, *Capitalism, Socialism, and Democracy* (Harper, 1942), Chaps. VI-IX.

7

to demand that incisive empirical work for which economists so monotonously beg. But I suspect that when our knowledge of economic growth has increased, we shall not be called upon to reverse all the conclusions reached by stationary analysis.

Let us put aside these and other possible complications and return to the concentration of industry. Industries vary greatly in their concentration, and we naturally seek to learn why. Three papers in this volume deal with important forces affecting concentration: the economies of scale, mergers, and taxation.

Since Cournot's time it has been recognized that at most only a few firms can usually survive in an industry in which the average cost of production of a firm declines as its size increases, and even today this is the popular explanation for concentration. Smith has summarized recent work on this subject, including the interesting efforts to estimate the costs of firms of different sizes from technological relationships between inputs and outputs. This latter type of approach has many attractions, especially in studies of the social (in contrast to private) economies of scale. But it also has two major defects. One defect is generally recognized: the method cannot be extended to selling, recruiting labor, financing, etc. Another defect is not always recognized: the economist is "solving" the problem of measuring economies of scale by turning it over to someone else, and yet it is fundamentally an economic problem.

Smith shows how difficult the problems of measurement are, even though he does not emphasize the point (the valuation of inputs) that I find most troublesome. Difficulty is not an adequate reason for abandoning a problem, but I think there are some positive reasons for determining economies of scale from changes in concentration over time rather than using economies to explain concentration. That is, those firm-sizes whose outputs are growing relative to the industry may be interpreted as having the lowest (private) costs. All comprehensive definitions of economies of scale ultimately imply that firms with the lowest costs prosper relative to other sizes of firms, and it is desirable to recognize this explicitly by defining the most efficient size as that which grows relative to other sizes. This interpretation does not inhibit research on the factors that lead to concentration, for one may still investigate the influence of plant size, of advertising, of the nature of the product, etc. In fact, I would consider it a merit of the reformulation that it divides a vast and complex problem into a series of more specific and manageable problems.

The merger of firms within an industry (putting aside "vertical" mergers) has been a major force in changing the firm structure of many industries. Mergers provide an interesting problem in measurement because of the peculiar basis for recording them: mergers leading to large firms, and acquisitions of all sizes of firms by firms that are already large, constitute the elements of newsworthiness which leads the financial press—and thus the historians of mergers —to record them. Absolute size, moreover, is commonly the test of "large" firms, although size relative to the industry is more relevant to questions of industrial structure. Because large firms are necessarily relatively few in number, perhaps on the order of one merger in a hundred is recorded, and the proportion no doubt varies through time and among industries. The available historical series on mergers, given by Markham, are thus sketchy to an extreme: long periods (before 1887, 1904-1918) have not been studied; size of firms has not been studied, or always recorded, for the variable points of truncation in reporting; horizontal and other mergers have not been distinguished; the industrial composition, when reported at all, is very crude; etc.

Much of the uncertainty over the causes and effects of mergers is attributable to this lack of information. For example, some economists believe that the improvements in transportation in the decades after the Civil War were an important factor in bringing mergers—chiefly because the expansion of market areas increased competition. Simple tests of the hypothesis are easy to devise: mergers should have come earlier in commodities whose production was geographically localized and in products (like ships and jewelry) for which transportation costs were relatively unimportant. We cannot, with our present empirical material, apply such tests.[4] A systematic recompilation of the historical record would be a vast task, but it would be labor well spent.[5]

Fifty years ago only one class of taxes was ever mentioned in studies of industrial organization: tariffs, "the mother of the trusts." Now taxes insist upon intruding into every branch of economic

[4] One basis for my belief that this particular explanation of mergers will not be found useful is that England had a wave of mergers at approximately the same time, although its regions became close-knit considerably before ours.

[5] When it is undertaken, particular attention should be paid to the timing of the several steps in mergers. The period between the initiation of negotiations and the formal merger or acquisition may be variable but substantial—indeed this is one reason, I believe, why the time series show considerable erratic short-run fluctuation.

analysis, and in a variety of forms and with a labyrinth of technical details sufficient to discourage casual generalization. Lintner and Butters' survey of the effects of income and estate taxes reveals the possibility that many significant influences on the industrial structure now flow from these taxes, and the same can be said of certain excises, payroll taxes, etc. Students of public finance may not welcome this new facet of their work: it is hard enough to devise a tax that will raise substantial revenue, be allocated equitably, counteract cyclical fluctuations, encourage efficiency and innovation, and keep the party in power, without adding a due regard for the preservation of competition.

One feature of the taxes Lintner and Butters discuss is that their effects appear to be related usually to the absolute rather than to the relative size of firm. The effects of these taxes upon concentration would therefore appear to be more powerful in industries in which the relatively large firms are large in absolute size, for then substantial absolute growth is required of new rivals before they can offer important competition (and it is absolute growth that taxes may retard). With this in mind it is interesting to compare changes between 1935 and 1947 in concentration in manufacturing industries classified by the absolute sizes of the largest firms. It would be preferable to measure size by assets in this connection, but value added is the most relevant measure available. The results of this tabulation are given in the accompanying table. The decline in con-

TABLE 1

Concentration Ratios in Manufacturing Industries, 1935 and 1947, Classified by Average Value Added in the Four Largest Firms, 1935

Value Added per Firm in Four Largest Firms, 1935	Number of Industries	Per Cent of Value of Product Produced by Four Largest Firms (concentration ratio)	
		1935	1947
Under $250,000	7	36.5	29.5
$250,000- 500,000	13	42.0	39.8
500,000- 750,000	14	41.7	37.7
750,000- 1,000,000	10	36.4	33.8
1,000,000- 2,500,000	37	43.4	42.3
2,500,000- 5,000,000	23	43.1	41.1
5,000,000-10,000,000	16	52.6	51.0
10,000,000-25,000,000	7	63.8	66.3
25,000,000 and over	4	70.7	70.7
Total	131		

Source: *The Structure of the American Economy*, National Resources Committee, 1939; *Concentration of Industry Report*, Dept. of Commerce, 1949.

10

centration was substantial in industries where the largest firms are absolutely small, but no decline occurred at the opposite end of the scale. Taxation may have been one of the significant influences in this pattern of change.

In the essays of Adelman and Edwards we leave the subject of horizontal concentration and explore other aspects of industrial structure. Adelman estimates by several procedures the quantitative extent of vertical integration in different firms and industries. We customarily view vertical integration as a technological problem: if a firm or plant produces an input it previously purchased, we say it has become more fully integrated. One difficulty with this approach is that it is applicable only if technology is stable. The National Bureau of Economic Research recently turned over publication of its books to the Princeton University Press, so we may say that it is now less vertically integrated. But if its researches should be televised—I have been informed of no such plan—no degree of program preparation corresponds to publication, so the change in vertical integration is indeterminable.

A quantitative measure of vertical integration comparable among industries must be monetary in nature, and the most common such measure is the ratio of value added (roughly, receipts minus purchases of materials) to value of product. This measure pertains only to intra-establishment integration when it is calculated from census data, and even then is subject to two serious ambiguities. The first is that when a plant produces a variety of products, with different ratios of value added to value, the extent of vertical integration varies with the composition of output, even if production processes do not change. The second ambiguity is that census industries frequently contain plants engaged in successive operations—motor vehicles is an extreme example—so the value of product contains much duplication.

Rather than enter into the problem of dealing with value-added data, we shall be content to notice that occasionally the Census of Manufactures reports information that is directly relevant to the extent of vertical integration. In each census, for example, there are reported the quantities of some commodities made and consumed in the same establishment and the quantities made for sale. Sample figures may be reproduced:

Year	Production of Sulfuric Acid, 50° Baumé, tons	Per Cent Made and Consumed in Same Establishment
1909	2,764,455	46.5
1919	5,552,581	40.0
1929	8,491,114	31.5
1939	7,711,487	33.2

It might be possible to make a general analysis of vertical integration by recasting census data in this form.

One may argue—as I would—that the fundamental basis of power of the conglomerate firm that Edwards describes is monopoly in the conventional sense. Some of the phenomena he describes are illustrations of well-known theoretical propositions, such as that individual monopolists of goods complementary in demand will make smaller aggregate profits if they act independently than will a single monopolist who takes account of the interrelationships in demand. Again, many aspects of the large, diversified firm's activities seem explicable if there are substantial difficulties in accumulating large amounts of equity capital; the capital market for small firms is possibly a strategic factor in a vast array of industrial practices.

But whatever its basis, the conglomerate firm poses new problems also. When large firms are cooperating in relatively concentrated industries, will they not also tend to cooperate in other industries where concentration is so low that normally competitive behavior would have been expected? Conversely, if the firms that are large in one industry are medium-sized or small in other industries, may not their differences in activity raise substantial difficulties in arriving at agreements in any one of the industries? We need to know which of the infinitely many possible constellations of related concentration in several industries are of empirical significance and to analyze their workings in detail.

Price behavior is so important an aspect of industrial behavior that apology is required, not that the conference had several essays in this area, but that there could not have been more. Still, the full-cost principle, price rigidity, and price discrimination are all sufficiently important, so the conference planning committee cannot be accused of gross neglect. I shall restrict my remaining comments to a problem on which all of these papers touch: How can one measure the relationship of price behavior to the structure of an industry and, in particular, to its concentration?

The output of a competitive industry is such that price equals long-run marginal cost. It is therefore natural to measure, or possibly even to define, the departure of an industry's price from the competitive level by the ratio of price to long-run marginal cost. Useful as this ratio is in the analysis of individual industries, there is unfortunately no known method of making tolerably comparable estimates for many industries so that one might correlate this measure with concentration data. For such broad surveys one is forced to employ a substitute measure.

The temporal rigidity of prices, with respect to either frequency or amplitude, has been the most popular substitute measure, and the vast literature on its use is discussed by Ruggles. For a time, price rigidity was hopefully taken as good evidence of noncompetitive behavior, but both economic theory and statistical studies have greatly weakened the confidence in this evidence. Monopolies may charge flexible prices in their own interests, and competitive industries may have periods of stable supply and demand conditions. The statistical work has shown little correlation between rigidity and concentration, but this work has been plagued by problems of data. Price data and production data are usually collected by different agencies, so that one must use (quoted) prices that are uncertain samples of the industry's real price structure or values of output which are influenced by changes in the composition of output.[6] Extreme price rigidity is inconsistent with competition, but beyond this the association is at best weak.

Since persistent and systematic price discrimination is also invariably associated with noncompetitive behavior of an industry, one might look to this area for measures. Yet price discrimination takes on a considerable variety of forms—geographical, product class, customer class, etc.—as the reader of Machlup's essay will be persuaded. (Machlup is apparently more optimistic than I on the possibility of also disentangling the motives which lead to price discrimination.) Some of the forms of price discrimination deserve study as possible bases for measures of noncompetitive behavior; in particular, the comparison of domestic and export prices might be feasible for a considerable number of industries.

The full-cost principle, in the only one of its numerous versions that I shall consider, states that prices are set equal to average variable cost plus a stable markup per unit of output. If this hy-

---

[6] Census value-of-product figures are possibly seriously biased because two components of output—interplant transfers and inventory additions—are often valued at cost.

pothesis is correct, we have a new measure of noncompetitive behavior because no competitive industry can adhere to such a formula in the face of large fluctuations in output. But if this theory is correct, then the conventional theory of imperfect competition, which makes demand a factor in price determination, is incorrect, and this dispute must first be settled. The settlement—presumably by a recourse to empirical tests—is difficult for two reasons. One is that the full-cost theory has many versions in addition to that stated above, as Heflebower shows, and its sponsors also differ considerably among themselves on the factors governing the markup on variable costs. The other difficulty is that both the conventional theory and the full-cost theories generally agree on the most easily tested predictions: the general correspondence between movements of price and costs, the similar movements of profits and output, etc. They differ qualitatively only in that the conventional theory affirms, and the full-cost theories deny, that short-run changes in demand will affect selling price even though prices of inputs do not change.[7] It is to be hoped that proponents of the full-cost theories will soon test its ability to predict price movements as compared with the conventional theory.

These various measures of price behavior do not of course constitute a complete listing.[8] The available measures, however, are usually either difficult to quantify or ambiguous in interpretation, and much work remains to be done here. Progress in the measurement of price behavior as an index of performance will in turn contribute greatly to improvements in the measurement and interpretation of concentration, for our interest in concentration is centered in its effects on the behavior of industries.

[7] Certain less prominent differences also exist. For example, on the conventional theory a monopolist is less concerned over the effect of current price on future demand if the commodity is perishable, whereas the full-cost theories make no such distinction.

[8] In addition to the popular measure, the ratio of price to average cost (or profitability), interesting experiments have been made with differences among firms in the level, and time and direction of change, of prices.

CENSUS PRINCIPLES OF INDUSTRY AND PRODUCT CLASSIFICATION, MANUFACTURING INDUSTRIES

MAXWELL R. CONKLIN

AND

HAROLD T. GOLDSTEIN

BUREAU OF THE CENSUS

1. *Introduction*

WHETHER concentration of industry (number of firms accounting for bulk of output of competitive products) can be measured and whether it can be related to profits and other economic characteristics depends on how the basic data are classified. The concentration ratio is profoundly affected, on an industry basis, by the range of products defined within the industry, and on a product group basis, by the detailed breakdown of products within the group. Generally the more detailed the definition of product, the more likely will be concentration of its output in a small number of firms. Thus the systems used for describing products and for grouping firms by their product outputs is fundamental to the analysis of economic concentration.

The classification used for organizing the nation's principal industrial statistics was not, of course, established chiefly to measure business concentration. The study of business concentration deals with the competitive nature of products and of firms producing them. This is only one characteristic of an industry; others are method of manufacture, types of facilities, and other physical or technological factors.

Comparison of product output concentration with data on employment, capital expenditures, inventory cumulation, etc., requires use of the establishment unit and data from establishments grouped into industries. In contrast, comparison of profits and other financial data with product output requires the use of the firm as a unit and data from firms grouped into industries. Industry data for establishments or firms are only rough approximations of measures of products or product groups. Such approximations derived from establishment units, of course, tend to be much closer than those derived from firms.

15

When firm, establishment, and product data are used to relate prices, profits, capital expenditures, inventory cumulation, etc., to output, a certain amount of noncomparability arises. This varies inversely with the degree of specialization of activity of establishments and firms in the particular product output. The choice of units is of course limited by the available data. Such data are often not sufficiently comparable to be useful and must therefore be carefully selected or adjusted. For example, practically no data will be available for a study of concentration and profits of a very detailed product such as 2-row corn planters. On the other hand, for textile fabrics, data for establishments and firms would approximate that for products fairly closely.

Available data on manufacturing activity useful for analyzing concentration may be divided roughly into three categories: (1) product output, published mainly by the Bureau of the Census, Department of Agriculture, Tariff Commission, Bureau of Mines, and by trade associations; (2) industry data (employment, earnings, output, capital expenditures, inventories, cost of materials, value added, etc.), derived from establishment reports, published mainly by the Bureau of the Census, Bureau of Labor Statistics (BLS), and on a limited basis by the Bureau of Old-Age and Survivors Insurance, and state employment security agencies; and (3) industry data (profits, income, sales, etc.), derived from firm reports, published mainly by the Department of Commerce (Office of Business Economics and Bureau of the Census), Bureau of Internal Revenue, Federal Trade Commission (FTC), and Securities and Exchange Commission (SEC). These data have been used in recent years in a number of attempts to measure concentration in manufacturing. They include such compilations as: Census of Manufactures industry tabulations by size of establishment; tabulations of census data showing subtotals for the largest 4, 8, 20, and 50 companies in each industry (1937 and 1947); tabulation of census data for 1937 showing proportion of total output accounted for by 4 largest producers for each of approximately 1,800 individual commodities; Temporary National Economic Committee (TNEC) investigations on concentration of economic power (1940); and FTC-SEC 1947 tabulations on largest companies in selected industry groups.

In addition to the above compilations, existing census records could be adapted to facilitate concentration analysis. For example, separate industries for cane and beet sugar could be combined into one; and separate industrial data could be prepared for companies producing farm freezers (part of the broader refrigeration and air-conditioning industry).

Industry data derived from the firm and establishment are directly comparable, of course, when the firm and establishment are the same, that is, for single-establishment firms, and when all of the establishments of a multi-unit firm are classified in the same industry. In manufacturing, single-establishment firms represent 80 to 90 per cent of the total number of establishments, but account for less than half of production. Analysis of census data indicates that the larger producers of particular products are frequently classified as firms in some other industry (air conditioning, margarine).

2. Industry Classification

PURPOSES, DEFINITIONS, AND CRITERIA

ONE of the main purposes of industry classification is to facilitate the compilation of data describing the magnitude and characteristics of the country's economic activity in an orderly manner and in terms of a manageable number of meaningful categories. The industry concept is useful in empirical statistical studies of the behavior of the economic system.

A classification of manufacturing activities by industry (rather than product) is needed because establishments and firms frequently are engaged in the output of more than one product (as defined in the classification system) and data for many input factors (employment, earnings, inventories, capital expenditures, etc.) are not generally reportable on a detailed product basis.

An industry classification is intended primarily for aggregating data for establishment units, rather than for firms. While data for firms may be summarized into the same industry categories, such data will generally represent aggregations of a greater variety of products than those derived from establishment units. In general, the larger the firms controlling establishment units, the less comparable will be the data from the different units. A huge food manufacturing firm engaged in activities scattered in many of the forty-odd food manufacturing industries, in can making, label printing, retail trade, and related fields, would be assigned to only one industry, say wholesale meat packing, on a firm basis. Its importance in that industry would be overstated by the relatively large part of its total activity which, if separable, would be assigned to other industries. On the other hand, the significance of that firm in each of the other industries, where it may be a leading producer, would be lost.

17

Concentration data in the other industries where some of the establishments of the firm would have been important would be less meaningful. By the establishment approach, the different major activities of the firm carried on at each of the establishments are allocated more closely among the various industries in which the activities are defined. It further makes it possible to correlate the firm's importance in any particular industry with its activities in other industries. An understanding and measurement of these interindustry relationships may be useful in interpreting the significance of business concentration.

The differences between industry concentration measures on an establishment and firm basis may be illustrated by 1947 data compiled from census and FTC reports.[1] Comparison of concentration measures by the two methods for selected industries is shown in Appendix Table A-1. Census establishment figures indicate that the largest four companies in the meat products industry accounted for a maximum of 38 per cent of the total shipments for the industry. From FTC corporate (firm) data, the largest four firms accounted for 69 per cent of the total net capital assets for the industry.

For most purposes, the basic units used in compiling manufacturing statistics are defined in the same way by the principal government agencies collecting establishment reports—Bureau of the Census, BLS, Bureau of Old-Age and Survivors Insurance, and Bureau of Employment Security.

Definition of industry. An industry is defined as a group of establishments primarily engaged in the same line or similar lines of economic activity. In the manufacturing field, the line of activity is generally defined in terms of the products made or the processes of manufacture used. On this basis, there may theoretically be thousands of manufacturing industries corresponding to the different types of products and the processes used in their manufacture. However, industries established in this manner would be too numerous to deal with and would not generally satisfy the criteria considered essential for a good system of industry classification.

In the 1947 Census of Manufactures, the *Standard Industrial Classification* (SIC) *Manual,* Volume I, *Manufacturing Industries,*[2]

[1] *Study of Monopoly Power,* report for H. Subcommittee, prepared by the Bureau of the Census from 1947 Census of Manufactures schedules, December 1, 1949. *The Concentration of Productive Facilities,* 1947, Federal Trade Commission, 1949.

[2] *Standard Industrial Classification Manual,* Vol. I, *Manufacturing Industries,* Bureau of the Budget, 1945.

was followed except for relatively minor modifications.[3] The manual lists a number of general guiding principles which were followed in the development of the industry classification system:

"1. The classification should conform to the existing structures of American industry;

"2. The reporting units to be classified are establishments, rather than legal entities or companies;

"3. Each establishment is to be classified according to its major activity;

"4. To be recognized as an industry, each group of establishments must have significance from the standpoint of the number of establishments, number of wage earners, volume of business, employment and payroll fluctuations, and other important economic features."[4]

The meaning of the first principle—that the classification should conform to the existing structure of American industry—may be made clear by an illustration. A system created entirely on the basis of materials used in the manufacturing process would not be satisfactory because many establishments produce the same end product from different materials. An example is gaskets: most establishments making this item produce rubber gaskets, leather gaskets, asbestos gaskets, etc., on the same premises. It would therefore be inappropriate to create separate industries for rubber, leather, asbestos, etc., gaskets.

In addition to the above principles, the classification should maximize the homogeneity or similarity of activity of the establishments in an industry. This means that a high proportion of the total activity of the establishments should be represented by the products, processes, or operations defining the industry. For example, the 1947 output of establishments in the malt liquor industry consisted entirely of malt liquors. On the other hand, only 68 per cent of the output of establishments in the cereals preparation industry consisted of cereal preparations, a large part of the other 32 per cent being represented by prepared feeds and grain mill products. The average "industry homogeneity" for all manufacturing establishments in 1947 was 90 per cent.

Homogeneity depends to some extent on the efforts made to ob-

[3] The differences between 1947 census and SIC classifications are explained in the 1947 Census of Manufactures volumes, Appendix E.

[4] *Standard Industrial Classification Manual*, as cited, p. iv.

tain separate establishment reports for locations engaged in two or more large-sized distinct activities (each industry classification being a distinct activity). Further, while an industry may be relatively homogeneous with respect to output of all products defining the industry, the industry may be defined on the basis of a variety of somewhat related products.

While the output of the establishments of an industry may to a high degree consist of the products of that industry, it may not represent a high proportion of total output of those products made by all establishments. This brings us to the related principle of "primary activity coverage," which requires that the establishments in the industry account for a large portion of the total activity defining the industry. For example, the total output of hydraulic cement is manufactured by establishments in the hydraulic cement industry. On the other hand, only 54 per cent of the total production of suspenders and garters is accounted for by establishments in the suspenders and garters industry, the remaining 46 per cent being made as secondary products by establishments in other industries. Some manufacturing industries are defined in terms of both product and type of operation or stage of production. In many of these industries, the primary product coverage may be low when the same product is defined as belonging to two industries which are distinguishable mainly in terms of operations. For example, although the beehive coke oven industry produces nothing but coke products, its coke production represents only 9 per cent of the total coke output. The other 91 per cent comes from the by-product coke oven industry.

Another criterion of industry classification structure is the extent to which the individual establishment within an industry tends to produce the full range of products primary to the industry. This implies that the activities of a significant number of the establishments are distributed among the various products, processes, or operations defining the industry. If any considerable number of the establishments concentrated on a single one of the activities among those defining the industry, such specialization would constitute a basis for further subdivision of the industry. For example, SIC industry 3543, *Metal-working machinery accessories*, includes establishments primarily manufacturing (a) dies, jigs, and fixtures on a "custom" basis and (b) standard small cutting tools. Very few establishments are engaged in both activities. This indicates that the two types of manufacturers do not belong in the same industry.

Summary distributions of industry size, homogeneity, and coverage are shown in Appendix Tables A-2 through A-5. For individual industries, see Census of Manufactures volumes.

From the foregoing discussion, it will be noted that primary emphasis in defining and describing the industry is on the supply side of the economic picture. Physical or technological structure and homogeneity of production are more important considerations in the classification system than close substitutability of demand for products. Although the industry generally represents a group of close competitors, producing close substitute commodities, the different commodities frequently cannot be substituted (lathe and drill press). Further, all close substitute commodities are not in the same industry. For example, tin cans and glass containers are close substitute commodities, but are defined in two different industries because of the differences in materials, process of manufacture, types of machinery, etc., that is, differences in supply characteristics.

Establishment. Given a system of industry classifications, it is then necessary to define the basic unit of industry classification: the establishment. The SIC manual defines an establishment as ". . . a single physical location where business is conducted or where services or industrial operations are performed; for example, a factory, mill, store, mine, or farm. Where a single physical location comprises two or more units which maintain separate payroll and inventory records and which are engaged in distinct or separate activities for which different industry classifications are provided in the SIC, each unit shall be treated as a separate establishment. An establishment is not necessarily identical with the business concern or firm which may consist of one or more establishments. It is also to be distinguished from organizational subunits, departments or divisions within an establishment."[5]

Perhaps to this definition, there ought to be added an economic flavor—a guiding principle, explicitly stated, that an establishment is an economic unit, and as such, is engaged in an activity of concern in management policy decisions. These decisions involve questions regarding rate of output, price policy, inventory cumulation, plant expansion, etc.

In summary, the establishment is an economic unit characterized by these elements: physical location, distinctive activity, reportability (e.g., ability to supply data on employment, payrolls, shipments, etc.), and management policy control.

In 1947 census practice, some flexibility was allowed in the appli-

[5] *Ibid.,* p. 1.

21

cation of the above rules. Where a company did not keep separate records for two or more establishments engaged in the same line of activity and located within the same county (but in different cities), a consolidated report was sometimes accepted and the plants counted as a single establishment.

The separate reporting of distinct lines of activity at the same location was also selectively applied. In particular instances—e.g., in the separation of blast furnaces from steel works, or of pulp mills from paper mills—reporting manufacturers were required to provide separate reports and in many cases somewhat arbitrary values were assigned to material transferred from one phase to another of an integrated industrial operation. For most industries outside the paper and products and some sections of the metals and products (including machinery) industries, consolidated reports were accepted and the plant classified in the industry accounting for the largest proportion of its shipments. Where, however, companies operated two or more establishments engaged in different lines of activity at different locations, separate reports were secured, even though this involved the assignment of estimated values for materials transferred from one plant to another.

The content of a particular industry may include both merchant and captive (whether or not separately located) establishments engaged in the same activity. In the manufacturing of some materials and components to be subsequently incorporated into end products, captive production (primarily for interplant transfer to other establishments of the same firm) may account for a significant part of the total. Since the demand for the output of captive plants is narrowly limited or controlled in contrast to the commercial market channels of merchant producers, it might be desirable, in a study of business concentration, to recognize instances where captive operations are important. Producers searching for buyers are much more closely competitive with each other than with captive establishments.

There were a total of 241,000 establishments in the 1947 Census of Manufactures: 206,000 independent or single-unit establishments (80 per cent of total number) accounting for 40 per cent of total value added for all manufacturing establishments; and 35,000 multiunit establishments operated or controlled by about 8,000 firms.

For Census of Manufactures purposes, the firm is identical with the establishment for single-unit manufacturing firms. Multi-unit establishment firms consist of the manufacturing establishments of the parent corporation as well as the manufacturing establishments

22

of all of its separately controlled (through stock ownership or otherwise) subsidiaries. The definition of the firm used by the Bureau is essentially similar to that used by FTC and SEC.

Auxiliary units and central administrative offices. Associated with the establishment concept is that of the auxiliary unit, which like the captive manufacturing plant, is a phenomenon chiefly of large business. These are elements of integration that tend to increase the total amount of production (and presumably profit) per unit of final output. The problem of classifying auxiliary units occurs particularly when such units are separately reported or separately located from "operating" establishments of the same firm. The main distinctions between an "operating" establishment and an auxiliary unit are: (1) an auxiliary unit is engaged in nonmanufacturing activity to facilitate the principal activity of establishments of the same firm; its existence depends on the establishments it serves; and (2) it is operated for the use of the firm's own establishments, that is, it is not operated commercially for other business concerns or individuals. The SIC manual does not provide specifically for separate auxiliary units; they are assigned to the industry of the establishments served. For example, a warehouse serving "operating" manufacturing establishments of the same firm has been classified by most agencies as an auxiliary unit in the manufacturing division; the SIC manual provides an industry for public but not for "captive" warehouses. On the other hand, a separate captive paper box manufacturing plant whose entire output is transferred to dress manufacturing plants of the same firm for packaging the dresses would be considered a manufacturing establishment, classified in the paper box industry. The SIC manual recognizes manufacturing for interplant transfer as a manufacturing activity.

The main types of auxiliary activities carried on for own use by the manufacturing establishments of a firm are: force account construction; power generation; warehousing and storage; repair and maintenance of own facilities and equipment; testing, research, and development work; buying operations; shipping and delivery operations; and garage operation.

The central administrative office of multi-unit manufacturing firms represents another type of unit in an establishment-reporting system. There are two schools of thought as to how these offices should be treated for classification purposes. One says that these units are engaged primarily in administration and management of the firm, and the classification system should recognize this by creating a separate management industry. The other school claims that these units serve (administer, manage, keep records, etc.) other establishments of the same firm just as the executive, administrative, and clerical employees of a single-unit establishment serve other parts of the establishment.

In the 1947 Census of Manufactures, the Bureau collected reports for central administrative offices but did not compile data for them along with that for "operating" establishments. The Bureau did not collect schedules for separate activities auxiliary to manufacturing (separate warehouses, garages, maintenance shops, etc.). It is expected that data for both auxiliary units and central administrative offices will be accounted for in the 1954 census.

Data from firms. Agencies collecting financial data use the firm rather than the establishment unit in compiling statistics by industry. The FTC and the SEC, in their quarterly financial report series, obtain reports from corporations. The classification unit may be a single corporation (independent or subsidiary), or a parent corporation consolidating data for parent and all subsidiaries in its annual report to stockholders. The Bureau of Internal Revenue data in the *Statistics of Income* series for corporations are based largely upon returns of separately incorporated entities. Consolidated returns for parent and subsidiary corporations are permitted in certain cases. They accounted for 6 per cent of net income of all returns showing net income in 1947.[6]

THE INDUSTRY CLASSIFICATION

THE *Standard Industrial Classification Manual* (SIC), Volume I, *Manufacturing Industries* (1945), was used with some minor modifications in the 1947 Census of Manufactures and subsequent annual surveys of manufactures. A description of the scope and characteristics of manufacturing establishments is contained in the introductions to the SIC manual and the Census of Manufactures volumes.

The manufacturing universe is divided into 21 major groups (designated by 2-digit codes), subdivided into about 150 industry groups (3-digit codes) which are further divided into some 470 industries (4-digit codes). Most of the industries are defined mainly in terms of establishments primarily engaged in manufacturing a specific product or group of products. In some instances, distinctions are made in terms of operations (examples: stamping, forging,

---

[6] *Statistics of Income for 1947*, Bureau of Internal Revenue, p. 2.

foundry, and machine shop industries); some, in terms of process of manufacture or stage of production (examples: sweaters made in knitting mill vs. cut-and-sew plants from purchased knit fabric; coke made in beehive vs. by-product ovens). Some industries are of a service type primarily servicing other manufacturing establishments, usually on a contract basis on materials owned by others (examples: dyeing and finishing textiles; apparel contracting; galvanizing, electroplating, etc., metal products; printing trade services). Important instances where the same products may be assigned to two or more industries on the basis of differing types or levels of production operations performed are listed in Appendix Table A-6.

APPLICATION OF THE INDUSTRY CLASSIFICATION

THE 1947 Census of Manufactures inquired about input (employment, manhours, earnings, cost of materials, inventories, capital expenditures, etc.) and output of products. Except for a few dozen industries, the product inquiries called for shipments (and sometimes, production) of a preprinted and precoded list of products of each of the industries. Additional information (process of manufacture, method of distribution, materials consumption, etc.) was requested, where necessary, to permit industrial classification of the establishments.

While the SIC manual establishes a system for dividing the universe of economic activities into smaller industry categories, it does not deal at length with specific application of the system in assigning industry classifications to establishments. It does provide that the establishment be assigned to an industry on the basis of its major activity, and the manual also states that ". . . in most cases, the industry assignment is determined on the basis of the principal product made in the establishment, but in a number of instances other criteria are used. . . ."[7] However, SIC does not prescribe the measuring rod (value of sales or receipts, value added, employment, etc.), nor any more specific method of applying the SIC system.

Theoretically, the major activity of an establishment would probably best be measured in terms of income produced or value added, but such information is generally not reportable in the detail necessary for determining an industry classification. In practice, the Bureau and most other establishment-report collecting agencies measure activity in terms of value of sales of products or receipts for services.

[7] *Standard Industrial Classification Manual*, as cited, p. 3.

In the 1947 census, an establishment was assigned to or classified in an industry generally on the basis of the principal products made. The products made by each establishment were grouped according to the industries to which they belong, and the group of products accounting for the largest part of the total value of shipments of the establishment determined its industry classification. This group of products is said to be the primary products of the establishment as well as of the industry which it defines; all other products made by establishments classified in the industry are referred to as secondary products.

In some instances, a knowledge of the types and value of products shipped was not sufficient for determining the proper industry classification of an establishment. It was also necessary to know the process used in the manufacture of the products, or the materials used, or other characteristics of the operations of the establishment. For example, an establishment primarily engaged in producing insulated copper wire was classified in Industry 3392, *Wire drawing*, if it purchased copper rods, drew the rods into wire, and insulated the wire, but classified in Industry 3631, *Insulated wire and cable*, if it purchased copper wire and insulated it. In both cases, the major product value of shipments would be insulated wire.

There are a number of limitations to the above method of assigning an industry classification to an establishment. In the first place, the assignment is based upon the plurality of a group of products (of an industry) having the greatest value. Thus an establishment can be classified in Industry A even if only a small proportion, say, 30 per cent, of its total shipments consists of products of Industry A, provided the value for that group exceeds the value for any other group of products in an industry classification. However, this situation probably does not occur very frequently, as evidenced by the 90 per cent average "homogeneity" (see above) for all manufacturing industries.

Further, the use of value of shipments as a measuring rod is sometimes inadequate in approximating income produced or value added. This occurs particularly for establishments engaged in two or more distinct activities crossing economic division lines (manufacturing, wholesale trade, retail trade, services, etc.). In many of these cases, the use of value of shipments may lead to misleading results since a dollar's worth of manufactured product shipments may not be equivalent in terms of income produced to a dollar's worth of, say, wholesale trade sales. For example, an establishment reporting the manufacture of motors valued at $1 million, and also the purchase and resale at wholesale of hardware at $1.5 million, would be classified in wholesale trade on the basis of value of sales. However, on the basis of income produced, one dollar's worth of manufactured product sales is probably more nearly equivalent to five or six dollars of wholesale sales, and therefore the establishment would be classified in manufacturing. Fortunately, the number of these borderline cases is undoubtedly limited to isolated establishments within certain industries and probably does not affect a significant portion of manufacturing establishments.

During the processing of the 1947 Census of Manufactures, a number of difficulties were encountered in arriving at establishment industry classifications. Many of the difficulties occurred in the borderland between the manufacturing and nonmanufacturing division— in the fringe industrial segments where establishments were engaged in manufacturing activities combined with nonmanufacturing activities or where a significant part of the output of manufactured products was attributable to establishments in nonmanufacturing industries. It was often a problem to distinguish manufacturing from nonmanufacturing classifications for establishments engaged in such activities as manufacturing and wholesaling of meat and poultry products; manufacturing dairy products and distributing fluid milk; manufacturing and sale at retail or wholesale of bakery products, confectionery, prepared feed, fertilizers, awnings, venetian blinds, window shades, etc; manufacturing millwork and lumber distribution; manufacturing and repairing truck bodies; sheet metal work and special trade contracting; fabricated structural steel production and general construction, etc.

The Bureau of the Census has been conducting annual surveys of manufactures on a sample basis since 1949. In many instances where only the current major activity is used as a basis for classification, a small actual change in activity may be reflected in an exaggerated change in industrial classification. For example, in 1947 an establishment with 1,000 employees shipping $10 million worth of products including $5.1 million worth of butter and $4.9 million of cheese would be assigned to the butter industry. If the butter and cheese figures were reversed in 1949, the establishment would be assigned to the cheese industry on a current activity basis. This would shift the whole 1,000 employees, $10 million shipments, etc., to the cheese industry, whereas actually the change affected only $200,000 of shipments, and approximately 20 employees. To avoid these abrupt and unrealistic fluctuations, the Bureau applied a "resistance" factor which would permit only significant changes in real activity to be reflected in industry code changes. The resistance factor was derived so as to minimize the combined errors of industry trend and current level, assuming equal importance (weights) for trend and level.

The resistance factor technique was applied to a universe of approximately 30,000 of the larger establishments in the 1949 sample survey of 45,000 establishments. Of these 30,000 establishments, primary activity changes occurred for 1,000 establishments. Application of the resistance factor prevented a change in code for 35 per cent of these 1,000 cases. For the 15,000 smaller establishments, the old (1947) codes were maintained, that is, 100 per cent resistance was applied.

As will be noted from the above discussion of the application of the industry classification, the nature and detail of information available are important factors in determining industry classifications of establishments. The detailed list of some 6,500 products and other inquiries on census schedules have resulted in establishment classifications often different from those assigned by other agencies.

For several years now the Bureau has been participating with other establishment-report collecting agencies (Bureau of Old-Age and Survivors Insurance, BLS, Bureau of Employment Security), under the sponsorship of the Bureau of the Budget, in attempting to achieve greater comparability of industrial statistics. An important beginning was the development of the SIC manual for use by government agencies compiling data from establishment reports. However, a standard classification system is not enough, by itself, to accomplish the desired level of uniformity. Among other things, the system must be uniformly interpreted, the classification units—establishments—must be the same, and the same classification must be assigned to identical units for a given time period. The agencies are at present directing their efforts toward these objectives.

3. Product Classification

THE 200-odd schedules sent to manufacturers contained an aggregate of some 6,500 different products for which the Bureau of the Census desired to collect shipments and, sometimes, production data.

A number of guiding principles were followed in the creation of the product list. An attempt was made to arrive at a balanced list of homogeneous products. In general, a product was not included if its 1939 production was valued at less than $2 million. On the other hand, product items which were reported in large volume by a large number of establishments in 1939 were split up in 1947 into a number of products, where feasible. In most cases, parts and accessories of machinery and equipment were listed separately from complete units. Distinctions were made in many instances between consumer and producer goods; for example, household washing machines, etc., were listed separately from commercial washing machines, etc. Finally, each product was set up so as to be assignable in its entirety as "primary" to a particular industry; that is, one part could not belong to one industry, and another part to another industry. For example, dress gloves were divided between leather and fabric gloves since establishments primarily making leather gloves were assignable to a different industry from those making fabric gloves.

Basically, the products were organized or grouped into a structure related to origin of production, that is, according to the industry primarily responsible for their output. This is in contrast to the 1946 Standard Commodity Classification which follows the sequence of the stage of production process. The latter system divides all products into three major groups: crude materials, fabricated basic materials, and end products. While the basic structures of the two systems are organized differently, at the detailed product level, they are comparable and consistent.

The 6,500 products were preprinted and precoded on the various schedules so that it was generally necessary to assign codes only when the respondent reported shipments of items not listed on his schedule. Such items were written in on blank lines by the respondent and were assigned codes corresponding to one of the 6,500 products of the system.

The term "products," as used in the Census of Manufactures, may have a broader or narrower content than in common usage. For example, automotive gasoline was reported as a single item. On the other hand, cotton broad-woven goods were distributed into nearly 200 individual "products" according to type of weave, width of fabric, and other specifications. For some items, e.g. bearings, it would have been desirable to obtain product information in much greater detail than that actually requested, but the extent to which the production of individual types and sizes is concentrated in one or two individual companies would have made it impossible to publish detailed data. Thus the 6,500 individual products included on the forms merely represent the number of items for which it was considered practical to publish census information.

Of the 6,500 items included on the forms, data were actually published for approximately 6,300. The balance were eliminated because their publication would involve disclosure of the activities of individual companies or because a number of important producers could not report products in the detail requested. A frequency distribution of the value of product shipments is shown in Appendix Table A-7.

To compile certain types of data, the 6,500 detailed products were condensed into approximately 1,000 broader classes of products. These product classes, with some modifications, were also used in collecting shipments data in the sample annual surveys of manufactures for 1949, 1950, and 1951.

The extent to which industry and product statistics can be matched with each other is indicated in transition tables (Table 5's, Census of Manufactures, Volume ii, Statistics of Industry) which show, on the one hand, the proportions by value of the primary and secondary products shipped by the industry and, on the other, the value of the primary products of the industry made as secondary products in other industries.

Following is an illustration of the relation between industry and product value data for the oleomargarine industry and the product, oleomargarine.

| | SHIPPED BY | | |
| | Oleomargarine Industry | Other Industries | All Industries |
PRODUCT	(millions of dollars)		
Total shipments of oleomargarine industry	215		
Oleomargarine (primary product)	173	64	237
Secondary products of oleomargarine industry	42		
Salad dressings	36		
Shortening and salad oils	3		
Other secondary products	3		

The above table shows that establishments in the oleomargarine industry shipped products valued at $215 million, only $173 million of which consisted of oleomargarine. On the other hand, total oleomargarine shipments amounted to $237 million of which $64 million was contributed by industries other than the oleomargarine industry.

In a classification system dividing the manufacturing field into some 470 separate industries to which establishments are assigned on the basis of their principal activity, a certain amount of over- lapping production by one industry of products of other industries is bound to arise. Such overlapping is particularly prevalent in such industry groups as apparel, furniture, and metal fabricating, where establishments within each group, employing the same basic types of machinery and fabricating operations, produce a wide variety of products belonging to a number of different industries. For 1947, the average amount of overlapping for all industries was approxi- mately 10 per cent in both directions, compared with from 15 to 20 per cent for the furniture and metal fabricating (except transpor- tation equipment) groups of industries. The greater the degree of overlapping, the less meaningful are the relationships between gen- eral and product statistics for the particular industry.

STATISTICAL APPENDIX

TABLE A-1

Comparison of Concentration Ratios Derived from *1947 Census of Manufactures*, Establishme
Reports and 1947 Federal Trade Commission Sample of Corporation Reports[a]

SIC Industry or Industry Group	Census of Manufactures: 1947 1947 Value Added, Total for Industry[b] (mill. $)	Census of Manufactures: 1947 Percentage of Total Industry Shipments by First Four Companies, 1947[c]	FTC Estimate Percentage of Total Net Capital Assets Owned by First Four Companies, 19
201, Meat products	$1,281	max. 38	69
202, Dairy products	595	max. 36	60
203, Canning and preserving	917	max. 29	39
204, Grain mill products	1,002	max. 28	36
2051, Bakery products, except biscuit, etc.	1,101	16	30
2052, Biscuit, crackers, and pretzels	265	72	71
2085, Distilled, rectified, and blended liquors	472	75	85
2111, Cigarettes	368	90	88
2232, Woolen and worsted fabrics	600	28	30
2271, 2273, Carpets and rugs	248	max. 49	58
2274, Hard-surface floor coverings, n.e.c.	83	80	94
281, 282, Industrial chemicals	2,006	max. 56	52
283, Drugs and medicines	749	max. 36	30
3011, Rubber tires and tubes	650	77	88
314, Footwear, except rubber	786	max. 28	47
321-323, Glass and glassware	713	max. 60	62
331, 332, Primary steel	3,780	max. 40	55
3334, Primary aluminum	65	100	100
3411, Tin cans and tinware	232	78	96
3431, Plumbers' supplies	156	35	74
352, Agricultural machinery	754	max. 52	75
357, Office and store machines	504	max. 61	74
371, Motor vehicles and parts	3,819	max. 54	71
372, Aircraft and parts	955	max. 58	44

a Industries selected are 23 of the 26 industries shown in the Federal Trade Commission repo
Census data are based on classification of individual establishments. To determine concentrati
ratios, establishments of same company in a particular industry were consolidated; a compa
could have establishments in many different industries. FTC data are based on classification
corporation as a whole (parent corporation and its subsidiaries), so that the corporation
classified in only one industry.

b Value added data for all establishments of industry listed to indicate size of the vario
industries.

c Percentages based on value of shipments of largest 4 companies in each SIC industry. Rat
shown for combinations of 2 or more industries represent a maximum possible percentage th
would be obtained if the first 4 companies of each of the industries of the combination we
identical. Ratios for these combinations are prefixed with the symbol "max." (maximum). Rat
are based on value of shipments, except for the following industry groups containing individe
industries with extensive duplication in shipments figures: 201, meat products; 2271 and 22
carpets and rugs; 331 and 332, primary steel; 371, motor vehicles and parts; 372, aircraft a
parts. Ratios for these industries are based on "value added" data.

Sources: *Census of Manufactures: 1947*, Bureau of the Census, Vol. II (value added dat
Study of Monopoly Power, a report for H. Subcommittee prepared by the Bureau of the Cen
from 1947 Census of Manufactures schedules, December 1, 1949; and *The Concentration of P
ductive Facilities, 1947*, Federal Trade Commission, 1949.

TABLE A-2

Frequency Distribution of Industries by Total Employment Size Class, 1947

Employment Size Class of Industry (thousands of employees)	Number of Industries	Number of Establishments (thousands)	Number of Employees (thousands)	Value Added by Manufactures (mill. $)
All industries, total	453	240.9	14,294	$74,426
Less than 1.0	9	.2	6	9
1.0– 1.9	24	1.6	34	219
2.0– 2.9	19	1.8	46	311
3.0– 3.9	20	2.1	68	394
4.0– 4.9	19	2.3	84	447
5.0– 9.9	95	17.6	709	3,942
10.0–24.9	118	40.0	1,869	10,009
25.0–49.9	70	50.9	2,521	13,635
50.0–99.9	52	51.9	3,523	18,974
100.0 and over	27	72.5	5,434	26,456

Source: *Census of Manufactures: 1947*, Bureau of the Census.

TABLE A-3

Frequency Distribution of Industries by Value Added Size Classes, 1947

Value Added Size Class of Industry (millions of dollars)	Number of Industries	Number of Establishments (thousands)	Number of Employees (thousands)	Value Added by Manufactures (mill. $)
All industries, total	453	240.9	14,294	$74,426
Up to $4.9	13	.6	12	46
5–$ 9.9	25	1.8	45	199
10– 24.9	60	8.4	249	1,097
25– 49.9	86	16.9	700	3,290
50– 99.9	83	21.7	1,162	6,090
100– 249.9	99	65.3	2,949	15,119
250– 499.9	57	52.0	3,648	20,158
500– 999.9	22	37.0	2,873	14,475
1,000 and over	8	37.2	2,656	13,952

Source: *Census of Manufactures: 1947*, Bureau of the Census.

TABLE A-4

Frequency Distribution of Industries by Degree of Homogeneity of Activity, 1947

Percentage Industry Homogeneity Class Interval[a]	Number of Industries	Number of Establishments (thousands)	Number of Employees (thousands)	Value Added by Manufactures (mill. $)
All industries, total	453	240.9	14,294	$74,426
50–59	1	.1	4	18
60–69	6	.9	50	439
70–79	37	7.4	520	2,772
80–89	129	60.6	3,767	19,238
90–99	255	162.0	9,400	47,820
100	25	9.9	553	4,139

[a] 1947 value of shipments of primary products of each industry as a per cent of the industry's shipments of all products. Average homogeneity for all industries is 90 per cent.
Source: *Census of Manufactures: 1947*, Bureau of the Census, Vol. II, *Statistics by Industry*, Table 5's.

TABLE A-5

Frequency Distribution of Industries by Percentage Coverage of Primary Activity, 1947

Percentage Industry Coverage Class Interval[a]	Number of Industries	Number of Establishments (thousands)	Number of Employees (thousands)	Value Added by Manufactures (mill. $)
All industries, total[b]	449	238.5	14,257	$74,252
Less than 50	19	3.5	366	1,737
50–59	9	3.3	86	479
60–69	19	5.7	216	1,231
70–79	50	18.2	838	4,226
80–89	110	60.0	3,195	16,458
90–99	207	118.2	7,423	38,212
100	35	29.6	2,133	11,909

a 1947 value of shipments of primary products by each industry as a per cent of shipments the products by all industries. Average coverage for all industries is approximately 90 per ce
b Excludes the following primarily service-type industries: 3465, enameling and lacqueri 3466, galvanizing; 3467, engraving on metal; and 3468, plating and polishing.
Source: *Census of Manufactures: 1947*, Bureau of the Census, Vol. II, *Statistics by Indust* Table 5's.

TABLE A-6

Principal Product Groups Primary to Two or More Manufacturing Industries[a]

Product Group (A)	Industries in which Primary (B)
Prepared meats	2011. Meat packing, wholesale
	2013. Sausages and other prepared meat products
Process cheese	2022. Natural cheese
	2025. Special dairy products
Flour, blended and prepared	2041. Flour and other grain-mill products
	2045. Blended and prepared flour
Sugar, refined	2062. Cane-sugar refining
	2063. Beet sugar
Knit apparel	2253-2255. Knit outerwear, underwear, and glove mills
	23. Various apparel industries
Waterproof outer garments	2385. Raincoats and other waterproof outer garments
	3099. Rubber industries, not elsewhere classified
Other apparel and fabricated textile products	23. Various apparel industries
Box shook	2421. Sawmills and planing mills, general
	2444. Wooden boxes (except cigar boxes)
Converted paper products	264-269. Paper product industries except pulp and paper board products[b]
Soap	2841. Soap and glycerin
	2842. Cleaning and polishing preparations
Fertilizers	2871. Fertilizers, manufacturing and mixing
	2872. Fertilizers, mixing only
Coke	2931. Beehive coke ovens
	2932. By-product coke ovens

34

TABLE A-6 *(Continued)*

Product Group (A)	*Industries in which Primary* (B)
Lubricating oils and greases	2911. Petroleum refining
	2992. Lubricating oils and greases not made in petroleum refineries
Laminated glass	3211. Flat glass
	3231. Glass products made of purchased glass
Glassware, decorated	321. Flat glass
	322. Pressed or blown glass and glassware
	3231. Glass products made of purchased glass
Ferroalloys and other additives	3311. Blast furnaces
	3313. Electrometallurgical products
Refined unalloyed nonferrous products	333. Primary smelting and refining, nonferrous metals
	334. Secondary smelting and refining, nonferrous metals
Nails and spikes	3392. Wire drawing
	3481. Nails and spikes
Wire, except insulated	3312. Steelworks and rolling mills
	335. Nonferrous rolling and drawing
	3392. Wire drawing
Fabricated wire products, except insulated wire	3392. Wire drawing
	3489. Wirework, not elsewhere classified
Insulated wire and cable	3312. Steel works and rolling mills
	335. Nonferrous rolling and drawing
	3392. Wire drawing
	3631. Insulated wire and cable
Fire-control equipment	1941. Sighting and fire-control equipment
	3831. Optical instruments and lenses

a Establishments primarily engaged in manufacturing products listed in Column A are classified in one of the two or more industries shown in Column B, on the basis of types of operations performed or materials used. For example, an establishment primarily manufacturing blended and prepared flour from grain milled at the same establishment is classified in 2041, Flour and other grain-mill products; from purchased flour, in 2045, Blended and prepared flour.

b Most of the industries in major group 23, apparel and other finished products made from fabrics and similar materials and in industry groups 264-269, paper converting industries, are defined in terms of establishments primarily engaged in making products from purchased materials (fabric for major group 23, and paper and paperboard for industry groups 264-269). The presumption is that if the establishments make the same products from their own materials (produced at the same establishment) they are to be classified elsewhere (weaving mill or pulp and paper mill industries).

Source: Bureau of the Census.

TABLE A-7

Frequency Distribution of Value of Individual Products Published in
Census of Manufactures: 1947

Value of Shipments Class Interval (millions of dollars)	Number of Products	Per Cent of Total Number of Products
All products, total	6,292	100
$ .0–$ 1.9a	1,539	24
2.0– 3.9	913	15
4.0– 5.9	630	10
6.0– 7.9	426	7
8.0– 9.9	384	6
10.0– 14.9	554	9
15.0– 19.9	361	6
20.0– 29.9	445	7
30.0– 39.9	251	4
40.0– 49.9	144	2
50.0– 59.9	89	1
60.0– 69.9	90	1
70.0– 79.9	80	1
80.0– 89.9	42	1
90.0– 99.9	38	1
100.0–199.9	170	3
200.0–299.9	54	1
300.0–399.9	33	1
400.0–499.9	14	x
500.0–599.9	6	x
600.0–699.9	4	x
700.0–799.9	6	x
800.0–899.9	3	x
900.0–999.9	5	x
$1,000.0 and over	11	x

a A large proportion of the products of small value are of the unavoidable "residual" type or of the type needed to simplify classifications or instructions for reporting other products.

x Means less than .5 per cent.

Source: *Census of Manufactures: 1947*, Bureau of the Census.

COMMENT

SOLOMON FABRICANT, National Bureau of Economic Research

ECONOMISTS belong to that hungry tribe of whom it is said that when shown a finger they try to seize the hand. Those of us concerned with business concentration do not admit the richness of the census for our purposes; we point only to the obvious fact that the census can be made richer—with no additional cost as far as we are concerned.

We ask, for example, for information on net capital assets, which would provide us with a more stable measure of size than does out-

36

put, value of product, or other flow items. It is true that some difficulties were encountered when the possibility of securing data on capital assets was explored in a pre-test of the 1947 census. However, if the census can secure useful information on capital expenditures, it is difficult to believe that it cannot at the same time secure useful information on capital assets.

More information on central offices and related activities would also be useful. Many of these offices straddle a variety of industries, and we need to know more about their relative importance before we can be sure we are measuring individual industries adequately. We need to know more also about ownership connections between industries, and not only within manufacturing but also between manufacturing and mining, trade, etc.; and central office information would help. A "distribution of sales" schedule also would help.

At present we are in some degree victims of the way in which the work of the Bureau of the Census is divided between its Industry Division and its Business Division—not to speak of its Agriculture Division. Ownership connections are broken when an enterprise is split between the Census of Manufactures and the Census of Trade. But even for enterprises entirely within manufacturing, our measures of business concentration depend on the classification of establishments followed by the Bureau of the Census. It would be informative, therefore, if the Bureau told us how its classifications compare with those implicit in various administrative rulings, such as those made by the Wage and Hour Division. And we ought to be given a clearer idea as to how congruent the census industries are with the clusters of establishments organized in trade associations and similar groups.[1]

Besides extending the census to provide additional data, the Bureau can produce a valuable body of source material merely by making new arrangements of data now in its files. Generally speaking, this means providing breakdowns and cross classifications of various sorts. Aggregates are only the beginning of information.

For example, we would like to know how individual establishments or enterprises change in size from one year or census to an-

[1] When discussing the classification question, Conklin and Goldstein mention a "resistance" factor to avoid "abrupt and unrealistic fluctuations" in the scope of industries. It would be interesting to know in which industries the resistance factor is most important. It would be well also if the Bureau of the Census indicated whether it expects to adhere to resistance factors even when a new census is taken, for apparently the factor has been applied so far only in moving forward from the 1947 census via the annual surveys.

other. Light on this question would be provided if for each industry we had a cross tabulation of establishments, by size in one year against size in another year, size being measured by value added, employment, or value of product, or—if the information were obtained—capital assets. It might not be necessary to do this for all establishments; a sample in each industry might be sufficient. If we had such information, we would know the extent to which establishments or enterprises shift into and out of the "top four," and could deal with one of the questions that Rosenbluth raises in his discussion of the time period. More generally, information would be provided about the shifts that occur in the position of individual firms wherever they may be in the size distribution. We might learn something also about the movement of establishments between industries; or within industries, of shifts in major product or extent of specialization.

Everybody knows the story of concentration in livestock purchasing. We could do with a few fresh examples of concentration in buying. What we need is a classification of a wide range of industries with respect to concentration in buying of various materials. I suspect that the census already has a fair amount of the basic data; perhaps all that is needed is to tabulate them in suitable form.

Suits mentions the relationship between product and industry. Tabulations already available in the Census of Manufactures provide information for narrow groups of industries. It would be desirable if, on occasion, the census could publish larger segments of the full product-by-industry tabulation that covers all industries and products.

Information already available could be organized to indicate how concentration in production of end products in a given industry is related to concentration in production of intermediate materials in that industry. We would like to know also how concentration in production is correlated with concentration of labor in trade unions in the same industry. Available information could probably be organized to show how frequently oligopolies face one another in their transactions.

Apart from the question of developing and extending our data, there is the problem of using the data most effectively to measure business concentration.

Value added or net value added has been suggested as superior to value of product in measuring concentration because materials and fuel differ in importance among establishments. However, even value added is not free of difficulties associated with varying degrees of integration. Companies that do their own construction and maintenance work or other auxiliary activities will necessarily have a larger value added than will concerns that do not, yet this kind of integration is largely irrelevant to our purpose. A further point: value added includes profits. When profits are high, value added will be high and so will profit rates. If we take value added as a measure of size and correlate it with the rate of profit, as we sometimes do, we may get spurious results. This is one of the reasons for asking that the census try to obtain information on capital assets.

A problem arises when using value of product in concentration measures because "captive" establishments transfer their output to affiliated establishments at assigned values. These values are usually lower than market values, as may be seen in the 1947 census statistics on the blast furnace industry, and the concentration ratios may be too low also. In any case, the presence of these "arbitrary" values—to use the term favored by Conklin and Goldstein—is disturbing. Perhaps better than value of product, then, is physical volume. One could omit "captive" establishments, as Conklin and Goldstein suggest; but what is really needed is knowledge of their importance, and of the extent to which shifts occur in the proportion between transferred and sold outputs.

It may be noted, further, that in some industries substantial quantities of goods are produced and consumed in the same industry. These goods will not find their value reflected in the total value of the output of that class of goods, since the total value will usually relate to the quantities sold.

Many of our concentration measures are based on industry classes as defined in the census and similar sources. Yet there may well be considerable competition between, say, manufacturing industries on the one hand and nonmanufacturing industries on the other. Thus the manufacture of canned fruits and vegetables is closely competitive not only with the manufacture of dried fruits and vegetables but also with the sale of fresh fruits and vegetables and with home canning. Another and perhaps better example is cheese or butter, which are (or used to be) produced on farms as well as in factories.

Whatever we do, difficulties will be encountered in getting up sensible concentration measures and using them. It must be emphasized, however, that these difficulties are not merely technical matters. They reflect phenomena of the economic world that are themselves worthy of study by economists. We need to know, for example, when auxiliary activities are taken on, when they are sloughed off. We need in fact a theory of auxiliary activity—recall Stigler's recent paper on specialization.

Another illustration is found in the type of analysis performed by Rosenbluth in which he distinguishes between changes in concentration within industries and changes in the weights of different industries and asks what has been the effect of each type of change on the over-all concentration ratio. A real question here is whether or not there is an economic relationship between these two "independent" factors. More specifically, is there any tendency for highly concentrated industries to grow less rapidly because they are more highly concentrated? A related question looks the other way along the line of causation. How does stage of growth of an industry influence the degree of concentration that characterizes it? Further, how does degree of concentration fluctuate with the business cycle? These questions, raised by Moses Abramovitz in an article now fifteen years old, still need looking into.

The stage we have reached in our study of concentration in business is much like the stage reached in the study of concentration of incomes a decade or so ago. At that time we thought the major question was the shape of the income distribution. We have since graduated to a higher level in which we worry about the factors that determine the position of a family in the income distribution and the bearing of that position on the division of income between savings and consumption. We seem to be approaching this new level of analysis in the present field. If we learn from the experience of investigators of income distribution, we should rise to the new level sooner.

FRANK J. KOTTKE, Federal Trade Commission

THE construction of a concentration ratio poses a problem in classification. Use of a single concentration ratio involves acceptance of two categories as comparable and relevant. Contrast of two or more concentration ratios generally predicates their comparability. The possibilities are great that the most readily available data are not comparable, or, though comparable, are not relevant to the problem at hand. Consequently, economists must take care to avoid the misuse of data in studies of economic concentration.

Publications of the Industry Division of the Bureau of the Census are the principal basis for concentration ratios for manufacturing activities in the United States. Conklin and Goldstein have rendered an important service in explaining precisely the classification principles on which such data are developed, and in indicating some of the considerations to be reviewed before any figure is incorporated in a concentration ratio. Many matters are involved in defining the categories of a census study. The Bureau of the Census must consider not only the interest of students of business concentration, but also the needs of other scientists, lawmakers, businessmen, and labor unions. The Bureau must consider the bases upon which informants can supply data, and also the importance of establishing specifications that all informants will interpret in the same way. Finally, the Bureau endeavors to accommodate its reporting program to those of other government statistical agencies. Even if there were only one concept of economic concentration, adjustment to these several needs almost certainly would leave much of the data less than ideal for the measurement of concentration.

A few comments on two of the industries listed in Appendix A illustrate difficulties for which a student of concentration must be on guard. Consider the dairy-products industry in 1947: The Federal Trade Commission (FTC) estimated that the four leading companies accounted for 60 per cent of the net capital assets, while the Bureau of the Census estimated that the four leading companies accounted for not more than 36 per cent of the value of shipments and interplant transfers originating in this industry.[1] Conklin and Goldstein imply that the difference is attributable to the procedure of the FTC in this particular study in assigning to one industry the entire capital assets of each parent company. Yet well over 90 per cent of the capital assets of the four leading dairy companies were directly related to the manufacture and distribution of dairy products. National Dairies had a minor commitment in frozen foods and salad products. Borden had seven chemical plants and eight special-products plants, but for the products of many of these plants, milk was an important raw material—viz., casein, milk sugar, beverage bases, and prescription foods. Carnation made its own cans and operated several feed mills. Another circumstance that might conceivably account for such a discrepancy is that the leading companies held large capital assets outside the continental United

NOTE: The views expressed in this comment are the writer's and not necessarily those of the Federal Trade Commission.

[1] The report of the Federal Trade Commission was issued August 24, 1949. The data on which the census ratios are based were released December 1, 1949.

States. But in 1951 (the closest year for which the information is available), less than 2 per cent of the assets of National Dairies was located abroad. Borden in 1947 operated in two Canadian provinces, and two of Carnation's thirty milk plants were in Canada: this would account for a difference of not more than a few percentage points in the two concentration ratios. The denominator for the FTC ratio, of course, included the value of nondairy assets, and of capital assets outside the continental United States, for all companies primarily engaged in manufacturing dairy products.

The difference between the FTC ratio of 60 per cent and the maximum ratio of Conklin and Goldstein is traceable to aspects of the dairy-products business not covered by the census data they employed. All establishments distributing fresh milk and cream, including those establishments for which the manufacture of dairy products was the more important part of their operations, were excluded in developing the census data.[2] Establishments for receiving milk, establishments for storing dairy products, and facilities for transporting dairy products all were excluded. The result is a concentration ratio based on a much more limited conception of the dairy-products industry than that which the FTC had in mind.

As another example, newspaper and business writers constantly refer to the "automobile industry." However defined, this industry provides employment for the largest group of manufacturing workers in the United States. The following are some of the concepts that may be considered relevant to a study of concentration in the automobile industry (with concentration measured, for convenience, in terms of the four leading companies):

1. The percentage accounted for by the four largest producers of the value (f.o.b. plant) of all passenger automobiles shipped during a year. A close approximation, for which data are available, is the per cent of new passenger-car registrations. The four largest companies accounted for 88 per cent in 1947.[3]

2. The percentage accounted for by the four largest producers of

2 In 1947, combination mercantile and manufacturing plants manufactured $1.7 billion of dairy products, whereas exclusively manufacturing plants accounted for $3.6 billion. In 1948, sales of milk dealers and dairy-product stores were $2.9 billion.

3 Registration data are from *Automotive News*, 1952 Almanac Issue, p. 32. The FTC suggested that 1948 production figures were preferable to those for 1947, as strikes, material shortages, and other factors seriously disturbed production in 1947. However, census data are available for 1947 but not 1948; consequently, Conklin and Goldstein had no choice but to use 1947.

the value (f.o.b. plant) of all motor vehicles shipped during a year. The term "motor vehicles" as used here includes passenger automobiles, ambulances, buses, and trucks, but not road-building equipment, self-propelled construction equipment, combat vehicles, farm machinery, locomotives, or motorcycles. The best approximation available is the per cent of new passenger-car and truck registrations. The four largest companies accounted for 85 per cent of such registrations in 1947.

3. The percentage accounted for by the four largest producers of the value of shipments (including miscellaneous receipts) of all establishments in which motor vehicle production is of greater value than output of goods primary to any other industry, as defined by the Bureau. The four leading companies here are those whose motor-vehicle establishments so defined, had larger shipments than did the establishments in the motor-vehicle industry controlled by any other combination of four companies. As of 1935 their share was 87 per cent. (Subsequently, the Bureau of the Census abandoned this concept of the industry.)

4. The percentage accounted for by the four largest companies of the value added by manufacture by establishments in which production of motor vehicles, motor-vehicle parts, or both motor vehicles and motor-vehicle parts is of greater value than output of goods primary to any other industry, as defined by the Bureau. Here the four companies are those whose motor-vehicle establishments so defined, added a larger value by manufacture than did the establishments in the motor-vehicle and parts industry controlled by any other combination of four companies. This is the measure used by Conklin and Goldstein. The share of the first four companies in 1947 was 56 per cent.

5. The percentage accounted for by the four largest companies of the net capital assets of all companies in which capital resources directed to the production of motor vehicles, motor-vehicle parts, or both motor vehicles and motor-vehicle parts are of greater value than those committed to any other industry as defined in sufficiently broad terms to facilitate classification of parent corporations in a single industry. With this approach, the leading companies are those having the largest net capital assets. This is the concept used by the FTC in its report on concentration.[4] The share of the four largest companies in 1947 was estimated at 71 per cent.

6. The percentage accounted for by the four largest companies of

---

[4] *The Concentration of Productive Facilities, 1947*, FTC, 1949.

the total assets of all companies in which capital resources directed to the production of motor vehicles, motor-vehicle parts, or both motor vehicles and motor-vehicle parts are of greater value than those committed to any other industry, as defined in sufficiently broad terms to facilitate classification of parent corporations in a single industry. Here the leading companies are those with the largest total assets. On this basis the share of the four largest companies at the close of 1947 was 68 per cent.

Concept 1 is, of course, a "product" concept. For purposes of market analysis, some economists might prefer to divide it into three or four price classes. Its purpose, and that of 2 and 3 as well, is to measure the fraction of the supply of a commodity provided by the largest companies. Concept 2 recognizes that automobiles, buses, and trucks generally are produced and distributed by the same companies, often with the same facilities. Some persons might consider this an industry concept, although in Bureau of the Census terminology it is a combination of certain "product classes."

Concept 3 corresponds to the census basis for measuring 1947 concentration in 440 of the 452 industries recognized in tabulations for that year. In measuring concentration, it serves as a substitute for 2. Sometimes it is a poor substitute, for reasons described by Conklin and Goldstein. However, the Bureau of the Census no longer recognizes a motor-vehicle industry, presumably because important integrated producers cannot develop satisfactory estimates of their production of motor-vehicle parts. For the motor-vehicle and parts industry, which it does recognize, value added by manufacture is used instead of value of shipments plus interplant transfers, since the motor-parts fraction of the latter would be counted again in the value of the assembled motor vehicles. This is concept 4. It gives weight to integration within a limited area of the motor vehicles industry, although it is not a complete measure of the extent to which motor-vehicle producers are integrated, even in that segment of their business classified as manufacturing.

Concept 5 is a measure of "total economic strength or productive potential."[5] So also is concept 6, which is identical in coverage but employs a different criterion of size.[6] In this they should be dis-

[5] *Ibid.*, p. 12.

[6] M. A. Adelman, among others, has urged total assets as preferable to net capital assets. The issues are developed in "The Measurement of Industrial Concentration," *Review of Economics and Statistics*, November 1951; John M. Blair, "The Measurement of Industrial Concentration: A Reply," and M. A. Adelman, "Rejoinder," both in *Review of Economics and Statistics*, November 1952.

tinguished sharply from concepts 1, 2, and 3, which are measures of the share of the supply actually accounted for by the largest producers. According to the reasoning of the FTC in presenting this report, a very large company may affect competition in its major line of activity not only through its current participation but also because of the other resources upon which it may draw. In many instances a very large company could transfer establishments currently engaged in other lines to the production of its principal product. Such reserve capacity is a significant circumstance, according to some students of oligopoly.[7] Establishments not susceptible to such a transfer generally bear a "vertical" relationship to the manufacture of the company's principal product: they supply materials and components, perform additional processing for certain end uses, distribute or service the product, or perhaps utilize by-products of the main operation. Ownership of such establishments may be a source of strength to a large company in its major line of activity.[8]

The Commission did not extend the analysis to the petroleum industry or to other industries where "capital assets . . . significant in relation to the size of the corporation [were considered to] contribute only indirectly to the corporation's position in the industry, and are not convertible to the industry in which the corporation is classified."[9] Also excluded were industries where one of the leading

[7] "A large corporation's productive equipment which is engaged in turning out products in 'other' industries may be convertible to the industry in which the corporation is classified. As was so strikingly illustrated by the experience of World War II, a very large proportion of modern technology is highly flexible and convertible. Hence, from the point of view of measuring a large corporation's productive potential, it might be unrealistic to exclude from the industry in which the corporation is classified that portion of its equipment which happens at the moment to be engaged in an 'outside' industry, but which could be quickly converted to the industry in which the corporation is classified." *The Concentration of Productive Facilities, 1947*, as cited, p. 10.

[8] The Commission cited as an example the ore boats of a large metal refiner, *ibid.*, pp. 9-10. A more recent report of the FTC staff describes the importance of vertical integration in certain situations: *Monopolistic Practices and Small Business*, 1952, pp. 21, 39.

[9] *Ibid.*, p. 11. Ratios on the primary steel industry were published only after comparison with industry data on capacity suggested that such limitations would not result in any serious overstatement of concentration. The Commission also relied on a special tabulation of the returns of the fifty largest manufacturing companies in the Census of 1937. As summarized by the staff of the Temporary National Economic Committee (TNEC), this tabulation (which suppressed the identity of companies and industries) showed that "the major portion of the total value of products of those companies was accounted for by the value contribution of relatively few products." Willard L. Thorp and Walter F. Crowder, *The Structure of Industry*, TNEC Monograph 27, 1941, Part VI, p. 609.

companies was classified in another industry, and industries where "specialization by one leading company on certain products, . . . by a second leader on other products, and so on, was so extreme that the figures for the industry as a whole were not significant."[10] The ratios published were "no more than estimates. . . . Errors, however, probably do not exceed a few percentage points. . . ."[11]

Thus for all economists who have occasion to construct measures of concentration, or to use measures developed by others, the Conklin-Goldstein paper is both an admonition and an aid. It is a warning that not all concentration ratios can be interpreted in the same way; it is a warning also that some data can contribute little to the measurement of concentration. The paper is valuable as a reference on the use of the Bureau's data on manufactures and on the interpretation of measures of concentration developed from such data.

But it seems to me that this informative paper holds lessons for producers of data as well as for consumers of data. For example, the comments on beet sugar and cane sugar and on tin cans and glass containers point up our lack of a description of the participation of an enterprise across many industries. Tabulations are desirable that would indicate the extent to which substitute commodities are (and are not) produced by the same companies, the proportion of the supply of a raw material that is captive to specific consuming industries, and the proportion of still other industries controlled by the companies producing their principal raw materials. Within recent months an encouraging beginning has been made on this problem by the Bureau of the Census in cooperation with the FTC. A still wider description of enterprises is desirable than can be afforded by a study of manufacturing alone. The concurrent censuses of the mineral industries, manufacturing, and trade in 1954 provide the opportunity for valuable tabulations. It is to be hoped that the Bureau is not denied the resources to derive from these censuses a description of the major structural features of our economy. Business decisions are made by *firms*, and the Bureau's publications will be made much more useful by explicitly recognizing that firms do not confine themselves to a single establishment, or to establishments in a single industry.

There is ample reason for revising many heterogeneous categories—both industries and product groups. Of the general characteristics of an industry named by Conklin and Goldstein—competi-

10 *The Concentration of Productive Facilities, 1947*, as cited, p. 14.
11 *Ibid.*, p. 13.

tive nature of products, competitive nature of firms, similarity of method of manufacture, similarity of facilities, "other physical or technological factors" (among them, presumably, significant size and sufficient enterprises to permit publication of data), and historical precedent—there are numerous cases in which historical precedent and a generalized complementarity of products seem the principal elements of cohesion. This observation deals only incidentally with the n.e.c., or "not elsewhere classified," genre. Such categories are inescapable, and cause difficulties only when one or more types of establishment in a given residual assume the importance of a separate industry. Food preparation, not elsewhere classified, with 1951 shipments exceeding $2 billion, is overdue for attention.[12] So also are four other n.e.c. industries with shipments exceeding $1 billion, and nine with shipments of less than $1 billion but more than $1/2 billion.

Given the industry concept, the problem that led to the "resistance factor technique" is inevitable once sampling is substituted for complete enumeration. This technique is the practice described by Conklin and Goldstein of not reclassifying an establishment to reflect a change in its primary activity where the discrepancy thereby introduced in the current level of the industry is smaller than the discrepancy avoided in the industry trend.[13] The fatal weakness of the present technique is that the entire body of industry data developed by a survey is incapable of interpretation. A better policy would be to return the industry to the Standard Industrial Classification concept, and to introduce a new concept, the "historical industry," in which all establishments would retain the same classification as in the last census year. An alternative is to abandon the publication of the survey data on industries appreciably affected by shifts in the primary activity of establishments, and to place greater emphasis on obtaining product statistics, which are not affected by the "resistance" problem.

The greater success of the 1951 and 1952 surveys in developing statistics on product classes than the 1950 or 1949 survey is most encouraging. Yet even for 1952, data are lacking for half the classes,

12 About two-thirds of the output of this "industry" is roasted coffee. Other important products are peanut butter, ground spices, ready-to-mix desserts, potato chips, and sweetening syrup and molasses.

13 Establishments with less than 100 employees have been continued in their 1947 industry without review. While there is little likelihood of such establishments shifting into or out of most industries, dairy and apparel industries would seem to be important exceptions.

47

and for many of the categories on which figures are supplied the standard errors are so large that the data are practically useless. In this situation the data on product class groups[14] are most welcome, but even these are not available for a third of the groups, and among those for which data are available the estimates frequently are subject to large standard errors.[15] Product statistics—detailed, current, and reasonably accurate—are important in so many ways that the Bureau of the Census should have vigorous support in its efforts to improve this phase of the annual survey of manufacture.

Daniel B. Suits, University of Michigan

THE proper evaluation of classifications can only be made in terms of the objective to be achieved by the use of the resulting classes, and different objectives generally require different classifications. These comments are restricted to classifications suitable for the measurement of concentration on the supply side of the market.

There are a number of attributes or yard sticks—capital, employment, sales, value added, production, etc.—by which we can, at least ideally, obtain a magnitude for each of a set of economic units (firms, establishments) and a total for the set. This total can then be compared with the total for any given subset of the units (the largest one, the four largest, etc.) or the magnitudes of the individual units may be somehow distributed and analyzed. But these measures and the concentration analysis based on them are not, so to speak, meaningful in their own right. They are, rather, indirect ways to approach the measure of something else, which we may call economic power over a market. They derive whatever validity

14 A "product class group" covers all products primary to a given industry. Thus, conceptually, there is a product class group corresponding to each industry recognized in census statistics. In the margarine example presented by Conklin and Goldstein, $237 million is the 1947 value of shipments of the product class group margarine, whereas $215 million is the value of shipments of the margarine industry. In this instance, margarine is the only product class in the group, but commonly there are several classes. For example, the product class group "canned and preserved products, except fish and meat" has nine product classes: canned fruits; canned vegetables and specialties; canned fruit juices; canned vegetable juices; canned baby foods; canned soups and poultry products; jams, jellies and preserves; and bulk fruit and vegetable juices.

15 For product classes, 158 of the 633 estimates are subject to a standard error of from 6 to 10 per cent of the estimate, and 118 estimates are subject to a standard error of 15 per cent. For product class groups, estimates are available for 154 categories where a group consists of more than one product class. Of these, 48 are subject to a standard error of 6 to 10 per cent, and 16 are subject to a standard error of 15 per cent.

they have from the extent to which they succeed in representing a given output market completely and to the exclusion of other output markets.

If each firm or establishment commonly exercised influence in only one market, the problems of defining product market classes and industrial classes would be the same. Unfortunately under any reasonable definition many establishments—not to say firms—participate in a number of different markets. Thus the appropriate classification of firms or establishments into industries involves a somewhat greater measure of adjustment and compromise than the classification of products into markets, which in turn does not lend itself to the ideal results we might prefer to obtain.

The appropriate classification of products is based on the competitive relations which hold among them. These competitive relations are not fixed, but change over time with alteration of productive techniques, consumer tastes, the introduction of new products, and doubtless in some cases the general level of business activity. Moreover, the competitive relations among products and firms differ in the long run, in which ultimately almost any firm is a competitor of any other, and the short run in which productive facilities are by and large fixed. It is the latter on which any given census focuses attention; thus our objective is a classification that will group together the products of rival productive facilities.

The commodity is merely the physical "embodiment" of the service of the establishment. The economic power possessed by an establishment inheres in the service it can provide, and to measure this service purely on the basis of the particular application being made of it at a given moment would be clearly wrong. Thus close technical substitutes, which are literally alternative embodiments of the same service, should be classified in the same product market. For example, a particular die-casting establishment that produces refrigerator door handles at one time and automobile radiator ornaments at another is part of a market in which similar facilities compete with each other over a wide range of uses. An appropriate classification of products must recognize these alternatives and identify them with a single market class of products.

There are, of course, all degrees of technical versatility and some recognition must be given this fact. Ideally we can conceive of using some minimum level of the elasticity of technical substitution as a criterion. Unfortunately, the basis on which to estimate these elasticities is seldom available and we are restricted to more readily observable characteristics of products. Two products can be considered technical substitutes if they are commonly produced in substantial amounts in the same establishment, by essentially the same equipment, technical process, and labor, and among which frequent variations in the proportion of output are observable. The existing census emphasis on the technical structure of production is a reflection of this criterion. Likewise, of course, it is the fact of technical substitutability that justifies our disposition to consider products of differing sizes and specifications as constituting a single market class. On the other hand we would consider as distinct two products found in the same establishments but produced by distinct technical processes. Variation among them represents alternative uses of working capital, but not of the fixed facilities themselves. Nor would joint products, appearing in effectively fixed proportions, generally be considered the same product. The establishments compete in the production of the output combinations, but frequently each product enters competition with others that are not subject to the same technical restriction. Cottonseed oil and cottonseed cake and meal, for example, each have important competitors and are therefore distinct. Where the several joint products do not have important "outside" rivals, however, they need not be separated.

The second way in which services substitute for one another is, of course, through the production of substitute products. Market classes should not distinguish among the production of different commodities that are close substitutes to the consumer. Ideally the appropriate measure here would be the cross-elasticity of demands among products, but again we must have reference to more readily observable criteria. Those commodities serving generally similar purposes, and among which users are frequently observed to vary the proportions of their purchases in response to price variations, may be defined as consumer substitutes.

Broad classes of products may be set apart "by eye," but final determination requires intimate technical knowledge of the structure of production, the nature of products and their uses, and familiarity with the habits of their consumers. It would obviously be of advantage if less subjective criteria could be applied, and substitutes identified by the behavior of their prices, sales, margins, etc., as actually observed in the market. The difficulties, however, are considerable, as the following example suggests.

The fact that the prices of close consumer substitutes should move together might serve as a necessary criterion for classification.

It is obviously not *sufficient* since prices may be kept together by substantial common cost elements, or even move together quite fortuitously. The absolute levels of most prices are highly correlated over wide cyclical changes, but the behavior of the price ratios can be analyzed.

In order to obtain a measure of price variation that is unaffected by the absolute levels of the prices and that also gives the same result no matter which price is selected as the denominator of the ratio, the coefficient of variation of the log of the price ratio is taken.[1]

In Table 1, ten commodity pairs are ranked in order of the stability of their price ratios. The two top ranking pairs—Texas and

TABLE 1

Variation in Price Ratios, Selected Pairs of Commodities, 1913-1939

Commodity Pair	Coefficient of Variation of Log of Price Ratio (Per Cent)
Packers' steer hides, native } Packers' steer hides, Texas }	1.7
Men's tan dress welt shoes, calf leather[a] } Men's tan dress welt shoes, side leather }	1.7[a]
Electrolytic copper ingot } #8 bare copper wire }	4.2
American medium salt } Granulated bulk salt }	6.2
6-foot crosscut saws } Granulated bulk salt }	8.4
Oleomargarine, white, Chicago } Butter, extra firsts, Chicago }	9.0
Bone black } Lamp black }	11.0
Currants } Raisins }	12.1
One-horse walking plows } Southern single warp cotton yarn }	12.9
Packers' steer hides, Texas } American medium salt }	21.2

[a] 1913-1929.
Source: Prices are Bureau of Labor Statistics wholesale prices.

native steer hides, and calf-leather and side-leather men's shoes— are, of course, close consumer substitutes, but are also closely related in production. They are followed by the production-related,

[1] The coefficient of variation is the standard deviation measured as a per cent of the mean. Thus it is unaffected by absolute levels. Using the log of the price ratios frees the measurement of the objection that price ratios are necessarily bounded at zero, but have no upper bound.

nonsubstitute pair, copper ingot–copper wire. Oleomargarine–butter shows slightly more price variability than bulk salt–crosscut saws, while bone black–lamp black and currant–raisins show only slightly less variability than one-horse plows–cotton yarn. A much greater number of price ratios would need to be examined before the merit of the method could be assessed, but it is clear that the behavior of quantities, production costs, and other data must be incorporated in the analysis before price behavior can be adequately tested.

Ideally we might hope to apply the criterion of substitutability to partition the universe of commodities into mutually exclusive classes so that (1) any pair of close substitutes fall in the same class and, (2) any two commodities in the same class are a pair of close substitutes. The first objective can always be achieved. It would, indeed, be satisfied by summarily lumping all goods in a single class. Moreover, forming the maximum number of product classes for which (1) will hold true will carry us a considerable way toward the attainment of (2). But the complete satisfaction of the second objective is not necessarily possible.

The difficulty is easily explained in terms of the logic of relations. In order to satisfy both (1) and (2) the relation "close substitute for" must, among other things be transitive.[2] That is if A and B and B and C constitute two pairs of close substitutes, it must follow that A and C are close substitutes.

Even among consumer substitutes, this transitivity does not always hold. Commodities are often arranged in "chains" where each is a close substitute for its immediate neighbors, but the nearness of substitution becomes less as we compare a given good with those farther away.[3]

When we have both consumer and producer substitutes, the difficulty is even greater. If A is a close technical substitute for B, while B is a close consumer substitute for C, A and C need bear no direct substitute relationship to each other, while the relationship between A and some fourth good, a close technical substitute for C, may be even more tenuous.

The magnitude of this problem should not be exaggerated. The

[2] The substitute relation must also be reflexive (any good is a close substitute for itself) and symmetrical (if A is a good substitute for B, then B is a good substitute for A). The three properties taken together mean that the relation "close substitute for" is an equivalence relation, i.e. that it will produce precisely the partitioning of the universe of commodities that we want.

[3] An obvious example of this in another context arises in spatial competition.

merit of discussing the underlying logic of classification derives from the light shed on the process of formulating and evaluating the most useful classes for the purpose at hand. If strict application of the criterion of substitution yields classes that are too heterogeneous, we can frequently subdivide them. This will put some substitute commodities in separate classes, and what is gained by increased homogeneity must be balanced against this loss. Wherever a relatively small amount of production serves as a bridge between two large and otherwise unrelated classes we are clearly justified in subdividing the classes. Where this is not the case, the balance of advantage probably lies with retaining the larger class as a whole.

The decision is again based on subjective considerations, but we can push them back a stage by making a class subject to subdivision if it contains a product which (1) if completely ignored would result in an increase in the number of market classes and (2) if its whole production were assigned to either of the resulting classes the measure of output concentration employed would not be substantially affected.

Aside from the considerable technical knowledge required, there is no reason why such a system of product classes could not be built up from census product detail. Census product classes on the most detailed level (e.g., bottled soft drinks, carbonated, containing kola extract; emulsified asphalt paving materials; builders' door locks, lock sets, and lock trim; etc.) are quite clearly suitable elements for such classification. In fact many of the larger census "bold face total" classes (e.g., soft drinks, total; paving mixtures and blocks, total; etc.) are themselves internally homogeneous with respect to substitution. On the other hand, even at the "bold face total" level there are classes which are not. (Professional furniture, total, includes both hospital bed springs and laboratory cabinets and cases, which are not close substitutes in either sense.) In some cases even those product classes that explicitly define census industries are elementary in this sense, but in general the system of classes must be built up from product classifications below the census industry level.

Where economic concentration is to be related to other variables obtainable only on a firm or establishment basis, the economic units themselves must be classified into industries which follow as closely as possible the lines of the product classes. This is done by assigning each establishment or firm to the industry in which the greatest portion of its output falls.

It is evident that industries based on market classes defined as above will differ somewhat from the existing census classification. In particular, establishments separated by the census solely on the basis of the material or technical process employed would appear in a single class. Moreover, although census emphasis on technical similarity tends to cause establishments in a single census industry to fall together in the "new" classification, doubtless some of them would be pulled apart. Even here, however, we should probably find that in most cases the readjustment of industry boundaries required to obtain adequate levels of homogeneity and coverage would result in their recombination.

The problems surrounding homogeneity and coverage arise primarily out of the nature of the firm's activities themselves and are not materially altered by changing the system of classification employed. An acceptable industry must be one for which both homogeneity and coverage, measured in terms of the products that define them, are high. Given fixed product classes, homogeneity and coverage tend to behave inversely. We can always increase the coverage of an industry by transferring into it establishments originally classified in other industries, but we generally do so at the expense of homogeneity. Where raw industrial classes must be adjusted, some compromise between the measures must be accepted.

It is this fact that would probably tend to recombine census industries which the strict application of product classification would split. A group of establishments, most of which were engaged in some production of each of two nonsubstitute commodities, would be split between the two classes involved. If, however, there are no other important substitutes for these commodities, combining the two raw classes would yield an industry of high coverage in terms of either product, while the homogeneity of the combination with respect to either product would be only slightly lower than when taken over the separate raw groups. As a matter of fact, I suspect that we would be disposed in such case to question the usefulness of the product distinction itself and combine the two sets of products into a single class.

In any case, the areas in which meaningful industry classifications are difficult or impossible to attain are precisely those in which existing census classifications are least meaningful, and for exactly the same reason. These are areas in which integrated and nonintegrated production are both common. Classification on the basis of substitutability of product only formally removes the distinction between integrated production and production carried on with purchased materials. Semifinished and finished products are substitute items of sale to the establishment producing both, but they are in no sense close substitutes in production. The integrated establishment clearly belongs in two distinct industries and whether classification is by the finished or the semifinished product, the result is unacceptable. We can gain high coverage or homogeneity in one industry only at the expense of a low measure in the other, and combining both reduces the homogeneity measure well below what could be obtained from either.

Ultimately, getting usable industry classifications in these areas depends on our ability to redefine establishments and obtain meaningful data from their separate departments. Where this cannot be done, the only alternative is to restrict our analysis of concentration in these areas to product data.

MEASURES OF CONCENTRATION

GIDEON ROSENBLUTH
QUEEN'S UNIVERSITY

A VARIETY of indexes of concentration have been used in the description and analysis of industrial structures. We shall review some of these measures, discussing their formal properties, their empirical relations to one another, and some of the significant economic findings that can be obtained with their help.

1. Main Classes of Indexes

THE term "economic concentration" has been employed in many different senses, and "indexes of concentration" have been constructed to measure a number of quite distinct characteristics of industrial structure. Our discussion will center on those indexes of concentration that measure the extent to which a small *number* of firms account for a large *proportion* of an industry's output. This definition is somewhat vague since it involves two variables, but it is sufficiently precise to permit a discussion of its economic significance and to distinguish it from other concepts of concentration.

Economic theory suggests that concentration as defined here is an important determinant of market behavior and market results. *Ceteris paribus,* monopolistic practices are more likely where a small number of the leading firms account for the bulk of an industry's output than where even the largest firms are of relatively small importance. Hence, in the explanation of business policy, the characteristics of an industry expressed in the concentration index are likely to play an important part. This relation to the degree of monopoly has motivated most of the empirical studies involving the measurement of concentration.[1]

[1] In some studies, however, concentration has been measured for large sectors of the economy that cannot be regarded as relevant to the problem of *market* behavior. The measurement by Gardiner C. Means of the importance of the largest 200 corporations in relation to the economy as a whole is perhaps the best-known example of an index of this type. A. A. Berle and G. C. Means, *The Modern Corporation and Private Property* (Macmillan, 1932), Bk. I, Chap. III. The significance of this index must be sought in theories that are broader in scope than the conventional economic analysis. The belief that democracy cannot survive where economic power is concentrated was cited by President Roosevelt as one of the bases for the investigations of the Temporary National Economic Committee (*S. Doc.* 173, 75th Cong., 3d Sess.), and probably implies the same concept of concentration as Mean's measure. The belief that the operation of an

57

It is not difficult for any imaginative investigator to develop a great many indexes to measure concentration in the general sense defined above. Our discussion will, however, be confined to measures that have actually been put to use in analyses of substantial bodies of statistical data.

A basic and very useful device for the description of concentration is the "concentration curve" used in the studies of the Federal Trade Commission.[2] The height of the curve above any point x on the horizontal axis measures the percentage of the industry's total size accounted for by the largest x firms. (Size of firms and industry may be measured in terms of output, employment, assets, or other variables.) The curve is therefore continuously rising from left to right, but rises at a continuously diminishing rate. It reaches its maximum height—100 per cent—at a point on the horizontal axis corresponding to the total number of firms in the industry (or making a product).

Three concentration curves are shown in Chart 1. A short, high curve indicates "high concentration," while a low-lying, long curve indicates "low concentration." When two curves cross, however, the lack of precision in our definition of concentration becomes apparent, and without refining the definition one cannot say which of them represents higher concentration.

The indexes measuring concentration as defined above are easily related to this curve. The most frequently encountered class of indexes can be represented by the height of the concentration curve above a given point on the horizontal axis. Thus, the percentage of output or employment accounted for by the leading four firms or the leading eight firms has been used in the analysis of American data,[3] and the percentage of output accounted for by the leading three firms has been used in Great Britain.[4]

---

independent personal business is a generally desirable way of life has been one of the motivations of antitrust legislation and of the special concern of government with "small business," and has prompted the measurement of "over-all concentration" as an indication of the portion of the economy closed to small business. This paper will not be concerned with such "broad" measures of concentration.

[2] See, for example, *The Concentration of Productive Facilities, 1947*, Federal Trade Commission, 1949, and *The Divergence Between Plant and Company Concentration, 1947*, FTC, 1950.

[3] E.g., *The Structure of the American Economy, Part 1*, National Resources Committee, 1939, Appendix 7; *Concentration of Industry Report*, Dept. of Commerce, 1949.

[4] H. Leak and A. Maizels, "The Structure of British Industry," *Journal of the Royal Statistical Society*, Vol. 108 (1945), pp. 142-199.

Instead of measuring the height of the concentration curve at a given horizontal distance from the origin, we can measure the horizontal distance to the curve at a given height. This is an inverse measure of concentration, increasing in numerical value as concen-

Chart 1

Concentration of Net Capital Assets, Three Industries, United States, 1947

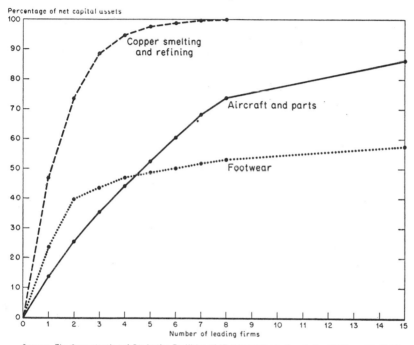

Source: *The Concentration of Productive Facilities, 1947*, Federal Trade Commission, 1949, pp. 28, 47, 79.

tration decreases. Thus, the number of plants required to account for 50 per cent of employment has been used by W. L. Thorp in a study for the Temporary National Economic Committee (TNEC)[5] and the writer has used the number of firms required to account for 80 per cent of employment in a study of industrial concentration in Canada.

These two classes of indexes can be criticized on the ground that they depend on only one point on the concentration curve, so that

[5] Willard L. Thorp and Walter F. Crowder, *The Structure of Industry*, TNEC Monograph 27, 1941, Part I.

there are many changes in the position of the curve that leave the index unchanged. The lack of a summary measure utilizing all points on the curve has therefore been lamented[6] and even offered as an argument for using a different concept of concentration.[7] But summary measures can be devised to measure concentration, just as they have been developed for other characteristics of size distributions. An ingenious measure of this type has been employed by O. C. Herfindahl in an investigation of concentration in the steel industry. It consists of the sum of squares of firm sizes, all measured as percentages of total industry size. This index is equal to the reciprocal of the number of firms if all firms are of the same size, and reaches its maximum value of unity when there is only one firm in the industry.[8]

These are the classes of measures that will be investigated in this paper. There is, however, an important class of concentration indexes that do not conform to our concept of concentration. The well-known Lorenz curve measures the cumulative percentages of output accounted for by various *percentages* of the number of firms.[9] Gini's concentration ratio is a function of the area between the Lorenz curve and the diagonal line the curve would follow if all firms were of equal size. It thus measures the extent to which a small *percentage* of all firms account for a large percentage of output, and does not measure concentration in our sense. The characteristic described by Gini's ratio and the Lorenz curve is often called "inequality," and that usage will be followed here, although some writers identify inequality as "relative" concentration and refer to concentration as defined by us as "absolute" concentration.[10]

[6] J. M. Blair, "Statistical Measures of Concentration in Business, Problems of Compiling and Interpretation" (paper presented at the Annual Convention of the American Statistical Association, December 29, 1950).

[7] J. Lintner and J. K. Butters, "Effect of Mergers on Industrial Concentration, 1940-1947," *Review of Economics and Statistics*, February 1950, p. 46.

[8] Orris C. Herfindahl, "Concentration in the Steel Industry" (Ph.D. dissertation, Columbia University, 1950). It should be noted that "summary" is a somewhat ambiguous term, and that in an important sense the measures based on intercepts of the concentration curve are also "summary measures." For example, a change in the size of any one firm will affect all such indexes as well as Herfindahl's index. It is true that many concentration curves and many values of Herfindahl's index are compatible with, say, the concentration of a given percentage of output in the leading four firms. But it is also true that many different values of the percentage concentrated in the leading four firms are compatible with a given value of Herfindahl's index.

[9] M. O. Lorenz, "Methods of Measuring Concentration of Wealth," *Journal of the American Statistical Association*, June 1905, pp. 209-319.

[10] Lintner and Butters, *loc. cit.*

Inequality is also identified with concentration in the work of R. Gibrat, who measures inequality of income-size distributions by the standard deviation of a normal curve fitted to the logarithms of income[11] and defines concentration as inequality of firm size.[12] There are many other measures of inequality, either based on intercepts of the Lorenz curve or summarizing the whole size distribution, and their properties have received more careful study, mainly in connection with the distribution of incomes, than has been devoted to the concentration indexes.[13]

Inequality is of course related to concentration, and an understanding of their relation is important. Given the number of firms, concentration increases with an increase in inequality; and given the degree of inequality, concentration decreases with an increase in the number of firms.[14] This proposition can be demonstrated in various ways. It follows directly from our definition of concentration as the extent to which a small *number* of firms account for a large percentage of output, and of inequality as the extent to which a small *percentage* of the firms account for a large percentage of output. The lack of precision in both definitions does not affect the precise relation between them. A consideration of the relation between the concentration curve and the Lorenz curve demonstrates the same proposition. The only difference between the two curves is that the first measures the cumulative number of firms along the

[11] Or the logarithms of the deviation of income from a given minimum.

[12] R. Gibrat, *Les inégalités économiques* (Librairie du Recueil Sirey, 1931), p. 206: "La concentration se définit et se mesure comme l'inégalité de répartition des entreprises suivant leur importance."

[13] Cf. Dwight B. Yntema, "Measures of Inequality in the Personal Distribution of Wealth and Income," *Journal of the American Statistical Association*, December 1933, p. 423.

[14] This algebraic relation among the three variables also implies, of course, that given the degree of concentration, inequality increases with an increase in the number of firms. It is not surprising, therefore, that some writers in this field have asserted that concentration is not affected by the number of firms but that inequality is so affected, while others have asserted the opposite. Mathematically, either statement can be correct if the right variable is held constant.

The misleading notion that measures of concentration are not affected by the number of firms arises in part from the fact that it is possible to calculate, for example, the percentage of output accounted for by the largest x firms without knowing the total number of firms (while this is not in general possible for measures of inequality). This is of great practical importance where complete and accurate statistics are not available. Many industries contain a large number of very small firms, so that total industry output (and hence the percentage accounted for by the leading four) can be estimated with great accuracy from a sample, while the total number of firms could be ascertained only at great cost.

horizontal axis, while the latter measures the cumulative percentage of firms.[15] Hence, if we compare two industries with the same number of firms any difference in their concentration curves must reflect a difference in their Lorenz curves. On the other hand, if we compare two industries with the same Lorenz curves, any difference in their concentration curves must reflect a difference in the number of firms, the industry with more firms having a longer and lower-lying concentration curve.[16]

A third class of concentration measures indicates neither concentration nor inequality as we have defined these concepts, but rather average firm size. In the study entitled *Economic Concentration and World War II*,[17] for example, the plants of an industry are grouped by size classes, size being measured in terms of employment, and the rising percentage of employment in the large-size classes is cited as showing increasing concentration. It is not quite clear whether the authors of this study (and others who have used similar data) have in mind a concept of concentration similar to ours and have made an error in their method of measurement, or whether they have in mind a concept of concentration that identifies it with absolute size. Again, there is, of course, a relation between these concepts. Given the size of the industry, a larger average firm size means fewer firms, and given the degree of inequality of firm size, fewer

[15] The original Lorenz curve measured the cumulative percentage of income on the horizontal axis and the cumulative percentage of the number of incomes on the vertical axis. Moreover, it started with the lowest incomes, while the concentration curve starts with the largest firms. By simply changing the axes and replacing x per cent by $100 - x$ per cent this curve can be transformed into one identical with the concentration curve except for the difference mentioned in the text.

[16] This relation between inequality and concentration can also be shown algebraically in terms of the three types of concentration indexes discussed above.

a. Herfindahl's summary index can be shown, by simple algebraic manipulation, to be equal to $(c^2 + 1) \div n$ where c is the coefficient of variation (standard deviation divided by mean) and n is the number of firms.

b. The index measuring the *number* of firms required to account for x per cent of output is equal to the total number of firms multiplied by the index measuring the percentage of firms required to account for x per cent of output. Here the indexes measure concentration and inequality inversely, so that, again, concentration increases with inequality and decreases with the number of firms.

c. The index measuring the percentage of output accounted for by the leading k firms is equal to $k \ (a/A) \div n$ where a is the average size of the leading k firms, A is the average size of all firms, and (a/A) can be regarded as a measure of inequality of firm size.

[17] *Economic Concentration and World War II*, Report of Smaller War Plants Corporation before Special Committee on Small Business, S. Doc. 206, 79th Cong., 2d Sess., 1946.

firms mean higher concentration. Hence one can say that, *ceteris paribus*, larger firms mean higher concentration. This is in fact frequently said, and the *cetera* are almost as frequently forgotten.

It is reasonable to assume that concentration as we have defined it is more directly relevant than either inequality or average firm size to problems of monopoly and business policy. An index of inequality may tell us that 10 per cent of the firms in an industry control 95 per cent of output, but it does not tell us whether this 10 per cent consists of one firm or perhaps a hundred firms, and surely a competitive pattern of behavior is much more likely in the latter case than in the former. Similarly, the size distribution may tell us that 95 per cent of employment is in firms with over 1,000 employees each, but there may be one such firm or there may be many, depending on the size of the industry, and the likelihood of competition will vary accordingly. In the extreme case in which one firm has a monopoly of the whole output, concentration will reach its maximum value, but inequality will be nil, and firm size may be large or small, as the industry may be large or small.

Concentration is not, of course, the only determinant of the degree of monopoly and perhaps not even the only relevant characteristic of an industry's size structure. Stigler has shown that the number of firms that are larger than a given percentage of the leading firm size *and* account for more than a given percentage of the industry is correlated with price flexibility.[18] Another variable that has been suggested is the height of the point on the concentration curve at which its second difference reaches a minimum. At this point the difference between successive firm sizes is greatest.[19] This measure may have some importance in those industries in which there are a few "giants" separated by a wide gap in size from the remaining firms in the industry, but many concentration curves do not have such a point at all.

2. Choice of an Index

WHILE elementary theoretical considerations suggest the relevance of our concept of concentration to the study of monopoly and business policy, they do not enable us to discriminate among the various indexes that have been used. The choice of measure may affect the outcome of an investigation since the different indexes involve dif-

[18] George J. Stigler, "The Kinky Oligopoly Curve and Rigid Prices," *Journal of Political Economy*, October 1947, p. 444.
[19] Cf. Blair, *op. cit.*, p. 8.

ferent scales of measurement, and even the ranking of observations by concentration level may vary with the index used. For example, in 1947 the percentage of fixed assets accounted for by the leading three firms was higher in cigarettes than in motor vehicles, but the percentage accounted for by the largest firm alone was higher in motor vehicles than in cigarettes.[20] In order to select one index as superior to others for a given purpose, careful empirical tests of carefully formulated hypotheses regarding the effects of concentration must be undertaken, and very little such work has been done to date. The research worker using any one of these indexes will therefore want to know how much his results might be altered by the use of another index. We shall examine this problem by comparing the behavior of various indexes when they are applied to the same body of data.

Our first exhibit is a comparison of concentration as measured by the percentage of fixed assets accounted for by the largest firm and the largest two, three, and four firms in a cross section of twenty-six industries for which data were published by the FTC.[21] The rankings of the industries by concentration level are compared in Table 1. It is evident that while many industries change their position in the array as the concentration index is changed, the general pattern remains the same. An industry with a "high" percentage of assets concentrated in the largest firm, in comparison with other industries, does not in general have a "low" percentage of assets concentrated in the largest two, three, or four firms. The similarity of patterns can be summarized by means of rank correlation coefficients. The Spearman correlation coefficients for the various pairs of rankings are as follows:

	CONCENTRATION IN		
	Largest Two Firms	Largest Three Firms	Largest Four Firms
Concentration in largest firm	.966	.924	.914
Concentration in largest two firms		.961	.939
Concentration in largest three firms			.984

The correlation among indexes of this type based on vertical intercepts of the concentration curve will of course decline as the distance between the two intercepts increases, but the above coefficients are all fairly high. Even when the number of the leading firms on which the index is based is well above four, a high correlation is

20 *The Concentration of Productive Facilities: 1947*, as cited, Table 3, p. 21.
21 *Ibid.*

TABLE 1

Ranking of Industries according to the Percentage of Net Capital Assets
Controlled by the Largest Firms, United States, 1947

Industry	Largest Firm (1)	Largest Two Firms (2)	Largest Three Firms (3)	Largest Four Firms (4)
Linoleum	1	3	3	4
Tin cans, etc.	2	1	2	2
Aluminum	3	2	1	1
Copper smelting and refining	4	4	4	3
Biscuits, etc.	5	8	11	11
Agricultural machinery	6	9	12	8
Office machinery	7	10	9	9½
Motor vehicles	8	7	10	12
Cigarettes	9	6	5	6
Plumbing equipment	10	5	7	9½
Distilled liquors	11	12	6	7
Meat products	12	11	13	13
Primary steel	13	16	16	17
Rubber tires	14	13	8	5
Dairy products	15	15	15	15
Glass and glassware	16	14	14	14
Carpets and rugs	17	18	17	16
Footwear	18	17	19	20
Industrial chemicals	19	19	18	18
Woolen and worsted	20	22½	24	25
Electrical machinery	21	20	20	19
Grain-mill products	22	22½	23	23
Aircraft and parts	23	21	21	21
Bread, etc.	24	25	25	24
Canning	25	24	22	22
Drugs and medicines	26	26	26	26

Source: Derived from *Report on the Concentration of Productive Facilities,
1947*, FTC, 1949, Table 3, p. 21.

obtained. This is shown by the comparison of concentration in the
largest four and eight firms in 1935 for a sample of 135 industries for
which employment-concentration indexes were published by the National Resources Committee.[22] The ranking of industries by the percentage of employment concentrated in the leading eight firms is
very similar to the ranking by the percentage of employment concentrated in the leading four firms, the correlation between the
rankings being .989.

[22] *The Structure of the American Economy*, as cited, Appendix 7, Table 1.
The sample was selected by taking every second industry in the table with a random start. Three industries for which concentration in the leading four firms
was not published and one for which concentration in the leading eight industries
was not published were omitted.

Concentration indexes belonging to three different families are compared in Table 2. The table shows, for a group of 96 Canadian manufacturing industries, estimates of (1) the percentage of employment accounted for by the leading three firms; (2) the number of firms required to account for 80 per cent of employment; (3)

TABLE 2

Comparison of Three Concentration Indexes, Selected Canadian Manufacturing Industries, 1948

Group and Industry	Index 1 Percentage of Employment Accounted for by Leading Three Firms	Index 2 Number of Firms Required to Account for 80 Per Cent of Employment	Index 3 Herfindahl's Index, Employment[a]
Foods, beverages, tobacco:			
Cigarettes, cigars, tobacco	84.5	2.1	.1797
Distilleries	84.2	2.5	.2400
Sugar refineries	68.3	4.1	.1805
Malt and malt products	66.2	3.6	.1111
Starch and glucose	64.6	4.0	.1000
Macaroni, etc.	59.9	5.6	.0714
Tobacco processing and packing	58.6	5.6	.1392
Wine	57.5	9.1	.1215
Slaughtering and meat packing	55.3	11.2	.1052
Processed cheese	49.2	7.4	.1053
Breweries	48.6	8.6	.0988
Biscuits and crackers	41.7	11.1	.0723
Condensed milk	35.6	12.0	.0377
Flour mills	34.9	22.0	.0604
Cocoa, confectionery, etc.	33.4	23.4	.0519
Fruit and vegetable preparations	32.4	72.3	.0398
Soft drinks	30.9	149.2	.0345
Bread and other bakery products	20.9	732.5	.0194
Butter and cheese factories	19.2	369.9	.0172
Prepared stock and poultry feeds	15.5	92.4	.0167
Fish curing and packing	14.9	132.5	.0175
Feed mills	3.4	469.8	.0022
Textiles, leather, fur:			
Cotton thread	94.3	1.8	.2975
Cordage, rope and twine	65.9	3.8	.1463
Carpets, mats, rugs	64.0	4.8	.1551
Belting, leather	62.2	6.5	.1435
Cotton yarn and cloth	59.8	5.1	.1317
Narrow fabrics, laces, etc.	53.8	10.3	.1085
Synthetic textiles and silk	48.7	11.3	.0945
Fur dressing and dyeing	41.1	9.1	.0852
Woolen yarn[c]	38.5	14.1	.0659
Corsets and girdles	37.1	13.9	.0654
Cotton and jute bags	36.7	12.8	.0685
Dyeing and finishing of textiles	34.3	12.9	.0635

TABLE 2 (*continued*)

Group and Industry	Index 1 Percentage of Employment Accounted for by Leading Three Firms	Index 2 Number of Firms Required to Account for 80 Per Cent of Employment	Index 3 Herfindahl's Index, Employment[a]
Woolen cloth	28.3	25.2	.0412
Tanning	26.5	19.3	.0438
Contractors, women's clothing	23.4	42.4	.0279
Leather gloves	20.9	30.5	.0311
Canvas goods	19.9	39.1	.0257
Hosiery and knitted goods	15.7	55.8	.0205
Miscellaneous leather products	13.8	80.2	.0145
Contractors, men's clothing	10.8	78.2	.0126
Boots and shoes, leather	8.5	109.6	.0087
Clothing, men's factory	8.2	155.4	.0078
Fur goods	5.6	282.1	.0040
Clothing, women's factory	4.0	517.0	.0023
Wood products:			
Excelsior	62.8	4.0	.1000
Coffins and caskets	43.4	14.5	.0759
Plywood and veneer	33.8	13.3	.0526
Flooring	32.0	12.8	.0641
Boats and canoes	17.0	92.7	.0117
Furniture	7.4	277.1	.0047
Sawmills	7.0	1,843.4	.0036
Planing mills, sash and door factories	4.6	377.0	.0035
Paper products:			
Roofing paper	60.5	6.3	.1406
Pulp and paper mills	27.8	22.5	.0448
Paper boxes and bags	16.8	57.6	.0196
Iron and Steel products:			
Pig iron	91.9[b]	2.6[b]	.2955[b]
Automobiles	87.5	1.7	.2181
Railway rolling stock	79.2	3.1	.2159
Aircraft	78.2	3.1	.2012
Steel ingots and castings	76.3[c]	3.4[c]	.2053[c]
Agricultural implements	63.4	4.4	.1377
Bicycles	80.6	2.9	.1546
Shipbuilding	32.3	13.1	.0626
Iron castings	19.8	45.9	.0267
Machine shops	6.2	229.6	.0046
Nonferrous metals:			
Aluminum	100.0 (1 firm)	.8	1.0000
Nickel	100.0 (2 firms)	.9[d]	.8957[d]
Nonmetallic minerals:			
Cement	100.0	1.2	.3333
Gypsum products	91.7	1.6	.2500

67

TABLE 2 (Continued)

Group and Industry	Index 1 Percentage of Employment Accounted for by Leading Three Firms	Index 2 Number of Firms Required to Account for 80 Per Cent of Employment	Index 3 Herfindahl's Index, Employment[a]
Glass	91.7	1.6	.2500
Artificial abrasives	86.7	2.0	.2000
Abrasive products	81.9	2.7	.1850
Petroleum products	80.1	2.99	.2195
Asbestos products	64.0	4.8	.1591
Coke products	52.7	5.7	.1204
Plate, cut, and ornamental glass	40.4	24.6	.0634
Cement products	11.7	119.2	.0118
Chemicals:			
Hardwood distillation	100.0 (2 firms)	1.0	.5000
Matches	97.9[e]	.9[e]	.8020[e]
Coal-tar distillation	91.7	1.6	.2500
Compressed gases	81.4	2.9	.2272
Soaps	74.6	4.1	.1885
Boiler compounds	66.7	3.7	.1562
Writing inks	66.3	3.8	.1629
Washing compounds	56.3	8.2	.1116
Printing inks	56.7	6.3	.1121
Vegetable oils	53.7	7.0	.1206
Polishes and dressings	36.0	12.1	.0677
Paints and varnishes	31.5	22.2	.0478
Medicinal and pharmaceutical preparations	19.7	49.4	.0238
Miscellaneous:			
Pipes and smokers' supplies	85.3	2.3	.2451
Umbrellas	83.5	2.7	.2416
Fountain pens and pencils	67.3	4.4	.1248
Buttons	48.9	8.8	.0992

a See p. 60 and footnote 8. Figures represent *minimum* estimates derived from grouped data on the assumption that firms within each size class are of equal size.

b Concentration measured in terms of blast-furnace capacity. Source: *The Primary Iron and Steel Industry, 1948*, Dominion Bureau of Statistics, Ottawa, 1949, p. 8.

c Concentration measured in terms of steel-furnace capacity. Source: *The Primary Iron and Steel Industry, 1948*, Dominion Bureau of Statistics, Ottawa, 1949, p. 13.

d Concentration measured in terms of value of sales of nickel producers. Source: *Moody's Industrials, 1949.*

e Concentration measured in terms of number of matches produced. Source: *Matches*, Report of Commissioner, Combines Investigation Act, Ottawa, Dec. 27, 1949, Ottawa, 1950.

Source: Estimates based on unpublished grouped firm-size distributions obtained from Dominion Bureau of Statistics.

Herfindahl's summary index measuring the sum of squares of firm sizes, expressed as percentages of industry size.

It is again apparent that the ordering of industries by concentration level is largely independent of the particular index employed. The Spearman rank correlation coefficient comparing indexes (1) and (2) is .981, the coefficient comparing indexes (1) and (3) is .980, and the coefficient comparing indexes (2) and (3) is .979.[23] Chart 2 is a scatter diagram of indexes (1) and (2), using a logarithmic scale

Chart 2

Comparison of Two Concentration Indexes, Selected Canadian Manufacturing Industries, 1948

x = estimated number of firms required to account for 80 per cent of employment.
y = estimated percentage of employment accounted for by leading three firms.

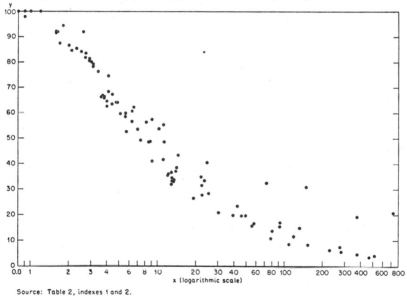

Source: Table 2, indexes 1 and 2.

for index (2). The chart indicates the close but nonlinear relation between the indexes.

These three comparisons suggest that in the analysis of cross-section data, the use of any one of the indexes considered here will result in substantially the same ordering of observations as any of the others. Analytical results that rest on the ordering of observations will not be greatly affected by the index used.

[23] The concentration indexes were estimated from unpublished firm-size distributions which were compiled by the Dominion Bureau of Statistics, Ottawa.

3. Comparison of Concentration in the United States and the United Kingdom

As AN example of the use of cross-section data on concentration we have made a comparison of the general level of concentration in the manufacturing industries of the United States and the United Kingdom. It is often said that the British economy is less competitive than that of the United States and it is of interest to see whether there is any basis for such a view in the size structure of business firms.

Reasonably comparable employment-concentration indexes for both countries are available for the year 1935.[24] The main difficulties in making a comparison are that the American indexes measure the concentration of employment in the leading four firms of each industry, while the British data deal with the leading three firms, and that the industrial classifications are not strictly comparable.

It is, of course, vital for a comparison of this sort that industries should be comparable in scope. In general, the more broadly an industry is defined, the greater will be the number of firms and the lower will be the apparent level of concentration. Inspection of the industrial classification of the United States Census of Manufactures and the United Kingdom Census of Production indicates, however, that the scope of the various "industries" is, on the whole, comparable in the two countries, although there are many differences of detail.

An over-all comparison can be made, without reconciling each individual industry classification, by studying the frequency distributions of industries by concentration level in the two countries. For this purpose the two different indexes used must be reconciled. There is of course no completely accurate method for comparing concentration in four firms with concentration in three firms, unless one knows the size of the fourth firm. We have made an estimate by calculating the straight-line regression of concentration in four firms on concentration in three firms for a group of twenty-five industries for which the necessary information was available.[25] Even

24 *The Structure of the American Economy*, as cited, *loc. cit.*, and Leak and Maizels, *loc. cit.*

25 *The Concentration of Productive Facilities*, as cited, Table 3, p. 21. One of the twenty-six industries included there is omitted from our calculation since it contains only three firms. The regression equation is $C_4 = 6.784$ per cent $+ .9913 \, C_3$ where C_4 is concentration in the leading four firms and C_3 concentration in the leading three firms, both expressed as percentages. The regression line fits the data very well, the correlation coefficient being .984. The 25 observations to which this line has been fitted range from 23.5 per cent to 95.3 per cent (con-

though the data for this regression equation are for 1947 instead of 1935 and measure asset concentration instead of employment concentration it is probably good enough for our purpose.[26] By applying the equation to the class intervals into which the British data were grouped, a comparable grouping of the American statistics could be achieved. The comparison is based on all British industries and a random sample of American industries.[27]

The results are summarized in Table 3 and Chart 3. The percentage of manufacturing industries with concentration ratios above any given level is higher in the United Kingdom than in the United States, and the same relation holds for the percentage of employ-

TABLE 3

Cumulative Frequency Distribution of Manufacturing Industries and Employment by Degree of Concentration, United States and the United Kingdom, 1935

Concentration Index[a]	Percentage of Industries		Percentage of Employment	
	U.S.	U.K.	U.S.	U.K.
Over 80	3	6	1	2
Over 70	8	13	2	7
Over 60	14	18	5	11
Over 50	22	28	14	19
Over 40	32	38	15	29
Over 30	49	57	28	46
Over 20	63	74	38	64
All industries	100	100	100	100

a Percentage of employment accounted for by leading 3 firms.

Source: For the United States, *The Structure of the American Economy, Part I*, National Resources Committee, 1939, Appendix 7, Table 1. (See footnotes 22, 27, above.) For the United Kingdom, H. Leak and A. Maizels, "The Structure of British Industry," *Journal of the Royal Statistical Society*, Vol. 108, 1945, pp. 142-199. Data for nonmanufacturing industries, as shown in Appendix XIII, were subtracted from the frequency distribution shown in Table IX.

centration in three firms). The equation cannot be expected to fit lower concentration levels, but this is not required since we group together all industries with concentration in three firms below 20 per cent and use the regression equation only to calculate the level of concentration in four firms corresponding to 20 per cent concentration in three firms.

26 The comparison of concentration in 1935 and 1947, discussed later in this paper, indicates that there has been little change in industry concentration indexes between the two dates. The application of the relation derived from fixed-asset concentration to employment concentration does not involve the assumption that asset and employment concentration are the same but only requires the weaker assumption that the difference between asset and employment concentration in four firms is .9913 times the difference between asset and employment concentration in three firms.

27 The sample is that used for the comparison of concentration in four and eight firms (note 22 above). One industry, excluded from the above comparison since concentration in eight firms was not available, is included here.

Chart 3

Cumulative Frequency Distribution of Employment in Manufacturing Industries by Degree of Concentration, United States and the United Kingdom, 1935

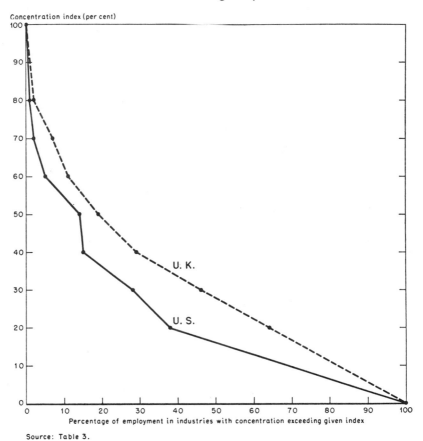

Source: Table 3.

ment. It is clear, therefore, that the general level of concentration is higher in the British industries.

The extent of the difference can be indicated in various ways. Interpolating between the values shown in Table 3, we find that the median industry has a concentration ratio of about 34 per cent in the United Kingdom and 29 per cent in the United States. Half of all employment is in industries with concentration ratios of over 28 per cent in the United Kingdom and over 16 per cent in the United States. The weighted average concentration indexes (using employment in each industry as weights) are 33 per cent for the United Kingdom and 19 per cent for the United States.

In both countries the level of concentration when judged by the cumulative distribution of employment appears considerably lower than when judged by the cumulative number of industries. This difference reflects a negative correlation between industry size and concentration level, which is generally found in cross-section data. The relation is shown more clearly in Table 4:

TABLE 4

Average Employment per Industry by Concentration Classes, United States and the United Kingdom

Concentration Index[a]	Average Number of Employees per Industry	
	U.S.	U.K.
Over 90	[b]	5,450
80–90	10,576	6,367
70–80	3,334	11,406
60–70	18,719	13,970
50–60	32,677	11,704
40–50	5,409	17,077
30–40	23,452	14,673
20–30	22,935	17,430
0–20	51,628	22,842
Average	31,275	16,397

[a] Percentage of employment accounted for by leading three firms.
[b] No industries in the U.S. sample in this class.
Source: For the United States, *The Structure of the American Economy, Part I*, National Resources Committee, 1939, Appendix 7, Table 1. (See footnotes 22, 27, above.) For the United Kingdom, H. Leak and A. Maizels, "The Structure of British Industry," *Journal of the Royal Statistical Society*, Vol. 108, 1945, pp. 142-199.

The negative correlation between industry size and concentration is not strong. It reflects the fact that on the average a large industry is more likely to have a large number of firms, and hence low concentration, than a small one.

An exact reconciliation of American and British classifications was possible for a limited number of industries, and for fifty-seven of these, concentration levels could be compared without resorting to the regression equation.[28] These industries are shown in Table 5.

[28] Since we know that the fourth firm in the United Kingdom cannot be larger than the average size of the largest three, we can be sure that United Kingdom concentration is less than United States concentration if the United Kingdom figure is less than three-fourths of the United States figure. Hence, the only cases in which a conclusive judgment is not possible are those in which the United Kingdom figure is less than the United States figure but greater than three-fourths of the United States figure.

TABLE 5

Comparison of Concentration in the United States and the United Kingdom, 1935,
57 Selected Manufacturing Industries

Industry Group (U.S. Classification, 1935)	Industry[a]	Percentage of Employment Accounted for by Leading Four Firms, U.S.	Percentage of Employment Accounted for by Leading Three Firms, U.K.
A. INDUSTRIES IN WHICH CONCENTRATION IN U.K. EXCEEDS CONCENTRATION IN U.S.			
ood and kindred products	Sugar, beet	62	72
	Liquors, distilled	50	74
	Condensed milk	44	94
	Liquors, rectified	42	57
	Flour and other grain-mill products	20	34
	Butter	19	22
	Feeds prepared for animals and fowls	15	32
	Confectionery	10	15
extiles and their products	Cordage and twine	29	32
	Rayon manufactures	19	80
	Dyeing and finishing cotton, rayon, and silk	16	24
	Knit goods	5	10
orest products	Matches	66	89
	Lumber and timber products, n.e.c.	4	7
aper and allied products	Wallpaper	46	90
rinting and publishing	Printing and publishing, newspapers	14	27
	Bookbinding	12	14
	Printing and publishing, book, music, and job	5	8
hemical and allied products	Soap	63	70
	Candles	58	77
	Fertilizers	31	34
	Perfumes, cosmetics, and other toilet preparations	18	20
	Drugs and medicines	18	19
roducts of petroleum and coal	Petroleum refining	38	82
tone, clay, and glass products	Cement	31	66
ron and steel and their products (not including machinery)	Nails, spikes, etc.	51	58
	Wrought pipe	43	71
	Gold and silver refining	49	71
lachinery, not including transportation equipment	Scales and balances	48	70
	Refrigerators and refrigerating apparatus	45	72

74

TABLE 5 (continued)

Industry Group (U.S. Classification, 1935)	Industry[a]	Percentage of Employment Accounted for by Leading Four Firms, U.S.	Percentage of Employment Accounted for by Leading Three Firms, U.K.
	Printers' machinery and equipment	30	38
	Pumps and pumping equipment	21	33
	Machine tools	14	26
B. INDUSTRIES IN WHICH CONCENTRATION IN U.S. EXCEEDS CONCENTRATION IN U.K.			
Food and kindred products	Vinegar and cider	39	13
Textiles and their products	Lace goods	33	11
	Hats, felt and straw, except millinery	29	9
Forest products	Cooperage	21	14
Chemical and allied products	Paints, pigments, and varnishes	28	16
Products of petroleum and coal	Coke-oven products	42	17
Leather products	Boots and shoes, other than rubber	21	9
Iron and steel and their products (not including machinery)	Files	83	42
	Firearms	79	49
	Saws	69	47
	Blast-furnace products	58	35
	Steel-works and rolling-mill products	46	22
	Wirework, n.e.c.	28	18
Nonferrous metals and their products	Needles, pins, hooks and eyes, and fasteners	65	30
Machinery, not including transportation equipment	Cranes, dredging and excavating machinery, etc.	34	22
Transportation equipment	Cars, electric and steam railroad	64	38
	Motor vehicles, bodies and parts	62	30
	Ship and boat building, steel and wooden, including repair	45	27
	Carriages, wagons, sleighs, and sleds	43	19
Miscellaneous industries	Optical instruments	65	13
	Musical instruments, parts and materials, piano and organ	48	24
	Umbrellas, parasols, and canes	38	18
	Sporting and athletic goods	35	22

a Names of industries as used by the Census of Manufactures: 1935.

Source: For the United Kingdom, H. Leak and A. Maizels, "The Structure of British Industry," Journal of the Royal Statistical Society, Vol. 108, 1945, Appendix III, and Final Report of the Fifth Census of Production, 1935 (4 volumes and General Summary Tables). For the United States, The Structure of the American Economy, Part I, National Resources Committee, 1939, Appendix 7, Table I, pp. 240-248, and Census of Manufactures: 1935, Industry Classification, Bureau of the Census.

Of the industries examined, thirty-three have higher concentration in the United Kingdom than in the United States, and twenty-four have higher concentration in this country. The average of concentration indexes (percentage of employment in the leading *three* firms) weighted by employment in each industry is 20 per cent for the United States and 25 per cent for the United Kingdom.[29] These findings confirm the impression gained from the over-all frequency distributions, that the level of concentration is somewhat higher in the United Kingdom.

How much of the difference in average concentration levels is due purely to differences in the relative importance of various industries in the two countries? If each industry in Britain had the concentration index of its counterpart in the United States, the weighted averages would be 20 per cent in the United States and 21 per cent in the United Kingdom. On the other hand, if each industry in the United States had the concentration index of its counterpart in the United Kingdom, the weighted averages would be 26 per cent in the United States and 25 per cent in the United Kingdom. The effect of differences in the relative size of industries on average concentration is therefore slight, and its direction depends on whether measurement is based on United States or United Kingdom concentration ratios. It follows that the difference in average concentration levels between the two countries reflects primarily the difference in concentration ratios for comparable industries.

Further analysis indicates that the sampled industries with lower concentration in the United States are larger in aggregate size, as well as more numerous, than those with lower concentration in Britain. Moreover, the average difference between the concentration indexes of the two countries is greater in the former group than in the latter. These findings are shown in the following tabulation:

	33 Industries with Higher Concentration in U.K. than U.S.	*24 Industries with Higher Concentration in U.S. than U.K.*	*Total*
Percentage of industries	58	42	100
Percentage of employment, U.S.	57	43	100
Percentage of employment, U.K.	56	44	100
Unweighted average concentration index:			
U.S.	25	41	32
U.K.	48	24	38
Difference	23	—17	6

[29] Average for the United States obtained by applying the regression equation shown in footnote 25 to the weighted average percentage concentrated in the leading *four* firms.

76

The conclusion suggested by the sample of fifty-seven "matched" industries is that the general level of concentration in British manufacturing industries is somewhat higher than in the United States because a majority of industries have higher concentration in the United Kingdom, and because in this majority group the inter-country difference in concentration is greater than in the minority having higher concentration in the United States.

These results can be taken only as suggestions since the sample is of course by no means random. The fifty-seven industries accounted for 32 per cent of manufacturing employment in the United Kingdom and 33 per cent in the United States. The weighted average concentration indexes for the United States and Britain are 20 per cent and 25 per cent respectively in the sample and 19 per cent and 33 per cent respectively for manufacturing as a whole. The sample therefore tends to understate the difference in concentration between the two countries.

4. Changes over Time

ARE the different concentration indexes also in substantial agreement when changes in concentration over time are measured? The evidence readily available for the investigation of this problem is more slender and less conclusive than that relating to cross sections.

Herfindahl's study of changes in concentration in the steel industry includes a comparison of his summary index with that measuring concentration in the leading four firms. Table 6 shows time series for concentration of pig-iron and steel-ingot capacity, based on his data.

The fluctuations in concentration shown in Table 6 are very small compared with the average difference in concentration among industries shown in Tables 2 and 5. The only large change in the time series is that associated with the formation of the United States Steel Corporation in 1901.

While the increase from 1898 to 1904 is reflected in all three concentration indexes, the subsequent small fluctuations are not so highly correlated as the variation among industries analyzed above. The rank correlation coefficient when Herfindahl's summary index is compared with the index of concentration in the leading four firms is .68 for pig iron and .72 for steel ingot. The rank correlation coefficient when concentration in the leading four firms and the leading eight firms is compared happens to be 1.00 for pig iron, but is only .53 for steel ingot.

The limited evidence of the steel industry suggests that while the different concentration indexes are in substantial agreement in measuring the relatively large differences among industries, their measurements of the small fluctuations in an industry frequently conflict. The index measuring concentration of capacity in the lead-

TABLE 6

Concentration of Capacity in the Iron and Steel Industry,
United States, 1898-1948

	PIG-IRON CAPACITY			STEEL-INGOT CAPACITY		
		Percentage Accounted for by			Percentage Accounted for by	
	Summary Index	Leading Four Firms	Leading Eight Firms	Summary Index	Leading Four Firms	Leading Eight Firms
Year	(1)	(2)	(3)	(4)	(5)	(6)
1898	.03	27.2	35.3			
1904	.16	48.4	56.7	.31	68.4	80.4
1908	.19	53.1	61.6	.25	64.5	77.2
1916	.17	53.9	62.5	.23	65.0	77.0
1920	.14	50.5	60.8	.18	56.7	67.4
1930	.19	65.6	77.3	.15	58.2	74.0
1938	.19	66.2	80.8	.16	63.0	79.2
1940				.16	63.8	80.3
1945	.18	66.6	82.0	.16	64.3	79.6
1948	.18	66.8	83.1	.15	63.9	79.6

Source: O. C. Herfindahl: "Concentration in the Steel Industry" (Ph.D. Dissertation, Columbia University, 1950). Columns 1 and 4 are from footnote 2, p. 44, footnote 2, p. 46, and footnote 1, p. 47, respectively. Columns 2, 3, 5, and 6 are computed from Table 6, p. 57, and Table 7, p. 58.

ing four firms agrees somewhat better with the index measuring concentration in eight firms than with the summary index.

A second source of data on changes in concentration is the *Concentration of Industry Report* published by the Department of Commerce. Here the percentage of value of output concentrated in the leading four and eight firms is given for 1935 and 1947, for 129 manufacturing industries which remained comparable between the two years.[30] Analyzing the direction of change of the two indexes between 1935 and 1947, we obtain the result shown in Table 7.

The two indexes are in substantial agreement with regard to the direction of change in concentration in individual industries between 1935 and 1947. In only 15 of the 129 cases does the evidence presented by the two indexes conflict. A judgment regarding the

[30] The report gives these data for 131 industries, but reference to the National Resources Committee's study indicates that in one of them (rubber, boots and shoes) the index listed for "eight firms" actually refers to a larger number of firms. Another industry was omitted by mistake.

change in concentration based on one index is therefore not likely to be contradicted by the other.

This conclusion differs from that based on the iron and steel industry, but we are dealing here with a large number of industries,

TABLE 7

Distribution of Industries by Direction of Change in Concentration Indexes, United States, 1935-1947

		CONCENTRATION IN FOUR FIRMS[a]			
		Increase	Decrease	No Change	Total
Concentration	Increase	49	8	0	57
in Eight Firms[b]	Decrease	7	64	0	71
	No change	0	0	1	1
	Total	56	72	1	129

a Percentage of value of output accounted for by leading 4 firms.
b Percentage of value of output accounted for by leading 8 firms.
Source: Compiled from *Concentration of Industry Report*, Dept. of Commerce, 1949.

only two years, and only two of the three indexes compared for the iron and steel industry. The average change in concentration from 1935 to 1947 is, however, not large, as will be shown below, and seems to be of the same order of magnitude as the fluctuations in iron and steel. It appears that in the great majority of industries, fluctuations in the index measuring concentration in the leading eight firms will generally agree with the movements of the index measuring concentration in the leading four firms, although some industries, such as steel ingot, will show very imperfect agreement.

5. *Change between 1935 and 1947*

THE fact that the average change in concentration between 1935 and 1947 was small is indicated in a rough way in the Department of Commerce's tabulation of changes in the concentration index, of which Table 8 is a summary.

It is possible, however, to obtain a more accurate idea of the general change in concentration between 1935 and 1947. This is a matter of considerable interest since there has been much speculation regarding the trend in concentration and the effect of the war. The above analysis suggests that if we can describe the general change in concentration by one index, such as the percentage accounted for by the leading four firms, our conclusions are probably also applicable, in broad terms, to the change in a number of other indexes,

TABLE 8

Number of Industries Showing Specified Changes in Concentration Index,[a]
United States, 1935-1947

	Increase	Decrease
Less than 5 per cent	32	35
5-9.9 per cent	17	10
10-19.9 per cent	5	22
20 per cent and over	4	5
Total	58	72

[a] Percentage of output accounted for by leading 4 firms.
Source: *Concentration of Industry Report*, Dept. of Commerce, 1949, Table v, p. 26.

such as the percentage accounted for by the leading eight firms.

On the basis of the percentage of output accounted for by the four leading firms, the general level of concentration in a given year can be described by a weighted average of industry-concentration indexes, the relative output of the industries being used as weights. For the group of industries for which the industrial classification of 1935 matches that of 1947 the weighted average of concentration indexes was 44.0 per cent for 1935 and 41.4 per cent for 1947. There has thus been a drop of 6 per cent in the average level of concentration as measured by this index.

This decline in concentration is the result of changes both in concentration within industries and in the relative importance of different industries. What has been the relative influence of these two factors?

The average change in concentration within industries can be measured by considering how the two weighted averages would compare if there had been no change in the relative size (value of output) of different industries. The relative sizes of industries were held constant at both their 1935 level and their 1947 level, and both systems of weights gave about the same result, as shown below:

	1935 Weights	1947 Weights
1935	44.0%	41.2%
1947	44.4	41.4

With both systems of weights there is a very slight average *increase* in concentration within industries between 1935 and 1947, amounting to less than 1 per cent. The drop in concentration between the two dates must therefore be ascribed entirely to the shift in the relative importance of different industries. The effect of this shift can be seen by reading along the *rows* of the above tabulation.

If all industry-concentration indexes had remained constant at their 1935 level, the shift in the relative importance of industries would have lowered the average from 44.0 per cent to 41.2 per cent. If concentration indexes had remained constant at their 1947 level, the shift in the relative importance of industries would have lowered the average from 44.4 per cent to 41.4 per cent.

We conclude that while there have been many changes in concentration in particular industries between 1935 and 1947, these changes have been small in most cases, and they show no unity of direction, the average change being close to zero. There has, however, been some increase in the relative size of industries with low concentration.[31]

These conclusions are again based on a nonrandom sample. The weighted average index of output concentration for 1935, as derived from this sample, is 44 per cent, while the corresponding index derived from the random sample of 136 industries used for the comparison with the United Kingdom is 35 per cent.[32] Industries with relatively high concentration are therefore overrepresented in the present sample, and our conclusions are misleading if there is a correlation between the level of concentration in 1935 and the change from 1935 to 1947. This possibility is investigated in Table 9, which indicates some association between high concentration (1935) and large decrease in concentration from 1935 to 1947, so that it appears that our sample, by overweighting the industries with high concentration, overstates the decrease in concentration.[33]

The bias in the *change* in concentration arising from the bias in the percentage distribution of the sample between concentration classes, as shown in columns 4 to 6 of Table 9, can be calculated by adding the products of columns 3 and 6. This procedure yields a bias of .90 index points, and adding this to the sample difference of

[31] The ten largest of the industries in the sample with lower-than-average concentration and greater-than-average increase in output are: soft drinks, malt liquors, poultry dressing, prepared animal feeds, pulp mills, paperboard boxes, lithography, sheet metal work, wire drawing, structural and ornamental products.
The ten largest of the industries with higher-than-average concentration and a smaller increase in value of output between 1935 and 1947 than the averages are: cereal preparations, malt, chocolate and cocoa products, cane-sugar refining, beet sugar, cigarettes, chewing and smoking tobacco, tires and inner tubes, tin cans and other tinware, welded pipe.
[32] These figures refer to concentration of output, while the comparison with the United Kingdom was based on concentration of employment.
[33] The observed association may reflect the well-known regression effect, and a grouping by 1947 index classes may show the opposite association.

81

–2.64 shown at the foot of column 3, we obtain a corrected difference of –1.74 index points between the average concentration indexes of 1947 and 1935. Using this corrected figure in conjunction

TABLE 9

Change in Concentration, 1935-1947, by Concentration Class, 1935,
Manufacturing Industries, United States

CONCENTRATION INDEX CLASS,[a] 1935	WEIGHTED AVERAGE CONCENTRATION INDEX			PERCENTAGE OF OUTPUT, 1935		
	1935	*1947*	*Difference*	*1935-1947 Sample*	*Random Sample*	*Difference*
	(*1*)	(*2*)	(*3*)	(*4*)	(*5*)	(*6*)
Under 10	6.38	7.43	1.05	2.9	17.8	14.9
10–20	13.80	17.87	4.07	11.4	21.1	9.7
20–30	25.63	24.13	—1.50	22.2	15.4	—6.8
30–40	36.79	37.11	.32	24.2	10.9	—13.3
40–50	44.58	44.83	.25	4.7	10.6	5.9
50–60	53.69	60.15	6.46	4.2	1.9	—2.3
60–70	67.56	63.59	—3.97	12.3	13.6	1.3
70–80	75.29	75.05	—.24	4.2	3.9	—.3
80–90	85.32	80.88	—4.44	13.5	4.7	—8.8
90 and over	92.00	70.10	—21.90	.4	0	—.4
Total or average	44.04	41.39	—2.64	100.0	100.0	.0

[a] Percentage of value of output accounted for by leading 4 firms.
Source: Computed from *Concentration of Industry Report*, Dept. of Commerce, 1949, Table 1, pp. 4ff.; *The Structure of the American Economy, Part I*, National Resources Committee, 1939, Appendix 7, Table 1; and *Census of Manufactures: 1935*, Bureau of the Census, Table 4, pp. 22ff.

with the average concentration index given by the random sample for 1935, we conclude that the average level of output concentration was about 34.8 per cent in 1935 and 32.9 per cent in 1947.[34]

[34] This procedure is based on the following considerations. The difference shown at the bottom of column 3 can be expressed algebraically as (1) $\Sigma\ c_{47}\ v_{47} - \Sigma\ c_{35}\ v_{35} = \Sigma\ (c_{47} - c_{35})\ v_{35} + \Sigma\ (v_{47} - v_{35})\ c_{47}$ where c is the weighted average concentration index in a given concentration class—columns 1 and 2—v is the proportion of output in a given class shown by the biased sample—column 4 for 1935—the subscripts refer to the two years, and the summation is over all concentration classes. An industry's concentration class is determined throughout by its *1935* concentration index.

The "correct" difference we seek is
(2) $\Sigma\ c_{47}\ v'_{47} - \Sigma\ c_{35}\ v'_{35} = \Sigma\ (c_{47} - c_{35})\ v'_{35} + \Sigma\ (v'_{47} - v'_{35})\ c_{47}$ where v' is the correct proportion of output in a given class—column 5 for 1935.

Since we do not know v'_{47} we assume that $v'_{47} - v_{47} = v'_{35} - v_{35} = e$—column 6.

It follows that $v'_{47} - v'_{35} = v_{47} - v_{35}$, and hence the second term on the right-hand side of equation 2 is equal to the corresponding term in equation 1.

Therefore, the difference between equations 2 and 1 is $\Sigma\ (c_{47} - c_{35})\ v'_{35} - \Sigma\ (c_{47} - c_{35})\ v_{35} = \Sigma\ (c_{47} - c_{35})\ (v'_{35} - v_{35}) = \Sigma\ (c_{47} - c_{35})\ e =$ the sum of products of columns 3 and 6.

This model involves a number of special assumptions (e.g., the assumption

The stability of concentration patterns shown by our sample has characterized a twelve-year period in which average plant size (in terms of employment) has increased by 21 per cent and total employment in manufacturing has increased by 73 per cent. This impressive increase in activity, the great technological advances of the period, the uneven wartime increase in plant capacity, the increased participation of government in economic activity, and all the other changes associated with the New Deal, war, and postwar readjustment have had remarkably little effect on the average level of industry concentration. The great expansion of industry size has been matched by increases in average firm size and/or in the degree of inequality of firm size within industries.

6. *The Dimensions of Measurement*

THE problems of measurement discussed in the preceding sections have been concerned with the *form* of the concentration index and with techniques for summarizing a large number of concentration readings.

Equally important, however, are problems concerning what might be called the "dimensions" of concentration. First, what is the appropriate business unit for the measurement of concentration? The plant? The firm? What degree of corporate control should define the firm? What about firms that operate in several industries? Secondly, what is the appropriate "scope" of an index? An industry (that is, group of plants or firms)? A product? A regional sector of an industry? How are industries or products to be classified? Thirdly, how should size be measured? In the preceding sections employment,

---

that the 1935-1947 sample correctly represents the average concentration index in each class, or that $v'_{47} - v'_{35} = v_{47} - v_{35}$) but it is nevertheless a fairly reliable and fast method of calculating the bias due to the association of high initial concentration and decreasing concentration.

This correction has not, of course, taken account of bias arising from other sources. Both new and rapidly growing industries and industries that are old and declining are likely to be in the group for which 1935 and 1947 classifications are not comparable, and hence omitted from the sample. The former are often divided and redivided by the statistician as they grow, while the latter, when they become small enough, are merged into the "other" or "miscellaneous" groups.

We may hazard the guess that the rapidly growing industries are characterized by decreasing concentration, and the decaying industries by increasing concentration (cf. TNEC Monograph No. 27, Part I, Chap. IV, especially pp. 58-59, 61-62). Over the period 1935-1947 the former undoubtedly predominated so that it seems likely that the over-all decline in concentration is greater than the corrected figure shown by the sample.

output, and fixed assets have all been used, and other measures, such as income, are possible. Finally, what is the best time period for the measurement of concentration; for example, output in a month? A year? A two-year period? These problems are, of course, to some extent interdependent. For example, if the index is based on products it would be difficult to use employment as the measure of size.

We shall not undertake an exhaustive discussion of these questions here. The most appropriate set of dimensions must depend on the particular problem in hand, and the set of dimensions actually used will depend only partly on what is most appropriate and very largely on the statistics that are available. In every empirical study of concentration the investigator will have to substitute what he can get for what he would like.

Instead of discussing the "optimum" set of dimensions we shall therefore comment on the empirical relation between some of the alternatives. Such comparisons must be of interest to any investigator forced to use "substitutes," and will also reveal important features of the industrial structure.

PLANTS AND FIRMS

THE statistics published by the National Resources Committee, *The Concentration of Industry Report* for 1947, and the firm-size data compiled by the Canadian Bureau of Statistics for 1948, all use "industries" that are defined as groups of *plants* with a common major product. The "firms" in these statistics consist of groups of plants under common ownership within such an industry. A firm that has plants in two industries as defined by the Census of Manufactures appears in the statistics as two firms.

If the industry classification is reasonably suitable for the study of monopoly, this definition of the firm and the industry is probably more appropriate for the measurement of concentration in particular markets than one which would throw all activities of the firm into the same industry. An incidental advantage for our present purpose is that this classification enables us to compare plant- and firm-concentration indexes having exactly comparable scope.

Firm concentration in an industry cannot be lower than plant concentration, but it may be higher if there are multiplant firms. Each firm has at least one plant, so that the collective size of the largest x firms cannot be less, but may be greater, than the size of the x largest plants.[35]

Two important questions can be answered by a comparison of plant and firm concentration for a cross section of industries. First, are plant and firm concentration correlated? If we have data concerning one, can we draw conclusions concerning the other? Secondly, how great is the difference between plant and firm concentration? If all multiplant firms were split up, and their plants made independent, how much lower would the level of concentration be?

Analysis of the Canadian statistics for 1948, for the sample of industries listed in Table 2, shows that the ranking of industries by firm-concentration index is very similar to the ranking by plant-concentration index. The Spearman correlation coefficient for the two rankings is .947. This analysis is based on employment concentration.[36]

The *difference* between plant and firm concentration is measured in Table 10 by the comparison of cumulative frequency distributions similar to those used in our comparison of concentration in

TABLE 10

Comparison of Plant and Firm Concentration in 58 Selected Canadian Manufacturing Industries, 1948

CONCENTRATION INDEX (Number of Firms or Plants Required to Account for 80% of Industry's Employment)a	PERCENTAGE OF EMPLOYMENT IN INDUSTRIES WITH HIGHER CONCENTRATION THAN THE SPECIFIED INDEX		Difference	Relative Difference
	Concentration by Firms	Concentration by Plants	$(2)-(3)$	$(4) \div (2) \times 100$
(1)	(2)	(3)	(4)	(5)
3	12	8	4	31
6	25	13	11	46
12	34	19	15	45
24	41	37	4	10
100	63	58	4	7

a High concentration indicated by low numerical value of index.
Source: Estimates made in unpublished study, "Concentration in Canadian Manufacturing Industries," from data supplied by Dominion Bureau of Statistics. Figures are rounded to nearest percentage point.

[35] Stigler has pointed out possible exceptions, such as the case where several firms jointly operate one plant, or successively operate one plant within the period on which the concentration measure is based.

[36] The index used is the number of the largest plants or firms required to account for 80 per cent of an industry's employment.

the United States and the United Kingdom. The table is based on a group of 58 industries in which concentration measured on a "national" basis can reasonably be expected to be related to price policy. Industries with a very heterogeneous product structure or products that are largely produced in other industries are excluded, as are industries with substantially separate regional markets and those in which imports or exports play a large role.

A comparison of plant and firm concentration that is to be relevant to problems of social policy must provide the answer to this question: If one takes a given concentration level as representing the maximum compatible with adequate competition, how large is the industrial sector with "excessive" firm concentration, and how much would it be reduced if all plants were independent? Table 10 answers this question for the concentration levels shown.

The table shows, for example, that 25 per cent of all employment is in industries in which fewer than six *firms* account for 80 per cent, but only 13 per cent of all employment is in industries in which fewer than six *plants* account for 80 per cent. Hence, if all plants were made independent, the total employment represented by "excessively" concentrated industries would be reduced by 40 per cent, as shown in column 5. If any concentration index between 3 and 12 is taken as representing the highest level that should be tolerated, a drastic "trust-busting" policy would reduce the area of "excessive concentration" by between one-third and one-half.

How far are these findings for Canada applicable to the United States? A comparison of plant and firm concentration in this country has recently been published by the Federal Trade Commission, but unfortunately it does not answer either of the questions we have asked above.[37]

A rough idea of the degree to which the Canadian results are applicable to the United States can, however, be obtained by comparing the number of plants per firm in the manufacturing industries of the two countries. The decile values of the number of plants per firm in the 96 Canadian industries on which our correlation of

[37] *The Divergence Between Plant and Company Concentration, 1947*, as cited. In this study the divergence between plant and company concentration is measured by the area between the plant and company concentration curves for the first fifty plants and firms, and is presented as an index, based on the median area as 100. It is impossible to tell from these statistics how closely plant and firm concentration are correlated, or how much the area of "excessive concentration" (on any given definition) differs when plant and firm concentration are compared.

plant and firm concentration is based are compared below with those for 452 United States manufacturing industries for 1947.[38]

| | Number of Plants per Firm | |
| | 96 Canadian Industries | 452 U.S. Industries |
Decile	1948	1947
1	1.00	1.00
2	1.00	1.01
3	1.01	1.02
4	1.02–1.03	1.04
5	1.05	1.06
6	1.09	1.10
7	1.17–1.18	1.15
8	1.31–1.32	1.24
9	1.75–1.81	1.52–1.56

The arrays are very similar, but the dispersion is somewhat greater in the Canadian sample than in the United States. It is reasonable to expect that great variation in the number of plants per firm will tend to reduce the correlation between plant and firm concentration, so that one may hazard the guess that the correlation is not likely to be worse in the United States than in Canada. One cannot, however, be so confident about the applicability to the United States of the divergence pattern shown in Table 10. In any case, there is no good reason for guessing, since the materials are available and the problem should be studied directly.

INDUSTRY AND PRODUCT CONCENTRATION

THE problems of industry and product classification and their suitability for the study of monopoly are discussed in other papers presented to this conference. It is obvious that since many firms produce more than one product, a difference between industry concentration and product concentration may arise. Without entering into the discussion of their respective merits for the study of monopoly, we may say a word about the mathematical relation between these two concepts.

Some writers have asserted that product concentration typically exceeds industry concentration. This is true if industries and products are defined in such a way as to make it true. If the product classification is more detailed than the industry classification, so that there are more products than industries, it is extremely likely, though not mathematically necessary, that product concentration

[38] Data for United States from J. I. Mills, *A Proposed System for Classifying Manufacturing Concerns by Size*, Dept. of Commerce and National Production Authority, 1951, Table III, pp. 75-84.

will be higher than industry concentration. The average product market will be smaller than the average industry, and if there is any degree of specialization among firms, the average number of firms producing a given product will be less than the average number of firms in an industry, so that concentration will tend to be higher. It is therefore not surprising that the general level of concentration in 1,807 manufactured products analyzed by W. F. Crowder in his study for the TNEC is considerably higher than the average level of concentration in manufacturing *industries* analyzed by Means for the National Resources Committee.[39] The product classification used by Crowder was much finer than the Census of Manufactures industry classification.

Suppose, however, that product and industry classifications are used that are strictly comparable; there is an industry corresponding to each product, the industry consisting of those firms that produce more of the given product than of any other product, by value. In this case there is no reason to expect a priori any bias toward higher or lower product concentration, and it is theoretically possible for all product-concentration indexes to be either higher or lower than the corresponding industry-concentration indexes.[40] An appreciable

[39] Thorp and Crowder, *op. cit.*, Part v, Table 1, p. 275, and *The Structure of the American Economy*, as cited, p. 115 and Appendix 7. About one-third of the *industries* analyzed in the latter study for 1935 had concentration indexes above 50 per cent, but over three-quarters of the *products* analyzed in the former study for 1937 were in this high-concentration class.

[40] Suppose there are two products, A and B, and two corresponding industries, each consisting of two firms. We measure concentration by the percentage of the industry or product accounted for by the leading firm. In model 1, output is distributed by firms, industries, and products as follows:

	INDUSTRY A				INDUSTRY B		
	Product A	*Product B*	*Total*		*Product A*	*Product B*	*Total*
Firm 1	90	10	100	Firm 3	10	90	100
Firm 2	80	20	100	Firm 4	20	80	100
Total	170	30	200	Total	30	170	200

Industry concentration is 50 per cent in both industries. Product concentration, however, is 90 ÷ 200 = 45 per cent for both products. Product concentration is, therefore, lower than industry concentration for all products and industries.

In model 2, output is distributed as follows:

	INDUSTRY A				INDUSTRY B		
	Product A	*Product B*	*Total*		*Product A*	*Product B*	*Total*
Firm 1	100	0	100	Firm 3	1	9	10
Firm 2	80	20	100	Firm 4	1	9	10
Total	180	20	200	Total	2	18	20

Industry concentration is again 50 per cent in both cases. But concentration in the production of product A is 100 ÷ 182 = 55 per cent, and concentration in

divergence of product concentration from industry concentration is of course not likely in those industries where the product accounts for the bulk of the industry's output and no large portion of the product originates outside the industry. Since industry-concentration data are often used as a substitute for product concentration, the percentage of the industry's output accounted for by the product and the percentage of the total product output produced outside the industry should be studied in interpreting such data.

OUTPUT, EMPLOYMENT, AND ASSETS

THE concentration statistics used in the preceding sections have employed value of output, employment, and fixed assets as measures of size. If we wish to know whether results obtained by the use of one of these variables are applicable to another, two questions must be answered. First, are there systematic differences in the level of concentration as measured by these three variables, and secondly, does an industry having high or low concentration (in relation to other industries) in terms of one of the measures also have high or low concentration in terms of another.

Output and assets concentration can be compared for a very limited number of industries by using the Department of Commerce *Concentration of Industry Report* and the FTC *Report on the Concentration of Productive Facilities, 1947.* For eleven industries the classifications appear to be comparable so that a comparison of concentration indexes can be made. Even for this limited group of industries the scope of the indexes is not strictly comparable, since in the FTC's study the "industry" consists of a group of firms, while the "industry" as defined by the Census of Manufactures and used in the Department of Commerce study consists of a group of plants and a "firm" consists of those plants *within an industry* that are under common ownership.

The comparison of assets and output concentration in eleven industries is shown in Table 11.

In this sample assets concentration exceeds output concentration. There are only two industries in which this relation is reversed—cigarettes and biscuits—and in the latter the concentration indexes differ by a negligible amount. The higher level of assets concentra-

---

product B is $20 \div 38 = 53$ per cent. In this example, therefore, product concentration exceeds industry concentration for all products and industries.

The Census of Manufactures contains many examples of industry-product relations such as those used in these models.

TABLE 11

Assets and Output Concentration, United States, 1947

INDUSTRY	CONCENTRATION IN THE LEADING FOUR FIRMS	
	Net Capital Assets	Value of Shipments
Primary aluminum[a]	100.0	100.0
Tin cans and other tinware	96.4	77.8
Linoleum	93.6	80.3
Rubber tires and tubes	88.3	76.6
Cigarettes	87.8	90.4
Distilled liquors	84.6	74.6
Plumbers' supplies	74.3	34.7
Biscuits, crackers, pretzels	71.4	71.5
Footwear (except rubber)	46.8	27.3[b]
Bread and other bakery products	30.6	16.4
Woolen and worsted goods	30.3	28.1

a The industry consists of three firms.
b Includes "house slippers." Output concentration index is estimated from the indexes for "footwear" (27.9) and "house slippers" (26.9) published separately by the Department of Commerce.
Sources: *Concentration of Industry Report*, Dept. of Commerce, 1949; *Report on the Concentration of Productive Facilities*, FTC, 1949.

tion reflects a positive correlation between firm size (in terms of fixed assets) and the ratio of assets to sales, within industries.

While assets concentration exceeds output concentration, the two are highly correlated, the (Pearsonian) correlation coefficient being .910.[41] The sample is of course very small, and the correlation for manufacturing as a whole may be appreciably higher or lower. The 95 per cent confidence limits for the correlation coefficient are about 0.65 and 0.97.[42]

The relation between output and employment concentration can be investigated with considerably greater confidence, for the National Resources Committee study for 1935 includes both output-

41 In the primary aluminum industry, output and assets concentration are of necessity equal since there are only three firms. This is an extreme illustration of the general proposition that the correlation between assets and output concentration is in large part due to the influence on both variables of variation in the number of firms.
The correlation coefficient for the ten industries other than primary aluminum is .898.
42 See F. N. David, *Tables of the Correlation Coefficient* (Cambridge, 1932) Chart II.
The confidence interval indicates that in samples of size 11 from a bivariate normal population with correlation coefficient less than .65 the probability of obtaining a sample correlation coefficient as high as .91 is less than 2.5 per cent, while if the population correlation coefficient is greater than .97, the probability of obtaining a sample coefficient as low as .91 is less than 2.5 per cent.

and employment-concentration indexes. The number of industries for which data are available is much greater, and the industries and firms are strictly comparable. A comparison of output and employment concentration was therefore made for the sample of 136 industries that were used for our comparison of concentration in the United States and the United Kingdom. This sample, it will be recalled, contains every second industry listed in the National Resources Committee tabulation of concentration data.

A graphic comparison of output and employment concentration is shown in Chart 4. The diagonal line drawn across the scatter

Chart 4

Concentration of Employment and Output in Leading Four Firms, 136 Manufacturing Industries, United States, 1935

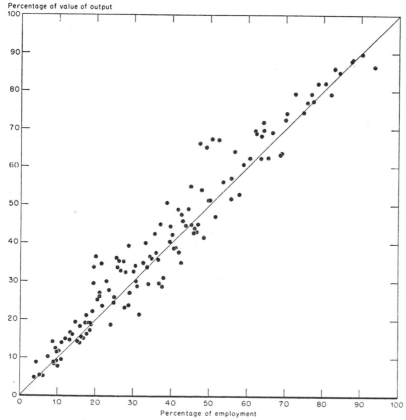

Percentage of value of output

Percentage of employment

Source: *The Structure of the American Economy*, National Resources Committee, 1939, Part I, Appendix 7, Tables I and II.

diagram is not a regression line fitted to the points, but is intended to show where the points would lie if output concentration were exactly equal to employment concentration in all industries. The diagram shows that the majority of points lie above this line, indicating that in most of the industries output concentration exceeds employment concentration. This tendency is, however, not overwhelming. In 48 of the 136 industries examined—over one-third of the total—output concentration is less than employment concentration, and in two industries they are equal. Nevertheless, there is a considerable difference between the weighted average indexes of output and employment concentration. The former (using value-of-output weights) is 35 per cent, while the latter (using employment weights) is 26 per cent.

The diagram also shows that output and employment concentration are highly correlated, so that the value of one can be used with great confidence for estimating the other. The rank correlation coefficient relating output and employment concentration is .958.

These two investigations suggest that while, in general, concentration in terms of fixed assets exceeds output concentration, which in turn exceeds employment concentration, the ordering of industries by concentration level is much the same, no matter which standard of size is used, so that the results of cross-section analyses based on one measure will also be applicable to the others. With respect to asset concentration, this conclusion is based on a very small sample and must be regarded as tentative.

THE TIME PERIOD

THE concentration statistics we have examined are all based on periods of one year, but it is not obvious that this particular period is the most suitable for the study of the structural factors that govern business policy. Stigler has suggested that the period is too short, since there is a random element in the year-to-year changes in a firm's output, so that a concentration index based on annual data may not adequately reflect the normal long-run size structure that is relevant to considerations of price policy. He has also suggested that an index based on a longer period would show lower values than one based on a year, since the averaging of fluctuations in individual firm sizes tends to lower their inequality.

Given a constant group of firms, an index based on a period of several years may be lower than the average of indexes for the component years if the ranking of firms changes during the period, and it would be of interest to investigate the actual importance of such changes for different industries and periods. Some evidence on this point is provided by Crowder's study of product concentration for the TNEC. Comparing the four leading companies in 1935 and 1937 for 262 products, he tabulated the extent to which the leaders coincided in the two years, as shown in the following summary:[43]

Number of Firms among the Leading Four in Both 1935 and 1937	Percentage of Cases (Products)
4	19
3	41
2	27
1	11
0	2
	100

Over the three-year period covered by this comparison, two or more of the leading firms were replaced by others in 40 per cent of the cases. This result certainly suggests that concentration indexes computed on a three-year basis would tend to be lower than the corresponding average of annual concentration indexes. Crowder suggests that the identity of the leading firms is more stable in old, well-established industries and in industries not subject to style or model changes than in others.

Granted that random year-to-year fluctuations in output are important and should not be reflected in the concentration index, the averaging or summing of output figures for individual firms may not be the best solution. The structural characteristics that a concentration index is intended to measure are not fixed; they may change over time, and one of the purposes of our indexes is to measure this change. In averaging firm sizes for several years one may average out not only random fluctuations but also real, long-term changes in industrial structure. This problem could perhaps be handled by the use of moving averages; an alternative solution would be to measure concentration for short periods, but in terms of a variable less subject to random fluctuations than output and employment. It would be reasonable to treat changes in *capacity* as representing structural changes that should be reflected in the index, and to measure con-

---

[43] We compiled this summary from the detailed data in Thorp and Crowder, *op. cit.*, Part v, Table 2C, pp. 495-505. In the text (p. 342) Crowder gives the number of products as 256 instead of 262 and the percentage of cases in which two of the leaders repeat as 7 instead of 27. The figure 256 is probably an error, and the figure 7 per cent certainly is, since his other percentages agree with ours.

centration in terms of plant capacity owned by each firm, thus eliminating the effect of fluctuations in the use of capacity.

At present we have no comprehensive data for either the measurement of concentration for longer periods than a year or its measurement in terms of capacity, and we can only speculate about the time period and measure of size most closely related to business policy. This is just one illustration of the need for better data and tests of carefully framed hypotheses, to be discussed in the next section.

7. Empirical Tests

WE DO not, as yet, know enough about the behavior of the various concentration indexes to be able to choose between them in investigating any given problem. Such knowledge can, however, be gained by using the indexes in empirical tests of hypotheses regarding the influence of concentration on business policy. Some, but very little, systematic work in this direction has been done to date.

Tests of this sort are not likely to discriminate effectively among the various indexes unless the concentration measures are used in conjunction with other determining variables, and the effects of the different variables are segregated as far as possible.

The danger involved in neglecting other variables is illustrated by an experiment we performed on a recent study by J. S. Bain. Bain finds a weak but significant association between profit rate and concentration index in a cross section of 42 industries, using the percentage of employment in the leading eight firms (taken from the National Resources Committee study) as measure of concentration. We found a very slightly better (inverse) association between his profit-rates data and the number of *plants* in each industry.[44] It

[44] Joe S. Bain, "Relation of Profit Rate to Industry Concentration, American Manufacturing, 1936-1940," *Quarterly Journal of Economics*, August, 1951, pp. 293-324, esp. Table I, p. 312 and pp. 311-17.

For this comparison we used Kendall's rank correlation coefficient, which is based on a comparison of all possible pairs of observations. We say that two variables—profit rate and concentration—"agree" in a pair of observations (industries) if their ranks are in the same order, e.g., if higher profit rate in industry A than in industry B is associated with higher concentration in industry A than in industry B. Supplementing Bain's data by the number of plants in each of the industries (from the 1935 Census of Manufactures), we can classify the pairs of industries by type of agreement as follows:

would be rash to conclude that the number of plants is as important a variable in the determination of profit rates as the concentration index used by Bain, but it is correct to conclude that very little can be said about the significant determinants of profit rates by testing one causal variable at a time. In this case a possible explanation might be that the number of firms has a certain independent influence (that is, that profit rates are higher if a given concentration index is due to a small number of firms rather than to a large number of firms and high inequality) and that the number of plants is highly correlated with the number of firms.

The conclusion is that we can learn what is a useful concentration index only in the process of learning more about the determinants of business policy and market results. In this field, as in many others, we require more tests of carefully formulated hypotheses regarding the joint effects of a number of variables.

COMMENT

Orris C. Herfindahl, Committee for Economic Development

These comments are directed at the finding that substantially the same ranking of industries is given by the three types of concentra-

		DISTRIBUTION OF PAIRS OF INDUSTRIES[a]		
		Concentration Index		
		Agreement with Profit Rate	Disagreement with Profit Rate	Total
Number of plants[b]	Agreement with profit rate	443	93	536.5
	Disagreement with profit rate	79.5	245	324.5
	Total	522.5	338.5	861

[a] The total number of pairs that can be obtained from 42 industries is 42 x 41 ÷ 2 = 861. Nine pairs having "ties" in one of the rankings are classified by assuming that each of the two possible orderings of the pair applies to "half" the pair.

[b] Agreement denotes association between fewer plants and higher profit rate.

Kendall's coefficient of rank correlation for concentration and profit rates is $(522.5-338.5) \div 861 = .21$, while the coefficient measuring the correlation between fewness of plants and profit rates is $(536.5-324.5) \div 861 = .25$. The tabulation shows that the slight difference between the values reflects the fact that there are 93 pairs of industries in which the number of plants agrees with profit rate but concentration does not, and only 78 pairs in which concentration agrees with profit rates while number of plants does not.

95

tion measures compared by Rosenbluth.[1] My remarks do not represent disagreement with his findings and evaluation of their significance, but serve to emphasize some points that were perhaps inadequately stressed in his paper.

Agreement among the ranks resulting from the use of these three measures of concentration does not, of course, permit the conclusion that the measures are good indicators of monopoly power or business policy. They may be equally poor indicators, suggesting differences among industries where none exist or even suggesting differences in the wrong direction. Lack of knowledge on this point should lead to caution in evaluations of Rosenbluth's study of concentration changes over time in the United States and his comparison of manufacturing industries in the United States and the United Kingdom. We cannot be sure whether limited differences in these concentration measures over time or between countries are important or not. This is not to say that such investigations, using measures whose significance for business behavior is not well understood, are not useful. After all, these measures came to be used because observation indicates, at the least, that some differences in the sizes of the coefficients are strongly associated with differences in the behavior of the industries' firms. Similarly, a showing of substantial change in concentration over a period of time is important because a part of the changes within industries will likely be indicative of changes in competition even though some of the changes in concentration are not.

In measuring concentration, the goal need not be, however, a measure whose every level corresponds to a different degree of competition. If we think of the measurement problem in terms of the concentration, numbers, and inequality framework used by Rosenbluth in his paper, the various combinations of number and inequality produce a concentration surface for a given measure. It is not necessary that the levels of this surface be in a one-to-one correspondence with the competitive behavior of the industry, for a significant improvement in the measurement of concentration would be represented by a partitioning of this surface into several sectors, each corresponding to a different degree of competitiveness.

We can be quite sure that the three types of measure under consideration in the paper do correspond with the competitiveness of

[1] The three types of measures are (1) the percentage of the industry's output accounted for by a given number of leading firms, (2) the number of leading firms required to account for a given percentage of the industry's output, and (3) a "summary" measure equal to the reciprocal of the number of firms in the industry times one plus the square of the coefficient of variation of the firm's outputs.

industry behavior for rather extreme values of the measures, but the area of uncertainty is sizable. So long as studies of the relationship between the values taken on by these measures and the behavior of the industries are lacking, the possibility is open that the measures do not take account of some significant aspects of the size distributions. In the case of the first two types of measures, there is some doubt that they give proper weight to the number of firms in the industry. The definitions of these measures do not include the number of firms, and the association between the measures and the number of firms is weak enough for the same level of concentration to be assigned to industries with possibly important differences in the number of firms.

From Rosenbluth's reformulations of types one and two measures, in order to show the relations among concentration, number, and inequality that are desirable in a measure of concentration, it may appear that the two measures do adequately reflect the number of firms. His purpose, however, was a demonstration of the desirable relationships and not that number is actually taken into account. Following Rosenbluth's suggestion, the type one measure—e.g. the percentage controlled by the top four firms—can be regarded as

$$\frac{4}{\text{Total no. of firms}} \quad \frac{\text{(average size of 4 largest)}}{\text{(average size of all firms)}},$$

with the right factor viewed as a measure of inequality and the left factor reflecting the number of firms. But this measure can also be viewed as

$$\frac{\text{average size of 4 largest}}{\begin{array}{c}\text{average size if 4 firms}\\\text{accounted for all output.}\end{array}}$$

The number of firms is not essential to calculation of the measure.

The type two measure can be viewed as $N\,(n/N)$, where n is the number of firms required to account for a given percentage of industry output and N is the total number of firms in the industry. But the total number of firms cancels out in this formulation so that again it is not essential to calculation of the measure.

The fact that these two measures reflect only one point in the distribution rather than the whole distribution also makes it possible for inequality to change, with number of firms constant, without affecting the measure of concentration, contrary to the relationships desired if we choose to measure concentration in terms of number and inequality. Suppose there are two industries with the firms' outputs distributed as follows:

INDUSTRY A		INDUSTRY B	
Firm Outputs	Cumulated Outputs	Firm Outputs	Cumulated Outputs
40	40	55	55
35	75	20	75
15	90	20	95
10	100	5	100
100		100	

Concentration is the same in both industries if it is measured by the percentage of output accounted for by the two largest firms or by the number of firms required to account for 75 per cent of the industry's output. Yet inequality is greater in industry B, unless special significance is attributed to the cumulated values for two firms.[2]

The fact that a measure can permit inequality to increase without showing an increase in concentration, number of firms remaining the same, is not necessarily a serious defect. Nor does a showing that the number of firms is not essential to the calculation of a concentration measure permit the conclusion that the measure is inadequate. It may be highly correlated with the number of firms or if it is not, the size distributions that it fails to distinguish may actually not differ in any respect significant for industry behavior.

The second possibility is not dealt with here, but the 1947 data from the Department of Commerce study of concentration in manufacturing can throw some light on the question of correlation between types one and two measures and the number of firms. It will be recalled that the rank correlations between type one measures for one, two, three, and four firms, based on the twenty-six industry FTC data, were all over .90. The lowest was .91, between one and four firms. The 1935 National Resources Committee data gave a correlation of .99 for measures based on four and eight firms, and the Canadian data gave a correlation of .98 between types one and two measures, using measurement axes of three firms and 80 per cent of employment, and a coefficient of .98 between type three and each of the first two types.

The 1947 Commerce data suggest that these measures would not be so highly correlated with measures that give more weight to the

2 The "summary" measure used by Rosenbluth, the sum of the squares of the percentage/100 outputs of the firms, does differentiate between the two industries because it depends on the outputs of all the firms. By this measure, concentration is .315 for industry A and .385 for industry B.

number of firms in the industry. These data give a rank correlation of .49 between the percentage of output accounted for by the four leading firms and the number of firms in the industry.[3] Perhaps more to the point is the range in number of firms at approximately the same level of concentration as measured by the percentage accounted for by the four leading firms.

The differences in number of firms for industries with approximately the same level of concentration are so great as to suggest that the type one measure fails to differentiate industries whose behavior may be distinctly different. Table 1 invites investigation of such

TABLE 1

Variation in Number of Firms in Industries
at Various Levels of Concentration

Per Cent of Industry Output Accounted for by Top Four Firms	Number of Industries in Class Interval	Number of Industries with Firms Less than Stated Number	Number of Industries with Firms Greater than Stated Number	Range in Number of Firms
90–100	11	3 under 13	3 over 33	3 to 50
80–89	20	6 under 16	6 over 33	9 to 93
70–79	28	8 under 24	8 over 68	13 to 249
60–69	35	9 under 31	9 over 80	14 to 346

Based on the 1947 Dept. of Commerce study of concentration in manufacturing.

questions as the following: What difference to the behavior of an industry does the presence of a fringe of smaller firms make? What is the significance of an increase in the number of firms for industries with various initial number of firms? Or, as Rosenbluth suggests at the end of his paper, does the number of firms have an "independent" influence on the behavior of an industry? And, of course, the number of firms is not the only aspect of the size distribution that calls for attention.

These remarks emphasize the importance of Rosenbluth's final conclusion that the way to find out how to measure concentration is to investigate empirically the relations between business policy and concentration indexes or their constituents. Knowledge of this sort is indispensable to the formulation of a satisfactory concentration index.

[3] This calculation is based on industries with 50 per cent or more of the output accounted for by the four leading firms.

ECONOMIC THEORY AND THE
MEASUREMENT OF CONCENTRATION

TIBOR SCITOVSKY

STANFORD UNIVERSITY

ECONOMIC theory might contribute in two possible ways to the development of a satisfactory measure or set of measures of concentration. The theory of price and general competitive strategy under conditions of oligopoly might provide guidance for choosing the measure that best distinguishes industries according to differences in their methods of competition. While I am not too familiar with this branch of economic theory, I doubt if it could be of much use at the present stage of its development, when—under the impact of Von Neumann's and Morgenstern's work on the general theory of strategy—it is in a state of ferment. Furthermore, I am not at all convinced that our main purpose in measuring concentration is (or should be) to distinguish among industries or economies according to their methods of price setting and competition. The public are concerned about industrial concentration, because they are concerned about its economic and political effects. The economist should, therefore, analyze at least the economic effects and assess their importance. Accordingly, measures of concentration should be evolved with a view to their usefulness in accomplishing this task. This criterion is very different from the criterion mentioned above, since the methods of price setting and competition brought about by concentration are neither the only nor necessarily the most important effects of concentration. Hence, the second possible contribution of economic theory is to make hypotheses as to the various effects of concentration. By so doing, it will indicate the various uses to which measures of concentration will be put and thus help to develop the most satisfactory measure.

I shall concentrate on this latter relation, and try to give a detailed statement of the various effects that the theorist would expect concentration to have. Also, I shall use this opportunity to make a few criticisms of some of the existing measures of concentration.

The discussion of the effects of concentration will have the useful by-product of providing an appraisal of some of the alternative measures of oligopoly power. Let us remember that measures of concentration, whether they try to measure the concentration of ownership, profits, or market policies within an industry, are only one among many possible indexes of oligopoly power. Another set of indexes aims at measuring oligopoly power by its effects. In this category belong the indexes developed by Lerner, Bain, Morgan, Papandreou, to mention only a few. I propose to deal with some of these at least in passing.

In discussions of the effects of industrial concentration, it is customary to distinguish between the distributive effects and the effects on the efficiency of economic organization; but each of these can be broken down yet further. In the case of the distributive effects of concentration, it is desirable to distinguish the effect of concentration on income distribution from its effect on the distribution of social and political power. In the case of the efficiency effects, the effects of concentration on resource allocation are usually stressed. Here we must distinguish the effects on resource and output allocation among different firms and industries from the effects on the way in which each individual firm combines its different productive resources. Furthermore, concentration may also influence the firm's internal administrative and engineering efficiency, and may affect technological progress. These six effects can be called the direct effects of concentration. Through its influence on income distribution, general efficiency (and hence labor productivity), and technological progress, concentration may also influence the level of employment; but since this is an indirect effect, wrought through the direct effects mentioned above, it will not be discussed further.

1. *Effect on Income Distribution*

INDUSTRIAL concentration has been attacked chiefly because of its effect on income distribution. Some attack it on equalitarian grounds, because concentration is generally believed to enhance the inequality of income distribution. Others feel that it is inequitable for anyone to receive a higher income than is necessary to call forth the supply of his type of services in the socially desirable quantities. In general, many resent the fact that in a world of monopolies and countermonopolies inequalities of income arise that have no economic justification or explanation but are caused by disparities in bargaining power. Furthermore, income distribution is not a matter of equity alone. Since it is one of the determinants of specialization and of the flow of primary resources into different uses, one can argue that income distribution is also a matter of efficiency—an efficient income distribution being defined as one that would bring about an efficient allocation of resources.

Industrial concentration may affect income distribution in a variety of ways. Concentration influences the profit margins and prices charged in product markets as well as the prices paid for resources in factor markets; and it can also affect income distribution by making it more expensive and generally more difficult for newcomers to enter the industry.

Statistical measures of the effects of concentration on income distribution have not yet been developed. An index, however, is provided by Bain's index of profit rates. In fact, it has been claimed that Bain's index measures not only this single effect of concentration but is a suitable index of concentration or oligopoly power itself. The aim of all concentration, it might be argued, is monopoly profit; and therefore the best way of measuring concentration is to measure the extent to which it achieves this aim. This argument would be valid if it were found that the other effects of oligopoly power were exerted through the same factors that influence profits and in a similar way.

2. Effect on Distribution of Power

THE next effect of industrial concentration I want to deal with is its effect on the distribution of social and political power. I shall consider this effect separately, partly because the distribution of social and political power is important quite aside from the effects it may have on income distribution, partly because concentration may affect income distribution and the distribution of social power in different ways, and partly also because value judgments may be different with respect to the two distributions.

It is sometimes argued, for example, that the increased concentration of business and of organized labor on the two sides of the labor market have just about offset each other as far as their effect on income distribution is concerned. If this is so, we would nevertheless regard the advent of collective bargaining on a nationwide scale as of the utmost political, social, and economic importance. Again, in our present-day society, when the power of the state is great and increasing, the individual's protection against abuses of this power might well lie in the social power of organized economic and other groups; and in this connection—as well as in many other connections—the political scientist might well be interested not only in the degree of concentration but also in how concentration is distributed among different social groups and economic interests.

103

3. *Effect on Resource Allocation*

THE next two effects of concentration have to do with resource allocation. Under pure competition, each firm would combine its resources in the best (socially most desirable) proportions and produce an output that stands in the correct (socially most desirable) relation to the output of all other firms and industries, because perfectly competitive prices reflect relative scarcities and demands correctly, and because each firm, guided by these prices, would aim at maximum profits.

Neither of these conditions is likely to be fulfilled under oligopoly.[1] When oligopolists sell at prices above marginal cost and oligopsonists buy at prices below marginal value, relative prices become unreliable as indexes of relative scarcities and relative demands; and the producers, whose policies are guided by market prices, may make socially undesirable decisions. In particular, too little will be produced and too few resources utilized in industries with high margins;[2] and too much will be produced and too many resources utilized in industries with low margins.

This is the chief effect of concentration on allocation; but it should be noted that it is the result of market imperfection in general rather than of concentration alone, which is only one of the many manifestations (or causes) of market imperfection. Furthermore, misallocation of resources is caused, not by the size of profit margins, but by the fact that they differ sharply among industries— though the best practical way of narrowing this difference might nevertheless be to lower the average profit margin.

To express the importance of this effect of concentration or of market imperfection we would want, ideally, a measure of society's loss chargeable to misallocation of resources. But we have hardly begun to take the first step toward laying the conceptual foundations on which statistical estimates of such social loss might be based.[3] In the interim, the best we can do is to use the margin between price and marginal cost as an index of this loss—or rather, some parameter of the frequency distribution of this margin. This is Lerner's well-known index of the degree of monopoly. A general

[1] The condition of profit maximization is discussed in section 5 below.

[2] Unless otherwise stated, the terms "margin" and "profit margin" refer throughout this paper to the margin between price and marginal cost, or between marginal value and price.

[3] See the work of Gerard Debreu in several Cowles Commission "Discussion Papers" privately circulated.

appraisal of this index will be given later, but I shall discuss some of the specific objections to it here.

One objection to Lerner's index of monopoly power is that its practical application presents formidable problems, because firms do not use marginal cost as an operational concept. The second objection is that Lerner's index shows the degree of monopoly power only in the product market and ignores the possibility of the firm's oligopsony power in factor markets.[4]

Both these difficulties, however, can easily be resolved in certain cases. In firms whose output varies in proportion with the input of variable factors (i.e. where the variable factors have fixed production coefficients) the margin between price and average variable cost (an operational concept!) can be used as an index of market imperfection both in the market where the firm sells and in the markets where it buys. In such firms, average variable cost and marginal cost would coincide if it were not for imperfect competition in factor markets; and the difference between average variable and marginal costs measures the weighted average degree of market imperfection faced by the firm in the factor markets. By adding this difference to the difference between marginal cost and price, which measures market imperfection in the product market, we obtain the margin between average variable cost and price as a measure of market imperfection in both product and factor markets. Dean's cost studies suggest that the special condition under which this amended form of Lerner's index could be used occurs in many industries.

A third objection to Lerner's index is that it measures market imperfection rather than monopoly or oligopoly power. The margin between price and marginal cost would not be zero even in the complete absence of oligopoly, which is only one of several factors that account for this margin. Accordingly, to measure the effects of oligopoly alone, two further indexes were developed, one by Rothschild and the other (along lines suggested by Triffin and Morgan) by Papandreou.[5]

The second effect of concentration on resource allocation also

---

[4] Lerner himself, unlike most other advocates of his index, was fully aware of this objection and met it in a way similar to that suggested in the next paragraph.

[5] Cf. K. W. Rothschild, "The Degree of Monopoly," *Economica*, February 1942, pp. 214-239; Theodore Morgan, "A Measure of Monopoly in Selling," *Quarterly Journal of Economics*, May 1946, pp. 461-463; A. G. Papandreou, "Market Structure and Monopoly Power," *American Economic Review*, September 1949, pp. 883-897.

results from the gap between price and marginal cost or marginal value; but it has to do with the proportions in which the individual firm combines its different productive resources. In short, it has to do with the method of production adopted by the firm. The margin between the price and marginal cost of productive resources tends to keep the socially most desirable method of production from being also the cheapest; and owing to the pyramiding of margins at successive stages of production, it might lead to a general bias against the use of capital equipment and other manufactured factors of production. Misallocation of this type must be distinguished from misallocation of the first type, discussed in the previous section, because, unlike the first type, it increases both with the average degree of market imperfection and with its dispersion, and also because vertical integration as well as bilateral concentration in factor markets are likely to restore the correspondence between the social desirability and the money cost of different methods of production.[6]

No attempts have as yet been made to appraise the importance of this type of misallocation and the social loss resulting from it, but the approach used in the case discussed in the last section must also be used here. Lerner's index, however, or any similar index is not applicable, because it cannot show the corrective influence of vertical integration or bilateral concentration.

4. *Effect on Efficiency of the Firm*

CONCENTRATION also affects the firm's internal administrative and engineering efficiency. Since this effect is exerted through the influence of concentration on the entrepreneur's desire to maximize profits, its consideration must be prefaced by a short discussion of profit maximization.

Under pure competition, the profit of the most profitable firm is supposed to be kept at or near zero by the free entry of newcomers. All the less profitable firms therefore are suffering a loss; and it is the whip-hand of this loss that keeps each entrepreneur on his toes and, so to speak, forces him to maximize his profit. By contrast, when restraints on or costs of entry to a monopolistic or oligopolistic market suspend the operation of the competitive forces that would tend to eliminate profits, then the failure to maximize profit

6 Cf. Lionel W. McKenzie, "Ideal Output and the Interdependence of Firms," *Economic Journal*, December 1951, pp. 785-803. See also my *Welfare and Competition* (Irwin, 1951), pp. 356-363 and 437-438.

may lead merely to lower-than-maximum profits instead of to the punishment of losses. The desire for profit may be strong enough, of course, to render even the threat of low profits enough to call forth the utmost effort to maximize profits; but the widespread criticism of the assumption of profit maximization suggests that there must be many markets in our economy in which the restraint on entry and consequent guarantee of monopoly profits removes or at least greatly weakens the desire to maximize profits.

What is the significance of the oligopolist's failure to maximize profits from the point of view of efficiency? I argued in section 3 that under imperfect competition even profit maximizing behavior would lead to inefficient resource allocation; and this situation may be rendered still worse by the firm's failure to maximize profits.[7] But, and this is more important, failure to maximize profits causes inefficiency also in another sense. It can be shown that profit maximization calls for efficiency in the internal administration and engineering setup of the firm, *whatever the nature and structure of the markets in which the firm operates.* Profit maximization therefore is desirable even if market imperfection interferes with efficient resource allocation; and it may well be one of the most important effects of concentration that by weakening the incentive to maximize profits it also weakens the management's incentive to enforce and maintain the firm's internal efficiency.

The internal inefficiency of the firm may take a variety of forms. On the technical side it may involve offering the consumer an unsatisfactory product, producing a given product with wasteful and old-fashioned methods, or simply not keeping up with technological progress. On the administrative side it may mean plain bad administration, the inadequate coordination of the firm's different activities and plants, or the unnecessary and wasteful expansion of the firm's administrative bureaucracy.

It is to be noted that profit maximization is a sufficient but not a necessary condition of the maintenance of internal efficiency in the firm. Management may be interested in efficiency per se, quite apart from its effect on profits; or, to put it differently, management may be interested in minimizing costs even if it is not anxious to maximize profits. I am rather skeptical, however, about this type of argument; and the experience of this country during World War II with the cost-plus type of contract suggests strongly that the profit

[7] It could conceivably lead also to better allocation, but this does not seem very likely.

motive is still the best if not the only guarantee of efficiency in the firm.

So far as I am aware, no attempts have been made to measure this effect of concentration.

5. *Effect on Rate of Technological Progress*

IN THE last two sections we were concerned with the effect of concentration on efficiency in a static sense and on the firm's inducement to keep step with the progress of its competitors. But concentration also affects the rate of technological progress, even though the importance and the direction of this influence is a matter of controversy. There is agreement only on the fact that basic scientific research has in our day become a very expensive operation, which can be indulged in only by large firms and well-endowed universities. Big business is therefore held to promote basic scientific progress.

Entirely separate from this is the problem of how soon a given state of scientific knowledge or a given rate of scientific progress will be put to industrial use. Here again bigness plays a role, although there are several conflicting factors. To begin with, the large firm has a greater inducement than the small firm to introduce methods of production requiring a high capital investment[8] and whenever improved productive methods happen also to require a heavy investment, it is the large firms that will put them into effect the sooner and the more readily. Secondly, there is the risk factor, which pulls in the opposite direction. It has been argued that an oligopolistic market is more risky than a freely competitive one; and it is also maintained (although on somewhat incomplete evidence) that large firms are more reluctant to engage in risky ventures than are small firms. It would follow from this that investment in innovations that involve a risk would be more readily undertaken by the small firm and in the freely competitive market. Thirdly, newcomers have more of an inducement than established firms to use the most up-to-date methods; whereas the adoption of the best available methods by established firms is governed and often retarded by the rate at which their existing equipment is wearing out. Since the distinction between established firms and newcomers usually coincides with that between large and small firms, this factor also tends to associate faster progress with the small firm. Common observation suggests that the first factor often has the upper hand

8 For the reasons see p. 111 below.

over the other two but for a definitive answer we must await here too a statistical study.

6. *Conclusions*

WE ARE now ready to draw certain conclusions about the measurement of concentration from this short review of its effects. It appears, to begin with, that a simple distinction can be drawn between measures of concentration on the one hand and all other indexes of monopoly or oligopoly power on the other hand. Monopoly and oligopoly consist of a power relation among the sellers or the buyers in a certain market; and this power relation depends largely on the number and size distribution of the competing sellers or buyers. Measures of concentration try to express the number and size distribution of competitors in terms of a one-parameter index, which could then be regarded as a direct measure of the degree of oligopoly.[9]

By contrast, all other indexes and proposed indexes of oligopoly or monopoly aim at measuring it indirectly by its effects. In view of the tenuous connection between numbers and size distribution on the one hand and the resulting oligopoly situation on the other, there is a great temptation to do this. Unfortunately, however, this procedure raises other, and I suspect worse, difficulties, which are due to the great variety of effects that concentration has. If concentration is to be measured by its results, which effect should be chosen for the role of the measuring rod? The answer would be easy if one effect were more important than all the others, or if all the different effects were closely correlated. However, there is good reason to doubt the latter; and the former is one of the questions we cannot yet answer.

Bain's index of profit rates therefore must be rejected, I think, as a general measure of oligopoly power—at least until statistical investigation has established that the most important influence of concentration is its effect on income distribution, and that the creation of monopoly profit is the main aspect of its redistributive effect. It is true that the size of profits is likely to be correlated with some of the efficiency effects of concentration; but there is at least one, which may well be among the most important, with which it is not correlated. It will be recalled that one result of concentration is the weakening of the competitive pressure under which the firm maximizes profits and maintains its internal efficiency for the sake of maximizing profits. It is obvious that Bain's index is inadequate as

[9] See, however, Fellner's discussion of this paper for a three-parameter index.

a measure of the effect of concentration on the firm's internal administrative and engineering efficiency.

Lerner's index must be rejected on similar grounds. This index, unlike Bain's, is aimed primarily at expressing the effects of concentration on efficiency; and it measures not an ultimate but an intermediate effect: the margin between price and marginal (or average variable) cost. But since concentration exerts its economic effects through two channels—margins and obstacles to entry—Lerner's index is also one-sided. It registers the influence of concentration on the allocation of output and resources among different firms and industries and would be acceptable as a general index of concentration only if this were the main effect of concentration. The index fails altogether to register the firm's internal efficiency, which has to do with obstacles to entry; it is an unsatisfactory measure of the distributive effects, which have to do both with margins and with obstacles to entry; and it also fails to show the effect of concentration on technological progress and on the choice of the firm's method of production. Rothschild's and Papandreou's measures, while interesting in some respects (especially Papandreou's), are also based on the firm's profit margin and must therefore be rejected on similar grounds.

7. Standards of Adequacy

WE CAN now at long last consider the proper subject of this Conference: measures of concentration in the strict sense of the word. Since these do not aim at measuring the *effects* of concentration, they can hardly be criticized for inadequacy on that score. But the foregoing discussion suggests that their main purpose is and must be to serve as a basis for a systematic statistical appraisal of the effects of concentration. Theory can only provide a list of these effects and indicate their nature. Ahead of us is the major task of verifying the surmises of theory and appraising the importance—absolute and relative—of each effect of concentration. It is clear that for this task a good measure of concentration is required; and it is by the standard of adequacy for this task that measures of concentration must be judged.

One of the problems raised is the choice of the most suitable quantity in terms of which to measure concentration. As far as I am aware, five such quantities have been suggested: employment, sales, value added, value of total assets, and "net capital assets." Theoretical considerations are helpful, I think, in making this choice. We should expect large firms to use more capital-using and small firms to employ more labor-using methods of production for at least three reasons. One is that the scope for using labor-saving machinery increases with size. The second is that large firms are likely to be in a better bargaining position vis-à-vis the producers of equipment and therefore obtain the latter at more favorable prices than do small firms.[10] The third reason is that the factor limiting the size of small firms is usually their limited access to capital, whereas the size of large firms is limited by various other considerations; and capital theory suggests that this difference in the limit to size encourages higher capital-using methods of production in the large firm.[11] Accordingly, we should expect a measure of concentration based on employment to understate, and one based on total or "net" capital assets to overstate the degree of concentration. This would leave sales and "value added" as the best measures of size; and since "value added" data are not available at present, we should conclude that the volume of sales is the most satisfactory basis for measuring concentration.

The use of sales for this purpose has been criticized, however, on the ground that it would show horizontal concentration but not vertical integration. Indeed, if the same index is to measure both horizontal and vertical integration, then employment, or assets, or—to take care of the problem raised in the previous paragraph—some average of employment and assets, would be a more suitable quantity in terms of which to measure the degree of concentration.

It is not at all certain, however, that it is desirable to express both horizontal and vertical integration with the aid of a single measure of concentration. If our sole concern were the effect of concentration on the distribution of income and of social and political power, a single measure might suffice. But if we are also concerned, as I think we should be, with the effect of concentration on efficiency, more than one measure is needed. For some aspects of efficiency we should expect horizontal and vertical integration to pull in opposite directions. Horizontal concentration can generally be expected to *worsen* efficiency in most respects; but vertical integration is likely to *improve* efficiency at least in the firm's choice of a method of production and in its combination of the different factors of production. This was argued in section 3. It is not my task to suggest a suitable index for measuring the degree of vertical integration; but I do

10 This is the bilateral concentration referred to in section 3.
11 Scitovsky, *op. cit.*, Chap. IX, Sec. 4.

think that if the aim of measuring concentration is to help assess its economic effects, horizontal and vertical concentration as well as their measurements should be kept strictly separate.

Another result that emerges from this analysis is the need for a measure of concentration that would show the fields in which and the degree to which concentration on one side of a market is matched by concentration on the other side of the same market. We know that in some though not all respects the effects of concentration are offset by the concentration of "countervailing power"; and it is clearly desirable that measures of concentration should be such as to enable their users to deal with this problem. I am fully aware of the difficulties that arise in this connection, mainly from the fact that the relevant statistics and much of our thinking on these matters are based on classification by industry; whereas the concept of bilateral monopoly or countervailing power refers to the individual market. It is not my task, however, to make concrete suggestions in this paper; and I shall confine myself to a mere statement of the economist's needs.

Finally, a few words might be said on the problem of finding a one-parameter index with which to express the shape of the distribution of an industry's total sales (or employment, or assets, etc.) among its members. There have been many attempts to solve this problem. To mention just a few: the percentage of an industry's total sales (or employment, etc.) concentrated in a fixed number of its largest firms—this number varying between four and eight; the number of the largest firms—or the percentage of all firms they represent—that among them produce a fixed percentage of the industry's total sales; the Gini index; the attempt, mentioned by Adelman, to fit a simple one-parameter function to a cumulated frequency distribution of size, and to use the parameter of this function as an index of concentration.

It is obvious, I think, that economic theory cannot offer much help in choosing among these and similar alternatives; and the little help it does provide is largely negative. I doubt, for example, if theory can help us choose from among the indexes of the type first mentioned. So far as I know, oligopoly theory does not tell us the maximum number of firms among which competitive behavior will still be oligopolistic. Similarly and for the same reason, we have no principle for choosing the fixed percentage of an industry's sales on which to base an index of the type mentioned second; nor do we have a criterion for choosing between the first and the second type.

As to Gini's index, it must be rejected, I think, because it indicates only the inequality of size distribution and is unaffected by the total number of firms; whereas absolute numbers are clearly relevant to monopoly power. The last-mentioned index, if it can be developed, appeals to me most; but on the basis of its elegance rather than on that of economic considerations. I must admit, however, that I am no specialist on oligopoly theory, which is relevant for choosing among these alternatives; and I should look for the definitive answer to these problems to Stigler or Fellner, who are specialists on the theory of oligopoly.

COMMENT

WILLIAM FELLNER, Yale University

SCITOVSKY'S analysis is concerned with how alternative measures of monopoly and of concentration relate to specific economic and social problems. I am in general agreement with his conclusions.

So-called measures of monopoly are essentially different from measures of concentration. Measures of monopoly relate to some property of monopoly, usually conceived of as an *effect* of this market condition. Measures of concentration tell us something about the *likelihood* that monopolistic (oligopolistic) behavior will become observable. All these measures possess significant limitations.

Among the many effects of monopoly, its influence on technological progress is certainly one of the most important and perhaps *the* most important. But no simple statement can be made about this aspect of the problem. It would be hopeless to try to express the influence of monopoly and competition on progress by the sort of measure Lerner has used for a definition of monopoly in terms of its effect on the allocation of resources on static assumptions. The effect on progress presumably does *not* grow monotonically with the "degree of monopoly" in the Lerner sense or in any other independently meaningful sense. It is much more likely that the circumstances most conducive to progress are characterized by some combination of competitive market characteristics with monopolistic ones.

For fuller understanding of the bearing of competition on progress we should know more about the relationship between the research efficiency (inventive efficiency) of the firm and its size. What is even more important, given the research efficiency of the firm we should have specific knowledge of the effect of monopoly and of competition on the quality of foresight and on the strength of the profit-incentive. For, if all firms *maximized* their profits on *correct* anticipations—including correct anticipations of the future rate of technological progress—then the speed with which given inventions are technologically introduced would be the same under monopoly as under competition.[1] Monopoly and competition influence the rate of progress by their effect on research efficiency, on the quality of foresight, and on the responsiveness of firms to the profit stimulus.

In view of these circumstances, it would be unreasonable to look for a "measure of monopoly" that would directly express the effect of monopoly and of competition on progress; and any measure by-passing this dynamic effect either is subject to the severe limitations of static analysis or is a concentration measure in disguise rather than a measure of monopolistic consequences. In empirical work it seems preferable to experiment with measures of concentration, rather than with measures of monopoly, by examining the question of what behavior is observable in markets characterized by different degrees of concentration.

Yet the difficulties standing in the way of the concentration-ratio

[1] A well-known proposition maintains that in a competitive industry new-comers enter with a new method (and force old firms to price below old total costs, according to the new method) as soon as new total cost falls short of old total cost, while a monopolist will adopt a new method only if new total cost is lower than old variable cost. This suggests that progress is slower under monopoly. But the proposition obviously implies that the competitive firms have wrong foresight and that they suffer losses. If they had known that new firms would enter with a new method, there would have been fewer firms in the industry, with the result that during the lifetime of the equipment of each firm the total cost would be recovered. During each such period (construction-to-scrapping period) the competitive output would be greater than the monopolistic, but this would merely express the "static difference" between competition and monopoly. The rate of progress (rate of increase of output) *from one such period to the next* would not depend on the character of the market structure if laboratory inventions were made at the identical rate, foresight were correct, and profits were maximized under all market structures. It is true, however, that the length of the construction-to-scrapping period *may* in certain circumstances depend on the market structure. This is probably not a very significant qualification. *The essential proposition here is that with identical laboratory efficiency, perfect foresight, and profit maximization, the difference between the monopolistic and competitive output is merely the familiar difference developed by static equilibrium theory for each successive period.* Aside from some complicating factors, which have no room in a first approximation, there would in these circumstances be no further difference such as would express itself in the growth or the diminution of the "static difference" from one period to the next. Hence there would be no difference in the rate of progress (cf. my discussion of this problem in the *Quarterly Journal of Economics*, "The Influence of Market Structure on Technological Progress," November 1951, pp. 556-577 and "The Test Which Inventions Must Pass: A Correction," May 1952, pp. 297-298).

approach are very considerable, too. One of these is that the approach requires distinguishing groups of firms (industries) from one another, in a fashion which implies a judgment on cross elasticities of demand or of supply. Another difficulty is that some significant consequences of monopoly cannot be measured in a way that permits correlation analysis between concentration ratios and monopolistic consequences. At best we can try to express the concentration characteristics and *some* market results numerically, and add to this a verbal discussion of the relationship between the numerical concentration characteristics and those aspects of market behavior that lend themselves poorly to numerical description.

A concentration ratio in the conventional sense is always a single "property" of an underlying function. The function expresses on the ordinate the cumulated share[2] of an increasing number of firms, with the firms arrayed from the largest to the smallest along the abscissa. For example, the share of the four largest firms is a single property of such a function. Considering that in an analysis of the effects of concentration on market results more than one property of these functions may prove significant, the present practice of basing the measures of concentration on a single property of the underlying function may block fruitful avenues. It seems to me that a somewhat fuller description of the characteristics of these functions could convey a good deal more information, without significant loss of simplicity.

Some convention of the following sort might, for example, prove convenient. Express the share of the largest firm as one number; list the number of the firms with shares exceeding, say, 10 per cent, and make this your second number; express, as your third number, the joint share of the firms with shares exceeding, say, 10 per cent; and add or omit a parenthetical (s) sign at the end of the symbol, depending on whether small firms with individual shares of less than, say, 1 per cent, do or do not jointly account for more than 10 per cent. For example, 20—3—52 (s) would mean that the largest firm has a share of 20 per cent, that the total number of firms with a share of more than 10 per cent is three, that the joint share of these three firms is 52 per cent, and that very small firms account for more than 10 per cent of the total. A symbol of this sort is not essentially more cumbersome than that which we habitually use for denoting the day of the year, and yet some symbol of this general character

[2] This may be the share in total output or in total employment or in any other significant variable.

may give a reasonably good picture of nearly the entire course of the underlying concentration function. In our illustration we would know that the share of the largest firm is 20 per cent, that the second and the third largest firm have individual shares of between 12 per cent and 20 per cent, and that firms which are very small[3] and which are fairly small[4] in relation to the biggest firm in the group *jointly* account for 48 per cent of the total. We would know also that the joint share of the very small firms is not entirely negligible, but we would not know the distribution as between "fairly small" and "very small" firms. (If this further information were considered essential, a fourth number could be added, in the parenthesis containing the letter *s*, and this number would disclose the joint share of the very small firms.)

If we could take it for granted that the underlying concentration function (cumulated distribution) is mathematically always of the same type, we might be able to summarize the essential properties of the entire function by, say, the value of a constant in its equation (or perhaps by the curvature of the function). M. A. Adelman discussed this question, along with other important ones, in his article in the November 1951 issue of the *Review of Economics and Statistics*. However, it seems unlikely to me that the same sort of function would fit reasonably well all or most of the concentration data. This is why I believe that a description of the kind here suggested might be more useful.

Scitovsky gave a constructive and revealing discussion of the relationship between measures of monopoly and measures of concentration on the one hand, and particular research objectives on the other. His discussion strengthens my conviction that measures of concentration, in spite of all their shortcomings, possess the advantage of being less specifically tailored to narrow objectives than are our measures of monopoly. I believe that one of the present shortcomings of measures of concentration would be reduced (perhaps eliminated) if in these measures we could summarize several essential properties of the underlying distribution.

CARL KAYSEN, Harvard University

SCITOVSKY's paper provides a lucid classification of the effects of concentration, and argues that measures registering only one of

---

[3] Possessing a share of less than 1 per cent.
[4] Possessing a share of less than 10 per cent but more than 1 per cent.

these effects—e.g. measures of profits, or measures of the discrepancy between price and marginal cost—are not good substitutes for direct measures of the number and size distribution of the competing sellers (buyers) in the market. Thus, in his view, the application of economic theory to the problem of measuring concentration supports the continuing attempt to find a good one-parameter summary of the size distribution of the most "appropriate" variable within the limits of the data. Scitovsky thinks this is sales.

This comment endorses a somewhat modified version of Scitovsky's conclusion, but on an entirely different view as to what economic theory shows. The application of price theory to the problem of the measurement of concentration suggests that more sophisticated and precise measures than those provided by any one-parameter summary of the size distribution of firms' sales are not worth the trouble of definition and computation. A simple index of the sort suggested can point to the existence of markets in which the presence and effects of oligopoly deserve detailed study; no more sophisticated measure calculable *without* such detailed study of the particular market can do any more.

This assertion rests on two bases. The first is provided by price theory in general; namely, that the delimitation of the market in which concentration is to be measured typically presents substantial problems and cannot be solved by recourse to Census classifications of industries or commodities. The market has both product and geographic boundaries; in neither product space nor geographic space are these boundaries sharp. To delimit the market in terms of products requires examination of both the chain of potential substitutes at various prices as seen by buyers and the widening circle of potential rival suppliers at various prices as seen by sellers. Similar problems arise in drawing the geographic boundaries of markets for the many commodities for which production is localized and transportation costs are significant. In general, the examination of the power of sellers (or buyers) in any particular market reveals a concentration of interrelated markets with influences of varying degrees of strength on the transactions in the particular commodity or service under examination. The more important of these influences must be included in defining the market relevant to the measure of concentration. Otherwise, an index of concentration would not serve to distinguish monopoly from product specialization.

The second basis of skepticism as to the utility of refined measures of concentration arises from the present state of the theory of oligopoly. This objection is more fundamental than the previous one, and would justify the standpoint of this comment if market boundaries always coincided with Census product definitions. Scitovsky says: "Monopoly and oligopoly consist of the power relation among the sellers or buyers in a certain market; and this power relation depends largely on the number and size distribution of the competing sellers or buyers. Measures of concentration try to express the number and size distribution of competitors in terms of a one-parameter index, which could then be regarded as a direct measure of the degree of oligopoly." The premise of this argument—that the power relation depends chiefly on the number and size distribution of competing sellers—must be denied. Many other features of the market are relevant to this "power relation." At least the following are of equal importance with the number and size distribution of sellers in many market situations: the rate of growth of demand over time, the character and speed of technological change, the degree to which sellers operate in other markets, the extent and nature of product differentiation, and the goals of individual firm policy—e.g. profit maximization vs. security. The failure of oligopoly theory in its present form to assist in the prediction of market behavior, or even to provide a framework for investigating particular markets, springs from its inability to take account of these and similar variables. It seems vain to expect that numbers and size distribution alone will explain market behavior, and therefore equally vain to hope for more from concentration measures than that they should provide a preliminary basis on which resources for further study should be allocated.

This comment is, of course, propaganda: propaganda for more studies of the operation of particular markets, and for elaboration of oligopoly theory to the point where it can begin to explain the results of such studies.

MEASURES OF MONOPOLY POWER AND CONCENTRATION: THEIR ECONOMIC SIGNIFICANCE

JOHN PERRY MILLER

YALE UNIVERSITY

THE purpose of this paper is to discuss the significance of various measures of monopoly power and concentration for both economic analysis and public policy. It is perhaps a sign of the immaturity of the science of economics that the notion should persist that the competitiveness of the economy or of a sector of the economy can ultimately be characterized by some single number or set of numbers. One might have supposed that theoretical and empirical developments in the last two decades would have brought home the essentially heterogeneous nature of our industrial structure and behavior.[1] But the illusion still persists in influential quarters that there is some simple key which will enable us to separate the monopolistic from the competitive. This paper is designed not to disparage progress to date but rather by underlining its limitations to suggest the magnitude of the task ahead.

1. *Aspects of Competition*

THE interests of economists in measures of monopoly and competition have been mixed. In part the interest has been in economic analysis, i.e. in distinguishing market situations according to such characteristics as the objective market conditions, the processes of decision making, or economic results. But much of the work in the field has been oriented quite understandably to issues of public policy, i.e. toward distinguishing desirable from undesirable market situations, workable from unworkable competition, etc. The policy approach may be at once both narrower and broader than the analytical. It is often narrower in that attention is focused on variables

---

[1] See, for example, Edward H. Chamberlin, "Monopolistic Competition Revisited," *Economica*, November 1951, pp. 343-362; Friedrich A. Hayek, *Individualism and Economic Order* (University of Chicago Press, 1948), Chap. 5; Joe S. Bain, "Price and Production Policies," in Howard S. Ellis, editor, *A Survey of Contemporary Economics* (Blakiston, 1948); John M. Clark, "Toward a Concept of Workable Competition," *American Economic Review*, June 1940, pp. 241-256; Arthur R. Burns, *The Decline of Competition* (McGraw-Hill, 1936); Clair Wilcox, *Competition and Monopoly in American Industry*, Temporary National Economic Committee, Monograph 21, 1940.

that are operationally measurable and upon identifying situations where it is feasible both politically and administratively to take action. Certain analytically significant factors may therefore be left out of consideration. But the policy approach may also be broader in some respects since it is concerned with such noneconomic aspects of market situations as the effects of market structures and practices upon political structures and the processes of political power, upon career opportunities and the processes of personnel selection, or upon the development of human personalities and the distribution of prestige. These noneconomic factors have bulked large in some of the discussions of antitrust policy, although little effort has been made to define with care the issues involved or to correlate kinds of market structures and practices with various political or social effects.[2]

Even when looking at the purely economic aspects of market situations, various economists have emphasized different aspects of the situations including:

1. *The objective characteristics of the market*, e.g. the number and size of the decision-making units, the ease of entry, the characteristics of the product, the characteristics of the buyers, and the rate of growth and age of the industry.[3]

2. *The power of the decision-making unit*, i.e. the kinds and extent of discretion available to the decision-making unit consistent with survival.

3. *The activities of decision-making units*, i.e. the exercise of discretion with respect to internal activities such as the use of resources, research and development, and investment policies and with respect to such external activities as the shaping of preferences, market development, pricing, procurement, and related trade practices.

4. *The economic effects of the activities of decision-making units*, i.e. the effects of economic activities in bringing about a mutual adaptation of wants and resources, including the rate of economic development, the allocation of resources and the efficiency with which they are used, and the allocation of income and wealth.

Differences in emphasis depend in part upon differences in the value orientation of various students. But more important are the differences in vision as to the nature of the competitive process, dif-

---

[2] It is clear from the legislative, administrative, and judicial history of our antitrust laws that noneconomic factors have played an important part in shaping policy in this area.

[3] See for example, Bain, *op. cit.*, pp. 160-161.

ferences that are likely to remain substantial until we develop a verified theory of market structures and behavior.[4] The limiting cases of markets characterized by perfect competition and perfect monopoly are reasonably well understood. But, although there has been a good deal of exploratory work in the areas between, these areas have proved relatively intractable to the traditional methods of economics.[5]

While the current body of theory provides a useful frame of reference for ordering empirical data and analyzing problems of policy, it is important to recognize certain limitations of this body of thought for the purpose at hand, limitations arising from the fact that the modern theory of the firm and market behavior is largely a by-product of efforts to refine the neo-classical theory of perfect competition. The essence of the perfectly competitive market is a condition in which the function of the firm is simply to adapt its input and output decisions in the light of market-determined prices. Significant deviations from the principle of profit maximization are incompatible with survival. Activities are confined, therefore, by the nature of the market structure to deciding the volume of inputs and outputs in light of the maximizing principle and to administering resources within the firm.

In an economy characterized by the Schumpeterian circular flow,

[4] In his summary-comments on a symposium conducted on the effectiveness of the antitrust laws, Dexter M. Keezer remarks ". . . one fact seems to emerge with increasing clarity. This fact . . . is that the concepts of competition and of a 'broadly competitive system' are so diverse that they offer wide latitude for difference of opinion as to the effectiveness of the antitrust laws . . . until we expose the various and complicated strands of our concepts of competition, and then put them together in a clear-cut design which we all understand and accept, our chances of charting clearly how well we are doing in preserving and protecting competition will be seriously compromised." "The Antitrust Laws; A Symposium," *American Economic Review*, June 1949, pp. 722-723.

[5] "Disencumbered, however, of all the limitations and taboos implied in the classical assumptions, the way is now open for the building up of a different type of economics. Instead of drawing its substance from arbitrary assumptions, chosen for their simplicity and unduly extended to the whole field of economic activity, our theory may turn to more pedestrian, but more fruitful methods. It will recognize the richness and variety of all concrete cases, and tackle each problem with due respect for its individual aspects. . . .

"We are rightly dissatisfied with the distorted picture of economic life which classical theory has bequeathed us. Subconsciously, however, we keep hoping for some other grand formula that would unravel as simply and elegantly the infinite complexity of our modern world. For economics to progress, it must give up its youthful quest for a philosophers' stone." Robert Triffin, *Monopolistic Competition and General Equilibrium Theory* (Harvard University Press, 1940), p. 189. See also William Fellner, *Competition among the Few* (Knopf, 1949), especially pp. 3-15.

it is assumed that individual preference scales, the body of knowledge, production functions, and the volume and efficiency of resources are fixed. It is usually further assumed that these variables are independent both of one another and of economic activity. Under less restrictive assumptions of an economy subject to fluctuation and secular change these variables may be conceived as subject to change. But in the case of perfect competition, such change is assumed to be exogenous to the firm. Even in such a world of change, the function of the firm in the perfectly competitive market is viewed as simply the adaptation of inputs and outputs to changes in market prices that in turn reflect changes in preference scales, the body of knowledge, production functions, and the supply of resources. The continuation of a condition of perfect competition is viewed as incompatible with activities by the firm designed to change these basic parameters of the system.

In the development theories of monopolistic or imperfectly competitive markets it has often been assumed that preferences, resources, the body of knowledge, and production functions are fixed or at least independent of the activities of the firm. As a result, the function of the firm has been conceived as that of adapting inputs and outputs in the light of these parameters and of specified conditions of interdependence between firms. The principal exceptions to this have been the attempts, as yet not too successful, to introduce advertising into the body of economic theory[6] and the work of Schumpeter who insisted on the innovating functions of the entrepreneur.[7]

In considering the various measures of monopoly power, it is important to bear in mind the limitations of the analytical models from which they arose, especially their preoccupation with price and output decisions to the exclusion of other activities. But the essence of much business behavior is the conscious attempt to shape preferences; to develop new resources; to seek, adapt, and add to the body of knowledge; to protect and extend market positions, thereby reshaping market structures; to influence interdependence by learning about the reactions of others and by affecting the expectations upon which others act.

[6] See especially Edward H. Chamberlin, *Monopolistic Competition* (Harvard University Press, 1933). Also George J. Stigler, *The Theory of Price* (rev. ed., Macmillan, 1952), pp. 207-209; N. S. Buchanan, "Advertising Expenditures; A Suggested Treatment," *Journal of Political Economy*, August 1942, pp. 537-557.

[7] Joseph A. Schumpeter, *Business Cycles* (McGraw-Hill, 1939), I, 2-3; *Capitalism, Socialism, and Democracy* (Harper, 1942), Chap. 8.

This view of the function of the firm implies that the processes of competition are infinitely more complex than is often assumed, and that the links between objective conditions, economic power, activities, and results are more involved than is often represented. Over a wide area of modern industry the important factor is the existence of a range of discretion often used in ways that violate the static assumptions. Our real interest is less in the *state of monopoly* or *competition* than in the *process of competing* and *monopolizing*. ". . . the modern theory of competitive equilibrium *assumes* the situation to exist which a true explanation ought to account for as the effect of the competitive process."[8] We should aim at devising measures characterizing not the *state of monopoly* but rather the *nature of the competitive process* conceived as a process of innovation and adaptation proceeding through time.

2. *Theoretical Indexes of Monopoly and Competition*

SEVERAL attempts to define theoretical indexes of monopoly power approach the problem from the point of view of the individual firm, although they can be adapted to the situation of a group of firms acting in concert. These indexes arise in general from the static theory of the firm and have the limitations attached thereto. With the exception of the Lerner index, the operational usefulness of these indexes is not great since they assume some knowledge of the elasticity or cross-elasticity of demand, knowledge that is generally hard to come by.

LERNER INDEX

PERHAPS the most famous of the indexes of monopoly power is that of Lerner,[9] $m = $ (price—marginal cost)/price. This index, m, may be equal to, greater than, or less than zero according as the product is sold at, above, or below marginal cost.

The Lerner index is clearly not a good indicator of differences in objective conditions of the market. To be sure, in the limiting case of a profit maximizing firm in equilibrium, the Lerner index is the inverse of the elasticity of demand and may, therefore, be taken as a characterization of the demand for the product of the firm. But in the case of a nonmaximizing firm it is no guide to the nature of demand.

8 Hayek, *op. cit.*, p. 94.
9 A. P. Lerner, "The Concept of Monopoly and the Measurement of Monopoly Power," *Review of Economic Studies* (1933-1934), pp. 157-175.

It is essentially an index of the extent of divergence from marginal cost pricing. As such it is an indicator of one aspect of the economic results of business behavior, and its significance depends on the relevance of marginal cost pricing as a condition of the desirable allocation of resources.[10] But at best the Lerner index is a limited index of results. While it indicates the divergence between marginal cost and price, it tells nothing about the extent to which market pressures or administrative action keep the costs at a minimum in the light of the existing body of knowledge, or to what extent competitive pressures stimulate costly sales effort and firms of uneconomic size, or to what extent the potentialities of technological development are being exploited. Although the Lerner index is designed primarily to indicate the effects of economic activities upon the allocation of economic resources, it has all the limitations of the static model from which it is derived. For a sector of the economy approaching the state of the Schumpeterian circular flow it may be reasonably useful, but even here it may fail to distinguish between firms operating along minimum cost functions and those which are not. For a world of fluctuation and growth its use is limited. Any given value of the index for a sector of the economy may be consistent with various total conditions of the sector and with various rates of change. The index makes no allowance for differences in activities of the firm in shaping preferences and developing resources, for different degrees of initiative in seeking, adapting, and adding to the body of knowledge, for various rates of fluctuation in the use of resources, or for various distributions of income and wealth and of gains and losses incident to change. Clearly, it tells us nothing about the distribution of power, whether economic or political, or about the other social and political repercussions of economic activity.

CROSS-ELASTICITIES OF DEMAND

BRIEFER mention will be made of several suggestions for distinguishing markets primarily on the basis of the conditions of demand for the product of the individual firm. While these proposals differ in detail, they are all concerned primarily with the discretion available to the firm to affect price or output.

[10] For discussion of this issue, see in particular Kenneth E. Boulding, "Welfare Economics," in Bernard F. Haley, *A Survey of Contemporary Economics*, II (Irwin, 1952); I. M. D. Little, *A Critique of Welfare Economics* (Oxford University Press, 1950); Nancy Ruggles, "The Welfare Basis of the Marginal Cost Pricing Principle," and "Recent Developments in the Theory of Marginal Cost Pricing," *Review of Economic Studies* (1949-1950), pp. 29-46, 107-126.

A frequent approach to the problem of monopoly power has been via the concept of the cross elasticity of demand.[11] If there are no close substitutes for the product X of a firm—that is, no other products whose price changes may affect the demand for X—the cross elasticities of demand for X with respect to all products are zero. This is the limiting case of perfect monopoly. At the other extreme is the case of pure competition where present units of demand will shift from one supplier to another upon the slightest difference in price. In this case the cross elasticities of demand for X with respect to the products of some rivals approach infinity. The more usual case is that in which the cross elasticities of demand for X with respect to the products of many other firms are zero but with respect to one or more is greater than zero but less than infinity.

This index, or cluster of indexes, is designed to indicate something about the range of discretion with respect to price available to the individual firm. While it is unambiguous in the limiting cases of perfect competition and a profit-seeking monopolist in static conditions, it is of doubtful significance in the intermediate range of cases or under conditions of change. It does not really indicate the range of effective discretion since it rules out of consideration relevant non-price factors and does not distinguish between alternative anticipations of rivals' reactions that may be crucial in markets with few firms. Thus, in the case of two firms selling a homogeneous product, the cross elasticities may be infinite. Yet it is well known that the behavior of the rivals and the resulting price and production policies may take any of several forms.[12] Moreover, this approach indicates nothing about non-price types of discretion, the objective conditions of the market, the firms' activities, or the results of such activities. In a world of fluctuation and change, this approach has all the other limitations discussed in connection with the Lerner index.

ROTHSCHILD'S INDEX

K. W. ROTHSCHILD has suggested an index of the degree of monopoly designed to show how far a particular firm controls the market for a commodity.[13] He defines his index as $m = (\tan a / \tan b)$ where

[11] Nicholas Kaldor, "Market Imperfection and Excess Capacity," *Economica*, February 1935, pp. 33-50; Stigler, *op. cit.*, pp. 205-207.
[12] Chamberlin, *op. cit.*, Chap. 3; Fellner, *op. cit.*
[13] K. W. Rothschild, "The Degree of Monopoly," *Economica*, February 1942, pp. 24-39. For discussion of this, see Joe S. Bain, "Measurements of the Degree

$d\ d'$ is the demand curve for the individual firm on the assumption that "competing firms do not change their price (or output)" and $D\ D'$ is the demand curve on the assumption that "other firms change their price (or output) in the same or some other predetermined way as the firm in question." This index presumes, then,

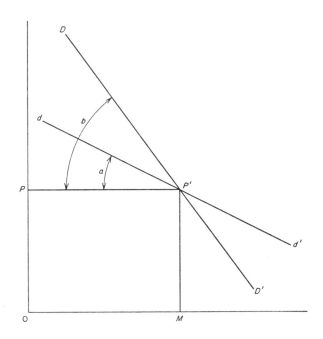

some knowledge or assumption concerning the reactions of other firms. It may be equal to or greater than zero and equal to or less than one. If the demand curve for the product of the individual firm is independent of the reactions of other firms, $d\ d'$ and $D\ D'$ coincide and the index is equal to one. If the firm is producing under purely competitive conditions so that its price is market-determined and completely independent of its own discretion, the index is equal to zero.

While this index has the advantage of making allowance for the reactions of rivals, it seems otherwise to have all the disadvantages and ambiguities incident to the approach through cross-elasticities.

of Monopoly: A Note," *Economica*, February 1943, pp. 66-68; K. W. Rothschild, "A Further Note on the Degree of Monopoly," *Economica*, February 1943, pp. 69-70; Theodore Morgan, "A Measure of Monopoly in Selling," *Quarterly Journal of Economics*, May 1946, pp. 461-463.

PAPANDREOU'S INDEX

PAPANDREOU, emphasizing the efforts of rivals to invade one another's markets, has proposed to measure the competitive relations among firms by two coefficients, one of penetration and one of insulation.[14] His coefficient of penetration, which measures the capacity of a firm to penetrate its competitors' markets by a price cut, takes into account both its capacity to attract customers and to match with units of supply the demand that stands ready to shift upon a price change. His coefficient of insulation is designed to measure the degree of nonresponsiveness of the actual volume of sales of a firm to price cuts initiated by its competitors. This approach has the advantage of recognizing the limits that the availability of capacity places upon competitive strategies, a factor neglected by the simple cross-elasticity approach. But otherwise this approach seems to suffer from most of the remaining limitations of the cross-elasticity approach, a fact that Papandreou clearly concedes.[15]

BAIN'S INDEX OF PROFITABILITY

JOE S. BAIN has been the principal proponent of the profit rate as a measure of monopoly power or "of deviations from competitive equilibrium." In his article of 1941[16] he proposed that the profit rate be defined as "in any short period the ratio of the net earnings of that period (quasi-rents less depreciation computed as indicated) to the replacement cost of service value of those assets of the firm which it could economically hold at a minimum and produce its present output." A comparison of the rate of profit so defined with the rate of interest "is therefore an indicator of the deviation of the earnings behavior of the firm from a selected norm. A deviation for a year or two is obviously significant of nothing more than that the firm operates in a cyclical economy. A persistent deviation over a period of years, however, is an indication of a failure of the competitive mechanism to force an approximation to equilibrium, and therefore a probable indication of monopoly or monopsony power, or less probably of pure competition with persistent impediment to entry."[17]

[14] A. G. Papandreou, "Market Structure and Monopoly Power," *American Economic Review*, September 1949, pp. 883-897.
[15] *Ibid.*, p. 897.
[16] Joe S. Bain, "The Profit Rate as a Measure of Monopoly Power," *Quarterly Journal of Economics*, February 1941, pp. 271-293.
[17] *Ibid.*, pp. 287-288.

It is clear that the Bain index may reflect the cumulative effect of several factors. For an economy in the state of circular flow it would reflect (1) profits incident to limitations upon entry into a given industry, whether the industry is "monopolistic" or purely competitive, (2) monopsonistic profits, and (3) the wasteful costs incident to investment in excess of the minimum necessary to produce present output.[18] In a world of economic fluctuation and secular change, the rate of profit would include as well (4) the effects of fortuitous change, (5) temporary profits and losses incident to the adjustment of the economy to exogenous changes, and (6) profits and losses incident to innovation.

The profit rate so defined is primarily an index of the gross effects of economic activity. It should be noted that since the rate of profit as defined by Bain involves an allowance for unnecessary expenditures with reference to the competitive norm, this profit rate has no necessary relation to the profit rate as viewed by business in a private enterprise economy. Bain emphasizes the significance of his index because of the effect of the profit rate "directly on the functional distribution of income, and indirectly on the propensity to consume, the level of employment, etc."[19] But in view of the synthetic nature of the Bain index, including as it does elements of unnecessary investment expenditures as well as profit in the usual economic sense, this index would seem to be of limited significance in these respects. Two situations with the same rate of profit in Bain's sense are consistent with different rates of profit in the usual sense and, therefore, with different effects on the distribution of income, the propensity to consume, the level of employment, etc.

The Bain index seems to be oriented primarily at welfare considerations, i.e. at providing some index of the efficiency with which resources are allocated and used. For purposes of both analysis and policy it is useful to separate the two components of the Bain index: (1) profits in the traditional economic sense and (2) unnecessary investment expenditures. The first component reflects the willingness and ability of owners of resources to respond to profit differentials and as such indicates in a rough way the effectiveness of the profit

18 It is not clear that Bain would remove from "costs" and add to the "profits" any *variable* expenditure which would be unnecessary in the "competitive norm," e.g. advertising, although this would seem to be consistent with his objective.
19 Bain, "Measurements of the Degree of Monopoly: A Note," as cited, p. 66.

stimulus in allocating resources *to* various sectors of the economy. It is a reasonably objective index. The second component is indicative in part of the effectiveness with which resources are organized *within* any sector, the extent of "wasteful" or "unnecessary" investment. As such this second component depends upon some comparison of the actual organization of resources within a sector with some "ideal" organization.

A normal rate of profit as measured by the first component is indicative of a low range of discretion consistent with survival. A high rate of profit associated with the first component of the Bain index may be indicative of either fortuitous circumstances, the imperfect adaptation of resources because of the time necessary for such adaptation, innovation, or a monopolistic or monopsonistic position. Since the first two must be ruled out as typically unimportant for long periods, a persisting high rate of profit requires further analysis to determine whether it arises from a more or less permanently entrenched position or from a monopoly position which is continually renewed by successful innovative effort. But although this component may be suggestive of the *extent* of discretion open to the firm, it tells us little about the *types* of discretion available.

The second component of the Bain index indicates the extent to which assets are held by a given firm or industry in excess of the minimum necessary to produce its present output. Clearly this reflects the wastes of investment due to excess capacity or "competitive" strategies. But it does not indicate whether there is "excessive" multiplication of products, nor does it indicate whether firms have found the most efficient method of production, nor whether the market is stimulating or retarding the improvement of products and processes. A normal rate of profit may be consistent with enlightened, progressive management working under aggressively competitive conditions or with inefficient, lethargic, routine management functioning in a protected position.[20]

[20] It should be noted in passing that despite the note of optimism in **Bain's** article of 1941 concerning the feasibility of approaching such an estimate of profits, I know of no attempts to date to do so. Bain's own efforts in his study of the Pacific Coast petroleum industry (*Pacific Coast Petroleum Industry*, 3 parts, University of California Press, 1944-1947), and his general study of the relation of profit rates to industrial concentration ("Relation of Profit Rate to Industry Concentration, American Manufacturing, 1936-1940," *Quarterly Journal of Economics*, August 1951, pp. 293-324) consider profits on "actual" rather than "economically necessary" investment.

3. *Ratios of Concentration*

A LARGE body of literature has developed in the last two decades on industrial concentration and its significance.[21] The concentration ratio is a common-sense approach, treating sectors of the economy at the level of the industry rather than at the level of the firm. But the industry concept raises serious classificatory problems of both a theoretical and practical sort, problems of delineating the boundaries of the industry in terms of the range of products and firms, and the geographical area to be included. These problems of classification are discussed in other papers in this Conference. It is sufficient to note that if the industry is defined too broadly, the concentration index may tend to understate the monopolistic potentialities of a situation; if it is defined too narrowly, the monopolistic potentialities may be grossly exaggerated.

The concentration ratio is, of course, a useful index of one characteristic of market structures. But the crucial question is whether there is any close correlation between the degree of concentration and the character of the competitive forces at work in a sector of the economy. An influential body of opinion holds that there is at least a rough correlation. This view holds that a combination of high concentration of output in a market with large size, measured in terms of the value of assets or number of employees, will generally be associated with monopoly rather than competition.

But what does the concentration ratio tell us? A low concentration ratio indicates a number of points of initiative and the existence of numerous alternatives available to buyers. It suggests that the range of discretion open to any one firm consistent with survival will be narrow. If there is relatively free entry and the absence of restrictive agreements, it is probable that there will be considerable pressure upon the firm to be efficient in its production, procurement, and marketing. Moreover, one would expect a general tendency for resources to flow in response to profit differentials. The concentration ratio will not, however, distinguish the kinds of competition,

21 See in addition to articles in this Conference, *The Structure of the American Economy*, National Resources Committee, 1939; Willard L. Thorp and Walter F. Crowder, *The Structure of Industry*, TNEC, Monograph 27, 1941; *The Concentration of Productive Facilities, 1947*, Federal Trade Commission, 1949; M. A. Adelman, "The Measurement of Industrial Concentration," *Review of Economics and Statistics*, November 1951, pp. 269-296; Corwin D. Edwards and others, "Four Comments on 'The Measurement of Industrial Concentration'; with a Rejoinder by Professor Adelman," *Review of Economics and Statistics*, May 1952, pp. 156-178.

i.e. between situations where competition takes the form of rivalry in price and those where it is deflected into sales effort or product differentiation. Moreover, it is in no way indicative of the opportunities and incentives to add to the body of knowledge or to develop resources. The most that can be assumed is that resources are responding to profit opportunities and that incentives to efficient use of resources within the firm are strong. Whether the environment promotes economic progress or whether it fosters "wasteful" non-price competition is open to question. How "workable" or "desirable" is the competition will depend upon further findings on these matters. But one can assume that output, efficiency, and innovation are not being restricted by the arbitrary decision of a few.

More serious difficulties arise in interpreting high concentration ratios. It is clear in such cases that the market has some monopolistic characteristics: it is not purely or perfectly competitive and there is some degree of mutual interdependence. But a typical view goes beyond this and assumes that the degree of discretion is substantial and that this discretion will be used for purposes detrimental to the best use of resources.

In a situation where the structure of the market, preference schedules, the supply of resources, and the body of knowledge can be taken as given or as subject primarily to exogenous change, it would be reasonable to assume that a high concentration ratio indicates monopolistic practices, i.e. practices restricting production or wasteful of resources. There are markets to which such a model may be applied without doing too great violence to the facts. The case of the cigarette industry, which has been well documented by two studies recently, is a case in point.[22] But even in a market approaching this state, it is not at all clear that there will be a high correlation between the degree of concentration and the degree of restrictiveness or waste. The degree of discretion, the activities of the firm, and the economic results will depend upon many factors. Among these will be the substitutability of products not included within the industry; the effectiveness of potential competition, which depends upon the availability of knowledge and resources and the costs of entry, and upon the character of patent control and the extent of equivalent inventions; the expectations concerning rivals'

[22] Richard B. Tennant, *The American Cigarette Industry* (Yale University Press, 1950) and William H. Nicholls, *Price Policies in the Cigarette Industry* (Vanderbilt University Press, 1951). In this case the principal exception to the circumstances envisaged by the typical static model is sales effort designed to shift preferences as between brands.

reactions and the competitive strategies resulting therefrom. Moreover, the extent and effect of economic power will depend not only upon the proportion of the market that a firm controls, but also upon the extent of integration of the firm and the point in the production and distribution process at which it is located. There is a substantial difference in the potential power of a firm or a few firms controlling the production of a basic raw material such as aluminum and the power of the large chains in the retail grocery field. The way this power is used in such cases and its economic effects likewise differ.

But in the modern economy in which the activities of the firm play an important part in economic change, the concentration ratio has further limitations. In such an economy the activities of the firm may be as important as the structure of the industry. It is crucial in considering highly concentrated industries to remember that the market itself is often an important variable in the competitive process. There is plenty of evidence in the last fifty years that the market positions of many dominant firms were insecure. A firm must be constantly alert to defend and enlarge its position. The question is how its position may be secured. For this reason, the concentration ratio must be regarded not only as one of the factors conditioning the current behavior of the market but also as one of the results of previous behavior. A high concentration ratio may be the result of aggressive, restrictive, and exclusive practices as in the case of many of the early "trusts," or it may be the result of control over strategic resources or patents. But it may also be the result of aggressive policies of innovation, market development, and cost reduction as in the aluminum industry.

The history of Alcoa is a significant case in point. It was virtually the sole domestic producer of virgin aluminum ingots from the beginning of the industry until World War II. Its discretion was limited only by rival products such as copper and steel, by imports of aluminum often limited by cartels and tariffs, and by the supply of secondary aluminum. There is no doubt that Alcoa had a wide range of discretion in many markets for a long period of time, although we are a long way from understanding the extent of this discretion.

But consider the other side of the picture. Alcoa was responsible for the development of a new basic material, and for continuous research into new uses for this material and new processes for its production. Any of the usual statistical measures of concentration in

132

industry during this period will show that this industry was from the beginning highly concentrated. Moreover, since the industry represented an increasing share of the economy, any overall index of industrial concentration would show *ceteris paribus* an increasing concentration. Yet the net impact of Alcoa was to increase competition by increasing the number of alternatives available to metal fabricators and consumers. Its effect was to increase the cross elasticities of demand for a wide variety of products, thereby narrowing the discretion available to producers of other materials for which it was a substitute.

These remarks are made without prejudice to the question of whether some other structure of the aluminum industry would have increased or reduced the competitive thrust of Alcoa or whether there are on balance good reasons of public policy to disapprove of the concentration of control of a basic material such as aluminum in the hands of a single firm, no matter how benevolent its intentions or beneficent its effects. I wish only to emphasize that sole reliance upon concentration ratios may lead to a distorted view of the competitive process. While the concentration ratio of an increasingly important industry remained virtually stationary at 100, the markets for metals were experiencing a dramatic increase in the competitive forces.

But the history of a firm developing a new product or a new method where there are no legal or other obstacles to entry need not be one leading to a high rate of concentration. A policy of short-run profit maximizing may lead instead to the multiplication of firms and a low rate of concentration, the innovator acting as an umbrella for the development of new competitors.[23] This contrasts with a policy of low prices and high volume that might result in high concentration. We would have to know a good deal more about these alternatives if we are to judge the relative merits in terms of economic or other effects. In the kind of world we live in behavior is not necessarily structurally determined by preference schedules, production functions, and the prices of the factors of production.

Skepticism about the significance of concentration as an index of monopoly behavior is reinforced by the limited studies of the effects of concentration that are available. Some of these are discussed in other papers. Mention may be made of a few. Alfred Neal in his study of price flexibility in the great depression concluded:

[23] Chamberlin, *op. cit.*, Chap. 5.

"First for the 1929-1933 period, there was a slight tendency, as has been claimed by proponents of the concentration thesis, for production to fall most where price fell least. (This relation does not obtain in the 1929-1931 period.) Neither price change nor production change, however, is to be explained by concentration. Rather, differential price changes are explicable by differential unit direct cost changes, and differential production changes are to be explained in terms of demand shifts which are a consequence of the nature of the demands concerned.

"Secondly, differential price behavior among industries for both comparisons (1929-1931 and 1929-1933) is to be explained for the most part by differential unit direct cost behavior rather than by concentration.

"Thirdly, concentration does not even explain the *difference* between actual price declines and those which could be expected on the basis of changes in direct cost. This conclusion is reasonable in view of the differences in cost structures among industries.

"In the fourth place, however, concentration did have a small but significant influence upon the decline in the difference between unit price and unit direct cost—the overhead-plus-profits margin. This margin tended to decline least where concentration was high; most where it was low."[24]

Similarly Ruggles in his paper in this Conference concludes with reference to the period 1929-1932 that "the major patterns of price behavior in the economy can be explained in terms of factors other than concentration."[25] Finally, although Bain found a correlation between concentration and the rate of profit for the period 1936-1940, his results are highly tentative.[26]

The crucial significance of the degree of concentration as a tool of economic analysis or as a guide to public policy has yet to be established. While it may be assumed that it is in the area of concentrated industries that the important cases of monopoly restrictions will appear, it has not been established that there is a unique correlation between the degree of concentration and either the degree of discretion available to the firm, the types of business practices pursued, or the character of the economic effects. This does not mean that further work may not show some relation between con-

[24] Alfred C. Neal, *Industrial Concentration and Price Inflexibility* (American Council on Public Affairs, 1942), pp. 165-166.

[25] See p. 488.

[26] Bain, "Relation of Profit Rate to Industry Concentration," as cited, pp. 293-324.

centration and important aspects of competition. Moreover, evidence on concentration may be administratively useful as a basis for preliminary screening of cases under review with an eye to possible antitrust proceedings or other policy action. But it appears both on a priori grounds and on the basis of such empirical evidence as we have that the extent of concentration is only one of several important variables to be examined, whether the interest is in economic analysis or public policy.

4. Some Suggestions for Further Research

ATTEMPTS to characterize various sectors of our economy in a meaningful way by simple indexes of concentration, profitability, and monopoly have not been very successful. There is a growing consensus that further progress in developing a meaningful theory of market structures and behavior lies in empirical work designed to test the significance of various hypotheses and to suggest new hypotheses of more relevance to the economic experience to which such a theory is addressed.

This field of economics, which has grown out of the very center of neoclassical economics, is at about the stage in which the field of business cycles stood in 1900, before the pioneering data collection and analysis of the National Bureau of Economic Research, the Harvard Committee on Economic Statistics, and other similar groups. But if we are to achieve an understanding of the competitive processes, we must develop a verified theory of market structure and behavior relevant to an economy in constant change. Such a theory should explain not only the processes by which wants and resources are mutually adapted, but also the constantly changing structure of markets and behavior by which this mutual adaptation is brought about. While intensive studies of individual firms, industries, and trade practices must play an important part in such a development, their usefulness would be immeasurably increased if they could be related to a broad, empirical analysis of the competitive process. At present the principal frame of reference is the vision of the static economy or the circular flow, in which change is treated as essentially exogenous to the system, and market structure and behavior are taken as structurally determined. This vision, the main contours of which date back to Adam Smith, represents a substantial contribution to economic thinking, which is still valuable for purposes of economic analysis. But while some are inclined to underestimate its usefulness, most will agree that this vision has serious shortcomings.

Whether we shall be able to devise a more fruitful vision of our economy remains to be seen.

An important step forward would be the development of an over-all picture of the changing contours of business structure and behavior in major sectors and subsectors of the economy. It should be feasible to develop for major sectors and subsectors a series of indexes reflecting the competitive processes over substantial periods of time. These indexes might cover such factors as (1) strategic aspects of industrial structure, e.g. numbers, size, concentration, rate of growth, and change in rank order of firms; (2) important aspects of industrial behavior, e.g. price and cost flexibility, price and cost trends, sales efforts, and technological and managerial innovation; and (3) important aspects of results, e.g. changes in the rate of investment, rate of output, gross margins, and profit rates and the development of new product lines. Clearly, much remains to be done in defining and constructing adequate indexes. But there are many data at hand that have not been fully analyzed for these purposes.

I urge such a sector analysis of industrial structure and behavior because of a belief that the competitive processes operate in somewhat different ways in various sectors and subsectors of the economy. Consequently, an analysis of the similarities and differences between sectors and subsectors and within sectors and subsectors may suggest fruitful hypotheses. It is a plausible hypothesis that various structural and behavioral characteristics of markets will have different effects depending on the sector or subsector of the economy in which they appear. Thus I suspect that high concentration will be associated with more serious monopoly effects in the mining and metal industries than in retail distribution. I suspect it will also be associated with more serious monopoly effects in industries where technological change is slow and comes from sources external to the industry than where technological change is rapid and is initiated within the industry. Such a sector analysis, in addition to providing a frame of reference for more detailed studies of individual firms and industries and assisting in the development of further hypotheses, should also aid in bridging the gap between micro- and macro-economic theory, a gap that has become increasingly serious.

It is beyond the scope of this paper to catalogue the variables that might prove significant in various sectors of the economy, but a few factors deserve more attention. In specifying the changing structure of an industry or sector of the economy, it may be useful to explore

136

not only the changing number, size, concentration, and degree of integration of firms but also changes, if any, in the rank order of the largest firms. Does the rank order of firms change more slowly in some sectors than in others? Are such differences related in any systematic way to other identifiable characteristics such as the importance of the control of raw materials or innovation and technological change? Are there any indications that frequent changes in rank order tend to stimulate the competitive factors?

Clearly, the effectiveness with which the competitive process is allocating resources should be a principal object of concern. In a freely competitive society one expects resources to be attracted to high-profit opportunities and to be repelled from low-profit opportunities. As an index of this tendency, one might explore the responsiveness of new investment to differences in the rate of profit. This suggests an index correlating the rate of new investment with the rate of profit on existing investment. Such an index would indicate the obstacles or resistances to freedom of entry and exit. Because new investment is more mobile than sunk investment, one might also expect to find a closer correlation in expanding industries than in unprofitable and contracting industries. One might explore the hypothesis that the degree of responsiveness of new investment to profit opportunities is inversely correlated with the degree of concentration, and also the hypothesis that the responsiveness is inversely correlated with the asset size of the individual firm. In any event, the extent to which the flow of new investment responds to profit differences should be a useful index of the allocative process in a market economy.

Further study of the short-run flexibility of prices, which is the subject of Ruggles' paper in this Conference, should be another aspect of the over-all description of the contours of market structure and behavior. Such a study might be supplemented with a study of fluctuations in gross margins, a measure that in some cases would serve as a first approximation to the Lerner index of monopoly power discussed above. Ruggles' paper suggests the usefulness of sector analysis for these problems and more particularly of the significance of fluctuations in costs as an explanation of differences in price flexibility. But how are we to explain differences in cost behavior? What part does concentration play in the differences between short-run fluctuation in prices of such different raw materials as minerals and metals on the one hand and natural fibers on the other? Are differences in the flexibility of wage rates due to differ-

137

ences in the organization of labor, to differences in the degree of concentration in the employing industry, or to both?

Clearly, some indexes of differences in the rate of technological change and innovation are called for. We need to develop some picture of the differences in the rate of technological change and innovation in various sectors of the economy and to test rival hypotheses concerning the effect of concentration and monopoly upon these processes.

The problem of technological change has, of course, many facets. What might we hope to measure? We would ideally like to know something about the rate of technological change and innovation in various sectors of the economy in comparison with the potential for such change. Such a study poses many serious problems. Expenditures on research and development suggest themselves immediately as one item on which data might be obtained. But before the significance of this would be clear we should need some studies of the economies of scale in research and development and of the advantages of integrating research and development with commercial exploitation and production. This suggests the need for case studies in the organization of research and development.

In some industries that have undergone considerable change of products it should be possible to acquire data on the extent to which the product mix has undergone change over a period of time, thereby indicating the extent to which the old products have been displaced by new. The rate of diffusion of new ideas might also be investigated. A study of the period elapsing between the state of an initial invention and the time at which it becomes commercially exploited and finally widely diffused would be useful. These and other variables seem worth exploring.

Two tentative hypotheses may be suggested that it might be possible to test from such data on technological change and innovation: (1) assuming that firms act independently in their technological and other decisions, the extent and speed of innovation will increase with the degree of concentration up to some critical point and will decline abruptly when the number of firms becomes very small, for example, one or two; and (2) in industries with high rates of innovation, the rank order of firms would change more frequently than where innovation is more gradual and less strategic.

A program of research along these lines would be a major undertaking. But a broad statistical picture of the anatomy of industry and the processes of competition in major sectors and subsectors of the economy is badly needed. Such an undertaking might well be the outcome of this Conference and the National Bureau of Economic Research might well serve as its focus.

COMMENT

JOE S. BAIN, University of California, Berkeley

MILLER has discussed the deficiencies of several measures of concentration that have been advanced in the last twenty years (most of them ten or more years ago), and has offered some suggestions for further work directed toward classifying and typing the market situations in which business firms operate.

With Miller's general view of the problem of classifying and typing market situations I am in substantial agreement. That is, I agree that we should distinguish, for purposes of classification, types of market structure, types of internal and market conduct of firms, and types of market performance or results emergent from the conduct of firms. (I am willing to add, if measurement is feasible at all, types of situations with respect to the "power" of firms.) I agree further that each of these things—structure, conduct, and performance—is in essence multidimensional, and that classification on any level will be correspondingly complex. I agree finally that in establishing classifications at each level and in looking for associations between types at different levels—certainly the crucial task— we should not limit ourselves to the classificatory systems and explanatory hypotheses put forth by static price theory. I may add that it is my impression that this general range of views is now shared by a large number of economists interested in the field of price studies.

Having said so much, I can scarcely disagree with Miller's major criticism of each of his "theoretical indexes" of monopoly. Each deals with only one dimension either of market structure (as for example in the case of simple cross elasticities, the Rothschild measure, or the Papandreou measure) or of performance (as in the case of the Lerner measure or my own profit measure), and as such it is insufficient. No single simple measure on any level will serve adequately to distinguish situations that may differ in many ways; a large number of one-dimensional measures must be used simultaneously to deal with a population of cases that differ in many dimensions. Precisely the same may of course be said of the measure of industry concentration. This view seems sound if hardly novel.

139

It may be suggested that a more charitable view of many individual measures of structure, conduct, or performance might be entertained if no one of them were expected to provide a self-sufficient classification of market situations. Detailed information on cross elasticities of demand among firms, for example, would be very useful—*along with many other sorts of information*—in typing market structures. In saying that each of many individual measures has a limited usefulness, it seems to me that Miller too much emphasizes the limitations and too little the positive usefulness. This same observation might be made about any relatively grandiose scheme of assembling data such as Miller suggests, wherein an array of individual partial measures, each with its limitations, would be discovered.

Two final comments may be added. First, although our ultimate goal may be a system of classification and explanation of markets and market performance which simultaneously comprehends numerous dimensions of market structure and conduct and which is adequately dynamic in its reference, a good deal may be discovered first by seeking for the partial associations of, for example, one aspect of market structure to one aspect of performance—and in this pursuit the usefulness of even static price theory as a source of hypotheses is not to be overly discounted.

Second, the outlines of the project of assembling data for empirical research that Miller puts forth are vague about some pertinent details. As these details are filled in, it will be found that the structure of the empirical research project—as regards definitions, procedures, hypotheses to be tested, and so forth—either will be arbitrary or *ad hoc* in character, or will be dependent upon some familiar or newly elaborated theoretical structure. Miller apparently eschews dependence upon existing theoretical structures, but he provides no systematic or established substitute. If the research effort he contemplates is to transcend the level of strictly pragmatic experiment, an extensive and thoroughgoing theoretical analysis should first be made in order to justify as fully as possible on an a priori level the definitions to be adopted and applied, the sorts of data to be collected, and the hypotheses to be tested. In this connection, traditional price theory, with all its limitations, may be surprisingly useful.

SURVEY OF THE EVIDENCE AND FINDINGS ON MERGERS

JESSE W. MARKHAM
PRINCETON UNIVERSITY

ONE authority has classified the literature on trusts, mergers, and consolidations according to the conclusions reached by various writers on the subject. His classification can be broadly summarized as follows:

1. Combinations reflect the desire and the ability of captains of industry to suppress competition. While proponents of this point of view unanimously agree that combinations are socially undesirable, they disagree on how long the undesirable effects last. Some hold that the creation of monopolies is, just as the socialists have long predicted, a final stage in the evolution of capitalism; hence monopoly will persist so long as capitalism survives. However, others hold that with the creation of each large combination go the seeds of its own destruction. This school argues that no man or group of men can long maintain control over the output of a commodity because of the inevitable supremacy of the laws of competition.

2. Combinations are not all-pervasive but arise only in those areas where control over transportation facilities and limited supplies of raw materials can be easily obtained, or where unwisely conceived legislation bestows monopoly power through tariff and patent protection and other means. Supporters of this view find an easy remedy to the combination problem in rigorous legal prohibitions and a reform of existing abuses.

3. Combinations are not a product of industry at all but of banking. To acquire control over all the assets in an industry requires far more liquid capital than any single manufacturing firm possesses. Hence the concentration of financial resources in large investment banks creates the "money trust" that is the mother of all others.

4. Combinations arise out of the chaos and wastefulness of small-scale enterprise and are merely a part of an evolutionary process in which the efficient survive and the inefficient are either absorbed or fall behind in the race toward lower production and distribution costs. Proponents of this view argue that "modern industrial conditions have demanded" that the "principle of combination be generally accepted."

5. Combinations represent the greatest invention and benefaction of this age or almost any other. Those who hold opposing views are "socialists, demagogues, blackmailers" and the like.

6. Mergers and combinations are legal, not social problems. Those who have reached this conclusion are primarily concerned with the problem of whether or not particular combinations are legal according to the antitrust laws.

The most observant student of the literature on mergers might easily conclude that this classification of schools of thought appeared in some recently published textbook on industrial organization—perhaps as recently as 1952. Actually it appeared in an article in 1901.[1] In the meantime the frequency distribution of views on the economic and social significance of mergers with respect to these classes has no doubt changed, but the range has not been significantly reduced—the extremes are still expressed. For example, a report of the House Judiciary Committee stated as recently as 1947, "The history of legislation previously adopted to prevent monopoly, the great increase in recent years of competition-destroying mergers, the damage to small business, the blighting of opportunity for our young people—all cry out for the enactment of legislation to stop the rising tide of monopoly."[2] In its 1948 report on mergers, the Federal Trade Commission sounded a similar note of alarm: "No great stretch of the imagination is required to foresee that if nothing is done to check the growth in concentration, either the giant corporations will ultimately take over the country, or the Government will be impelled to step in. . . ."[3] On the other hand, recent textbooks on business finance indicate a widely-held view that mergers have come about largely to reduce the cost of production, distribution, administration, etc.; and where the authors of such texts pass judgment on the social significance of mergers, the reader is frequently more impressed with their desirable than with their undesirable consequences.

There is no simple explanation for this persistence of divergent schools of thought. Admittedly, as it will be shown later, the available data on mergers are far from complete. In the face of incomplete data, economists might be expected to behave a little like the six blind men of Indostan and develop entirely different appercep-

[1] Charles J. Bullock, "Trust Literature: A Survey and Criticism," *Quarterly Journal of Economics*, February 1901, pp. 167-216.

[2] H. Rep. 596, 80th Cong., 1st Sess. amending Secs. 7 and 11 of Clayton Act, June 17, 1947.

[3] *The Merger Movement, A Summary Report*, Federal Trade Commission, 1948, p. 68.

tions about something big—whether it be elephants or mergers. The data, however, are not so faulty as this. The principal causes of divergent conclusions on mergers lie elsewhere. High on the list among these appears to be the willingness to accept, without fully testing it, a single simple explanation for why firms merge. Mergers, however, are not monolithic in character. Some have been born of monopoly and have been socially undesirable; others have been an integral part of competitive adjustment and may have been highly desirable; still others have had no recognizable effect on either industrial structure, market behavior, or anything else outside the particular firms involved. If this point, unspectacular though it may be, can be clearly demonstrated through an appraisal of the known data, this essay will have served its principal purpose.

1. Some Fundamental Shortcomings in Research on Mergers

ALTHOUGH some merger operations can be squeezed into theoretical maximizing models, the paths of economic theory and merger literature have rarely crossed.[4] Its nontheoretical nature hardly distinguishes the literature on mergers from that on many other economic phenomena. Nevertheless it has probably accounted for considerable disorganization of research efforts. Researchers, having no set of hypotheses as a point of departure, have relied principally upon the arts of description and enumeration. Accordingly, the vast body of merger literature shows the lack of cohesive purpose that may have followed from empirical testings of merger theory.

It is probably for this reason that mergers have been associated so closely with the monopoly problem. In fact, early authorities defined mergers to include only those combinations of formerly independent firms that resulted in substantial increases in market control.[5] In this area at least, economists had available some fairly crude tools of analysis and a long-standing observation on merger as a means of monopoly growth. Adam Smith as long ago as 1776 had observed the businessman's propensity to turn convivial conversations into trade conspiracies. Obviously, one way for businessmen to conspire is to merge their respective firms. In truth, the early pools and trusts might

[4] For two of the few discussions of mergers and theory see George J. Stigler, "Monopoly and Oligopoly by Merger," *American Economic Review*, Supplement, May 1950, pp. 23-34, and his "The Division of Labor is Limited by the Extent of the Market," *Journal of Political Economy*, June 1951, pp. 185-193, especially pp. 190-191.

[5] Shaw Livermore, "The Success of Industrial Mergers," *Quarterly Journal of Economics*, November 1935, pp. 70-71; and H. R. Seager and C. A. Gulick, Jr., *Trust and Corporation Problems* (Harper, 1929), p. 1.

be conveniently viewed as conspiracies par excellence. More recently, Adam Smith's observation has been formalized into price models giving a rationale for the merger, combination, or association of firms. Nearly every elementary textbook contains tools of analysis which may be used to show how a combination of all firms in a previously competitive industry can, at least in the short run, give rise to monopoly profits, higher prices, and a reduced rate of output.

Trusts and combinations formed before 1894, such as the sugar, oil, tobacco, cordage, linseed oil, cotton oil, whisky, and lead trusts, as well as some of the later mergers, clearly were instruments of market control. They therefore conform to the Smithian rationale. It is equally clear, however, from a priori reasoning and the available data, that this rationale explains only a small part of the merging process. Merger, as ordinarily defined, reflects the operation of many economic forces and, correspondingly, gives rise to almost any number of end results.

A second shortcoming of research on mergers arises from definitional problems and biases. It is evident of course that the composition and size of any list of mergers depend upon the definition of merger adopted. Thus the Twelfth Census, by using a rather restricted definition, recorded the formation of only 170 mergers between 1890 and 1900. By combining lists based on several definitions, Shaw Livermore compiled a master list for the same period comprising 231 mergers.[6] The difference between the two lists is 61 mergers, or 36 per cent of the total number included on the smaller list.

Moreover, nearly all the tabulations of early mergers were based primarily upon those mergers which, in the eyes of the researchers, loomed large in the world of business;[7] and none of them includes mergers involving a capitalization of less than $1 million. In omitting small mergers, all the lists for the 1887-1904 period overstate the proportion of mergers having monopoly as their goal and accordingly understate the proportion of mergers formed for other purposes. The number of such omissions is not known but it must have been large. According to a frequency distribution of mergers by capitalization constructed in 1899, the modal class of mergers was no greater than the $1-$5 million group; it may have been smaller.[8] Hence all the lists of early mergers deal only with the upper half of the frequency distribution. The upper half, however, contains a dispropor-

[6] *Ibid.*, pp. 70 ff.

[7] See the discussion in the next section.

[8] A. S. Dewing, *The Financial Policy of Corporations* (4th ed., Ronald, 1941), pp. 924-925, note b.

tionately large share of mergers that resulted in substantial market control.

Another shortcoming of research on mergers stems from statistical ambiguities inherent in most measures designed to show the impact of mergers on concentration. If, as is usually done, researchers concentrate their attention upon the change in ownership of *fixed* assets attending mergers, the conclusion that mergers increase concentration of control in some sense is inescapable. It does not necessarily follow, however, that control over *total* assets has become more concentrated. Whether or not it has depends upon how the merger was performed. Where one corporation acquires the assets of another for cash (a method of merging, according to the FTC, used frequently in recent years), the surviving corporation simply reduces liquid assets and increases fixed assets by a corresponding amount; the selling corporation reduces fixed assets and increases liquid assets. Total assets for neither firm changes. On the other hand, where mergers occur by simply fusing ownership, such as through stock exchanges, statutory proceedings, and holding company arrangements, and no exchange of assets among firms is involved, it seems fairly safe to conclude that they increase concentration of control over total assets. Asset transfers among corporations and ownership fusions, therefore, may not have the same effect on concentration of control. However, a distinction between the two is seldom made in merger analysis.

Finally, the literature has dealt only with those portions of the component firms going into the merger and has neglected those portions left over. No merger is ever quite complete in the sense that the resultant firm is exactly the sum of its previously independent parts. Before merging, each firm had a president, a board of directors, a comptroller, and other officers usually associated with entrepreneural decision making. Regardless of the number of firms merging, the surviving firm still has but one president, one board of directors, one comptroller, etc. Hence, while mergers increase the quantity of assets controlled by the entrepreneurs of surviving firms, they also free entrepreneurs to create new firms with new assets elsewhere. In short, merger is a means of contraction and exit as well as of expansion, and its total impact on the structure of industry may largely depend upon which motive is dominant.

These may be only fringe issues, or they may be extremely significant. We will not know which until the scope of merger investigations has been expanded to include more than balance sheet items, and until theorists have provided a more useful definitional and conceptual framework for merger research. However, there is much that we do know, or at least have good reasons for concluding we know, about the social and economic importance of mergers.

2. *Cyclical Behavior of Mergers*

MOST students of mergers have apparently concluded that mergers are timed closely with the business cycle.[9] This conclusion, however, is based entirely upon the rather superficial observation that 1899 and 1929 were peaks in both merger formation and business activity, and that the most recent flurry of mergers occurred in a period of wartime and postwar prosperity. What purpose would be served by testing the validity of this thesis is not entirely clear, but a few observations are in order. A study of the cyclical behavior of mergers may furnish clues to the pattern of collusion. Moreover, the cyclical aspects of merger activity may suggest dominant motives for merger. Finally, cyclical patterns of merger activity may have important implications for public policy. For example, if it can be clearly demonstrated that mergers are a product of booms (or a product of a depression-prosperity sequence), effective control over merger activity may be sought through fiscal measures as well as through the antitrust laws.

Unfortunately, the collecting of data on mergers has itself been explosively cyclical. The available data relate almost entirely to those periods in which the number of mergers formed per unit of time is believed to have been unusually high. About the period 1904-1918 we know only that the number and size of mergers formed must have been too insignificant to attract even casual attention. Hence, quantitative analysis of the cyclical behavior of mergers must be confined largely to those periods recognized as merger movements. Any conjectures about "normal" and "slump" periods of merger activity must be based upon data for the 1930's, a decade that holds out little promise as a meaningful reference point from which to measure anything—especially mergers.

Furthermore, data for the 1887-1904 merger period are a product of truncated sampling and are not comparable with those of later

[9] The frequency of such assertions makes substantiation of the statement hardly necessary. However, for typical observations made after each of the three major merger movements, the reader is referred to Luther Conant, Jr., "Industrial Consolidations in the United States," *American Statistical Association Publications*, Vol. 7, March 1901; Willard L. Thorp, "The Persistence of the Merger Movement," *American Economic Review*, Supplement, March 1931; and *The Merger Movement, A Summary Report*, as cited, p. 18.

years. Annual series for mergers occurring before 1904 have been compiled by Moody, Conant, Watkins, and the Bureau of the Census.[10] They all use the industrial consolidation, combination, or "trust" as units of measurement, and build their series upon rather restricted definitions of these terms. None of the lists include mergers having a total capitalization of less than $1 million. The Bureau defines a combination as "a number of formerly independent mills which had been brought together into one company under a charter obtained for that purpose." By a strict interpretation of the Bureau's definition its series would include only those consolidations created by new charters, i.e. statutory combinations. A cross check of its list with other lists, however, reveals that it contains a fairly large number of conventional mergers. Moreover, the Bureau specifically stated that its list includes several holding companies.[11] However, it does not include "many large establishments that grew up by the erection of new plants or *the purchase of old ones*" (italics added). Thus the Bureau's list probably does not include those mergers resulting from the outright purchase of one firm's assets by another. It does comprise all known statutory mergers, some conventional mergers, and several holding companies, having capitalizations of $1 million or more. The number of mergers omitted is not known but it must have been substantial, since other lists covering the same time period (which are themselves limited to mergers involving capitalizations of at least $1 million and are therefore incomplete) include over one and one-third times as many.[12]

Conant's series covers industrial consolidations as defined in their "narrow Wall Street sense" having authorized capitalizations (the sum of bonded indebtedness and authorized common and preferred stock) of $1 million or more. Accordingly all railroads, public utilities, and similar fields, and all small consolidations were excluded from Conant's series by definition. Watkins' series is also limited to consolidations having capitalizations of at least $1 million and includes most of those appearing on Conant's list. Moody's list includes

[10] John Moody, *The Truth about the Trusts* (Moody Publishing Co., 1904); Conant, *op. cit.*; Myron W. Watkins, *Industrial Combinations and Public Policy* (Houghton Mifflin, 1927); and *Twelfth Census of the United States*, Bureau of the Census, Vol. VII, Part 1, pp. xxv ff.

[11] *Twelfth Census of the United States*, as cited, p. xxvi. For two widely different views on what types of combinations the Bureau's list does include, see Morris A. Adelman, "The Measurement of Industrial Concentration," *Review of Economics and Statistics*, November 1951, pp. 293-294, and comment on this paper by George W. Stocking, *The Review of Economics and Statistics*, May 1952, pp. 163-164.

[12] See below a comparison with Livermore's list.

only those consolidations having *issued* capitalizations of at least $1 million and therefore omits some of those listed by both Conant and Watkins.

For the years 1890-1900, the period covered by all four series, the Bureau of the Census lists 170 consolidations; Conant lists 212; Watkins, 172; and Moody, 155. A master list compiled by Livermore from these and other lists for the period 1890-1904 includes 377 combinations.[13] When from this list is deducted the highest estimate of the number of consolidations (146) formed in the years 1901-1904, 231 are left for the period 1890-1900, or 9 per cent more than Conant, 36 per cent more than the Bureau, 34 per cent more than Watkins, and 49 per cent more than Moody list for the same period. It is not known how many mergers or consolidations were omitted from Livermore's list because they were not strictly industrial in character, had capitalizations of less than $1 million, or were simply overlooked, but the number must have been significant. For example, a frequency distribution by capitalization of 259 industrial consolidations believed to have been in existence in 1899 shows that the modal capitalization did not exceed the $1-$5 million class, and that 43 consolidations had a capitalization of exactly $1 million.[14] The distribution suggests that a considerable number of consolidations must have been capitalized at less than $1 million. Moreover, the 259 consolidations include no public utility, mining, or local enterprises. On the other hand, some of the consolidations appearing on all the lists were probably no more than "paper incorporations."[15]

The only continuous data on mergers for the 1919-1939 period were compiled by Thorp from the daily reports of the Standard Statistics Co.[16] The series shows the net number of concerns disappearing quarterly and annually in manufacturing and mining through mergers and acquisitions. According to Thorp, the record is neither complete nor very accurate, but should serve as a measure of cyclical behavior and trend tolerably well.[17] The FTC, using reports made by Moody's Investors Service and Standard & Poor's Corp. as primary sources of data, has extended Thorp's quarterly series of net disappearances through mergers and acquisitions through the fourth quarter of 1947.

[13] *Op. cit.*, pp. 70 ff. The annual series is not available.
[14] Dewing, *op. cit.*, pp. 924-925, note b.
[15] *Ibid.*, p. 924, note a.
[16] Willard L. Thorp and Walter F. Crowder, *The Structure of Industry*, Temporary National Economic Committee, Monograph 27, 1941, pp. 231-234.
[17] *Ibid.*, p. 232.

TABLE 1

Industrial Mergers in the United States, 1887-1904 and 1919-1947

	NUMBER OF MERGERS				Highest Number Reported	TOTAL CAPITALIZATION (millions of dollars)		
ar	Conant	Watkins	Census Bureau	Moody		Conant	Watkins	Census Bureau
87	8		0	1	8	$ 216.2		$ .0
88	3		0	2	3	23.6		.0
89	12		9	5	12	152.2		97.0
90	13	11	11	2	13	155.2	$ 137.6	119.5
91	17	13	9	7	17	166.2	133.6	141.2
92	10	12	10	7	12	193.4	170.0	124.2
93	6	5	7	7	7	239.0	156.5	180.4
94	2	0	4	3	4	30.4	.0	17.4
95	6	3	5	6	6	107.3	26.5	124.5
96	5	3	5	5	5	49.9	14.5	29.9
97	4	6	7	5	7	81.0	75.0	99.5
98	20	18	20	12	20	708.6	475.3	623.8
99	87	78	79	74	87	2,244.0	1,886.1	1,696.8
00	42	23	13[a]	27	42	831.4	294.5	237.7
01		23		46	46		1,632.3	
02		26		63	63		588.9	
03		8		18	18		137.0	
04		8			8		236.2	

DISAPPEARANCES THROUGH MERGER AND ACQUISITION[b]

	QUARTER				
	1	2	3	4	Total[c]
1919	57	82	147	125	438
1920	209	186	188	166	760
1921	184	99	80	122	487
1922	86	53	82	76	309
1923	84	67	44	105	311
1924	110	71	87	85	368
1925	124	104	127	175	554
1926	286	236	171	146	856
1927	161	247	220	213	870
1928	197	315	242	274	1,038
1929	349	395	312	160	1,245
1930	204	237	156	189	799
1931	163	142	87	71	464
1932	7	102	46	40	203
1933	19	43	33	12	120
1934	19	25	34	23	101
1935	36	27	38	24	130
1936	39	25	27	32	126
1937	32	27	29	31	124
1938	32	20	22	33	110
1939	24	22	16	25	87

149

TABLE 1 (*Continued*)

1940	29	49	31	34	143
1941	24	25	26	47	122
1942	19	17	31	52	119
1943	48	47	49	77	221
1944	69	72	77	102	320
1945	57	54	77	139	327
1946	97	132	109	75	413
1947	98	97	77	125	397

Total 1940-1947   2,062

a Through June 30.

b All but 104 disappearances from mining and manufacturing. Capitalization data not available.

c Annual totals larger than sum of quarterly figures because exact dates of some mergers were not known.

Source: 1887-1904 data: Luther Conant, Jr., "Industrial Consolidations in the United States," *American Statistical Association Publications*, Vol. 7, March 1901; Myron W. Watkins, *Industrial Combinations and Public Policy* (Houghton Mifflin, 1927); *Twelfth Census of the United States*, Bureau of the Census, Vol. VII, Part 1, pp. xxv ff.; John Moody, *The Truth about the Trusts* (Moody Publishing Co., 1904). 1919-1939 data: Willard L. Thorp and Walter F. Crowder, *The Structure of Industry*, Temporary National Economic Committee Monograph 27, 1941, p. 233. 1940-1947 data: *The Merger Movement, A Summary Report*, Federal Trade Commission, 1948, estimated from chart 2, opposite p. 18.

Since the available merger data are incomplete, biased, and probably subject to errors other than those of sampling, the annual merger series shown in Table 1 and Chart 1 probably contains several spurious cycles. However, since there is no promising method for separating the spurious ones from the real, we shall count them all. The 1887-1904 segment of the merger series contains 3 cycles and 6 turning points, while over the same period the National Bureau of Economic Research recorded 5 reference cycles and 10 turning points (excluding 1887 and 1904).[18] Five of the 6 merger-cycle turning points coincide with reference-cycle turning points; however, one merger-cycle peak (1891) coincides with a reference-cycle trough. The Fechner-Weber index of correlation[19] between general business activity and mergers for the seventeen-year period is .65. (If the total

[18] Arthur F. Burns and Wesley C. Mitchell, *Measuring Business Cycles* (NBER, 1946), p. 78.

[19] The formula for the Fechner-Weber index is as follows: $I = (C - D)/(C + D)$, where C is the total number of years in which the directional movements of the merger series and of business activity coincide, and D is the total number of years in which they move in opposite directions. The Fechner-Weber index for two time series moving at random should equal zero. I am indebted to my colleague Nicholas Georgescu-Roegen for calling the Fechner-Weber index to my attention.

150

capitalization series instead of the one based on the number of mergers is used, 7 merger-cycle turning points out of 9 coincide with reference-cycle turning points, and 3 fall between reference-cycle turning points.) The 1919-1947 segment of the merger series contains 2½ cycles and 6 turning points between 1919 and 1939, while over the same period there occurred 5 reference cycles and 11 turn-

Chart 1
Industrial Mergers and Business Cycles, 1887-1904,
and 1919-1947

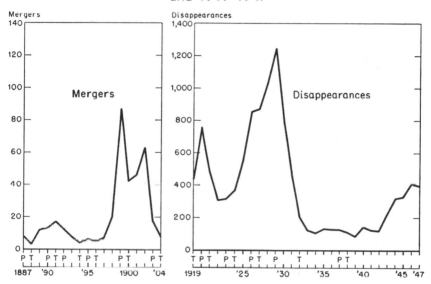

P's and T's indicate reference cycle peaks and troughs.
Source: Table 1.

ing points.[20] Only 2 of the 6 merger-cycle turning points coincide with reference-cycle turning points and the other 4 fall between reference-cycle turning points. The Fechner-Weber index of correlation between mergers and general business activity is .20.

These data do not give strong support to the thesis that merger cycles are timed closely with business cycles. The correlation between mergers and general business activity for the 1919-1939 period is only a little better than that which would be expected of two

[20] Reference-cycle turning points recently calculated by the NBER for the war and postwar years cannot be used. Only two reference-cycle turning points occur between 1938 and 1947 (the terminal year of the merger series)—a peak in February 1945 and a trough in October of the same year. See Robert A. Gordon, *Business Fluctuations* (Harper, 1952), p. 216.

time series moving at random. While the Fechner-Weber index shows that over the period 1887-1904 mergers and business activity generally moved in the same direction, the apparent high correlation is subject to several important qualifications. The 1888-1894 merger cycle appears to have been unrelated to general business activity. The initial trough, the peak, and the final trough of the cycle all coincided with troughs of reference cycles. Hence the high value of the Fechner-Weber index for the period 1887-1904 is almost wholly accounted for by the identical directional movements of the merger series and the business cycle for all years between 1897 and 1904. Because of the great difference in amplitudes between merger cycles and business cycles over this period, the high index of directional correlation is of doubtful significance. The merger wave of 1897-1904 comprised an era. No other merger wave of comparable scope and size is to be found in the annals of American economic history. By way of contrast, the two business cycles of 1897-1900 and 1900-1904 were relatively insignificant. Neither of them is included among the major business cycles in the United States; both are generally regarded as minor waves superimposed upon the expansion phase of a major cycle culminating in 1907.[21] Over the same period the turning points in stock-price cycles (with the exception of 1901) also coincided with those of the merger cycles. Moreover, as it will be shown later, between 1897 and 1903 stock prices and mergers were subject to the same pronounced cyclical swings. Hence, merger activity between 1887 and 1904 seems to have been tied more closely to stock-price movements than to general business fluctuations.

The cyclical aspects of mergers occurring over the 1919-1941 period have been subjected to close statistical examination by Weston.[22] While he questions the fruitfulness of regarding mergers as having occurred in cycles at all, Weston correlates merger activity with the Federal Reserve Board (FRB) index of industrial production, the wholesale price index, and the Dow-Jones industrial stock price index. A summary of his results appears in Table 2.

Of the three variables investigated by Weston, industrial stock prices appear to have been most closely related to merger activity. The correlation coefficient between the number of disappearances per year and the Dow-Jones industrial stock price annual averages was .676; the coefficient was significant at the 1 per cent probability

21 See Alvin H. Hansen, *Business Cycles and National Income* (Norton, 1951), pp. 24, 28-29.
22 J. Frederick Weston, *The Role of Mergers in the Growth of Large Firms* (University of California Press, 1953).

level. Correlation between mergers and industrial output and between mergers and wholesale prices was much weaker.

This evidence of colinearity between stock-price movements and merger activity tempts one to accept as valid one partial explanation of mergers; namely, that rising security prices stimulate merger activity by making possible large gains to promoters through asset revaluations. This explanation seems all the more acceptable when it is noted that the 1897-1904 and 1923-1934 merger movements rode

TABLE 2

Correlation between Mergers and Industrial Production, Wholesale Prices, and Industrial Stock Prices during the Interwar Period

	Correlation Coefficient[a]	Level of Significance
Mergers and industrial production	.434	Significant at 5%; not significant at 1%
Mergers and wholesale prices	.453	Significant at 5%; not significant at 1%
Mergers and industrial stock prices	.676	Significant at 1%

[a] Weston also investigated multiple regression relationships and obtained the following regression equation:

$$X_1 = -446.15 - 440.39X_2 + 3.7414X_3 + 8.4544X_4$$

where X_1, X_2, X_3, and X_4 are respectively the number of mergers per year, and the industrial production index, stock prices, and wholesale commodity prices. Weston found the multiple correlation coefficient to be .82 and statistically significant at the 1 per cent level. Only the relationship between the number of mergers and stock prices was found to be clearly significant. Letter from J. Fred Weston, Nov. 10, 1952.

Source: J. Frederick Weston, *The Role of Mergers in the Growth of Large Firms* (University of California Press, 1953).

to their respective peaks on crests of rapidly rising stock prices of corresponding magnitudes. Like most simple explanations of complex phenomena, however, this one also leaves a great deal unexplained. For example, stock prices registered one of their most rapid gains in history between the fourth quarter of 1932 and the fourth quarter of 1933; over this period, however, the quarterly volume of mergers decreased. Moreover, recent findings[23] suggest that the relationship between stock prices and merger activity for the 1942-1947 period did not conform to that for the period 1919-1941. Hence, it would be unwise to ascribe more to the statistical findings than they clearly show, namely: that merger activity seems to be much more closely associated with fluctuations in stock prices than with those

[23] J. K. Butters, John Lintner, and W. L. Cary, *Effects of Taxation on Corporate Mergers* (Harvard University Press, 1951), p. 312.

in general economic activity and wholesale prices; moreover, all great upswings in stock prices have not brought on corresponding upswings in merger formation; and the most recent flurry of mergers occurred while stock prices were moderately steady.

The cyclical aspects of mergers, therefore, may tentatively be summarized as follows: (1) The widely expressed view that mergers are causally connected with general economic fluctuations is only weakly supported by the available statistical data. (2) The relationship between merger activity and wholesale price movements lends no support to the hypothesis that mergers are motivated by generally declining prices brought on by outbreaks of competition. In fact, for the years 1919-1941 merger activity and wholesale prices tended to rise and fall together. (3) When correlated with reference cycles, industrial production, industrial prices, and stock prices, merger activity appears to have been much more strongly associated with the latter than with any of the other three. However, stock prices and industrial production have usually followed similar cyclical patterns. Hence causal relationships between either of these and merger activity are difficult to infer from statistical analysis. Such an inference is all the more precarious because no allowance can be made for the average time interval separating decisions to merge and the mergers themselves.

These conclusions alone would justify special treatment of each period of high merger activity on the grounds that each merger movement may possess features peculiar to itself. Moreover, if mergers are to be appraised according to their impact on the structure of industry, special treatment of each wave of mergers is necessary.

3. The Early Merger Movement: 1887-1904

ALTHOUGH contemporaries of the period may have differed about the purposes and the ultimate significance of the 1887-1904 combination movement, on one point they were in accord—the movement took on phenomenal proportions. It gave rise to a stream of economic literature which by 1920 was probably equal in volume to those on the industrial revolution, international trade, or the business cycle. Complete books on the movement by Moody, Ely, Dewing, Jenks, von Halle, Ripley, van Hise, Montague, LeRossignol, Nolan, Collier, and a host of others had appeared before 1920.[24] In

24 John Moody, op. cit.; R. T. Ely, Monopolies and Trusts (Macmillan, 1900); A. S. Dewing, Corporate Promotions and Reorganizations (Harvard University Press, 1914); J. W. Jenks, The Trust Problem (McClure, Phillips, 1900); Ernst von Halle, Trusts, or Industrial Combinations and Coalitions in the United

the decade following there appeared such standard works as those by Seager and Gulick, Watkins, Jones, Curtis, Basset, Tippetts and Livermore, and others.[25] If to all these were added the journal articles, pamphlets, newspaper reports, and public records that focused their attention upon the early combination movement, the aggregation would constitute a private library of no mean size.

The early combination movement, therefore, was of extraordinary social and economic importance. Historians have recorded it as an era and economists consider it the period when the pattern of concentration characteristic of twentieth-century American business formed and matured.[26]

However, we do not know the extent to which those changes in the form of American enterprise that occurred during the early merger period were in fact a product of mergers; nor, one must sorrowfully add, is it likely ever to be fully determined. It was not until the appearance of Nutter's recent study[27] that the extent of concentration as early as 1899 could be compared with that of subsequent years. By 1899, however, the early combination movement had already reached its peak. Since the change in concentration between 1887 and 1899 for the whole economy has not yet been ascertained, we would not know what impact mergers had on concentration over this period even if we could assume they accounted for it all.

Moreover, concentration in ownership of productive resources and monopoly power in the market sense, while never quite the same,[28] had little in common prior to 1893. One need only compare railroad mileage maps for selected years between 1870 and 1893 to sense the significant spatial transformation that markets underwent in the

---

States (Macmillan, 1895); W. Z. Ripley, *Trusts, Pools and Corporations* (rev. ed., Ginn, 1916); C. R. van Hise, *Concentration and Control* (Macmillan, 1912); G. H. Montague, *Trusts of Today* (McClure, Phillips, 1904); J. E. LeRossignol, *Monopolies Past and Present* (Crowell, 1901); E. J. Nolan, *Combinations, Trusts and Monopolies* (Broadway Publishing Co., 1904); W. M. Collier, *The Trusts* (Baker Taylor, 1900).

[25] Seager and Gulick, *op. cit.*; Watkins, *op. cit.*; Eliot Jones, *The Trust Problem in the United States* (Macmillan, 1929); Roy E. Curtis, *The Trusts and Economic Control* (McGraw-Hill, 1931); William R. Basset, *Operating Aspects of Industrial Mergers* (Harper, 1930); Charles S. Tippetts and Shaw Livermore, *Business Organization and Public Control* (Van Nostrand, 1932).

[26] Cf. Paul T. Homan, "Trusts," *Encyclopedia of the Social Sciences*, Vol. 15, (Macmillan, 1931), Vol. 15, p. 114.

[27] G. Warren Nutter, *The Extent of Enterprise Monopoly in the United States, 1899-1939* (University of Chicago Press, 1951).

[28] For a clear discourse on the differences between the two, see Adelman, *op. cit.*, pp. 269 ff.

short span of about twenty years. As late as 1870 virtually the entire
United States, except what is now known as the Trunk Line Territory, was a mass of unconnected local markets. Between 1870 and
1900 railroad mileage in the United States increased from 52,922
miles to 194,262 miles, an increase of 268 per cent. Over the same
period freight rates fell from 18.2 mills to 7.3 mills per ton-mile, or
over 60 per cent. Between 1882 and 1900 the ton-miles of traffic
carried by railroads in the United States increased from 39.3 billion
to 141.6 billion, or 260 per cent.

There are no ready means for relating this tremendous growth of
transportation facilities and reduction in transportation costs to the
growth in size of particular markets. However, it can be crudely
estimated that the area served by the average manufacturing establishment in 1900 was about 3.24 times as large as it was in 1882.[29]
Market extension begets specialization; and specialization requires
that the relatively inefficient give way to the relatively efficient. Accordingly, by simply applying the logic of comparative cost analysis,
low-cost producers probably drove out some high-cost producers
during the period 1870-1900. And since market extension reduces
the values of the less efficient firms' fixed assets (possibly even to
zero), buying out may well have implemented the driving out process, thereby increasing concentration in ownership.[30] Moreover,
market expansion must have given considerable impetus to the per-
fection of mass-production as well as mass-marketing techniques,
all of which stimulated growth in the size of firms.

Hence, not all the increase in concentration or the ascendancy of
bigness during the early combination period can be attributed to
the formation of combinations. However, of all those forces unleashed in the latter part of the nineteenth century that tended to
make for larger size and greater concentration, the industrial combination was clearly the most important. According to Moody,[31]
318 industrial combinations formed prior to 1904 involved over $7
billion in securities issues and 5,288 distinct plants. While Moody's

29 Between 1882 and 1900 the physical volume of manufactured production in
the United States doubled and ton-mile shipments increased 3.6 times. The
average radius of all market areas, therefore, increased 1.8 times. Hence (from
$A = \pi r^2$), the area served by each production center must have increased by
3.24 times. Physical volume of production from Edwin Frickey, *Production in the
United States, 1860-1914* (Harvard University Press, 1947), p. 54; ton-miles data
from "Railway Statistics Before 1890" (mimeographed), Interstate Commerce
Commission, 1932.
30 It does not follow, however, that monopoly in the market sense increased
also; in fact, it may well have decreased.
31 *Op. cit.*, p. 486.

list includes some duplications, it errs on the under side; the number of combinations omitted almost certainly exceeds the number counted twice. It can be roughly estimated that the 1887-1904 combination movement accounted for approximately 15 per cent of the total number of plants and employees comprising manufactures in 1900.[32] The greater part of the movement, in terms of capitalization, the number of consolidations, and the number of plants involved, occurred during the eight-year period 1897-1904 (see Table 3). The

TABLE 3

Number of Trusts Formed and Capitalization and Plants Involved for Specific Periods before 1904

	Number of Trusts	Per Cent of Total	Capital- ization (mill. $)	Per Cent of Total	Number of Plants	Per Cent of Total
Up to 1890	23	7	$ 504.2	7	663	12
1890–1896	38	12	501.0	7	398	8
1897–1904	257a	81	6,146.1	86	4,227	80
Total	318a	100	$7,151.3	100	5,288	100

a Includes 13 in process of reorganization in 1904.
Source: John Moody, *The Truth about the Trusts* (Moody Publishing Co., 1904).

single year 1899 accounted for 87 combinations representing a total capitalization of $2.24 billion,[33] or nearly 25 per cent of all the combinations known to have occurred between 1887 and 1904.

Neither numbers of combinations nor amounts of capitalization involved are good measures of the growth of size or market control. For example, the formation of a single combination—the United State Steel Corp. in 1901—reportedly involved 785 plants and $1.37 billion, or over 60 per cent of the total capitalization of the 87 combinations formed in the peak year of 1899, and 19 per cent of the total capitalization and 14 per cent of all the plants involved in all the combinations recorded for the 1887-1904 period. Obviously, therefore, even the larger mergers comprise a heterogeneous class.

[32] The list of 185 combinations compiled by the Bureau of the Census accounted for 8.4 per cent of all manufacturing employment in 1900. This list includes less than one-half the combinations known to have occurred up through 1904. The Bureau recorded 296,440 manufacturing establishments and 512,191 factories and hand and neighborhood industries for the year 1900; the number of plants exceeded the former but was not as large as the latter. However, for what it is worth, the number of plants affected by combinations was 18 per cent of the total number of establishments and 10 per cent of the total number of factories and hand and neighborhood industries recorded by the Bureau in 1900.
[33] Conant, *op. cit.*, pp. 7-9.

157

Nevertheless, a significant percentage of the larger horizontal mergers possessed one common feature: they increased concentration of control over their respective markets. The mean share of the total domestic market controlled by 22 mergers studied by the Industrial Commission was 71 per cent.[34] Of 92 large mergers studied by Moody, 78 controlled 50 per cent or more of the total output of the industry; 57 controlled 60 per cent or more; and 26 controlled 80 per cent or more.[35] While more recent students of the early merger movement have detected some serious errors of overstatement of control in Moody's data,[36] they have not challenged the essential features of Moody's conclusions. Even in the absence of comprehensive pre-merger period data, therefore, it seems safe to conclude that a significant number of the large horizontal mergers greatly increased the size of particular firms and their proportionate control over both total productive capacity and the market, however defined. In the steel, tobacco products, petroleum refining, sugar refining, nonferrous metal smelting, shoe machinery, typewriter, and other industries, it is quite clear that mergers transformed oligopolistic or competitive markets into markets dominated by partial monopolists frequently controlling over 50 per cent of total output. In short, the aim of such mergers clearly must have been monopoly, although it was never perfectly achieved and rarely if ever displaced anything resembling perfect competition.

It does not follow, however, that either greater relative size or market control motivated a majority of the 1887-1904 mergers. At least, if motive can be at all inferred from results, it is tautological to describe the period as one of "merger for monopoly";[37] i.e. it suggests a motive for only those mergers that produced dominant firms. Many early mergers, however, obtained no significant degree of market control. Hence, it must be concluded that they were either highly unsuccessful in their purpose or were formed for other reasons.

In 1935 Shaw Livermore compiled a master list of mergers formed between 1890 and 1904.[38] (By this time the record should have been fairly complete.) While Livermore was principally concerned with

[34] *Report on Trusts and Industrial Combinations,* Industrial Commission, 1901, Vol. XIII, *passim,* esp. pp. xvii-xviii.
[35] Stigler, "Monopoly and Oligopoly by Merger," as cited, p. 29; quoting Moody, *op. cit.*
[36] Cf. Livermore, *op. cit.,* pp. 68 ff. See also the discussion below.
[37] Cf. Stigler, "Monopoly and Oligopoly by Merger," as cited, p. 27.
[38] Livermore, *op. cit.,* pp. 68-96.

measuring the financial success of mergers, he made some observations on why they were successful. After eliminating duplications, Livermore's list contained 377 mergers that showed promise of conforming to his definition, i.e. gave rise to firms with sufficient power to influence their respective markets. Mergers easily recognized at the outset as nonmonopolistic in character, therefore, never appeared on the original list. Thirty-eight mergers were then dropped from the list because they were strictly local and so small that they obviously had obtained *no* greater market influence through consolidation. Of the remaining 339 mergers, careful study showed that only 155 had resulted in the creation of firms with enough power *markedly to influence the market,* and only a select minority of these had obtained before 1910 any *considerable degree of monopoly control.*[39] Livermore later identifies his "select minority" as the 16 out of a total of 146 successful mergers that owed their success to monopoly control or unfair and vexatious practices.[40]

Further study of Livermore's list of 155 "influential" mergers, however, shows that considerably more than 16 attained an initial dominant position in their respective industries. One hundred and thirty-two of them appear on Moody's list of "trusts,"[41] seventy of

[39] *Ibid.,* pp. 71-75. The terms "power markedly to influence the market" and "considerable degree of monopoly control" are somewhat confusing. While they appear to be roughly equivalent terms, in their context they were clearly designed to mean different things. To eliminate this source of confusion, Mr. Livermore has furnished the following additional information: "What I meant by . . . 'somewhat less than half could rightfully claim to be mergers with power enough to influence markedly conditions in their industry' was about as follows: Some companies possess the ability to draw executives away from competitors by offering either a better salary or more power; they are the first in their industries to introduce new technology; they are the leaders in changing the location of plants to reduce shipping and marketing costs; they devote earnings to new equipment and methods, which keep them a step ahead of competitors in operating costs; they tend to be the leaders in setting wage patterns; they are the most prominent voices in industry groups or associations. This is what I meant by influencing conditions and being 'successful.' It is not the strength or leadership which can be defined as truly monopoly power or oligopoly power, as economic theorists define those terms, that is, there is no clear-cut ability to restrict output, to raise prices above the bulk-line cost situation in the industry, or the power to exclude or eject competitors. By 'any considerable degree of monopoly control' I intended to refer to the possession of monopoly power in the theoretical sense in which economists use it. That is, this small group *did* possess the kinds of power indicated above which American theorists associate with the concept of monopoly. Note that I said 'in considerable degree' to assure the reader that this little group did not possess absolute monopoly power in the old-fashioned sense." Letter dated September 29, 1952.

[40] *Ibid.,* pp. 87-88.

[41] Moody, *op. cit.,* pp. 453-469.

which Moody estimates as having obtained control over 40 per cent or more of their markets. However, the evidence that Moody's estimates greatly exaggerate the extent of control obtained by 19 of the 70 mergers is sufficiently strong to warrant dropping them from the monopoly group.[42] For 47 of the remaining 51 mergers it can either be verified that they obtained over 40 per cent of their respective markets or the evidence that they did not do so is too weak to justify shifting them to the nonmonopoly group.[43] The three remaining mergers appearing on both Moody's and Livermore's lists—American Ice, National Candy, and International Mercantile Marine—raise special problems of classification. Both the American Ice and National Candy mergers involved only a small percentage of their respective industries' total capacities. However, American Ice brought together 80 per cent of the ice capacity located along the Hudson and Kennebec rivers and the National Candy Co. obtained control

[42] Moody's estimates of market control obtained through merger were frequently based upon statements made by promoters prior to the merger. Census data and other evidence show the per cent of control stated by Moody to have been either exaggerated or inapplicable in about two dozen mergers. For example, the New England Yarn Co., listed by Moody as controlling from 20 to 40 per cent of the yarn industry, never controlled more than 389,000 mule spindles and 194,000 frame spindles, or only about 3 per cent of the active spindles in the United States at the time the merger was formed. Moody listed two shipbuilding mergers as controlling over 50 per cent of their "local" markets while the shipbuilding market was essentially an international one. The American Hide and Leather merger was listed as controlling about 55 per cent of the upper leather industry although the merger brought together only 22 of the 407 establishments producing upper leather in the United States at the time of the merger. International Steam Pump and Allis-Chalmers were listed as having control over 80 per cent and 50 per cent respectively of the "heavy steam power machinery of all kinds"; one must obviously be dropped. The same is true of several copper refining and cast iron and sewer pipe mergers. Other mergers erroneously listed as having obtained control over as much as 40 per cent of their respective markets are United Button Co. (merging only 3 out of 238 button establishments), Virginia-Carolina Chemical Co. (phosphate), U.S. Leather, U.S. Envelope, American Glue, Standard Sanitary, and National Enameling and Stamping.

[43] Some, however, might be considered borderline cases: Moody lists U.S. Cotton Duck as having obtained control over from 45 to 65 per cent of the cotton duck market. The company's total sales in 1902, comprising a wide variety of cotton textile products, amounted to less than one-half of the total value of cotton duck alone sold in the United States for the year 1900. Moreover, Dewing's study shows the merger to have been promoted for purposes of promoter's profits rather than market control. (Dewing, *Corporate Promotions and Reorganizations*, as cited, p. 376.) The percentages of market control obtained by the American Fork and Hoe, Corn Products Refining, National Asphalt, American Car and Foundry, Harbison Refractories, and National Fireproofing mergers appear also to have been overstated by Moody.

over about 55 per cent of the candy-producing capacity located in ten Midwestern cities. The former, because ice markets are essentially local, initially obtained considerable monopoly control over the market in which it sold; the latter, for opposite reasons, probably did not. Moody lists the International Mercantile Marine merger as having obtained control over 40 per cent of Atlantic shipping lines, but states elsewhere that ". . . it must be plain to even the most superficial observer today [shortly after the merger] that the entire trouble with the Shipping Trust is its total lack of a monopoly advantage. It is subject to free and open competition from companies which are fully as well equipped, and in addition have important advantages themselves in the shape of government subsidies and less weighty capitalizations."[44] It is doubtful therefore that the merger's actual control over Atlantic shipping lines ever came close to 40 per cent, although the object of the merger seems clearly to have been monopoly.[45]

About 51 of Livermore's mergers, therefore, obtained control over 40 per cent or more of their respective industries. To these may be added 8 that Moody included but Livermore omitted.[46] About 24 additional mergers neither clearly obtained substantial market control nor failed to do so. Some of them (Pressed Steel Car, American Colortype, American Soda Fountain, Electric Vehicle Co., and American Felt) involved only two or three plants, while others (Eastman Kodak and Pope Manufacturing Co.) involved many more. Moody lists 19 of them among his lesser industrial "trusts," a term he uses to designate all mergers. Livermore apparently includes these 19, along with 5 other mergers not listed by Moody, among those that obtained no monopoly power before 1910. In the face of inadequate or conflicting information in each case, we may arbitrarily assign about one-half of Livermore's 24 to the group of mergers for monopoly, thereby bringing the total number of such mergers to approximately 71. Hence, out of every 5 mergers ostensibly monop-

---

[44] Moody, op. cit., p. 107.   [45] Ibid., p. 98.

[46] Moody recorded 9 "trusts" that do not appear on Livermore's list as having obtained 50 per cent or more control over their industries. One of these, The Expressage Corp., was not a merger. The other eight were American Caramel Co., California Fruit Canners Association, Casein Company of America, Borden's Condensed Milk Co., Computing Scale Company of America, Rubber Goods Manufacturing Co., Standard Table Oil Cloth Co., and U.S. Bobbin and Shuttle Co. Livermore may have dropped the first 4 of these 8 mergers from his original list on the grounds that they were small or involved only a few local plants while they competed in national markets. There are no apparent grounds for his having failed to include the last 4.

161

olistic in character, only 1 resulted in considerable monopoly control. Either one of two conclusions seems inescapable: (1) if the purpose of all mergers was monopoly power, 4 out of every 5 were unsuccessful in obtaining their initial objective, or (2) many mergers were formed for other purposes.

Stigler has observed that theory would lead us to expect mergers for monopoly to be characterized by the fusion of the leading firms in a given industry simultaneously.[47] Most mergers that resulted in substantial market control were in fact formed by simultaneously joining together the leading firms (Stigler notes one prominent exception—Standard Oil). At the time many mergers were formed, therefore, the participants must have known that they were not obtaining substantial control over their respective industries. To deduce motives from results is perhaps not the best logic—since some who sought monopoly through merger may have failed. Nevertheless, it is certain that many mergers formed during the early merger movement did not have monopoly power as their principal objective and, accordingly, must be explained on other grounds.

The literature provides convincing evidence that the abnormally large volume of mergers formed in 1897-1900 stemmed largely from a wave of frenzied speculation in asset values. Several students of the early merger movement agree that excessive demand for securities was an impelling force in the mass promotion of mergers after 1896. Average stock prices increased from $40 in the second quarter of 1897 to nearly $80 by the fourth quarter of 1899.[48] Most of this rise in stock prices occurred between mid-1897 and the closing months of 1899. The new and lucrative market gave rise to a new type of entrepreneur—the producer of mergers.[49] His method of ex-

47 "Monopoly and Oligopoly by Merger," as cited, p. 26.

48 Dow-Jones industrial stock average. Rumblings of a speculative avalanche were recorded by students of the early merger period as early as the middle 1880's, but the avalanche was periodically checked by the uncertain outcome of elections, the free silver issue, and short-lived panics. It broke forth in full fury at the end of the Spanish-American War. For a fairly detailed discussion of these and other forces at work in the 1890's, see Conant, op. cit.; see also the address of Henry D. Baker in *Chicago Conferences on Trusts* (The Civic Foundation of Chicago, 1900), p. 340.

49 Stigler has expressed a similar view, but with the important difference that he calls the new type of entrepreneur a producer of monopolies. Stigler, "Monopoly and Oligopoly by Merger," as cited, p. 30. His interpretation is of course correct for the 71 (approximately) large mergers that resulted in substantial market control. For the most part, however, students of the early merger movement have assigned the professional promoter a much less important role than early investigatory agencies found him to have played. See *Preliminary Report*

ploiting the market was conceptually simple. The discounted values of expected future earnings (frequently inflated by promoter advertising) greatly exceeded the prevailing book values of assets. The formation of a merger or holding company afforded promoters and participating industrialists an opportunity to float additional securities issues against the same assets, thereby increasing the supply of securities by the difference between the amounts of the old and new securities issues. This difference, which was also the difference between the amounts of the old and new asset valuations (usually expressed as "good will"), was the promoter's gross profit. If the added inducement of monopoly could be offered the stock-buying public and the participating firms, the merger was, of course, that much easier to promote. For about four-fifths of the mergers involving capitalizations of $1 million and over formed between 1890 and 1904, however, this additional inducement appears to have been unnecessary.

The high incidence of failure among early mergers attests to their general speculative character. Presumably a large proportion of the profitable mergers were provided with a real basis for merger (market control or production and distribution economies) while a corresponding proportion of the unprofitable ones were not. The professional promoter was likely to have played a less important role in the formation of mergers falling in the former than in the latter group.[50]

---

on Trusts and Industrial Combinations, Industrial Commission, 1900, Vol. 1, pp. 15-16.

[50] This hypothesis finds its origin in a very simple line of logic. The mergers that actually turned out to be profitable operating firms were *expected* to be more profitable than those that did not. Where expectations of operating profitably were high, however, less professional promotional services were needed. While readily available data on this point include a very small proportion of the total number of mergers, they seem generally to support the hypothesis. Ten mergers that were either promoted by banks, syndicates, or other persons outside the industry, or gave rise to large promotional profits, were early failures (National Starch, United Starch, Glucose Sugar Refining Co., American Bicycle, American Malting, New England Cotton Yarn, Mt Vernon-Woodbury Cotton Duck, U.S. Shipbuilding, Atlantic Rubber Stores, and Asphalt Co. of America). Of 11 mergers in which outside promoters played a negligible role, 7 were successes (Standard Oil, DuPont, American Sugar Refining, National Cash Register, International Harvester, International Shoe Machinery, and Aluminum Corp.), 1 was a limping success (International Paper), 1 was a rejuvenated success (National Salt), and 2 were early failures (National Wallpaper and National Glass). Data for 4 other mergers can be used, depending on the aspects of the mergers given emphasis, either to support or refute the hypothesis. Promoters of 2 additional successes, American Tobacco and American Can, received large promoters

Several attempts have been made to measure the success of the early mergers in terms of their relative profitability. Dewing, after comparing the actual profits of mergers with their expected profits and with the profits previously made by the independent firms comprising the mergers, concluded that only one-seventh of the larger mergers were successful.[51] However, Dewing's analysis is weak on several counts and tends to understate the proportion of mergers that were successful: (1) His conclusions were based on a sample of 35 mergers, less than one-tenth of the number of mergers known to have occurred between 1890 and 1904. (2) His pre-merger profits data were principally those reported in prospectuses and financial journals just before the merger occurred and therefore had probably been subjected to considerable window dressing. Moreover, his pre-merger profits data included the relatively profitable years of the late 1890's, while his post-merger data were for the decade beginning around 1900 and included the panics of 1903-1904 and 1907. (3) Most of the expected abnormal earnings were probably capitalized at the time the merger was formed, thereby increasing the annual charges against earnings over subsequent years. Moreover, estimated earnings in some cases were calculated from pre-merger estimates of *rates* of return. Accordingly, had *any* of the mergers earned the expected profits or rates of return they would have been remarkably profitable. Nevertheless, 5 of Dewing's mergers recorded earnings equaling or exceeding expected earnings, and 6 others recorded earnings that fell just a little short of their expected earnings.

More comprehensive studies of the profitability of mergers have been made independently by Shaw Livermore and the National Industrial Conference Board.[52] Both reach substantially the same conclusions but Livermore's analysis is cast in more quantitative terms (see Table 4). His study shows that 146 out of a total of 328 mergers were unquestionably successful. Of these, 130 owed their success (and profitability) to rapid technological and managerial improve-

---

profits in the form of common stock. However, the promoters of each were associated with their respective industries and did not, as was frequently the case, sell their securities soon after the mergers were formed, thereby leaving the industry and taking their promotional gains in cash. Outside promoters played a minor role in 2 additional failures, U.S. Leather and National Cordage. However, bankers who engineered the financial plans for both received large underwriting fees. Cf. Dewing, *Corporate Promotions and Reorganizations*, as cited, p. 538; Jones, *op. cit.*, pp. 283-299; and Seager and Gulick, *op. cit.*, *passim*.

51 A. S. Dewing, "A Statistical Test of the Success of Consolidations," *Quarterly Journal of Economics*, November 1921, pp. 84-101.

52 Livermore, *op. cit.*, pp. 68-96; *Mergers in Industry*, N.I.C.B., 1929, pp. 28-119.

ment, promotion of quality brand names, development of new products or entry into a new subdivision of the industry, and to commercial exploitation of research. The remaining 16 owed their success to monopoly control or "unfair and vexatious practices." Promotional gains, expected monopoly profits, or a combination of both probably provided the dominant motives for some of the mergers falling in the latter group.[53] In the formation of many of the 130

TABLE 4

Success of Mergers Formed between 1888 and 1905

	Number of Mergers Studied	Per Cent of Total
Successes	146	45
Limping successes	28	9
Rejuvenations	13	4
Failures	141	43

Source: Shaw Livermore, "The Success of Industrial Mergers," *Quarterly Journal of Economics*, November 1935, pp. 75, 77.

mergers that owed their subsequent success to extraordinary entrepreneural ability, however, professional promoters probably played a subordinate role to business entrepreneurs.

Of the remaining 182 mergers studied by Livermore, 141 clearly were failures. Thirteen rejuvenations were saved from being classified as complete failures only because original ownership interests were not entirely eliminated. In the rejuvenating process—which in most cases commenced soon after the date of the merger—original capitalization was greatly revised, original management replaced, and ownership interests seriously reduced. As mergers, therefore, they should be added to the number of failures, bringing the total to 154. Twenty-eight limping successes underwent minor reorganization, but their ownership interests and managements did not change. Since they survived virtually intact for at least twenty-five or thirty years they clearly cannot be counted as failures.

Hence, 154 out of 328 mergers, or 47 per cent, turned out to be failures, 53 of which failed soon after they were formed. When it is considered that mergers represent not entirely new and untried ventures but fusions of firms that have already survived their uncertain years of infancy, such a high incidence of failure suggests that promotional rather than operational gains motivated the formation of a large number of them.

[53] See U.S. Steel, American Tobacco, and American Can, note 50.

As one would expect, the merger-creating industry did not thrive for long. Bankers, industrialists, and the stock-buying public, on whose support the promoter relied, soon had their expectations shattered. In the eighteen-month period preceding October 1903, the market value of 100 leading industrial stocks shrank by 43.4 per cent.[54] Much of this shrinkage was undoubtedly a downward adjustment of stock prices to reflect the difference between *expected* and *actual* earnings. The result was the "Rich Man's Panic" of 1903, by which time the early merger movement had run its course.

So much, then, for the motives behind the 1887-1904 merger movement. In summary, nearly one-half of the recorded mergers appear to have been unquestionably profitable ventures. A reasonable inference is that a large proportion of these were motivated by market control and production and distribution economies. About one-fifth of the mergers resulted in dominant firms controlling from nearly one-half to nearly all of their respective markets. These and some others that sought a high degree of market control and failed must have had monopoly as their goal. These two overlapping groups, while accounting for perhaps no more than one-half of the total number of recorded mergers, contain the larger mergers with which the literature has identified the movement. However, about an equal number of moderately large mergers were decidedly unprofitable, 53 of which failed soon after they were formed. Many in this group probably were products of the promoter, hastily put together for purposes of obtaining promotional rather than operational profits. The smaller mergers having capitalizations of less than $1 million were overlooked by those who recorded the early movement. There are no available data that suggest the reasons why they were formed or how they affected the structure of their respective markets. While they did not loom large in the business world, they appear to have been numerous and an integral part of the 1887-1904 merger wave.

Why the movement occurred when and as it did defies precise answers. In view of the moderately high positive correlation that exists between merger activity and stock prices,[55] it is worth pointing out that the movement conformed closely to a general statistical pattern. The great flurry of mergers following 1897 also fits neatly into Schumpeterian business cycle theory. Schumpeter considered merger as a form of innovation. According to his theory, neighborhoods of equilibrium were spawning grounds for innovations, and

[54] Moody, *op. cit.*, quoting the *Wall Street Journal*, October 24, 1903.
[55] See Table 2.

1897 was a neighborhood of equilibrium for all the various cycles. Hence the 1897-1904 merger movement is twice-blessed: it fits both a statistical and a theoretical model. But this explains neither its form nor scope. Here the literature relies heavily on institutional factors: (1) The Sherman Act of 1890 made collusion illegal and put an end to the trustee device, thereby forcing industrialists seeking market control to resort to complete fusion of their separate companies. (2) The 1880's marked the development of the modern capital market, a prerequisite to the flotation of large issues of securities. (3) Important changes in state incorporation laws also occurred during the 1880's—the requirement of unanimous agreement of stockholders was eliminated, limitations on capitalization and area of operation were relaxed, and restrictions on mergers were removed. This was useful groundwork. The passage of the Holding Company Act by the State of New Jersey in 1888, with subsequent further liberalizations of the act in 1889, 1893, and 1896, provided the capstone. (4) The *Northern Securities* decision made it evident in 1904 that the merger avenue to monopoly was also closed.

Hence, both economic and institutional factors were favorable for a merger movement of some kind sometime after the mid-1880's. Conditions were particularly favorable for several years following 1896. The collapse of the stock market and the *Northern Securities* decision of 1904 brought these favorable conditions to an abrupt end. Those who seek a more rigorous formulation of causation than this will probably have to go beyond the existing body of merger literature.

4. The 1919-1930 Merger Movement

No ONE has yet written the "Truth about Mergers" for the 1920's. For the most part the small body of literature on the movement that does exist is cast in fairly dispassionate tones. It condemns with restraint the "devouring octopuses," the "bloodsuckers of competition," and the "pillagers of enterprise" who allegedly had wrought such irreparable damage a quarter of a century earlier, and praises with less ardor the handiwork of those who sought to build pillars of economic efficiency.[56] In comparison with mergers and combina-

[56] It should not be inferred from this that economists are in full agreement on either the intensity or the social significance of merger formation during the 1920's. Dewing views merger as a subordinate feature of the rising tide of business that culminated in 1929. (See Dewing, *The Financial Policy of Corporations*, as cited, p. 929.) On the other hand, Stocking and Watkins view the period as having "practically duplicated the situation at the turn of the century. . . ." (See G. W. Stocking and Myron W. Watkins, *Cartels or Competition?* [Twentieth Century Fund, 1948], p. 16, note 11.)

tions of the 1890's, those of the 1920's were much less spectacular. Accordingly, they were described in less picturesque language.

This does not mean, however, that the second wave of mergers was completely dwarfed by its predecessor. On the contrary, in absolute numerical terms it was larger in size. Between 1919 and 1930 nearly 12,000 public utility, banking, manufacturing, and mining concerns disappeared from the American economy through mergers, more than twice the number of *plants* absorbed in all the industrial combinations recorded up to 1904 (see Table 5). The 11,852 absorptions included approximately 2,100 mergers, or about five times the number of mergers recorded for the earlier wave. Moreover, between

TABLE 5

Concerns Disappearing from Manufacturing, Public Utilities, and Banking, 1919-1930

	Number of Firms in Operation, 1929 (1)	Number of Concerns Disappearing 1919-1928 (2)	1919-1930 (estimated)a (3)	Per Cent Total Concerns Disappearing (4)
Manufacturing:				
Food	57,500	835	1,120	1.9
Metals	27,900	1,770	2,373	8.5
Lumber and paper	47,800	419	562	1.2
Chemicalsb	8,100	1,175	1,577	19.5
Textiles and apparel	29,700	401	538	1.8
Other (includes mining)	86,563	1,391	1,865	2.2
Total manufacturing (and mining)	257,563	5,991	8,035	3.1
Public utilities	6,355c	2,757d	n.a.	43.3
Banks (Federal Reserve System)	8,052e	1,060	n.a.	13.2
Total	271,970	9,805	11,852	4.4

n.a.=not available.

a Assumes mergers occurred among industry groups in 1929-1930 in same proportion as 1919-1928.

b Includes products of petroleum and coal.

c Number of reporting establishments in 1922. By 1932 the number of reporting establishments had been reduced to 3,429. See *Statistical Abstracts of the Fifteenth Census*, Bureau of the Census, 1930.

d 1928 estimated from data for first three quarters.

e 1930.

Source: Concerns disappearing are from Willard L. Thorp, "Facts about the Consolidation and Merger Movement and the Concentration of Industry," *Mergers, Consolidations and Affiliations* (General Management Series 92, American Management Association, 1929), p. 10. Thorp's data for the period 1919-1928 (column 2) were adjusted to include the years 1929 and 1930 (column 3). The number of operating firms in each of Thorp's industry groups in 1929 was calculated from Dept. of Commerce data. See Melville J. Ulmer, "Industrial Patterns of the Business Population," *Survey of Current Business*, Dept. of Commerce, May 1948, p. 15.

1919 and 1929 the number of chain distributors in 26 kinds of business increased from 8,500 to 20,000, and, between 1919 and 1930, 1,591 chains identified with the 26 kinds of business made 10,519 store acquisitions.[57] Hence, by any previously (or subsequently) established standard of measurement, the second wave of mergers was large. Why the literature has left it so completely overshadowed by the 1887-1904 wave of mergers and consolidations, therefore, must be explained on grounds other than its absolute size. There are several obvious reasons.

First, between one-quarter and one-third of the 1919-1930 mergers occurred in industries where the question of monopoly was not applicable. Of 11,852 concerns known to have disappeared through mergers, about 24 per cent were public utility and 9 per cent were banking concerns. While the extent to which banking was left to competitive regulation in the 1920's is not entirely clear, the Federal Reserve Act of 1913 gave member banks something approaching a public utility status. Moreover, all banks were subject to certain regulatory provisions of state banking laws. Public utilities, of course, except in the State of Delaware, had long since been regulated by public authority. Hence, only two-thirds of the mergers involved firms operating in sectors of the economy where competition was expected to regulate.

Second, the larger horizontal mergers, on balance, may well have stimulated as much competition as they stifled. Stigler has characterized mergers during the period as having typically transformed near monopolies to oligopolies;[58] the dominant firm left the field clear for firms of the second and lower levels to launch their own merger programs instead of seeking to regain a lost dominant position for itself. In some cases circular dependency may have replaced dominant firm control; in others it may have replaced moderately independent action; in still others independent action may have replaced dominant firm control. Hence the net effect on competition of the 1919-1930 horizontal mergers is not nearly so clear as that of the large horizontal combinations of the earlier merger movement.

While mergers in the 1920's increased oligopoly, oligopoly provided a motive for no more than a small fraction of them. Merger for oligopoly presupposes an extremely high order of oligopolistic

---

[57] *Report of the Federal Trade Commission Relative to the Growth and Development of Chain Stores*, S. Doc. 100, 72d Cong., 1st Sess., 1932, pp. 6-7. 61-62.
[58] "Monopoly and Oligopoly by Merger," as cited, p. 31.

169

rationalization—a much higher order than events or logic can support. The rationale of merger for oligopoly under highly competitive conditions would probably run something like this: (1) Intense price competition is undesirable. (2) It can be eliminated by reducing the many firms in an industry to a few. (3) I know this and all my many rivals know this. Accordingly (4) I will collect a large fraction (say one-sixth) of the industry together by merger, and assume that five of my rivals will do likewise. (5) After the formation of all (six) of the mergers we can rationalize prices. Until more is known about the much simpler phenomenon of pricing among the few, it seems best not to rely upon this line of reasoning for an explanation of mergers.

The above rationale is also partly applicable and equally as unreliable under conditions of near monopoly (the starting point in Stigler's analysis), when the unmonopolized sector of the industry comprises many smaller firms. Moreover, when the dominant firm controls considerably more than one-half of the entire market, oligopoly by merger is impossible. However, if the industry comprises a partial monopolist controlling 50 per cent of the market or less and not many smaller firms, one or several of the latter may prefer oligopoly to complete domination and may also find the transformation relatively easy to perform. Mergers by Bethlehem and Republic in the steel industry, cited by Stigler to support his conclusion, may also be cited here as a case in point. There were others, but the extent to which oligopolies sprang up in the 1920's by the merger route can easily be exaggerated. Of 22 oligopolistic industries studied by Weston, 5 were made oligopolies by court dissolution or by pressure of government investigation, 9 by merger, 5 by internal growth of rivals, and 3 by a combination of internal growth and merger. Accordingly he concludes that mergers, while an important cause, accounted for less than half of the number of oligopolies studied.[59]

Third, mergers of all kinds in the 1920's typically embraced a relatively small proportion of the total firms in their respective industries and, for one reason or another, firms that had not previously competed with each other. The number and per cent of concerns disappearing through merger from each broad industry group appear in Table 5. Although data for broad industrial classifications are not very illuminating, they measure in a rough fashion the incidence of merger activity during the period 1919-1930. In absolute

[59] Weston, *op. cit.*, p. 64.

terms, merger activity in manufacturing was highest in the food, metals, and chemical industries,[60] these three groups having accounted for 5,070 of the 6,170 disappearing firms that can be identified with any particular industry group. However, the proportion of total active firms disappearing was significant in only the metals and chemicals industries (column 4).

The shortcomings of the data shown in Table 5 hardly require elaboration but, until both disappearances and census data have been broken down into much finer classifications, quantitative measurement of the effect of the 1919-1930 merger movement on the structure of all industries can proceed no further. Other data scattered throughout the literature, however, suggest the effect mergers had on the structure of some of them. In the food industries, merger-created firms were largely of the chain- and conglomerate-firm variety. National Dairy, General Foods, General Mills, and several bakery chains—Continental, Ward, and Purity—all date from this period. In the copper industry, mergers extended vertical integration. In 1922 Anaconda merged with American Brass; the merger subsequently acquired other finished goods producers, notably the Detroit Brass and Rolling Mills. In 1929 Kennecott Copper acquired Chase Companies, Inc., Phelps-Dodge acquired Habirshaw Cable and Wire and the American Tube Works in the early 1930's. In chemicals, where Allied Chemicals and Dye and Du Pont are the best examples, mergers were mostly of the conglomerate firm type.

While such illustrative cases permit no sweeping generalizations, they suggest that a large portion of the mergers formed in the 1920's brought together firms producing totally different lines of products, the same products in noncompeting territories, or firms engaged in different stages of fabrication. They contributed to a concomitant increase in concentration of control of assets,[61] but it is much less certain that, on balance, they measurably affected monopoly power in specific market areas. At least in the dairy industry, where merg-

[60] Stigler concluded from changes in the number of establishments in central offices between 1919 and 1937 that merger activity was highest in the food, paper and printing, and iron and steel products industries. Where similar industrial classifications can be compared, his conclusions are supported by the above data. It should be pointed out, however, that changes in establishments in central offices measure total expansion, and are therefore not very good measures of merger activity for periods when internal growth was significant. "Monopoly and Oligopoly by Merger," as cited, p. 31.

[61] It has been fairly conclusively established that concentration of control of assets increased between 1924 and 1929, the six-year span that includes most of the merger activity associated with the second merger movement. See Adelman, op. cit., p. 285.

ers were particularly numerous, they did not prevent violent out-breaks of price competition in milk production and distribution in the early thirties.[62]

Fourth, the second great wave of mergers was accompanied by a fairly steady decline in price levels, a remarkable increase in the national income, and a rising level of employment. While the writer does not mean to imply that these concomitant phenomena were beneficial effects of mergers, they have long been regarded as in-compatible with pervasive monopoly growth.

Fifth, horizontal merger in the 1920's, like that of the earlier movement, was probably increased by major developments in trans-portation and communication. Between 1910 and 1930 the economy assimilated a new system of transportation—the motor vehicle. In 1910 passenger motor vehicle registrations in the United States totalled only 468,500, and motor truck registrations only 10,000; by 1930 passenger motor vehicle registrations had reached a total of 26,545,281, and motor truck registrations 3,486,019.[63] This new trans-portation system tended to break down small local markets in two ways: it provided sellers with a new means for extending their sales area, and it made consumers considerably more mobile. The 1920's also marked the rise of the home radio, a medium particularly amen-able to advertising national brands. Between 1922 and 1928 the radio audience in the United States increased from 75,000 to 40 million and the value of radios and accessories sold per year, in the face of declining prices, increased by 980 per cent.[64]

Finally, except where mergers were motivated by production and distribution economies (centralized chemical research, chain distri-bution, etc.) they appear to have been largely inspired by the pro-fessional promoter. This explains in part why the merger movement followed the pattern it did. According to Dewing, "In the period before 1929, much more than in the earlier period, consolidations were attempted in order to deal better with merchandising prob-lems. Rubber factories and stationery factories were brought to-gether merely because both rubber goods and stationery could be sold in drug stores, washing powder and breakfast foods because

62 Cf. *Nebbia* v. *New York*, 291 U.S. 502 (1934), and subsequent cases involv-ing the constitutionality of state regulation of milk prices.

63 D. Philip Lockin, *Economics of Transportation* (Irwin, 1947), pp. 666-667.

64 Dwight D. Farnham, "Types of Consolidations and Mergers in America and Europe," in *Mergers, Consolidations and Affiliations* (General Management Series No. 92, American Management Association, 1929), p. 18.

both were found on the shelves of grocery stores."[65] In some cases the promoter could probably give convincing evidence that merger would be profitable, either because it made for lower buying, production, or distribution costs, or because it furthered product differentiation through national brand advertising, or both. In others, where the advantage of merger was not so evident, he found his product more difficult to sell. In such cases promoters (principally investment bankers) resorted to high-pressure salesmanship. Thorp, who has probably devoted more careful study to the period than anyone else, has summed up the merger movement of the 1920's as follows:

"Many mergers, and some acquisitions, involve the flotation of new securities. In periods like 1928 and early 1929, when there is almost an insatiable demand for securities, the merger movement will be certain to flourish. Its most active sponsor is the investment banker. Reputable business houses merely carrying on their business under their existing organization bring a very slight volume of new securities for the banker to handle. But if they can be brought together into a new organization it may mean a large flotation of stock. During 1928 and 1929 some investment houses employed men on commission who did nothing but search for potential mergers. One businessman told me that he regarded it as a loss of standing if he was not approached at least once a week with a merger proposition. A group of businessmen and financiers in discussing this matter in the summer of 1928 agreed that nine out of ten mergers had the investment banker at the core."[66]

This wave, then, like that of the closing years of the 1890's, rode to its peak on a crest of rising stock market prices. While oligopoly (with and without product differentiation) and distribution and production economies undoubtedly motivated some of the mergers, others certainly had promoters' profits as their principal objective. In any case they seem to have given little impetus to monopoly growth, although they are reflected in a concomitant increase in concentration of control of assets. It is not surprising, therefore, that the public's reaction to the merger movement of the 1920's was not more rigid enforcement of the Sherman Act, but the enactment of the Securities Act of 1933, the Securities Exchange Act of 1934, and the Holding Company Act of 1935.

[65] *The Financial Policy of Corporations*, as cited, p. 929.
[66] "The Persistence of the Merger Movement," as cited, pp. 85-86.

5. *The 1940-1947 Merger Movement*

I⠀T WAS stated earlier that researchers on mergers have tended to act like the six blind men of Indostan—on examining different parts they reach different conclusions about the whole. For the most recent merger movement, however, this analogy is not applicable. Two studies have been made of the 1940-1947 mergers, one by the FTC and the other by Butters, Lintner, and Cary.[67] Initially, the two appeared to have reached entirely different conclusions on the effect of recent mergers on concentration although they analyzed almost identical data.[68]

According to FTC's report, 2,450 concerns were known to have disappeared from mining and manufacturing through merger and acquisition in the period 1940-1947 (see Table 6, col. 3). The report emphasized that this was a minimum estimate since it was based on "a sample drawn principally from reports of acquisition of the larger corporations."[69] The Commission's data therefore were incomplete and tended to underestimate the proportion of acquisitions made by small concerns. In textiles, an extreme case in point, its sample showed a total of 154 concerns acquired, whereas *Textile World* showed an additional 388 concerns acquired, most of which represented small-business enterprises acquired by small-business enterprises. Nevertheless, from its sample data summarized in Table 7 the Commission concluded (1) "that the preponderant number of firms have been acquired by the very largest corporations" and (2) "that fully 93 per cent of all the firms bought out since 1940 held assets of less than $5 million, and 71 per cent had less than $1 million of assets."[70]

Just what conclusions on concentration the Commission drew from these data have been a matter of considerable debate. The relevant statements appearing in the report are as follows:

"No great stretch of the imagination is required to foresee that if nothing is done to check the growth in concentration, either the giant corporations will ultimately take over the country, or the Government will be impelled to step in. . . ."[71]

67 *The Merger Movement, A Summary Report*, as cited; and Butters, Lintner, and Cary, *op. cit.*

68 For negligible differences in the two sets of data, see John Lintner and J. Keith Butters, "Effect of Mergers on Industrial Concentration, 1940-1947," *The Review of Economics and Statistics*, February 1950, p. 34, note 9 and p. 39, note 23.

69 *The Merger Movement, A Summary Report*, as cited, p. 17.

70 *Ibid.*, p. 28.   71 *Ibid.*, p. 68.

Per Cent of Total Firms Disappearing through Merger and Ratio of Net Increase in Firms to Disappearances, Manufacturing, Mining, and Other, 1940-1947

(firms in thousands)

Industry	Firms in Operation (1)		Increase in Number of Firms, 1940-1947 (2)	Total Firms Merged or Acquired, 1940-1947 (3)	Per Cent of Total Firms (1947) Disappearing (4)	Ratio of Net Increase to Disappearances, 1940-1947 (5)
	1940	1947				
Manufacturing:						
Food and kindred products	54.0	57.0	3.0	.369	.6	8.13
Textiles and apparel	23.5	39.0	15.5	.154	.4	100.65
				(.542)[a]	(1.4)[a]	(28.60)[a]
Paper and allied products	2.5	3.0	.5	.084	2.8	5.95
Printing and publishing	37.7	41.7	4.0	.028	.7	142.86
Chemicals and allied products[b]	7.4	9.8	2.4	.369	3.8	6.50
(Petroleum and coal products)	(.9)[c]	(.9)	(.0)[d]	(.157)	17.4	.00[e]
Rubber products	1.3[e]	1.5	.2[d]	.025	1.7	8.00
Leather products	3.2	5.2	2.0	.019	.4	105.26
Metals and metal products	25.9	49.8	23.9	.241	.5	99.17
Nonelectrical machinery	15.8[c]	17.2	1.4[d]	.167	1.0	8.38
Electrical machinery	3.6[c]	4.1	.5[d]	.105	2.6	4.76
Transportation equipment	3.1[c]	4.2	1.1[d]	.149	3.5	7.38
Lumber and furniture	33.0	64.2	31.2	.050	.1	624.00
Stone, clay, and glass products	5.5	14.6	9.1	.064	.4	142.19
Other manufacturing	f	4.8		.036	.8	f
Total manufacturing	215.5	316.3	100.8	1.887	.6	53.42
Mining and quarrying	27.2[c]	29.6	2.4[d]	.071	.2	33.80
Other nonmanufacturing	3,161.1[c]	3,502.4	341.3[d]	.104	g	3,281.73
All industries	3,403.8	3,848.3	444.5	2.062	.1	215.56
				(2.450)[a]		

a Including 388 additional acquisitions reported in Textile World.
b Includes products of petroleum and coal.
c Number of active firms are those reported as of June 30, 1946. Not available for previous years.
d Increase between June 30, 1946, and Dec. 31, 1947.
e No net increase in number of firms; 157 absorptions.
f Cannot be put on comparable basis with 1947.
g Less than .01 per cent.
Source: Survey of Current Business, Dept. of Commerce, May 1948, and The Merger Movement, A Summary Report, Federal Trade Commission, 1948.

"Either this country is going down the road to collectivism, or it must stand and fight for competition. . . . Crucial in that fight must be some effective means of preventing giant corporations from steadily increasing their power at the expense of small business."[72]

"The importance of external expansion [mergers, consolidations, etc.] in promoting concentration has never been more clearly revealed than in the acquisition movement that is taking place at the

TABLE 7

Size of Acquiring and Acquired Concerns, 1940-1947

Size of Acquiring and Acquired Concern in Terms of Millions of Dollars of Assets	Acquisitions Made by Acquiring Concerns	Concerns Acquired
Under $1	239	1,468
$1–$4	365	455
5– 9	264	58
10–49	590	66
Over $49	604	15
Total	2,062[a]	2,062[a]

a Does not include 388 additional acquisitions in the textile industry reported in *Textile World.*

Source: *The Merger Movement, A Summary Report,* Federal Trade Commission, 1948.

present time—a movement which is strengthening the position of big business in several ways."[73]

"The evidence thus points clearly to the conclusion that, insofar as its impact on concentration is concerned, the outstanding characteristic of the current merger movement has been the absorption of smaller independent enterprises by larger concerns."[74]

These statements in the Commission's report appear to add up to an initial conclusion by the Commission that concentration was significantly increased by the 1940-1947 mergers. Accordingly, Butters and Lintner, since their own study led them to a contrary conclusion, announced their results as essentially a reversal of the Commission's findings.[75] Whereupon Blair and Houghton, speaking on behalf of the Commission's report, replied that they had made no general statement about the effect of mergers on concentration and "Indeed, if the Commission had made any general statement on this point, it would probably have concluded, based on its own data, that the recent mergers have *not* substantially increased concentra-

[72] *Ibid.*, p. 69.   [73] *Ibid.*, p. 25.   [74] *Ibid.*, p. 28.   [75] *Op. cit.*, pp. 30-48.

tion in manufacturing as a whole."[76] With the divisions of research in the FTC and the Harvard Business School finally in substantial agreement that the 1940-1947 mergers had little pervasive effect on industrial concentration, the case can fairly be considered as closed. The evidence, however, is worth reviewing.

Data compiled by Butters and Lintner representing acquisitions totaling $3 1/3 billion show that for the 1940-1947 period merger was a more important source of relative growth for small than for large companies. Acquiring companies having assets of $100 million or more had an average growth through merger of 2.3 per cent; companies having $50-$100 million assets had an average growth through merger of 13.8 per cent; the $10-$50 million companies, 18.7 per cent; the $5-$10 million companies, 33.4 per cent; the $1-$5 million companies, 68.1 per cent; and companies having assets of less than $1 million increased their size through merger by 142.3 per cent. From this it can safely be concluded that mergers were a much less important source of relative growth for large companies *that made acquisitions* than for small companies *that made acquisitions.*[77] But what was the effect of mergers on the relative growth of *all* firms in each size class? Here again, the Butters and Lintner data show that the larger the size of firms the less important mergers were as a source of relative growth. If the fairly reasonable assumption were made that the estimated $1 2/3 billion of assets of unreported acquisitions were made largely by firms having total assets of less than $10 million, then *all* companies having assets of less than $10 million expanded through merger by 10.1 per cent, whereas *all* firms having assets of $10 million or more expanded through merger by only 6.3 per cent.

The remaining conclusions reached by Butters and Lintner may be summarized as follows: (1) Virtually all the firms disappearing through mergers and acquisitions for the period 1940-1947 were small companies (a conclusion reached earlier by the FTC). Accordingly, mergers of large firms with large firms, so pronounced in earlier merger movements, did not occur. (2) For all manufacturing and mining the Gini coefficient increased from .809 to .816 through merger, or only .007 in eight years. (3) Among the 1,000 largest manufacturing firms, the lower 500 grew relatively more through

[76] John M. Blair and Harrison F. Houghton, "The Lintner-Butters Analysis of the Effect of Mergers on Industrial Concentration, 1940-1947, A Reply," *Review of Economics and Statistics*, February 1951, p. 67.

[77] Cf. *ibid.*, p. 66.

merger than the upper 500. Within the largest 1,000 firms, there-fore, mergers produced some deconcentration.

Data showing the percentage of total firms disappearing through merger from mining and manufacturing and from each major manu-facturing group in the years 1940-1947 are presented in Table 6. They support the conclusions reached by Lintner and Butters. In all manufacturing and in 8 of the 15 manufacturing industry groups less than 1.0 per cent of the total number of firms disappeared through merger. In 6 of the remaining 7 groups the number of dis-appearances through merger amounted to only 3.8 per cent or less of the groups' respective populations. Only in the petroleum and coal products group was the number of disappearances through merger relative to the total firm population significantly high (17.4 per cent).[78] For all industries, the number of firms disappearing through merger amounted to less than 0.1 per cent of the total number of firms in operation in 1947.

In comparison with earlier merger movements, therefore, the 1940-1947 movement was exceedingly small. The individual firms disappearing through merger were small and disappearances were relatively few in number. The average annual number of disappear-ances in mining and manufacturing for the eight-year period was 258, or barely over one-third the average annual number of disap-pearances for the thirteen-year period 1919-1931, considerably less than the number of disappearances recorded for any year in the period 1919-1931, and exceeded by only 55 the number of disappear-ances occurring in the depression year of 1932.

What is more important, however, merger activity in 1940-1947 was dwarfed by other forms of growth. In the eight-year period total assets of mining and manufacturing corporations increased by more than 10 times the estimated $5 billion involved in all mergers in mining and manufacturing. In 5 out of 15 manufacturing industry groups the net increase in the number of active firms between 1940 and 1947 was over 100 times the number lost through merger. Only in the petroleum and coal products industry, where no net in-crease occurred, was the ratio of the net increase in firms to disap-pearances through merger less than 5 to 1. In all manufacturing, the ratio of the net increase in firms to the number of firms lost through merger was 53.42 to 1; in mining, the ratio was 33.80 to 1.

[78] This was also the industry group in which acquiring firms showed the low-est percentage growth in assets by acquisition. Hence, the 157 absorbed firms must have been extremely small. See Lintner and Butters, *op. cit.*, p. 43.

When viewed against these overriding forces, some doubt is cast upon the propriety of characterizing the 1940-1947 mergers as a "merger movement." Unfortunately, the English language provides us with no descriptive term for movements of a diminutive sort. But if previous (and future) merger movements are still to be associated with waves of mergers, the 1940-1947 movement might be viewed as a ripple.

Judged by their results and the circumstances under which they occurred, the recent mergers patently did not have monopoly as their goal. Furthermore, they were accompanied by no spectacular rise in stock market prices; accordingly, the professional promoter appears to have been conspicuously inactive. Hence two prominent historical motives for merger played little or no part in the formation of mergers during the 1940's. Probably the wartime and postwar flurry of mergers had no pervasive motives at all, other than those associated with conventional business transactions.

Fortunately, this assessment can be carried beyond the stage of mere conjecture. Stigler explains a sizable number of the wartime and postwar vertical mergers in terms of attempts to circumvent price controls and allocations, and supports his conclusions with an explanatory hypothesis.[79] In their careful case-by-case investigation of why firms merged, Butters, Lintner, and Cary found that taxation, management, and investment considerations prompted most owners to offer their firms for sale; the desire for a new product, plant, or production organization, or for greater vertical integration prompted other business firms to buy them.[80] These reasons of course are always operative in varying degrees, and probably accounted for most of the 226 average disappearances per year through merger for the period 1930-1939. It is not so surprising that this annual average should have increased by nearly 15 per cent during the war and immediate postwar years. As Butters et al. have shown, high wartime and postwar income and estate taxes and the relatively much lower capital gains tax motivated the sale of about 9.7 per cent of the total number of firms disappearing through merger between 1940 and 1947. Moreover, aside from taxes, vertical integration, and other wartime business considerations, businessmen (and economists as well) during 1940-1947 held widely different views about the economic prospects for the years ahead. Pessimists who

[79] "The Division of Labor is Limited By the Extent of the Market," as cited, pp. 190-191.
[80] Op. cit., pp. 201-240.

179

foresaw a long postwar recession should have been quite willing to dispose of their stock of assets at prices somewhere below the then prevailing reproduction costs. Contrariwise, optimists seeking additional plants, for whatever purpose, should have been equally willing to buy them at those prices. While it may be argued correctly that this rationale does not explain very much, it should be borne in mind that there is not a great deal to be explained.

6. *Summary of Conclusions on Mergers*

AN EFFECTIVE appraisal of the findings on mergers requires considerable candor. The literature reflects the views of men who stand as much as a half-century apart in time and at opposite ideological poles. To combine the findings of researchers holding opposing ideologies and conflicting preconceptions produces a synthetic logic that will probably please no one. Nevertheless, the synthesis leads to conclusions that all the available data support. It is not expected that all will accept them, but they may serve as a first approximation to the "truth about mergers" until the whole truth is known.

1. Contrary to what is perhaps the most frequently advanced explanation of merger, relatively few mergers appear to have had market monopolization as their goal. Monopoly was unquestionably the aim of about one-fifth of the larger combinations formed between 1887 and 1904, but has played a dormant role over the past half-century. The fact that examples of merger for monopoly appearing in even the current literature are taken exclusively from the 1887-1904 period convincingly confirms this point. Standard Oil, United States Steel, American Tobacco, and others of this era still epitomize the merger for monopoly. Oligopoly had supplanted partial monopoly in at least 22 industries by the 1930's, and had supplanted near-competition in several more. However, merger was the instrument by which oligopoly was fashioned in only 9 of them, and the number in which oligopoly provided the dominant motive for merger was still less.

This does not suggest that merger has resulted in an insignificant amount of monopoly control or concentration. The conversion of approximately 71 important oligopolistic or near-competitive industries into near monopolies by merger between 1890 and 1904 left an imprint on the structure of the American economy that fifty years have not yet erased. Moreover, many mergers obviously not motivated by monopoly nevertheless may have increased concentration and lessened competition. For the sake of historical and statis-

180

tical accuracy, however, it should be made clear that most mergers left no such imprint.

2. The most important single motive for merger at the peaks of merger movements seems to have been promotional profits. The waves of mergers in 1897-1899 and in 1926-1929 rode to their respective peaks with concomitant rapidly rising stock prices. Both periods were marked by easy money and a securities-hungry public. This environment gave rise to a new type of entrepreneur—the producer of mergers. In some cases the promoter already headed one of the merging firms; in others he came from the outside. Sometimes he combined a sufficient number of firms to significantly affect the industry's structure. More often, as was true of the 1920's, he did not. Original owners were paid sometimes in stock and sometimes in cash. Whatever the differences in scope and procedure, promoter-created mergers appear to have had one common feature—the whole was greater than the sum of its parts. The difference between the two was the promoter's profits.

3. A large number of mergers have been prompted by the prospects of neither monopoly gains nor promoters' profits, but have simply reflected ordinary business transactions among entrepreneurs. Mergers or acquisitions of this sort are one means whereby some entrepreneurs make their exit from an industry, selling their undepreciated assets to other entrepreneurs. The underlying reasons behind such liquidations and acquisitions may be unlimited in number.

Regrettably, the literature on mergers is confined largely to the three merger movements that it identifies. Accordingly little is known about mergers as a normal aspect of business behavior except that they occur all the time. Even in the period 1930-1939 the average number of disappearances annually was 226, just slightly lower than the annual average for the period 1940-1947. Since 1930 most mergers appear to have been of the ordinary business variety in that they had neither monopoly nor promotional gains as their objective. Hence, whether the outcropping of mergers and acquisitions in 1940-1947 took on the size and form of a movement or merely reflected a quickened pace in asset transfers among entrepreneurs is not entirely clear. However, contemporary literature argues in favor of the former.

4. Finally, some mergers have undoubtedly come about as adjustments to major innovations having a rapid and pervasive effect on the entire economy. The principal evidence in support of this conclusion, however, is that if one uses it as a premise, the timing of

intense merger activity is consistent with it: the first great wave of mergers followed a period of rapid railroad building, and the wave of the 1920's came with the rise of motor car and motor truck transportation and a new advertising medium, the home radio. From the logic of comparative costs, it would be expected that these innovations would cause some small local enterprises eventually to give way to larger and more efficient firms. However, mergers and acquisitions could hasten the process.

*　*　*　*　*

A half-century ago economists held widely different views on the causes and social significance of mergers and combinations. This is neither discomforting nor surprising. The phenomenon was new and its causes largely unexplored. Each formed his opinion out of his own ideology and out of what he saw; but the early merger movement was big, and no one saw it all.

The mid-twentieth-century student of industrial organization, however, can do far better than choose his flag and wave it vigorously. Admittedly there is much that still is not known about mergers, but if the findings reveal anything, they show that the causes and consequences of merger are complex and diverse. For purposes of framing and administering a public policy committed to maintaining competition, the broad implication of this conclusion is obvious. It means that while some mergers impair a competitive enterprise system, others may be an integral part of it. The choice, therefore, is not whether to condemn or sanction them all, but how to design appropriate criteria for judging which is which. If this essay has served to bring economists into substantial agreement on this point, it will have fulfilled its principal purpose. To those who have had no occasion to review the literature on mergers, recent and past, this may appear as a much less ambitious task than it is.

COMMENT

WALTER ADAMS, Michigan State College

MARKHAM has done a commendable job in surveying the evidence and findings on mergers. He has summarized, digested, and assimilated the major contributions made in this controversial field, and come up with the significant—yet exceedingly modest—conclusion that the "causes and consequences of merger are complex and diverse." While Markham's paper is generally beyond reproach, his analysis is subject to some major limitations and criticisms.

1. Markham examines so many divergent aspects of the merger problem, that the central issue—the effect of mergers on concentration—is buried in a welter of detail. He gives inadequate attention to the conspicuous role of mergers in the concentration of economic power, a concentration which, by 1947, found 139 companies owning 45 per cent of all manufacturing assets. Moreover, the effect of mergers on this phenomenal concentration seems to be seriously understated.

The record shows that there were three distinct merger movements since 1890. The first, and largest, lasted from 1897 to 1904; the second, from 1920 to 1931; and the third, from 1940 to 1947. By the end of the first movement 300 industrial combinations covering most major lines of production had been formed. These combinations, according to generally accepted estimates, controlled fully 40 per cent of the nation's manufacturing capital. Of these consolidations 78 controlled 50 per cent or more of their respective industries, 57 controlled 60 per cent or more, and 26 controlled 80 per cent or more.[1] This wave of merger activity was so gigantic as to "give American industry its characteristic twentieth century concentration of control."[2] It was so pervasive in its effects primarily because the consolidations formed during this period "very frequently included most, if not all, of the already largest companies in the industry,"[3] companies which themselves had been formed by mergers between previously leading industrial giants.

It is with a measure of satisfaction that Markham offers the finding that subsequent merger movements were progressively smaller. We are told that in its percentage effect on concentration, the merger movement of the 1920's fell short of the earlier movement, and that the wave of mergers during the 1940's should not even be dignified as a movement but rather be "viewed as a ripple." These conclusions—as Markham readily admits—are not startling. More important, however, they should not give rise to complacency among public policy makers.

[1] George J. Stigler, "Monopoly and Oligopoly by Merger," *American Economic Review*, Proceedings, May 1950, p. 29.

[2] P. T. Homan, "Trusts," *Encyclopedia of the Social Sciences* (Macmillan, 1931), Vol. xv, p. 114.

[3] J. K. Butters, J. Lintner, and W. L. Cary, *Effects of Taxation on Corporate Mergers* (Harvard University Press, 1951), p. 289.

It is undoubtedly true that the assets of the largest companies participating in the earliest merger movement frequently increased by several hundred per cent, while the maximum growth of a $100 million company during the recent movement amounted to no more than 22 per cent. It is true that the effect of mergers has become relatively smaller in the highly concentrated industries. But this is to be expected.[4] The larger the base, the smaller the percentage effect of any change in size. The more highly concentrated the industry, the smaller will be the relative increase in concentration as a result of acquisitions by giant firms. This does not mean, however, that mergers should no longer concern those who regard excessive concentration as a potential danger. It does not mean that we can accept with equanimity even the small increase in concentration which future merger movements may inflict on the economy. Markham could have done us a signal service by emphasizing why the more recent merger movement could not possibly have assumed such gigantic proportions as its predecessors. He might have pointed to the truism that, given the high level of concentration prevailing in 1904, later merger movements were smaller simply because there were smaller worlds to conquer.

2. Markham, because of his uncritical acceptance of the Lintner and Butters findings, offers the unsubstantiated, doubtful, and controverted conclusion that, during the merger movement of the 1940's, "the larger the size of firms the less important mergers were as a source of relative growth." This conclusion is grossly misleading because of two statistical biases in the Lintner and Butters approach.

The first bias, according to Blair and Houghton, "stems from the difference in size of the acquiring firm. Since the average size of the acquired firm bought by smaller companies is about the same as that bought by large companies, . . . the addition of this relatively constant increment inevitably results in a higher percentage figure for small than for large companies. Thus, if each of the size classes had made exactly the same number of acquisitions (assuming a relatively constant size of acquired firm), the percentage gain for this reason alone would have been higher for the smaller than for the larger firms."[5]

The second bias compounds the first and involves using as a base

[4] For a plausible explanation of this phenomenon, see Stigler, *op. cit.*, p. 31 ff.

[5] J. M. Blair and H. F. Houghton, "The Lintner-Butters Analysis of the Effect of Mergers on Industrial Concentration, 1940-1947: A Reply," *Review of Economics and Statistics*, February 1951, p. 65.

only those companies which made acquisitions during the relevant period. Here it is quite clear that mergers were a more important source of growth for the small companies *which made acquisitions* than for the larger companies *which made acquisitions*. What is not established, however, is the fact that small companies *as a group* increased their assets more as a result of merger than did the large companies *as a group*. This, the really crucial question, has not as yet been conclusively answered and remains the subject of controversy.[6] Markham, however, conveys the impression that the controversy has been settled and that "the divisions of research in the FTC and the Harvard Business School finally [are] in substantial agreement."

3. Markham, in following Lintner and Butters, offers yet another conclusion which has doubtful significance and misleading implications. He states that, from 1940-1947, "For all manufacturing and mining the Gini coefficient [of relative concentration] increased from .809 to .816 through merger, or only .007 in eight years," thus implying that relative concentration increased very little during this period. He does not explain the Gini index, nor do Lintner and Butters offer more than a footnote reference to an article by Dwight B. Yntema[7] in which the Gini index is discussed. While the reading of footnote references is not always rewarding, an examination of this one did provide some interesting and significant insights.

First, Yntema repeats Dalton's warning that it is better "not to rely upon the evidence of a single measure, but on the corroboration of several."[8] Then, with the purpose of analyzing the nature of corroboration among six concentration indexes which he considered acceptable (including the Gini index), Yntema selected ten wealth

[6] On the basis of their evidence, Blair and Houghton conclude that: "Mergers of all manufacturing and mining companies, 1940-1947, were a much less important relative source of growth for those large companies which made acquisitions than for those smaller companies which made acquisitions, but were a much more important relative source of growth for large companies as a whole than for smaller companies as a whole." *Ibid.*, p. 66.
Markham, by contrast, contends that during the latest merger movement, "*all* companies having assets of less than $10 million expanded through merger by 10.1 per cent, whereas *all* firms having assets of $10 million or more expanded through merger by only 6.3 per cent." Following Lintner and Butters, Markham bases his conclusion on the assumption that there was an *estimated* $1 2/3 billion of unreported asset acquisitions, and that these acquisitions were made largely by firms with total assets of less than $10 million.
[7] Dwight B. Yntema, "Measures of the Inequality in the Personal Distribution of Wealth or Income," *Journal of the American Statistical Association*, December 1933.
[8] *Ibid.*, pp. 428-429.

distributions and seven income distributions for study. He found that "the expected corroboration among the several coefficients in adjudging the extent of inequality has failed to materialize, since there is little uniformity in the ranking of any one wealth distribution or any one income distribution."[9] The dispersion coefficients agreed in giving first rank to one income distribution, but contradicted each other in ranking the six other income distributions. On the basis of his study, Yntema therefore offered the tentative conclusion that no one index can be considered reliable, and that if a choice between indexes had to be made, three of the six acceptable coefficients were preferable to the Gini index. Yet it was the Gini index which Lintner and Butters used, after citing Yntema as a reference, and which Markham now offers the reader without explanation or reservation.[10]

4. Markham, because of his singular preoccupation with over-all concentration, tends to understate the effect of mergers in *particular industries* and on *particular products*. The emphasis is on the forest, and little concern is shown for the trees—in spite of the fact that some of these have recently grown to be giants. The focus is almost exclusively on aggregates, probably on the assumption that significant concentration in any *one* segment would inevitably affect the general index for *all* segments. Unfortunately this assumption is unwarranted.

The structure of the industrial economy is such that quite a number of important mergers would have to occur in the highly capitalized industries in order to affect significantly the level of concentration in manufacturing as a whole. The fact is that most of the heavily capitalized industries—such as steel, petroleum, etc.—were already highly concentrated prior to the outbreak of the recent merger movement. Under such circumstances it was unlikely that further increases in concentration would take place in these industries. After all, once the conditions of oligopoly have been established, the oligopolists have little opportunity or incentive to extend their degree of market control. As the Federal Trade Commission points out:

"Intensive merger activity can hardly be expected to take place in those industries which have already become so highly concentrated that there remain only a relatively few small competitors still

9 *Ibid.*, p. 431.

10 I am indebted to a brilliant young statistician, Ingram Olkin of Michigan State College, for his valuable comments on the various concentration indexes.

available for purchase. It is difficult, for example, to conceive of any further widespread merger activity taking place in such industries as steel, rubber tires, copper, glass, and many other highly concentrated fields."[11]

Granted that this statement is correct, granted also that only through sizable mergers in such fields can the level of over-all concentration be significantly affected, then the real problem becomes: the effect of mergers in industrial fields that were once primarily among the "small business" segments of our economy. Most of these fields—foods, textiles, etc.—have relatively small capitalization as compared to such industries as steel, petroleum, etc. Hence each of these "low-capitalization" industries could become almost completely monopolized without significantly affecting the concentration index for manufacturing as a whole. This is the crucial point which Markham never makes. This is also the reason why Markham's conclusions are potentially a deadly weapon in the hands of the careless public policy student or the special-interest-serving legislator.

Markham is, of course, aware of the concentration trends in many highly competitive industries, especially textiles.[12] There mergers have prominently facilitated the integration movement which, according to most observers, has been almost revolutionary. As one student puts it:

"While some sections of the industry have not been greatly affected, the proportion of the industry now embraced by the large integrated organizations is so considerable as to make them the characteristic form of industrial organization. 'Stabilized competition' . . . is increasingly becoming evident in the major segments of the textile industry."[13]

On another occasion, Markham himself has recognized that, as a result of large-scale integration,

"Many large textile fabric producers now by-pass the intermediate markets between them and the end-product fabricators. In the process, independent converters, selling agents, and commission merchants have lost a large share of their traditional importance. A considerable part of the movement toward combining textile fabric production, converting, and selling may be traced to forward and

[11] *The Merger Movement, A Summary Report*, Federal Trade Commission, 1948, pp. 21-22.

[12] See Markham's excellent article, "Integration in the Textile Industry," *Harvard Business Review*, January 1950.

[13] S. Barkin, "The Regional Significance of the Integration Movement in the Southern Textile Industry," *Southern Economic Journal*, April 1949, p. 395.

187

backward integration *which resulted from transfers in mill ownership*,"[14] i.e., mergers.[15]

It is now agreed that the merger movement in this industry has resulted in increased concentration. Thus the balance sheet assets controlled by the four largest cotton manufacturers increased from 12.1 per cent of the total in 1937 to 19.6 per cent in 1947. Over the same period their share of total productive capacity rose from 4.9 to 10.7 per cent. In 1947 employment concentration ratios in some segments of the industry were even higher, as for example in cotton (13.2 per cent), woolen and worsteds (28 per cent), and silk and rayon (24 per cent).[16]

While the FTC conservatively states that "it is too early to appraise the ultimate effects of the merger movement on competition in the textile industry,"[17] one of the industry's own trade journals is less reticent. Says *Textile World*:

"Belief is prevalent that the industry is entering an era of larger mill groups and that consequently fewer men will control the majority of its equipment and its products. Some extremists even forecast that the time is coming when a mere five or six companies will dominate the textile field just as has come to pass in the automobile industry."[18]

Similar concentration has resulted from mergers in other "low-capitalization" industries without affecting the concentration index for manufacturing as a whole. Butters, Lintner, and Cary, for example, concede that "the increase in concentration in the broadly defined 'food and kindred products' industry is predominantly attributable to the activities of the four large distilling companies. The acquisitions of these four companies accounted for about one-half the number and assets of all the acquisitions of all companies with assets of over $50 million in the food and kindred products group."[19]

14 Markham, *op. cit.*, p. 86 (emphasis supplied).

15 The Cotton Textile Institute estimates that, in the years 1940-1946 inclusive, approximately 20 per cent of the industry's capacity (164 companies owning 4.4 million spindles and more than 88,000 looms) changed ownership. "On the one hand, the basic producers of gray goods [such as Burlington Mills] were expanding forward into finishing operations, while on the other hand, the various fabricators engaged in the latter stages of operation [such as M. Lowenstein & Sons, J. P. Stevens & Co., Ely & Walker Dry Goods Co.] were moving backward into the gray-goods field." *The Merger Movement, A Summary Report*, as cited, p. 55.

16 See Markham, *op. cit.*, p. 86.

17 *The Merger Movement, A Summary Report*, as cited, p. 58.

18 *Ibid.*, p. 58 gives this quotation from the *Textile World*, July 1946, p. 101.

19 Butters, Lintner, and Cary, *op. cit.*, p. 301.

As a result of this merger activity, the Big Four: (1) substantially enhanced their position with respect to inventories of aging whiskeys; (2) gained control of virtually the entire tight cooperage capacity in the country; and (3) acquired wineries holding approximately half of all the wines then aging.[20] All told, the four leading distillers, as of 1947, held 84.6 per cent of the industry's total assets.

Steel drums are another case in point. The recent absorption of practically the entire industry by the major steel producers is a striking example of how mergers can bring about the almost complete disappearance of a typical small business industry. In the words of *Iron Age*:

"Long, long ago, in 1939, before the words postwar and planning were wedded, the manufacture of heavy steel barrels and drums was a rather volatile business firmly in the hands of a large number of highly individualistic entrepreneurs. Most of these fabricators had started on a precarious shoestring and were justifiably vocal in their pride of success in the classical Horatio Alger Pluck and Luck Tradition. [By 1944, however] . . . the purchase of Bennett Mfg. Co., Chicago, by the United States Steel Corp. pretty well completed the capture of the entire barrel and drum business by major steel producers."[21]

Mergers had placed 87 per cent of barrel and drum capacity in the hands of the steel giants.

To summarize, then, it seems apparent that mergers can have considerable effect on concentration in particular industries and in the manufacture of specific products without affecting the general concentration index for manufacturing as a whole. Since the latter is heavily weighted in favor of the "high-capitalization" industries, a whole segment of the manufacturing economy might be monopolized without producing substantial changes in the over-all level of concentration. Markham would have done well to offer the reader this caveat as a "significance test" for his data on mergers and concentration.

5. Finally, it is regrettable that Markham gives only the scantiest consideration to the influence of public policy (or the lack of it) on mergers. He makes passing reference to the *Northern Securities* case, but fails to mention the crucial *E. C. Knight* decision. Yet it was this decision which provided the first significant test of the

[20] See *The Merger Movement, A Summary Report*, as cited, p. 64; also "The Big Wine Deal," *Fortune*, September 1943.

[21] *Iron Age*, September 21, 1944, p. 103; quoted in *The Merger Movement, A Summary Report*, as cited, p. 46.

Sherman Act's effectiveness in combatting mergers. It was this decision ("manufacturing is not commerce") which reassured lawyers and businessmen that mergers in manufacturing and mining were quite safe under the new law. It was this decision—combined with President Cleveland's subsequent statement that it made trusts a state rather than a federal problem—which served as a powerful impetus to the merger movement of the late 1890's. On the basis of the available evidence it appears that public policy—both the "favorable" ruling in the *Knight* case and the "adverse" dictum in the *Northern Securities* case—had a profound influence on the scope and limits of this admittedly gigantic merger movement. The public policy on mergers during this period might, therefore, have received more prominent attention in the Markham analysis.

Finally, Markham contends that mergers have caused little, if any, increase in over-all concentration during the last twenty years. If we assume, *in arguendo*, that this contention is valid, the implications are rather significant. For it was during this period that Section 7 of the Clayton Act was rendered practically meaningless by the so-called merger loophole. It was during this period that incipient monopolists found it perfectly legal to acquire the assets of competing companies, even if the effect was to substantially lessen competition.

Yet it is argued that concentration during this period did not increase as a result of mergers. If this be so, here indeed is an eloquent testimonial to the dynamism and competitiveness of the American economy. Here indeed is a graphic manifestation of centrifugal forces in the economy—holding their own despite a public policy which left the highway to monopoly unblocked and unguarded. One can only speculate on the degree of *deconcentration* that might have taken place had the merger loophole been closed in 1930 instead of 1950. One can only wonder about the effects of an alternative public policy that would have prohibited, rather than facilitated, the use of the monopolist's favorite instrument for the achievement of market control.

It seems to me that further investigation may well reveal that mergers are not inevitable, either technologically or economically; that they are not merely the product of promoters' dreams and rising stock prices; but rather that their occurrence is intimately connected and inextricably intertwined with the permissive, protective, or promotive policies of government toward the monopolization of the economy.

190

MERGERS

GEORGE W. STOCKING, Vanderbilt University

I THINK for the most part that Markham's paper reflects a painstaking and discriminating review of the literature, fairness and good judgment in evaluating its findings. He not only reviews the literature but he does some research on his own and adds to our knowledge and understanding of the several combination movements that have characterized American industrial history during the past seventy-five years. On the significance of mergers he comes to the middle-of-the-road conclusion that some mergers have been socially desirable, some have had no effect on market structure or behavior, and some have been socially undesirable. With that conclusion no one will quarrel.

Having acknowledged the generally high quality of Markham's analysis, I shall turn to his specific findings, some of which seem to me to be quite untenable.

FUNDAMENTAL SHORTCOMINGS OF RESEARCH ON MERGERS

MARKHAM recognizes four fundamental shortcomings of research on mergers. First, no theory of mergers has been developed. "Researchers, having no set of hypotheses as a point of departure, have relied principally upon the arts of description and enumeration." A lack of hypotheses, he thinks, has led to the improper conclusion that mergers have generally resulted in monopoly and that monopoly has been their goal. Second, mergers have ordinarily been defined in terms of this objective, with the result that many mergers which neither strove for nor attained monopoly have been ignored. Third, although most merger studies have been designed to throw light on industrial concentration, they have ignored the fact that when a corporation acquires the assets of another corporation for cash, as is sometimes done, this has not increased concentration of control over total assets. The surviving corporation reduces its liquid assets and increases its fixed assets by a corresponding amount; the selling corporation reduces fixed assets and increases liquid assets. Total assets have not changed and control over assets has not been centralized. Fourth, just as a merger may free liquid assets for investment elsewhere, so it is likely to free entrepreneurial talent for application elsewhere.

Within the limits of his assumptions Markham is correct in both these latter points. But in acknowledging that a merger which involves an exchange of liquid for fixed assets increases the concentration of fixed assets, Markham apparently denies or belittles its relevancy. As he puts it: "If . . . researchers concentrate their attention upon the change in ownership of *fixed* assets attending mergers, the conclusion that mergers increase concentration of control *in some sense* is inescapable." (Last italics supplied.) If a merger should involve *only* a transfer of liquid assets for fixed assets, total assets have, of course, not been changed; but the corporation that no longer has fixed assets has in effect withdrawn from the industry. And that is where Markham leaves it. Meanwhile the firm that increased its fixed assets has presumably increased its share of the market, and that is the significant development in a study of industrial concentration.

In discussing the effect that mergers have on the use of entrepreneurial talent Markham says: ". . . while mergers increase the quantity of assets controlled by the entrepreneurs of *surviving* firms, they also free entrepreneurs to create new firms with new assets elsewhere." (Italics supplied.) Here he clearly implies that mergers reduce the number of firms and concentrate assets, as indeed he does in developing the point that they don't, when he says: "Where one corporation acquires the assets of another for cash . . . , the *surviving* corporation simply reduces liquid assets and increases fixed assets by a corresponding amount; the *selling* corporation reduces fixed assets and increases liquid assets." (Italics supplied.) This apparently implies that only one firm *survives*. If so, inevitably the total assets in the industry have been concentrated. This may sound like a retreat to logomachy, but actually it strikes at the heart of an issue: Do mergers within a particular industry *tend* to concentrate the control of assets in that industry? I believe they do, and I infer that Markham recognizes that they do. Exceptions, I believe, would be rare.

Markham's criticism of researchers on mergers for their failure to proceed from and test formal hypotheses seems plausible enough. This would be the scientific method. And its more frequent use by social scientists might contribute to a more orderly analysis of their problems. But while its use may contribute to the discovery of truth, it does not guarantee it. Social scientists deal with far more complex phenomena than do physical scientists and they are less well equipped to do their job. When men deal with social phenomena, they are themselves a bundle of preconceptions. I doubt that students who have relied on description and enumeration in their study of the early combination movement and concluded that the movement had monopoly as its goal would have saved themselves from this conclusion merely by having adopted it as an hypothesis to test. Testing such an hypothesis involves definition, classification, and counting. Defining and classifying involve judgments, and as Alexander Pope put it,

> 'Tis with our judgments as our watches; none
> Go just alike, yet each believes his own.

Judgments of social phenomena are influenced by one's conception of "the true, the good, and the beautiful." Monopoly is generally associated with evil; bigness, with either good or evil, depending on one's preconceptions. Bigness may approach monopoly. How far must it go to get there? That depends on the judge. A skilled craftsman can prove that in every log there is a beautifully sculptured Madonna. His conception of beauty, his skills and tools are such that to get inside the wood he carves the statue.[1]

Having indicated the basic shortcomings of the literature on mergers, Markham examines the widely held notion that mergers are "timed closely with the business cycle." To do this he compiles a merger time series based on Conant, Watkins, the Bureau of the Census, Moody, and Thorp and correlates his series with the peaks and troughs of reference cycles. He concludes that "these data do not give strong support to the thesis that merger cycles are timed closely with business cycles." He then summarizes Weston's findings on the relation of merger activity to industrial production, to the index of wholesale prices, and to the Dow-Jones index of stock prices and cautiously and tentatively accepts the conclusion that rising security prices stimulate merger activity. With somewhat less caution he infers from these statistical relationships a motive for mergers— the desire of promoters to profit through asset revaluations. Recognizing that "causal relationships . . . are difficult to infer from statistical analysis," however, and that each merger movement may possess unique features, he analyzes in turn each of the major merger movements—1887-1904, 1919-1930, and 1940-1947— not merely to ascertain their causes, but to determine their impact on the structure of the economy.

THE GREAT COMBINATION MOVEMENT: MOTIVES FOR MERGER

In analyzing the first and greatest merger movement, 1887-1904, he

[1] See Nicholas Georgescu-Roegen's comments on Guy H. Orcott's "Toward Partial Redirection of Econometrics," *Review of Economics and Statistics*, August 1952, p. 211.

concludes, and I believe correctly, that of all the "forces unleashed in the latter part of the nineteenth century that tended to make for larger size and greater concentration, the industrial combination was probably the most important." Proceeding on the assumption that motives may be inferred from results, he turns from the general to the particular. In doing so he analyzes and, on a basis of some independent research, amends the findings of Shaw Livermore[2] and John Moody.[3] Markham finds that "out of every 5 mergers ostensibly monopolistic in character, only 1 resulted in considerable monopoly control." And from this he observes that either of two conclusions is inescapable: "(1) if the purpose of *all* mergers was monopoly power, 4 out of every 5 were unsuccessful in obtaining their initial objective, or (2) many mergers were formed for other purposes." (Italics supplied.)

The other purpose which he thinks was predominant was to make money by promoting mergers. "The literature," he finds, "provides convincing evidence that the abnormally large volume of mergers formed in 1897-1900 stemmed largely from a wave of frenzied speculation in asset values." It brought forth a new type of entrepreneur— the maker of mergers who sought not monopoly but promoter's profits.

LIVERMORE ON MERGERS FOR MONOPOLY

IN THIS and many of Markham's other generalizations I find little with which to quarrel. It is the preciseness of his conclusion on the role of monopoly in mergers that disturbs me. His finding that only one-fifth of the mergers in the early combination movement achieved power over the market is a neat and comforting figure to those who frequently argue that there is little evidence that mergers have made the American economy less competitive, and I would not be surprised if this figure became a part of the folklore of students of industrial combination. If it does, I think the finding will have done a disservice. Therefore I wish to examine it minutely and critically. As originally presented in his paper before the Princeton Conference, Markham's conclusion rested wholly on Shaw Livermore's study of the financial success of industrial mergers. Livermore was not primarily interested in the objectives of mergers but in their consequences. Since the merger movement at the turn of the century

2 Shaw Livermore, "The Success of Industrial Mergers," *Quarterly Journal of Economics*, November 1935, pp. 68-96.
3 John Moody, *The Truth about the Trusts* (Moody Publishing Co., 1904).

has been so intimately associated with the monopoly problem, he included in his study only mergers that gave rise to firms with sufficient power to influence their respective markets. He omitted mergers that at the outset could clearly be recognized as nonmonopolistic. Starting with 409 mergers he dropped *"more* than seventy . . . as not being true mergers in any sense of that term, as formed prior to the period under examination, as foreign corporations, or as obviously included by error."[4] After a more careful analysis of the remainder, he divided them into a primary group and a secondary group. The firms in the secondary group, although formed by merger, were later "little different from thousands of other corporations."[5] The primary group constituted *somewhat less than half of the total.* This primary group, presumably consisting of about 156,[6] Livermore characterizes as "mergers with power enough to influence *markedly* conditions in their industry." (Italics supplied.) I take this to mean mergers achieving power over the market; and, although I would attach no importance to the specific figure, I would conclude from Livermore's analysis that almost 50 per cent of his original list of "true" domestic mergers formed between 1888 and 1905 achieved what may be loosely described as "monopoly power."

Markham read the record differently and based his initial calculation of one-fifth on what to me is a baffling statement. Livermore's full characterization of the primary group is as follows: "Somewhat less than half [that is, of all his true domestic mergers] could rightfully claim to be mergers with power enough to influence *markedly* conditions in their industry; of these a select minority possessed, before 1910, any considerable degree of monopoly power."[7] (*Sic,* italics supplied.) The last clause of this statement obviously does not say what it means and what it means, therefore, is conjectural. But two other statements which Livermore makes indicate rather clearly that the last clause of the above-quoted sentence should have read: "of these *only* a select minority possessed, *after* 1910, any considerable degree of monopoly power." For at page 76 Livermore states: "The criticism [that the success of mergers was due to the exercise of monopoly power] is seen not to be fair if it be recalled

---

4 Livermore, *op. cit.,* p. 71. (Italics supplied.) Markham reduces the 409 by 70 to get 339.

5 *Ibid.,* p. 72.

6 Livermore's carelessness in manipulating simple statistical data is reflected in his references to this primary group at various places in his discussion as numbering 157 (p. 72), 150 (p. 75), 155 (total in his Table 1, Appendix A), and 156 (total in his Table 1 in text, p. 75).

7 *Ibid.,* p. 72.

that monopoly power was largely lost *after* 1910, except for a handful of companies . . . , by the growth of new competition or because of legal interference." And again at page 90, he says: "Nor was monopoly power, *after* the first decade, the means by which earnings were obtained." (Italics supplied.) Markham, as he presented his paper at the Princeton Conference, paraphrased Livermore's enigmatic statement to read: ". . . only 155 had resulted in the creation of firms with enough power *markedly* to *influence the market,* and only a select minority of these had obtained before 1910 any *considerable degree of monopoly control.*" Reasoning correctly that a "select minority" must be less than one-half (of 155), Markham reached his conclusion that only one "of every five mergers ostensibly monopolistic in character [of the total of approximately 339] . . . resulted in considerable monopoly control."

To clear up the enigma which my criticisms raised, Markham wrote Livermore, asking him to explain the difference between mergers "with power to influence markedly conditions in their industry" and mergers with "any considerable degree of monopoly power." Livermore, seventeen years after his original confusing statement, in a letter dated September 29, 1952, cleared up the enigma in the ingenious manner set forth in Markham's footnote 39. Whether this is a tribute to a lively imagination or to a remarkable memory, the wayfaring reader may decide. But to me it is a slender reed on which to rely. And Markham appropriately discarded it.[8]

MARKHAM ON MERGERS FOR MONOPOLY

BUT he did not discard the one-fifth. On the contrary, he has made a valiant effort to establish it by his own independent research. I think he has failed. The job he set himself was to classify—more accurately, to reclassify—and count. His counting can be no more accurate than his classifying. Reclassifying the combinations of a half century ago as monopolistic or nonmonopolistic without having

[8] Markham has appropriately quoted Livermore on Livermore; I also should like to do so. In *Business Organization and Public Control* (2d ed., Van Nostrand, 1941), jointly authored by Livermore and Charles S. Tippetts, at page 472 the authors make it indisputably clear that Livermore in his earlier article, "The Success of Industrial Mergers," had found that approximately one-half of all his mergers had in Livermore's judgment achieved monopoly power, for about these mergers they state: "Two groupings were made: one of 156 companies included all concerns which attained some degree of dominance in their respective industries, and perhaps corresponded to the popular conception of trusts; the other consisted of remaining minor consolidations, which never achieved the prominence necessary to the exercise of *real* control." (Italics supplied.)

made detailed case studies or discovered new evidence is apt to be illusory, the more so since neither Moody nor Markham clearly states his standards for classifying. Apparently Markham accepts control of 40 per cent of output as the dividing line between monopolistic and nonmonopolistic combinations.[9] Some may question the validity of this. It is of course arbitrary and its justification might well depend on the structure of that portion of the industry remaining outside the combination. But in judging the validity of Markham's classification I shall accept this standard.

Markham takes Moody's list of trusts as his point of departure. He finds plenty wrong with it. Foremost is the vagueness and unreliability of Moody's sources. But Markham's sources are also vague and I fear not always reliable, and his procedure at times seems arbitrary. He finds that "the evidence that Moody's estimates greatly exaggerate the extent of control obtained by 19 of . . . 70 mergers is sufficiently strong to warrant dropping them from the monopoly group." In dropping them Markham relies on "census data and other evidence." What other evidence, he does not specify, nor does he cite census sources. He drops American Hide and Leather, characterized by Moody as "the upper leather trust," incorporated May 3, 1899 to consolidate the plants and business of twenty-two companies operating fourteen plants in New England and eight in New York, Wisconsin, and Illinois. Moody states that at the time of consolidation the companies "*were said* to represent 75% of the upper leather business of the United States."[10] (Italics supplied.) That obviously is not very convincing authority. Markham apparently rejects it because of its vagueness and because "the merger brought together only 22 of 407 establishments producing upper leather in the United States at the time of the merger." That it had only 22 of 407 establishments is not to me a convincing reason for deciding that American Hide and Leather had less than 40 per cent of the market for upper leathers. Obviously the relative size of the establishments and of the markets they served are the critical factors and on these both Moody and Markham are silent.

Moody characterizes United States Leather Company, incorporated February 25, 1893, as "the leather trust." He finds that U.S. Leather acquired twenty-five plants controlling from 60 to 75 per cent of the "industry."[11] Moody does not define "industry," but we

9 See Markham, note 42 and text just above.
10 Moody, *op. cit.*, p. 225. Moody later states that at the time of writing (1904) the proportion of the industry controlled was "now about 55%," p. 226.
11 *Ibid.*, p. 281.

know that U.S. Leather was the country's leading producer of sole leather. According to Lewis H. Lapham, its vice president, who testified before the Industrial Commission about eight years after U.S. Leather was organized, it initially acquired "perhaps one-half of the sole-leather business of the United States" and at the time of his testimony had about the same percentage.[12] In the light of this testimony I do not understand why Markham drops U.S. Leather from the monopoly group. He offers no explanation, merely stating that Moody "erroneously" listed it as having obtained more than 40 per cent of its market.

Moody characterizes International Steam Pump Company, incorporated March 24, 1899, as "the steam pump trust." He finds that International consolidated ownership of seven companies specializing in steam pumps and that it controlled 90 per cent of "the steam pump industry."[13] International also produced products other than steam pumps and according to Moody accounted for 80 per cent of "heavy steam power machinery of all kinds."[14] Moody characterizes Allis-Chalmers, which consolidated four firms—two with plants in Illinois, one with a plant in Wisconsin, and one with a plant in Pennsylvania—as "the machinery trust" and states that the new company controlled about 50 per cent of this "industry." This industry Moody describes as consisting of "heavy machinery, such as steam power engines, mining machinery, rock and ore breakers, cement, saw mill and flour mill machinery, etc."[15] Markham, ignoring Moody's statement that International produced 90 per cent of the country's steam pumps and assuming that "heavy steam power machinery of all kinds" is identical with "heavy machinery, such as steam power engines, mining machinery, rock and ore breakers, cement, saw mill and flour mill machinery, etc.," incorrectly concludes that either International or Allis-Chalmers must be dropped from the monopoly classification. Moody does not regard these categories as identical, and Markham offers no evidence that they are. Lacking evidence that they are, we have no basis for challenging Moody's percentages and hence no basis for dropping either company.

And so it goes. I have not checked Markham's authority or evidence for reclassifying each of the nineteen combines which he charges Moody with having erroneously classified. Indeed I could

[12] *Report on Trusts and Industrial Combinations*, Industrial Commission, 1909, Vol. XIII, p. 686.
[13] Moody, *op. cit.*, p. 256.   [14] *Ibid.*, p. 257.   [15] *Ibid.*, pp. 209-210.

not do so, because Markham does not cite specific authorities or offer specific evidence for most of them. But I have checked enough of them to conclude that the one-fifth figure at which he has been aiming is a shaky target. He has not hit it.

Moreover, Markham's conclusions at best are based on counting, not weighing. The percentage of mergers that achieved power over the market is not a very significant figure to students of industrial structure. I agree with Markham that probably none of the available lists of mergers is all-inclusive. They scarcely could be since they purport to include only mergers of significance to market structure and behavior. By searching for all the unrecorded little mergers, "the cats and dogs," and thereby increasing your denominator without increasing your numerator (those achieving monopoly power), you could progressively reduce the percentage of mergers that sought or achieved monopoly power; but the more mergers you found the less significant your figures would be to the influence of mergers on industrial structure.

I do not want to do Markham any injustice in making these comments; and I hasten to add that if students of his paper exercise the commendable caution that he does in evaluating the significance of his findings, his findings will have helped, not hurt, in understanding motives for mergers. He recognizes that the motives are often complex, and he is probably correct in concluding that by sheer count most mergers have not acquired monopoly power. But, as he points out, the merger movement "between 1890 and 1904 left an imprint on the structure of the American economy that fifty years have not yet fully erased." With this I agree, although I believe it is an understatement. But it is not an understatement that some students will recognize as such.

EFFECT OF THE GREAT COMBINATION MOVEMENT ON CONTEMPORARY INDUSTRIAL STRUCTURE

LIVERMORE and Tippetts think that the influence of the great combination movement on contemporary industrial structure has been exaggerated. As they put it, "The *continued* importance of the mergers created in 1888-1905 . . . has not been generally understood by the public."[16] And they point out that only 40 to 45 per cent of the 100 largest industrial corporations of any year since 1925 were originally created during the great merger era. To get even a percentage this large, they count each successor of the oil and tobacco

[16] Livermore and Tippetts, *op. cit.*, p. 474. (Italics supplied.)

combinations as a separate large company. As indeed they should. But having first done so, they then reject this procedure. They find that by counting them "genealogically as derived" from one merger they can reduce to one-third the percentage of contemporary large industrial corporations originating in the first great combination movement. And this they do. Finding further that only 5 per cent of our "largest" industrial companies are the result of mergers since 1905, they conclude that well over half of "our largest industrial companies today are the clear *result of 'natural' growth by reinvestment of their own profits. . . ."*[17] I think this statement inaccurate and misleading. In refuting it, I also have done a little counting. Such counting involves judgment; and with my preconceptions what they are, I count differently than do Livermore and Tippetts. I have taken Berle and Means' list of the 100 largest industrial corporations and classified them as having originated in mergers or having got into the list wholly because of internal growth. I find that 75 of the 100 originated or grew substantially by merger, and most of them originated during the 1888-1904 period. The discrepancy between Livermore and Tippetts' findings and mine is explained partly but not wholly by their treatment of units segregated from their parent by antitrust proceedings, e.g. the several Standard Oil companies. Since each of these achieved the dominant position it now occupies in its limited market area under the parent company's ruthless determination to dominate the entire national market by buying out or killing off competition, I see no reason for not treating each included in the "100" list as having originated by merger. Livermore and Tippetts do not reproduce the statistical data on which they based their calculation. Nor do I. My classification is based in part on secondary sources, e.g. Moody's *The Truth about the Trusts,* and in part on independent research. I do not attach much importance to my precise figure of 75 per cent. But I attach less importance to Livermore and Tippetts' contradictory figure that well over half our largest industrial companies (as of 1932, the date of the first edition of their book) are the clear result of " 'natural' growth by reinvestment of their profits." In truth, I fear this idea is also becoming a part of our folklore. Jacoby, for example, in discussing the relation of mergers to the contemporary size of our giant corporations states:

"Another fundamental misconception is that business mergers have been the most important cause of the growth of giant enter-

[17] *Ibid.,* p. 475.

prises and industrial concentration. A forthcoming empirical study demonstrates, to the contrary, that between 1905 and 1948 two-thirds of the increase in the total assets of the largest American manufacturing corporations in the most highly concentrated 'industries' was due to internal growth and that only one-third was achieved through acquisition of assets from other firms. Prohibition of *all* business mergers between 1900 and 1948 would have changed only to a minor extent the degree of concentration found in these industries in 1948."[18]

This statement may be accurate but it is misleading. Jacoby's reference is to J. Frederick Weston's study, *The Role of Mergers in the Growth of Large Firms*.[19] Weston does indeed conclude that only "approximately one-fourth of the growth of the 74 firms studied was *directly* accounted for by mergers. If assets of the initial year for firms which were formed by combinations are classified as acquisitions, about one-third of the growth then becomes external growth."[20] (Italics supplied.) But Weston does not come to the uncritical conclusion that internal growth has been the major cause of industrial concentration. He recognizes that the first merger movement led to a high degree of concentration in a great many industries and that "although the *absolute* size of present day oligopolists is due only in small part to either earlier or later acquisitions, the *relative* position of these firms is accounted for mainly by the merger movement at the turn of the century."[21] Weston also recognizes that although the combined assets of original mergers today represent a relatively small part of the total assets of the merged companies, if the merger movement had not taken place, the assets of the many separate companies that were combined might well have shown a rate of growth comparable to that of the combination; and he recognizes that in the absence of the merger movement assets as large as those now under the control of a single company might well have been under the control of as many companies as went into a particular merger. In short, he recognizes that the potential internal expansion of each of the merged companies has been merged into the actual internal expansion of the combination and, hence, that the merger may be indirectly responsible for the overwhelming size of many present-

[18] Neil H. Jacoby, "Perspectives on Monopoly," *Journal of Political Economy*, December 1951, p. 526.

[19] J. Frederick Weston, *The Role of Mergers in the Growth of Large Firms* (University of California Press, 1953).

[20] *Ibid.*, p. 30.

[21] *Ibid.*, p. 49.

day corporations which ostensibly have grown primarily by internal expansion.

NUTTER ON MONOPOLY

WEIGHING, I repeat, is more important than counting in determining the significance of the early combination movement to industrial monopoly. In this regard Nutter found that as early as 1899 (before the great combination movement had spent its force) monopolistic industries accounted for 32 per cent of the total income derived from manufacturing in the United States and about 40 per cent of the income derived from mining.[22] I do not regard Nutter's findings as definitive. His definition of monopoly is necessarily a loose one and his classification of industries involves judgment. Students familiar with Nutter's work will recall that he compares the extent of monopoly in 1899 with the extent in 1937. In both years he classifies coal and petroleum (which he lumps together) as competitive industries. In view of the controls which state and federal governments had set up over petroleum production (in 1937 in Texas, which accounts for almost one-half the total domestic production of crude oil, the Texas Railroad Commission determined the right to drill, the location of wells, and the allowable production for each well), to classify it as competitive in 1937 seems to me indefensible. Its classification as competitive in 1899 is certainly more logical, inasmuch as Standard Oil of New Jersey had never accounted for more than 23 per cent of the domestic crude oil output in any one year. Nevertheless, Standard, as the largest purchaser of crude oil, controlling virtually all the country's pipelines and refining and marketing about 90 per cent of the country's domestic output of petroleum products, must have exerted a great influence over oil prices. If petroleum were shifted to the monopoly category in Nutter's classification, it would have increased significantly his figures on the extent of monopoly in mining. Students in evaluating Markham's finding that only one-fifth of the mergers in the period 1888-1904 obtained monopoly power should bear in mind Nutter's findings, inadequate though they may be, that 32 per cent of the total income derived from manufacturing and 40 per cent of the income derived from mining originated in monopolistic sectors of the economy. Nutter, of course, was not measuring the effect of mergers on industrial structure but the extent of monopoly, however achieved. It is a safe

22 G. Warren Nutter, *The Extent of Enterprise Monopoly in the United States, 1899-1939* (University of Chicago Press, 1951), Table 9, p. 40.

bet, however, that in manufacturing and mining as of 1899 virtually all "monopolies" had achieved their power through mergers.

THE ROLE OF THE PROMOTER

MARKHAM emphasizes the role of the promoter in both the first and the second merger movements and thereby performs a service to industrial history. He is undoubtedly on sound ground in concluding that corporate promotion and stock market speculation as a business had a great deal to do with the scope and the duration of these merger movements. But it is risky to infer that because mergers take place in periods of rising stock values, the opportunity to make money by promoting mergers is the basic cause of mergers. Whether you accept the hypothesis that the primary object of the first combination movement was to restrict competition by concentrating control over industry or prefer the hypothesis that it was to make money by promoting mergers, you must recognize that the best time to realize either goal is during a period of rising stock prices. Either hypothesis is consistent with Markham's findings. Actually, as Markham at times recognizes, the motives are complex. It is therefore difficult—and perhaps unrewarding—to try to separate them. The investment banker has frequently played the dual role of promoter and stabilizer.

Edwards makes this clear in discussing developments in the railway field.[23] By the late 1880's many railway lines had been consolidated into railway systems. Investment banking houses had played an important role in this development. But ruthless competition had wrecked many a road, and railway securities had accordingly suffered. To remedy this situation, in January 1889 J. P. Morgan invited the leading railway executives and the leading investment bankers to his Madison Avenue home to discuss the problems of the railway business. At the conclusion of the meeting he made the following significant public announcement:

"I am authorized to say, I think, on behalf of the banking houses represented here that if an organization can be formed practically upon the basis submitted by the committee, and with an executive committee able to enforce its provisions, upon which the bankers shall be represented, they are prepared to say that they will not negotiate, and will do everything in their power to prevent the negotiation of, any securities for the construction of parallel lines, or the

[23] George W. Edwards, *The Evolution of Finance Capitalism* (Longmans, 1938).

extension of lines not approved by that executive committee. I wish that distinctly understood."[24]

Edwards in commenting on this development states: "The financial press of the time referred to this meeting as 'the bankers' triumph and the presidents' surrender.' This conference signified the transfer of control of the railroads from the hands of the industrial capitalist to those of the investment banker."[24]

The professional promoter and more particularly the investment banker, both of whom played a prominent role in organizing and financing mergers in the late 1890's, were undoubtedly interested in making money by selling securities; but the investment banker was also interested in stabilizing security values by stabilizing markets. This is clearly indicated in the organization of the United States Steel Corp. The twelve concerns that went into United States Steel were themselves consolidations. It was a combination of combinations. Several of the original concerns had obtained a large proportion of the country's total capacity for producing the particular products each made. Some were partially integrated. Shortly before the birth of United States Steel, several of the leading consolidations had projected expansion programs each into the market of the other. The bankers precluded an impending "battle of the giants" by uniting these rivals in a single control. In doing so they reaped promotion profits estimated at $62,500,000. Obviously, here both control of the market and promotion profits played important roles. This of course is a dramatic case and certainly not typical. But, although it may sound like the rattling of old bones, it should make clear the risk in attributing any merger to a single motive.

THE 1919-1930 MERGER MOVEMENT

IN DISCUSSING the significance of the merger movement of the 1920's to market structure and behavior, Markham draws six conclusions: (1) from a fourth to a third of the mergers of this period were in fields for the regulation of which society does not rely on competition—banking and public utilities; (2) the larger horizontal mergers may on balance have stimulated rather than stifled competition; (3) the mergers typically embraced relatively small firms in their respective industries and for the most part these firms had not previously competed; (4) the movement was accompanied by a fairly steady decline in price levels; (5) improvements in transportation and communication encouraged the movement; and (6) when not

24 *Ibid.*, p. 174.

initiated by production and distribution economies, the mergers were largely inspired by professional promoters.

On observations 1 and 5 I make no comments. The others, I believe, involve judgments as well as facts; and with the implications of the judgments some students may not agree.

I for one do not believe that Markham's discussion warrants his generalization that the larger horizontal mergers on balance may have stimulated rather than stifled competition, or indeed that it warrants any generalization on this issue. Moreover, his discussion of this issue confuses me somewhat. Markham criticizes Stigler's thesis that the 1919-1930 merger movement transformed markets dominated by a single firm into oligopolistic markets, largely on the grounds that the movement was not deliberately designed to create oligopolistic market structures. But he apparently accepts Stigler's conclusions that a decrease in the relative importance of dominant firms and a growth through merger of rival firms made 1920 markets oligopolistic rather than monopolistic, and he apparently infers from this that competition may have been intensified. But he also challenges the idea that the oligopolistic market structures created in the 1920's were primarily the product of mergers. As he puts it: ". . . the extent to which oligopolies sprang up in the 1920's by the merger route can easily be exaggerated." I agree. To support this observation Markham cites Weston's study, stating:

"Of 22 oligopolistic industries studied by Weston, 5 were made oligopolies by court dissolution or by pressure of government investigation, 9 by merger, 5 by internal growth of rivals, and 3 by a combination of internal growth and merger. Accordingly he concludes that mergers, while an important cause, accounted for less than half of the number of oligopolies studied."[25]

This summary represents, I believe, an unwitting misuse of Weston's findings—findings which themselves are not wholly accurate. In the first place, Weston is not concerned specifically with mergers *during the 1920's*. His is a broader question: How did each of 22 oligopolistic structures in the contemporary economy get that way? The 5 industries in which he finds that oligopoly resulted from dissolution decrees or government investigation and the pressure of public opinion are: tobacco, agricultural implements, petroleum, corn products refining, and aluminum.[26] While economists generally will probably accept Weston's characterization of these industries as

[25] See Weston, *op. cit.*, pp. 35-37. [26] *Ibid.*, Appendix E, Table 14.

205

oligopolistic, some students of industrial history will recognize, as Markham fails to do, that developments during the 1920's are not responsible for their basic structure; and some will deny that mergers did not have a significant influence in making them oligopolistic. The International Harvester Company, organized in 1902, merged the five leading makers of harvesting machines and thereby obtained a virtual monopoly in their manufacture. In 1903 International produced 92.4 per cent of all binders made in this country, 87.7 per cent of all mowers, and 80 per cent of all rakes. These are *harvesting machines*. They are also *agricultural implements*. By 1918 International had lost a lot of ground to its rivals, producing in that year only 65.3 per cent of the domestic output of binders, 59.5 per cent of the mowers, and 57.5 per cent of the output of rakes.[27] Moreover, by 1918 International had become a full-line company turning out the whole range of major agricultural implements, and its leading rivals had similarly broadened the scope of their operations. International's share of the farm implement business was far less than its share of harvesting machines. In short, oligopoly, not monopoly, characterized the farm implement business as early as 1918. Both internal growth and mergers had influenced this development. Under the 1918 dissolution decree International divested itself of three relatively unimportant lines of harvesting machinery, but this had little effect on the industry's basic structure. It accentuated but did not create oligopoly.

The Standard Oil Co. of New Jersey was dissolved following the Supreme Court's decision in 1911. The dissolution decree changed the ownership of thirty-three Standard Oil subsidiaries, but it did not immediately affect their control. The forces which by the middle of the 1920's had changed the structure of oil refining and marketing from monopoly to oligopoly were numerous and complex, but we would certainly have to look beyond the dissolution decree to segregate and analyze them. Neither Weston nor Markham does this.

The dissolution decrees following the Supreme Court's decision in the *American Tobacco* case of 1911 transformed a monopoly market into oligopoly, an event quite apart from the 1920 merger movement. And it is interesting that oligopoly immediately resulted in competition in the sale of cigarettes.[28] But the record and the court's

27 Myron W. Watkins, *Industrial Combinations and Public Policy* (Houghton Mifflin, 1927), p. 128.
28 William H. Nicholls, *Price Policies in the Cigarette Industry* (Vanderbilt University Press, 1951), pp. 45-57; George W. Stocking and Myron W. Watkins, *Monopoly and Free Enterprise* (Twentieth Century Fund, 1951), p. 140.

finding in the second *American Tobacco* case indicate that during the 1920's cigarette pricing, with Reynolds as the price leader, was noncompetitive—conforming, though somewhat loosely, to what might be termed the ideal Chamberlinian oligopolistic solution—that is, to monopoly pricing.

Glucose was sold by oligopolists during the 1920's, but not because of a dissolution decree. Under consent decrees entered in 1915 and in 1919, following antitrust litigation, the Corn Products Refining Co. had divested itself of its interest in Penick & Ford, Ltd., and in two obsolete glucose plants, two candy plants, and a starch plant. During the 1920's eleven companies sold corn products—starch and glucose. Only one of these, Penick & Ford, Ltd., stemmed from the dissolution, and several were organized long before the decrees. Available evidence indicates that the industry customarily collaborated through the Corn Derivatives Institute to restrict competition.[29] Weston's fifth illustration of oligopoly replacing monopoly as a result of court decisions or public pressure came long after the 1920's. It was not until 1945 that Judge Learned Hand delivered the Second Circuit Court of Appeals' opinion in *United States* v. *Aluminum Company of America*, and Alcoa has never been dissolved. Reynolds Metals and Kaiser's Permanente, as makers of aluminum ingots, were the offspring of World War II.

Nor are Weston's "oligopolies by merger" wholly 1920 products. Notable exceptions include ammunition, steel, rubber, whiskey distilleries (nonexistent during the Prohibition 1920's). In truth, I believe that Weston's study throws little if any light on Markham's problem—the effect of *the 1920 merger movement* on market structure and behavior.

Markham's third observation—that the 1920 mergers typically embraced a small proportion of the total firms in their industries, firms which had not previously competed with each other—may be correct; but his evidence does not wholly support his finding. National Dairy, for example, he classifies as of the "chain- and conglomerate-firm variety" and implies that its organization had little effect on the structure of the market in which it operated. Painstaking research would be required to explore this hypothesis fully. But easy-to-get information reveals that National Dairy acquired

[29] Government's petition filed April 6, 1932 against Corn Derivatives Institute and its fifteen corporate members (mimeographed; obtained from the Dept. of Justice, Antitrust Division). A consent decree was entered the same day. See *The Federal Antitrust Laws with Summary of Cases, 1890-1951* (1952 ed., Commerce Clearing House), Case 382.

the Kraft-Phoenix Cheese Co. in 1929, which represented a 1928 merger of the nation's two largest cheese producers, together selling about two-fifths of the cheese consumed in the country.[30] National Dairy did not consolidate the country's cows; but by merging rival dairies in local communities or by acquiring leading local milk distributors (many of which represented recent mergers), by 1930 it was selling from 18 to 81.5 per cent of the fluid milk sold in each of sixteen selected city markets.[31]

Markham says that mergers in the copper industry extended vertical integration. This is correct. It is also true that by buying out rivals, Anaconda, Kennicott, Phelps Dodge, and American Smelting and Refining increased their combined share of domestic copper-fabricating capacity from 20 per cent in 1920 to 80 per cent in 1940.

In chemicals, Markham concludes that mergers were mostly of the conglomerate firm type and offers Allied Chemical and Dye and Du Pont as examples. Unfortunately economists do not have a standardized definition of a conglomerate firm. Markham's classification of Allied Chemical and Dye as a merger of the conglomerate firm type is accurate in the sense that the merged companies had engaged in some noncompetitive activities and in that Allied Chemical produced a range of products far greater than that of any of its constituents. But if Allied Chemical were typical of the merger movement of the 1920's it would certainly be misleading to characterize the mergers of that period as primarily of the conglomerate type. Allied Chemical centralized control over five companies— General Chemical, Barrett, Solvay Process, Semet-Solvay, and National Aniline and Chemical. As early as 1910 there had been a community of interest among four of these, which apparently had as one of its objectives the lessening of competition. General Chemical, a merger of the early combination period, brought together in 1899 twelve of the country's makers of sulfuric acid. Barrett had for many years operated as an agent for the sale of by-product ammonia. In this way it had eliminated competition among by-product producers accounting for about four-fifths of the domestic output. It was also the country's leading purchaser of coal tar and its leading maker of coal tar products. Solvay Process was the sole domestic producer of ash under the Solvay process, but through Semet-Solvay it made and sold coke ovens and also produced coal tar and its deriva-

[30] See "Consolidated Cows," *Fortune*, May 1934, pp. 77-84, 170-178.
[31] See William H. Nicholls, *Imperfect Competition within Agricultural Industries* (Iowa State College Press, 1941), Table 10, p. 72.

tives. In 1910 General Chemical, Barrett, and the two Solvay companies organized Benzol Products Co. to make aniline oil. Before 1917 Semet-Solvay, General, and Barrett each produced dyestuffs. In that year they segregated their dyestuff business and merged it with the business of Benzol Products and with that of other important dyestuff makers to form National Aniline and Chemical Co. In 1919 National supplied more than half the domestic consumption of dyestuffs. Allied Chemical, organized in 1920, brought under a single management competitive and complementary branches of basic chemical manufactures and by doing so became the leading producer in several fields. In 1937, according to Wilcox, Allied produced ". . . some 28 per cent of the coal tar, 40 per cent of the aluminum sulfate, 45 per cent of the soda ash, 66 per cent of the ammonium sulfate and benzol, and all of the sodium nitrate made in the United States."[32]

The story of Du Pont is better known, particularly its rise to power in explosives. While its 1920 acquisitions may have been largely designed to round out its production of chemicals, its acquisitions were not wholly of noncompeting lines. In 1924 it acquired the General Explosives Co. and in 1927 the Excelsior Powder Manufacturing Co. In 1928 it acquired the assets of Grasselli Chemical Co., a rival producer of chemicals and explosives. But its merging of competitive rivals for the most part belongs to an earlier era. However, as late as 1917-1918, after it had acquired an important stock interest in General Motors, it acquired the paint and varnish business of Harrison Brothers and Co., Beckton Chemical Co., Cawley, Clark & Co., the Bridgeport Wood Finishing Co., Flint Varnish and Color Works, and the New England Oil, Paint and Varnish Co. These, of course, gave it no monopoly of the paint and varnish business, but only the earliest, if any, of these acquisitions can appropriately be characterized as of the conglomerate type.

Markham's fourth observation—that the 1920 merger movement was accompanied by a fairly steady decline in price levels, a remarkable increase in the national income, and a rising level of employment—is sound. Moreover, Markham wisely refrains from drawing any inferences from this except to point out that such prosperity has long been regarded as incompatible with monopoly. I am no expert on business cycles, but I believe that the experts would acknowledge that World War I engendered powerful inflationary

[32] Clair Wilcox, *Competition and Monopoly in American Industry*, Temporary National Economic Committee, Monograph 21, 1940, p. 201.

forces throughout the business world, forces which had not spent themselves with the short and severe 1920-1921 depression. Mergers during the 1920's, even though they may have changed market structure and behavior, certainly did not stop these expansive forces.

Prosperity brought a prolonged stock market boom; and, as Markham points out, this created an environment favorable to the flotation of securities on a scale essential to a large-scale merger movement. When the expansive forces had spent themselves, the stock market collapsed and the dismal decade of the 1930's followed. The ensuing economic environment was not conducive to a large merger movement, but it did encourage all sorts of output-restriction schemes, at first by law under National Industrial Recovery Administration, later by voluntary cooperation. I surmise that the 1920 merger movement with its reduction in the number of sellers facilitated this domestic cartel movement.

For his sixth observation—that except when the 1920 mergers were motivated by production and distribution economies they appear to have been largely influenced by the professional promoter—Markham relies largely on Thorp. This is good authority and I have no quarrel with it. But I believe that both Markham and Thorp may underestimate the influence on the movement of (1) the corporate quest for security through integration and (2) the introduction of new methods of merchandising. Both of these are complex phenomena and I can only touch on them.

1. By the 1920's, business generally had come to appreciate the advantages of integration. Some of these grew out of a shortening of processes or elimination of waste motions in a mechanical sense. Others relate to the increased financial security gained by control of supplies and market outlets from the raw material to the consumer in markets characterized by various sorts and degrees of imperfections. Integration in the oil industry illustrates both types. Without going into details, let me call attention to the fact that by 1930 nearly all the specialized subsidiaries of the dissolved units of the Standard Oil Company had become fully integrated concerns. Some had reached back to their crude oil supplies, others had reached forward to their product markets. Independent companies had experienced a similar development and, for the most part, integration had involved the acquisition of established enterprises.

2. By the 1920's, new methods of merchandising had encouraged an increase in the scale of operations. These new methods had two aspects: (a) mass distribution with low profit margins; (b) a differ-

210

entiation of product with increased reliance upon the press and the radio in selling. Mass distributors had to be large. To maximize the advantage of radio and periodical advertising it may be necessary to sell your product wherever people read or listen. Both these developments encouraged larger firms and hence mergers.

To call attention to these influences is not to deny the importance of the investment banker in the merger movement of the 1920's. But as previously indicated, his motives in both the earlier and the 1920 movement were frequently multiple.

THE 1940-1947 MERGER MOVEMENT

WHILE the literature of this movement is not so voluminous as that on the movement at the turn of the century, it has engendered as much heat. This heat has reached the point of incandescence and has shed some, but I think not enough, light. It seems fairly clear that the recent merger movement has not increased industrial concentration in the technical sense in which it is now being used, i.e. the proportion of assets, output, or employment in various industrial segments accounted for by a specified number of firms. It is also clear that internal expansion has overshadowed mergers as a source of individual growth during this period. But, as Markham points out, census data do not tell the whole story. Unless births in the business population of a particular and relatively narrow segment of industry exceed deaths through merger, the number of sellers in that segment declines. Census figures which revealed a decrease in concentration ratios might therefore conceal a trend toward industrial oligopoly. Unfortunately census data are frequently too general to tell us what is happening in particular markets. According to the *Survey of Current Business*[33] the number of firms in chemicals and allied products showed an increase from 7,400 to 9,800 between 1940 and 1947. Yet in 1947 the Smaller War Plants Corp. found that four or fewer companies accounted for the entire output of 102 products. The four leading producers accounted for 70 per cent of the output of 100 additional products.[34] These data indicate high concentration ratios, but tell us nothing about trends. I do not mean to imply that the 1940-1947 merger movement had anything to do with this. I merely point out that unless census figures are available

[33] Dept. of Commerce, May 1948, p. 15.
[34] *Economic Concentration and World War II*, Report of Smaller War Plants Corporation before Special Committee on Small Business, S. Doc. 206, 79th Cong., 2d Sess., 1946, pp. 183-192.

for narrow categories they do not tell us what is happening in "markets" as distinct from "industries." And even available data indicate that recent mergers have in fact increased concentration in some markets—liquor, for example.

Some of us who believe in free enterprise have been encouraged by the tremendous increase in the business population and by the spirit of business rivalry that has pervaded the entire economy since World War II. But some who point with pride to such statistics fail to recognize that the growth is differential. Without having the figures before me, I suspect that it is greatest in local service and distribution industries, least in basic manufactures. Moreover, while I hope that the spirit of business rivalry will endure, it has yet to meet a real test. Nearly everyone likes competition when consumers are long on dollars and short on goods, because nearly everyone prospers. Capitalistic enterprise with its heavy fixed charges flourishes in an expanding economy; it languishes in recession. This, I suspect, suggests the real significance of the business cycle to the spirit of enterprise. Live-and-let-live policies, although perhaps not mainly a product of depression, as Jacoby has insisted,[35] are greatly encouraged by it. They need not increase the number of mergers, and they often prove inadequate to prevent price competition. But given the proper environment, they grow like the green bay tree. Herein lies a dilemma of capitalism. Businessmen and some economists view with concern, if not alarm, high government expenditures, high taxes, unbalanced budgets, all of which have created the postwar environment in which business has flourished. Whether or not competition can survive without these luxuries is a matter of conjecture.

[35] Neil H. Jacoby, "Perspectives on Monopoly: A Rejoinder," *Journal of Political Economy*, June 1952, p. 258.

SURVEY OF THE EMPIRICAL EVIDENCE
ON ECONOMIES OF SCALE

CALEB A. SMITH

BROWN UNIVERSITY

AT THE outset the reader should be warned that only after what may seem an over-long introduction have I attempted to carry out the commission assigned me: to survey the available empirical information on the variation of cost with size of plant and company, to appraise the validity of the literature on economies of large-scale production, and to indicate what generalizations it will support.

The time available proved inadequate to anything approaching a comprehensive review of the scattered and uneven material. Only a sample of the literature on economies of large-scale production has been consulted and summarized and a very limited appraisal of individual studies undertaken. The validity of the available empirical information on the variation of cost with size of plant has been weighed in general on the total information, rather than in detail.

Based on the survey, the conclusion is that the generalization that available empirical information supports are indefinite and disappointing. In part, this is because much information in government and trade association files has never been studied[1] but in part I suspect a more fundamental difficulty.

Whenever the best answer to any question adduced by empirical investigators tells them little, the question should be re-examined. Because I was disappointed in the answers to the question, "What generalization will the empirical evidence on economies of scale support?" I undertook the introductory analysis comprising so much of this paper. This re-examination may be divided into two parts.

[1] So far as I have been able to discover, very little information obtained by the national war agencies which might throw substantial light on this subject has been compiled and published in a usable form. The only exception of any importance is the Office of Price Administration Economic Data Series published by the Office of Temporary Controls. The material here presented, while it seems worthy of more study than it has received, is certainly less significant than the data we had reason to hope might emerge from the OPA files. The most needed research job today in the field of the relation of cost to size of plant and firm would be one done by a government agency with full access to the data accumulated during the war. If one of the small business committees of Congress, for instance, would put a modest research staff to work on this task, a monograph of very great value probably could be produced.

First, what sort of problems arise when we seek empirical evidence of a relationship developed in deductive theory?

Second, what related questions might have more significant answers?[2] These two questions will be examined in some detail in the following Introduction to this discussion.

1. *Introduction*

THE effort to obtain empirical evidence of relationships which have been developed in deductive economic theory encounters two sets of problems. The first centers around the widespread but fundamental misconception as to the nature of em/pirical facts. Certain empirical facts—the length of a table (under specified conditions), for instance—can be defined operationally. (That is, the process of measurement against a specified standard of length may be described.) Such facts have validity for any use where the operational process of measurement and the standard used are acceptable.

But there is another sort of empirical fact which has meaning only in terms of a complicated conceptual framework. That a particular empirical study shows or does not show economies of scale is an example of this. Only in terms of a carefully delineated concept can we say that particular evidence shows or does not show economies of scale. The Introduction to this paper first considers the concept of economies of scale and distinguishes this from concepts with which it easily may be confused in empirical work.

The second set of problems centers around the elimination of variations in cost which do not result from differences in size of plant or firm. Simplifying assumptions are essential to the development of theoretical concepts. Inevitably, however, each simplifying assumption blocks the path toward an empirical investigation of the relationship which the theory states. In empirical investigation the complexities cannot be removed by a simple declarative sentence; nor can the empirical economist—like his empirical brethren in the laboratory sciences—remove complicating factors by carefully regulated experiments in which the factors are held constant. The second subsection of the Introduction to this paper discusses some of the more serious problems posed by factors other than scale which influence costs in the empirical studies of economies of scale.

The final subsection of the Introduction considers some questions

[2] The author claims no originality in questioning the question asked. Such questions have been posed by the authors of some of the studies surveyed in the preparation of this paper.

closely related to economies of scale, in the hope of finding a more promising line of inquiry.

To give some precision to this discussion, economies of scale may be defined as equivalent to a falling long-run average cost function.[3] These economies can be considered either with respect to size of plants or of firms. The long-run average cost function of economic theory shows the long-run relationship between average cost and the output of one homogeneous product.

Questions of definition arise with respect to the terms "average cost" and "size." Average cost includes (in the economist's definition) the imputed cost of capital or any other services supplied by the owners. Empirical data generally follow accounting practice and exclude dividend payments and other payments of "profits" to owners from costs. Unfortunately, there is no reason to assume that costs covered by dividends are the same for all plants or firms making the same product. In fact there are reasons to think that there may be systematic variations in these costs with size of firm. Salaries of owners who are officers of corporations which show little relation to value of services rendered pose a similar problem of a possible systematic variation between costs recorded by accountants and the economist's costs for firms of different size. When using empirical material to test economic theory, we must not forget these different concepts of cost.

To measure size in empirical studies of economies of scale is even more difficult. The measurement of output is unequivocal only if the output is homogeneous. In practice we do not find either plants or firms which, during a period of growth from small-scale to large-scale, produced one homogeneous product, nor do we find a group of plants or firms of widely different size which produce a single homogeneous product.[4] Output of plants and firms is in fact heterogeneous to a very substantial extent. Since the definition of economic theory has little relation to reality, let us explore the implicit definition of common usage.

When we talk about the size of a plant or firm we ordinarily mean its capacity to turn out its entire product mix, not its capacity to

[3] The long-run average cost function is the envelope curve to the short-run average cost functions. Thus the capacity or size of a plant or of a firm is that output for which the short-run cost function and the long-run cost function coincide.

[4] The reader should not conclude that data from even such plants or firms would, without surmounting further problems, yield an empirical counterpart of the theoretical long-run cost function.

215

turn out one specific product. When we talk about cost in relation to size we ordinarily mean the cost of a specific product. We thus pose two problems: (1) What do we mean by cost for one of a group of products? (2) What are we doing when we relate the cost of one product to capacity to produce a multiplicity of products?

The cost of a number of products produced by a firm can be determined only on the basis of arbitrary allocations. In practice, empirical studies of economies of scale have accepted the cost allocations made by the firms studied. Unfortunately, the cost accounting techniques used by business are not nearly so highly standardized in most industries as are income accounting techniques. These have been subjected to at least two powerful standardizing influences which have not affected cost accounting techniques: the rules of the Bureau of Internal Revenue, and the pronouncements of the American Institute of Accountants, which shape accounting practices through the institution of outside auditors. In spite of the standardizing influences to which income accounting techniques are subject, the lack of comparability of balance sheet and income statement data of different firms lead the author of a well-known text on financial statement analysis to issue this warning: "The figures of one enterprise may be compared with those compiled for another only with great care. The combination of the financial statement data of different enterprises for statistical studies is usually unsatisfactory."[5]

It is extremely unlikely that the cost figures obtained from the accounting records of a group of firms are really comparable. The student of empirical data on economies of scale is seldom in a position to make the figures comparable; he can only hope that there will be no incomparability systematically related to size. The dangers in using cost accounting figures in empirical studies of economies of scale are, I believe, greater than most economists realize, because their lack of familiarity with accounting practice leads them to underestimate the uncertainties of cost data.

The second problem posed by the comparison of cost for one product with size measured in terms of a multiplicity of products is a conceptual one. What relation, if any, is there between the concept of economies of scale as defined in economic theory (a relation between cost and size in plants or firms producing homogeneous out-

[5] John N. Meyer, *Financial Statement Analysis* (2nd ed., Prentice-Hall, 1952), p. 44.

216

put) and either (1) the concept of a relation between the cost of producing one of many products and the size of plants or firms measured in terms of composite output, or (2) the concept of a residual relation between cost and size after allowing for the effect of variations in other dimensions of output?

If the product mix of the composite output for the different observations of cost and size is highly similar, then we are seeking a relationship which might be regarded as similar to the concept of economies of scale as defined in economic theory. The problem is to distinguish sufficiently similar product mixes from those which are diverse. Here we must rely upon our own judgment and that of the investigator.[6]

Even if we accept similar product mixes[7] as the output in a study of the long-run cost output relation, the problem of measuring output remains. If all the elements of the product mix occurred in the same proportion at all different sizes of plant or firm any element might be used as the measure of output, and we might as well regard the output as homogeneous. The real problem of measurement of output arises because the elements of the product mix occur in different proportions for the different observations of cost and size. The use of a number of different dimensions of size, which might appear to be a way around this problem, is explored later and found to be generally impractical. Perhaps the most practical method of measuring the amount of somewhat heterogeneous product mix is to use the familiar though arbitrary common denominator of economics—money value. We may at times wish to question price as a measure of output but at least it has the merit of being a market evaluation.[8]

There are at least two ways to get around the two problems posed

[6] Unfortunately, once an economist discovers data which might be used for an empirical study he is strongly inclined to use them, if it is at all possible, and to present the study "for whatever it is worth." Others, less familiar with the problems posed by the basic data, are likely to overrate the significance of the study.

[7] What should be meant by product mix similarity? To require similar percentages of identical products would be too restrictive. Product mixes might better be regarded as highly similar even though no product in one is homogeneous with any part of the other if all the products are highly similar and are produced in highly similar percentages. Thus the output of Fords and of Chevrolets might be regarded as similar product mixes.

[8] The use of this common denominator has the added practical advantage that general price-level changes will tend to move an observation of cost and size more or less along the function rather than almost at right angles to it as would occur if a physical measure of output were used with a money measure of costs.

217

by cost allocation and the relation between the cost of one part of output and size in terms of a composite measure of output. The first is to study the relation between cost per composite unit of output and scale in terms of the composite unit, i.e. if money value is used as the composite unit, the cost of a dollar of output at various dollar scales of output. The second is to regard output, and hence size of plant, as having many dimensions. Each of these routes around the problems will be explored in some detail.

The difficulties with studies of cost per dollar of output in relation to capacity measured in dollars of output are obvious. Different firms may charge different prices for the same product. More serious questions arise when the price differences between similar products do not fairly represent differences in the "quantity" of output. In spite of these obvious difficulties, studies relating cost per dollar of sales to dollar capacity for plants or firms which have similar product mixes may be preferable to those seeking to relate cost for a particular product to either a physical or a dollar measure of capacity. Further, the data needed to determine costs per dollar of output in relation to scale measured in dollars of sales are more generally available than are data needed to determine the relation between costs per unit of a particular physical output and size, though empirical economists have been afraid to use them. This reluctance may rest on no more secure basis than a greater familiarity with variations in price for the same product than with variations in costs allocated to the same product by different cost accounting systems or with the variability of product mixes within an industry.

The second way around the problems posed by cost allocation and by relating cost of a part of output to capacity to produce many different products is to regard output as having many dimensions. In a study of costs for airlines, Allen R. Ferguson explores this method.[9] Dr. Ferguson, in summarizing his study, says that it "avoids the assumption of a homogeneous product and deals explicitly with the problems of varying the quality and the product mix of output."[10] Explicitly, the product is not conceived of as simply ton-miles or passenger-miles; speed and length of flight are introduced as measures of output characteristics. The introduction of additional dimensions of output results in complications which are more than computational.

9 Allen Richmond Ferguson, "A Technical Synthesis of Airline Costs" (Ph.D. dissertation, Harvard University, 1949).
10 Ibid., Summary of thesis, p. 1.

On the surface, the problem of measuring somewhat heterogeneous output appears to be more manageable conceptually when the idea of several dimensions of output is introduced, but here new problems arise. First, what is the significance of one of several dimensions of output? Second, can the data support statistical procedures for separating the effects of variations in several dimensions?

We must realize that not all dimensions of output measure the size of plant or firm. It is easy to conceive of a scale relationship between costs per ton mile and "capacity" in ton-miles in which all other dimensions of output are held constant; but to conceive of the relation between costs per mile per hour and capacity in miles per hour *as a scale relationship* is bizarre. (Incidentally, capacity in miles per hour is a dimension for which cost increases rapidly with large "scale.") The whole problem of what is meant by "scale" is cast in a different light when viewed as the dimensions of a single output. The usual notion of a larger plant or firm involves the production of a greater number of identical units of output. It is better to regard the other dimensions of output as elements in the heterogeneity of output. Interesting relations between cost and any of these dimensions of output may be discovered empirically, but they should not be regarded as cost-size relations.

It may be suggested that empirical study should seek an over-all relationship between cost and all the various dimensions of output and size. One phase of this complex would be the cost-size relation. Output has too many dimensions to make this approach seem promising as an empirical method of deriving a cost-size relation. Ordinarily, observations are too few to indicate the shape of a cost-size relation after allowing for the effect of many other variables.

The multiplicity of dimensions of product is fantastic. Simply in terms of its physical characteristics, a product always has more than one dimension, and the dimensions of a product cannot be so limited. Among its other dimensions are consumer and trade acceptance of the brand name and the characteristics of its distributive system. Thus, although it may be possible to describe the outputs of a steel rolling mill by many fewer dimensions than the number of products, even the minimum number of dimensions probably would leave the problem of deriving a cost-output function statistically unmanageable.

Competing products may have quite different dimensions in these respects. The possibility of having a larger firm or plant may depend upon the existence of different dimensions for the product of the large-scale firm. A good example of the different nonphysical dimensions of competitive products is found in a study of costs incurred by fourteen manufacturers of rubber tires. The data are presented in the *Survey of Rubber Tire and Tube Manufacturers.*[11]

In August 1943 for the 6.00-16 4-ply synthetic rubber passenger car tire the selling, general, and administrative expense for the four largest manufacturers was 65 cents more per tire than for the ten other manufacturers studied. This 69 per cent higher cost indicates a different dimension of the product. Whether or not we enjoy listening to the "Firestone Hour" we must recognize that it helps give the Firestone tire a different dimension; that is, it makes it a different product. The higher cost of selling and administration is not just the result of the larger size of the firm, but of expenses undertaken to differentiate the product. These expenses may be necessary in order to have the larger firm or they may be profitable only for the larger firms. If the former, then the data may be regarded as revealing the cost-size relation for firms producing this product. On the other hand, if they are not necessary to the maintenance of the larger firms but are profitable for the larger firms though they wou'd not be profitable for smaller firms, the data pertain to two products too dissimilar to reveal a cost-size relation.

2. *Methods Used to Handle Cost Variations from Causes Other than Economies of Scale*

IDEALLY, empirical evidence on economies of scale should be obtained by observing the variations in cost associated with different scales of plant or firm with all other cost influences constant. Since it is obviously impossible to find any such situation, the relation between average cost and the scale of plant or firm must be sought by other means. Two methods of study have been used which may be characterized as the statistical approach and the engineering approach.

In the statistical approach, the costs of the plant or firm as a unit or the costs allocated to some type of output are related to size. Other influences on cost either are ignored or allowed for by such techniques as deflation or multiple correlation. Though the details will not be discussed here, some inherent weaknesses of this approach will be considered.

11 Office of Temporary Controls, OPA Economic Data Series 10, 1947. A portion of this data is presented in an article by John M. Blair, "Does Large Scale Enterprise Result in Lower Costs?" *American Economic Review*, May 1948, p. 149.

First, statistical data show costs in relation to scale for the many different technologies actually used by plants or firms for which sufficient empirical evidence is available to make it possible to include them in a statistical study. If the technologies used by the different plants varied only because different sizes of plant require different technology, the data would be appropriate. But technology varies from plant to plant for other reasons. For example, some plants are old, others newly built while technological horizons have changed from year to year. Further, technologies were selected at various times because of different relative factor prices, or because of different demand expectations, etc. Statistical studies have limited significance because they regarded all or most of the plants or firms currently classified as part of the "industry" as sufficiently homogeneous in technology to warrant grouping them together to derive a long-run cost function.

Another difficulty with the statistical approach is that it assumes that each cost-size observation used represents a point on the long-run cost function; that is, that every output studied is the optimal output for that plant or firm. This is an heroic assumption, but most studies make no attempt to eliminate any observations because they represent obviously nonoptimal outputs. There is, perhaps, a tacit assumption that at any one time all plants or firms are operating in the same relation to optimal output and that their nonoptimal function is similar to the optimal cost function. Simply to state these assumptions reveals their inherent dangers.

In the engineering approach, each element of the production process is studied to discover the relation between inputs and outputs at different scales for that process. The input-output relations of the processes are then combined to give the over-all input-output relations. The introduction of prices for the inputs transforms these relations into cost-output relations. Since this method of study is less familiar, two studies of economies of scale made from the engineering point of view will be discussed as examples of the method. These studies are presented in unpublished doctoral theses written independently but at about the same time at Harvard.

The first of these studies, already mentioned, was submitted in April 1949 by Allen Richmond Ferguson and is entitled "A Technical Synthesis of Airline Costs." The second, "Engineering Bases of Economic Analysis," was submitted in August 1949 by Hollis B. Chenery. Both studies apply parts of the great mass of engineering observations of the relations between inputs and outputs to an

221

analysis of over-all cost functions of both the short- and long-run variety. The technique of using engineering laws in discussions of economies of scale is not new[12] except in the thoroughness and precision with which it is applied, but this exact use opens exciting new vistas for the further study of economies of scale which can be made on the basis of the empirical relations developed by engineers.

Chenery, in the summary of his thesis, says, "The purpose of this study is to determine the usefulness of physical laws for the economic analysis of production. It seeks to develop a method by which the type of calculation made by engineers in designing plants and equipment may be used to derive the general relations among productive factors expressed in the production function of economic theory."[13]

Ferguson's conception of the subject for investigation, though it is essentially the same, is broader. He is concerned not only with the "technical" but also with the "institutional determinants of the amount of each type of input required and [with] ascertaining the quantitative input-output relationship so determined."[14] The author recognizes that the institutionally determined input-output relations are subject both to arbitrary changes and to changes which may be induced by a large or sudden change in this input or in other inputs. However, the inclusion of what have sometimes been called human engineering relations in the purview of engineering studies considerably broadens the usefulness of the technique.

Studies made by economists on the basis of observations by engineers avoid the problem which arises from the fact that the existing plant was built when different technological horizons existed, but they have similar limitations. They have been over-oriented toward the study of input-output relations in the elements of the presently utilized productive processes because these relations are the only ones thoroughly investigated by the engineers. The authors have recognized explicitly the fact that this narrowed the economic significance of their studies. The importance of this limitation is greatest if a change in scale or factor prices makes it more economical

[12] Economic discussions frequently have pointed out engineering laws which may lead to either economies or diseconomies of scale, e.g. that heat loss is proportional to the square of any one dimension while volume is proportional to the cube.

[13] Hollis B. Chenery, "Engineering Bases of Economic Analysis" (Ph.D. dissertation, Harvard University, 1949), Summary, p. 1.

[14] Ferguson, *op. cit.*, p. 2.

to adopt techniques, the input-output relations of which have not been studied. Furthermore, engineering studies show ideal rather than actual relations of size and cost. This is good or bad, depending on what we want the cost function to reveal. Finally, the relation of factor cost to scale, if not explicitly studied, further limits the usefulness of the engineering studies.

The problem of cost and size of plant is more susceptible to study through the engineering approach than is the problem of cost and size of firm because the relations between the plants which make up a firm do not lend themselves to engineering study. These relations probably are dominated by the more or less unique considerations for each aggregation of plants into a firm.

3. The Question to Which We Seek an Answer

WHEN we ask the supposedly precise scientific question, what is the relation of cost to size of plant or firm, we are usually concerned in fact with finding answers to questions which appear less precise: Are giant firms more efficient or do they prosper because of "unfair" advantages? How much saving does the public get from giant firms? How?

Examination of the data that are available and that conceivably might be available shows that we cannot hope to make very satisfactory empirical studies of the long-run cost function. I believe that if we asked the student of the data to tell us in detail just what cost differences exist between different types and sizes of plant and firm and what causes, if any, he could discover for those differences, the information would go farther to clarify the practical questions to which we seek answers than would studies of the relation of cost to size.

4. Comments on a Sample of the Empirical Studies

BEFORE venturing on a statement of the generalizations which the empirical evidence warrants, some comments on a sampling of the material which has become available since 1940 will be presented. Earlier material on the subject was sampled in *Cost Behavior and Price Policy*,[15] published ten years ago by the National Bureau of Economic Research. This discussion provides, in my opinion, an adequate treatment of the material prior to 1940. The material published since 1940 enables us to fill in some portions of the picture

---

[15] Committee on Price Determination, Conference on Price Research, National Bureau of Economic Research, New York, 1943.

drawn there. We still lack sufficient data for confident and precise generalization.

In 1941 the Temporary National Economic Committee Monograph 13, *Relative Efficiency of Large, Medium-Sized, and Small Business*, a study prepared by the Federal Trade Commission was published. This presents substantial material each part of which, however, is rather briefly and superficially analyzed. The results show that, in general, medium-sized business[16] is most efficient in the industries and instances studied. The material on costs of individual plants and companies in a number of industries shows that very seldom (1 out of 59 cases for companies, and 2 out of 53 cases for plants) did the largest plant or company show the lowest costs. These results, unfortunately, prove little since the much greater number of medium-sized, small and very small plants and companies included biases the results. This may be, in part, the result of more frequent accounting abnormalities among small and medium-sized businesses. Furthermore, we should expect to find that some small or medium-sized plants or companies had especially favorable cost conditions. These facts—coupled with a lack of detailed discussion and analysis of the material presented— (much of it rather sketchy) prejudice the scholarly mind against accepting the conclusions which seem to follow from the data in the monograph.[17]

On the other hand, a second look at the data reveals somewhat better evidence in support of the idea that small or medium-sized business is more efficient. (1) "On the average, over one-third of the companies in every array" and "over one-third of the plants in each cost array had . . . costs lower than that of the largest company" or "plant."[18] (2) When data for companies or plants grouped according to size were used, in ten out of eleven cases when companies were studied, and in all five cases when plants were studied, the medium-sized group showed lowest costs.[19] (3) A few quick calculations on some of the cost data presented in arrays but not included in the grouped data mentioned above, show instances—although

16 The classification "medium-sized" is sometimes strained, e.g. Chrysler is called medium-sized when clearly the significant difference between Chrysler and Ford is in degree of vertical integration.

17 For a reasoned and highly critical review of this monograph see John M. Blair, "The Relation between Size and Efficiency of Business," *Review of Economic Statistics*, August 1942, pp. 125-135.

18 *Relative Efficiency of Large, Medium-Sized and Small Business*, Temporary National Economic Committee, Monograph 13, 1941, p. 12.

19 *Ibid.*, p. 12.

not an overwhelming predominance of cases—in which grouping the plants or companies would result in the medium-sized plants showing the lowest costs. The mass of data is so great and the conclusion of lower costs for medium-sized plants or companies so general that in spite of the fact that almost every individual study is subject to serious criticism it is necessary to give considerable weight to the findings.

There may be a bias in the data on cost and size of firm which prejudices our conclusions. It is entirely possible that, although almost always we find costs for the largest firms higher than for a group of medium-sized firms, it is not general. In those industries where cost continues to decrease with increasing size it is probable that all the medium-sized firms either have become giants and swallowed the other medium-sized firms or they have failed or shrunk into small firms. If this is the case, the sound generalization is not that medium-sized firms have, in general, lower costs than do large firms, but that in industries where both medium-sized and large-sized firms are found, the costs of the medium-sized firms are probably lower than those of the large firms. (But, let us not forget that "medium-sized" here includes the Chrysler Corporation.)

A study by Steindl presents some interesting ideas and evidence on the general subject of size of plants and firms although it offers little bearing directly on our question. He shows, by the use of data from the *Statistics of Income*, that capital intensification accompanies increasing size of firm for all manufacturing industry as a group, for mining, for trade, and for most of the major subgroups of manufacturing. He rejects as unlikely the possibility that this showing of greater capital intensity for larger firms is caused only by differences in the products produced by small and large firms or by greater vertical integration of larger firms.[20] Steindl devotes a considerable part of his study to demonstrating that with capital intensification, the profit rate will fall beyond a certain point even if cost per unit of output continues to fall. He thus offers a possible explanation of the declining profit rates frequently found by Crum[21] for the largest corporations in any industry which is consistent with the idea that unit costs are lower for larger companies. He also explores suggestively certain difficulties the large firm may face be-

[20] Joseph Steindl, *Small and Big Business* (Monograph 1, Oxford University Institute of Statistics, 1945), pp. 23-25.
[21] William Leonard Crum, *Corporate Size and Earning Power* (Harvard University Press, 1939).

cause of imperfect competition or oligopoly. The high selling and administrative costs of the four largest tire manufacturers, discussed earlier, is an example of this problem. He re-analyzes the material on the growth of concentration in manufacturing and shows that although the percentage of wage earners in manufacturing establishments with over 1,000 wage earners hardly changed from 1919 to 1937, establishments with 250 to 1,000 wage earners gained substantially relative to establishments with fewer than 50 wage earners.[22] This loss by small manufacturing business he regards as a significant continuance of the concentration pattern which was so marked before and during World War I.

Steindl, in his discussion of capital intensity, highlights the association of size with capital intensity. He asserts that "large-scale economies are in reality *technically* inseparable from capital intensification, so that the greater plant, if it is to make use of large-scale economies, has also to use a greater proportion of capital to labor."[23] While we may admit readily that many large-scale economies require much capital there seems no a priori reason why a small-scale plant using the best available technology and facing the same relative factor prices should use relatively less capital.

Greater capital intensity in large-scale plants could result if small-scale plants have inadequate capital resources, or if their managers believe they can find more profitable uses for capital in horizontal expansion rather than in capital intensification. If few small-scale enterprises want to put capital into intensive investment, the capital-intensive technology for small-scale plants will not be as adequately developed and the appropriate capital-intensive machines will not be readily available to them. There are, also, other reasons why small-scale technology may be less well developed in general than large-scale technology. On the basis of all these factors, we may conclude that, if capital intensification, as a rule, leads to lower unit costs, a systematic difference in the capital intensity of the technology between plants of different sizes may prejudice seriously the unit-cost size relations which we discover empirically.

Many numbers of the Office of Price Administration Economic Data Series published in 1947 by the Office of Temporary Controls contain material on cost and size of firm.[24]

[22] Steindl, *op. cit.*, Figure 1, p. 49.   [23] *Ibid.*, p. 22.

[24] Study 10, on rubber tire and tube manufacturers, cited earlier, shows costs divided into several categories for nine products for two size groups of firms. Study 7 on retail furniture stores shows operating expenses as a percentage of

In a paper presented at the December 1947 meetings of the American Economic Association, John M. Blair analyzed data for several industries which show the lowest cost for groups of plants or companies smaller than the largest group.[25] On the basis of this evidence he seems ready to make the generalization that both plants and firms which are larger than the lowest cost size are found in practice in a substantial number of industries. His conclusion is especially interesting in view of his attack, referred to above, on the similar conclusions drawn in the TNEC Monograph 13. It should be noted that he attaches great significance to the growth of new "decentralizing" techniques which have improved the position of plants and firms of less than maximum size.

A study by Florence[26] presents a great deal of information on subjects related to that here under survey. He shows that in many industries the predominant size of plant is not large. More specifically, he shows that highly localized industry generally has medium-sized plants. If predominance of a plant size less than that of the largest firms may be taken as an indication of a certain sort of efficiency (even if not of lowest average cost) for medium-sized firms, his data clearly establish substantial areas in which medium-sized firms are "efficient."

There also is scattered evidence, some of it of very high quality, on the relation of cost and size. Unpublished Harvard doctoral theses by Ferguson and by Chenery have already been mentioned. There are undoubtedly similar theses at other universities. Other Harvard theses on this subject include:

John B. Lansing, "An Investigation into the Long-Run Cost Curves for Steam Central Stations," 1948, in which he concludes, "For a station under [theoretically ideal] conditions the answer is clear, 'No, the long-run cost curve does not turn up.' The important

---

sales for three size groups in metropolitan and nonmetropolitan areas. Study 12, on fresh fruit and vegetable wholesalers, gives cost figures for four cost categories for five size groups of wholesalers for each of three types of wholesaler. Study 13, on women's underwear and nightwear, gives cost figures for two different years by five cost categories for six size groups of manufacturers. Study 26 on grocers retail chains and wholesale, gives expense as a percentage of sales by size groups for a considerable number of time periods. Other studies in this series contain similar data. Detailed appraisal of this mass of material would be a major task which, so far as I know, has not been undertaken.

25 Blair, "Does Large Scale Enterprise Result in Lower Costs?" as cited.

26 P. Sargent Florence, *Investment, Location, and Size of Plant* (Cambridge, 1948).

question is different: what factors tend to make long-run cost curves turn up?"[27]

Morris A. Adelman, "The Dominant Firm," 1948, a study of the Great Atlantic & Pacific Tea Co. A chart from a revision of this thesis supplied by the author shows a regular decline with increasing size in practically all elements of costs for the company's super-markets.

Raymond G. Bressler, Jr., "City Milk Distribution," 1946. Also a study, *Economies of Scale in the Operation of Country Milk Plants*, published in 1942 by the New England Research Council on Marketing and Food Supply in cooperation with the New England Agricultural Experiment Stations and the Department of Agriculture, and an article "Research Determination of Economies of Scale," *Journal of Farm Economics*, August 1945. The emphasis in Bressler's thesis is on the analysis of the elements of the costs of urban milk distribution with regressions fitted to scatters between short-run variations in output and cost. Observations on the long-run cost function are derived from these short-run considerations.

Finally, mention should be made of three largely unexplored sources of empirical evidence. First, the publications of the Agricultural Experiment Stations contain a substantial volume of evidence on this subject pertaining not only to agriculture but to first stage assembling and processing. Second, the engineering journals contain occasional articles giving empirical relations. The data often are not described carefully but a thorough search would reveal much interesting information. An example is an article by J. G. Berger, "Does a Laundry Cut Costs by Buying or by Generating Its Electricity?"[28] The article presents "Curves A and B [which] indicate cost of purchased and generated power based on actual average laundry experience." The curves show falling cost per kw. hr. with increasing size for both with generated power cost falling below purchased power at 3,700 kw. hr./month and—what is more significant—still falling appreciably at 15,000 kw. hr./month, the largest size shown.

The third neglected source is the data compiled and published by the agencies regulating railroads and public utilities. A careful study of a part of this data has been made by my colleague, George H. Borts, in a thesis at the University of Chicago. Borts develops

[27] P. 56.
[28] *Power*, July 1946, p. 457.

long-run production functions in railroading, showing declining costs with increased size up to the maximum size.[29]

5. Conclusion

IT is both difficult and dangerous to generalize on the basis of the scattered and heterogeneous empirical material on economies of scale. The following generalizations, however, appear to be warranted by the evidence I have examined in the preparation of this paper and in my connection with the preparation of Chapter X of the National Bureau of Economic Research's study "Cost Behavior and Price Policy."

1. With increasing size of plant, at least from small to medium size, average cost of production declines as size increases if factor costs are held constant.

2. There is no substantial evidence that the decline in unit costs stops before the maximum size of plant available for study if factor costs are held constant and the product is the same. On the other hand, the little evidence available does not refute the idea that the long-run cost curve even with factor prices constant turns up at some attainable size. We can hardly hope to find an answer to this question as to whether there is in practice a plant so large that the costs of producing a specific product increase even if factor prices are held constant because:

a. Factor costs, especially labor costs, seem to vary with size of plant. Generalization is hazardous and must be based primarily upon studies not concerned with determining the long-run cost function because most of the studies of the long-run cost function have not given this problem careful consideration. Generally, wage rates are found to be higher in the larger plants while probably raw materials (exclusive of assembly costs) and almost certainly capital, are cheaper.

b. Assembly costs and distribution costs per unit decline for a time with increasing size of plant but usually start to increase within the range of size of plant available for study.[30]

These increases in factor prices and in assembly and distribution

[29] See also his articles "Production Relations in the Railway Industry," *Econometrica*, January 1952, and "Increasing Returns in the Railway Industry," *Journal of Political Economy*, August 1954.

[30] This conclusion is based primarily on studies of plants engaged in first stage agricultural processing, but there is no evidence to indicate that it is not generally applicable.

costs result in cost increases which make it impractical to build plants which might be large enough to have higher average cost. Therefore, we have no opportunity to study the costs of such giant plants.

The hypothesis that the long-run cost function for the production of a product typically turns up at some very large size cannot be subjected to empirical verification. Even if one or two products should be found for which the cost elements which are supposed to be impounded in *ceteris paribus* do not in practice increase so as to prevent practical businessmen from expanding and the giant plants which they then built showed higher unit costs (*ceteris paribus*), it would be foolhardy to generalize on these instances. Furthermore, if the range in size of plants in practice stops (because factor prices and assembly and distribution costs increase) within the range in which the cost of producing a specific product is still decreasing when factor prices are held constant, the hypothesis that the long-run cost function eventually turns up is not very meaningful even if it could be proved. The fact that there is no substantial evidence that the long-run cost function for plants does not continue to decline up to the largest sizes found in practice if factor prices are held constant (a generalization apparently justified by the evidence) seems to have much greater significance for economists.

3. With increasing size of firm, the best documented generalization about average cost is that when factor costs are not held constant and outputs which are not the same but are sold competitively are considered as similar, costs decline with increasing size of firm up to a rather high point but that frequently and perhaps generally beyond a certain size of firm, costs again increase. But there is no satisfactory basis for distinguishing types of product for which the long-run cost function of the firm rises within the range of firm size actually found in practice.

COMMENT

Milton Friedman, University of Chicago

I have great sympathy with Caleb Smith's conclusion that the right questions have not been asked of the data on the costs of firms of different sizes. My quarrel with him is that he does not go far enough. I believe that cross-section contemporaneous accounting data for different firms or plants give little if any information on so-called economies of scale. Smith implies that difficulty arises because the observed phenomena do not correspond directly with the theoretical constructs; because there is no single, homogeneous product, and so on. I believe that the basic difficulty is both simpler and more fundamental; that the pure theory itself gives no reason to expect that cross-section data will yield the relevant cost curves. Some of the bases for this view are suggested by Smith in his discussion, but he stops short of carrying them to their logical conclusion.

NO SPECIALIZED FACTORS OF PRODUCTION

LET US consider first the simplest theoretical case, when all factors of production are unspecialized so there are numerous possible firms all potentially alike. This is the model that implicitly or explicitly underlies most textbook discussions of cost curves. For present purposes, we may beg the really troublesome point about this case—why there is any limit to the size of the firm—and simply assume that there is some resource ("entrepreneurial ability") of which each firm can have only one unit, that these units are all identical, and that the number in existence (though not the number in use) is indefinitely large, so all receive a return of zero.

In this case, the (minimum) average cost at which a particular firm can produce each alternative hypothetical output is clearly defined, independently of the price of the product, since it depends entirely on the prices that the resources can command in alternative uses. The average cost curve is the same for all firms and independent of the output of the industry, so the long-run supply curve is horizontal, and hence determines the price of the product.[1] In the absence of mistakes or changes in conditions, all firms would be identical in size, and would operate at the same output and the same average cost. The number of firms would be determined by conditions of demand. In this model, the "optimum" size firm has an unambiguous meaning.

Suppose this model is regarded as applying to a particular industry. Differences among firms in size (however measured) are then to be interpreted as the result of either mistakes or changes in circumstances that have altered the appropriate size of firm. If "mistakes" are about as likely to be on one side as the other of the

[1] This neglects some minor qualifications, of which two may deserve explicit mention: first, the irrelevance of the output of the industry depends somewhat on the precise assumptions about the source of any increased demand; second, strictly speaking, the supply curve may have tiny waves in it attributable to the finite number of firms. On the first point, see Richard Brumberg, "*Ceteris Paribus* for Supply Curves," *Economic Journal*, June 1953, pp. 462-463.

"optimum" size, the mean or modal size firm in the industry can be regarded as the "optimum"; but there is no necessity for mistakes to be symmetrically distributed, and in any event this approach assumes the answer that cross-section studies seek.

What more, if anything, can contemporaneous accounting data add? Can we use them to compute the average cost curve that was initially supposed to exist? Or even to determine the size of firm with minimum average cost? I think not. Consider a firm that made a "mistake" and is in consequence, let us say, too large. This means that the average cost per unit of output that would currently have to be incurred to produce the firm's present output by reproducing the firm would be higher than the price of the product. It does not mean that the current accounting cost is—even if there have been no changes in conditions since the firm was established, so that original cost corresponds to reproduction cost. If the firm has changed hands since it was established, the price paid for the "good will" of the firm will have taken full account of the mistake; the original investors will have taken a capital loss, and the new owners will have a level of cost equal to price. If the firm has not changed hands, accounting costs may well have been similarly affected by write-downs and the like. In any event, cost as computed by the statistician will clearly be affected if capital cost is computed by imputing a market return to the equity in the firm as valued by the capital market. In short, differences among contemporaneous re-corded costs tell nothing about the *ex ante* costs of outputs of different size but only about the efficiency of the capital market in revaluing assets.

In the case just cited, data on historical costs would be relevant. However, their relevance depends critically on the possibility of neglecting both technological and monetary changes in conditions affecting costs since the firms were established. A more tempting possibility is to estimate reproduction costs. This involves essentially departing from contemporaneous accounting data and using engineering data instead, in which case there seems little reason to stick to the particular plants or firms that happen to exist as a result of historical accidents.

Under the assumed conditions, the unduly large firms would be converting themselves into smaller ones, the unduly small firms into larger ones, so that all would be converging on "the" single optimum size. Changes over time in the distribution of firms by size might in this way give some indication of the "optimum" size of firm.

SPECIALIZED FACTORS OF PRODUCTION

THE existence of specialized factors of production introduces an additional reason why firms should differ in size. Even if output is homogeneous, there is no longer, even in theory, a single "optimum" or "equilibrium" size. The appropriate size of firm to produce, say, copper, may be different for two different mines, and both can exist simultaneously because it is impossible to duplicate either one precisely—this is the economic meaning of "specialized" factors. Or, to take another example, Jones's special forte may be organization of production efficiently on a large scale; Robinson's, the maintenance of good personal relations with customers; the firm that gives appropriate scope to Jones's special ability may be larger than the firm that gives appropriate scope to Robinson's. It follows that in any "industry," however defined, in which the resources used cannot be regarded as unspecialized, there will tend to be firms of different size. One could speak of an "optimum distribution of firms by size," perhaps, but not of an "optimum" size of firm. The existing distribution reflects both "mistakes" and intended differences designed to take advantage of the particular specialized resources under the control of different firms.

The existence of specialized resources not only complicates the definition of "optimum" size; even more important, it makes it impossible to define the average cost of a particular firm for different hypothetical outputs independently of conditions of demand. The returns to the specialized factors are now "rents," at least in part, and, in consequence, do not determine the price, but are determined by it. To take the copper mine of the preceding paragraph, its cost curve cannot be computed without knowledge of the royalty or rent that must be paid to the owners of the mine, if the firm does not itself own it, or imputed as royalty or rent, if the firm does. But the royalty is clearly dependent on the price at which copper sells on the market and is determined in such a way as to make average cost tend to equal price.

The point at issue may perhaps be put in a different way. The long-run conditions of equilibrium for a competitive firm are stated in the textbooks as "price equals marginal cost equals average cost." But with specialized resources, "price equals marginal cost" has a fundamentally different meaning and significance from "price equals average cost." The first is a goal of the firm itself; the firm seeks to equate marginal cost to price, since this is equivalent to maximizing its return. The second is not, in any meaningful sense, a goal of the firm; indeed, its avoidance could with more justification be said to be its goal, at least in the meaning it would be likely to attach to average cost. The equality of price to average cost is a result of equilibrium, not a determinant of it; it is forced on the firm by the operation of the capital market or the market determining rents for specialized resources.

Consider a situation in which a group of competitive firms are all appropriately adjusted to existing conditions, in which there is no tendency for firms to change their output, for new firms to enter, or for old firms to leave—in short, a situation of long-run equilibrium. For each firm separately, marginal cost (long-run and short-run) is equal to price—otherwise, the firms would be seeking to change their outputs. Suppose that, for one or more firms, total payments to hired factors of production fall short of total revenue—that average cost in this sense is less than price. If these firms could be reproduced by assembling similar collections of hired factors, there would be an incentive to do so. The fact that there is no tendency for new firms to enter means that they cannot be reproduced, implying that the firms own some specialized factors. For any one firm, the difference between total receipts and total payments to hired factors is the rent attributable to these specialized factors; the capitalized value of this rent is the amount that, in a perfect capital market, would be paid for the firm; if the firm were sold for this sum, the rent would show up on the books as "interest" or "dividends"; if it is not sold, a corresponding amount should be imputed as a return to the "good-will" or capital value of the firm. The equality between price and average cost, in any sense in which it is more than a truism, thus reflects competition on the capital market and has no relation to the state of competition in product or factor markets.

For simplicity, the preceding discussion is in terms of a competitive industry. Clearly, the same analysis applies to a monopolistic firm with only minor changes in wording. The firm seeks to equate marginal cost and marginal revenue. The capital market values the firm so as to make average cost tend to equal price. Indeed, one of the specialized factors that receives rent may be whatever gives the firm its monopolistic power, be it a patent or the personality of its owner.

It follows from this analysis that cross-section accounting data on costs tell nothing about "economies of scale" in any meaningful sense. If firms differ in size because they use different specialized resources, their average costs will all tend to be equal, provided they are properly computed so as to include rents. Whether actually computed costs are or are not equal can only tell us something about the state of the capital market or of the accounting profession. If firms differ in size partly because of mistakes, the comments on the preceding simpler model apply; historical cost data might be relevant, but it is dubious that current accounting cost data are. And how do we know whether the differences in size are mistakes or not?

THE DEFINITION OF COST

THE preceding discussion shares with most such discussions the defect of evading a precise definition of the relation between total costs and total receipts. Looking forward, one can conceive of defining the total cost of producing various outputs as equal to the highest aggregate that the resources required could receive in alternative pursuits. Total cost so estimated need not be identical with anticipated total revenue; hence *ex ante* total cost, so defined, need not equal total revenue. But after the event, how is one to classify payments not regarded as cost? Does some part of receipts go to someone in a capacity other than as owner of a factor of production?

All in all, the best procedure seems to me to be to define total cost as identical with total receipts—to make these the totals of two sides of a double entry account. One can then distinguish between different kinds of costs, the chief distinction in pure theory being between costs that depend on what the firm does but not on how its actions turn out (contractual costs), and the rest of its costs or receipts (noncontractual costs). The former represent the cost of factors of production viewed solely as "hired" resources capable of being rented out to other firms; the latter represent payment for whatever it is that makes identical collections of resources different when employed by different firms—a factor of production that we may formally designate "entrepreneurial capacity," recognizing that this term gives a name to our ignorance rather than dispelling it.

Actual noncontractual costs can obviously never be known in advance, since they will be affected by all sorts of accidents, mistakes, and the like. It is therefore important to distinguish further between expected and actual noncontractual costs. Expected noncontractual costs are a "rent" or "quasi-rent" for entrepreneurial capacity. They are to be regarded as the motivating force behind the firm's decisions, for it is this and this alone that the firm can seek to maximize. The difference between expected and actual non-contractual costs is "profits" or "pure profits"—an unanticipated residual arising from uncertainty.

Definitions of total costs that do not require them to equal total receipts generally define them as equal either to contractual costs alone or to expected costs, contractual and noncontractual, and so regard all or some payments to the "entrepreneurial capacity" of the firm as noncost payments. The difficulty is, as I hope the preceding discussion makes clear, that there are no simple institutional lines or accounting categories that correspond to these distinctions.

Smith mentions the possibility of relating cost per dollar of output to size. Presumably one reason why this procedure has not been followed is that it brings the problems we have been discussing sharply to the surface and in consequence makes it clear that nothing is to be learned in this way. If costs *ex post* are defined to equal receipts *ex post*, cost per dollar of output is necessarily one dollar, regardless of size. Any other result must imply that some costs are disregarded, or some receipts regarded as noncost receipts. Generally, the costs disregarded are capital costs—frequently called "profits." The study then simply shows how capital costs vary with size, which may, as Smith points out, merely reflect systematic differences in factor combinations according to size. One could with equal validity study wage costs or electricity costs per unit of output as a function of size.

The use of physical units of output avoids so obvious an objection; clearly it does not avoid the basic difficulty and, as Smith points out, it introduces problems of its own. The heterogeneity of output means that any changes in average cost with scale may merely measure changes in the "quality" of what is taken to be a unit of output. Insofar as size itself is measured by actual output, or an index related to it, a much more serious bias is introduced tending toward an apparent decline of costs as size increases. This can most easily be brought out by an extreme example. Suppose a firm produces a product the demand for which has a known two-year cycle, so that it plans to produce 100 units in year one, 200 in year two, 100 in year three, etc. Suppose, also, that the best way to do this is by an arrangement that involves identical outlays for hired factors in each year (no "variable" costs). If outlays are regarded as total costs, as they would be in studies of the kind under discussion, average cost per unit will obviously be twice as large when output is 100 as when it is 200. If, instead of years one and two, we substitute firms one and two, a cross-section study would show sharply declining average costs. When firms are classified by actual output, essentially this kind of bias arises. The firms with the largest output are unlikely to be producing at an unusually low level; on the average, they are clearly likely to be producing at an unusually high level, and conversely for those which have the lowest output.[2]

SIZE DISTRIBUTION OF FIRMS

IT MAY well be that a more promising source of information than cross-section accounting data would be the temporal behavior of the distribution of firms by size. If, over time, the distribution tends to be relatively stable, one might conclude that this is the "equilibrium" distribution and defines not the optimum scale of firm but the optimum distribution. If the distribution tends to become increasingly concentrated, one might conclude that the extremes represented mistakes, the point of concentration the "optimum" scale; and similarly with other changes. Whether, in fact, such deductions would be justified depends on how reasonable it is to suppose that the optimum scale or distribution has itself remained unchanged and that the emergence of new mistakes has been less important than the correction of old ones. None of this can be taken for granted; it would have to be established by study of the empirical circumstances of the particular industry, which is why the preceding statements are so liberally strewn with "mights."

THE RELEVANT QUESTION

I SHARE very strongly Smith's judgment that one of the main reasons why the evidence accumulated in numerous studies by able people is so disappointing is that insufficient attention has been paid to why we want information on so-called economies of scale; foolish questions deserve foolish answers. If we ask what size firm has minimum costs, and define "minimum costs" in a sense in which it is in a firm's own interest to achieve it, surely the obvious answer is: firms of existing size. We can hardly expect to get better answers to this question than a host of firms, each of which has much more intimate knowledge about its activities than we as outside observers can have and each of which has a much stronger and immediate incentive to find the right answer: much of the preceding discussion is really only a roundabout way of making this simple point.

---

[2] This is the general "regression fallacy" that is so widespread in the interpretation of economic data.

But surely studies of this kind are not really directed at determining whether existing firms make mistakes in pursuing their own interests. The purpose is quite different. It is, I believe, to predict the effect on the distribution of firms by size of one or another change in the circumstances determining their interests. The particular question may well suggest relevant criteria for distinguishing one kind of cost from another, and in this way enable cross-section accounting data to provide useful information. For example, Smith discusses studies supposedly showing that assembly and distribution costs rise with the size of plant whereas manufacturing costs decline. This finding might be decidedly relevant to predicting the effect of a decline in transportation costs on the distribution of firms by size. Or, again, the fact that some firms may use different combinations of factors from others may be due to identifiable differences, geographical or otherwise, in the prices of what in some sense are similar factors. The combinations of factors employed by different firms may then be relevant information in predicting the effect of changes in factor prices. This is the implicit rationale of some of the studies of production functions.

In many cases, the changes in circumstances that are in question are less specific. What would be the effect, for example, of repealing the Sherman antitrust laws on the distribution of firms by size? Of eliminating patents, or changing the patent laws? Of altering the tax laws? As Smith says, there must be much evidence available that is relevant to answering such questions. Unfortunately, as he recognizes, the generalizations assembled by him at the conclusion of his paper do not make much of a contribution; in the main, they simply confirm either the absence of obvious discrepancies between the existing size of firms and the size that is in their own interests or the effectiveness of the capital market in writing off mistakes

EFFECTS OF TAXES ON CONCENTRATION

JOHN LINTNER AND J. KEITH BUTTERS

HARVARD UNIVERSITY

Two of the important characteristics of the American economy in recent years have been high "concentration" and high taxes.[1] High concentration is well established, whether concentration is measured in terms of employment, total assets, net capital assets, profits, sales, or even research expenditures; whether one looks to the economy as a whole or to many of the more important areas in the economy; and whatever the definition or index used to measure concentration.[2] Similarly, there can be no doubt that by any historical standards both corporate and personal income taxes have been very heavy during the past ten to fifteen years.

It is obvious that this second condition—high taxes—cannot account for the first—high concentration. The economy was already highly concentrated by the turn of the century, well before either the corporate or personal income tax was introduced. Nor can the generally rising trend of tax rates since 1909 explain the trend in concentration over the last two generations. Even though imperfections and gaps in the data counsel caution, the best available evidence establishes a rather strong presumption that there has been no increase in over-all concentration over the last fifty-year period and indicates that there probably has been some decrease in concentration over this period, at least so far as manufacturing is concerned.[3] Such broad stability (i.e. zero or negative trend) cannot be readily explained by secularly rising taxes. Neither can the known fluctuations in the degree of concentration within this half-century be readily or consistently explained by concomitant changes in tax rates within the period.[4]

[1] In this paper we make no attempt to examine all potentially significant features of the tax structure. In particular we do not examine the effects of such presumably transitory features of the tax law as the current excess profits tax and accelerated amortization of emergency facilities.

[2] See M. A. Adelman, "The Measurement of Industrial Concentration," *Review of Economics and Statistics*, November 1951, pp. 269-296, and the references there cited, as well as the discussion of Adelman's study in the May 1952 issue of the *Review*. See also "Measures of Concentration" by Gideon Rosenbluth in this volume.

[3] Adelman, *op. cit.*

[4] After their introduction in 1909 and 1913, taxes quickly reached high levels during World War I and remained far above previous peacetime levels in the

The historical record points to the general conclusion that the prevailing levels and the broad changes in concentration have been primarily determined by nontax considerations. It suggests that taxes were only one factor—and perhaps not a very important one— in the whole complex of forces affecting the level of concentration and shifts in this level. Nevertheless, there is real point in examining whether taxes have tended, and are tending, to increase or diminish the level of concentration from what it otherwise would have been, i.e. whether the *thrust* of taxes on balance has been, and is, positive or negative. Taxation is recognized and accepted as a major instrument of public policy, and its impact on the competitive structure should be given due consideration along with its other effects in framing policy. Moreover, taxes are currently at very high levels, and unless the international situation improves substantially, they are likely to continue high; if they are sustained indefinitely at current levels, their effects may well be substantially more severe than they appear to have been in the past. In this connection it should be recalled that, barring the 1917-1921 period, high effective and marginal tax rates on income are a development of the last ten to fifteen years.

Ideally, in attempting to analyze the net effect of taxes on concentration, we should know all the basic factors and conditions controlling changes in the level of concentration and be able to measure the relative importance of each (with due allowance for their interactions). Then, if we could determine the net effect of taxes on each of these controlling considerations, we should be in a position to push the analysis through to specific conclusions regarding the changes in concentration attributable to the tax structure. Unfortunately, this background analysis of the forces primarily and directly determining concentration simply does not exist in the complete and precise form necessary for an analysis in these ambitious terms.

---

early 1920's; concentration seems to have increased between 1909 and 1924, but imperfections of data again make it impossible to know definitely how much. The broad positive association between general trends in tax rates and levels of concentration, however, did not continue. Concentration definitely increased between 1924 and 1929 during a period of substantially unchanged corporate tax rates and declining personal income tax rates. Taxes were successively raised throughout the 1930's and have been at very high levels during the early 1940's to date, but there is evidence that concentration was actually less in the late 1940's than in the early 1930's, and numerous studies suggest that over-all concentration in manufacturing was reduced during the high tax period of the 1940's.

The scope of the present paper, therefore, is limited to an examination of the effect of taxes on a few of the more important determinants of concentration. Successive sections appraise in general terms the effects of taxes on (1) the formation and early growth of new firms and enterprises, (2) management incentives to growth and expansion, (3) relative rates of growth of different sizes of firms through retained earnings, (4) the availability of outside funds to finance expansion for larger and smaller concerns, and (5) the effects of taxes on mergers.

In large part, this report represents a summary and synthesis of the various studies bearing on the present subject that the present authors have undertaken over the last seven or eight years. New material, however, is introduced in the section dealing with the effects of taxes on the relative rates of growth of larger and smaller firms through retained earnings, and the authors also hope that the recasting of the earlier analysis, designed to bring it to bear directly on the problem of corporate concentration, will prove helpful.

The effects of taxes on three different types or measures of concentration will be considered. The first is the usual "concentration ratio," which will be taken as a measure of "absolute concentration" because it measures the proportion of assets (or sales or some other base factor) accounted for by some *absolute* number of the largest firms in an industry or industry group.[5]

The second measure of concentration used is a measure of *relative* concentration or "inequality." In contrast with usual measures of absolute concentration, relative concentration measures the different percentages of all assets held by various proportions of all companies. It is a more general measure than the concentration ratio because it summarizes changes in concentration occurring throughout all asset-size classes rather than solely within the top size classes.[6] It is also a very flexible measure that can be applied to various sections of the distribution.

[5] When applied to individual industries, the ratio of the assets or sales of the largest four firms to the total assets or sales of all firms in the industry is what is usually measured, though the ratio of the largest eight or some other number to the relevant total for all firms is sometimes used. In dealing with large groups such as all manufacturing, we measure changes in absolute concentration in terms of the change in the proportion of assets held by the number of firms which happen to have individual assets in excess of $50 million or $100 million in the benchmark year.

[6] We have used the Gini Concentration Ratio to measure relative concentration in our statistical work; in geometrical terms this measures the inequality shown in the Lorenz diagram.

Finally, in the section on mergers we are also concerned with a much broader and looser concept of concentration—one which simply reflects the fact that previously existing assets become "concentrated" into the hands of a smaller remaining total number of firms whenever mergers occur, inasmuch as they necessarily involve the disappearance of the acquired companies and reduce the total number of firms.

1. *Formation and Early Growth of New Firms*

THE first segment of our analysis deals with the effect of taxes on the formation and early growth of new firms—roughly up to the point at which they become capable of profitable operations. The importance of this phase of business development hardly needs to be stressed. The continued formation of successful new firms is needed to replace existing business units that fall behind or drop out of the competitive race. Even more important, new firms are needed to develop new ideas, techniques, and products that can potentially offer effective competition to established firms. A high birth rate of new firms is required to prevent an increase in concentration, because mortality rates are higher for small firms than for larger enterprises and because the mortality of new firms is high. In particular, any reduction in the rate of formation of new firms would tend to increase the share of total output accounted for by a fixed number of large firms (absolute concentration) and to "concentrate" the total of all activity among a more limited number of firms.

Taxes may affect the formation and early growth of new firms in two ways. First, they may dull the *incentives* needed to induce people to undertake to establish new business concerns. Secondly, taxes may impair their *ability* to do so by restricting the supply of capital required to finance the formation and early growth of new firms. We shall consider these two types of effects separately.

So far as incentive effects are concerned, our conclusion is that tax considerations generally do not play a critical role at this stage of development of a business organization. At least until the enactment of the present excess profits tax,[7] the effect of taxes on profit prospects appears typically to have been given little conscious consideration by the individuals actually responsible for the organization of new enterprises. We recognize, of course, that new firms will seldom be started at all if their founders do not expect them to be

[7] We have done no empirical work on this topic since Korea.

profitable, and with rare exceptions their survival as well as their subsequent growth will depend upon their ability to earn a profit; but the precise amount of this expected profit does not usually have an important bearing upon the decision to undertake the business. When a new business is organized, only the crudest estimates of its profit potentialities can be made, even when the growth potential seems to be great. The impossibility of estimating profits prospects with any degree of precision at this stage of a corporation's development tends to preclude a careful evaluation of the effect of taxes on these indefinite profits prospects—unless tax rates approach confiscatory levels and are expected to remain there..

Another factor diminishing the importance of the incentive effects of taxes in the formative stages of a new business is that the kind of individuals who are interested in organizing new businesses are often motivated to a marked degree by nonpecuniary considerations. They tend to be aggressive, confident of their ability to succeed, anxious to be their own boss, and desirous of developing a new "idea" in which they are intensely interested. If the organizer's primary interest is in the satisfaction of creating something new and in the power that goes with a successful business development, as it often is, tax considerations tend to be viewed as of only secondary importance.

While taxes do not generally appear to have an important effect on the *desire* of individuals to start new enterprises, they may have a pronounced effect on their *ability*, i.e. on their financial capacity, to do so. Practically speaking, a minimum amount of ownership capital is essential to the formation of every new business, however small. In the very early stages of a new business, this capital must usually be supplied from the personal resources of the individuals directly interested in the business, or by their immediate relatives and friends; outsiders typically have little interest in new ventures until they have developed to the point where they give real indications of being potentially profitable. Consequently, unless the individuals immediately concerned can accumulate the minimum amount of capital needed to start the enterprise, the chances are that it will never be organized. By making such accumulations more difficult, the tax structure has a significant, though limited, effect on the formation and early development of new enterprises.

After the initial developmental phases of a new enterprise have been completed and the promoters have demonstrated that they have a potentially salable product or service, the feasibility of raising outside capital from disinterested sources is often greatly increased. Generally, also, the stage of "getting into production" is one at which substantial new financing is required; in most industries, it is a rare new venture that can pull itself up by its own bootstraps and become a stable, revenue-producing enterprise of significant size without having to draw on outside capital in the transition from a developmental to a producing organization. A critical test for many enterprises is their ability to raise additional equity capital at this stage of their growth.

At this stage, as well as in the early formative and developmental stages, the only possible sources of equity capital are those supplied from outside the enterprise. Until the business develops an independent earning power of its own—and frequently for a long period thereafter—it will absorb rather than "throw off" capital. For an operation of significant size, moreover, the task of getting into production is likely to require larger amounts of financing than can be raised from the immediate resources of the promoter and his associates. At this point in their development, therefore, numerous (perhaps most) expanding companies have to turn to disinterested private investors, acting individually or through an investment organization, for outside capital. To the extent that taxes affect the capacity and willingness of investors to put money in small, growing enterprises at this phase of their growth, therefore, they are likely to have an important effect on the continued existence and rapidity of expansion of such companies. If the needed capital is not forthcoming, the alternatives are likely to be to sell out—often to a larger competitor—or to strive to continue the development with inadequate resources and the almost inevitable consequence of ultimate failure.

The effects of taxes in this respect, however, are mixed and complex, and it is difficult to appraise their net impact. So far as the personal income tax is concerned, the high rates of this tax on individuals with large incomes obviously reduce the capacity of these individuals to accumulate funds for equity investment, and the evidence indicates that the willingness to make such investments is heavily concentrated in the very small fraction of individuals in the economy with large incomes. In this respect, the personal income tax clearly tends to increase the cost of equity capital to growing enterprises by reducing the potential supply of such funds, as compared to a tax structure bearing less heavily on the upper income classes. (It should be noted in passing, however, that the effects of the income tax structure in this regard are not as severely repressive as is often claimed because of the variety of ways in which individuals can accumulate large amounts of new investable funds without being subject to the full impact of the personal income tax rates.)

At the level of investment *policy* (as contrasted with investment capacity), however, the situation is more complex. To the extent that the tax structure reduces the potential *income* yield from investments in growing enterprises, the effects of the income tax will further compound the previously noted effects on capacity to invest. To the extent, however, that the motive for investing in small, growing enterprises is to make capital gains—and this is probably the dominant motive—the tax structure has a quite different impact. In this case, the large differential between the upper bracket rates on ordinary income and the favorable rates (not exceeding 26 per cent) on long-term capital gains often operates as a positive attraction to investments in growing enterprises.

The strength of this inducement will be particularly strong for venturesome investors who are not averse to taking substantial risks of capital loss, provided that the compensating opportunities for capital appreciation are sufficiently great, and for companies with outstanding growth prospects. The same inducement will be much weaker for more conservative investors who place less of a premium on capital appreciation in relation to the risk of capital loss, and for companies offering more limited prospects for capital appreciation.

It is hard to say where the over-all balance lies, but it is fairly clear that, at the level of investment *policy* effects, taxes tend to reduce the flow of capital to some types of small companies but to increase it for others. The latter companies—those with outstanding growth prospects—though small in number are of strategic economic importance, since they are the organizations that have the potentiality of challenging the established industrial leaders.[8]

So far as the corporate income tax is concerned, its effects at this stage of a company's growth are obviously limited to its repercussions on the willingness of investors to supply outside capital; the

---

[8] For a detailed discussion of the analysis covered in the preceding paragraphs see J. Keith Butters and John Lintner, *Effect of Federal Taxes on Growing Enterprises* (Harvard Business School, 1945) and J. Keith Butters, Lawrence E. Thompson, and Lynn L. Bollinger, *Effects of Taxation: Investments by Individuals* (Harvard Business School, 1953).

corporate income tax has no effect on internal sources of financing until the company reaches a profitable stage of operations and has exhausted any loss carry-overs accumulated during its formative period. Theoretically, the corporate income tax should have a powerful repressive effect on the willingness of outsiders to furnish equity capital to companies in this stage of development. Practically, however, our belief (based, however, on empirical inquiries conducted before the enactment of the current excess profits tax) is that this repressive effect is much less pronounced than has generally been anticipated on theoretical grounds.

The reasons are essentially the same as those explained in the earlier discussion of management incentives. In the early stages of a company's growth, the range of error in estimating its eventual profit potentialities is so great that adjustments for the impact of corporate taxes on these profit potentialities are difficult to make and often are given little attention. As a company reaches more and more advanced stages of development, however, and as it becomes possible to estimate its profit potentialities more precisely, the role of the corporate tax becomes increasingly significant. It goes without saying that the higher the corporate income tax rate, and the more severe the impact of special corporate taxes (such as the undistributed profits tax in 1936 and 1937 and the current excess profits tax) on growing enterprises, the more repressive will be the effects of the corporate tax structure on such companies.

In summary, the balance of the above tax effects on new and growing enterprises in the preprofits stage of their development is difficult to strike with assurance, but it seems fairly clear that the over-all impact is to penalize this class of company in comparison with the established industrial leaders. (This judgment is hardly subject to question so long as an excess profits tax with high marginal rates is expected to remain in effect.) The tax structure of recent years has tended to reduce the number of new firms organized and carried through the "development of idea" stage, thereby maintaining concentration at a somewhat higher level than it would otherwise have been. Beyond the initial developmental stage, but before the attainment of profitable operations, the tax structure has exerted an influence in the same direction by restricting the capacity of upper bracket individuals to accumulate new investable funds and, to a lesser degree, by the damping effect of the corporate income tax on profit expectations. But against these effects must be set the positively favorable influence of the disparity between the low capital gains rates and the high marginal rates on ordinary income in increasing the willingness of venturesome individuals to invest in highly promising new ventures.

The one statement that can be made with positive assurance is that no sweeping conclusions apply without exception to all types of firms. The tax factors do not operate all in one direction, nor do they affect all types of firms with equal force. On balance, it would seem that the mixture of stimulating and repressive effects, and the great importance of nontax considerations at early stages in a company's growth, are such that the tax structures of recent years (pre-1950) have not greatly influenced levels of concentration. Insofar as there are tax effects at this stage, however, our judgment is that their net impact has been in the direction of increasing industrial concentration.

2. Incentives for Expansion

IN THIS and the following two sections, we shall be concerned with the effects of taxes on concentration by way of their effects on the growth of existing companies that have reached the stage of profitable operations. We can, therefore, treat the total number of firms as being constant. Under these conditions it follows that both absolute concentration (the concentration ratio) and relative concentration (inequality) will be unchanged if the relative rates of growth of all firms are identical, and both measures or aspects of concentration will be increased if the effect of taxes is to favor the relative growth rates of larger as compared with smaller firms.

The effect of taxes on incentives for growth for firms of any size depends critically upon the ratio between (a) the size of the new investment undertaking and (b) the minimum reasonably assured income of the company resulting from its established operations over the period within which losses may be offset against income. In cases where the latter exceeds the former, the mean expectation of profits (as a percentage of the initial investment) is reduced in proportion to the tax rate.[9] Moreover, the profits expected if the undertaking is successful, the probable losses if it is unsuccessful, and the net amount of investment at risk are also simply reduced in propor-

[9] It may also be noted that the dispersion of the outcomes contemplated is reduced by the tax, and this should be counted as some positive inducement to invest in the (probably common) cases where corporate management is subject to some risk aversion.

tion to the tax.[10] We have found that managements often consider each of these magnitudes, as well as the expected return (summarizing both probable profits and losses together) in appraising new investments. The condition stated above is important because the restrictive effects of the tax on investment incentives will be much less severe when it is satisfied than when it is not.

Most of the individual investment projects of large well-established firms meet the conditions specified. A large number of investment projects considered by small firms will doubtless also fall into this category. Flat rate taxes will damp incentives to undertake *these* investments no more seriously for the smaller than for the larger firm.

But such investment projects do no more than maintain the orderly growth of a company. Smaller firms frequently have major investment decisions under consideration, which are large in relation to their current size and to any reasonably assured income arising from their current operations.[11] Such major investments are of the greatest social consequence. They are the investment projects that make possible the extraordinarily rapid growth of smaller firms. They are also the undertakings that "carry them out of their class" and, provided they are successful, enable them to make significant inroads upon the established positions of their larger and stronger competitors. These are consequently the investments that are particularly significant from the point of view of a dynamic competitive structure—i.e. from the standpoint of both industrial concentration and of competitive behavior.

But investment undertakings that are large in relation to the reasonably assured income of the company are precisely the ones for which the incentives are severely impaired by high corporate tax rates. In the first place, where the individual investment project is larger than the reasonably assured income from other operations

[10] The phrase "in proportion to the tax" used in the text implies a standard of reference in which there was no tax. This choice was made largely as a matter of expositional convenience. The conclusions developed in this paper are equally valid with respect to the differential effects of increases in tax rates, although the factor of proportionality involved is a little more complicated, being not merely the tax rate as in the former case, but rather the ratio of (a) the difference in the two rates to (b) one minus the initial rate.

[11] There are doubtless similar cases involving what would be generally considered to be "large firms" (in an absolute sense), but in view of the extent of multiplant and multiproduct operations among such firms, the proportion of investments falling in this category for "large" firms must be small relative to the proportion for smaller firms.

within the loss-offset period, the mean profit expectancy is reduced *more* than in proportion to the tax rate. Any profits that may be made if the major new investment proves successful will be taxed in full, but income available from other operations would be inadequate to cover potential losses if the undertaking is unsuccessful.[12]

Although the expectation of profit is only one of many motives leading a management to make an investment, most investments will probably not be undertaken without the prospect of some minimum rate of profit in compensation for the risk and effort involved. While an outsider cannot set a numerical value to this rate in each given case, the important fact is that in most cases such a minimum rate exists. Once profits have fallen below this level these ventures will not be undertaken, even though they may be attractive from other points of view. If taxes reduce expected profits below this level in a large number of cases, a substantial volume of employment may be lost.

Moreover, the amount of investment at risk will not, in these cases, be reduced in proportion to the tax rate; indeed, where the source of other income is removed because other operations must be suspended in order to undertake the new development, the amount of new investment at risk will be unaffected by the tax rate. But even this statement unduly minimizes the matter. In situations where the decision to embark on the new undertaking involves serious risk of incurring bankruptcy in the event of failure, the possible loss to the company from major new undertakings would be the entire value of the total investment of the company and not simply the amount specifically invested in the particular project itself. Since the loss to the owners of the company could exceed the amount invested in the new development, the rate of loss computed as a percentage of the new investment could exceed

[12] In the event that the new investment involves the commitment of the entire operations of the firm, there will be no income at all available from other sources against which losses could be offset if the new development is not successful, and the entire loss would have to be borne by the company; but the profits, if realized, would still be taxed in full. In this event, highly favorable mean expectations of profit before tax can readily become negative—i.e. turn into mean expectations of *loss*—in the face of high flat-rate corporate taxes.

Even where there is reasonably assured income from the company's existing operations (but this income would not fully cover potential losses on the new investment) expected profits will be reduced much more than in proportion to the increase in the tax rate. In making these estimates, provision must, of course, be made for the effect of the carry-back and carry-over provisions.

100 per cent. On the other hand, if the company itself has a thin equity position and the expansion was financed mostly with borrowed funds, the actual loss of the owners, in the event of bankruptcy, might be less than the dollar amount invested in the new development.

Finally, to make matters still worse, a high tax would not only lower the net return if the venture were successful, but it would also cut down on the probability of a successful outcome. Major new investment undertakings by smaller firms with limited capital resources are such that any serious hitch in the program may spell complete failure. In major experimental undertakings, it is common experience that there will be many blind alleys and unexpected delays before success is achieved. But each dead-end street adds to the capital that must be committed before the project is completed. High taxes bite deeply into the capital supply of small firms. Since one of the major elements of risk for a small firm is the danger of being caught short of capital and thus of having to abandon a project on the verge of success, high taxes may drastically reduce the prospect of success to a small firm. On the other hand, the large company has much greater leeway for experimentation and mistakes.

In summary, high flat-rate corporate income taxes severely discriminate against major investment expansions (and relatively in favor of minor expansions) because they reduce their probability of success and because they reduce the expected returns on these investments much more severely. The higher the tax, the more severe is the discrimination in each of these respects. Given the greater relative frequency of major expansions in the investment plans of smaller firms, it follows further that high flat-rate corporate income taxes discriminate with special severity against the growth of smaller independent firms and relatively, at least, in favor of larger, established companies. Consequently, the effect of high corporate income taxes on concentration by way of their effect on incentives for growth is to preserve prevailing degrees of concentration and over time to result in higher levels of concentration than would otherwise have existed. In this connection the effect of a progressive corporate income tax or of an excess profits tax would be much more pronounced than that of a flat-rate income tax.

One final point, however, needs to be emphasized in appraising the severity and seriousness of this thrust of the corporate income tax toward greater concentration. The desire of an aggressive business management to expand may be so intense that expansions will be undertaken in spite of the repressive effect of high taxes. Many such managements may be imbued with the spirit to go through with their plans, "come hell or high water." High taxes may cause such men to fail; they are unlikely to prevent them from trying. But, quite obviously, although this consideration modifies the *extent* of the repressive effect of the tax, it does not compromise the *fact* that the effect of the tax is more severe on smaller firms and that the tax tends to some degree to increase concentration.

The personal tax structure may, in some cases, significantly modify the effects of corporate taxes on management decisions to expand. The *net* effect of personal tax factors will depend on the particulars of a given case. Our analysis of the complex interactions involved may be found elsewhere.[13] In general, we conclude that, except possibly for wealthy individuals with widely diversified investments, it does not seem probable that the possibility of obtaining limited loss offsets against personal income taxes will ease the burden of the corporate tax to any appreciable degree. In cases in which the owners have invested a large percentage of their personal assets in a single business endeavor, the personal tax structure probably accentuates the repressive effect of the corporate tax.

If a business is organized as a proprietorship or partnership, the personal income tax greatly reduces the incentive of its owners to undertake major expansions—perhaps more so than the corporate tax impedes expansions by small corporations. The highly progressive rates of the personal income tax strike with full force at the profits resulting from a partnership expansion. But if the expansion is unsuccessful and results in business failure, the partners' personal assets as well as their business assets and perhaps also their jobs will be in jeopardy. Moreover, because of the progressive nature of the personal income tax, the *more* successful the venture, the *larger* would be the government's share in the profits. But the risk of loss remains, and even in the relatively favorable case where other income is available against which partnership losses could be offset, the deduction of losses from this income would result in tax savings in lower surtax brackets, whereas additional income from the partnership would throw the taxpayer into higher surtax brackets. Moreover, under these circumstances the individual partner to some degree would be risking his entire personal assets for a rela-

---

[13] Cf. Butters and Lintner, *op. cit.*, pp. 36-39.

251

tively small potential income from the partnership; this income would be taxable at high surtax rates. All in all, under most circumstances the partnership form of organization does not appear very attractive for small enterprises with a large potential growth, even in comparison with the present high taxation of corporate profits.[14]

3. Ability to Finance Growth from Retained Earnings

THE second way in which taxes can affect relative rates of growth of larger and smaller firms is through their effect on the ability to finance expansion by retained earnings. In actual practice, this is likely to be even more important than the effect of taxes on investment incentives. Managements can and often do ignore adverse incentive effects resulting from high taxes, but they cannot safely ignore any substantial impairment of necessary supplies of capital to finance expansion. A company that does not have and cannot get the funds to finance an investment program is effectively stopped, however optimistic its appraisal of profit prospects.

Retained earnings have long been a major source of funds for financing growth of American industrial corporations. This is clearly shown in the history of individual companies and industries, including many of our most rapidly growing smaller firms as well as many of our leading large corporations. Terborgh's data[15] for all nonfinancial corporations show that retained earnings amounted to over 75 per cent of the aggregate net expansion in physical assets (including inventory) during the years 1925-1929 inclusive, and over 60 per cent of such expansion in 1939-1941.[16] Corresponding esti-

[14] In this connection it is pertinent to note that one method of tax relief frequently proposed for small businesses is to allow them to compute their tax liabilities on a partnership basis, although they are organized as corporations. This privilege may be of considerable value to the owners of a corner grocery store or of a local service station. But, unless personal tax rates on incomes of, say, $10,000 and over are reduced much more than now appears feasible, it would ordinarily be of little value to small companies with prospects for large-scale growth.

[15] Data from worksheets for The Bogey of Economic Maturity (Machinery and Allied Products Institute, 1945), Chart 14, p. 145, kindly supplied to us by the author and used with permission. Retained earnings have been adjusted upward to allow for profits disclosed by audit less resulting additional taxes. If both depletion and "inventory profits" are included in retained earnings, and outlays are correspondingly adjusted, the ratio is 79.5 per cent; if both are excluded, the ratio is 79.0 per cent; if the inventory valuation adjustment is made but depletion included, the ratio is over 81 per cent.

[16] If both inventory profits and depletion are excluded from both numerator and denominator, the ratio is 61.2 per cent; if both are included, 67.5 per cent.

mates of the Department of Commerce show that the retained earnings of all nonfinancial corporations in the four years 1947-1950 amounted to about 80 per cent of the net increase in plant, equipment, and inventory in these recent years of extraordinary expansion.[17] Similarly, Dobrovolsky's recent tabulations of the National Bureau's samples of large and of small and medium-sized manufacturing corporations shows that, for both size groups of firms, retained earnings substantially exceeded net physical asset expansion not only in the late 1920's but again in the years 1939-1943.[18]

The great and continuing importance of retained earnings in financing business growth strongly suggests that the effects of taxes on concentration may be more important through this channel than through any other. In this connection, it should also be noted that retained earnings have been far larger than all the assets involved in corporate mergers, which frequently have been said to be a major determinant of concentration even in recent years. The total amount of assets involved in *all* mergers in manufacturing and mining during the eight years 1940-1947 was on the order of $5 billion; assuming that mergers have continued at the peak rates of 1945 and 1946,[19] the total would be raised to perhaps $8 billion by the end of 1951—a sum over a twelve-year period just about equal to the earnings retained by manufacturing corporations in the single year 1948, and only a modest fraction of the total retained during the full twelve-year period.

What then is the distribution of retained earnings by size of firm? And what has been the effect of taxes on this distribution? Since our main concern is with the effect of income taxes, and unprofitable firms pay no income taxes, we shall confine our analysis to the retained earnings of *profitable* corporations. Moreover, in order to deal specifically with the sector in which the issue of concentration is most important,[20] our statistical analysis will be confined to manufacturing industries.

[17] Data from *Economic Report of the President*, January 1952, pp. 203, 172. Without inventory valuation adjustments, the ratio is 83.8 per cent; after these adjustments, 79.8 per cent. Depletion is included in both cases.

[18] Sergei P. Dobrovolsky, *Corporate Income Retention, 1915-1943* (National Bureau of Economic Research 1952), pp. 74 and 79.

[19] Our tabulations indicate that assets acquired in mergers were greatest in these two years, averaging about $750 million. For sources, cf. J. K. Butters, J. Lintner and W. L. Cary, *Effects of Taxation on Corporate Mergers* (Harvard Business School, 1951), Chap. IX.

[20] Cf. Adelman, *op. cit.*, pp. 286-287.

Analysis of data in *Statistics of Income* shows the following relationships:

1. As would be expected, the distribution of retained earnings among profitable manufacturing corporations is highly concentrated. In 1947 and 1948, for instance, only 0.4 per cent of all profitable manufacturing corporations had assets of more than $50 million, but these companies had 30.6 per cent and 42.1 per cent of all earnings retained in the two years. At the other end of the scale, the 96.7 per cent of companies with assets under $5 million accounted for only 38.9 per cent and 29.7 per cent of the retained earnings of profitable manufacturers in the two years.

2. Even so, retained earnings were *less* concentrated than were total assets, net worth, profits, or even sales. Illustrative data for 1947 and 1948 are given in Table 1.

TABLE 1

Percentage of Various Totals for All Profitable Manufacturing Corporations Held by Companies with Assets over $50 million and $100 million, 1947 and 1948

	COMPANIES WITH ASSETS OVER $50 MILLION		COMPANIES WITH ASSETS OVER $100 MILLION	
	1947	*1948*	*1947*	*1948*
Retained earnings	30.6	42.1	23.1	34.5
Net worth	50.2	52.5	42.5	44.2
Total assets	49.8	52.7	42.1	44.4
Profits before taxes	38.7	47.8	30.9	39.3
Profits after taxes	39.0	48.1	31.2	39.7
Gross business receipts	40.2	42.6	32.7	35.7
Number of corporations	.4	.4	.2	.2

Source: *Statistics of Income*, Dept. of the Treasury, Part II; data supplied in correspondence.

3. This conclusion is strikingly confirmed by Table 2, which shows that *in every year* from 1931 through 1948 (the last year for which data are available) the average retained earnings of profitable smaller manufacturing companies consistently constituted a much larger percentage of their net worth,[21] than did the retained earnings of larger companies.[22] In twelve of the eighteen individual

[21] Incidentally, they also quite consistently constituted a larger percentage of their total assets.

[22] The purely statistical significance of the relationship may be judged by the rank-X^2 test with 8 degrees of freedom (cf. Milton Friedman, "The Use of Ranks to Avoid the Assumption of Normality Implicit in the Analysis of Variance," *Journal of American Statistical Association*, December 1937, pp. 675 ff.). Fisher's tables show that there is only one chance in 100 that observations drawn at

TABLE 2

Retained Earnings as a Percentage of Net Worth, All Manufacturing Corporations with Net Income, 1931-1948

(asset size classes in thousands of dollars)

Years	Total	Under $50	$50–$100	$100–$250	$250–$500	$500–$1,000	$1,000–$5,000	$5,000–$10,000	$10,000–$50,000	$50,000–$100,000	$100,000 and over	$50,000 and over
1931	.2	7.3	4.5	2.9	2.3	1.7	1.6	.7	.1			1.0ᵃ
1932	.3ᵃ	4.1	2.9	2.8	2.0	1.7	1.1	.6	.0			1.4ᵃ
1933	1.7	5.7	5.8	5.7	5.6	5.3	4.0	3.8	1.8			.2ᵃ
1934	2.0	5.1	5.4	5.7	4.9	3.7	2.1	3.0	.9			1.4
1935	2.9	6.8	6.0	5.6	5.1	4.5	3.6	2.3	1.6			2.5
1936	1.6	5.4	3.6	3.4	3.1	3.5	3.3	2.9	1.9	1.4	.3ᵃ	.0
1937	1.6	4.7	3.7	3.1	2.9	3.1	2.8	2.4	1.5	.6	.8	.8
1938	1.7	6.9	6.3	5.1	4.1	3.5	2.6	2.0	1.3	.9	.7	.8
1939	3.1	8.7	7.9	6.9	5.9	5.3	4.5	3.9	3.2	2.2	1.5	1.6
1940	4.1	9.6	8.2	7.5	6.6	6.5	5.8	4.7	4.0	4.2	2.5	2.8
1941	5.9	14.4	12.2	11.2	10.1	9.8	8.4	7.3	5.7	5.7	3.5	3.9
1942	5.7	15.3	11.7	10.2	9.2	9.0	8.4	7.8	7.0	5.6	2.8	3.2
1943	5.9	16.8	11.7	9.9	8.8	8.6	8.3	7.7	7.0	6.2	3.8	4.1
1944	4.5	19.5	13.0	10.4	8.5	7.8	7.4	6.4	5.2	4.6	2.0	2.3
1945	2.8	18.3	13.1	9.8	8.0	7.2	5.9	4.3	3.4	2.5	.1ᵃ	.2
1946	7.5	22.5	20.4	18.4	17.4	17.2	14.5	10.8	8.2	5.9	1.3	2.0
1947	9.5	18.0	16.7	15.5	15.2	15.5	15.1	12.7	10.5	9.2	5.1	5.8
1948	9.2	16.0	14.1	12.7	12.2	12.2	11.9	11.1	10.0	8.4	7.2	7.4

ᵃ Negative retained earnings resulting from an excess of dividends over net profit after taxes.
Source: Computed from *Statistics of Income*, Dept. of the Treasury; 1947 and 1948 supplied by correspondence.

years the ratios of retained earnings to net worth decline from size class to size class with no exceptions; in the remaining years, the irregularities were minor.[23]

The persistency of the relationships found between ratios for different sized groups in every one of the eighteen years strongly suggests that these relationships represent continuing characteristics of profitable firms.[24] Moreover, firms with ability to grow are likely to be the more consistently profitable firms over a period of years because they are likely to be the ones with the better products and managements. These firms are also likely to be even *more* profitable and retain an even *higher* percentage of those profits than profitable small firms in general, and *a fortiori* higher than profitable larger firms.

Thus there can be little doubt that consistently profitable smaller firms have been able to finance a more rapid rate of growth from retained earnings than larger profitable companies. The importance of this fact with respect to corporate concentration is obvious: retained earnings among profitable manufacturing corporations have been a potent factor tending to deconcentrate the manufacturing sector of the economy.[25] But the degree of its importance can appropriately

random from a parent universe in which the true mean rate of retained earnings was the same in all size classes would yield an X^2 as great as 20.09. Since the observations in Table 2 give an X^2 based on this null hypothesis of 140.31, the conclusion that retention rates are related to size of firm is clearly indicated.

Corresponding tests of the hypothesis that the observed data were drawn from a universe in which the ratios progressively declined without exception from size group to size group show it to be quite "consistent" with the data.

[23] It may also be noted that the average of the ratios for the prewar years 1931-1940, and also those for 1941-1948, declines from size class to size class without exception.

[24] In our judgment, the persistence of these relationships, together with the considerations brought out in the rest of this paragraph, persuasively establish the broad conclusions reached despite any technical qualifications that might be thought necessary due to the changes in the makeup of the profitable group of firms from year to year. Such shifts would, of course, be due to the fact that the firms in any size group that are profitable in one year may not have been so in others. Other shifts, of lesser potential significance to our conclusions, will occur as some firms move from one size group to another because of profits or losses, changes in outside liabilities, or capital accounts.

It should also be noted that the ambiguity of data for small companies (taken up later) does not affect the validity of the ratios of retained earnings to net worth, since any understatement of "true" profits implies an equal and offsetting understatement of "true" withdrawals via dividends.

[25] It is necessary to emphasize that this conclusion relates simply to the effects of retained earnings of *profitable* firms; specifically, it does *not* extend to the

be emphasized. Such differences in rates of growth are *cumulative*, and the differences in growth over a period of years—and hence the amount of *deconcentration* affected—will be substantially greater than the rates of retained earnings on net worth by themselves would suggest.[26]

Such considerations, along with the extraordinary consistency of the decline in the retained earnings to net worth ratio with increasing size of firm, leave little doubt that here is one of the major factors tending positively to reduce prevailing levels of concentration.

This conclusion is further emphasized by the evidence that retained earnings are a much more important source of funds to finance expansion for smaller than for larger concerns. Not only are retained earnings larger in relation to net worth and assets for profitable small corporations,[27] but smaller companies generally have much less access to outside capital than larger companies. Generally speaking, small companies can expect to be able to float stock only in limited periods of booming markets and even then often only on relatively unfavorable terms. In contrast, large, established concerns, in addition to their ability to float common stock with much greater ease than smaller companies, can often sell preferred stocks or bonds. These alternatives are available to smaller concerns only on a limited scale, on considerably more expensive terms, and at great risk to the common stockholder.

---

effects of all retained earnings (positive and negative) of all firms, whether profitable or not, on concentration. Unpublished data show that the negative retained earnings of *unprofitable* firms have consistently been much larger in relation to net worth and total assets for small than for large firms; *their* effect has therefore been to *increase* concentration. But this is not relevant to the present paper since, as emphasized earlier in the text, we are concerned with the effects of (income) *taxes* on concentration; only profitable firms pay taxes; therefore taxes affect concentration through retained earnings only insofar as they affect the retained earnings of *profitable* firms.

[26] As a specific illustration, the retained earnings to net worth ratio in 1947 for companies with assets between $1 and $5 million was 15.1 per cent—or not quite three times the 5.1 per cent ratio for firms over $100 million. But, if these ratios were maintained for as little as ten years, net worth of the smaller firms would have increased 308 per cent—or nearly five times the 64 per cent increase of the largest size group of companies. Similar calculations using the (still higher) retained earnings ratios of smaller size groups of firms would show even greater contrasts. While no particular significance is attached to these specific figures, they do serve to illustrate the important cumulative effects involved.

[27] They are also markedly and regularly larger in relation to *total* internal sources of funds for investment, which include such noncash expenses as depreciation and depletion allowances and other accruals as well as retained earnings, than for larger firms.

Finally, even when available, outside capital is likely to be less *acceptable* to smaller firms than to larger. This reaction is attributable to the generally more onerous terms already mentioned and also to the fact that the owner-managers of small firms are frequently unwilling to weaken their control position and freedom of action by acquiring equity capital. Such control-conscious managements are sometimes unwilling to incur the risks and restrictions involved in issuing senior equity and debt securities or in other forms of borrowing. The importance attached to control considerations depends both on management attitudes and objectives and upon such factors as how widely the company's stock is distributed.

The fact that retained earnings are a more critical source of funds for financing expansion for smaller than for larger companies leads to a further conclusion of major consequence to our analysis: high corporate income taxes will restrict the growth of smaller firms more severely than that of larger companies—and thereby tend to increase concentration—*even if* their relative impact on growth from retained earnings alone were the same for all sizes of firms. Because of the greater importance of retained earnings to smaller firms, an unshifted corporate income tax could have a neutral or favorable effect on concentration only if it were found to restrict the internally financed growth of large firms much more severely than that of smaller companies.

What, then, has been the effect of taxes on the relative ability of larger and smaller firms to grow through retained earnings? Analytically, it can be shown that higher as compared with lower corporate income tax rates will restrict potential internally financed growth more than in proportion to the differences in the rates.[28] Moreover, this restriction is *cumulative* in character and will be more severe (a) the longer the tax is in effect, (b) the higher the initial rate of the tax, (c) the higher the rate of profit earned by the company, and (d) the more conservative the dividend policy of the company in question before the tax increase. Consequently, a high flat-rate corporate income tax—or an increase in the rates of this tax—will restrict the growth of smaller firms more than that of larger firms, and thus serve to increase concentration, if two conditions are fulfilled: (1) the smaller firms are earning a higher

[28] Detailed proofs of these propositions, as well as illustrations of their impact and detailed studies of individual companies having outstanding growth records, have all been given in Butters and Lintner, *op. cit.*, Chap. VI, and John Lintner, *Tax Restrictions on Financing Business Expansion* (Ph.D. dissertation, Harvard, 1946), Chap. III and Appendix B.

rate of profit before tax than the larger firms and (2) the smaller firms are paying out a smaller proportion of their net income as dividends than large concerns.

For companies with assets of over $1 million, the statistical evidence regarding the effect of the tax laws since 1931 on concentration is unequivocal: in every year their effect was consistently and markedly to *increase* concentration within this size range. The significance of this finding is indicated by the fact that this size range in 1948 included about 10,000 manufacturing concerns.[29] Given the size of the economy and the character of most of our more important industries, it is clear that the absolute and relative size of the firms in these size classes are matters of major consequence for all those aspects of concentration most closely related to competitive practices and performance.

The evidence in question may be summarized as follows: (1) Within these size classes smaller profitable firms quite consistently enjoyed markedly higher rates of profit before taxes on net worth than larger sized firms.[30] In 1946-1948, for instance, profitable companies with assets of from $1 million to $5 million averaged virtually 30 per cent on net worth before taxes, while companies over $100 million averaged about 16 per cent, and the decline from size class to size class was quite regular and marked in virtually all of the eighteen years analyzed. (2) Effective tax rates on smaller firms in this size range were quite consistently as high and generally higher than for the larger firms. (3) With even greater regularity throughout this eighteen-year period, smaller firms retained a larger proportion of their disposable income than did larger concerns.

For instance, in the ten years 1931-1940, profitable firms with assets of between $1 million and $5 million retained an average of 27.6 per cent of their profits after taxes while firms with assets over $5 million retained 7.86 per cent. In the postwar years 1946-1948 the smaller firms retained 74.3 per cent, while the larger group retained less than 50 per cent. The share retained declines between every pair of size classes over $1 million in every one of the ten years 1939 through 1948 and, as shown in Table 3, aberrations in

[29] In this year there were 9,228 companies showing net profits and 936 with deficits or 10,164 for the total number of companies submitting balance sheets and having assets over $1 million.

[30] The available evidence indicates that this same pattern is found in the separate major divisions and individual industries within manufacturing as a whole. See W. L. Crum, *Corporate Size and Earning Power* (Harvard University Press, 1939). Spot checking for later years also confirms the relationship.

TABLE 3

Retained Earnings as a Percentage of Net Profits after Taxes, All Manufacturing Corporations with Net Income, 1931-1948

(asset size classes in thousands of dollars)

Years	Total	Under $50	$50-$100	$100-$250	$250-$500	$500-$1,000	$1,000-$5,000	$5,000-$10,000	$10,000-$50,000	$50,000-$100,000	$100,000 and Over	$50,000 or More
1931	2.6	63.4	51.4	36.8	29.7	21.2	21.1	7.6	1.7	12.0[a]		12.0[a]
1932	4.8[a]	44.0	40.5	39.4	29.0	24.0	16.9	7.7	.2	26.9[a]		26.9[a]
1933	28.4	65.4	74.7	69.0	67.8	62.3	52.9	45.8	24.2	4.6[a]		4.6[a]
1934	24.9	46.2	57.9	60.7	51.0	38.9	24.3	33.1	11.7	18.1		18.1
1935	29.4	62.0	60.1	54.5	49.1	41.7	35.9	22.9	15.8	27.3		27.3
1936	16.0	42.0	30.6	28.4	26.1	29.4	29.0	25.7	19.0	13.4	3.7[a]	.1
1937	17.0	35.8	32.1	27.1	25.8	27.4	25.8	23.4	15.6	6.9	9.8	9.3
1938	23.7	58.4	61.3	51.7	45.9	40.0	32.5	26.9	19.1	12.0	12.1	12.1
1939	35.1	68.7	67.1	60.7	52.8	49.4	42.9	39.3	34.9	26.6	21.4	22.5
1940	41.7	72.5	66.9	62.3	56.7	55.3	50.7	44.4	40.8	37.1	30.5	32.1
1941	50.0	80.0	77.5	73.5	68.5	65.6	59.5	55.8	49.0	43.8	36.3	38.0
1942	55.2	84.2	81.3	76.1	70.8	69.4	66.1	62.7	59.7	52.4	37.1	40.2
1943	57.9	83.9	79.0	73.9	70.2	69.4	66.8	63.8	59.5	54.8	47.2	48.6
1944	49.6	86.5	79.6	76.5	71.8	66.8	65.8	59.9	52.7	49.1	28.4	32.2
1945	38.1	87.8	84.0	77.7	72.6	67.6	60.8	49.4	42.4	32.6	2.4[a]	4.7
1946	58.9	86.1	86.5	83.8	80.0	79.4	75.7	66.4	59.1	50.5	19.7	27.0
1947	62.9	85.8	84.0	81.9	79.9	77.3	75.4	68.7	63.7	60.4	46.5	49.2
1948	61.8	85.3	84.3	80.3	76.6	74.6	71.3	66.8	63.2	56.2	53.7	54.1

[a] Negative retained earnings resulting from an excess of dividends over net profit after taxes.

Source: Computed from *Statistics of Income*, Dept. of the Treasury; 1947 and 1948 supplied by correspondence.

earlier years are few and minor.[31] This relationship is also found with similar consistency in a marked degree on a *marginal* as well as an average basis.[32]

The extent to which the tax structure encourages concentration among firms with assets of more than $1 million may be roughly indicated in the following way. During the eight years 1941-1948 the average rate of retained earnings on net worth of companies in the $1-$5 million group was 10.0 per cent; for companies over $100 million, 3.2 per cent. If there had been no tax, and if the companies would have retained the same percentage of the funds that were paid in taxes as they retained from their actual disposable income,[33] these rates of retained earnings would have been raised to 20.6 per cent and 5.9 per cent respectively. By using their average actual retained earnings rates, we may compute that average companies in the $1-$5 million bracket would have grown over a ten-year period by 159.3 per cent of their initial size, if they were to have been continuously profitable. Using the computed rates under an assumption of no taxes, the corresponding ten-year growth would have been 550.9 per cent. The restriction in growth due to taxes for these smaller firms may, therefore, be taken as 390 per cent of their initial size. On the basis of the same set of assumptions,[34] for companies over $100 million, the restriction in growth due to taxes would have been only 40 per cent of their initial size. Under these assumptions, taxes may be estimated to have deprived smaller firms of relatively about ten times as much growth as larger firms.[35] These estimates,

[31] For the 18 years 1931-1948, with firms over $50 million combined in one class, the table yields an Xr^2 of 48.33, in comparison with a value of 11.34 based on the null hypothesis (1 per cent level using 3 degrees of freedom) and a maximum value of 54.00 obtainable from such a table in the event of perfect consistency. Beginning with 1936 it is possible to separate the firms with over $100 million in assets. The thirteen years 1936-1948, with five columns and four degrees of freedom, the maximum value of Xr^2 assuring perfect consistency would be 52.00, the table yields a Xr^2 of 50.648, and the "one-per cent level" is 13.28.

[32] This statement is based upon regressions, for each size group separately, of dividends against profits after taxes for the years 1934-1941 (except 1936-1937) and also for 1942-1948.

[33] These percentages were 67.7 per cent and 33.3 per cent respectively.

[34] In addition to the assumptions already stated, this entire set of illustrated calculations assumes that the corporate income tax is unshifted, that the demand for the companies' products and the percentage rate of net income before taxes would not be affected by the level of the tax, and that new issues and retirements of stock would be made in the same dollar amounts. For discussion of the reasonableness of these assumptions, cf. Butters and Lintner, *op. cit.*, pp. 87-88.

[35] If instead of using average propensity to retain earnings, we use the marginal

of course, need to be adjusted downward to allow for such factors as the greater variability of earnings rates among smaller firms, but even in their present rough form they are sufficient to indicate that this effect of the tax structure probably is of major consequence.

The statistical evidence regarding the effect of taxes on concentration is considerably less clear for firms with assets of less than $1 million. In the first place, while the rate of profit earned before taxes by profitable firms generally declined with increasing size up to $1 million before the war, the wartime pattern was mixed; in the three postwar years for which data are available, average reported rate of profit tended to increase modestly with size of firm within this range. Since, however, reported profits generally tend to be substantially below "true" profits among firms with assets of less than $1 million,[36] the significance of these "reported" relationships is, to say the least, ambiguous.

Second, due to exemption features and to preferential tax rates for small companies, the average effective rate of tax on reported profits generally tended to increase with size of firm up to about the $1 million asset level, with the progression being especially marked after 1940. This apparent progression of effective tax rates with increasing size of firm would be even more marked if tax liabilities were related to "true" profits earned by firms in these size classes. On the other hand, the share of reported profits after taxes paid out in dividends consistently and markedly increased with increasing size of firm throughout the period,[37] but the pattern that would

---

propensities based on regressions for the years 1941-1948, then the computed (average) retained earnings ratios in the absence of taxes become 23.5 per cent and 8.4 per cent respectively. Over ten years the smaller companies' growth would have been 725.2 per cent of their initial size and the larger companies' growth would have been 124 per cent. Larger companies on this basis lost a growth of 87 per cent of their beginning size as a result of taxes while smaller companies lost 566 per cent or relatively seven times as much.

[36] See Joseph L. McConnell, "Corporate Earnings by Size of Firm," *Survey of Current Business*, Dept. of Commerce, May 1945, pp. 6-12, and Sidney Alexander, "The Effect of Size of Manufacturing Corporation on the Distribution of the Rate of Return," *Review of Economics and Statistics*, August 1949, pp. 229-235.

Both McConnell and Alexander find on the basis of independent tests that the understatement diminishes progressively with increasing size of firm; McConnell finds it "insignificant" for groups of firms having assets over $1 million (*op. cit.*, p. 8) and Alexander also finds it to be quite small in the $1-$5 million and larger groups.

[37] For what it is worth, we may note that this relationship was as marked and regular in the under $1 million size classes here being considered as it was among firms having assets over $1 million.

be formed by the economically relevant magnitudes is in doubt.

Such considerations would suggest that, because of the favorable tax treatment accorded smaller firms, the tax structure on balance has restricted the growth of small firms somewhat less than that of larger firms *within* the $1 million and under asset size class; its net effect within this size class may have been to facilitate some small deconcentration of the corporate structure. Before this conclusion is accepted as final, however, appropriate allowance must be made for the fact that the more vigorous and progressive companies will have higher rates of profit (and presumably more conservative dividend policies) than the average profitable company in their size group. Such firms probably were subject to effective and marginal tax rates that were as high as those on larger firms, since the tax concessions accorded smaller firms were based upon the dollar amount of profit. The impact of the tax structure on such companies, therefore, has tended to *increase* concentration even in the size groups having assets of less than $1 million.[38]

In the absence of further data and much more exhaustive analysis, it is not possible to strike a definite and firm balance between these considerations. But insofar as our concern with concentration is focused upon those aspects of competitive structure most closely related to probable market behavior, the subgroups of small firms noted are disproportionately important because these companies have the best chance of offering an effective challenge to large, well-established concerns. There is consequently a real possibility that the tax structure has been no more than neutral and may even have tended to increase effective concentration among firms having assets of less than $1 million. This probability is of course much increased when the impact of the existing excess profits tax is taken into account.

When our conclusions regarding the effects of taxes on concentration among firms having more than $1 million in assets and among those of smaller size are combined, it seems clear that the tax structure on balance tended to increase concentration insofar as its impact upon opportunities for internally financed growth are concerned. This conclusion seems clear whether one looks to the decade of the 1930's, to the war years, or even to the early postwar years. In view of the effect of relative rates of growth of profitable

[38] As previously explained, the same rate of tax will penalize the growth of such very profitable firms more severely than that of larger, less profitable companies.

firms on concentration and the critical importance of retained earnings in financing such growth, this conclusion is of major significance to our analysis.

Restrictions placed by high corporate taxes on expansion from retained earnings may be offset in part by increased reliance on outside financing. To the extent that this occurs, the restrictions due to the tax on the *total* amount of investment and growth in the economy are reduced, but the effects on concentration are worsened. As previously noted and as discussed in detail below, outside capital is generally available on less restrictive terms to large firms than to small. Moreover, managements of large companies typically are less reluctant to resort to outside financing than are managements of small companies. In terms of the effects of taxes on concentration, therefore, we may conclude not only that the internally financed growth of larger corporations is restricted relatively much less than that of smaller companies by income taxes, but also that for the larger companies relatively more of this restriction is "made up" through outside financing than is the case for smaller companies. For both reasons, corporate income taxes have markedly tended to increase concentration.

4. *Availability of Outside Capital*

IN ADDITION to their differential effects on incentives to expand and upon ability to finance expansion from internal sources, taxes can affect relative rates of growth of larger and smaller firms—and thereby concentration—by altering the availability of outside capital needed to finance growth. The effects of taxes on the availability of outside capital arise largely from considerations developed in previous sections.

Our consideration of the effects of corporate taxes on the availability of outside capital can best be focused on the more promising smaller concerns. The problem is of less practical importance for other smaller concerns because of their limited access to outside capital in any event, and the effect will be similar, though less marked.

It has been shown that a high corporate tax would sharply lower the profit expectancy of a risky expansion undertaken by a small company, and, in addition, would greatly reduce the potential expansion from retained earnings of a growing company over a period of years. But the principal attraction offered by the stock of small companies undertaking venturesome developments is the prospect of high profits and rapid growth. A high corporate tax, by limiting these prospects, would almost inevitably hold down the value of the stock of such companies.[39]

The practical effect of lower stock prices would be to make expansions financed by outside capital much less attractive to existing stockholders. These stockholders would be required to surrender an increased percentage of their ownership interest in their company as a price for a given amount of new capital. If the existing management or stockholders insisted on maintaining a specified percentage ownership in order to protect their control position, the deterioration in the *terms* on which outside capital could be obtained would reduce, often substantially, the *amount* of new capital which could be raised. This reduction in the available outside capital would increase the chances of failure in the whole investment undertaking.[40]

In this respect a high corporate tax would seriously worsen the position of a growing firm in competition with its more stable established competitors. The point may be illustrated by considering the relative effects of, say, a 25 per cent and a 50 per cent corporate tax rate on a vigorous, small, growing enterprise (Company S), and on a well-established, large competitor (Company L), which, it is assumed, has reached its full growth and is expected to operate at a relatively constant volume and level of profitability for some years to come. Since the larger competitor's net income is not needed to finance expansion, it is paid out in dividends to stockholders. For purposes of discussion, assume also that the full burden of the tax is borne by stockholders and that the stock of Company L would sell at the same multiple of its annual earnings after taxes, irrespective of the level of the tax rate. Under these circumstances a higher tax rate would reduce the price of the stock of

[39] Stock prices *in general* will not necessarily decline in proportion to the decline in (expected) net income resulting from an increased tax. Conceivably, the capital seeking the higher return available on equity investments may be sufficiently large and determined to cause the stock market to find its equilibrium at a higher price-earnings ratio with a high corporate tax than with a lower corporate tax. Even admitting this possibility, however, it is highly probable that a high corporate tax would result in a lower level of stock prices *in general* than would a lower tax. If this probability holds for stock prices in general, it may be regarded as a virtual certainty for highly speculative stocks in which the risk of complete loss is great.

[40] See above, p. 256 *et seq.*

Company L approximately in proportion to the decline in its income resulting from the higher tax. A 50 per cent tax rate, for instance, would result in a 33⅓ per cent lower price on the stock of Company L than would a 25 per cent tax rate.[41]

Under the same circumstances, however, a 50 per cent tax, as compared with a 25 per cent tax, would cause a much greater relative deterioration in the price of Company S's stock. The market valuation of its stock is presumably determined by offsetting the discounted value of the potential earning power of the company against the risks faced by the company—risks which are obviously much greater for Company S than for its established competitors. As already noted, the cumulative effect of a higher tax on such a growing company would reduce its future earning power much more than in proportion to the decline in income resulting from the tax in any given year. In addition, the higher tax would increase the risks of such a venture. For instance, the very survival of a growing company in a competitive industry, let alone its expansion, depends in large measure on its ability constantly to improve its products and to increase the efficiency of its operations. To the extent that taxes cut into the company's limited capital supply, the necessary improvements will be more difficult to introduce.

It should be noted in passing that, in addition to cutting down the retained earnings of Company S and making outside capital less accessible, a high corporate tax would indirectly decrease the borrowing power of the company. The ability of a company to borrow depends largely on the strength of its net worth and working capital positions. Increased tax payments would obviously weaken both of these positions. The resulting reduction in borrowing power would constitute a much more serious limitation on a small, growing company than on a large, established company.

To summarize, in addition to curtailing drastically the potential earnings power of Company S in future years, a high corporate tax would increase the risks confronting the company. Such a tax, on the other hand, might even make the future of Company L more

41 Suppose that Company L earns $4 million a year before taxes, that it has 4 million shares of capital stock outstanding, and that its stock sells at 10 times its annual earnings. With a corporate tax rate of 25 per cent, net income after taxes would be $3 million and the price of the stock would be $7.50 a share. With a corporate tax rate of 50 per cent, net income after taxes would be $2 million and the price of the capital stock would be $5 a share, 33 1/3 less than with a 25 per cent tax.

secure. It would lessen the intensity of the competition that established companies would face from small but rapidly growing competitors. The combined effect of all these considerations makes it appear almost certain that a high tax rate would depress the price of Company S's stock and its ability to borrow much more than that of its well-established competitors.[42]

The importance of this fact is still further accentuated when the relative need of the two companies for outside capital is compared. Even with a very high tax rate, an older, established company often would have large amounts of funds available from its noncash expenses. Indeed, the level of corporate taxes might have little effect on the actual operations of a company that had reached its full growth; higher taxes might simply mean lower dividends for stockholders.

Vigorously growing small companies, on the other hand, typically cannot rely to an equivalent degree on funds becoming available in the form of depreciation and other reserves. They must depend primarily on retained earnings and outside capital for funds with which to purchase new assets and to finance the introduction of new processes and techniques.

The general conclusion indicated by all these considerations is that after a new business has reached the stage of profitable operations, high corporate taxes exert a strongly repressive effect on expansion financed either by retained earnings or by the acquisition of outside capital, and thereby serve to increase concentration.

The effects of the personal tax structure upon the availability of outside capital to business enterprises is analytically similar to the discussion already presented in Section 1 and need not be repeated in full at this point. It should, however, be noted that investor motivations for the purchase of the stock of large, established companies may differ substantially from those for investments in small, growing companies. In particular, the desire to obtain a good *income* yield is likely to be a much more important consideration in the purchase of the stock of a large, established company than that of a small, growing company. On the other hand, the capital gains

[42] This comparison, for purposes of simplicity of presentation, has assumed that a corporate tax is not shifted to consumers or wage earners and that the price-earnings ratio of the stock of Company L would be unaffected by the level of the corporate tax rate. Neither of these rigid assumptions, however, is essential to the logic of the argument. So long as Company S and Company L are equally affected, the conclusions of the text hold.

motivation is relatively more important as a reason for the purchase of unseasoned stocks issued by small, growing companies.

Generally speaking, as we have already noted, the high marginal income tax rates tend to discourage investors from purchasing relatively risky assets such as common stocks, provided that the motivation for the purchase is to obtain an adequate income yield. On the other hand, the large differential between the income tax rates and the capital gains rates tends to stimulate the purchase of securities believed to offer good prospects of capital appreciation. On the assumption that opportunities for capital appreciation are regarded by investors as being relatively greater for investments in promising small companies than for investments in the stock of large, established companies, it could be argued with considerable force that the existing personal income tax structure tends to narrow the relative advantages of the established company in obtaining outside equity capital over that of its small but more rapidly growing competitors. If this reasoning is accepted, it follows that this aspect of the personal income tax structure tends to offset somewhat the overall impact of the tax structure that seems definitely to be in the direction of promoting greater industrial concentration.

5. *Effect on Concentration via Mergers*

THE tax structure exerts two important pressures on the owners of many closely held businesses to sell out or merge[43] with other (usually larger) companies. The first of these tax incentives is to sell out a closely held business to lessen the impact of the estate tax. The sales in this case may be caused by the liquidity problems that would be encountered in meeting estate tax liabilities if the business were still in the estate at death or by uncertainties regarding the valuation of the business for estate tax purposes. The second tax incentive is for the owners to sell out a closely held successful business in order to lessen the impact of income taxes. The motivation for such sales typically is to get profits out of the firm by the capital gains route. This is often an attractive alternative to having the profits distributed as dividends subject to the full individual income tax rates or to leaving the profits in the company and having them possibly subject to penalty taxes under Section 102.

43 Throughout this paper, the term "merger" is used in a very broad sense to refer to all combinations of formerly independent companies and not in a restricted legal or technical sense. In other words, we use the word "merger" interchangeably with the phrase, "sale or purchase of business enterprises."

The liquidity problem is how to raise the cash with which to pay the estate tax. Unless the owner has sufficient funds outside his closely held business to cover his estate tax and to meet his other liquidity needs, he is likely to feel compelled to dispose of part or all of his closely held stock during his lifetime. If he dies without doing so, his executors may be forced to make the sale after his death.

While most owners of closely held businesses of any size have to give this matter serious thought, the circumstances under which liquidity needs create strong pressures to sell are much more specialized than is often realized.[44] The great bulk of small companies— most of those with assets of less than $1 million and many considerably larger—are eliminated because no single stockholder will be subject to such large estate taxes that he will be forced to make sales that would not otherwise have occurred for the purpose of putting his estate in order. At the other extreme, most very large companies have sold stock to the public at some stage of their growth and thereby created a market for their securities. It is in between these ranges—say, especially in the $5 million to $25 million asset class—that the greatest density of sales for liquidity reasons is found.

In addition to liquidity problems, uncertainty as to the valuation which the Treasury will place on the stock of closely held companies in determining estate tax liabilities is frequently mentioned as a factor tending to force owners of closely held enterprises to sell out in anticipation of estate tax problems. An unreasonably high valuation will, of course, increase the size of the estate taxes and aggravate the severity of liquidity problems arising in connection with the tax.

The main reason for this uncertainty is simply that there is no objective test that can be applied to determine the value of the stock of closely held companies in the absence of trading of the securities of the company in question. Impartial experts often differ by wide margins in their estimates of the fair market value of such securities.

The evidence we have seen does not justify the conclusion that the Treasury is deliberately or consistently unfair in the valuation it places on the securities of closely held companies.[45] Numerous

[44] See Butters, Lintner, and Cary, *op. cit.*, Chap. ii, esp. pp. 60-71.
[45] As many instances have been cited to us in which Treasury valuations were on the low side of the range of reasonable doubt as on the high side. The most frequently expressed opinion of informed individuals has been that Treasury

businessmen, nevertheless, *believe* that an unreasonably high valuation is ordinarily placed on the securities of closely held companies by Treasury agents, and isolated instances of such valuations undoubtedly do occur. Regardless of the dubious factual foundation for this belief as to *general* Treasury policy, the fact that it is widely held and the risk of encountering a high valuation in any individual instance adversely influence the willingness of businessmen and investors to hold the securities of closely held companies— especially as the owners grow older and become more conscious of impending estate tax problems. In general, however, valuation problems do not appear to have been a major reason for the sale of closely held enterprises.[46] They seem more frequently than not to be of secondary importance in relation to other tax motivations for sale, especially liquidity considerations, and to nontax motivations.

The impact of the estate tax on the owners of closely held companies is reinforced by the combined effects of high income taxes and of low capital gains tax rates. As already noted, if owners of closely held companies are to pass their holdings on to their heirs, they must accumulate large amounts of liquid assets in order to provide for the payment of their estate taxes and for their other liquidity needs. The personal income tax along with the double taxation of dividends often makes the accumulation of such funds in adequate amounts prohibitively costly if not impossible. This difficulty has been substantially mitigated for many though not all owners of closely held companies by the Revenue Act of 1950.[47]

In addition to making it unattractive for the owners of closely held companies to retain their holdings, the tax structure further abets the decision to sell by providing very favorable tax treatment in the event that the owners decide to sell out. The gains from

---

agents ordinarily will agree to a reasonable valuation provided the taxpayer's case is carefully and effectively presented.

46 The greatest concern over Treasury valuation policies is found among owners of so-called "one-man" companies, i.e., companies which would lose much of their value when their owners ceased to direct their affairs. In view of the extraordinarily difficult problem of measuring the contribution of the owner's personal services to the value of such enterprises, unreasonably high valuations are not improbable when these contributions are large. Occasionally, the fear of unreasonably high valuations under these circumstances appears to have constituted a major reason for sale; even in these instances, however, it is not altogether clear how much of the owner's worry really had to do with death taxes as such and how much with the effects of *death* itself.

47 Cf. Butters, Lintner, and Cary, *op. cit.*, pp. 28-34. The relief provision introduced by the Revenue Act of 1950 was further modified by the Revenue Act of 1951.

such sales are capital gains and hence are taxed at a maximum rate of 26 per cent. If the sale takes the form of a tax-free exchange of securities, the owner may be able to transfer his holdings to readily marketable securities of high investment quality without incurring any taxes at all on the transaction. Thus, while funds taken out of the business as dividends may be taxed at rates as high as 92 per cent under the 1951 act, owners may convert the stock of their companies into cash or marketable securities at a tax cost ranging from zero to a maximum of 26 per cent of the gain on the sale.

Even when no attention is paid to the estate tax, perhaps because the owners are still young, the income tax structure itself may be a major factor in inducing the owners of closely held companies to sell out. This inducement will be especially strong for owners of rapidly growing companies that have developed a substantial capital value but still represent highly risky investments. Entirely apart from tax considerations, the temptation is great for the owners of such companies to cash in their gains and to invest them in less risky form while the opportunity is still available.

To the degree that the opportunity for further gains through retaining holdings is curtailed by heavy taxation—including the corporate income tax, possibly Section 102, and the personal income tax on amounts distributed as dividends—the incentive for the owners of rapidly growing companies to play safe and cash in the gains already attained at capital gains rates will be correspondingly strengthened. The rate increases of the Revenue Acts of 1950 and 1951 have substantially augmented this incentive to sell out as has, under many circumstances, the excess profits tax imposed in 1950.

Another factor that makes a sale to a large company more likely, especially if Section 102 taxes are involved, is that the tax penalties and risks confronting the purchasing company often are much less severe than those confronting the potential seller. Such a purchaser ordinarily need not be concerned about Section 102 taxes. The greater financial resources of large companies tend to reduce many of the risks encountered by a smaller, less well-established company; and, if losses should be incurred, a large purchaser would be more likely to be able to offset them against other sources of taxable income than would the existing owners. For all these reasons, a closely held company often has a substantially greater value to a potential purchaser than to its existing owners. A large purchaser, therefore, is likely to be able to offer a price so favorable that the existing

271

owners will feel that it would be foolhardy to decline the opportunity to consolidate their position by cashing in their gains.

These two combined tax effects—the estate tax and the income
tax, sometimes complicated by Section 102—have undoubtedly been
a major factor motivating the merger or sale of many independent
enterprises. But it would be incorrect to stress the importance of
this fact too strongly. For the conditions under which these tax
effects exert their full force are highly specialized and apply to only
a small proportion of all small and medium-sized companies. And
even when tax incentives are important, they are not necessarily
controlling. The problem of whether or not to sell out a closely
owned business is very complex and embraces the whole range of
human motivations and interests. Frequently such matters as the
desire to retire; to avoid the ever-increasing red tape involved in
managing an independent enterprise; to provide for management
succession; to become associated sometimes as an officer or director
with a nationally known company; to achieve competitive advantages; to consolidate risky investments; and a host of similar reasons
may far overshadow tax considerations—even when the conditions
needed to make tax considerations important are met. Moreover, in
some cases where the tax pressures are strong, they can be substantially relieved or bypassed by various courses of action other
than sale of the business to another company.[48]

In our recent study of these problems, we were able to divide eighty-
nine of the mergers covered in our field interviews into two categories: (1) those in which taxes were of major importance, and (2)
those in which they were of lesser or negligible importance, if any
attention at all was given to them. In general, mergers have been
included in the former category only when the owner with good
reason was consciously and seriously concerned about his tax problems and when other motivations for sale did not dwarf the tax
worries of the owner.

This classification indicated that for the period since 1940 taxes
have been a major reason for sale for about two-fifths, or a little
more, of the transactions in which the selling company had assets
of between $15 million and $50 million as of the date of sale, for
between one-fourth and one-third of the companies sold in the $5-
$15 million asset size class, for a little over one-fifth of the companies
in the $1-$5 million class, and only rarely for the sale of companies

[48] These alternatives are discussed in Butters, Lintner, and Cary, *op. cit.*, Chaps.

with assets of under $1 million. These fractions obviously represent only approximations of the percentage of tax-motivated sales as we have defined this concept, but within reasonable limits they provide a basis for appraising the relative role of taxes as a motivating force for recent merger activity.

By combining these conclusions with our aggregate data on reported mergers for 1940-1947, we have been able to make estimates of the over-all role of taxes in recent merger activity involving manufacturing and mining companies. Subject to a fairly wide margin of error, our estimate is that taxes were of major importance for something less than one-tenth of the total number of mergers of manufacturing and mining companies reported in the financial manuals for the years 1940 through 1947. About one-fourth of the mergers involving selling companies with total assets of over $1 million fall in this category. In terms of total assets rather than of numbers of companies, taxes appear to have been a major reason for sale in the mergers involving a little over one-fourth of the total assets of *all* companies sold in such transactions and about one-third of the assets of all companies sold with assets of over $1 million. The larger fraction for total assets transferred reflects the greater relative importance of taxes as a motive for the sale of large companies than of small companies.

To say that taxes were a major reason for sale, however, is *not* to say that the sale was caused by the tax motivation in the sense that the merger would not have occurred in its absence. Often there were several reasons for sale of approximately equal importance in the minds of the owners, and it was impossible to say that any one of them was in itself decisive. Thus the figures presented in the preceding paragraphs, subject to the margin of error inherent in our data and procedures, represent maximum estimates of the role of taxes as a cause of merger activity. They overstate to an unknown but probably large degree the sales in which tax motivations were clearly the decisive factor.

In some cases in which taxes were decisive in the *immediate* decision to sell, other nontax causes, such as the lack of adequate management succession, might have forced the owners to sell out at a later date. From the *long-run* viewpoint the effect of taxes in such cases might more properly be described as accelerating the sale rather than as causing a sale that would not otherwise have been made. For this reason, also, our figures on tax-motivated sales undoubtedly overstate the *long-run* effect of taxes as a cause for the sale of independently owned companies.

Nonetheless, if mergers in recent years had markedly increased over-all concentration, tax-motivated mergers were numerous enough to justify a conclusion that these tax factors gave a significant thrust toward higher levels of general concentration. This would be true both because tax-motivated mergers were more frequent among larger firms being sold, and also because large companies were disproportionately active buyers of other firms.

But the evidence is clear that the effects of merger activity in recent years on prevailing over-all levels of concentration were relatively minor. Since there now seems to be general agreement on this point, the evidence need not be reviewed here.[49] It, therefore, follows that tax-motivated mergers have not contributed significantly to increases in over-all levels of concentration, though they may have been of considerable importance in a few limited industrial areas of which the distilling industry is perhaps the outstanding example.

6. *Conclusions*

OUR general conclusion is that the tax structure of recent years has tended to increase levels of concentration within the corporate sector of the economy and among all business firms, but that these tax effects have been of relatively moderate proportions. This is not to say that the level of concentration itself has increased. As we have repeatedly stressed, taxes are only one factor among many that have affected the level of industrial concentration, and it appears highly probable that the nontax factors at work have been considerably more powerful than the tax factors. We leave it to other participants in this conference, however, to appraise the direction and scale of over-all changes in the level of industrial concentration. Our conclusion is simply that the net effect of the tax structure has been to produce higher levels of concentration than would otherwise have obtained.

The high rates of the corporate income tax during recent years appear to have been by far the most important feature of the tax

49 See, for instance, Jesse Markham's paper in this volume, p. 141. It should be noted that these conclusions are based on analysis of data through 1947, originally prepared in connection with studies published in 1950 and 1951. Data on numbers of mergers through 1950 confirm that there was no significant change up to that time. We have made no investigation, however, of the effects of the much greater rates of merger activity since Korea.

structure tending to increase the level of concentration. To the extent that this tax has not been shifted, it has restricted the growth of successful small companies much more severely than that of larger concerns. This conclusion applies to the effects of the tax on the availability of outside capital as well as on internally financed growth, although the latter is of greater importance. This restrictive effect of the tax has been especially marked with respect to the growth and growth potential of the more vigorous and promising concerns with the best chance of effectively challenging the established positions of their dominant competitors.

The personal income tax structure, on balance, appears to have had a much less marked effect on industrial concentration. True, the high rates at which ordinary income is taxed have tended in the various ways noted to increase the level of concentration. The relatively favorable treatment accorded long-term capital gains, however, has tended to offset some of these effects; in particular, it has tended to increase the supply of venture capital available to companies with outstanding growth prospects. When these counteracting effects are offset against each other, it appears unlikely that the personal tax structure as a whole has exerted a powerful effect in either direction on industrial concentration, though on balance it has probably tended to increase rather than to reduce existing levels of concentration.

COMMENT

DANIEL M. HOLLAND, National Bureau of Economic Research

FROM their extensive investigations, over a number of years, in the general area of the economic effects of taxation, Lintner and Butters have distilled those findings pertinent to the problem of concentration. We are indebted to them for this valuable and stimulating summary. My comments are largely peripheral, either dealing with qualifications already made by the authors or else factors that for good reason were not included within the scope of their studies.

1. The authors have struck a rich vein in the section on retained earnings although the qualification that they make in their text is important enough to be repeated here. Their analysis deals with the effect of taxation on the growth of profitable firms via retained earnings and not with the net effect of growth via retained earnings on concentration. Their investigation focuses on profitable firms only. But, as the authors tell us in a footnote, it is more important for

the ultimate effect on concentration to know the net relationship between retained earnings and growth for both profitable and unprofitable firms in each asset size class.

In connection with the findings about profitable firms, since the *Statistics of Income* classifications are based on the annual profit or loss experience, and since this is likely to be much more varied over a period of years for small than for large firms, it would be desirable to check their findings with a continuous sample of small and large firms. (This is more easily said than done. Such a sample would be difficult to set up for small firms, since the successful ones would grow into new asset size classes and, hence, out of the sample.)

The estimates of potential growth through reinvested earnings are admittedly rough, but indicative. I would like to suggest a refinement in their computation, albeit one that will not change the results substantially. As I understand it, the ratio of retained earnings to net worth for profitable corporations in the asset size class $1-$5 million was estimated assuming no corporation income taxes and applied over a ten-year period. With no corporation income tax and with the same retention rates as before assumed, there would have been an increase in the size of the average company in this class of 550 per cent. But this rate of growth is rapid enough and the time period long enough for this average size of corporation to become so large before the end of the ten-year period that it would be greater than the average size in the next highest asset class at the start of the period. Logically, therefore, the retention characteristics of this higher group should be attributed to the initially $1-$5 million average corporation at this point, and from here on its annual rate of reinvestment would be lower, so it would not grow as rapidly as the illustrative figures claim.

This same type of consideration—the decline in the rate of retention and hence deceleration in the rate of growth of profitable corporations as they grow larger—should be kept in mind as qualifying the authors' statement about the difference in retention rates for small and large corporations and the illustration which follows. "Such differences in rates of growth are *cumulative*, and the differences in growth over a period of years—and hence the amount of *deconcentration* affected will be substantially greater than the rates of retained earnings on net worth by themselves would suggest." This qualification, of course, does not change the principle established by Lintner and Butters, but it moderates its strength.

2. One of the most important reasons for using the concept of

276

concentration and measuring it is the presumed relation (which it is one of the tasks of this conference to clarify) between concentration and the extent of monopoly and market control.

For this purpose the relevant industry group for which to measure concentration should be closely related to a product or group of similar products—an industry classification more refined than the broad groups used by Butters and Lintner in their merger studies. With industries broken down into a larger number of groupings, rather large increases in concentration for some could be consistent with relatively slight changes in concentration measured for broader groups. For the aggregate results in the broad industry group could mask divergent movements in the components of the group.

A further point would show up more clearly from the data for specific industry groups. True enough, the general pattern of retention ratios that characterizes manufacturing as a whole—the decline in the ratio of retained earnings to net worth as asset size increases—is still discernible, but, as would be expected, there is much less regularity as among asset size classes, and wide differences among industry groups. Significant differences among industries show up also in the relative size and importance of small and large firms. This means that corporate income tax effects on growth potential will vary significantly with different industries. To assess this range of difference, I have made a few haphazard and crude calculations with the 1946 data. The results are interesting. They do not, in any sense, contradict Lintner's and Butters' findings; they merely point up the desirability of examining specific industry groups.

With the 1946 ratio of retained earnings to net worth (assuming no corporate tax, no change in total earnings, and a division of earnings between retentions and dividends in the same proportion as post-tax earnings were actually divided) compounded over a ten-year period for each of the asset size classes in an industry, concentration, as measured by the percentage of net worth accounted for by the five largest firms, would change to a different degree depending on the industry.[1] In the case of tobacco manufactures, for ex-

[1] The figures which follow are, at best, illustrative. Expiation for the numerous statistical sins committed in their calculation is claimed on this basis. Among the more venial is that no allowance is made for changes in asset size and, hence, retention ratios over time. Among the major sins is the use of the 1946 retention ratio alone rather than an average for a number of years, and the failure to make any allowance for the fact that the number of small firms would increase relative to the number of large firms if the corporation income tax were rescinded.

ample, the concentration ratio would have changed from 72 per cent of net worth accounted for by the five largest firms to 68 per cent. For nonferrous metals and their products there would have been a much greater decline—from 54 per cent to 16 per cent. No precision is claimed for these figures. They are intended to be no more than indicative. While they prove nothing, they do bring out the importance of directing attention to specific industry groups.

3. There is another reason why tax influences on concentration might profitably be studied on a more refined industrial classification basis. Certain provisions of the tax laws have highly differential effects on different industries and special types of taxes, of course, affect particular industries. For example, it is sometimes claimed that the high federal excise taxes on liquor that must be financed by the manufacturer create a need for an amount of working capital large enough to make it difficult for new firms to be started and to survive. (On the other hand high taxes on whisky allegedly encourage to a sizable extent the activities of a particular type of firm—bootleggers—about which we know next to nothing but which is liable to be relatively small, and this probably leads to lower concentration. The data, however, are almost impossible to collect for tax purposes, let alone for analysis.) It has also been claimed that by reducing relative price differentials a flat tax of eight cents per package on ordinary size cigarettes regardless of the price per pack, makes price competition from "economy" brands difficult, if not impossible.[2]

4. What can we conclude about the effects of taxation on concentration as a result of the work of Lintner and Butters? In brief summary, in the authors' own words, we have been told that:

a. "insofar as there are tax effects" at the formation and early growth of new enterprises stage, "their net impact has been in the direction of increasing industrial concentration."

b. ". . . the effect of high corporate income taxes on concentration

[2] These problems have recently been taken out of the area of allegation and into that of analysis in a very interesting thesis by Horace J. DePodwin, "Discharging Business Tax Liabilities" (Ph.D. dissertation, Columbia University, 1953). After a careful review of the problem, DePodwin concludes that heavy excise taxes especially those levied at a flat rate that must be paid before the commodity is sold (as is the case with the present stamp taxes of eight cents per pack on cigarettes and $10.50 per gallon on whisky), exercise a significant force tending to increase concentration. Particularly noticeable, he finds, has been the effect of excise taxation on concentration in the liquor and tobacco industries. (Elimination of the pre-payment feature of liquor and tobacco excise taxes and substitution of payment on a quarterly basis has been provided for in the Internal Revenue Code of 1954.)

by way of their effect on incentives for growth is to preserve prevailing degrees of concentration and over time to result in higher levels of concentration than would otherwise have existed."

c. In connection with the relative rate of growth of firms of different sizes through retained earnings, "corporate income taxes have markedly tended to increase concentration."

d. When analyzed from the point of view of availability of funds . . . "the over-all impact of the tax structure . . . seems definitely to be in the direction of promoting greater industrial concentration," with the capital gains tax provision of the personal income tax pulling in the opposite direction, however.

e. Analytically, both the personal and estate tax structure provide incentive to merger, and tend to increase concentration. But "tax-motivated mergers have not contributed significantly to increases in over-all levels of concentration" though they may have been of greater importance in some specific areas of which "the distilling industry is perhaps the outstanding example."

We know, therefore, that there are a number of powerful arguments for thinking that the effect of the federal tax system is in the direction of increasing concentration. Yet in the one category where it was possible to measure tax effects—in connection with mergers—it was found that concentration was very slightly affected over the period 1940-1947. From 1931-1947 and from the turn of the century to 1947 as well, over-all concentration appears to have changed little (see M. A. Adelman's article in the November 1951 *Review of Economics and Statistics*). Can we conclude, then, that the tax pressures toward increasing concentration may seem powerful in theory but are weak in practice? I do not think so. Nor do I think that we need conclude, as do Butters and Lintner, that "these tax effects have been of relatively moderate proportions." In only one of their analytical categories have they demonstrated this quantitatively. For the rest their argument is qualitative. In the present state of our knowledge of the dynamics of concentration, a tenable alternative proposition could be that in the last ten or fifteen years a significant decline in concentration would have developed had not the tax system pushed strongly in the opposite direction.

5. Analysis of the effects of the existing tax system on concentration is an important task and has been expertly performed by Lintner and Butters. But it is only part of the job. Implicit in it is this comparison: the effects of our present tax structure compared with what would have been likely to happen in the absence of taxes. But,

accepting the government's expenditure level and the need to finance at least a major part of it by tax revenues, we are brought up against a somewhat different comparison, one which involves the differential effects on concentration of the existing tax system compared with alternative tax structures. Here the possibilities are legion, but the point usually boils down to this: What will be the net effect on concentration of expanding receipts from tax A and contracting receipts from tax B by a similar amount? Lintner and Butters did not essay this task. I think it follows from their analysis, however, that were the corporation income tax to play a lesser role in our revenue structure and the personal income tax to raise a commensurately greater amount of revenue, the effect on concentration would be salutary.

CONCEPT AND STATISTICAL MEASUREMENT OF VERTICAL INTEGRATION

M. A. ADELMAN
MASSACHUSETTS INSTITUTE OF TECHNOLOGY

WE OFTEN speak of a firm as being highly integrated vertically, of one industry as being more integrated than a second, of either a firm or an industry as becoming more integrated or less integrated in the course of time. Once we speak in terms of greater and less, we have spoken in terms of quantity and have indicated the need of measuring quantity.

This need is emphasized by the fact that one commonly used measure of size and of concentration, the amount of sales, has a well-known shortcoming. This measure does not indicate the degree of vertical integration; for example, a manufacturer selling $1 million worth of goods is a much larger firm than a retailer selling the same amount. Firms of such dissimilar structure should not be classified together upon the basis of size of sales. It is a mistaken though common practice to analyze firms statistically by computing the percentage of their sales that is allocated to research, wages, or other purposes. Also, it is a regrettable fact that the "concentration ratios" developed by the Temporary National Economic Committee can be stated only in terms of sales; however, as a measure of oligopoly rather than of concentration, this is not nearly so objectionable. Furthermore, ambiguities arise when attempts are made to measure the trend of concentration through time.[1]

It seems clear that there is some kind of relationship, at least of a formal kind, between integration and concentration. The object of this paper is to develop the formal relationship as an aid to the study of the real one. Accordingly, two requirements have been set up for defining any measure of vertical integration. First, it must be an extension of, and consistent with, accepted economic doctrine. Second, it must be operational and capable of statistical treatment. Two such measures will be proposed and used here. Their use suggests that size is positively correlated with the degree of vertical integration, but the relation is not a simple one.

1. Ratio of Income to Sales

THE first proposal employs the concept of the ratio of income to

[1] M. A. Adelman, "The Measurement of Industrial Concentration," *Review of Economics and Statistics*, November 1951, pp. 272, 291.

sales. Every firm is confronted by a choice between purchasing or selling on the one hand and additional processing[2] on the other: make *or* buy, sell *or* process further. The decision depends upon the particular economies of each course of action. Through vertical integration the firm by-passes or, more accurately speaking, encompasses a market nexus. Administrative direction replaces the bargaining of the market. In the widest sense all firms, even small ones, are vertically integrated in that they could conceivably be divided into two or more firms, earlier stages selling to the later.[3]

Now, were all firms and industries *completely* integrated, there would be no sales except to final consumers. A tableau of the Leontief type[4] (but arranged on a firm rather than on an establishment basis) would be collapsed into the lowest line and the extreme right-hand column. The total sales of business firms to consumers would be equal to the income originating in the business sector of the economy. There is, of course, a whole family of income measurements, each with a different degree of netness; but assuming consistency in use, complete vertical integration would mean that the ratio Y/S (where Y denoted income, and S sales) would equal unity. The less integrated the business system, the more interfirm transactions there would be, the larger would S become, and the smaller would be the ratio.

If the firm instead of the whole economy is considered, the situation is largely but not wholly the same. The sales of the firm, whether to consumers or to other firms, are equal to the total income generated up to that point of sale. The income originating within the firm is its own contribution to that total. Thus the ratio Y/S defines the degree of integration only up to the point of sale and takes no account of operations past this point. For example, suppose that in a given industry there are three firms: a primary production firm, a manufacturing firm, and a distribution firm; each contributes one-third of total value added by the industry. The primary producer—on the unrealistic assumption that he buys nothing from other firms—would have a ratio of 1.0; the manufacturer, a ratio of .50; the distributor, one of .33. If the manufacturer integrated backward to absorb primary production, the new

[2] The word "process" or "make" means any productive activity, not merely extractive or manufacturing activity.

[3] R. H. Coase, "The Nature of the Firm," *Economica*, November 1937, p. 389.

[4] W. W. Leontief, *The Structure of American Economy* (Harvard University Press, 1941), pp. 15-20, and Tables 5 and 6.

firm would have a ratio of 1.0; if he integrated forward to absorb distribution, the new firm would have a ratio of .67.

Thus the ratio of income to sales, when calculated for the single firm, does not have the simplicity and accuracy it has when calculated for the whole business economy. The nearer we go to primary production, the less sensitive the index becomes to changes in the degree of integration. This is a serious limitation, but it can also be turned to good use. Thus, if our completely integrated primary producer has integrated forward and his ratio of income to sales has actually decreased, it follows that he must now be very asymmetrical, with the later stages buying a considerable amount from outside sources. Again, if two firms of apparently identical function show a significant difference in ratios, the identity must be spurious.

The measure of integration in an industry is in concept midway between those involving the economy and the firm. Thus, if every individual producer in the industry were completely integrated or if, as a special case of complete integration, the industry were monopolized, there would be no sales within the industry. But if the industry were finely subdivided into as many firms as there were successive processes, the amount of sales would be very much larger. Thus the ratio of sales to value added is again an index of the degree of vertical integration. But for the industry the ratio reflects two separate characteristics: one is the "stretch" of the whole industry from material entry to product exit; the other is the degree of subdivision between these two points. And for the purposes of any particular investigation, it may make a good deal of difference which characteristic is responsible for the ratio.

2. Ratio of Inventory to Sales

A SECOND proposed or alternative measure of vertical integration is the ratio of inventory to sales. The longer the production line and the more successive processes are operated by one firm, the higher the ratio. This is a derived measurement rather than a direct one. There is no limiting value which would signify complete integration, and all figures are of purely relative significance. The accuracy of this measure would probably be improved if it included only goods in process, since this would be closer to the length of the production line. The ratio of inventory to sales has one particular virtue as a measure of integration: it is not distorted by the nearness of the firm to primary production; the other ratio or measure is. On the other hand, the ratio of inventory to sales is more susceptible to meaningless comparisons.

3. *Divergent, Convergent, and Successive Functions*

AT THIS point it is useful to consider an earlier attempt at quantitative measurement of integration, both horizontal and vertical. Monograph 27 of the Temporary National Economic Committee classified multiplant firms into five broad types.[5] The most common type consisted of firms performing a "uniform function"; this illustrates the most obvious form of horizontal integration. The least common type engaged in "unrelated functions," or conglomerate integration. Of the 5,600 multiplant firms recorded by the Bureau of the Census in 1937, 2,100 controlled plants in more than one industry, but only 95 firms controlled plants without visible functional relationship among themselves. Even this number the monograph considers as an overestimate resulting from the lack of time and money to delve further.[6] Types of integration involving "uniform" and "unrelated" functions are outside the scope of this study. The other three broad classifications may be considered in detail, since they are involved to some extent in this analysis.

The "divergent functions" performed by one group of firms include: (a) "Joint products," which are defined as goods made from the same raw material or subassembly. This would seem to be horizontal rather than vertical integration. (b) "By-products," which are really joint products as commonly defined in economic theory; that is, they are technically inseparable, so that the firm cannot produce one without the other. The possession of an establishment for further processing a by-product is vertical integration. (c) "Like processes," or producing goods which are different in the physical and market sense, such as woolen and cotton woven goods. This constitutes horizontal integration.

The "convergent functions" of another group are also subdivided: (a) "Complementary products," where two or more specialized plants supply the several components of the finished product. (b) "Auxiliary products," where one plant supplies a product or products of another. Both of these seem to involve that progression from earlier to later stages of production which constitutes vertical integration and would be reflected in our two ratio measurements. (c) "Like

[5] Willard L. Thorp and Walter F. Crowder, *The Structure of Industry*, Temporary National Economic Committee, Monograph 27, 1941, Part II, Chap. 3.
[6] *Ibid.*, pp. 206-207.

markets," where physically unlike products result. This would be classified as horizontal integration.

The "successive functions" of the fifth group illustrate vertical integration in the narrowest sense.

The monograph lists, by major industrial groups, the number of central offices (of multiplant firms) operating in each group, according to the function of the central office. Although this information is interesting, it is not a measure of the degree of integration. Each central office was counted once, whether it controlled two establishments or two hundred; there is no indication of the number of employees or of the amount of value added by the establishment controlled by the central office. The total number of establishments involved is not given. Even if these data were available, this would by no means solve the problem. A "plant" is sometimes an arbitrary grouping and may as properly be called two (or more) as one. A single plant does not necessarily perform a single function or produce a single product. Thus most large firms in the rubber industry would on common-sense grounds be considered vertically integrated, but the integration or the succession of functions takes place within very large plants, so that the mere counting of plants and of central offices performing vertical functions would not indicate vertical integration.[7]

4. *Statistical Data*

WITH these various concepts in mind, we turn to the statistical evidence. Table 1 summarizes census data on multiplant production, which reflect both horizontal and vertical integration for 1939 and 1947. The change between these years is not significant; the number of establishments of the multiplant firms, as would be expected in so expansionary a period, did not increase as much as the total number of establishments of all firms, but the percentage of value added of multiplant firms[8] scarcely diminished. The establishments of the multiplant firms are substantially larger than the average establishment in terms of the number of employees and still larger in terms of value added. Thus since multiplant production is unmistakably associated with size and also with vertical and horizontal integration, these data constitute evidence of some positive association between

[7] *Ibid.*, pp. 196-197.
[8] This is not a measure of change in concentration, however, because the census does not give us the total number of manufacturing firms or the number of multiplant firms for either year.

size and vertical integration. But this association is extremely loose; nothing more precise can be obtained from the census data.

Table 2 presents a comparison of the income-sales ratios for a sample of 183 large manufacturing corporations, and Table 6 shows the same comparison for the manufacturing corporate universe. The sample was selected from available data in annual reports; for this reason the proportion of income thus accounted for varies widely among industries. For both the sample and for the universe, the denominator of the ratio is sales. This would require for strict comparability a similarly gross concept of income; hence the best numerator would be one which comprehends the whole spread between purchases of goods and services from other firms and sales. Unfortunately, such data are available in only a few of the corporate reports; therefore, income has been defined as the total of (a) payrolls, including supplemental employee payments and "fringe" benefits, (b) profits before federal income taxes, (c) interest, and (d) depreciation.

For the universe and the industry subdivisions, the denominator is corporate sales as estimated by the Department of Commerce.[9] The numerator is, in effect, income originating in the corporate sector by major industrial groups.[10] The largest element is the Commerce estimate of "wages and salaries" by industry. For each industrial grouping, the estimate has been multiplied by a factor repre-

[9] The advantage of using Commerce data arises from their conformity with the national income concept. But they are based on *Statistics of Income*, Bureau of Internal Revenue; and to the extent that corporate income tax returns are not completely consolidated, certain amounts appear as sales which are really intracorporate transfers. Hence there must be an upward bias in the sales figure and a downward bias in the Y/S ratio.

The extent of this bias is suggested by comparison of *Statistics of Income* with the *Quarterly Industrial Financial Report Series, 1949*, Federal Trade Commission and Securities and Exchange Commission, since large corporations in the latter are completely consolidated. For all manufacturing, the *Quarterly Industrial Financial Report Series, 1949* total is about 15 per cent below that of the Bureau of Internal Revenue. Unfortunately, there seem to be some factors other than consolidation involved here. The discrepancy is least in the big-business industries and largest in the small-business industries, although the importance of consolidation is just the contrary. It has so far proved impossible to devise an adjustment.

[10] This is the first attempt to construct such a table, so far as I am aware, and some revision is necessary before it can be considered satisfactory. Such refinement would be well worth while, in my opinion, because these statistics could then be used for other purposes—most notably to extend John Lintner's valuable study of corporate profits and national income, *Corporate Profits in Perspective* (American Enterprise Association, Inc., 1949).

senting the corporate share of total employee compensation in the industry. The factor is derived largely from *Census of Manufactures, 1947* and from some miscellaneous subsidiary sources. Corporate interest is the figure taken from the Bureau of Internal Revenue reports, since the Commerce estimates of interest are much too net— they measure "the payments less the receipts of relevant payer groups" rather than the interest outpayments of corporations, with which we are concerned. Corporate profits are those estimated by the *Quarterly Industrial Financial Report Series,* since the adjustments made by the Department of Commerce to fit the national income concept make its estimates less comparable with the sample and the Bureau of Internal Revenue data were not available at the time of writing.

There is a question as to whether interest should be counted as income originating within the firm, since it might be considered simply a payment for services, perhaps comparable with a payment for electric power service. Our view is that creditors should be counted as members of the corporate family. Profits plus interest include the return on the property of the corporation; to exclude interest would be to have income determined by the fortuitous effect of the company's particular capital structure, which is a matter largely of the discretion of management.

Corporate reports usually do not show the amount of rents and royalties paid out, but these items would be excluded in any event, since they are payments for services by outside persons or agencies. If the firm bought rather than rented, it would be more highly integrated and the return to capital would be higher; similarly, the firm has a choice between paying patent royalties or setting up a research department, so that payment would be shifted from royalties to salaries and to property income. Nor is the matter different in the case of the firm without any such choice. The best-known example of this is found in shoe machinery,[11] where the payments to the lessee of shoe machinery are clearly to be imputed to the latter.

No two corporate reports are exactly alike, and a host of small adjustments were necessary to keep the data comparable. An important defect of Table 2 results from the volatility of corporate profits over time and their variability among firms. The more capital-intensive the firm and the higher the ratio of property income to

---

[11] *United States* v. *United Shoe Machinery Corp.,* Commerce Clearing House, 1953, par. 67,436.

labor income generated, the wider the margin of possible error. And the more unsettled the general price level, the less precision of meaning do the profit data have: for this reason, the year 1949 was used in Tables 3A, 3B, and 4. If there were a systematic and strong association between size and profitability, there might be as a diminished echo an association between size and vertical integration. This does not seem to be the case during periods of high employment.[12]

For most branches of manufacturing, the Commerce industry groupings are at least as broad as the fields of activities of the large corporations in the sample. But some difficulties were encountered. Employee income, which is the major part of total income, is given on an establishment basis in our national income statistics, so that employee income originating in the nonmanufacturing activities of a predominantly manufacturing concern appears in the nonmanufacturing sector. But corporate profits, as recorded by the Bureau of Internal Revenue and adapted by the Department of Commerce, are shown by firms and not by establishments. This is comparable to the reports used in our sample but not comparable to the other national income statistics.[13]

The best procedure might have been to estimate, for each nonmanufacturing industry, the total of all activities operated by concerns predominantly engaged in manufacturing, in order to obtain a "mixed" universe comparable with the "mixed" sample. Since this was impossible, it was necessary to include in the activities of certain manufacturing industries those of the whole nonmanufacturing industry which supplies them, as explained in the notes to Table 3A.

Table 4 presents the ratio of the value of inventories to sales computed from data given in *Statistics of Income* for the years 1940 and 1949. Since inventories are a relatively unstable item of assets, affected not only by changes in business activity and in price but also by anticipations of both, it is desirable to choose years when these were at a minimum. During 1940 the sum of the absolute values of the inventory valuation adjustment, for all corporations and for each component of the business economy, was the lowest for any year of the period 1929-1951 (with the exception of 1935, for which

[12] Joseph L. McConnell, "Corporate Earnings by Size of Firm," *Survey of Current Business*, Dept. of Commerce, May 1945, and "1942 Corporate Profits by Size of Firm," *Survey of Current Business*, January 1946; Sidney S. Alexander, "The Effect of Size of Manufacturing Corporation on the Distribution of the Rate of Return," *Review of Economics and Statistics*, August 1949, pp. 233-235.

[13] *National Income Supplement, 1951, Survey of Current Business*, Dept. of Commerce, p. 85.

statistics are not otherwise as satisfactory).[14] The data for 1940 are unsatisfactory for two reasons: (1) 1940 is more than a decade past; (2) because consolidated tax returns were not permitted between 1934 and 1941, the figures result in an artificial equalization of firm size and an artificial increase in sales. For these reasons, it is desirable to use data for a later year. There was the smallest inventory distortion for 1949 of all nonwar years since 1940.

5. Size Associations

TABLE 1 suggests that large corporations are more integrated vertically than are small corporations; this is not satisfactorily verified in Table 2. The reasons for this inconclusive result are fairly obvious: (a) the diversity within each two-digit industry group and (b) the small number of corporations within each subgrouping. Certain such subgroups are purely formal or residual; for example, the group "Stone, clay, and glass" contains four diverse and noncomparable kinds of enterprise.

Some of the industry detail is comparable, however. In meat packing and in dairy products, there seems to be a mild association between size and degree of integration. The rest of the food firms and the tobacco firms are too diverse in their output to allow any meaningful comparison. No textile group shows any trend. No relation is observable in paper production or in chemicals, rubber, or petroleum refining. The homogeneity of the major oil companies is striking, but Standard Oil of California is substantially more integrated than any other. In primary iron and steel, among the first eight concerns, there appears to be a positive relation; and the same may be said of electrical machinery, if we exclude a rather specialized firm like Raytheon.

The transportation equipment group is perhaps the most interesting. It has long been known that General Motors (like Ford) is considerably more integrated than Chrysler; according to the table, this is in the proportion of 5 to 3. Yet one would hesitate to conclude that there was any tendency *in general* for larger automobile companies to be more integrated than smaller, for there is no significant difference between Chrysler and the other, much smaller, automobile assemblers (even if Nash-Kelvinator is disregarded as being too much a part of the electrical machinery group). The large parts makers like Briggs, Budd, and Borg-Warner are, as was to be expected, more integrated than the automobile builders other than General Motors.

[14] *Ibid.*, Table 22.

TABLE 1

Corporate Multiplant Firms by Manufacturing Industry Groups, 1939 and 1947
(PERCENTAGES REFER TO TOTAL OF INDUSTRY GROUP)

Industry Group	ESTABLISHMENTS OPERATED Number		ESTABLISHMENTS OPERATED Per Cent		Per Cent of All Production Workers		Per Cent of All Wages and Salaries		AVERAGE NUMBER OF PRODUCTION WORKERS In Corporate Multiunit Establishments[a]		In All Others	
	1939	1947	1939	1947	1939	1947	1939	1947	1939	1947	1939	1947
Food and kindred products	9,273	8,016	21.2	20.1	53.3	54.1	n.a.	54.9	46	74	11	16
Tobacco manufactures[b]	119	211	15.6	19.3	73.3	78.9	n.a.	80.9	539	386	51	25
Textile mill products	1,921	1,742	29.8	21.4	59.5	55.0	n.a.	54.1	335	364	97	80
Apparel and related products	1,431	1,669	7.1	5.4	28.1	23.9	n.a.	19.5	148	139	29	25
Lumber and lumber products (except furniture)[c]	1,957	2,169	16.1	8.3	39.6	30.3	n.a.	33.9	80	83	23	17
Furniture and fixtures[c]	463	459	9.1	6.0	27.4	26.1	n.a.	27.5	115	161	30	29
Paper and allied products	1,275	1,422	38.9	34.7	66.3	68.6	n.a.	69.2	138	188	44	46
Printing and publishing	1,223	1,202	4.9	4.1	25.2	29.3	n.a.	32.6	67	107	10	11
Chemicals and allied products	3,047	2,858	33.1	28.4	77.7	73.3	n.a.	72.0	73	120	10	17
Petroleum and coal products	643	614	65.0	44.3	92.9	85.5	n.a.	85.9	152	236	21	32
Rubber products	161	180	27.1	20.6	69.4	74.7	n.a.	76.7	520	890	85	78
Leather and leather products	627	647	17.9	12.2	48.9	44.5	n.a.	41.4	256	240	58	42
Stone, clay and glass products	1,835	1,520	26.1	13.0	57.7	55.7	n.a.	58.8	90	149	23	18
Primary metal industries[d]	(571)	1,261	21.7	23.5	54.7	77.2	n.a.	77.5	223	618	51	56
Fabricated metal products[e]	(1,318)	1,523	13.7	9.1	44.0	47.4	n.a.	47.0	144	256	29	29
Machinery (except electrical)	1,253	1,559	13.2	8.7	52.2	53.4	n.a.	53.0	218	426	30	35
Electrical machinery	441	885	21.9	22.3	67.0	73.2	n.a.	74.7	389	529	54	55
Transportation equipment	564	615	26.8	16.6	80.6	80.4	n.a.	81.3	986	1,290	70	63
Instruments and related products[e]	183	275	16.0	10.6	50.5	58.1	n.a.	59.2	211	384	39	33
Miscellaneous manufactures[e]	505	992	6.6	7.0	27.6	33.8	n.a.	35.6	103	135	19	20
Total	29,500	29,566	16.0	12.3	54.6	54.8	n.a.	56.4	146	221	29.4	25

See page 292 for footnotes.

TABLE 1 (continued)

(dollars in thousands)

Industry Group	Per Cent of Total Value Added by Manufacturers		Average Value Added by Manufacture				Average Value Added per Production Worker			
			In Corporate Multiunit Establishments a		In All Others		In Corporate Multiunit Establishments		In All Others	
	1939	1947	1939	1947	1939	1947	1939	1947	1939	1947
Food and kindred products	57.7	59.4	$ 218	$ 669	$ 43	$115	$ 4.7	$ 9.0	$ 4.0	$ 7.3
Tobacco manufactures b	87.7	89.9	2,581	2,720	67	75	4.8	7.1	1.3	3.0
Textile mill products	59.5	55.7	564	1,710	163	368	1.7	4.7	1.7	4.6
Apparel and related products	24.8	20.6	240	548	55	120	1.6	3.9	1.9	4.3
Lumber and lumber products (except furniture) c	42.0	35.4	146	407	39	67	1.8	4.9	1.7	3.9
Furniture and fixtures c	30.5	30.1	287	904	66	133	2.5	5.6	2.2	4.6
Paper and allied products	70.5	72.7	481	1,469	128	293	3.5	7.8	2.9	6.4
Printing and publishing industries	29.3	33.4	423	1,186	53	102	6.3	11.1	5.1	9.2
Chemicals and allied products	77.4	74.8	477	1,405	69	187	6.5	11.7	6.6	10.8
Petroleum and coal products	92.6	83.4	973	2,738	144	432	6.4	11.6	6.7	13.6
Rubber products	72.8	75.6	1,895	5,474	255	457	3.5	6.1	3.0	5.9
Leather and leather products	49.9	43.2	464	1,024	102	187	1.8	4.3	1.7	4.5
Stone, clay, and glass products	67.1	63.0	333	956	58	84	3.7	6.4	2.5	4.8
Primary metal industries d	62.5	78.1	646	3,570	107	308	2.9	5.8	2.1	5.5
Fabricated metal products e	45.7	47.4	469	1,530	88	170	3.2	6.0	3.0	6.0
Machinery (except electrical)	50.8	51.4	799	2,578	117	232	3.7	6.1	3.9	6.5
Electrical machinery	72.5	75.3	1,643	3,315	175	311	4.2	6.3	3.2	5.6
Transportation equipment	83.2	81.3	2,646	7,758	196	355	3.3	6.0	2.8	5.7
Instruments and related products e	57.8	60.4	962	2,371	134	184	4.6	6.2	3.4	5.6
Miscellaneous manufactures e	28.0	37.0	261	780	48	100	2.5	5.8	2.5	5.0
Total	59.4	58.2	$ 497	$1,464	$ 65	$147	$ 3.4	$ 6.6	$ 2.2	$ 5.8

291

n.a. = not available.   *Notes to Table 1*

a "Production workers" and "multiunit" are designations used in 1947. They are treated as equivalent to the "wage earners" and "controlled by central office" designations used in 1939.

Multiunit establishments include only those owned by corporations. Those owned by individuals and partnerships have been classified with "all others," because they resemble the latter much more closely. In 1947 two industry groups, "electrical machinery" and "miscellaneous manufactures," include under multiunit all types of organization in order to avoid disclosure. In both groups, however, the distortion is negligible.

b This includes in 1947 the designation "tobacco stemming and redrying," which was not included in 1939 and for which no 1939 figures are available. Of 1,086 firms in "tobacco manufactures," 163 were in this subgroup; therefore the data for the two years are not completely comparable.

c These industry groups were reclassified from 1939 to 1947, and as a consequence a retabulation of 1939 data was necessary. In a few cases figures for the individual industry groups were not available. The error introduced on account of this difficulty is, however, less than 10 per cent.

d These industry groups were reclassified from 1939 to 1947. Because of the disclosure rule, data for certain of the industries for 1939 were not available; hence the total given here is incomplete and not comparable with the 1947 data. Where the column entries are ratios rather than absolute numbers, the 1939 entries can be considered as a sample, although probably not a representative one, of the 1939 industry group.

Source: *Census of Manufactures: 1939*, Bureau of the Census, Vol. I, Chap. v; *Census of Manufactures: 1947*, Vol. I, Chap. IV.

Table 4 is based on the complete universe of manufacturing corporations, and the trend which is indicated in Tables 2 and 3 is much more striking here. Table 4 shows that in every case there is a strong trend toward higher ratios between the value of inventories and sales as the size of the firm increases. But for total manufacturing and for fifteen out of twenty industry groups in 1949,[15] firms with the largest inventories had a lower ratio than the group immediately preceding. Possibly this might be explained by the correlation of LIFO (last-in, first-out) accounting (which would understate inventories) with size of firm.[16] But the same tendency is observable in thirteen industry groups for 1940, despite the artificial equalization of firm size. Assuming, at least for the sake of the argument, that a more normal period would show the same phenomenon, how can this be interpreted? One explanation might be that, where the marketing of the product becomes an important consideration, the advantages of carrying a full line impel the larger firms not only to process to completion but also to buy semifinished products and to

[15] This is true also for 1948, although the data for that year have been omitted.

[16] J. Keith Butters, *Effects of Taxation: Inventory Accounting and Policies* (Harvard University Press, 1949), Chap. II.

(dollars in millions; ratios in per cent)

CODE	NAME OF FIRM	Sales	Wages and Salaries	Profits before Taxes	Interest Paid	Depreciation	Total Excluding Depreciation	Total Including Depreciation	Ratio of Income to Sales Excluding Depreciation	Ratio of Income to Sales Including Depreciation
						INCOME				
	Food and Kindred Products									
201	Swift and Company	$2,213	$249	$46	$3	$13	$298	$311	13.4	14.1
201	Armour and Co.	1,848	203	2	6	8	211	219	11.4	11.9
201	Wilson and Co.	709	75	7	1	3	83	86	11.6	12.1
201	Cudahy Packing	559	49	−7	1	2	43	45	7.6	8.1
201	John Morrell	293	30	a	1	1	31	32	10.5	10.9
202	National Dairy	898	157	57	2	15	216	231	24.0	25.7
202	Borden Co.	614	110	35	1	10	146	156	23.7	25.4
202	Beatrice Foods	192	26	8	a	1	34	35	17.8	18.2
202	Pet Milk(b)	138	19	7	a	2	26	28	18.8	20.3
203	California Packing Co.	169	45	16	a	4	62	66	36.6	39.1
204	General Mills	410	44	18	a	3	62	65	15.1	15.9
204	Corn Products Refining Co.	145	26	23	a	3	49	52	33.4	35.9
205	National Biscuit(b)	296	101	39	a	6	140	146	47.3	49.3
205	Sunshine Biscuit	101	27	13	a	1	39	40	39.0	39.6
205	Continental Baking	154	51	9	a	2	60	62	39.1	40.3
206	American Sugar Refining	277	23	13	a	2	37	39	13.2	14.1
206	National Sugar Refining	132	8	4	a	a	13	13	9.5	9.8
206	American Crystal Sugar Co.	32	6	3	a	1	8	9	25.1	28.1
208	Schenley Industries	201	48	40	3	4	92	96	45.6	47.8
208	Brown Forman Distributors	27	4	7	a	1	11	12	42.4	44.4
208	Anheuser-Busch	135	30	24	a	4	53	57	39.4	42.2
209	General Foods	475	69	45	1	5	114	119	24.1	25.1
	TOTAL SAMPLE	$10,018	$1,400	$409	$19	$91	$1,828	$1,919	18.2	19.2
	Tobacco									
2111	P. Lorillard	$85	$8	$11	$1	$1	$20	$21	23.4	24.7
2111	Philip Morris(d)	131	11	25	2	1	38	39	29.3	29.8
	Total Sample	$216	$19	$36	$3	$2	$58	$60	26.9	27.8

See page 301 for footnotes.

293

TABLE 2 (continued)

CODE	NAME OF FIRM	Sales	Wages and Salaries	Profits before Taxes	Interest Paid	Depreciation	Total Excluding Depreciation	Total Including Depreciation	RATIO OF INCOME TO SALES Excluding Depreciation	Including Depreciation
						INCOME				
	Textiles									
221	J. P. Stevens Co.	$278	$71	$35	n.a.	$4	$106	$110	38.1	39.6
221	Pacific Mills	99	27	6	a	2	33	35	33.6	35.4
222	West Point Manufacturing	84	23	10	a	1	33	34	39.5	40.5
223	Dan River Mills	65	26	5	n.a.	2	31	33	47.5	50.8
227	Bigelow Sanford Carpet Co.	67	26	5	a	1	31	32	45.5	47.8
227	Alexander Smith	70	29	3	n.a.	1	31	32	44.2	45.7
227	Armstrong Cork	163	54	17	n.a.	5	71	76	43.4	46.6
	Total sample	$826	$256	$81		$16	$336	$352	40.7	42.6
	Lumber									
242	Weyerhaeuser Timber Co.	$156	$49	$39	n.a.	$11	$88	$99	56.3	63.5
242	Long Bell Lumber	81	20	11	a	4	31	35	38.5	43.2
	Total Sample	$237	$69	$50		$15	$119	$134	50.2	56.5
	Furniture									
251	Simmons Co.	$110	$38	$9	a	$1	$48	$49	43.2	44.5
	Total Sample	$110	$38	$9		$1	$48	$49	43.2	44.5
	Paper									
261	International Paper	$416	$94	$89	n.a.	$15	$183	$198	44.1	47.6
261	Crown Zellerbach	168	45	34	a	6	80	86	47.4	51.2
261	St. Regis Papere	144	33	24	$1	4	58	62	40.2	43.1
261	Champion Paper and Fibre	81	27	16	a	3	44	47	54.3	58.0

261 West Virginia Pulp and Paper	88	27	14	a	5	42	47	47.1	53.4
261 Rayonier	49	15	9	a	3	25	28	51.5	57.1
264 Marathon Corp.	60	23	7	a	3	30	33	50.3	55.0
267 Container Corp. of America	115	24	15	n.a.	3	38	41	33.4	35.7
Total Sample	$1,121	$288	$208	$1	$42	$500	$542	44.6	48.3
Chemicals									
282 E. I. duPont	$1,025	$335	$334	n.a.	$57	$669	$726	65.2	70.1
282 Dow Chemical	200	61	41	$2	20	104	124	51.9	62.0
282 Allied Chemical	364	86	62	n.a.	17	147	164	40.5	45.1
282 Monsanto	166	45	28	1	9	74	83	44.5	50.0
282 Hercules Powder	121	38	17	n.a.	6	55	61	45.1	50.4
282 American Home Products	148	35	19	a	2	54	56	36.5	37.8
282 Air Reduction	90	27	11	1	4	39	43	43.0	47.8
282 International Minerals	53	14	7	a	3	21	24	40.1	45.3
282 Liquid Carbonic	38	16	2	a	2	18	20	47.4	52.6
282 Diamond Alkali	48	17	5	a	3	22	25	45.3	32.1
282 Virginia-Carolina	60	11	6	a	2	18	20	29.3	33.3
282 Commercial Solvents	33	8	5	n.a.	1	13	14	40.1	42.4
282 U.S. Industrial Chemicals	51	8	1	a	1	10	11	19.5	21.6
283 Abbott Laboratories[b]	74	20	19	a	1	39	40	52.6	54.1
283 Merck and Co.	74	22	11	n.a.	3	34	37	46.1	50.0
283 E. R. Squibb	82	18	12	a	1	30	31	36.3	37.8
283 Rexall Drug[b]	154	36	4	1	2	41	43	26.5	27.9
284 Colgate Palmolive	204	34	16	n.a.	2	50	52	24.5	25.5
289 Eastman Kodak	396	187	76	a	17	263	280	66.3	70.1
289 General Aniline and Film	80	33	5	1	3	38	41	47.5	51.3
289 American Viscose	195	71	34	n.a.	11	104	115	53.5	59.0
289 Celanese Corp.	171	61	34	3	11	98	109	57.1	63.7
Total Sample	$3,827	$1,183	$749	$9	$178	$1,941	$2,119	50.7	55.4

TABLE 2 (continued)

CODE	NAME OF FIRM	Sales	Wages and Salaries	Profits before Taxes	Interest Paid	Depreciation	Total Excluding Depreciation	Total Including Depreciation	RATIO OF INCOME TO SALES Excluding Depreciation	Including Depreciation
	Petroleum and Coal									
2911	Standard Oil (N.J.)	$2,892	$537	$442	$10	$184	$988	$1,172	34.1	37.1
2911	Standard Oil (Ind.)	1,158	219	139	7	44	364	408	31.4	35.2
2911	Socony Vacuum	1,227	228	116	5	42	349	391	28.4	31.9
2911	Texas Company	1,077	168	158	5	59	331	390	30.7	36.2
2911	Standard Oil (Calif.)	743	131	181	3	76	315	391	42.4	52.6
2911	Gulf	970	168	113	5	52	286	338	29.5	34.8
2911	Shell	816	159	102	3	48	264	312	32.3	38.2
2911	Sinclair	584	86	74	4	36	165	201	28.1	34.4
2911	Phillips	486	84	60	3	30	147	177	30.2	36.4
2911	Sun	462	98	31	a	21	129	150	27.8	32.5
2911	Atlantic Refining	446	78	33	1	27	112	139	25.1	31.2
2911	Tidewater	355	51	34	a	22	86	108	24.0	30.4
2911	Continental Oil	315	34	46	a	18	81	99	25.6	31.4
2911	Standard Oil (Ohio)	255	41	22	1	12	65	77	25.3	30.2
2911	Union Oil (Calif.)	200	34	22	2	25	58	83	29.1	41.5
2911	Skelly	164	16	32	a	13	49	62	29.8	37.8
2911	Richfield	123	20g	25	1	9	46	55	37.0	44.7
2911	Lion	66	9	12	1	4	22	26	33.3	39.4
299	Koppers Co.	191	50	12	1	5	63	68	33.0	35.6
299	Flintkote Co.	68	20	9	a	2	29	31	42.9	45.6
	Total sample	$12,598	$2,231	$1,663	$52	$729	$3,949	$4,678	31.3	37.1

			Rubber							
3011	Goodyear Tire	$634	$190	$42	$4	$20	$237	$257	37.3	40.1
3011	U.S. Rubber	518	184	23	3	13	210	223	40.4	43.1
3011	Firestone Tire	580	167	35	2	15	205	220	35.3	37.9
3011	General Tire and Rubber	93	29	2	a	2	31	33	34.0	35.5
	Total sample	$1,825	$570	$102	$9	$50	$683	$733	37.4	40.2
			Leather							
314	International Shoe	$199	$77	$19	n.a.	$2	$97	$99	48.7	49.7
	Total sample	$199	$77	$19		$2	$97	$99	48.7	49.7
			Stone, Clay, and Glass							
322	Pittsburgh Plate Glass	$281	$88	$59	n.a.	$7	$147	$154	52.2	54.3
322	Libbey Owens	134	46	38	n.a.	6	84	90	62.4	67.2
322	Anchor Hocking	71	27	8	a	2	35	37	49.0	52.1
3241	Lone Star Cement	64	14	16	n.a.	2	30	32	47.0	50.0
3241	Lehigh Portland Cement	41	12	10	n.a.	2	23	25	55.2	61.0
3272	U.S. Gypsum	138	26	35	n.a.	5	61	66	44.1	47.8
3272	National Gypsum	59	16	9	a	2	26	28	44.2	47.5
3292	Johns Manville	163	61	22	a	5	83	88	51.1	54.0
329	Minnesota Mining	115	32	24	n.a.	5	56	61	49.0	53.0
329	Harbison-Walker	43	17	8	n.a.	2	25	27	57.9	62.8
329	Carborundum Co.	39	19	1	a	1	21	22	53.8	56.4
	Total sample	$1,148	$358	$230		$39	$591	$630	51.5	54.9

TABLE 2 (continued)

CODE	NAME OF FIRM	INCOME							RATIO OF INCOME TO SALES	
		Sales	Wages and Salaries	Profits before Taxes	Interest Paid	Depreciation	Total Excluding Depreciation	Total Including Depreciation	Excluding Depreciation	Including Depreciation
	Primary Iron and Steel									
331	U.S. Steel	$2,293	$946	$295	$2	$97	$1,243	$1,340	54.2	58.4
331	Bethlehem Steel	1,267	477	171	5	33	654	687	51.6	54.2
331	Republic Steel	652	207	81	2	15	291	306	44.5	46.9
331	Jones and Laughlin	386	147	35	2	17	184	201	47.5	52.1
331	National Steel	425	105	77	1	13	183	196	42.9	46.1
331	Youngstown Sheet and Tube	335	85	52	1	10	137	147	40.9	43.9
331	Armco Steel	341	99	51	2	10	152	162	44.4	47.5
331	Inland Steel	346	88	41	2	10	131	141	37.9	40.8
331	Wheeling Steel Corp.	143	58	14	1	6	73	79	50.6	55.2
331	Colorado Fuel and Iron	138	51	16	a	3	68	71	48.9	51.4
331	Crucible	99	43	2	1	3	45	48	45.4	48.5
331	Allegheny Ludlum Steel Corp.	106	40	3	n.a.	2	43	45	41.0	42.5
331	Pittsburgh	80	33	1	a	2	35	37	43.4	46.3
331	Sharon Steel Corp.	90	29	5	a	2	34	36	38.3	40.0
331	Lukens	56	17	4	a	1	21	22	37.7	39.3
331	Granite City	46	10	5	a	1	15	16	32.1	34.8
331	Alan Wood	36	11	4	a	2	15	17	41.0	47.2
331	Copperweld	43	10	3	a	1	13	14	29.5	32.6
331	Interlake Iron	57	8	10	n.a.	2	18	20	19.3	35.1
331	Continental	23	7	2	n.a.	1	9	10	41.1	43.5
331	Rotary Electric	17	3	2	a	a	5	5	30.6	29.4
331	Detroit Steel	28	3	5	n.a.	1	8	9	28.7	32.1
	Total sample	$7,007	$2,477	$879	$19	$232	$3,377	$3,609	48.2	51.5
	Primary Nonferrous Metals									
332	Aluminum Co. of America	$347	$143	$41	n.a.	$16	$184	$200	52.9	57.6
332	Calumet and Heclab	47	14	7	a	2	22	24	46.4	51.1
332	Scovill Manufacturing	74	34	4	n.a.	3	37	40	49.9	54.1

3411	American Can	$468	$112	$48	a	$11	$160	$171	34.2	36.5
3411	Continental Can	336	86	19	$2	7	107	114	32.0	33.9
343	American Radiator	206	70	29	a	3	99	102	47.7	49.5
343	American Steel Foundries	75	27	11	n.a.	1	38	39	50.4	52.0
349	Yale and Towne	57	24	2	a	1	26	27	45.8	47.4
	Total sample	$1,142	$319	$109	$2	$23	$430	$453	37.7	39.7
	Machinery (except Electrical)									
352	International Harvester	$909	$325	$94	$1	$19	$420	$439	46.2	48.3
352	Deere and Co.	362	91	70	1	6	162	158	44.8	46.4
352	Allis-Chalmers	351	100	33	1	3	134	137	38.1	39.0
357	National Cash Register	167	106	23	1	4	129	133	77.6	79.6
352	Caterpillar Tractor	255	77	30	1	5	108	113	42.2	44.3
357	Remington Rand	148	82	17	2	5	100	105	67.4	70.9
352	J. I. Case	156	45	30		3	75	78	48.2	50.0
357	Burroughs Adding Machine	82	54	11	n.a.	1	65	66	78.8	80.5
356	Link Belt	88	35	13	n.a.	1	47	48	53.5	54.5
352	Oliver Corp.	101	30	10	a	3	41	44	40.2	43.6
3551	Food Machinery and Chemical	82	26	7	a	3	33	36	39.9	43.9
356	Fairbanks Morse	78	27	3	a	1	31	32	40.3	41.0
353	Dresser Industries	81	21	6	a	2	28	30	34.2	37.0
353	Bucyrus-Erie	62	16	11	n.a.	1	27	28	43.4	45.2
	Total sample	$2,924	$1,035	$358	$7	$57	$1,400	$1,457	47.9	49.8
	Electrical Machinery									
361	General Electric	$1,614	$650	$204	$5	$47	$858	$905	53.1	56.1
361	Westinghouse	946	376	111	4	14	490	504	51.8	53.3
366	Western Electric	858	348	69	2	17	420	437	48.9	50.9
366	Radio Corp. of America	396	141	42	1	7	184	191	46.4	48.2
366	Electric AutoLite	218	75	18	1	4	94	98	43.3	45.0
366	Sylvania Electric	103	39	5	1	2	45	47	43.6	45.6
366	Raytheon Manufacturing	56	26	2	a	1	28	29	50.2	51.8
	Total sample	$4,191	$1,655	$451	$14	$92	$2,119	$2,211	50.6	52.8

TABLE 2 (continued)

CODE	NAME OF FIRM	Sales	Wages and Salaries	Profits before Taxes	Interest Paid	Depreciation	Total Excluding Depreciation	Total Including Depreciation	Ratio Ex- cluding Depre- ciation	Ratio In- cluding Depre- ciation
							Income		*Ratio of Income to Sales*	
	Transportation Equipment									
371	General Motors	$5,701	$1,441	$1,125	$9	$110	$2,574	$2,684	45.1	47.1
371	Chrysler	2,085	349	213	a	19	563	582	27.0	27.9
371	Studebaker[h]	503	110	23	1	3	133	136	26.3	27.0
371	Nash-Kelvinator[h]	364	86	45	1	3	132	135	36.3	37.1
371	Packard	213	40	13	n.a.	3	53	56	25.0	26.3
371	Willys-Overland	142	34	5	n.a.	2	39	41	27.3	28.9
371	Fruehauf Trailor	78	22	4	1	1	27	28	34.3	35.9
371	Mack Trucks	78	29	—6	a	2	23	25	29.9	32.1
371	Kaiser-Frazer	104	41	—39	2	11	43	14	41.3	13.5
371	Briggs Manufacturing	338	123	22	n.a.	5	146	151	43.0	44.7
371	The Budd Company	267	82	26	1	5	108	113	40.6	42.3
371	Borg-Warner	252	68	36	a	4	103	107	41.0	42.5
371	Thompson Products	108	41	9	a	2	50	52	46.9	48.1
371	Eaton Manufacturing	102	27	13	n.a.	1	40	41	39.5	40.2
371	Houdaille Hershey	53	23	3	a	1	26	27	49.4	50.1
371	Stewart Warner	55	22	4	n.a.	1	26	27	46.7	49.1
372	Boeing Airplane[b]	307	135	24	a	1	159	160	51.7	52.1
372	Bendix Aviation	183	79	18	n.a.	3	97	100	53.0	54.6
372	North American Aviation	124	69	12	a	1	81	82	65.0	66.1
372	Douglas Aircraft	117	68	11	a	2	79	81	67.1	69.2
372	Lockheed	118	63	7	a	1	69	70	59.0	59.3
372	Grumman	60	23	7	n.a.	a	31	31	51.4	51.7
373	Newport News Shipbuilding and Drydock	78	35	8	n.a.	1	43	44	55.3	56.4
374	Pullman, Inc.[l]	286	63	13	n.a.	2	76	78	26.4	27.3
374	American Locomotive	147	39	9	a	2	48	50	32.5	34.0
374	Baldwin Locomotive	119	35	6	a	1	41	42	34.4	35.3
374	Westinghouse Air Brake	76	30	16	n.a.	1	46	47	60.6	61.8
374	American Parts Shoe	98	30	6	n.a.	3	37	40	39.8	43.5

Instruments

3821	The Sperry Co.	$116	$63	$8	a	$2	$72	$75	61.9	64.7
384	Johnson and Johnson	136	40	16	n.a.	2	55	57	40.6	41.9
	Total sample	$252	$103	$24		$4	$128	$132	50.8	52.4

Miscellaneous

3983	Diamond Match	$76	$23	$5	a	$1	$29	$30	37.7	39.5
3989	Remington Arms	38	17	3	n.a.	1	20	21	53.3	55.3
	Total sample	$114	$40	$8		$2	$49	$51	43.0	44.7

n.a. = not available.
a Less than $500,000.
b 1950 data.
c Sales figures are exclusive of federal excise taxes.
d Fiscal year ending March 31, 1950.
e 1947 data.
f Corporate sales figures are exclusive of federal and state taxes on gasoline and lubricants.
g Estimated.
h 1951 data.
i 1948 data.
Note: The industry code numbers approximate those used in the Census of Manufactures, Bureau of the Census. Total income is computed from unrounded data so that subtotals will not necessarily add to totals.
Source: Annual reports.

301

TABLE 3A

Ratio of all Corporate Income to all Corporate Sales by Manufacturing Industry Groups, 19.
(dollars in millions; ratios in per cent)

Industry Group	Wages and Salaries	Profits before Taxes	Interest Paid	Total Income	Sales	Rati Inc to S
Food and kindred products	$4,103	$1,600	$71.2	$5,775	$36,167	1(
Tobacco manufactures	218	250	20.6	488	1,714	2(
Textile mill products	3,134	596	31.6	3,761	10,602	3!
Apparel and related products	2,086	142	7.4	2,235	7,896	2(
Lumber and lumber products (except furniture)	970	228	7.6	1,204	3,061	3!
Furniture and fixtures	1,218	97	6.6	1,320	3,082	4:
Paper and allied products	1,496	547	22.6	2,066	5,301	3(
Printing and publishing	2,444	249	13.3	2,707	6,067	4
Chemicals and allied products	2,504	1,475	38.7	4,017	13,355	3(
Petroleum and coal products	2,041	2,446	126.8	4,614	18,450	2!
Rubber products	785	181	10.1	977	3,088	3.
Leather and leather products	900	83	5.6	988	2,750	3
Stone, clay, and glass products	1,421	522	8.7	1,952	3,917	4
Iron and steel and their products	6,123	2,042	83.1	8,253	19,921	4
Nonferrous metals and their products	1,604	477	28.2	2,109	5,587	3.
Machinery (except electrical)	4,635	1,305	21.9	5,962	13,139	4
Electrical machinery	2,496	629	16.6	3,140	8,466	3
Transportation equipment	4,426	2,199	16.0	6,642	18,963	3
Miscellaneous manufactures	1,366	290	18.3	1,673	3,229	5

Source: *Census of Mineral Industries: 1939*, Bureau of the Census; *Statistics of Income for 1946*, Bureau of Internal Revenue; *Quarterly Industrial Financial Report Series* for 1946 and 1949, Federal Trade Commission and Securities and Exchange Commission; *Census of Manufactures: 1947*, Bureau of the Census; *National Income Supplement, 1951, Survey of Current Business*, Department of Commerce.

Derivation of the data for mixed mining-manufacturing industries: The industry group "Iron and steel and their products" includes the iron-ore mining industry and part of the bituminous-coal mining industry, while "Nonferrous metals and their products" includes nonferrous metal mining. The data for the narrower definitions of these industry groups, excluding the mining industries, were obtained in the following manner: (1) Wages and salaries for 1949 were taken from the *National Income Supplement, 1951, Survey of Current Business*. (2) To this figure was applied the ratio of corporate to total wages and salaries, derived from a previous amalgamation of figures for the individual industries of *Census of Manufactures: 1947*, into those for industry groups corresponding to "Iron and steel and their products" and "Nonferrous metals and their products." In 1947, 97 per cent of all wages and salaries paid in the iron and steel industry and 95 per cent in nonferrous metals were paid by corporations. It was assumed that there had been no change up to 1949, and the *National Income Supplement, 1951* total industry group figures were so divided. (3) Profits before taxes were also taken from the *National Income Supplement, 1951*, and adjusted upward 2 per cent to compensate for the discrepancy between figures in the *National Income Supplement, 1951* and in the *Quarterly Industrial Financial Report Series*, the latter being used for most of the other industry groups. (4) Interest paid in 1949 was derived as follows: Interest paid in 1946 was obtained from the *Statistics of Income for 1946* and inflated according to the percentage change in interest-bearing liabilities, obtained from a sample of published reports, from 1946 to 1949.

To the figures obtained for the narrow industry definitions for iron and steel and their products and for nonferrous metals and their products were added those for appropriate portions of the mining industries. The procedures used for computing figures for metal mining and bituminous coal mining were similar to those outlined above, with the exception of the second step. An estimate of the approximate division between corporate and noncorporate shares of wages and salaries was made, using the *Census of Mineral Industries: 1939.* This is the most recent source of any figures or statistics of this kind, although at some future date a new census of mining will be published in conjunction with the 1950 census. Corporate firms paid 94 per cent of the total payrolls in bituminous coal mining and 95 per cent in metal mining. Since there were no later figures or indications that these percentages had been substantially altered, they were applied to the 1949 data in the *National Income Supplement, 1951.*

Metal mining data were divided between iron and steel and their products and nonferrous metals and their products on the basis of the proportion of the wages and salaries paid by iron mines to the total industry wages and salaries. Thus, 30 per cent of industry wages was paid in iron and steel and 70 per cent in nonferrous metals. Approximately 19 per cent of wages paid in bituminous coal mining was assumed to be paid in 'the iron and steel industry on the basis of the ratio of coal production to coal used in iron and steel production in 1949.

The figures for the industry group "Petroleum and coal products" were derived in the same way as the figures for the majority of the industrial groups. However, the figures for crude petroleum and pipeline transportation industries were added to this group. The data for the crude petroleum and natural gas industry were obtained in the same manner as those for iron and steel and nonferrous metals, again with the exception of the second step of the procedure. Corporate firms paid 88 per cent of total wages and salaries. For pipelines the figure was an estimate based on data in *Petroleum Facts and Figures, 1950,* American Petroleum Institute, and the 1939 census; corporations paid about 94 per cent of the total. The classification of natural gas was removed from the crude petroleum and natural gas industry and natural gas transmission from pipelines by using the ratio of gas wells to oil wells and to oil and gas wells in 1939, as given by the *Census of Mineral Industries: 1939.* The resulting figures were checked by later figures given in *Petroleum Facts and Figures, 1950.* Thus, 94 per cent of wages paid in each industry was credited to the industry group "Petroleum and coal products."

assemble on a large scale. This is particularly true of the automobile companies; indeed, the most striking decline of the ratio in the top size classes, both in 1940 and in 1949, is observable in the automobile group.

However, if we are too cautious to accept the idea of an actual decline in the degree of vertical integration as one approaches the top size class, it does seem clear that we cannot speak of any observable increase. It may not be too farfetched to say that, even if such a trend toward a decline existed, we would not know it. After all, there are only about 140 manufacturing firms with total assets

TABLE 3B

Illustration of the Derivation of Corporate Income and Sales
by Manufacturing Industry Groups, 1949
(*dollars in millions*)

Food and Kindred Products

Operation and source	Data
1. Total wages and salaries, 1949, Department of Commerce, *National Income Supplement, 1951*	$4,632.00
2. Total wages and salaries, 1947, *Census of Manufactures*	3,789.00
3. Corporate wages and salaries, 1947, *Census of Manufactures*	3,357.00
4. Line 3 divided by line 2	88.60%
5. Line 4 multiplied by line 1: estimated corporate wages	$4,103.00
6. Profits before taxes, 1949, *Quarterly Industrial Financial Report Series, 1949*	1,600.00
7. Corporate interest paid, 1946, *Statistics of Income, 1946*	59.30
8. Long- and short-term indebtedness, 1st quarter 1947, *Quarterly Industrial Financial Report Series, 1947*	1,708.00
9. Long- and short-term indebtedness, 4th quarter 1949, *Quarterly Industrial Financial Report Series, 1949*	2,092.00
10. Line 9 divided by line 8	1.2%
11. Line 7 multiplied by line 10: estimated interest paid 1949	$ 71.20
12. Income originating in corporate business: lines 5 plus 6 plus 11	5,774.00
13. Corporate sales, 1949, Department of Commerce, *National Income Supplement, 1951*	36,167.00
14. Ratio of income to sales: line 12 divided by line 13	.1597%

Source: *Statistics of Income for 1946*, Bureau of Internal Revenue; *Quarterly Industrial Financial Report Series, 1946* and *1949*, Federal Trade Commission and Securities and Exchange Commission; *Census of Manufactures: 1947*, Bureau of the Census; *National Income Supplement, 1951*, *Survey of Current Business*, Department of Commerce.

TABLE 4

Ratio of Value of Inventories to Gross Sales by Manufacturing Industry Groups
and Asset Size Classes, 1940 and 1949

Asset Size Class (thousands of dollars)	Total Manufacturing 1940	1949	Food and Kindred Products 1940	1949	Beverages 1940	1949
I. Under $50	.007	.075	.050	.042	.080	.094
II. $50-$100	.104	.094	.064	.053	.078	.097
III. 100-250	.124	.105	.078	.063	.093	.091
IV. 250-500	.147	.116	.089	.065	.109	.101
V. 500-1000	.164	.127	.099	.070	.141	.113
VI. 1000-5000	.191	.148	.123	.083	.128	.122
VII. 5000-10,000	.216	.167	.145	.107	.250	.146
VIII. 10,000-50,000	.224	.175	.160	.102	.267	.222
IX. 50,000-100,000	.260	.173	.221	.119	.417	.196
X. Over $100,000	.194	.157	.181	.094		.224
Total	.189	.152	.116	.091	.177	.177

TABLE 4 (continued)

Asset Size Class (thousands of dollars)	Tobacco Manufactures		Textile Mill Products		Apparel and Related Products	
	1940	1949	1940	1949	1940	1949
I. Under $50	.116	.148	.073	.064	.056	.053
II. $50-$100	.162	.197	.114	.094	.083	.085
III. 100-250	.220	.191	.137	.113	.104	.103
IV. 250-500	.195	.199	.165	.126	.146	.121
V. 500-1000	.300	.238	.189	.138	.151	.138
VI. 1000-5000	.347	.408	.219	.169	.206	.157
VII. 5000-10,000	.238	.286	.272	.184	.295	.192
VIII. 10,000-50,000	.521	.409	.327	.223	.247	.193
IX. 50,000-100,000	.433	.486	.355	.234		.249
X. Over $100,000	.424	.490		.184		
Total	.421	.502	.233	.179	.129	.131

Asset Size Class (thousands of dollars)	Lumber and Lumber Products (except furniture)		Furniture and Finished Lumber Products		Paper and Allied Products	
	1940	1949	1940	1949	1940	1949
I. Under $50	.098	.081	.117	.099	.102	.075
II. $50-$100	.140	.108	.159	.126	.114	.096
III. 100-250	.170	.125	.176	.126	.125	.103
IV. 250-500	.191	.144	.195	.143	.141	.109
V. 500-1000	.229	.157	.210	.152	.155	.110
VI. 1000-5000	.243	.186	.236	.159	.178	.118
VII. 5000-10,000	.189	.179	.257	.190	.176	.141
VIII. 10,000-50,000	.262	.164	.260	.161	.182	.138
IX. 50,000-100,000		.151	.272	.186	.145	.130
X. Over $100,000	.154	.069			.202	.117
Total	.208	.157	.208	.148	.167	.125

Asset Size Class (thousands of dollars)	Printing and Publishing		Chemicals and Allied Products		Petroleum and Coal Products	
	1940	1949	1940	1949	1940	1949
I. Under $50	.044	.042	.122	.120	.061	.064
II. $50-$100	.067	.055	.130	.112	.045	.053
III. 100-250	.080	.063	.128	.108	.052	.060
IV. 250-500	.090	.071	.156	.105	.072	.062
V. 500-1000	.094	.083	.183	.122	.107	.074
VI. 1000-5000	.108	.097	.195	.141	.103	.075
VII. 5000-10,000	.071	.094	.223	.157	.164	.101
VIII. 10,000-50,000	.071	.086	.195	.172	.169	.137
IX. 50,000-100,000	.107	.077	.216	.171	.171	.115
X. Over $100,000	.043	.046	.138	.166	.185	.131
Total	.082	.080	.182	.157	.174	.127

305

TABLE 4 (*continued*)

Asset Size Class (thousands of dollars)	Rubber Products		Leather and Leather Products		Stone, Clay, and Glass Products	
	1940	1949	1940	1949	1940	1949
I. Under $50	.081	.083	.091	.090	.125	.098
II. $50-$100	.126	.091	.109	.101	.127	.094
III. 100-250	.133	.086	.125	.107	.146	.100
IV. 250-500	.153	.103	.170	.117	.163	.096
V. 500-1000	.158	.087	.202	.149	.154	.107
VI. 1000-5000	.165	.115	.306	.175	.187	.132
VII. 5000-10,000	.193	.102	.218	.217	.237	.168
VIII. 10,000-50,000	.327	.207	.271	.181	.239	.172
IX. 50,000-100,000		.290	.296	.252	.138	.156
X. Over $100,000	.250	.199		.247	.144	.101
Total	.229	.177	.215	.166	.183	.136

Asset Size Class (thousands of dollars)	Iron, Steel, and Their Products		Nonferrous Metals and Their Products		Primary Metals	
	1940	1949	1940	1949	1940	1949
I. Under $50	.101	n.a.	.099	n.a.	n.a.	.066
II. $50-$100	.127	n.a.	.122	n.a.	n.a.	.063
III. 100-250	.147	n.a.	.137	n.a.	n.a.	.076
IV. 250-500	.159	n.a.	.159	n.a.	n.a.	.095
V. 500-1000	.181	n.a.	.180	n.a.	n.a.	.103
VI. 1000-5000	.207	n.a.	.191	n.a.	n.a.	.133
VII. 5000-10,000	.218	n.a.	.173	n.a.	n.a.	.143
VIII. 10,000-50,000	.219	n.a.	.211	n.a.	n.a.	.170
IX. 50,000-100,000	.293	n.a.	.233	n.a.	n.a.	.151
X. Over $100,000	.277	n.a.	.277	n.a.	n.a.	.156
Total	.229	n.a.	.201	n.a.	n.a.	.151

Asset Size Class (thousands of dollars)	Fabricated Metal Products		Electrical Machinery and Equipment	
	1940	1949	1940	1949
I. Under $50	n.a.	.096	.149	.131
II. $50-$100	n.a.	.114	.142	.147
III. 100-250	n.a.	.125	.155	.151
IV. 250-500	n.a.	.142	.155	.159
V. 500-1000	n.a.	.155	.182	.172
VI. 1000-5000	n.a.	.172	.201	.184
VII. 5000-10,000	n.a.	.196	.205	.190
VIII. 10,000-50,000	n.a.	.186	.212	.174
IX. 50,000-100,000	n.a.	.160		.125
X. Over $100,000	n.a.	.166	.223	.199
Total	n.a.	.165	.206	.184

TABLE 4 (continued)

Asset Size Class (thousands of dollars)	Machinery (except Electrical and Transportation Equipment) 1940	1949	Automobiles and Equipment (except Electrical) 1940	1949
I. Under $50	.131	.108	.112	.117
II. $50-$100	.162	.137	.130	.139
III. 100-250	.177	.155	.125	.128
IV. 250-500	.198	.187	.175	.165
V. 500-1000	.206	.193	.159	.145
VI. 1000-5000	.250	.224	.152	.188
VII. 5000-10,000	.286	.236	.187	.147
VIII. 10,000-50,000	.310	.247	.153	.161
IX. 50,000-100,000	.296	.237	.180	.151
X. Over $100,000	.355	.245	.117	.103
Total	.267	.228	.132	.116

Asset Size Class (thousands of dollars)	Transportation Equipment (except Automobiles) 1940	1949	Other Manufacturing 1940	1949	Manufacturing Not Allocable 1940	1949
I. Under $50	.112	.097	.105	.106	.126	n.a.
II. $50-$100	.118	.141	.145	.124	.142	n.a.
III. 100-250	.152	.153	.163	.133	.158	n.a.
IV. 250-500	.186	.178	.188	.148	.164	n.a.
V. 500-1000	.220	.163	.208	.166	.213	n.a.
VI. 1000-5000	.273	.186	.254	.193	.201	n.a.
VII. 5000-10,000	.235	.248	.328	.196	.266	n.a.
VIII. 10,000-50,000	.288	.179	.293	.205	.327	n.a.
IX. 50,000-100,000	.495	.241		.299		n.a.
X. Over $100,000	.307	.244	.311			
Total	.335	.220	.230	.174	.191	n.a.

Asset Size Class (thousands of dollars)	Ordnance and Accessories 1949	Scientific Instruments, Photographic Equipment, Watches, Clocks 1949
I. Under $50	.169	.137
II. $50-$100	.205	.114
III. 100-250	.195	.188
IV. 250-500	.107	.177
V. 500-1000	.423	.229
VI. 1000-5000	.220	.239
VII. 5000-10,000	.674	.260
VIII. 10,000-50,000	.321	.277
IX. 50,000-100,000		.300
X. Over $100,000	.378	.228
Total	.352	.249

n.a. (not available)
Source: *Statistics of Income* for 1940 and 1949, Bureau of Internal Revenue. Complete tabulations for years following 1947 were unpublished in 1952. Access to the unpublished data was by courtesy of Joseph R. Pechman of the Treasury Department.

over $100 million; within the group, the variation from lowest to highest is over 4,000 per cent; and if we subdivide by industries, the samples become, in almost every case, so small as to lose any reliability. Or, what amounts to the same thing, the large firm is so much a historically individual one that the general influences are merged and hidden in the particular situation. And, of course, the large firms often cross industry boundaries, which makes the samples even less reliable.

6. *Trends over Time*

TABLES 5 to 8 measure the trend of integration through time. Table 5 indicates no perceptible change in the degree of vertical integration among manufacturing plants (not firms) since 1849; Table 6, covering all firms since 1929, also shows no change. This is our only evidence for the long-term trend of integration over large areas of the economy. It is obvious but bears repeating that these are broad averages that indicate nothing about individual subgroups.[17]

Table 7 measures vertical integration of the U.S. Steel Corporation since 1902. Fortunately, both variants of income are available: (1) the spread between total sales and total payments to other firms and (2) the total of wages, profits before taxes, interest, and depreciation. There are no significant discrepancies between the two series shown in columns 4 and 12 in Table 7. As noted earlier, the ratio of income to sales is much more sensitive to changes in backward integration than to changes in forward integration. If U.S. Steel had become more integrated after 1902, it would probably have been forward integration, for it began operations nearly self-sufficient in raw materials. Hence an increase in the ratio would be evidence of a real increase in integration greater than the apparent increase. But no significant increase is discernible. U.S. Steel has acquired many companies since 1902 and built many plants for itself, but it is no more nor less self-sufficient, that is, no more nor less dependent on the market, than it was fifty years ago.

However, this stability of the statistics is consistent with at least two hypotheses. Suppose that the product mix of U.S. Steel changed, with products requiring relatively little fabrication replacing products requiring much fabrication. This would tend to lower the ratio. But over the same period, suppose also that U.S. Steel acquired more capacity in later stages, becoming more integrated vertically and increasing its ratio of income to sales. Two such opposing

17 See the three principal qualifications discussed below.

tendencies could exist and precisely offset each other, leaving the ratio unchanged. This hypothesis is certainly not absurd, but until it is supported by further evidence, it is less tenable than the much simpler hypothesis that there has not been much change in the vertical integration of U.S. Steel.

Table 8 presents the results (omitting the computation) for ten major steel companies other than U.S. Steel. The data are not amenable to any formal manipulation, but for the larger producers, from Bethlehem to Inland, there seems to be no marked trend over time. Some of the smaller companies, like Wheeling Steel Corporation, may be increasing their degree of vertical integration.

Certain qualifications must be borne in mind when using data of this kind.[18] The ratio of value added to value of products or of income to sales can be affected not only by the integration of manufacturing processes but also by three broad types of fortuitous developments which are discussed below.

1. The first of these involves price movements. The price changes of raw materials, manufactured fuels, and imported semimanufactures purchased may differ from the price movements of manufactured goods. An increase in the prices of raw materials purchased would result in a change of roughly the same order of magnitude in value of products but would have a much smaller effect, and that only of an indirect kind, upon value added. Over the long run, this is not an important qualification, because there is no reason to believe that since 1849 the long-term price movements of raw materials and other purchases have differed significantly from the long-term movement in prices of manufactured goods. The only way to test this hypothesis is to compare the statistics on agricultural and nonagricultural prices; the comparison does not support such a hypothesis.

However, it is obvious that the short-term price movements of manufactured products differ markedly from those of nonmanufactured raw materials. This is essentially a cyclical movement. If the census of manufactures were taken annually, or oftener, comparisons could be made from peak to peak or trough to trough. Since this is not the case, one might look for cyclical movements which happened to coincide roughly with the census years. A better procedure would be to take averages of prices for decades or for overlapping decades, as the National Bureau of Economic Research

[18] My obligation to Maxwell R. Conklin is great, but he bears no responsibility for any errors in the following discussion.

usually does. It is a nice question how many such overlapping decades one needs to consider. In general, the less variable the ratio, the fewer the number of observations needed to establish its constancy apart from random fluctuations.

2. The second possible distortion of these ratios would be caused by shifts in the pattern of output.

a. First, it might be the case that in each individual industry integration was, say, decreasing but that there was a shift from the less to the more integrated industries. In such a situation the ratio for every industry would show a decline, although the ratio for manufactures as a whole might be stable or even show an increase. Each individual industry would be becoming less integrated, but the economy as a whole would be becoming more integrated.

b. In the second situation, if the industries in which the prices of materials consumed were very high were to expand more rapidly than those industries in which the prices of materials were very low, the ratio of value added to value of products would decrease, and vice versa. This would be not a paradox but a statistical mirage. However, there are two reasons for doubting that the results would be significantly distorted in this way. First, a constant shift from lower- to higher-priced raw materials, or vice versa, would, over the years, be reflected in an upward or downward movement of raw material prices relative to others. This must be the case, if the average of raw material prices is a weighted average. Second, even if there were a real possibility of such distortion occurring between any two given industries, it would become of negligible importance when scores or hundreds of groups are involved. The larger the number of separate forces, the less the influence of random events.

3. Finally, the Bureau of the Census may classify as two plants a production unit that was treated as a single plant in earlier censuses. The effect of such action would be to increase the value of products without any increase in value added. It is hardly conceivable that such distortions could affect the figures for manufactures as a whole, but they might well be significant for a given minor industry group.

In summary it can be said that the ratio of income to sales as a measure of integration may be distorted by random "errors" (in the statistical, not the computational, sense), and it certainly is distorted by cyclical divergences in price movements. Obviously, comparisons among small industrial groups are dangerous unless it can be established that each group is homogeneous in all aspects which may affect the ratio. Even for all manufactures, comparisons over a short period are misleading as often as not.

Our aim at this point is not the measurement of secular trend but the much more modest objective of determining whether the trend differs significantly from zero. For this very limited purpose the length of the time period, especially for Tables 5 and 7, makes it difficult to imagine an accumulation of random errors which would just offset some tendency one way or the other, leaving the horizontal trend line we are able to observe. For more precise answers, the ratio must be adjusted in various ways; if these adjustments cannot be made, the ratio cannot be used.[19]

The ratio is, even for the individual firm, an aggregative measure in that it reflects the net outcome of all internal and external forces influencing the degree of vertical integration. It indicates nothing about any particular market or source of supply.

7. Paradoxes of Technical Change

THE statistical measures of vertical integration proposed here are not necessarily better or worse than the more traditional concepts. But they are different from those measures and do not serve only as an approximation to them. Furthermore, the ratio Y/S depends on a certain concept of *size* in economics; if that concept is unacceptable, the ratio is invalid.

The size of any part of the economic world is defined as the amount of income generated there or of factor cost absorbed.[20] Measurement of the size of fixed assets by the cost of acquisition (adjusted for price changes if need be) is only a variant of the income approach: it is the cumulation of past factor cost totals. Size is a value magnitude, and relative size is a ratio of two or more values.

Thus, it appears that the large firms' percentage of total value added is about the same as their share of total employee compensation (see Table 1). The large firms use more capital per employee but

[19] Because the meaning of the total "value of products" standing alone is limited and because this figure was continually misused over the years, the Bureau of the Census, after extensive consultation, reluctantly decided not to publish the figure for the 1947 and later censuses of manufactures. The Bureau has, however, informed the author that "the 1947 ratio, as compared to that for 1939, does not show evidence of increasing integration of plants."

[20] For our purpose, we need not consider the problem of income at market value or factor cost.

TABLE 5

Ratio of Value Added by Manufacture to Total Value of Products,
Selected Years, 1849-1939
(dollars in billions; ratio in per cent)

Year	Total Value of Products	Value Added by Manufacture	Ratio of Value Added to Total Value
1849	$ 1.0	$ 0.4	40.0
1859	1.9	0.8	42.1
1869	3.4	1.4	41.2
1879	5.4	2.0	37.0
1889	9.4	4.2	44.7
1899a	13.0	5.7	43.8
1899b	11.0	4.6	41.8
1904	14.3	6.0	41.9
1909	19.9	8.2	41.2
1914a	23.4	9.4	40.1
1914b	23.0	9.2	40.0
1919	60.0	23.7	39.5
1921	41.6	17.3	41.6
1923	58.2	24.6	42.3
1925	60.8	25.7	42.3
1927	60.3	26.3	43.6
1929	68.0	30.6	45.0
1931	39.8	18.6	46.7
1933	30.6	14.0	45.8
1935	45.0	18.6	41.3
1937	60.7	25.2	41.6
1939	56.8	24.7	43.5

a Old basis.
b New basis.
Source: *Census of Manufactures*, Bureau of the Census. Data for 1947 are not available. See discussion in text.

no more capital per unit of wage. If the measure of capital intensity is the hybrid ratio of value units to physical units, then large firms are more "capital intensive"; if the measure is the ratio of two value units, they are not. The latter ratio seems more meaningful and useful. In this case, it has a clear implication for the study of cost behavior. The cost structures of large and small manufacturing firms are not significantly different; large firms do not usually have higher overhead or capital costs, and lower labor costs, per unit of output than do small firms in the same broad industrial group.

Some paradoxes arise in studying technical change. Suppose that the steel industry installs the continuous casting process, eliminating the pouring of steel ingots, reheating, and rough shaping before fabrication. Costs and prices would fall, in the long run, by about the same amount; so would Y and S, and hence the ratio Y/S, as shown in tables such as 7 and 8, would decline; steel manufacture

TABLE 6

Ratio of all Corporate Income to all Corporate Sales, 1929-1951
(*dollars in billions; ratios in per cent*)

Year	Sales	Total Income	Ratio of Income to Sales
1929	$138.6	$45.2	32.6
1930	118.3	38.2	32.3
1931	92.4	28.1	30.4
1932	69.2	18.3	26.4
1933	73.0	17.2	23.5
1934	89.6	23.2	25.9
1935	102.0	27.0	26.5
1936	119.5	32.0	26.8
1937	128.9	37.3	29.0
1938	108.6	32.0	29.4
1939	120.8	36.0	29.8
1940	135.2	42.2	31.2
1941	176.2	56.5	32.0
1942	202.8	72.9	35.9
1943	233.4	88.2	37.9
1944	246.7	90.8	36.8
1945	239.5	82.8	34.6
1946	270.9	87.2	31.1
1947	347.8	105.8	30.4
1948	388.7	121.4	31.2
1949	370.1	116.5	31.5
1950	423.9	131.2	31.0
1951	484.9	152.3	31.4

Source: *National Income Supplement, 1951, Survey of Current Business*, Department of Commerce; *Survey of Current Business*, July 1952, Tables 12, 29.

would be said to be less integrated. Most of the reduction would come in capital costs; the labor used might well be more skilled and highly paid; the steel industry would be less capital-intensive and more labor-intensive.

Another example: a grocery supermarket is a larger and costlier distribution unit than any of the stores it replaces. Yet the cost of moving a given unit of food through the supermarket is roughly half that of moving it through a service store;[21] hence an integrated distributor who was also a manufacturer (as a few chains are) became less integrated by changing to supermarkets. And the wages of clerks are greater per unit of "output" in a supermarket than in an old-fashioned store, so the glittering modern supermarket is more labor-intensive than its predecessor.

Such decreases in integration, I would maintain, are genuine and

[21] The reason is not only that capital and labor are used much more efficiently but also that the consumer has taken over the function of collection of goods, of delivery, and to a considerable extent, of holding inventory.

TABLE 7

Ratio of Two Variants of Income to Sales, U.S. Steel Corp., 1902-1952

(dollars in millions; ratios in per cent)

Year	Purchases (1)	Sales (2)	Income A (Margin) (2—1) (3)	Ratio of Income A to Sales (4)	Wages and Salaries (5)	Profits after Taxes (6)	Federal Income and Excess Profits Taxes (7)	Profits before Taxes (6+7) (8)	Interest Paid (9)	Depreciation (10)	Income B (5+8+9+10) (11)	Ratio of Income B to Sales (11÷2) (12)
1902	$160.8	$423.1	$262.3	62.0	$120.5	$90.3		$90.3	$21.3	$27.8	$259.9	61.4
1903	164.1	398.2	234.1	58.8	120.8	55.4		55.4	25.6	29.3	231.1	58.0
1904	142.3	324.9	182.6	56.2	101.0	30.2		30.2	30.1	18.2	179.5	55.2
1905	151.1	409.2	258.1	63.1	128.1	68.6		68.6	29.8	28.0	254.5	62.2
1906	168.7	484.0	315.3	65.1	147.8	98.1		98.1	29.4	35.6	310.9	64.2
1907	169.1	504.4	335.3	66.5	160.8	104.6		104.6	29.4	35.1	329.9	65.4
1908	104.9	331.6	226.7	68.4	120.5	45.7		45.7	31.3	23.8	221.3	66.7
1909	138.4	441.1	302.7	68.6	151.7	79.0		79.0	31.5	31.8	294.0	66.7
1910	157.1	491.8	334.7	68.1	175.0	87.4		87.4	30.6	32.5	325.5	66.2
1911	146.3	431.7	285.4	66.1	161.6	55.3		55.3	31.1	27.8	275.8	63.9
1912	214.3	533.9	319.6	59.9	189.6	54.2		54.2	32.6	33.7	310.1	58.1
1913	191.6	560.8	369.2	65.8	207.5	81.2	$ 1.9	83.1	33.3	34.0	357.9	63.8
1914	153.7	412.2	258.5	62.7	162.7	23.4	1.2	24.6	33.2	26.6	247.1	59.9
1915	189.8	523.7	333.9	63.8	177.3	75.9	1.8	77.7	32.8	34.3	322.1	61.5
1916	265.3	902.3	637.0	70.6	263.9	271.5	12.2	283.7	32.0	43.0	630.2	69.8
1917	345.9	1,284.6	938.7	73.1	347.9	224.2	233.5	457.7	31.0	83.3	919.9	71.6
1918	339.2	1,344.6	1,005.4	74.8	453.0	125.3	274.3	399.6	30.7	98.8	982.1	73.0
1919	364.5	1,122.6	758.1	67.5	479.7	76.8	52.0	128.8	30.1	89.9	728.5	64.9
1920	413.6	1,290.6	877.0	68.0	581.8	109.7	37.5	147.2	29.3	80.0	838.3	65.0
1921	249.9	726.0	476.1	65.6	332.2	36.6	2.4	39.0	28.5	40.1	439.8	60.6
1922	334.7	809.0	474.3	58.6	323.4	39.6	2.5	42.1	28.4	47.1	441.0	54.5
1923	377.4	1,096.5	719.1	65.6	470.4	108.7	15.8	124.5	28.0	56.9	679.8	62.0
1924	266.9	921.4	654.5	71.0	443.8	85.1	11.6	96.7	27.3	53.2	620.8	67.4

Year												
1925	333.6	1,022.0	688.4	67.4	458.2	90.6	13.3	103.9	27.1	61.6	650.8	63.7
1926	346.7	1,082.3	735.6	68.0	469.3	116.7	17.1	133.8	26.8	70.4	700.3	64.7
1927	323.1	960.5	637.4	66.4	412.7	87.9	11.5	99.4	26.1	64.4	602.6	62.7
1928	338.4	1,005.3	666.9	66.5	402.9	114.1	15.0	129.1	25.7	73.2	630.9	62.8
1929	350.0	1,097.4	747.4	68.1	410.2	197.5	17.2	214.7	14.9	69.8	709.6	64.7
1930	234.8	828.4	593.6	71.7	371.7	104.4	12.0	116.4	5.6	63.8	557.5	67.3
1931	187.2	548.7	361.5	65.9	258.4	13.0	0.1	13.1	5.5	50.4	327.4	59.7
1932	141.8	287.7	145.9	50.7	138.5	−71.2	0.1	−71.1	5.3	41.6	114.3	39.7
1933	161.4	375.0	213.6	57.0	167.9	−36.5	0.1	−36.4	5.2	45.3	182.0	48.5
1934	140.5	420.9	280.4	66.6	214.8	−21.7	2.6	−19.1	5.1	46.4	247.2	58.7
1935	191.2	539.4	348.2	64.6	253.9	1.1	3.9	5.0	5.0	49.8	313.7	58.2
1936	287.5	790.5	503.0	63.6	339.0	50.5	11.2	61.7	4.9	59.0	464.6	58.8
1937	342.6	1,028.4	685.8	66.7	447.1	94.9	29.5	124.4	5.1	64.1	640.7	62.3
1938	228.3	611.1	382.8	62.6	294.4	−7.7	2.9	−4.8	8.3	50.3	348.2	57.0
1939	293.5	846.0	552.5	65.3	386.5	41.1	13.0	54.1	9.3	63.4	513.3	60.7
1940	358.3	1,079.1	720.8	66.8	454.3	102.2	26.3	128.5	13.6	72.6	679.0	62.9
1941	604.6	1,622.3	1,017.7	62.7	628.3	116.2	118.7	234.9	6.0	98.6	967.8	59.7
1942	673.4	1,863.0	1,189.6	63.9	782.7	71.2	153.1	224.3	6.2	128.2	1,141.4	61.3
1943	730.6	1,972.3	1,241.7	63.0	912.9	62.6	84.3	146.9	6.3	134.0	1,200.1	60.8
1944	814.4	2,082.2	1,267.8	60.9	957.2	60.8	65.0	125.8	5.0	139.0	1,227.0	58.9
1945	670.1	1,747.3	1,077.2	61.6	825.5	58.0	30.0	88.0	3.5	123.4	1,040.4	59.5
1946	560.4	1,496.1	935.7	62.5	704.5	38.6	32.0	120.6	4.8	68.7	898.6	60.1
1947	839.4	2,122.8	1,283.4	60.5	903.6	127.1	91.0	218.1	2.5	114.0	1,238.2	58.3
1948	1,008.9	2,481.5	1,472.6	59.3	1,035.7	129.6	109.0	238.6	2.4	146.0	1,422.7	57.3
1949	885.7	2,301.7	1,416.0	61.5	945.9	165.9	126.0	291.9	2.3	119.7	1,359.8	59.1
1950	1,118.8	2,956.4	1,837.6	62.2	1,170.4	215.5	234.0	449.5	2.2	143.9	1,775.0	60.0
1951	1,327.9	3,524.1	2,196.2	62.3	1,374.5	184.3	398.0	582.3	2.0	162.1	2,121.0	60.2
1952	1,307.6	3,137.4	1,829.8	58.3	1,322.1	143.7	117.0	260.7	1.9	176.9	1,761.6	56.1

Source: *Annual Report* for 1950 and 1952, U.S. Steel Corp. Data in column 7 supplied by U.S. Steel Comptroller's Office. (They vary slightly from *Study of Monopoly Power*, House Subcommittee on Monopoly Power, Serial No. 14, Part 4-13, Exhibit S-239, p. 570.)

TABLE 8

Ratio of Income to Sales, Ten Major Steel Companies, 1905-1952

(per cent)

Year	Bethlehem Steel	Republic Steel	National Steel	Armco Steel	Youngstown Sheet and Tube	Jones and Laughlin	Inland Steel	Wheeling Steel Corp.	Sharon Steel Corp.	Allegheny Ludlum Steel Corp.
1905	47.6									
1906	31.4									
1907	27.5									
1908	38.1									
1909	45.7									
1910	49.8									
1911	47.7									
1912	48.1									
1913	51.0									
1914	51.2									
1915	32.2									
1916	54.7									
1917	51.3									
1918	51.0	43.6								
1919	64.1	48.1								
1920	59.6	50.6								
1921	57.0	24.5								
1922	54.3	39.9								
1923	56.0	53.2								
1924	56.4	53.9								
1925	56.4	48.8		55.1						
1926	56.7	52.9		53.5						
1927	58.2	52.7		49.8						
1928	57.4	n.a.		44.0						
1929	58.6	n.a.								

Year										
1930	59.2	39.5	35.6							
1931	55.0	39.3	32.7							
1932	47.1	34.4	39.0							
1933	52.6	41.6	39.6							
1934	56.8	45.0	40.9							
1935	59.9	47.6	41.4	46.6						
1936	58.4	46.8	41.4	46.3		47.2				
1937	57.6	49.2	42.3	48.3		47.3				
1938	60.1	48.9	38.7	48.8		49.0	48.3			37.7
1939	56.8	51.1	42.3	45.5		50.4	50.6			44.8
1940	55.6	50.1	41.8	45.9	47.9	46.8	52.5	49.9	35.8	47.3
1941	57.6	49.7	44.4	46.9	50.8	n.a.	50.3	49.5	43.1	47.0
1942	59.6	52.1	44.4	49.6	46.9	47.2	56.1	50.3	43.0	48.5
1943	60.8	46.6	42.6	44.3	42.5	45.2	54.2	50.4	42.0	48.3
1944	62.3	48.4	44.8	43.7		43.9	52.3	51.8	42.1	50.2
1945	59.9	45.9	44.3	41.5	40.8	41.7	48.3	48.2	43.6	48.3
1946	61.4	50.4	48.4	50.5	45.3	42.6	53.2	54.0	43.9	52.7
1947	53.2	47.6	46.2	47.3	44.3	42.8	52.5	56.4	43.7	49.3
1948	53.4	47.8	44.3	47.9	45.8	41.5	49.8	56.8	44.4	47.8
1949	54.9	49.8	47.1	50.3	45.0	40.8	51.4	54.2	40.2	42.7
1950	58.1	51.4	51.8	50.2	47.5	41.9	52.6	59.7	43.9	44.1
1951	56.2	50.8	48.3	50.1	43.0	42.1	53.2	59.4	44.5	45.1
1952		47.3		44.5	41.0	37.2	49.3	56.3	39.5	42.8

Note: Fully consolidated statements were used for all companies. Where reported, total employment costs (including social security taxes and fringe benefits) have been included. Sales figures are net in all cases.

not merely statistical. If the input of resources necessary for a given process should decline and the process occupy less economic space relative to earlier processes than it formerly did, then the firm would rely more on the market and less on its own contribution for the final product. It would be less self-sufficient and less integrated.

The same paradox relates to labor or capital intensiveness. It is difficult to avoid the impression of capital intensiveness when the operating units are physically large and impressive. But, again, size in economics is not a physical but a value dimension, and in our capital-rich civilization we can and do treat as cheap, because they are plentiful, capital instruments which are scarce and therefore expensive in other societies. In commenting on the ancient protectionist argument against cheap foreign labor, one wit has pointed out that foreign protectionists might with equal logic inveigh against being flooded with the products of cheap American capital. I suspect that research would show many American exports and perhaps exports as a whole to be really labor-intensive, as that term is defined here.

8. *Possible Correlation with Expansion*

ASSUMING, then, that the ratios of income to sales and of inventory to sales are logically sound, what interpretation can be made of the apparent rough correlation between size and the degree of vertical integration?

George J. Stigler has come nearer than anyone else to formulating a law of vertical integration.[22] Treating integration as the opposite of specialization, Stigler expects disintegration to be characteristic of an expanding industry, integration of a contracting one. As the industry (the market) expands, economies of scale become possible in the various processes and these tend to split off to be separately performed. Hence, in the absence of attempts at market control, there should be decreasing integration; this would be reflected in falling ratios.

Stigler doubts that we need a distinctive theory of vertical integration; this leads me to interpret the above situation as a pattern of industry development rather than a logical necessity. As a pattern, it is plausible and will doubtless be borne out in many instances. But in my opinion Stigler's analysis (correctly) contrasts a mature or large-scale industry with a small-scale industry, *not* an expanding

[22] "The Division of Labor Is Limited by the Extent of the Market," *Journal of Political Economy*, June 1951, pp. 185-193.

industry with a contracting one. The distinction between process and result seems to be of crucial significance: I would guess that an expanding industry is more highly integrated than a relatively stable one. If we start with an industry in its earliest years, when it is an innovation, it is at first adapted to and fills a niche in the existing structure of markets and of factor supply. It is essentially a rearrangement of known and available resources. Few can discern its large possibilities for growth and for pushing the capacity of supplying industries and firms. The railroads were originally feeders to canals and turnpikes, and, later, pipe lines and trucks were considered as feeders to railroads; the automobile was a rich man's toy; wireless transmission of signals was intended for ship-to-shore telegraphy; and many other examples might be given.

As the firms and their industry grow, they do so under the forced draft of demand chronically in excess of supply at prevailing prices. This economic tension is transmitted to the factor markets as the firms bid not only for increasing amounts but for changing composition of factors. As larger quantities are needed, some factors become relatively scarce and substitution must be resorted to, often by painful trial and error. Economies of scale now appear, as Stigler rightly insists; my point is that they appear unforeseen and generally lagging behind a keenly felt need. A sluggish response will often force the growing firm to provide its own supplies and/or marketing outlets.

It may be regarded as axiomatic that integration takes place only in response to imperfections of competition in supplying or receiving markets. A firm does not normally integrate into a market where it can buy unlimited quantities at the going price and where the producers are receiving a normal (or subnormal) return. A firm does integrate into a broadening market whose service is scarce and expensive. The scarcity and the high price may be the result of monopoly control in the invidious sense, by a single seller or by a group whose several minds have but a single thought. But the scarcity may exist simply because of the time lag in supplying the new factor. A small, uncertain, and fluctuating supply is peculiarly subject to recurrent "corners" and extortion. Also, there may be considerable monopoly profit. Even when this is not the case, if the factor is expensive or unsuitable, so that it takes additional costly processing before being ready for use or is uncertain in amount, the impact on the expanding firm is much the same. Thus the very expansion of demand which induces economies of scale in the associated markets also induces the firms in the growing industry to occupy the associated markets. Once established, the pattern perpetuates itself, unless the (private) diseconomies of integration are considerable.

An industry in rapid growth throws the process into boldest relief, but it is only the most extreme example of a more general problem. Given an expanding and changing economy, there must necessarily at any instant be a host of markets out of equilibrium into which it becomes profitable to integrate. This would explain the existence of vertical integration even in the absence of attempts to pre-empt an essential resource in order to prevent competitors from using it or to insure the "right" kind of price policy at later stages.

Given imperfect competition and no sharply defined loci of least-cost output, so that a firm may be well away from the optimum scale without ceasing to exist, then the half-forgotten history of an industry plus the power of inertia may largely explain its existing pattern of vertical integration. Chance alone may be no small part of the explanation. Imagine an industry comprising n stages with no economies or diseconomies of vertical integration. The joining of functions would then be purely random. There would be 2^{n-1} possible varieties or degrees of vertical integration; the "average" firm would encompass $(n+1)/2$ stages, with $\sqrt{n-1}/2$ standard deviation.[23] Thus, with only a half dozen stages, one would find 32 possible patterns; the average number of stages encompassed would be $3\frac{1}{2}$, but this could be in any one of several patterns; furthermore, there would be one chance in three of any given firm encompassing less than $2\frac{1}{2}$ or more than $4\frac{1}{2}$ stages.

9. *Four Developmental Patterns*

THE foregoing sketch is not, I think, inconsistent with the evidence. The smallest firms appear to be specialists in a particular process. As the firm grows, it does not merely duplicate its activities; it takes over additional functions, performing some of the services it formerly purchased. Hence, both ratios would increase. But for the firm which has grown into a large part of its available market, the trend to self-sufficiency may be reversed by the marketing necessity to carry a full line. Hence the firm purchases many finished or nearly finished goods to be marketed in conjunction with those it processes over a greater length of production line. This decreases the two ratios, but even with this reversal the large firm is more integrated than the small. A similar development takes place in the

[23] My thanks on this point are due to Robert M. Solow.

fully developed industry, where with the passage of time certain diseconomies of integration are slowly realized and certain functions are discontinued. For any growing industry or firm, the trend is to increasing integration, but this is counteracted both by the constant growth of new, less integrated industries and firms and by the reversal of the trend in highly mature industries.

Thus we have about four developmental patterns of vertical integration. For any given firm at any given time, they may be mutually exclusive but not over longer periods. Nor are they exhaustive. It would be most unfortunate if we looked for *the* typical pattern and tried to make of it a general theory of vertical integration. What we need is to increase our knowledge of various patterns and to multiply hypotheses while trying to practice some orderly housekeeping among them. The ratios proposed here, when used in conjunction with other evidence, may serve as useful tools in this task.[24]

Appendix

CERTAIN sources other than those discussed above were investigated, but they proved unworkable. They are briefly indicated in this Appendix, as a warning to those interested in further research in this area. *The Structure of the American Economy*[25] contains two interesting tabulations of census data. One of them concerns the 200 largest manufacturing concerns, grouped by fives; the other gives concentration data (the largest four and the largest eight producers) in several hundred industries. For each group the value added and also the value of products is indicated. Unfortunately, the latter is given on a combined rather than consolidated basis, so that sales are overstated, in ratio loosely proportional to the number of plants. It is impossible to calculate and allow for bias from this source, since a firm with many horizontally related plants would show little or no overstatement, while a plant with even two vertically related plants might show a very large overstatement. If Monograph 27[26] showed the number of establishments involved in the several relationships discussed above, it might be possible to calculate the bias; unfortunately, as already seen, the monograph shows only the number of central offices (firms) involved.

Another source which was not useful was tabulation by the Office

---

[24] Cf. the able Ph.D. thesis by Frederick E. Balderston, *Scale, Vertical Integration, and Costs in Residential Construction Firms* (Princeton University Press, 1953).

[25] Leontief, *op. cit.*

[26] Thorp and Crowder, *op. cit.*

of Price Administration of wartime manufacturing corporate finance, which was published by the FTC in 1947.[27] The basic trouble with these data, for our particular purpose, is that the gross is too gross, and the net too net. Only purchases of raw materials are indicated, so that the spread between total purchases and sales includes more than value added by the firm. Proceeding contrariwise, corporate profits are available, as well as interest; but the wage total is incomplete and a very large part of total cost is unclassified general manufacturing expense. Hence, income generated is understated. Another defect, for our particular purpose, is that certain large subsidiaries were not consolidated with their parents; this results in an overstatement of sales.

Monograph 27 also presents concentration data for 1,807 narrowly classified industries, each producing what approximates a "product" in the market sense. Unfortunately, concentration is given in terms of sales in dollars and in physical units but not in terms of value added, so that no ratio can be calculated.

Finally, there are the tables computed for the Celler Subcommittee from the 1947 census.[28] Here, too, concentration is shown in terms of sales, except for twelve industries for which it is given in terms of value added. Nowhere, however, do we have both.

[27] *Report on Wartime Profits and Costs for Manufacturing Corporations*, FTC 1947.
[28] Letter from the Secretary of Commerce to Representative Emanuel Celler, December 1, 1949, Table v appended.

COMMENT

IRSTON R. BARNES, Federal Trade Commission

VERTICAL integration is normally understood to refer to an organization of production under which a single business unit carries on successive stages in the processing or distribution of a product which is sold by other firms without further processing. Vertical integration results in by-passing a market or having a position on both sides of the market: making a product instead of buying it, carrying it to a later stage instead of selling it. Thus, bringing together under one managerial direction a raw material producer and the manufacturer using that raw material, a producer of an intermediate product and a manufacturer using that intermediate product, or a

NOTE: The views expressed in this comment are the writer's and not necessarily those of the Federal Trade Commission.

manufacturer of the finished product and a distributor of that product, are examples of vertical integration. In a practical sense, integration must be examined with respect to the particular product or products which a firm manufactures, not with respect to products generally; full integration with respect to all products which a manufacturer fabricates probably exists nowhere in the real economy.

It is, of course, commonplace that a large proportion of industry involves two or more successive steps in production which might theoretically, though not practicably, be split among two or more producers. However, attention is generally focused on those situations where successive stages of production are brought under a single managerial supervision and where markets are by-passed or straddled.

It is not fruitful for present purposes to make a prolonged inquiry as to whether vertical integration is fundamentally different, either in objectives or in consequences, from other coherent forms of integration. We may simply note in passing that the questions raised by all coherent forms of integration are essentially similar.

RATIO OF INCOME ORIGINATING TO SALES

STATISTICAL attempts to measure vertical integration have yielded less than satisfactory results. After noting many of the deficiencies, Adelman proposes two measures of vertical integration. He would measure vertical integration by the ratio of income originating within the corporation (or within the industry) to its sales. He also offers an alternative measure of integration: the ratio of inventory to sales.

Throughout his paper Adelman appears to identify his concept of integration with the measures which he advocates. These measures are offered as general-purpose yardsticks, and the implication is that the magnitude measured may be accepted as an accurate index of integration for any and all purposes.

Adelman appears to be drawn to his proposed measures because theoretically and conceptually the larger the value added by the manufacturer, or the greater the income originating within the firm, the farther the firm carries its processing of the product. Unfortunately this conceptually neat identification of integration does not yield results which are useful in resolving the real problems which arise with respect to integration.

Adelman recognizes most of the deficiencies inherent in the application of his two measures; yet he nevertheless advocates the refinement of the statistical series which he uses and holds out the hope that the measures may be made to work. Where the author has been so diligent in pointing out the deficiencies in his own analytical tools, it is somewhat gratuitous for the critic to affirm the defects which have been noted. Nevertheless, a skepticism amounting almost to conviction that Adelman's ratios of income originating to sales and of inventory to sales will not prove useful in resolving the practical problems associated with integration prompts a warning that others refrain from following this path. In short, neither of these measures of integration yields reliable or consistent results. Indeed, each reflects a complex of factors, many of which—such as the profit level of the firm or industry—are quite unrelated to integration.

Some of the deficiencies associated with the income-sales ratio may be examined briefly:

1. Adelman offers a theoretical example of integration involving a primary producer, a manufacturer, and a distributor, each of which by assumption contributes one-third of the total value of the product. The application of the income-sales ratio yields an index of 100 for the primary producer, 50 for the manufacturer, and 33 for the distributor; yet by definition all are equally "integrated." In this instance the ratio reflects the stage in the productive process which is being measured rather than the degree of integration. This characteristic alone deprives the index of any real value in making comparisons between industries or even in comparing different producers in the same industry, where they are not at exactly the same stage in the productive process.

The question commonly arises as to what effect an acquisition or merger has upon the degree of integration before and after the merger. The same example illustrates another deficiency. If the manufacturer absorbs the primary producer, that is, if he integrates backward, the index of integration increases from 50 to 100 and the manufacturer is fully integrated. On the other hand, the primary producer, whose index of 100 indicates that he is already fully integrated, might absorb the manufacturer; if so, the index of integration would still be 100. However, if the manufacturer absorbs the distributor, that is, integrates forward, an equal degree of forward vertical integration yields an index of 67. Thus in these instances the index of integration measures, not the degree of integration but the direction of integration, yielding higher magnitudes for backward integration than for forward integration.

2. The infirmities revealed by the theoretical example lead Adel-

man to conclude that comparisons are possible only when dealing with the same economic function or with closely similar functions, and he warns against comparing the integration of a mining company with that of a retailer. Yet there will seldom exist that similarity or identity of function which would render the use of this index dependable. Indeed, it is the fundamental purpose of vertical integration to combine different functions, and different mergers will effect different combinations of functions. However, the index is not available for these simple and direct comparisons. If one knows enough to use the income-sales index with safety, he knows more that is significant about the companies concerned than the index can ever reveal.

3. A high index of integration as indicated by the income-sales index may reflect the intensiveness of the productive process as well as the vertical extension of the productive operation over successive stages. The employment of skilled labor and expensive machinery normally gives rise to a greater value added by the manufacturing operations, even though only a single productive stage is involved. Thus, without calculating the index of integration, we should expect to find a higher index for a watch company than for a company engaged in a relatively simple metal-fabricating operation.

4. Income originating, or value added, includes sales less expenditures for raw materials, fuel, and power. Specifically it includes corporate profits. Hence the greater the corporate profits, the higher the degree of integration which the index will show, and, conversely, the larger the corporate losses, the lower the degree of integration which the index will record. Thus, of two companies carrying on identical manufacturing operations, the more successful will show a higher index of integration. In this instance differences in the indexes of integration measure differences in the competence of management or in the profit-making possibilities of the two companies. Hence the index is not a reliable measure of integration even with respect to two companies operating at the same stage in the same industry.

The lack of comparability between companies performing the same function renders Adelman's caution against comparisons between companies in different industries somewhat misleading. In fact, the same lack of similarity which he accepts with respect to interindustry comparisons is inevitably present within most two-digit industries. Furthermore, comparisons might be rendered invalid by integration which carries different companies in the same industry across different industry lines. In short, a statistical measure of integration which is applicable only within the narrowest confines has very limited utility. Many critical questions respecting integration which demand answers refuse to be neatly pigeonholed, as the proposed index would require.

5. When the income-sales measure is applied to reveal changes in integration from year to year, new difficulties are encountered. Differential changes in the level of prices introduce aberration. Without any change whatever in the productive processes carried on within the firm, a lower index of integration may result from an increase in the costs of materials, fuel, and power. Or without any change in the physical processes of production, a higher index of integration may result from an increase in the prices at which the product is sold, from a greater increase in prices than in costs, or from a greater reduction in costs than in prices.

6. Adelman presents an array of indexes of integration for two-digit industries. In the light of the deficiencies already noted, comparisons between industries have no discoverable significance. Moreover, the two-digit industries comprehend so many different productive operations that it may not be assumed that the industry's index is an average which is characteristic of any of the companies comprising the industry.

7. Adelman presents a tabulation of the indexes of integration for the U.S. Steel Co. from 1902 to 1950. To the uncritical reader, the index yields curious results. The index is lower during the depression years than during the years before and after the depression. What changes in the realities of integration occurred during these years is not known, but if there were no changes, the same results might be expected from changes in cost-price relationships.

RATIO OF INVENTORY TO SALES

AN ALTERNATIVE index of integration, the ratio of inventory to sales, is presented as a derived measure of integration. The theoretical justification lies in the observation that the longer the productive line and the more successive processes performed within the same firm, the higher the ratio will be. Adelman notes that this measure is "more susceptible to meaningless comparisons" than the income-to-sales ratio. His warning is necessary, for this ratio appears to be no better than the income-to-sales measure. It is subject to many of the objections already considered as well as to a number of additional deficiencies. Only three new objections are commented on here:

1. The inventory-sales index is simply the ratio of inventory to sales without respect to the stage at which the inventory is held. Thus, if the inventory is at the final-product stage, the index could be as high for the unintegrated producer of the final product as for an integrated producer whose operations cover several stages in production.

2. The index yields confusing results where the productive process is continuous. If there are no intermediate products or if production moves continuously, as in some of the chemical and paper companies, the amount of the inventory is minimized. Hence the more highly integrated producers, whose visible inventory consists primarily of low-value raw matcrials, may show a lower index of integration than a partially integrated firm whose first inventories are in the form of intermediate products. An index which makes a partially integrated firm appear to be more highly integrated than a fully integrated firm is a measure which should be discarded, not refined.

3. The index of integration will vary according to the marketing practices of companies within the same industry. For example, if they are successful in moving finished cars directly from the production line to their dealers, the larger and more highly integrated automobile manufacturers may show lower indexes of integration than smaller, less integrated competitors who are less successful in inducing their dealers to carry their inventories.

In summary, it does not appear that either of the two ratios proposed, income originating within the firm to sales or inventory to sales, can be helpful in dealing with any of the real problems of vertical integration, whether the problems arise with respect to specific firms or to industries.

A SIMPLE PROPOSAL

MANY problems in connection with vertical integration relate to the effects of such integration upon a competitive organization of industry and upon competitive markets. Some of these problems can be illuminated by the development of measures which would show the degree to which different companies are dependent upon markets at specific stages in the processes of production and distribution. An unambiguous and simple measure of the degree of vertical integration of the individual firm with respect to different market levels

327

can be constructed for any product or class of products, with separate measures showing the degrees of forward and backward integration. To make the example specific, one might seek to measure integration with respect to the pulp-producing and pulp-consuming operations of a paper company. In this instance one would measure the interplant transfers of pulp by the company as a percentage of its total shipments and interplant transfers of pulp; this would supply an index of the degree of forward integration. Or, the consumption of pulp by a paper company from its own pulp mills might be expressed as a percentage of its total consumption of pulp. This would reflect the degree of backward vertical integration. This measure would facilitate comparisons of the degree of integration of different companies in the same industry and would be equally serviceable in showing the degree of integration of the same company at different periods of time.

Where suitable universe data are available, as they are in the paper industry, the same type of measure may be used to determine the degree of vertical integration between successive market levels or between the same markets at different periods of time. Or, one may compare the degree of vertical integration of specific companies with the degree of vertical integration for the market as a whole.

The complement of the measure of vertical integration for an individual company shows its dependence on the market for sales or purchases of the products in question. The complement of the measure of forward integration indicates the degree to which the producing firm at any particular stage is dependent on the market for the disposition of its product. The complement of the measure of backward integration shows the degree to which any consuming unit in the company depends upon the open market to supply it with the product in question.

The complement of the measure of forward vertical integration for the market as a whole states the percentage of the industry's output of the product which is available to open-market purchasers. And the complement of the measure of backward vertical integration for the market shows the percentage of the consumption of the material or product which is derived from open-market purchases.

No statistical measure of vertical integration is without its disadvantages. Two immediately apparent disadvantages of the measure here proposed may be briefly noted:

1. Suitable universe figures are collected for only a limited num-

ber of industries, and within those industries for only a limited number of products. Thus, figures for total shipments or for the total of sales or purchases in markets, particularly regional markets, may not be available.

2. The measurement of interplant transfers does not yield an unambiguous figure, for different companies, even within the same industry, may value their interplant transfers on different bases. The valuation of interplant transfers is essentially a matter of managerial decision. Some companies value interplant transfers at cost, others value them at market price at the time of the transfer, and others appear to split the final sales price according to an individual management formula.

The principal advantages of the proposed alternative measure arise from the fact that it is concerned with real problems of integration:

1. The percentage of market measure will yield consistent results both through time and as applied to different companies.

2. Full forward or backward vertical integration with respect to a product will yield an index of 1. This would mean that a company sold none of its output of the product in question on the open market or made no purchases of material on the market.

3. A company selling all its output of a product and using none of it, or buying all its requirements of a product, would have a vertical integration measure of zero.

4. The indexes are additive, that is, the individual company fractions can be totaled to give a sum which indicates the degree of market integration. Thus, if the degree of vertical integration for some of the largest producers or consumers of a product is known and if corresponding figures are available for the market, it is possible to infer the degree of vertical integration for other companies as a group. This may be helpful in characterizing particular markets, and it may also illuminate some of the competitive problems facing other producers and consumers in that market.

5. The percentage of market index can be applied either to quantity figures or to dollar figures, whichever are available.

6. The index will not be distorted by changes in price levels, since equivalent values are used for any given period of time.

7. Finally, the percentage of market index expresses the commonly accepted concept of vertical integration rather than defining vertical integration in terms of the measure employed.

There are many problems relating to vertical integration where judgments must rest on some fairly reliable measure of the position of individual companies with respect to other companies and to the market as a whole. The critical questions relating to vertical integration must be asked before suitable measures of integration can be devised. Further work in the construction and refinement of measures of integration should await a clinical examination of the problems of vertical integration and should be directed at yielding useful and unambiguous results.

CONGLOMERATE BIGNESS AS A SOURCE OF POWER

CORWIN D. EDWARDS

UNIVERSITY OF VIRGINIA

THE concept of "conglomerate bigness" is a useful tool for probing into problems customarily neglected. Economic thinking about questions of business organization has been concerned with markets for products, has assumed that business behavior in each market is explicable as an effort to maximize profits there, has interpreted monopolistic markets as involving the exercise of varying degrees of monopoly power by one or more business enterprises, and has appraised problems of monopoly power in the light of certain conceptions of monopolistic exploitation, on the one hand, and certain conceptions of business efficiency, on the other. The growth of diversified large enterprise[1] has made this conceptual scheme

[1] The term "conglomerate" has been used negatively in economics to refer to a business that is neither horizontally homogeneous nor vertically integrated, but the meaning of the term is not clear because the concepts of horizontal and vertical integration are imprecise and because there are also other forms of structure. More than 1,800 of the 5,625 central office companies covered by Monograph 27 of the Temporary National Economic Committee (1941) performed "divergent" or "convergent" functions. The term "divergent" was applied to functions in which unlike products emerge from a given material or process. The term "convergent" was applied to functions in which different materials or products were brought together to serve a particular need or market. Once these patterns are recognized, it is hard to be clear about the meaning of horizontal and vertical integration; for vertical integration may spread out horizontally, both backward toward the raw material and forward toward the consumer. A concern performing divergent functions may produce a series of joint products or byproducts and may integrate the production of any of them vertically down to the ultimate consumer. In connection with any of them, it may perform convergent functions by producing articles that are complementary or auxiliary, or that pass through the same distributive channels, or that reach the same customers. In connection with any of the secondary commodities, it may integrate vertically back to the raw material, and at any stage in the backward integration may take on new divergent functions that carry it into a new range of products. Thus there may be lines of functional congruity among business activities that at first glance sprawl across functions apparently unrelated; and where there is no such congruity, it probably could be introduced by adding appropriate intermediate activities. The true conglomerate is relatively rare.

Furthermore, the concept of a conglomerate is defective because it is derived from physical rather than operational characteristics. In practice, similarities in the business process may make activities functionally coherent as readily as similarities in basic materials or physical productive processes. For example, the limited-price variety store sells goods that have no common origin or destina-

insufficient as a basis for the description and appraisal of business conduct. A concern that produces many products and operates across many markets need not regard a particular market as a separate unit for determining business policy and need not attempt to maximize its profits in the sale of each of its products, as has been presupposed in our traditional scheme. It may classify its products into such categories as money-making items, convenience goods, and loss leaders, and may follow different policies in selling the different classes. It may possess power in a particular market not only by virtue of its place in the organization of that market but also by virtue of the scope and character of its activities elsewhere. It may be able to exploit, extend, or defend its power by tactics other than those that are traditionally associated with the idea of monopoly. Public problems created by its activities may be of such a character that both the traditional idea of monopoly power and the traditional idea of internal efficiency are insufficient to give insight into the pros and cons of the policy issues.

Where these circumstances prevail, there is advantage in an abstraction that throws a spotlight upon a part of the situation that cannot be described and appraised in the traditional way. The conglomerate firm is such an abstraction. As a business type, a conglomerate can be as large as one chooses to conceive it without thereby acquiring a monopoly of any product and without deriving from its size the efficiencies that are traditionally associated with mass production. Thus the term conglomerate becomes a device for examining problems of size and power apart from the traditional focus upon monopoly and efficiency.

In making this examination, we should not forget the artificial character of the abstraction. If we find that bigness brings power and power creates public problems, we must remember that, where the large enterprise takes a form resulting in monopoly, the impact of bigness is likely to be superimposed upon the impact of monopoly. We must also remember that coherence and incoherence of business function are usually so intermingled as to make it difficult for a public agency to take action appropriate to the problems of size

---

tion because the specialized business techniques of supplying customers with convenience goods at low prices and with low markups can be applied to a considerable range of commodities.

Thus the term conglomerate does not express a clearly defined type of enterprise, but is useful in calling attention to problems associated with significant degrees of incoherence in business function.

without producing collateral effects upon the internal functioning of the concern.

In what follows, I shall treat the problem of the conglomerate as synonymous with the problems of bigness in business enterprise and of diversification in business activities. I shall not attempt to cover all aspects of bigness or of diversification, but shall limit myself to consideration of the respects in which these attributes of business enterprise may jeopardize the interests of suppliers, competitors, or customers. This treatment of the subject should not be understood to imply that all large and diversified enterprises give rise to the problems I shall discuss nor to deny that such enterprises, as a class, also have other and more desirable attributes than those with which I am presently concerned. Though I can illustrate the points I shall make, I have no way of measuring the frequency and relative importance of the phenomena to be discussed. I shall draw illustrative materials not only from business structures that would be generally recognized as conglomerate but also, and perhaps chiefly, from those aspects of other business enterprises which appear to relate to diversity of operation or total size rather than to a proportionate place in particular markets. Such points as I shall make are, in my opinion, appropriate to bigness and diversity whether or not these are associated with monopoly. I shall, however, try to distinguish between monopolistic power (that is, power expressed in control of a particular market for a particular type of product) and power derived from bigness (that is, power that may inhere in a large enterprise) even if there is no such market control.[2]

[2] I shall use the monopoly concept in the sense it had in the older economic theory and still has in our antimonopoly laws, rather than in the later meaning given it by the theory of monopolistic competition. Although for some purposes any departure from the competitive pattern of traditional economic theory may usefully be described as monopolistic, the term monopoly cannot be stretched so thin if it is to describe a category of cases to which a special type of public policy is applicable. For such a purpose, monopoly ends where effective control of the market ends; and a concern may be nonmonopolistic even if it is substantially larger than many of its business rivals and even if it is one of so small a number of concerns that its competition takes the form of activities directed at identified enterprises rather than of adjustment to the play of anonymous forces. One effect of the use of this concept of monopoly is that, in an industry divided between several large companies and a considerable number of much smaller companies, advantages enjoyed by the large companies are treated as relevant to the bigness of these concerns rather than to the limited monopoly power enjoyed by them. Since the advantages in question are similar to those enjoyed by large concerns in settings to which even the broadest definition of monopoly could not easily be applied, this treatment is believed to be justified. But it is not crucial to the argument; for even if all differentials of

1. *Bigness and Power*

BIGNESS in a business enterprise is not a precise concept. The big
concern may be big in several different ways:

1. Its assets, its income, its expenditures, its sales, or its employment may constitute a substantial part of the total for all business
or of the subtotal for a broad range of economic activity such as
manufacturing or retail trade.

2. Its holdings or its operations may be much larger than those
of other successful business enterprises.

3. It may fall into a category of concerns capable of undertaking
activities or using forms of organization that would not be feasible
for smaller business enterprises.

The size and rank of large enterprises may differ according to the
method of measurement used, and many concerns may look big
or little if they are compared, respectively, with smaller and with
larger enterprises. Where exact measurements are sought, these
difficulties are vexing. There has been controversy, for example, as
to whether growth of second-line big companies relative to both
smaller companies and first-line big companies is to be conceived as
an increase or a decrease in business concentration.

But to examine the types of power associated with bigness, precise measurement is not needed. It is enough to speak of concerns
which would lie near the top of the business pyramid of size regardless of the measure used and regardless of the placing of the
boundary line between the big and the little. The large concern
in this sense is one among a relatively small number of companies
each of which possesses resources and carries on operations on a
scale substantially greater than most business enterprises.

An enterprise that is big in this sense obtains from its bigness a
special kind of power, based upon the fact that it can spend money
in large amounts. If such a concern finds itself matching expenditures or losses, dollar for dollar, with a substantially smaller firm,
the length of its purse assures it of victory. In encounters with
small enterprises it can buy scarce materials and attractive sites,
inventions, and facilities; pre-empt the services of the most expensive technicians and executives; and acquire reserves of materials
for the future. It can absorb losses that would consume the entire
capital of a smaller rival. The advantage that lies in this difference

power within a single market are described as aspects of monopoly, manifestations of power based upon an aggregate position in a series of markets must
still be considered.

of scale is not offset by the fact that the large operations of the large enterprise require purchases on a large scale, present more complex managerial and technical problems, and result in larger net revenues or deficits. Moment by moment the big company can outbid, outspend, or outlose the small one; and from a series of such momentary advantages it derives an advantage in attaining its large aggregate results.

Closely associated with differences in financial strength is a difference between the attitudes of large concerns toward one another and their attitudes toward smaller business enterprises. A large concern usually must show a regard for the strength of other large concerns by circumspection in its dealings with them, whereas such caution is usually unnecessary in dealing with small enterprises. The interests of great enterprises are likely to touch at many points, and it would be possible for each to mobilize at any one of these points a considerable aggregate of resources. The anticipated gain to such a concern from unmitigated competitive attack upon another large enterprise at one point of contact is likely to be slight as compared with the possible loss from retaliatory action by that enterprise at many other points of contact. There is an awareness that if competition against the large rival goes so far as to be seriously troublesome, the logic of the situation may call for conversion of the warfare into total war. Hence there is an incentive to live and let live, to cultivate a cooperative spirit, and to recognize priorities of interest in the hope of reciprocal recognition. Those attitudes support such policies as refraining from sale in a large company's home market below whatever price that company may have established there; refraining from entering into the production of a commodity which a large company has developed; not contesting the patent claims of a large company even when they are believed to be invalid; abstaining from an effort to win away the important customers of a large rival; and sometimes refusing to accept such customers even when they take the initiative.

Similar policies by a large company toward a small one are seldom encountered. The small concern's business is limited geographically, or in the commodities it covers, or in the classes of customers with which it is concerned, or in some other way; and the large company can seldom be seriously injured by aggressive tactics which the small one may undertake, or by retaliatory or disciplinary tactics which may be employed against it by the small company. The large company is in a position to hurt without being hurt. The attitude of the small company may range from eager deference to defiant independence; but, whatever its quality, it will take the policies of the large concern into account. The attitude of the large company may range from generosity through indifference to peremptory exercise of authority; but, whatever its quality, the policies underlying it will not be substantially modified by the probable course of action of small companies except in cases in which the small companies act in concert.

This aspect of the power of large concerns becomes more conspicuous as the diversity of operations becomes greater, that is, as the likelihood that the large concern has monopoly power in any particular market becomes less. When the large company spreads across many products throughout a wide geographical area and covers a series of stages in production and distribution, its opportunities for multiple contacts with other large concerns are at their greatest, and the advantage to be derived from an effort to get the best of another large company at a particular point is least evident. Similarly, such a company has the maximum chance to discipline or destroy any particular small company by a localized attack without serious inconvenience to itself, and has the minimum vulnerability to attack from a single small company. Monopoly prosecutions under the antitrust laws have contained frequent evidence of the use of local price-cutting by large nationwide companies to discipline localized competitors; but the opportunity to use such tactics usually depended, not upon monopolization of the national or regional market, but upon a difference in the resources and geographic spread of the aggressor and the victim. In recent decades, the antimonopoly agencies and the legislative bodies have received many complaints from specialized producers or distributors who assert that their business has been seriously injured by price reductions on their specialty that have been made by diversified business enterprises using the specialty as a loss leader. The diversified concern employing loss leader tactics often appeared to have no significant degree of monopoly power.

Differentials in size rather than in monopoly power are the source of such advantages. The large concern has a special status, even though it may operate in an industry so large that its percentage of the total market is small. The small enterprise lacks these advantages even though it may operate in an industry so small that it has a practical monopoly from which it derives other types of advantages. The consideration of the large company for other large companies and its authority over small companies can be seen in dealings with suppliers, distributors, and competitors alike, in each of the fields of operation in which the large concern is substantially engaged. If a concern as large as DuPont sells various products for which its share of the market ranges from 100 per cent to 5 per cent, it may monopolize some of these products and not others; but even where it sells only a small part of the total supply, the fact that the seller is very large is likely to be a source of significant power.

2. *Manifestations of Power: Discrimination*

ONE important way in which bigness contributes to power is by creating opportunities for self-sufficiency. A concern that uses any component of its products in quantities sufficient to constitute the whole output of an efficient establishment could produce the component instead of purchasing it. A concern that sells producer's goods in quantities sufficient to supply the requirements of a processing establishment could discontinue the sale and undertake the processing itself. A concern that sells a commodity or a group of commodities in quantities sufficient to supply the requirements of a distributive organization could undertake its own distribution instead of selling to distributors. A concern whose operations are extensive enough to permit it to spread its risks could provide its own insurance. A concern big enough to keep a transport service reasonably busy could operate its own transportation facilities instead of buying commercial transportation.

To the extent that these potentialities for self-service are actually realized, the large concern becomes not only large but vertically integrated. However, the mere existence of the capacity to integrate vertically, even where the opportunity is not seized, is likely to be a source of bargaining advantage. To continue to do business with the potentially self-sufficient enterprise, a supplier or customer must offer terms no less advantageous than the concern could achieve through integration. Thus, unless the law prevents, the large enterprise is in a position to receive discriminatory treatment as compared with smaller enterprises with which it may be in competition as a buyer or seller of goods or services. The discrimination is likely to appear not only in transactions for products and services in which the large concern has a monopoly or monopsony position, but also in the purchase or sale of any other product or service as to which the large concern is capable of self-sufficiency.

The advantage thus obtained by large concerns is particularly evident in their relations with suppliers. The most prevalent form of discrimination is a price differential. The potentially self-sufficient buyer is in a position to buy at prices whose ceiling is direct production cost plus a reasonable allowance for the minimum overheads involved in producing the quantities that he buys. He need not pay prices that include costs of selling, costs of intermittent operation due to the vagaries of the market, costs of stand-by equipment, costs of equipment bought at previous higher price levels, or high rates of profit. Indeed, his advantageous position may induce the seller to regard his purchases as a windfall increment, to rely upon other purchasers for overhead and profit, and to supply him at little more than the direct costs of production. Differentials in prices quoted to big buyers may come to be so taken for granted that these buyers need not make overt use of bargaining power in order to obtain a discriminatory advantage.

Another important form of discrimination is a preferential status for large buyers or sellers when customary trading relationships are disturbed. When production is not sufficient to fill all orders, a large buyer is likely to be more adequately and promptly supplied than a small one. Refusal to serve the large customer means cutting off a relatively large part of the seller's total sales. It involves the risk that the large buyer may be permanently lost to some other seller who can tide him over the emergency, or that, by integrating vertically, the large buyer may permanently cease to buy on the open market. To reduce sales by depriving small buyers permits a more flexible adjustment to the shrinking market, with less risk of future loss of business; and from time to time it enables a seller to acquire the fabricating facilities of a small customer at a valuation determined by the customer's distress.

Similarly, when demand is low and customers are scarce, distributors are likely to prefer the well-known products of large sellers to the less familiar products of smaller sellers. The large seller tends to hold his market, and the small seller must either suffer a sharper reduction in volume or retain his position by a deeper cut in prices. The large distributor or processor may be able to acquire, at a distress valuation, the productive facilities of certain small suppliers who cannot weather the storm.

Thus, in buyers' and sellers' markets alike, there may be incentives and opportunities for vertical integration involving acquisitions of small concerns by large ones; and there may also be advantages of preferred status for large concerns that make no acquisitions.

Discrimination between large and small buyers may appear, not only in prices and in continuity of trading relationships, but also in many other aspects of terms of sale. Examples are the privilege of selecting the best quality from a stock that varies in quality; more generous credit terms; less rigorous allowances for returned goods; provision of containers and package units appropriate to the buyer's type of business; and provision of sales aids, demonstrators, and technical advice. The privilege of choosing the best quality illustrates a type of case in which a similar concession cannot be granted generally and therefore, if granted at all, is likely to be extended to the most important customer. Preferential credit terms illustrate a class of cases in which only the large customer is likely to be thought important enough to be individually considered as a possible exception to a general policy. Provision of special containers is illustrative of cases in which there may be technical difficulties or prohibitive costs in varying the seller's practice unless the volume of sale that is subjected to the variation is relatively large. Generosity in returned goods allowances is representative of discriminatory concessions that are made, without inherent logic, because the large buyer's good will seems too important to be hazarded upon small matters. The common element in such varying types of preference is that bigness is translated into buying advantages which give the large concern a head start over its smaller rivals in the competitive race.

There is also a tendency to transfer risks and costs from the large enterprise to those who deal with it. During NRA, protests against the working-hour provisions of the upholstery code brought out the fact that the ability of automobile companies to operate with minimum inventories of upholstery rested upon the willingness of upholstery manufacturers to make large deliveries on short notice and to permit last-minute cancellation of orders by their automobile manufacturer customers, even though such changes of plan raised the costs of production and made it necessary for upholstery manufacturers to carry large inventories of fabrics for automobile upholstery. Such extreme examples of transfer of risk are presumably few and are likely to appear only where a large company's operations are so concentrated as to be of crucial importance to the concerns that deal with it. But there are many instances less suggestive of monopoly power in which the large concern buys or sells in accord with a standard contract form of its own devising, designed to impose upon others rather than itself such risks of the transaction as may arise from delays in shipment, loss in transit, damage not due to negligence, and the like.

Since discriminations and preferences tend to be granted to the large concern in each of the many different fields in which it might become self-sufficient, their cumulative effect is likely to be more significant than is apparent in the individual instances separately considered. A substantial buying advantage, associated with unusual security of buying relationships and with a tendency on the part of suppliers and customers to accept risks and burdens which could be assumed either by the seller or by the buyer—these may contribute significantly to the business success of the large enterprise.

3. *Manifestations of Power: Tie-in Selling*

WHERE a large enterprise markets a variety of goods, one way in which it may express its power as a seller is by the tie-in sale. Some of its products may enjoy a monopoly position. In such cases, a tie-in sale is a device to extend the power of the monopoly over other articles not monopolized. But tie-in sales may also be used in selling a product that enjoys a high degree of consumer acceptance, even if this product is in competition with other highly acceptable products and constitutes a portion of the total supply too small to be an expression of monopoly power. Similarly, a commodity that is peculiarly scarce or available only from scattered sources may be sold under a tie-in arrangement even if a substantial number of producers compete in the sale of the scarce article. Any influence, competitive or monopolistic, that might permit a seller to charge a relatively high price for a commodity may be used instead to enhance the sale of his other products by tie-in devices. The seller may refuse to sell his preferred items separately, but, instead, may make it a condition of their sale that buyers accept other goods which they do not want or which they prefer to obtain elsewhere.

The scope of such tie-in arrangements varies widely. In some instances, two or more selected items are tied together, and the purpose appears to be to sell an increased volume of the item that is hardest to sell. In other instances the tie-in may apply to all of the seller's products that can be distributed or used by a given class of buyers. The effects of such a comprehensive tie-in, and probably its purposes, are to bring about a coordinated distribution of the seller's full line, to make the buyer more dependent upon the seller by increasing the seller's importance as his source of supply, and to interfere with sales to the buyer by other sellers who can offer only part of the line.

Closely related to the tie-in sale is the exclusive dealing arrangement. In some instances, the requirement that a seller's full line be taken is sufficient to prevent the buyer from also acquiring the products of rival sellers. In other instances, the seller may refuse to sell to buyers who also make purchases from his competitors, or may stipulate in a formal contract that the buyer will turn to the seller for all of his requirements. Alternatively, the seller may establish a system of discounts of such a character that the buyer's failure to purchase his full requirements from one source would be unduly expensive. Any of these arrangements may be sufficient to close the buyer's door to rival sellers. In instances in which the buyer is large and powerful, an exclusive dealing arrangement may work in reverse to prevent a seller from finding more than one customer in a particular field, and to deprive the buyer's competitors of access to the pre-empted seller.

Not all exclusive dealing arrangements and tie-in arrangements are manifestations of power. Some tie-in arrangements are designed to safeguard quality by providing suitable auxiliary commodities or services. Some exclusive dealing arrangements are designed to provide an incentive for efforts which are hazardous or slow in producing results, by assuring the concern that makes the effort that it will also reap the reward.

Some exclusive dealing arrangements are extensions of monopoly power. Where there is a dearth of alternative sources of supply, the exclusive arrangement shuts rival buyers out of the market, and extends monopoly from the seller's level of business activity to the buyer's level as well. Where there is monopsony power, the reverse effect may appear.

But other instances of exclusive dealing are likely to reflect the cumulative importance that the seller (or the buyer) has derived from his bigness, from the multiplicity of his products (or market outlets), and from his ability to integrate vertically and thus expose the buyer (or seller) to new competition. In cases where there is neither monopoly nor monopsony, an exclusive arrangement may give a large seller or buyer an advantage from the closeness of the tie that is established with concerns on the other side of the market. A distributor dependent upon a single source of supply is likely to be more docile than one who has a free choice. He is likely to observe the seller's wishes as to resale prices, display of goods, and similar matters, and to give all his energy to promotion of the seller's products. A producer dependent upon a single buyer is likely to conform closely to that buyer's desires as to delivery dates, product specifications, and the like. Once dependence is well established, the dependent concern cannot effectively resist price changes that narrow its operating margins to enhance the profits of the concern upon which it depends.

Moreover, when a substantial buyer and a substantial seller have made an exclusive arrangement, other enterprises, aware of the shrinkage of the open market and desirous of forestalling risks to the continuity of their supply or to the adequacy of their market outlets, often protect themselves by making similar exclusive arrangements. The principal concerns on each side of the market pair off as dancing partners, and there is likely to be a remainder of smaller enterprises that must accept the disadvantages and risks incident to purchase and sale in a thin market.

4. *Manifestations of Power: Reciprocal Favors*

WHERE large and powerful concerns encounter each other as seller and buyer, there is sometimes a reciprocal exchange of favors, by which each of the great enterprises strengthens the other.

The most common form of such a relationship is probably reciprocal buying. A reciprocal buying arrangement may arise either through formal contract or through an informal understanding that may be scarcely distinguishable from a mere policy of cultivating the good will of a large customer. The essence of the arrangement is the willingness of each company to buy from the other, conditioned upon the expectation that the other company will make reciprocal purchases. The goods bought are typically dissimilar in kind, and in the usual case could be obtained from other sources on terms which, aside from the reciprocal purchases, would be no less advantageous. Where such a relationship is well established, it prevents the competitors of each company from selling to the other company, and affords to each company whatever increase of size and strength can be derived from an assured place as supplier to the other.

Purchase and sale relationships are by no means the only, and probably not the most significant, reciprocal arrangements. Large companies occupying related but different fields may work out arrangements for the reciprocal exchange of technology, for the joint enjoyment of transportation facilities, or for the joint development of sources of raw material.

Arrangements for joint ownership of transportation facilities or productive facilities fall into two broad classes. One, which eliminates direct competition between the cooperating companies, is a part of the monopoly problem rather than the problem of bigness. The other consists in joint activity by companies engaged in different lines of business at a point where the activity will contribute to the operations of each company. Thus, a petroleum refiner and a chemical manufacturer may pool their interest in developing a petro-chemical process for which neither possesses all of the needed technology and resources. Again, a paper manufacturer and a lumber manufacturer may collaborate in developing a logging railroad. In instances such as these, monopoly is not necessarily promoted. Indeed, projects may be undertaken that would not otherwise get started so promptly, if at all; and different groups of companies may undertake several such projects in competition with one another. Nevertheless, the broad effect of such alliances is that the strength of each participating company contributes to the position of the other participants in the projects. The benefits of the venture are not likely to be made generally available, either by allowing all interested parties to participate in the investment or by letting them buy the products or services on equal terms. If there are few opportunities to launch similar projects or if the cost of such an undertaking is beyond the reach of small companies, the fact that the venture is a partnership of big users of the product, rather than a cooperative project by all users or an enterprise designed to sell to all comers, deprives third parties of opportunities that might otherwise be open to them. Such partnerships among the big companies are likely to foster industrial progress, but at the same time to sharpen the differentials in power between the big and the little.

Arrangements for exchange of technology usually enable each participant to enjoy the collateral uses of the other participant's inventions, so far as these are applicable to its own field, without an increase in its own expenditures for research. To its own patents it can add the patents it obtains in the exchange, thus strengthening the hedge of patents which it has available to prevent its competitors from using its technology or to control the conditions under which they use it. When the technologies and patent rights of the partners to a comprehensive technological exchange have been thoroughly intermingled, each concern acquires, in practice, a veto upon the right of the other to work out similar technological exchanges with third parties, since such exchanges could not possibly be confined to the technology of one of the two parties exclusive of the technology of the other. Where such a reciprocal veto is enjoyed, each partner has an incentive to persuade concerns with which it is negotiating to make appropriate alliances with the other partner that will delimit fields of operation or establish mutually agreeable terms upon which to operate in overlapping fields. Consequently, technological partnerships tend to grow into complex systems of mutual accommodation among large business enterprises, within which the permissible sphere of activity of each enterprise is defined with ever-increasing precision as one agreement after another establishes a boundary, or a mutually satisfactory joint occupancy, between that enterprise and some other enterprise with reference to additional products and additional markets.

Reciprocal exchanges of technology may take place between small companies as well as large, but such exchanges are kept narrow by the limited research and the limited patent holdings of the small concerns. The typical pattern appears to be one in which large companies make broad exchanges among themselves and smaller companies are gradually fitted into the pattern through technological exchange arrangements with some one of the large companies, usually accompanied by commercial understandings as well. In such a system, the advantage of the large concern is apparent in the scope of its alliances and the tightness of the patent fences that it can build. This advantage is often further demonstrated, however, by the terms of the technological agreement between the large company and the small; for such agreements frequently contain provisions obligating the small company to convey to the large one the improvements it may make upon the large concern's patented processes, without reciprocal obligation as to the large company's improvements upon the small company's processes. In most such arrangements, the large company acts as an assembly point for technological knowledge and for patent rights, but each small company obtains only a segment of what has been assembled. The small companies are thus fitted into the interstices of the technological pattern established by agreements among large companies.

In summary, the large enterprise has advantages over the small in its capacity to spend money or take losses at any selected point at which it encounters a small rival, in its enjoyment of discriminations and preferences, in its ability to control distributors, customers, and sources of supply by tie-in sales and exclusive dealing arrangements, and in its opportunities to strengthen its position through exchange of favors with other large enterprises.

These various advantages may be important enough to assure the survival and growth of big concerns, relative to small ones, whether or not the big are functionally as efficient as the small.

5. *Nonmarket Uses of Power*

BY VIRTUE of its size, the large concern also has substantial advantages in activities that lie outside the processes of production and sale. These advantages are particularly evident in litigation, politics, public relations, and finance.

The large company's advantage in litigation is derived from the fact that it can afford to maintain its own law office and to disregard the costs of litigation in determining its legal tactics. In general, the big companies hire the best lawyers. In general, they do not hesitate to start lawsuits, to defend lawsuits, or to appeal cases that they have lost. In general, they do not skimp expenses incident to the thorough preparation of their side of a case. Small companies may have weaker counsel, may prepare a case less thoroughly, and may be less tenacious of their full legal rights.

These differences have important practical consequences. They not only tend toward a fuller protection of the legal rights of large companies but also enable them to win bargaining victories based upon their advantages as litigants even where there is no sound legal basis for the victories. The records of antitrust proceedings contain impressive evidence that certain patents held by large companies were not believed by the holders to be legally valid, but were nevertheless serviceable as parts of a system of asserted legal rights which gave the large company a protected position. Every patent may be the basis for a lawsuit, and an enterprise holding 500 patents has great capacity for legal harassment of those it may accuse of infringement, whether or not the patents are eventually found to be valid. Moreover, if some of the patents are good, acknowledgment of the validity of the rest may be one of the provisions of a license under the good patents, and thus consent may be invoked to bolster the weak parts of the patent holdings. Moreover, the holder of a patent may choose to sue not only the manufacturer who infringes it but also the customer who buys from that manufacturer. By adopting a policy of instituting such suits, the

345

large concern can force the customers of its small rival to stop dealing with him unless they are willing to buy a lawsuit with their purchase. Thus the effect of a boycott may be created by a persistent litigant whether or not the patent upon which he relies is eventually sustained in the courts.

In exploiting patent claims, the general financial strength of the large company furnishes a strong base for its aggressiveness in litigation. If a small concern accuses a large one of infringing patents, the contingent liability associated with a possible adverse verdict is unlikely to affect the large company's credit or to induce it to compromise a doubtful case. A single small concern's patents can seldom cover more than a minor segment of a large diversified concern's business activity. When the large company sues the small, however, the alleged infringement may apply to the small company's whole business or to a large part of it, and the contingent liability may be so great as to impair the small company's opportunity to borrow money for current operations. Under these circumstances, the large company may be able to strike a strong bargain even though it has a weak case.

Patent litigation is merely illustrative of the advantage a large company is likely to enjoy in litigation arising out of questions about the interpretation of contracts and about the validity of titles to land, claims of damage from unfair business conduct, and similar matters. The law courts may be used as a basis for an attack upon a competitor or potential competitor or as a bargaining device in dealing with suppliers and customers. Recourse to law may supplement, or be a substitute for, the strategies of the market. Current advantages may be transformed into contractual rights in such a way as to establish an enduringly protected business position.

The political strength of the great concern is likewise an aspect of its ability to spend money. Large companies start with certain initial political disadvantages because they are in the spotlight, because there is some suspicion of their power, and because small companies are more numerous. However, the large company can often overcome its handicap and obtain a decided advantage by political expenditures. The campaign contributions of large companies and the occasional case of direct or indirect bribery are probably the least significant sources of the large company's political power. More important, the large company spends whatever money is needed to argue effectively on behalf of its interest where a political issue affects it. To know what decisions affecting a particular business interest are pending in Congress, in the many administrative agencies of the federal government, and in state governments is a task for one or more full-time persons. The work of many people may be required in assembling facts and preparing persuasive arguments relevant to these decisions. Detailed acquaintance with governmental processes is necessary to know what official will actually formulate a particular decision. Close attention to timing is indispensable if the case for a particular business interest is to be presented to that official at a time neither so early that he will disregard it nor so late that he cannot use it. Large concerns are increasingly skilled in these processes, primarily because they take such work seriously and do it on a large scale. While some smaller business interests make a comparable showing through associations set up for the purpose, the experience of a Washington official is that small companies generally find out what is happening too late and prepare their case too scantily and hastily to be fully effective where their interests conflict with those of large companies. A government policy may be designed in broad terms to be neutral as between large and small business or to give preference to small business and yet may be translated into a series of decisions not fully expressive of the policy because the presentation by large companies of fact and persuasive argument relevant to each decision has not been sufficiently offset by similar presentations by small companies.

The political advantages of large companies are significant because of the increasing tendency of businessmen to seek from government laws and administrative rulings that directly affect business activity. Tariffs, labeling laws, licensing laws, taxes, subsidies, health regulations, and the like are invoked in an effort to give one type of enterprise or product an advantage over another.

The large concern has an advantage in public relations like its advantage in politics. It must overcome an initial suspicion based upon its size, although this suspicion is blended with admiration for success and presumption that success reflects efficiency and usefulness. Large companies have developed a wide variety of techniques for winning public respect and sympathy by devices ranging all the way from ballyhoo to substantial contributions of public service. By institutional advertising, they tell the public directly and indirectly how good they are. By speeches, pamphlets, and subsidized studies, they present to various audiences reasoned statements of their points of view. By a wide variety of devices they cultivate contacts with people who are influential in community affairs, in journalism, and in education. They participate in charities, educational projects, and many other nonprofit activities well regarded by the public. Increasingly, they use public opinion research, psychological findings, and careful analyses of group interests to develop well-planned and heavily financed campaigns for the purpose of achieving specific objectives in public relations. There was such a campaign a few years ago, for example, by segments of American business that desired legislation to modify the law applicable to basing point systems.

Many of these devices are not new, and few, if any, are used exclusively by large business enterprises. However, they cost money, and the large concern, being able to spend substantial sums in this way, and to employ expert advice as to how to do it, is capable of guiding a substantial part of public opinion to such views as it may think desirable. Within wide limits, it can buy its own reputation. Good repute, in turn, may be used for market advantage, political advantage, or advantage in controversies with other economic groups.

The large concern also has an advantage in finance. It is a large user of the services of commercial banks and investment banks, keeps large sums on deposit, and therefore receives the consideration given a valued customer. Being well known throughout a wide area, it has an unusually broad field of choice of banks to deal with. If its operations are widely diversified, the consequent diversification of risk is attractive to those who extend credit or place investments.

These characteristics of large companies give them a preferred status in financial transactions to such an extent that the operations of investment bankers and of important commercial banks have been planned with the large company in mind. Investment bankers, particularly, have not developed procedures appropriate to small-scale flotations. The federal government has repeatedly sought to encourage the establishment of financial institutions better suited to the requirements of small business, especially in the provision of equity capital, but has not succeeded in eliminating the institutionalized advantage of the large concern.

Moreover, there appear to be important instances in which certain large companies have preferential access to the funds of certain financial institutions. Such access may mean not only greater ease in borrowing money but also a reluctance on the part of the financial institution to finance companies whose business policy is regarded by the favored customer as unsound or dangerous. Moreover, the favored customer's loans may be protected at times when

348

its business position is precarious or when credit is stringent. Such protection is peculiarly likely if the financial commitments to the favored company are so heavy that its fall would be a blow to the credit of the financial institution itself.

The significance of advantages in access to credit is apparently great, for some of our largest companies have been developed in close affiliation with important banks, and many others have become interconnected with large banks by interlocking directorates and interlocking stock holdings.

Thus, in various ways, bigness and diversity may become a source of special advantage. Certain advantages spring from bigness when the bigness is concentrated in a single industry but falls short of monopoly there; certain advantages inhere in bigness regardless of the degree of internal coherence in the enterprise; others may increase or diminish as the activities of the enterprise become more diverse. Traditional concepts of monopoly are insufficient in analyzing the character and extent of these advantages.

How much importance should be attached to the advantages derived from bigness is not clear. That an effort should be made to curb the exercise of some types of power derived from bigness is, to me, obvious. That unless such an effort is successful big companies are likely to have a larger place in the economy than would be justified by their relative functional efficiency is a reasonable inference. No conclusion can be drawn, however, as to whether or not a progressive concentration of economic activity in the big companies is to be anticipated. Bigness is only one source of power. The effective balance of power in industry is the result of the interaction between the power of the big and other types of power, including, for example, the monopoly power that may be exercised by concerns that are not big and the power that small concerns may derive from organized association. Moreover, the trend of economic organization is not determined by power alone. A tendency for bigness to generate power and for power to enhance bigness may be offset in various ways—by a technological trend toward decentralization, bureaucratic inefficiencies associated with excessive size, sustained public encouragement of small enterprise, selective public action against concentrations of power, and many other influences. The trend of concentration is determined by many forces and cannot safely be predicted from an analysis of one alone.

Some of the important consequences of bigness depend, not upon the power of certain large enterprises, but upon the relative place

349

of large-scale business organization in the economy as a whole. The farther we move toward an economy of a few large business units, the less we can count upon automatic competitive adjustments to harmonize production, demand, prices, and costs. In a big diversified company the checks and balances upon which economic theorists have relied for the protection of the public interest do not operate in the traditional way. The diversification of the large concern minimizes risk by setting loss in one part of the business against profit in another and thereby providing an automatic business risk insurance. This kind of stability is one source of strength for such a concern. In economic terms, however, such a spreading of risks sets aside the effect of changes in prices, costs, and profits as guides to economic activity and as selective factors in assuring the survival of well-designed and well-conducted operations and the elimination of ill-designed and ill-conducted ones. The essential feature of the spreading of risks is that the profits from one activity shall subsidize the continuance of another. In such a system, the selective forces of competition are ineffective; activities are selected and adjustments made within diversified concerns by managerial decisions as to the extent of subsidy.

Doubtless there is a possibility that the management of such an enterprise, desiring to maximize profits, will reduce or eliminate the unprofitable activities and expand the profitable ones. However, even if the broad strategy of the company does not make the continuance of unprofitable activities desirable, the chance to eliminate them is no greater than the ability of management to detect them. Within the diversified company a considerable number of expenditures take the form of overhead costs or joint costs when they would be directly attributable to particular types of activity if the same operations were carried on by specialized companies. The allocation of many of these costs is the result of a policy decision more truly than it is the source of one, and consequently the accuracy with which the profits from different types of activity can be determined tends to decrease as activities become more diversified. Furthermore, the large diversified company may not establish a system of records detailed enough to segregate income, costs, and profits by lines of activity. The FTC recently sought to obtain from the largest manufacturing companies the value of their shipments of each 5-digit product class from each plant. A considerable number of the companies were unable to give important parts of even so limited a body of information except on an estimated basis. To the extent that the data are not available, managements cannot be expected to provide through managerial decision the type of adjustment that competition between companies can no longer make. Thus one effect of diversification is to promote the survival of groups of business activities that are historically or strategically related, so long as somewhere in each group there are enough profitable activities to support the unprofitable ones.

Apart from these effects of bigness upon the functioning of the market, the replacement of small business enterprises by large ones has significant consequences for personal opportunity and for the process of making business decisions. So far as our economic organization takes the form of a small number of large enterprises, the points at which decisions of business policy are made are relatively few, and each policy decision applies to a relatively wide area of business activity. This necessarily means that a few business executives carry responsibility for basic business decisions, while the executives down the line in the large concern have limited discretion within the boundaries set by the decisions of their superiors. Entrepreneurship becomes scarce, and much of what was once entrepreneurship is converted into bureaucracy. Insofar as diffusion of ownership is associated with bigness, the persons making entrepreneurial decisions at the top of large corporations may be guided less by the simple pursuit of profit and more by a miscellany of considerations reflecting their personal attitudes and the various pressures that focus upon them, of which the pressure of the owner's interest is only one. Moreover, a small proportion of the persons who hold responsibility as business executives can reach the top, and the ascent to final authority in some business enterprise is up a few very long ladders.

That part of the business community is organized in this manner seems to me to furnish no ground for concern, provided it is a small enough segment of the whole to be effectively checked by other types of business organization. But if the business community should come to be typically thus organized, the impact of the institutional change would be far-reaching. Its general direction would be toward an authoritarian system of business, within which the significant checks and balances would be, not those of the market, but whatever safeguards might be built into the structure of the corporation or into the relations between the corporation and the state.

The important questions as to this kind of institutional change are highly controversial: How important can large enterprises become before there is a significant change in our institutions? Do large enterprises now have, or is there danger that they will have, this degree of importance?

COMMENT

GEORGE W. STOCKING, Vanderbilt University

ECONOMISTS in their study of the economics of the firm have used simplified models. On the basis of their rigorous assumptions, these models afford a coherent and consistent theory of entrepreneurial behavior. Despite the unreality of their underlying assumptions, they are useful in analyzing price behavior in industrial markets. The prevalence of numerous and complex monopoly elements in the world about us makes the purely competitive model seem wholly unreal, yet it still affords a useful norm with which to compare actual conditions and by which to evaluate the significance of departures from the norm. The Chamberlinian models make a closer approach to reality by taking account of two significant characteristics which differentiate the real world from the nineteenth century neoclassical economists' conception of it—few sellers and differentiation of product. But these, too, have necessarily been simplified models, helpful in understanding aspects of entrepreneurial behavior but inadequate to explain all the ramifications of market behavior under the complex conditions of modern business. In truth, business behavior is too complex and varied to permit of a single generalized explanation. As John M. Clark has pointed out in trying to classify markets, hundreds or thousands of combinations are possible.[1]

The tool makers, as well as the tool users, are aware of the shortcomings of their instruments and are constantly striving to perfect them. Edwards, recognizing the inadequacies of generalized monopoly theory to explain fully the concrete and intricate industrial situations that have come within his experience, has made a fresh approach. In doing so he points out that the economists have appraised "problems of monopoly power in the light of certain conceptions of *monopolistic exploitation,* on the one hand, and certain conceptions of *business efficiency,* on the other." (Italics supplied.) What he means by the appraisal of "monopoly power in the light

[1] John M. Clark, "Toward a Concept of Workable Competition," *American Economic Review,* June 1940, pp. 241-256.

of certain conceptions of monopolistic exploitation" and its relevance to his subsequent discussion, I can readily understand. What he means by the appraisal of "monopoly power in the light of . . . certain conceptions of business efficiency" is more obscure. I infer that he has in mind the argument that the economies of mass production in many industries permit so few firms that each will have some power over the market, and this is one of my assumptions in commenting on his discussion.

Like monopoly, the conglomerate as he uses the term is an abstraction, useful because it "throws a spotlight upon a part of the situation that cannot be described and appraised in the traditional way." His conglomerate, the chief attributes of which are bigness and diversification, "can be as large as one chooses to conceive it without thereby acquiring a monopoly of any product and without deriving from its size the efficiencies that are traditionally associated with mass production. Thus the term conglomerate becomes a device for examining problems of *size* and *power* apart from the traditional focus upon monopoly and efficiency."[2] (Italics supplied.)

With this tool in hand Edwards examines various manifestations of business power which he thinks are the product of size unassociated with monopoly, and various aspects of size which he thinks are not associated with efficiency. I propose to test some of his specific illustrations or arguments in the light of these two criteria. Specifically, I shall concern myself with two questions: Does the power of Edwards' conglomerate inhere in its size and diversification (as he thinks) or stem from an element of monopoly (as I argue)? Does its size reflect economic efficiency or a search for efficiency? In applying the first test I shall resort to conventional theory. In applying the second I shall have in mind the distinctions made by E. A. G. Robinson in his discussion of the optimum firm: (1) the technological optimum; (2) the managerial optimum; (3) the marketing optimum; (4) the financial optimum; and (5) the security optimum.[3] In arguing that Edwards' conglomerate may

[2] Since presenting his paper at the Princeton Conference, Edwards has added a footnote to it (note 2) expressly limiting his interpretation of the monopoly concept to "the sense it had in the older economic theory and still has in our antimonopoly laws, rather than in the later meaning given it by the theory of monopolistic competition." This limitation excludes all that Chamberlin and his refiners have brought within the scope of neoclassical monopoly theory and thereby enhances the apparent theoretical significance of Edwards' concept of "conglomerate power," although Edwards readily concedes that its actual significance lies in dealing with concrete market situations.

[3] E. A. G. Robinson, *The Structure of Competitive Industry* (rev. ed., London: Nisbet, 1935), Chap. 2.

reflect a search for one of these optimums, I do not mean to imply that the optimum scale of operation as judged by these criteria, with a single exception, is so large as necessarily to eventuate in monopoly. That exception is the security optimum. A firm in a competitive industry may enhance its security by joining a cartel or by monopolizing the market. The security optimum, in short, may be inconsistent with competition. The other optimums, although falling short of monopoly, may contribute to an oligopolistic market structure, and this I believe is likely to lessen the vigor of competition, although generalization about their consequences may be risky. My criticism of Edwards is that in the illustrations he cites either the size of the conglomerates reflects economic efficiency or their power reflects monopoly.

As Edwards sees it, bigness has a "special kind of power," based upon the fact that a big concern can spend money in large amounts. "In encounters with small enterprises it can buy scarce materials and attractive sites, inventions, and facilities; pre-empt the services of the most expensive technicians and executives; and acquire reserves of materials for the future." All of these advantages I believe can be expressed in traditional terms with a gain, not a loss, in clarity. Apparently it is the indivisibility and the limited supply of the better raw material deposits, the more attractive sites, the new inventions, and the more expensive technicians and executives that account for the inability of small firms to buy them. Exceptional factors, scarce and indivisible, may have such a high differential rent that they can be used economically only when their total cost is distributed over a large output. That is to say, only large firms can afford to buy them. Here business efficiency is a function of size. If without achieving monopoly power big firms pay more for these factors than their economic rent, they cannot long survive in competition with their smaller rivals. The problem is thus reduced to one of monopoly exploitation, one of efficiency, or both.

"Closely associated with differences in financial strength is a difference between the attitudes of large concerns toward one another and their attitudes toward smaller business enterprises." Big firms manifest a live-and-let-live attitude towards each other not displayed by any of them towards their smaller rivals. But is relative size the significant variable? Or is it power over the market? "The interests of great enterprises are likely to touch at many points [geographical or points of diversification], and it would be possible for each to mobilize at any one of these points a considerable aggregate of resources. The anticipated gain to such a concern from unmitigated competitive attack upon another large enterprise at one point of contact is likely to be slight as compared with the possible loss from retaliatory action by that enterprise at many other points of contact." This situation suggests the well-known monopolistic solutions of division of markets and division of fields. And even if such do not take place, the live-and-let-live policy can readily be brought within the scope of oligopolistic theory. The problem apparently is one of fewness of sellers or relative, not absolute, size.

"This aspect of the power of large concerns becomes more conspicuous as the diversity of operations becomes greater, that is, as the likelihood that the large concern has monopoly power in any particular market becomes less. . . . The large company . . . has the maximum chance to discipline or destroy any particular small company by a localized attack without serious inconvenience to itself, and has the minimum vulnerability to attack from a single small company." Again, neither absolute size nor diversification seems to be the significant variable, but relative power. Local price cutting to destroy a rival is a long-recognized monopoly device. And unless the large firm can (1) recapture the temporary losses involved in the price war by above-normal (monopoly) returns elsewhere on the same or some other product, (2) eventually obtain a local monopoly by driving out its little rival, or (3) force the rival to follow its price leadership, what has it profited? Surely all this can be brought within traditional monopoly theory. Why does the little firm need disciplining in the first place? Presumably because it has cut prices. Below what? Below competitive levels or below noncompetitive prices charged by the little company's sole rival? The little company, unless it is more efficient than the big or unless the big company as price leader has been charging monopoly prices, has nothing to gain in the long run by price cutting. Traditional theory seems adequate to explain this behavior.

"One important way in which bigness contributes to power is by creating opportunities for self-sufficiency." The big nonintegrated concern, Edwards believes, can use the threat of integration in bargaining with either its suppliers or its distributors and thereby get better terms than its smaller rivals can get, at the expense of those from whom it buys or to whom it sells. Although the motives prompting entrepreneurs to integrate their business may be complex, if one assumes profit maximization as the goal of business enterprise the economics of integration can be succinctly stated.

355

Integration may lower costs by economizing in the use of some factors, by eliminating some steps in the process of production, or by insuring a more even flow of materials. Here an increase in size through integration brings greater efficiency: the technological optimum is large. It may bring greater security in the short run by guaranteeing that supplies will be available when they are wanted and in the long run by freeing a concern from reliance on the decisions of those who have no stake in the nonintegrated enterprise. It may stabilize profits by freeing an enterprise from the ill effects of uneven price movements at different levels of the productive process. It may relieve a firm of the necessity of paying tribute to a monopolistic supplier. In each of these illustrations an increase in size brings greater security; that is to say, the security optimum is large. It may lower administrative expenses by using managerial talents more effectively: the managerial optimum is large. By bringing a manufacturer closer to the ultimate consumer, integration may insure a more certain and continuous market for his product at profitable prices: the marketing optimum is large. Thus all of these advantages may be comprehended under the traditional concepts of monopoly power and efficiency of scale. By integrating, firms may increase their profits by escaping from the power of others or by reducing their costs, or they may obtain greater security. If this analysis is correct, Edwards is wrong in attributing to a conglomerate as such the power to exploit suppliers or distributors by threatening to integrate. If a conglomerate is obtaining materials from a supplier at a competitive price, it has no economic advantage in integrating unless integration lowers costs or brings greater security. If it lowers costs or brings greater security, these are advantages inherent in size. This of course is not to argue that large, integrated firms do not possess monopoly power, but to argue that their power inheres in an element of monopoly, not in integration *per se*. Nor is it to argue that the nonintegrated conglomerate may not buy on such scale as to have monopolistic power. If the situation is one of bilateral monopoly or oligopoly, the conglomerate may by threat of integration get its goods for less than the little buyer can hope to do.

Edwards recognizes that *some* tie-in sales may stem from monopoly power, "but tie-in sales may also be used in selling a product that enjoys a high degree of consumer acceptance, even if this product is in competition with other highly acceptable products and constitutes a portion of the total supply too small to be an expression of monopoly power." Surely this is a typical case of product differentiation comprehended by the Chamberlinian concept of monopolistic competition and characterized many years earlier by Veblen as a monopoly of prestige (see note 2). No firm could exact a tie-in contract for products sold in a purely competitive market. A monopolist of one product in great demand may use his monopoly power to sell other products which otherwise he could not so profitably sell. But a conglomerate without monopoly power could not do so.

Similarly, the practices which conglomerates resort to of extending reciprocal favors, exchanging patents, and owning transportation facilities or developing raw materials or new processes jointly can be explained in the traditional terms of monopoly power or economic efficiency. Firms may exchange patent rights either to increase their efficiency by a more complete use or development of technology or to monopolize markets or for both purposes. They may pool resources to develop new processes, to find new sources of raw materials, or to provide joint transportation facilities because by doing so they reduce risks in conducting large-scale enterprise. They do so because they believe that the security optimum is large.

A rose by any other name will smell as sweet. But this is not merely a problem of nomenclature. To designate a plant as a rose may identify it to the undiscriminating man in the street. But the horticulturist or expert gardener will find it edifying to know whether the particular rose in question is of the polyantha, the Noisette, or the hybrid perpetual class. Different care may be required in growing each class.

Edwards' conglomerate, as I understand his discussion of it, is a firm that is large and diversified but whose size and diversification do not reflect a quest for efficiency and whose power over the market cannot be explained in traditional terms of monopoly or oligopoly. If antisocial power inheres in the conglomerate purely because it is large and its activities are diversified, I should think Congress should limit by statute the right of firms to grow indefinitely and to diversify. Such a policy might seem to have the advantage of simplicity, but it raises the questions of how big is too big and how varied may a firm's activities become without constituting a social menace? Our antitrust policy may need overhauling to bring it into harmony with the complex structure of modern industry, but I am not convinced that the conglomerate as such is a useful target at which to aim.

Despite these criticisms, I think Edwards' discussion enriches the

357

literature by calling attention to the many and complex ways in which monopoly power may be exercised—and therefore in showing antitrust agencies what to look for—and to the various factors which make for an increase in size; and I think he breaks new and important ground in his discussion of the nonmarket uses of power, be it conglomerate or monopoly. Some of his ideas on this issue, too, can be fitted within the traditional concepts, but to so fit them might tend to conceal rather than reveal their social and economic significance. For example, as Edwards points out, large companies can afford to maintain elaborate law offices or use expensive lawyers. Small firms cannot. This might be regarded as an economy of scale, but it also may be contrary to the general welfare because, as Edwards makes clear, the large companies not only can win their *lawsuits*, they can win *bargaining victories* even when they have no sound legal or economic basis for doing so. Such power tends to keep small companies small and to make big companies bigger with no social *quid pro quo*. Similarly in politics and more particularly in public relations, bigness brings advantages to those possessing it quite apart from its relation to economic efficiency. And I suspect not the least of them is the power to mold individual thinking and thereby to create public opinion. The modern techniques of mass communication—the periodical, the radio, television, and the privately made propaganda film—are giving our giant corporations a subtle and ominous power, a power over the human mind. They are enabling the big and powerful corporation with a vested interest in a particular pattern of business control to shape attitudes, arouse prejudices, coin good will, form public opinion, create habits of thought, with their readers and listeners unaware that their ideas are being fabricated for them.

The giant corporation is indeed one of the most significant institutional developments of all time. I would agree with Edwards that it is an instrument of power—social, economic, and political. About its origin, the factors making for its growth, the factors which influence the decisions of its managers, and the exercise of its power, we know too little. I would also agree with Edwards that traditional tools of analysis are inadequate to an understanding of these phenomena. The key figure in contemporary theory is the enterpriser. But the enterpriser is a conceptual product of simpler institutional arrangements. Traditionally he was both owner and decision-maker. The modern corporation has brought a separation of these functions. Thus the large corporation has acquired power not exercised by those who own it. Corporate executives, although not insensitive to pecuniary considerations, may be more interested in security than in maximizing earnings. The corporation affords a way of life for those who run it. They have power and prestige which they want to preserve and enhance. Although they cannot ignore market considerations in their decision-making, neither can they ignore the impact of their decisions on their organized labor force, the public, and the politicians. In brief, they may be more concerned with a socio-political than with a pecuniary calculus. Contemporary theories of entrepreneurial behavior may be institutionally obsolete. What we need is a new "conceptual framework," to use the jargon of our profession, in our study of business enterprise. But I am not convinced that Edwards' conception of the conglomerate is the answer to our problem. I am convinced, however, that Edwards' informed and realistic appreciation of the social, political, and economic significance of bigness (whether it be described in terms of the conglomerate or monopoly) and the clarity with which he presents his views represent an important contribution to an understanding of the problem.

FULL COSTS, COST CHANGES, AND PRICES

RICHARD B. HEFLEBOWER

NORTHWESTERN UNIVERSITY

THE vigorous debate over full-cost and over theories which relate price changes to cost changes has brought about neither their rejection nor their general incorporation into received doctrine. When Hall and Hitch[1] in their report on the interviews with British businessmen by the Oxford Economists' Research Group attracted the attention of other economists to the theory of full-cost pricing, it was hailed by many as an original and practical theory of price determination. Actually it was not new, for in varied forms it had long occupied a place in business school texts and in the moralistic and expository statements of businessmen.[2] To the extent that economists were not aware of this pricing procedure,[3] that indicated their ignorance if not disdain of "business" literature. But in the 1930's economists were in a more receptive mood for such heresy as the full-cost pricing idea. During those years of declining demand the flexibility of prices in the markets where sellers were numerous compared to the rigidity of those in concentrated industries called for explanation.[4] At the same time developments in theory pointed to the indeterminacy of price in markets where sellers are few. The solution of that enigma which Hall and Hitch derived from their questioning of businessmen was that "in pricing they try to apply a rule of thumb which we shall call 'full cost.' "[5] While this theory

[1] R. L. Hall and C. J. Hitch, "Price Theory and Business Behaviour," *Oxford Economic Papers*, No. 2, May 1939. Reprinted in T. Wilson and P. W. S. Andrews (eds.), *Oxford Studies in the Price Mechanism* (Oxford, 1951). Further references to this study will be to the reprinted volume.

[2] Indeed, a quite full exposition had been presented in 1924 by a businessman, Donaldson Brown, in his "Pricing Policy in Relation to Financial Control," *Management and Administration*, February 1924, pp. 195-198, 283-286, 417-422.

[3] That is, in unregulated markets. In publicly controlled pricing, the building of prices on costs, as in the "fair return on fair value" tenet in public utility regulation, has long been accepted. Another example is "cost-plus" pricing of military goods. Somewhat analogous is the (average) cost-difference defense of price differences under the Robinson-Patman Act. The repeated attempts to require that maximum prices during the World War II and post-Korea crises be set on the basis of total costs, or of change in total cost from the date at which prices were frozen, indicate the hold of this doctrine on the business community.

[4] That much of this difference, for various reasons, was more apparent than real, or that it might reflect differences in cost-change experience, need not detain us here.

[5] Hall and Hitch, *op. cit.*, p. 113.

provided a rationale for the immunity of prices to demand changes when unaccompanied by cost changes, it did not gain wide acceptance as a substitute for orthodox marginal analysis. In the years since 1940 the relation of costs to pricing policies has been further investigated empirically[6] and has been subjected to the close scrutiny of theorists.[7] As a consequence parts of price theory have been re-examined and some economists would assign to full cost a definite role in economic doctrine.[8]

The task here is to appraise (1) the empirical evidence and (2) the theoretical significance of full-cost pricing and of other theories which at least appear to relate prices only to costs. Before this can be undertaken, the meaning of the full-cost doctrine must be delineated. Then the empirical evidence in support of such theories will be appraised; this will lead to some comments on research methods and needs. Whether or not empirical proof is established, the theoretical significance of the full-cost ideas will be explored. Some comments will be offered as to whether these ideas disprove or give empirical content to marginal analysis and some observations will be made about the empirical study of certain problems of oligopoly.

1. *What is Full-Cost Pricing?*

THE term "full-cost" pricing does not have precise meaning nor does it refer to a clearly delineated group of ideas about price determination. In part, this reflects an inevitable reduction of precision when theoretical and empirical work are blended or when disputants representing these two approaches enter into debate. In

---

[6] E.g. C. C. Saxton, *The Economics of Price Determination* (Oxford, 1942), and R. A. Lester, "Shortcomings of Marginal Analysis for Wage-Employment Problems," *American Economic Review*, March 1946, pp. 63-82. Joel Dean, *Managerial Economics* (Prentice-Hall, 1951), pp. 444-450 and A. R. Oxenfeldt, *Industrial Pricing and Market Practices* (Prentice-Hall, 1951), pp. 156-164, give some support to this doctrine. Quite different in approach is A. C. Neal's *Industrial Concentration and Price Inflexibility* (American Council on Public Affairs, 1942).

[7] E.g. Fritz Machlup, "Marginal Analysis and Empirical Research," *American Economic Review*, September 1946, pp. 519-554. William Fellner, *Competition among the Few* (Knopf, 1949), pp. 153-157 and 224-225, and "Average-cost Pricing and the Theory of Uncertainty," *Journal of Political Economy*, June 1948, pp. 249-252. E. A. G. Robinson, "The Pricing of Manufactured Goods," *Economic Journal*, December 1950, pp. 771-780. R. F. Kahn, "Oxford Studies in the Price Mechanism," *Economic Journal*, March 1952, pp. 119-130. Tibor Scitovsky, *Welfare and Competition* (Irwin, 1951) Chap. XIII. E. H. Chamberlin, "Full-Cost and Monopolistic Competition," *Economic Journal*, June 1952, pp. 318-325. R. F. Harrod, *Economic Essays* (Harcourt, Brace, 1952) pp. 157-174.

[8] Notably Fellner, Scitovsky, Chamberlin, and Harrod, in above citations.

part, also, it reflects the mixing of two analyses: the level of equilibrium price and the conditions of change of price—a mixing which has been usual in other theoretical analyses but of questionable value in oligopoly analysis, as Sweezy pointed out.[9] It is particularly so where the analysis is approached empirically. For these and other reasons, further analysis will be facilitated by exploring assumptions, clarifying terminology, and indicating the variety of theories which fall under, or are akin in important attributes to, the full-cost principle. This will mean that the discussion will include more of recent price theory than the term "full cost" may connote.

Stated briefly, but in a form which involves the essential attributes of many variations of the idea, the full-cost principle holds that the firm (s) set its (their) prices with regard only to total unit costs at some assumed volume rate.[10] As such the theory is a direct challenge to two tenets of generally accepted economic theory; i.e. (1) that demand as well as supply conditions, or costs, enter into price determination (for which Marshall used the "two blades of the scissors" analogy); and (2) that the rational solution of all price problems requires the equating of *marginal* revenue and *marginal* cost.[11] Whether the heresy is as great as it appears, particularly in Harrod's formulation, will be clarified by exploring the following topics: (1) meaning of "full cost," (2) short-term pricing, (3) price setting or price changing, (4) influence of demand, (5) full-cost or gross-margin pricing, and (6) types of markets.

MEANING OF "FULL COST"

CONTRASTING the term "full cost" with marginal cost does not explain adequately the meaning of the former. The idea implies average cost, for it includes variable and fixed costs. Whether a profit is considered as a cost, or as part of a gross margin added to part or all of direct costs, or is specifically included as a net margin above costs, a return on investment is part of the pricing formula.[12]

[9] Paul M. Sweezy, "Demand Under Conditions of Oligopoly," *Journal of Political Economy*, August 1939, pp. 572-573.

[10] It makes no difference whether "normal" profit is considered to be added to a cost or to be itself a cost. Indeed, it is often included in a gross margin over part or all of direct cost.

[11] In contrast to marginal analysis, full-cost pricing is full-unit-cost pricing without regard to demand. Viewed from the usual theoretical framework, it could result in a price that maximizes profits only by accident, not by design.

[12] Indeed, the profit rate may be computed as that which will yield a target rate of return on investment at normal volume. The procedure is described by

Since most firms are multiproduct, the accountants' allocation of common costs, and of costs distributed over time as well, are accepted at face value. Or differential margins over direct costs (which have evolved out of some complex of common cost allocations and the intensity of competition in the sale of various products[13] or items) may be used in arriving at full cost.

But these parts of the definition leave unsettled the impact of factor prices and of volume rates on costs under given technology. The average total cost could be that experienced historically, or expected, or considered "normal." Ordinarily, either present or expected prices of important factors are used. But the impact of volume rate on conversion or handling costs per unit is either assumed to be nominal or is disregarded by assuming an average or "normal" volume.[14] In a few cases reference is made to expected volume; indeed Harrod's argument involves the assumption of a plant scale reflective of expected average volume at a full-cost price.[15] With this exception, and with particular reference to those who relate full-cost to short-term pricing, the doctrine disregards the possible impact of the level of price set on volume and hence on unit costs. The reasoning is a one-way street from costs to price, with no reverse influence.

SHORT-TERM PRICING

FULL-COST pricing is used by many writers as a short-term price theory.[16] This is not short-term in the formal sense of cases in which

Dean (*op. cit.*, pp. 448-449) and an elaborate application shown in Homer Vanderblue, "Pricing Policies in the Automobile Industry," *Harvard Business Review*, Summer and Autumn, 1939.

[13] Note how the cost formula itself comes to incorporate demand influences, a fact which becomes increasingly evident in the following pages.

[14] This is typically the volume rate assumed in the "standard cost" system of the firm or a cost system which provides norms for testing operating efficiency or for making choices between alternative uses of facilities. Saxton (*op. cit.*, pp. 52-53) found that among the British firms he surveyed the most typical view was that 80 to 85 per cent of capacity constituted "normal" volume. On the basis of his study of American practice, Dean suggests that 75 per cent is regarded as normal.

[15] Harrod, *op. cit.*, pp. 160-161.

[16] This seems to be an appropriate interpretation of Dean's explanation (*op. cit.*, pp. 145 and 149) and is pointed out specifically by Saxton (*op. cit.*, pp. 29-37). The short period is also the center of attention of Hall and Hitch (*op. cit.*, pp. 109, 120-122, and 124). This deduction rests in considerable part on the fact that while they emphasize the competitive influences on the size of the margin between direct costs and prices this margin is assumed not to change in the short run. On the other hand, Harrod (*op. cit.*, pp. 159 ff.) seems to look upon full cost as a long-term principle.

the firm's plant and equipment remain unchanged. Instead the reference is to pricing for a specific contract, for a planning or budgeting period, or for a season or model period. Even more clearly these doctrines deal with the change of price from its preexisting level.[17]

PRICE SETTING OR PRICE CHANGING

THE full-cost doctrine and the related ideas examined here appear as explanations both of the level of the price for a commodity at a given time and of the conditions under which that price will or will not be changed. Sometimes this distinction is not made clearly, as if it were not important.[18] Theorists particularly are inclined to disregard the distinction. The setting of prices in the strict meaning of the term is not an important part of the pricing problem.[19] What most people mean by price setting is the procedures and forces by which the existing level of price was determined. For Hall and Hitch concluded: "The height of price . . . is determined on the 'full cost' principle. . . ."[20] Harrod argues that the firm will plan its plant size to be that which at optimum operating rate, the output can, on the average of good times and bad, be sold at a full-cost price.[21] Andrews has a statement which except for the reference to plant scale amounts to the same when he says "that the price which a business

[17] Andrews' theory reverses the emphasis, however. He is concerned primarily with the long-run price, which he finds to be equal to direct costs plus a competitively determined gross margin. Then, in the short run, prices change only with movements of direct costs or under extreme circumstances by a larger amount when adherence to the gross margin breaks down. Thus Andrews' theory becomes one of the dominance of long-term considerations over short-term conduct. For details see his *Manufacturing Business* (Oxford, 1949).

[18] Dean refers to "Surveys of actual business practice in setting prices" (*op. cit.*, p. 444) and to price setting for "specifically designed" goods (p. 445). Presumably he would include price changes according to cost changes in what he calls "cost plus" pricing. Oxenfeldt (*op. cit.*) deals explicitly only with price setting.

[19] J. T. Dunlop and E. M. Martin in their study of the International Harvester Company report: "Consideration of prices for most items . . . centers around changes from established levels. A decision not to change a quoted price in some circumstances where the market situation has changed radically may be as significant a decision as one in which an important price change is made. Only in those instances where a complete new line, such as a new tractor, is introduced, is it necessary to consider the price of an implement de novo." (D. V. Brown and others, *Industrial Wage Rates, Labor Costs and Price Policies*, Temporary National Economic Committee, Monograph 5, 1940, p. 80.)

[20] Hall and Hitch, *op. cit.*, pp. 122-123. Later we shall refer to their hastily added modifications of this principle.

[21] Harrod, *op. cit.*, pp. 159-161.

will normally quote for a particular product will equal the estimated average direct cost of production plus a [gross or] costing-margin."[22] Such rules are most often used to explain that prices will change ordinarily when factor prices move. On the other hand, it is agreed that selling prices will ordinarily not reflect demand variations unassociated with, or greater than, factor price movements.[23] For this reason the analysis here is broadened to include investigations which are directed solely to the price change problem, such as that of A. C. Neal.[24]

THE INFLUENCE OF DEMAND

BUT further consideration of these cost explanations of prices shows that the cost rules themselves contain, or in application are modified for, demand influences. In direct relation to the height of cross elasticities of demand among rivals' products, the gross margin used by the individual firm reflects not its own indirect costs but rather the margin it finds by experience to be desirable in light of costs and market conduct of its rivals. For longer-term pricing, Harrod specifically refers to the firm's long-term demand curve, which he assumes to be quite flat.[25]

Once the price exists, all proponents of the cost-to-price theories agree that price will not be changed because volume rises or falls moderately, except when a rival decreases the price first. Otherwise, the benefits of favorable demand will be enjoyed in the form

[22] Andrews, *op. cit.*, p. 184. Andrews does not consider this to be "full cost" for reasons to be given below.

[23] Hall and Hitch say on page 124: "This does not mean that there will be no tendency for the prices of these goods to fall in depressions and rise in booms, but simply that there will be no tendency for them to fall or rise more than the wage and raw materials cost." Andrews says that the manufacturer will "maintain his price so long as his costs [direct costs plus costing margin] re-. main unchanged." He states also: "The manufacturer will not willingly cut his price, *apart from the extent to which it will reflect cost changes*, when markets are weak and demand is falling" (*op. cit.*, p. 180. Italics supplied).

[24] Neal, *op. cit.*

[25] Harrod, *op. cit.*, p. 160. The last part of the incomplete sentence from Hall and Hitch quoted above reads: ". . . conditioned by such historical accidents as (a) the size and efficiency of the firms in the industry at the time price stability was achieved, and (b) the extent of their optimism and of their fear of potential competitors as measured by the percentage addition for profits" (*op. cit.*, p. 123).

Andrews repeatedly warns of the competitive influences on the size of the "costing-margin," or the gross margin between direct cost and price. For example, "The costing-margin, and with it the business man's price, will thus be arrived at by competition . . ." (*op. cit.*, p. 159).

of the larger volume, for price is assumed to be above marginal cost, at least until the output rate rises to the point that "stressing of the plant" develops.[26] On the other hand, the impact of lower sales, at least down to a point where the firm's financial security is threatened, will be minimized by a drive for cost-cutting and by cost deferment. Beyond that, losses will be absorbed out of profits.[27] But there are limits to this immunity from short-term, industry-wide demand movements. Thus Hall and Hitch found that, of the firms interviewed, there were "a few admitting that they might actually charge more [than "full cost"] in periods of exceptionally high demand, and a greater number that they might charge less in periods of exceptionally depressed demand."[28] Similarly, Vander-blue, after describing General Motors' elaborate cost-plus price computations notes: "This price, once set, must stand the test of the market place in competition with cars produced by other companies. Merely having a cost guide to judgment does not assure that the market will pay a price that will return this cost (plus a profit), however carefully the cost analysis has been made. . . . In practice the final quoted or *Prevailing Price* has generally been below *Standard Price* [full-cost price] and only occasionally above."[29]

FULL-COST OR GROSS-MARGIN PRICING

MUCH of what is called full-cost pricing, or cost-plus pricing, and most of the analyses which relate price changes to cost changes could better be termed "gross-margin pricing." Generally, this gross margin above direct costs is not related to the remaining costs of the firm. As already noted, Andrews considers the size of such margins to be a function of rivals' costs, but other writers take such margins as data which require no explanation.

Application of the same margin to a number of products has been stimulated by the common-cost allocation problem. In addition, the facility with which repetitive pricing problems can be handled, once the gross margin is adopted, explains its wide use not only in the distributive trades[30] but also in manufacturing where the variety of items is great and in constant flux. It is also used in

---

[26] Saxton, *op. cit.*, pp. 103-104.

[27] Saxton elaborates the cushion role of profits (*ibid.*, pp. 131-132).

[28] Hall and Hitch, *op. cit.*, p. 113.

[29] Vanderblue, *op. cit.*, pp. 396 and 397.

[30] This is stressed as an aspect of "cost-plus" pricing by Oxenfeldt (*op. cit.*, pp. 157-164) and presumably would be included in Fellner's discussion of markup pricing (*op. cit.*, pp. 154-155).

the thin-margin agricultural processing industries, which experience frequent and wide movements of raw materials prices.[31] A more general application is to relate product price movements throughout the manufacturing industries to movements of prices of factors which enter into direct cost. This explanation of price change runs through the work of the Oxford Group and is the major point made by Neal.

TYPES OF MARKETS

THE structure of the markets and the relationship found among sellers, while a fundamental part of such doctrines as those examined here, are frequently not discussed explicitly. There is a strong tendency to speak of the firm as "setting its price," as though every firm were a monopolist. But when other parts of the discussion are considered, there is reference to rivals' reactions.

The writers in this field seem to have had a variety of market situations in mind. Hall and Hitch were studying oligopolistic markets primarily, but they did not differentiate definitely between respondents who were parties to price agreements and those whose relation to rivals was that of "quasi-agreement," to use Fellner's term. Thirteen of their thirty-eight respondents were members of "large-numbers" industries.[32] Saxton identifies the dominant price-leader cases[33] and trade association price-fixing activities.[34] Andrews does not follow the customary classification of markets but is concerned with cases in which "an established business will have a more or less clearly defined market, and will be protected from the efforts of would-be competing businesses to cut into that market."[35] Harrod states specifically that he is not concerned with markets where oligopoly is present, but with those in which entry is so easy that sellers cannot for long charge more than full cost.[36] Dean does not specify the types of markets but his illustrations cover a wide range of situations. Oxenfeldt also seems to have a number of types of markets in mind but draws most of his illustrations from the distributive trades where sellers are numerous.

With full-cost and cost-change price theories being applied to such a variety of markets it will be necessary at points in the fol-

[31] Indeed, the whole concept of hedging against raw material price movements in these industries is based on the assumption of a similarity of movement of those prices and of the prices of the products made from them.

[32] Hall and Hitch, *op. cit.*, p. 119, Table 6.

[33] Saxton, *op. cit.*, p. 125. [34] *Ibid.*, p. 12.

[35] Andrews, *op. cit.*, p. 153. [36] Harrod, *op. cit.*, p. 161.

lowing sections to make clear the type of market to which the discussion refers.

IN THE sections which follow we shall be concerned with ideas which hold that prices are established at the level of (or are changed or not changed) according to the level (or change or nonchange) (1) of some type of average total costs or (2) of a gross margin over direct costs. While it is implicit in all of these theories that prices stem directly from sellers' decisions and do not emerge from impersonal market processes, the emphasis is not on "setting prices" but rather on the level which emerges from a whole series of decisions as to whether or not to change prices. Whether or not particular theories surveyed can be properly denoted "full cost" will not be of concern.

The empirical evidence and the theoretical significance, if any, will be reviewed with respect to each of the following topics:

1. The relation of costs to output rate as shown by empirical evidence and as viewed by managements.

2. Full cost and the level of price under oligopoly, both when overt collusion is present and when it is not.

3. Cost formula or gross margin pricing in the distributive trades and in manufacturing where frequency of product change or variety of items produced call for numerous price decisions.

4. Price effects of factor price and demand changes which involves a generalized explanation of the impact on prices of movements of direct costs.

2. The Relation of Costs to Output Rate

NUMEROUS assumptions as to the relation between volume rate and unit costs underlie the various theories being considered here. A typical assumption (sometimes made explicitly) is that, within the output range relevant for short-term pricing, the marginal cost curve is quite flat.[37] The reference may be to a cost-output relation analogous to the economist's static cost function. Or, as we shall see, the view of the cost-output relation may stem from an expected concomitance between output changes and non-static factors which influence the level of costs. Then, where the assumption of horizontal marginal costs is not made explicitly, it is clear that the cost

[37] Harrod makes this point most emphatically (op. cit., p. 154 and Figure 2 on p. 170).

changes with volume changes are not considered to be of sufficient magnitude to outweigh the advantages of a price based on cost at one assumed volume rate, usually at some concept of a "normal" rate.

EMPIRICAL EVIDENCE ON COST FUNCTIONS

THERE is now significant evidence to the effect that, in manufacturing operations at least, marginal costs do not vary for a fairly wide range of output rates. The area of flatness of marginal costs extends downward from the neighborhood of the output for which the plant was designed to as much as 30 per cent below that point. That marginal costs are horizontal in this range has been demonstrated almost without exception in statistical investigations of cost experience[38] and has been supported in a number of studies of expected effects of volume on costs as derived from accountants' and engineers' cost estimates.[39] Saxton concludes on the basis of discussion with entrepreneurs that: "There is a range of output starting from a point as much as 10 per cent or 15 per cent below 'normal' output to a point as much above 'normal' output, over which marginal cost is fairly constant."[40] Nicholls finds that there is no significant evidence for other than a linear relation between labor inputs and output in meat packing.[41] Andrews' investigations lead him to conclude that average direct costs are constant over a wide range of output because business finds that favorable and unfavorable influences associated with volume changes tend to offset each other and hold direct costs constant.[42]

MANAGERIAL VIEWS OF COST-OUTPUT RELATIONS

INDEED, it is such a mixture of static forces and expectations of con-

[38] For references to these investigations and a summary and critique of the findings, see: Committee on Price Determination, Conference on Price Research, *Cost Behavior and Price Policy* (National Bureau of Economic Research, 1943), pp. 81-101 and 109 and Hans Staehle, "The Measurement of Statistical Cost Functions: An Appraisal of Some Recent Contributions," *American Economic Review*, June 1942, pp. 321-333. For a more extensive presentation of a number of these studies, see Joel Dean, *Statistical Determination of Costs with Special Reference to Marginal Costs* (University of Chicago Press, 1936). For a briefer exposition and some additional cases, see Dean's *Managerial Economics*, as cited, pp. 272-296.

[39] Summarized in *Cost Behavior and Price Policy*, as cited, pp. 101-102.

[40] Saxton, *op. cit.*, p. 96.

[41] W. H. Nicholls, *Labor Productivity Functions in Meat Packing* (University of Chicago Press, 1948), p. 24.

[42] Andrews, *op. cit.*, pp. 102-109.

currence between volume changes and cost-influencing events which dominate managerial notions about the relation of operating rate to costs. Managements note the relation between volume changes and the individual efficiency of workers, the attentiveness of supervisory personnel to their tasks, and the general alertness or carelessness about costs.[43] It is observed that larger volume and the ability to delay deliveries and still keep the business, affect the length of runs and hence, by tending toward lower costs,[44] work in opposition to reduced individual efficiency of workers. The quality and prices of factors generally, not merely of labor, are often correlated positively with output rate. Clearly, the view of managements in respect to cost-volume relationship involves a mixing of static and other considerations.[45] It is not necessary here to enter into the debate as to whether particular cost-influencing factors are static or otherwise. Our concern is with management's views of the problems.

Management's conclusions on the relation between volume rate and costs seem to reflect the variety of conditions under which they experience stable or rising costs. Getting more volume than that for which the plant was designed is recognized as possible, but not ordinarily by adding small increments of such variable factors as labor. Instead, it is accomplished by postponement of normal shutdowns for cleaning or for repairs and by putting normally idle, inefficient units into operation. Actually, businessmen appear to relate rising costs at higher output rates to lower quality of factors[46] or higher price for them, both of which reflect the high level of demand for factors. Such costs will be incurred to meet orders of valued customers, to meet war demands, or to face similar situations; but these conditions of rising marginal costs are beyond the range of output for which short-term, price-output plans are ordinarily made.[47]

[43] The present writer has frequently found the response to the question, "What do you do when sales volume falls off?" to be "We get busy on our costs."

[44] *Cost Behavior and Price Policy*, as cited, p. 84. In the present writer's judgment, this explains much of the increased output per man in such industries as textiles, steel, and rubber tires between 1939 and 1942.

[45] This is the way Saxton (*op. cit.*, pp. 101-102) analyzes the problem without specifically pointing to the difference between the two concepts of marginal costs. The Committee on Price Determination (*Cost Behavior and Price Policy*, as cited, p. 113) recognizes the difference but recommends the usage which reflects the effects of both static and other influences.

[46] This may affect wastage of material or percentage of product failing to pass inspection. These were two major causes of rising costs during the war in metal-working firms who appealed to the Office of Price Administration for price relief.

[47] Andrews (*op. cit.*, pp. 109-110) contends that such "extraordinary" costs do not enter into pricing.

371

The difficulties faced in cost accounting and the practices adopted, as typified by "standard cost" systems, contribute to a horizontal view of marginal costs and to the quoting of a single total cost figure by management.[48] In such systems direct costs are computed by multiplying "standard" physical inputs of direct factors per unit of output by prices of factors. Sometimes part of indirect costs are assigned in a similar fashion. All unassigned costs are included in a "loading factor," which is computed from an estimate of what these costs would be for a group of products or for the enterprise as a whole at a "normal" volume. Often the loading is translated into a percentage of part or all of direct costs at the "standard" volume rate. Consequently neither direct costs nor overhead costs are analyzed as dependent on actual or expected volume but on "standard" volume. Of course managements are fully aware of the spreading effect of higher volume on unit overhead costs; the addiction to price discrimination attests to this. But the horizontal view of the direct cost curve remains.[49] Corollarily, direct costs are presumed to change by the amount that factor prices move. Because total costs are typically estimated by a percentage add-on to direct costs, total costs also are presumed to change in proportion to factor price movements.[50]

The break-even charts, which are so popular in business circles,[51] show unit variable costs as constant over a range from near zero to 100 per cent of "capacity," and fixed costs per unit of product as falling along a straight line.[52] Such rigidity of classification of costs into fixed and variable costs outdoes economic textbooks in misrepresenting the facts about costs. Right or wrong, these charts portray businessmen's thinking and particularly their assumption that unit variable costs do not change with volume. For our purposes the conclusion seems clear that there is a substantial volume range within which marginal costs, particularly as viewed by managements, are approximately constant, given constant factor prices.

[48] Relevant attributes of "standard costs" and their relation to management's appraisal of operations, but not their limitations as a guide to pricing, are explained succinctly by W. W. Cooper, "A Proposal for Extending the Theory of the Firm," *Quarterly Journal of Economics*, February 1951, pp. 87-109.

[49] Scitovsky (*op. cit.*, pp. 309-314) incorporates this conclusion into price theory.

[50] Anyone who participated in wartime price fixing realizes the strength of this business belief.

[51] See *Cost Behavior and Price Policy* (as cited, pp. 104-108) and Dean (*op. cit.*, pp. 326-338), who refers to charts for particular enterprises.

[52] That these charts do show total costs as falling with volume is not inconsistent with what was said about standard costs, for the latter disregard volume changes. Actually, break-even charts are not used primarily for price setting but for showing impact of different prices or of volume rates on profits.

The theoretical significance of constancy of marginal costs lies in its relation (1) to the conditions of equilibrium and (2) to what happens to prices when demand changes.

1. Presumably the barrier to an indefinite increase of output and reduction of prices lies in the fact that marginal costs do rise when output is pushed beyond the range ordinarily involved in pricing. While some recognition of this fact was noted above, this appears only as a general limit on competitive maneuvers. Managements policies are interpreted as designed for a "normal" volume short of this point.

2. As long as the firm's demand moves within the range in which its marginal revenue curve intersects the horizontal segment of the marginal cost curve, the level of that intersection does not change. Whether or not the price at which that quantity could be sold does change depends on whether the firm's revenue curve retains the same elasticity as it shifts.

3. Full Cost and the Level of Price under Oligopoly

DETERMINATION of where an oligopolistic price will fall between the upper limit of that of a monopoly and the lower limit of a competitive equilibrium was the objective of the study from which the full-cost pronouncement first appeared. Probably most persons still look upon the full-cost doctrine as a guide to how the level of the price is determined, although, as observed above, attention has veered toward the cost-change problem. But an exposition which runs in terms of conduct of one firm involves the problems of what happens when rivals' costs or other relevant attributes differ. This difficulty hounds the full-cost disciples as it has those who offer other approaches to a theory of oligopoly price.

THE EMPIRICAL EVIDENCE

RARELY has so much debate been set off by a proposal for which such meager supporting evidence has appeared. Hall and Hitch summarized the interviews with a nonrandom sample of thirty-eight businessmen, a substantial portion of whom confessed that they did not adhere, or adhered only under favorable demand conditions, to the full-cost principle.[53] In Saxton's study of fifty firms by questionnaire, thirty-six said they fixed prices on standard or on estimated

---

[53] It is understood, however, that their conclusions were based upon a much more extensive program of discussion with businessmen and unpublished studies of particular industries by the Oxford Research Group.

costs,[54] but he found the answers to questions as to how demand considerations affected prices to be so varied that results were not tabulated. Dean concludes from his unpublished studies that "a majority of businessmen set prices on the basis of cost plus a 'fair' profit percentage."[55] Published studies of particular companies[56] and of the metal-container[57] and rayon[58] industries give credence to pricing on full cost. In two recent analyses of the cigarette industry, Tennant asserts that "Prices appear to be set on some principle of markup over cost. . . ,"[59] but one does not find a similar conclusion in Nicholls.[60] Nor does full cost appear as an explanation of price performance in extensive studies of industries which rank quite high in concentration such as newsprint,[61] Pacific Coast petroleum refining,[62] and farm machinery,[63] or in briefer reports on industries which are much less concentrated, such as those making shoes[64] and textiles.[65]

The fact that questionnaire and interview surveys covering a number of industries have often led to full-cost pricing conclusions, while full-blown studies of particular industries usually have not, calls

[54] Saxton, op. cit., p. 181, question 19.

[55] Dean, Managerial Economics, p. 445. Dean refers here only to manufacturing businesses operating under conditions of oligopoly or a high degree of product distinctiveness.

[56] See p. 367 above with respect to Vanderblue's report on General Motors. Oxenfeldt (op. cit., p. 181) cites a similar policy statement by a Ford official. Price decisions in these cases are clearly tempered by current and prospective demand.

[57] In this industry five-year contracts (used before the recent antitrust decision) provided tin can prices at a specified margin above future announced prices of tin plate. C. H. Hession, Competition in the Metal Food Container Industry 1916-1946 (privately printed, 1948), pp. 223 ff.

[58] Jesse W. Markham (Competition in the Rayon Industry [Harvard University Press, 1952]) specifically denies the existence of a full-cost policy (pp. 187-190) but the evidence he quotes has to do with year-to-year relations between total unit cost and prices. The same evidence which shows stability of the unit profit margin from 1931 to 1940, except for high- or low-volume years, may in fact indicate a policy of pricing on full cost at some normal or average volume.

[59] R. B. Tennant, The American Cigarette Industry (Yale University Press, 1950), p. 364.

[60] W. H. Nicholls, Price Policies in the Cigarette Industry (Vanderbilt University Press, 1951). The summary of price policies appears in Chaps. XIII and XIV.

[61] J. A. Guthrie, The Newsprint Paper Industry (Harvard University Press, 1941), especially pp. 106-120.

[62] Joe S. Bain, The Economics of the Pacific Coast Petroleum Industry (California University Press, 1945), Vol. II, especially pp. 285-298.

[63] Dunlop and Martin, op. cit., pp. 80-97.

[64] Ibid., pp. 15-22.   [65] Ibid., pp. 50-53.

for a comment on methods of investigation. The inherent weaknesses of the questionnaire method have been emphasized elsewhere.[66] That businessmen's responses to questions about their policies are taken at face value without definite checking as to their conduct is disconcerting. But more basic is the question as to whether price determination can be studied by any method that short-cuts a deep understanding of the particular market.[67] Managements rarely meet the simple question of how cost or demand affects price. Questions and answers are out of context unless they are considered as part of the complex in which the firm and industry operate. Even such elementary concepts as "product" may be vague otherwise, and often the relevant data, which are rarely up to the statistician's dream, cannot be handled judiciously without such a background. Consequently, with survey results supporting to some degree, but intensive studies of industries not corroborating, it seems best to conclude that the wide use of full cost in determining the level of price under "quasi-agreement," as distinct from formal collusion, has not been demonstrated.

WHOSE COSTS ARE APPLICABLE

A MAJOR problem in a noncollusive oligopoly is that of how two or more rival firms with different costs can, in fact, price on a full-cost basis. This problem is not always recognized, and where it is, the solutions offered are diverse. Hall and Hitch, except where rivals' costs are similar, fall back on a price leader's use of full cost;[68] or they state that "the effect of 'competition'" is "to induce firms to modify the margin for profits which could be added to direct costs and overheads so that approximately the same prices for similar products would rule within the 'group' of competing producers."[69] Except insofar as the margins so determined are then applied to other products, this is not full-cost pricing in the sense of the determinant of the level of price. Indeed, the somewhat different and more elaborate analysis of Andrews is not full-cost in this sense either, for he repeatedly emphasizes the competitive determination of the gross margin over direct costs.[70] Saxton seems to conclude that in all industries which depart very far from the competitive

---

[66] E.g., by Machlup, *op. cit.*, pp. 536-538.
[67] J. S. Bain thinks not ("Price and Production Policies" in H. S. Ellis [ed.] *A Survey of Contemporary Economics* [Blakiston, 1948], pp. 163-165).
[68] Hall and Hitch, *op. cit.*, p. 120.
[69] *Ibid.*, p. 113.
[70] Andrews, *op. cit.*, pp. 145-204.

model either price leadership or various degrees of collusion exist.[71] Tennant does not explain how the differential cost problem is solved in the cigarette industry, but a pattern of differential margins does develop and price changes to correct a margin change must be initiated by a price leader.

PRICE LEADER'S USE OF FULL COST

INDEED, the full-cost idea as an explanation of a price leader's conduct is quite persuasive, although again the empirical evidence is sparse. Reference here is to the "dominant" rather than the "barometric" price leader, for the latter has to do with price change in response to factor price or demand movements. The dominant leader must fix a level of price, relative to costs primarily, to which other sellers will adhere because it is to their advantage or because of fear of consequences of noncompliance. Such a price leader needs an objective guide and his own costs are the major ingredient of such a guide. The net margin must reflect the level of prices which will hold lesser rivals in line and discourage disruptive entry. This is another way of saying that the dominant firm's own costs, or even that of a noncolluding oligopolist, is the best guide to the long-run demand of the firm.[72] Dean describes a convincing case of this sort,[73] and Saxton stresses similar situations[74] but seems to find that consultation usually strengthens the leadership.[75] The fact that the market share of the price leader usually falls[76] indicates a tendency to err on the high side in fixing prices.

FULL COST PRICING UNDER COLLUSION

EVEN more persuasive is the role of full cost in collusive arrangements. Although the evidence is scattered, it appears with respect to so many diverse arrangements and its logic is so clear that firm conclusions can be reached. Saxton concludes that full cost guides British trade association price policies operating in the absence of governmental prohibitions.[77] Hall and Hitch had referred to the publication of standard costs by such associations and stated that "firms in the industry were urged to use the 'standard' costs in ap-

[71] Comments of this sort appear at several points in his chapter on "Price Fixing and Price Policy."

[72] Machlup, *op. cit.*, pp. 543-546.

[73] Dean, *Managerial Economics*, pp. 439-442.

[74] Saxton, *op. cit.*, pp. 129-130 and 139-144.   [75] *Ibid.*, p. 126.

[76] A. R. Burns, *Decline of Competition* (McGraw-Hill, 1936), p. 142.

[77] Saxton, *op. cit.*, pp. 139-143.

plying the full cost principle."[78] Similar efforts toward pricing on the basis of the average of the full costs of rival firms have been made by American trade associations within the narrower limits imposed by the antitrust laws.[79] The rush to full-cost pricing when those laws were suspended during the days of the National Recovery Administration and the incorporation of the average of full costs of the region into bituminous coal price fixing under the Bituminous Coal Act of 1937[80] show the attraction to this guide when agreement is possible.

The significance of full costs as a guide to the determination of the level of price goes beyond cases of overt agreement. The literature on "quasi-agreement" and the realistic emphasis on consultation of the sort not detectable directly by the antitrust agencies have amplified the area to which such a tangible, workable guide to similarity of price conduct as full cost is applicable. Thus, although the industries involved in recent basing point cases have been found guilty of "implied conspiracy" because of identity of delivered prices and the imperviousness of those prices to changed market conditions, the evidence does not show the guides by which the price level was determined. But one can suspect that something akin to full cost was involved.

HARROD'S MODEL

WHILE Harrod's quite complete and explicit model of full-cost pricing does not, as he develops it, fall in the present section, it can be fitted in easily. He has in mind a producer of a differentiated good whose main concern is with preventing entry. That is analogous to the price leader's problem both as to entry of new sellers and as to shares of established sellers.

The keys to Harrod's model are: (1) Plant size and type are not those which yield maximum economies of scale, but those which have lowest cost for an output rate which, on the average, can be sold at a full-cost price. (2) Short-term marginal costs are constant over the range within which volume would ordinarily fluctuate. (3) In its price policy (both long-term and short-term) the firm considers only its long-term revenue curve. At quantities less than that which the plant was designed to produce, the long-term demand

[78] Hall and Hitch, op. cit., p. 113, note 2.
[79] Burns, op. cit., pp. 45-74.
[80] D. H. Wallace, Economic Standards of Government Price Control, Temporary National Economic Committee, Monograph 32, 1941, pp. 274-298.

curve is considered to be close to horizontal at a price equal to full cost. This is the price which would discourage entry.

Putting these ingredients together, Harrod finds an equilibrium at full cost with the long-term demand tangential to the average cost curve of the plant actually built. This leads to the conclusion: "So long, therefore, as we are subject to the proviso that the entrepreneur dare not charge a price above full cost without rendering his market vulnerable, the 'full-cost' criterion gives the same answer as the marginal criterion."[81]

Aside from the presumed greater stability of the equilibrium and the lack of excess capacity, which stem from designing the plant at less than the economic optimum scale, the whole of this argument rests on forestalling entry. Thus, the full-cost argument becomes that of using one's own costs as a guide to the level of price maintainable over a long period, and of using this as a guide to short-term as well as to long-term policy.

Once, however, one admits close rivals into the analysis (as Harrod must), there arises the question raised repeatedly here as to whether firms plan that way, or whether varied cost-price relations for the various firms develop on the basis of experience. The presence of rivals, and of interaction among them, cannot be avoided for most important situations.

SUMMARY

THE conclusion which emerges is that full cost as a determinant of the level of price is most significant where the market structure approximates a pure oligopoly. In such cases price decisions involve collusion in the sense of a high degree of "conjectural interdependence" typically aided, perhaps, by consultation.

4. Cost-Formula or Gross-Margin Pricing in Repetitive-Pricing Operations

IN A number of manufacturing industries and in the distributive trades generally, the variety of items sold or the frequency of change in what is sold requires that many price or output decisions be made. Typically some kind of formula is adopted as a procedure in which part or all of direct cost at current or expected factor prices constitutes a base on which is superimposed a margin, usually in percentage form, to cover other costs and profit. Although the generality of such procedures, usually carried out by persons far down in

---

[81] Harrod, *op. cit.*, p. 162.

the administrative hierarchy of the firm, has been amply demonstrated empirically, the relation of prices so computed to prices asked and adhered to is much less clear. Here we shall explore two types of cases: (1) cost formulas in certain flexible-product manufacturing industries and (2) the use of markups in the distributive trades.

COST FORMULAS FOR PRICING

THE manufacturing industries in which the variety and changing character of products require that frequent price decisions be made include the metal casting, stamping, and forging industries, mechanical rubber goods, specialty paper manufacturing, and doubtless many nonbasic chemical businesses. In some of these the product wanted by two customers is rarely the same. In others the variety of items wanted by users is wide and changing, or newness may be initiated by the manufacturer. In many of these goods, e.g. castings, price is agreed upon before the order is given. But these formulas are also used in connection with pricing the numerous "new" or varied products of metal-working or other plants turned out in advance of sale.[82] On the production side, typically, the labor and to a large degree the plant also are adaptable to a variety of items and to frequent change of items. Usually the costs which are not directly assignable to the item being priced constitute a high proportion of total costs in the enterprise, but there are important exceptions to this condition.

In such businesses, pricing formulas applicable to the enterprise, or separate formulas for product areas, have evolved in which price is computed as a multiple of estimated direct cost, or as a multiple of direct labor cost to which direct material costs are added. Examples are provided by Dean[83] and appear frequently in accounting and business management journals. During World War II the Office of Price Administration approved the use of formulas of this sort which manufacturers had used in a "freeze" period as the device for determining ceiling prices where the goods to be sold were not analogous to those produced in the "freeze" period.[84]

[82] Obviously in both types of situations referred to here, one use of the cost formulas is to choose between whether to take an order or make an article for future sale. But cost-price comparisons of this sort are part even of the pure competition model.

[83] Dean, *Managerial Economics*, pp. 446-447.

[84] An example is found in the machinery price regulation, Maximum Price Regulation No. 136. Thousands of pricing formulas of this sort were filed with Office of Price Administration (OPA), and even more price computations were made by

DISTRIBUTIVE TRADE MARKUPS

A SIMILAR procedure prevails in the distributive trade markups on invoice cost,[85] which differ among categories of goods or even among individual products.[86] Markups provided under manufacturers' list prices are quite uniform not only among manufacturers who occupy similar market positions in the sale of a given product line such as tires[87] but also for a category of goods such as appliances.[88] Where retail prices are set by individual stores, there is substantial variation in margins on particular items,[89] but these disparities are much less when type and location of store are defined narrowly.

DETERMINANTS OF FORMULAS AND MARKUPS

SUCH pricing formulas or gross margins need not be full cost in the sense that the individual firm or even the industry relates them to the cost of particular products or items. In the manufacturing industries referred to here, most costs other than for direct labor and materials are common for a family of products or for all of the products sold by the enterprise. In the distributive trades practically all costs other than for goods bought for resale are common for a department and many for the enterprise as a whole. For such manu-

their use. So far as the present writer knows, no analysis of the structure of these formulas has been published. Some comments on the experience with their use in price control are contained in *Historical Reports on War Administration: Office of Price Administration*, No. 8, "Problems in Price Control: Pricing Techniques," pp. 85-90 and No. 6, "Studies in Industrial Price Control," pp. 101-176, but in the judgment of this writer they fail to bring out the major reason why such pricing formulas proved to be loose price control. See p. 383 below.

[85] Actually most of these margins are expressed as a percentage of selling price rather than of invoice cost.

[86] There are notable exceptions for trades such as those handling perishables where price movements and possibilities of loss are frequent. In fresh fruit and vegetable wholesaling and fresh fish wholesaling, dealers tend to buy for what they have to pay and sell for what they can get, with the spread over a period of time being enough to cover costs.

[87] This is shown in exhibits filed by the Department of Justice in case 126-193 Criminal, Federal District Court for Southern District of New York. Companies other than the Big Four provided larger initial margins, but these were "traded away" so that in the end retail prices were lower on brands of small companies.

[88] This again was shown by the experience in price control, in which the present writer participated. However, the commodity areas where margins, as shown by price lists, are quite uniform are also those in which departures from lists are frequent and responsive to demand conditions.

[89] See *Survey of Retail Sellers of Apparel and House Furnishings*, Office of Temporary Controls, OPA Economic Data Series 9, where the range of margins for each category of goods is shown.

facturers the only available data are standard or actual costs for a group of products, or for the distributive trades the storewide expense rate.[90] Under these circumstances cost formulas or gross margins replace allocations of common costs in sellers' thinking about prices.

Such formulas and gross margins are affected by competitive influences but by what process and how promptly is not clear. In the distributive trades, margins on particular items and even for enterprises tend to reflect the services offered. Within a given trade or even in an individual store, margins vary widely on different products handled[91] but, as was noted above, these differences can rarely be related to cost differences. Presumably, such margin differences reflect competitive experience. Certainly margins do change on occasion, particularly as new types of businesses take on the line.[92] Such competitive forces also affect pricing formulas in manufacturing, a fact which has been generalized by Andrews in this discussion of forces shaping the "costing margin" which is added to direct cost to determine price.[93]

TESTING THESE PROCEDURES UNDER CHANGED CONDITIONS

THE empirically demonstrated fact that cost formulas and gross margins enter widely into pricing operations is open to two types of misinterpretations. One is that these procedures replace managerial attempts to gain by adjusting prices for factors not reflected in formulas or margins—a statement preferred for present purposes to the term, "profit maximization." The other is that prices are actually set by such procedures and maintained. These two points are in a sense the same; the first deals with the consistency between an observed administrative procedure and the theory of price. The second is a question of fact as to whether prices do accord with the formulas.

The development and repetitive application of procedures by which prices are actually set, and which consequently govern the

[90] This means all expenses, except cost of goods bought for resale, expressed as a percentage of net sales.

[91] Thus the OPA fixed margins on particular items of dry groceries sold in large stores which conformed roughly with the trade's experience. For a given type of store, margins varied from a low of 6 per cent of invoice cost to a high of 25 per cent, while the over-all gross margin of large chains was about 16 per cent of cost of goods. In other trades the variation is less.

[92] The selling of drugstore and tobacco store items by chain food stores has had this effect on margins on these items formerly sold only in the first stores.

[93] Andrews, op. cit., pp. 163-180.

sellers' volume, is not, per se, inconsistent with pecuniary motivation. A fresh recomputation of all factors in the situation need not be made each time another order is taken or a shipment of goods for resale received. The issues rather are (1) whether such procedures have been worked out (or evolved) so that, for the conditions for which they were designed, they are consistent with the theory of the firm; and (2) how, if at all, the procedures are revised when a change in those conditions would warrant their modification.

Where a pricing method is repeatedly applied, as is undoubtedly the fact in those manufacturing and distributive industries just considered, one can claim that the test of the market has endorsed the procedures. These industries are in the competitive zone as industries have been classified.[94] Presumably their pricing methods are the result of rivalry among firms who have different views as to the variables or who are doing business in different ways.[95]

But it is still possible that, with firms uncertain as to their demand situation or as to costs for individual products, prices will be too high or too low on such individual products. The price of nails at a hardware store or of sugar at a grocery—two very low-margin items—may not reflect the maximizing of retailers' profits on those items. This is important with respect to the resource allocation and rationing functions of the prices of those commodities. But in examining whether the distributive trades are efficient or how they carry on their business as a whole (i.e. how they adapt to cost and demand conditions), the adjustability of their over-all gross margins is a more fruitful subject of inquiry.[96] Indeed, retailers view their business as selling a retail service, not by items handled but for an outlet as a whole.[97]

Let us now consider the repetitive application of a pricing procedure which, by an adaptive process, came to represent a rational reaction to cost and market considerations. Such conduct is appropriate so long as those conditions obtain. Obviously, changing the rules or making exceptions from them involves persons in the upper echelon of a firm's command; indeed, that is their pricing job.[98] What evidence is there on this question?

[94] E.g. George J. Stigler, in *Five Lectures on Economic Problems* (Macmillan, 1950), pp. 55-57, and Clair Wilcox, "On the Alleged Ubiquity of Oligopoly," *American Economic Review*, Proceedings, May 1950, pp. 70-73.

[95] Andrews, *op. cit.*, pp. 163-180.

[96] Cf. Richard B. Heflebower, "An Economic Appraisal of Price Measures," *Journal of the American Statistical Association*, December 1951, pp. 467-478.

[97] This theme is developed by M. A. Adelman in an unpublished manuscript on the A. & P. Company.

[98] The rule-making rather than rule-applying role of top management is stressed

Undoubtedly, a thorough examination of pricing formulas which consist of cost computations would show the frequency of their violation in the direction of lower prices. The same companies who filed with OPA pricing formulas which provided large margins over direct costs proved to be content with prices on large-volume items which by the same accounting procedures, would cover only manufacturing cost with no margin for general overhead or profit.[99] To say that such was the pricing on a large order and that reduction in expected overhead would leave a profit margin merely shows that pricing does not follow the formula. Another piece of evidence which points to the same conclusion is the way in which these companies sought to get higher ceiling prices relative to costs by modifying what they made. When they changed the product significantly, they were allowed to use their pricing formula to compute the price ceiling. Quite generally, prices so computed were more profitable than prices for the particular castings, stampings, or types of machinery they had sold at the date to which "freeze" prices applied.

Actually, I would hazard, such formulas are used only when there is no competitive reason for doing otherwise. Consequently, I would hazard also, the profit and loss statements of companies who flaunt such formulas would show, even in good times, that on their over-all business they obtained a far smaller markup over direct costs than is provided in the formulas. In times of low demand such after-the-fact proof would show, I think, still smaller markups on direct cost. So far as I know, there has been no systematic study of this sort.

An interpretation of distributive margins, on which there are more data, cannot be made without simultaneously considering operating cost and dollar-volume movements. Fixed percentage margins become widely varying dollar margins when the level of invoice costs changes substantially. Thus the approximately 16 per cent (of invoice cost) store-wide gross margin of large food chains in 1939, as found by OPA, yielded about 18 per cent more dollars to cover operating expenses and profits in 1941 because the wholesale cost of food had advanced that much.[100] Dollar costs advanced also, but by a smaller percentage, so profits rose. When dollar sales fall, the

by A. G. Papandreou in "Some Problems in the Theory of the Firm," in B. F. Haley (ed.), *Survey of Contemporary Economics* (Irwin, 1952), Vol. II, pp. 185-191.

[99] Examples the writer noted included automotive crankshafts and fractional horsepower motors for original equipment sales.

[100] Actually, as is pointed out in note 101, the percentage gross margins of these stores declined from 1939 to 1941.

reverse happens. Typically, the concomitance of the movement of the level of invoice prices to which percentage margins apply and of factor prices entering into operating expenses becomes an important qualification of the idea that margins have a rigidity unrelated to operating cost and demand developments.

Space cannot be taken here for a full analysis of this sort, but some suggestive figures can be given. In Table 1, it is noted that in men's clothing stores the gross margin fell 1.4 percentage points

TABLE 1

Gross Margins as a Percentage of Net Sales of Selected Types
of Retail Stores, 1936-1941 and 1947-1951

Year	Men's and Boys' Clothing Stores[a]	Department Stores[b]	Large Furniture Stores[c]
1936	37.0	36.5	
1937	36.2	36.4	32.4
1938	35.6	36.4	28.5
1939	36.7	36.9	28.6
1940	n.a.	37.0	29.0
1941	37.3	38.2	31.8
1947		35.4	39.7[d]
1948		35.6	38.9[d]
1949		35.2	38.5[d]
1950		36.5	39.8[d]
1951		35.3	38.9[d]

n.a. = not available.

[a] OPA Economic Data Series 22, Office of Temporary Controls, Table 9. Figures are for 56 identical stores.

[b] Annual surveys of *Operating Results of Department and Specialty Stores* (Harvard Business School).

[c] Annual survey of *Retail Furniture Store Operating Experiences and Departmental Activities* (National Retail Furniture Association).

[d] Not comparable with prewar figures because some expenses then considered to be part of cost of goods have, more recently, been included in operating expenses.

from 1936 to the depression year 1938 and then rose 1.7 percentage points by 1941. Similar changes in gross margins for furniture stores occurred. Those for department stores did not reflect the recession of 1938 but did expand by about 1.5 percentage points by the prosperous year of 1941. A contributing factor was that markdowns from original asking prices, which varied by size of store from 6.9 to 11.4 per cent of sales in 1938, fell to only 5.3 to 6.4 per cent in 1941. A similar sort of development in automobile retailing was that the *gross loss* on used automobiles traded in by a group of dealers fell from 8.2 in 1939 to 6.4 per cent of sales in 1941.[101] But the gross

[101] OPA Economic Data Series 19, Office of Temporary Controls, 1947, Table 9. This means that less of the rigid new car margin was traded away in the

margin of four major food chains, who are in a highly competitive business, was about one percentage point less in prosperous 1941 than in 1939.[102] On the other hand, the stability of postwar margins (as shown in the table), even when goods were short at going prices, does attest to the failure of margins to expand just because demand is high.

These data all suggest that margins prove to be less rigid than they appear to be; but further analysis would have to consider cost movements, the timing of entry, elasticity of capacity, and a series of other points. All that can be concluded here is to suggest that margin pricing in the distributive trades is less uniform among sellers, and less rigid over time, than has been asserted.

5. Factor-Price and Selling Price Changes

A MORE generalized form of the cost approach to price changes than those involving precise formulas and gross margins is that which sees selling-price movements geared to cost changes, particularly those which reflect movements of labor rates and material prices. Such theories apply to industries in which price decisions and price changes are infrequent as well as to those in which they are numerous. The doctrines apply both to industries in which direct costs are a moderate proportion of prices and to those in which the margin over direct costs is narrow. They are applicable both to highly concentrated industries with strong price leadership and to those with substantially less of both attributes.

That selling prices are responsive to substantial movements in direct costs is orthodox theory, but the doctrine being considered here differs in two regards: (1) In value theory the price changes by less than the change in marginal cost by an amount determined by the slopes of the marginal cost and marginal revenue curves. Here, however, the price change corresponds—some say in absolute amount and some say in a percentage—to the change in direct costs. The effect on volume is considered inconsequential or is disregarded. (2) Selling prices are presumed not to respond to demand move-

---

prosperous year 1941. Margin on used cars is expressed here as gross loss because what was received for the used cars when resold was less than what had been allowed on them as trade-ins.

Although it cannot be documented in a comparable fashion, one can conclude safely that a comparable oscillation of realized margins occurs between good and bad times for most "big-ticket" consumer goods. Hence the apparent rigidity of the "margins" provided by manufacturers' retail list price and discount arrangements is illusory.

[102] OPA Economic Data Series 26, Office of Temporary Controls, 1947.

ments when the latter do not correspond in direction and degree to factor-price change.

FROM a theoretical critique aimed at the limited assumptions and static nature of the doctrines of E. H. Chamberlin and Joan Robinson, Neal arrives at the conclusion that under "realistic" conditions selling prices can be expected to reflect movements of prime cost when that term has been enlarged to include "user cost."[103] By the latter is meant "the change in the value of the facilities of the firm due to operating, as opposed to not operating, during the week. 'Facilities' is a very broad term which covers plant, goods in process, inventory, access to markets, customer relationships, good will, and similar items."[104] Neal says further: "User cost, which may be *positive* or *negative*, expresses the net result of selected factors which are not included within the Chamberlin-Robinson type of analysis."[105] When demand falls, user cost rises and vice versa. Since, in the thinking of management, user cost is added to marginal costs,[106] a demand decline, for example, tends to raise marginal costs with given factor prices; and a resistance to price reduction is built. Consequently, Neal concludes that margins over direct costs tend to be rigid, and such product price changes as do occur will be a reflection of direct cost changes and not of the structure of the market.

Neal then offers extensive statistical proof of his thesis from the 1929-1933 experience. He found a high correlation between price changes "expected" (on the basis of the movement of direct costs) and price changes which occurred from 1929 to 1931 and from 1929 to 1933.[107] At the same time there was only a low correlation between price changes and the degree of concentration in the respective industries.

The statistical part of Neal's study has all of the weaknesses and merits of the census data used in developing the measures of expected and of actual price change. The latter are census indexes of prices in which the price for each period is found by dividing reported value of products by units of output. Thus a "census index" is a variable rather than a fixed weight index. The value of product data presumably reflect price concessions[108] and also the numerous

---

103 Neal, *op. cit.*, Chap. III. 104 *Ibid.*, pp. 58-59.
105 *Ibid.*, p. 71. 106 *Ibid.*, pp. 65-66.
107 *Ibid.*, p. 124. The Pearsonian coefficient of correlation between the two series was plus .85 for the 1929-1931 period and plus .92 for the 1929-1933 price changes.
108 A major possible source of error is that they are on a plant basis and the

product composition shifts which firms make when demand changes. Because different items in a product line provide different margins over cost, these product-mix shifts can change the sellers' realizations relative to costs and change what buyers on the average pay for goods, even though the price of individual items remains unchanged. Neal thinks that this characteristic of a census index is a defect of his study, but for some purposes the present writer holds that this is a merit.[109] It should also be noted that product-mix shifts, which often reflect buyers' choices, affect such a measure and hence the index shows not merely responses to movements of direct cost but also reflects the influence of demand changes.

Presumably firms following Neal's thesis would make overt price changes for identical goods in proportion to direct-cost changes. But a comparison of movements of Neal's census indexes with changes of comparable wholesale price series would show, I am certain, that the latter dropped less from 1929 to 1933. So what Neal's measure demonstrates is that the adjustments of quoted prices, plus price concessions and modification of product quality and of composition of product groups, brought about changes in average realization per unit for product groups which were about the same in percentage as changes in direct costs.

DIRECT COSTS PLUS "COSTING MARGIN"

ON THE basis of studies of business behavior, nearly all of which are unpublished, Andrews concludes that businessmen change prices when, and in the short period ordinarily only when, direct costs change; that is, he holds that prices consist of varying direct costs plus a "costing margin" which reflects experience with what can be obtained above direct costs.[110] The argument depends on the view that manufacturers usually sell to other businesses and that customary relations between a manufacturer and these other businesses are not only greatly valued but also give a market share which cannot be altered materially in the short run, at least by means which do not have longer-run adverse consequences for the initiator. But a change in price which accords with changes in direct costs, since these cost movements tend to be uniform in impact, does not change shares;

---

reporting companies' statements of value of products in intracompany transfers must be accepted.

[109] Heflebower, *op. cit.*

[110] To get the whole of Andrews' argument, *op. cit.*, Chap. v should be examined.

and a proportionate price change would not be interpreted as a competitive maneuver.

DEMAND ASSUMPTION IN THESE PROPOSALS

WHILE both Neal's and Andrews' proposals appear in the first instance to be cost approaches to prices, they actually depend heavily on the expected reactions of rivals. In this their analysis is somewhat analogous to the "kinked" demand curve idea but not entirely so. Neal includes more than the expectation of rivals' prompt response to a price cut in his user cost concept. To some degree he, Andrews even more so, and Harrod explicitly so,[111] look upon short-period market conduct as being governed by longer-period demand considerations. Among these are each firm's high regard for the affiliation of customers and the conviction that market share cannot be built quickly or solidly by overt price maneuvers.[112]

Some comments on Stigler's statistical testing of the "kinked" demand curve follow logically from this discussion of the doctrines of Neal and Andrews. Stigler finds that in seven industries examined "there is little historical basis for a firm to believe that price increases will not be matched by rivals and that price decreases will be matched."[113] He assumes that the kinked demand curve can be observed from the actual conduct of the firms; while its promulgators, particularly Sweezy,[114] interpreted it as an imagined curve, whose contour varies according to a number of influences such as the percentage of the industry's capacity utilized. Presumably a price increase would not take place if the kink were sharp and unfavorable. That price increases by one firm are generally followed by others might mean nothing other than that they occur only when the kink is eliminated by collusion, by orders above capacity, or by substantial increases in factor prices, influences not considered in this test by Stigler. Furthermore, in his later test of frequency of price change, no consideration is given the experience of such industries as petroleum refining, starch manufacture, and the tire industry with changes in factor cost.[115] These comments cannot be

[111] Harrod, *op. cit.*, p. 162.

[112] This interpretation of Andrews' theory is brought out by M. J. Farrell in a note in the *Economic Journal*, June 1951, pp. 423-426. For a view similar to Andrews', see R. A. Lester, "Equilibrium of the Firm," *American Economic Review*, March 1949, pp. 478-484.

[113] George J. Stigler, "The Kinky Oligopoly Demand Curve and Rigid Prices," *Journal of Political Economy*, October 1947, reprinted in G. J. Stigler and K. E. Boulding (eds.), *Readings in Price Theory* (Irwin, 1952), p. 425.

[114] Sweezy, *op. cit.*, *Political Economy*, XLVII (1939), pp. 568-573.

[115] Stigler, *op. cit.*, p. 429.

carried further, for the only purpose here is to suggest that substantial movements of direct costs may remove the "kinks," as do effective price leadership or collusion.

To return to the demand assumptions made but not developed by Neal and Harrod (i.e. their explanation of why price changes do not follow short-period demand movements), they can be turned into an explanation of why stability can exist when marginal costs[116] are below price as they must be at times when prices do not follow demand changes. Neither Chamberlin[117] nor Mrs. Robinson[118] find the explanation in inelasticity of the firm's demand curve. They attribute failure to change prices with demand movements to adherence to a code which amounts to agreement. Andrews, on the other hand, stresses the impact of longer-term considerations of the firms individually on their short-term conduct. Furthermore, Mrs. Robinson does not note that such views as those of Andrews, to which she makes reference, are also an explanation of why competition can exist when most of the time sellers have some excess capacity. This problem becomes particularly acute when marginal cost curves are flat over a wide range. But failure to exploit idle capacity in the short run, according to Neal, Andrews, and Harrod, results not merely because of rivals' expected reactions to price cuts but also because reducing the margin over direct costs is inconsistent with longer-term objectives of the firm.

REACTION TO DEMAND CHANGES

AN IMPORTANT corollary of the doctrines being examined here is that prices are not revised when demand rises or falls. The exceptions occur when there is a concurrent movement of direct costs or when the demand change is sizable and prolonged. Otherwise, nonresponsiveness of quoted prices is supported by general observation and by the literature of the rigid-price controversy of the 1930's. That it is less true of transaction prices has been amply documented for a few industries;[119] but the extent of price concessions, the reclassifications of customers, and the adjustments in freight charges and services rendered which go on with demand variations are little

116 Marginal costs as used here excludes Neal's user costs.
117 Chamberlin, op. cit., pp. 318-325.
118 Joan Robinson in Monopoly and Competition and Their Regulation, edited by E. H. Chamberlin (Macmillan, 1954), pp. 245-251.
119 A notable example is the Bureau of Labor Statistics study made for the OPA and reported in "Labor Department Examines Consumers' Prices of Steel Products," Iron Age, April 25, 1946.

appreciated. The present writer has found few exceptions to the rule that transaction prices vary to some degree relative to quoted prices when the latter do not move in response to demand.

Beyond that, variations in product specifications and in volume of sales (in channels of sale or of items in the line which provide wide as opposed to narrow margins) occur in the direction of movements of demand. Consequently, realizations from the composite of items and channels of sales vary relative to direct costs even though transaction prices, as well as quoted prices, remain unchanged. Of course, transaction prices also tend to vary relative to quoted prices. Altogether demand has a greater impact on the gross margin over direct costs than is shown by quoted prices, or even transaction prices.[120]

After all of these qualifications—and they are important—there remains the fact that when demand varies there is a marked "stickiness" of quoted prices and probably also, but to a lesser degree, of transaction prices. Realizations move sluggishly by price concessions and by the indirect means stressed in the preceding paragraph. But according to the doctrine examined here this "stickiness" is less or nonexistent when substantial changes in direct costs occur.

This general pattern of reaction to factor price movements by overt selling price changes, but to demand changes by means which work more slowly and indirectly to affect the level of realization, is promising, but interpretation of this kind of price performance requires much further work. Among the difficulties of interpretation is the fact that prices of raw materials are themselves often a reflection of demand. The close association between the prices of vegetable oil and of shortening, for example, may mean that the former reflect the demand for the later. Furthermore, the frequency of sizable changes in the price of raw materials may be important, or the structural aspect of the market (or the character of the product which facilitates "agreement" or makes nonovert price adjustments easy or difficult) may be relevant in spite of Neal's findings from the use of crude data. Finally, cases in which movements of factor prices and of demand are not concurrent will be particularly useful in sorting out the cost influences on prices and realizations from those of demand.

6. Concluding Comments

THE full-cost doctrine and the other theories which relate price

[120] This argument is developed further in Heflebower, *op. cit.*

change to direct-cost movements are attempts to deal constructively with price theory as applied to markets which fall between the competitive and the monopolistic. These ideas clearly reflect the impasse reached in the attempts to develop oligopoly theory within the neoclassical framework.[121] But these doctrines also reflect dissatisfaction with the assumptions underlying the theories of monopolistic and imperfect competition, both as to the number of assumptions needed and as to the accuracy of those used. The corrections Neal proposes are presented as providing a more accurate empirical content for marginal cost and marginal revenue curves than that often assumed.[122] Indeed, Harrod's model not only provides views as to the shapes of cost and revenue curves different from those usually stated, but is a model of part of a larger revision of the theory of imperfect competition. Andrews goes further, for he prefers to drop the marginal framework in deriving generalizations about industrial markets.[123] Part of his reason for this, and the dissatisfaction of others with neoclassical theory, arise from what they consider to be the preeminently static character of that theory. Particularly serious is the way uncertainty is handled[124] or disregarded. Adapting marginal theory to encompass more variables and to make it dynamic tends to make it meaningless.[125] But the postwar marginalist controversy need not be revived here.

On the positive side, neither the full-cost doctrine in its more precise form nor the similar ideas reviewed here, yet constitute a fully developed or demonstrated body of price theory. The empirical work from which the theories stem has been spotty in quality and in its representation of situations. The theoretical deductions from empirical observations leave many questions unanswered. Even traditional concepts, such as "capacity" and "cost," have been difficult to use empirically or have been given new usage without adequate explanation. For this reason, and because the usual theoretical

---

121 This is stated explicitly by Hall and Hitch (*op. cit.*, pp. 109-112) and is an element in Fellner's solution via "limited joint profit maximization" (*op. cit.*, pp. 146-157). Chamberlin (*op. cit.*) adopts the full-cost doctrine as one way out of the stalemate.

122 Neal (*op. cit.*, Chaps. III and IV).

123 See his essay in *Oxford Studies in the Price Mechanism*, as cited, pp. 171-172.

124 See R. A. Gordon, "Short-Period Price Determination," *American Economic Review*, June 1948, pp. 280-281.

125 "Refuge in subjective interpretations of the cost and revenue functions is certainly no answer. It leaves theory saying that businessmen do what they do because they do it." *Ibid.*, p. 287.

framework has not always been used in exposition, the theoretical interpretation has often been confusing, particularly to readers steeped in neoclassical doctrine. Part of the problem of clarity also stems from the simultaneous exposition of an underlying tendency and of its qualifications. This seems an unavoidable burden when the conclusions are based on empirical work in contrast to deductive theorizing where complexity is controlled by the assumptions made.

Despite these limitations, two valuable but not fully demonstrated hypotheses run through the literature on this theory. One has to do with market policy in a situation of present uncertainty both about rivals' reactions to price moves and about future developments impinging on the group. Under such circumstances, firms may place more faith in cost guides than in considerations ordinarily viewed as reflecting demand. The implications of such an hypothesis for both the level and the conditions of change of prices need not be developed here. The second hypothesis concerns the adoption of a short-term policy which reflects both longer-term cost and demand considerations. This requires reconsideration of what is maximized in the short run and of the short-term corrective role of prices in industrial markets. Both hypotheses suggest important aspects of the task which still remains, that of the development of satisfactory, empirically verifiable models.

COMMENT

Ronald Coase, University of Buffalo

Heflebower's paper is largely devoted to what has become known as the full-cost principle, which holds that producers set prices "with regard only to total unit costs at some assumed volume rate." It implies both that cost alone matters in pricing, and that what is taken into account on the cost side is not the change in total cost associated with a change in output, but some sort of average or computed cost. I have also been asked to discuss Machlup's paper, which is on the theory of price discrimination. In this theory it is taken for granted that producers in fixing prices take into account demand conditions in the various markets in which they sell their products, and the argument runs, broadly speaking, in marginal terms. It is clearly a theory which, if the full-cost principle applied generally, could have no relevance because the practices which it describes could not exist. The organizers of this conference have so contrived things that if I am to take Machlup's paper seriously, it is first necessary that I should reject the full-cost principle. Fortunately, I found Heflebower's discussion of full-cost pricing extremely congenial and the reader need not expect that I will argue that the pricing practices so vividly described by Machlup exist only in his own imagination.

I have implied that Heflebower rejected the full-cost principle. Perhaps this is too strong. But I had the impression, at the end of reading his paper, that if the full-cost principle was still standing, it was only because it was supported by two old gentlemen, one of whom was certainly Demand and the other of whom looked uncommonly like Marginal Analysis. It is clear from Heflebower's masterly survey that many of the arguments used by supporters of the full-cost principle are in no way inconsistent with orthodox economic theory. Much of what has been called full-cost pricing, as Heflebower indicates, would be better termed "gross-margin pricing," and in so far as the determination of the gross margin is discussed, there seems to be little doubt that it is influenced by demand considerations. It would be idle to pretend that present-day economic analysis is not in need of improvement, but it does not seem sensible to expect that such an improvement will be achieved by denying the importance of demand conditions in the determination of price.

I think the full-cost principle has seemed attractive to many economists because of their discovery of the work of the cost accountant and of the part it plays in business decisions. At first sight the practices of the cost accountant do seem to be inconsistent with the assumptions of normal economic theory. But this feeling ought not to persist if one realizes that in a large or complicated organization there is a need for some cost accounting system. In any large organization in which individuals using resources do not know the alternative use to which these resources could be put (so that they cannot choose whether they should be used in this way or that but only whether they should be used in this way or not), it will usually be necessary, if the organization is to run smoothly, to attach cost figures to the use of particular resources. You get the whole paraphernalia of machine-hour rates and similar figures. Heflebower gives a long list of industries in which cost formulas are used.

Economists are very liable to be impressed by the fact that the cost accounting figures will often not reflect the receipts which would accrue through the use of a factor in another way and that their use for pricing or for other business decisions will give results different from those which we would expect from our ordinary economic analysis. But it should not be assumed that there do not

393

exist within a business organization means for correcting the position when the action to which the cost accounting figures would lead is obviously absurd. R. S. Edwards of the London School of Economics has emphasized that one ought also to examine what happens *after* the cost accountant has prepared his figures. And in a recent article, he gives some interesting examples illustrating his point of view.[1] Heflebower argues in much the same way. He tells us that "a thorough examination of pricing formulas which consist of cost computations would show the frequency of their violation in the direction of lower prices." And in connection with a closely related point, he observes: "The present writer has found few exceptions to the rule that transaction prices vary to some degree relative to quoted prices when the latter do not move in response to demand."

I am quite willing to accept as a purely descriptive statement about business behavior that a businessman fixes prices by adding to direct cost a "reasonable" margin for profit (or to cover what is termed overhead). But as it now seems to be agreed, and this is in accordance with Heflebower's observations, that this margin varies from firm to firm, from product to product, and from time to time, I cannot help feeling that what is considered a "reasonable" margin is closely related to what the businessman thinks he can get. I make this statement subject to the understanding that the businessman cannot usually make a separate decision for each product (so that a rule of thumb is needed), that these rules of thumb, if they are to be useful, must be observed for some time, and that the businessman often has no exact knowledge of his demand and cost conditions. I am not willing on the basis of the arguments brought forward so far to abandon ordinary marginal analysis (taking account of demand) as a first approximation. It is clearly not the whole story and there is need for much more research on business behavior. But we should not be disappointed if a good deal of economic theory turns out to be usable after our investigations are completed.

A. G. Papandreou, University of Minnesota

The major issue of the full-cost principle controversy seems to be: What is the nature of the challenge to the "tenets of generally accepted economic theory" presented by the "discovery" that business

[1] R. S. Edwards, "The Pricing of Manufactured Products," *Economica*, August 1952.

firms do, in fact, in many cases employ rules of thumb in pricing their products?

In its strongest and most extreme form the challenge might be interpreted to mean that the economic theorist's rational-action models are not useful analytical devices for prediction of behavior; that business firms behave in a nonrational fashion; and that they are dominated by custom and by arbitrary socially established standards. Those who take this extreme position must face the burden of establishing the proposition that the nonrational models lead to predictions of firm behavior at least as good as those derived from rational-action models. Closely associated with this burden, however, is another and somewhat more difficult task. If the standards and rules of thumb (markups, margins, etc.) employed by firms in the pricing process are not invariant, if they are subject to change on short notice, it becomes necessary for the advocates of the nonrational approach to offer a theory—no matter how simple—that accounts for the standards and rules of thumb employed by firms at any one time. They must be in a position, in other words, to predict *which* rule of thumb will be employed by *what* firms at *what* time and place. The attempt to do so, I am convinced, will make it necessary for them to fall back upon a rational-action model of one sort or another—and the differences between their practice and that of the theorist will become imperceptible. My conviction is not founded on the notion that only rational-action models are capable of yielding useful predictions in the social sciences; rather it stems from the notion that in the rationalistic-scientific culture of twentieth-century industrial society nonrational models of behavior are not apt to lead to useful results. This may be much less true of consumer behavior than it is of business behavior, as is indicated by the relative success of formulations of nonrational models of consumer behavior (i.e. the Keynesian consumption function). Be that as it may, I should be willing to give up my rational-action tool kit if the advocates of nonrational behavior models could either establish a high degree of invariance for the standards and rules of thumb they claim business firms employ, or offer a theory that accounts for changes in these standards and rules of thumb. Until they do either one of these things, the economic theorist may disregard their attack upon his methods of theory construction.

It is well known, of course, that the full-cost principle in all of its many forms can be incorporated easily into a rational-action model. Linearity of the cost function, the cost of changing price, and uncertain expectations may easily explain why management uses rules of thumb as a "procedural step"—to use Heflebower's terminology—in the process of independent profit maximization. In oligopolistic markets, collusive and quasi-collusive resolutions of the "game" may also account effectively for the employment of rules of thumb within the rational-action frame of reference. All this is too well known to require further discussion on my part.

Does this mean, however, that, since the theorist can "fit" certain observed patterns of behavior into his analytical frame of reference, economists may consider the challenge nonexistent and proceed to rest on their laurels? It seems amply clear to me that this is not the case. The task of the theorist, as I see it, is not to "explicate" reality; rather, it is to construct analytical models that permit him to predict reality. This implies the need for operational concepts and operationally meaningful propositions—propositions, that is, which refer to empirical data. It is not sufficient for us to "account" for observed patterns of business behavior. We must be in a position to make a prediction about business behavior. Our success in this regard has been only moderate. Too many of us are satisfied too much of the time with an "accounting" for or an "explication" of observed behavior. Altogether too little effort is being expended toward the development of operationally meaningful theories. In this, I believe, lies the challenge presented to us by the advocates of the full-cost principle. Even though their criticisms are misdirected, and even though their constructive work has not borne much fruit, they have served to focus our attention on the vital need for constructing useful theory—theory, that is, which is capable of yielding predictions about empirical reality.

CHARACTERISTICS AND TYPES
OF PRICE DISCRIMINATION

FRITZ MACHLUP

THE JOHNS HOPKINS UNIVERSITY

THE literature on price discrimination is widely scattered over the different fields of economics, and the references to problems of discrimination made by various specialists have long remained un coordinated. We find these references in discussions of rate-making problems in Transportation and Public Utilities; antitrust problems in Industrial Organization; problems of unfair competition in Marketing; dumping in International Trade; basing-point and delivered-price problems in Government Control of Business; problems of output determination in Pure Economic Theory. An attempt will be made here to draw some of these separate studies together in a more comprehensive picture.

1. The Essential Characteristics of Price Discrimination

To BEGIN with definitions and conceptual arguments is sometimes inexpedient, and usually uninspiring. Our present task, however, will be clearer if we do not defer an attempt to define our subject.

THE DEFINITION

PRICE discrimination is sometimes defined as the practice of a firm selling a homogeneous commodity at the same time to different purchasers at different prices. Almost every word of this definition needs to be qualified.

1. "Selling to different purchasers": We ought to add "buying from different sources of supply" (because there is price discrimination in buying as well as in selling) and "leasing and hiring."

2. "Commodity": This should include services as well as goods, productive factors as well as products.

3. "At the same time": This means "under given conditions." The transactions surely need not be simultaneous; indeed, there is temporal discrimination, such as between Sunday rates and weekday rates, matinee and evening prices, peak rates and off-peak rates, season and off-season prices.

4. "Homogeneous": The commodities need not be homogeneous; they may be differentiated in many ways and, indeed, in several types of price discrimination differentiation is of the essence.

5. "At different prices": To sell different qualities or products with different marginal cost at the same price, or to buy different qualities or factors of different efficiency at the same price, is also discriminatory. And while there may be price discrimination without price differences, there may be differential pricing that is not discriminatory.

6. "Firm": We may have to take a group of firms, perhaps an entire industry, into account to establish the existence of price discrimination. For example, a single firm may participate in a discriminatory scheme by serving different consumer groups through different (subsidiary) distributor firms to whom it sells at a uniform price but whom it induces to resell with different markups. Or several railroads may set combined through-rates which are discriminatory in comparison with other rates charged by the same or other lines.

A comprehensive definition must be somewhat vague to avoid excessive clumsiness. Price discrimination may be defined as the practice of a firm or group of firms of selling (leasing) at prices disproportionate to the marginal costs of the products sold (leased) or of buying (hiring) at prices disproportionate to the marginal productivities of the factors bought (hired). The chief vagueness in this definition lies in the word "disproportionate." We shall not now attempt to be more specific, but merely to clarify the case of a discriminating seller. Most firms produce several products (or at least several product qualities) and can sell them at discriminatory prices. That is, they discriminate in favor of the buyers of some products and against the buyers of others if the prices of the latter include a higher markup over marginal cost than the former. In the process of this discrimination a multiproduct firm will "switch" some of its productive capacity from the production of the relatively higher-priced to the production of the relatively lower-priced products—just as a single-product firm which practices price discrimination in the sale of a homogeneous commodity "switches" some of its output from the less-favored to the more-favored markets.[1] This "switching" of the use of capacity or of output produced is, of course, merely metaphoric, that is, descriptive of an imagined transition from a situation in which no discrimination is practiced to one that involves discrimination; the "switching" is a metaphor used to picture a comparison between two situations.

[1] The market that is charged the higher price is, for that reason, called less favored although the firm will surely "favor" (in the sense of prefer) sales to this market.

Extension of the concept of price discrimination from the pricing of homogeneous products—or, at least, of technologically similar products—to the pricing of altogether different products whose only relationship with one another lies in the fact that they are produced under the same management or control, will probably be protested as an illegitimate departure from tradition. I submit that it is a logical step. The explanation of price making for "different" products follows exactly the same principles as the explanation of price making for the same or "similar" goods that can be sold to separate groups of buyers. To confine the concept of discrimination to homogeneous products has one great advantage: their marginal cost may be supposed to be the same, so that price differences are sufficient evidence of discrimination. But once we decide to treat "slight" differences in the products under the heading of price discrimination—and of course we must then take account of cost differences—there is no analytical reason for drawing lines between various degrees of technological differences and of cost differences. Rational price determination for the different products of a multiproduct firm facing markets with different demand elasticities is price discrimination in the wide sense of the word proposed here.

Not much depends, however, on the acceptance or rejection of the extension of the concept proposed here. Only a question of classifying and labeling is involved. This paper, of course, would be shorter if I had been satisfied with the narrower concept of price discrimination, but I shall save much space by confining myself to selling price discrimination and leaving buying price discrimination for another occasion.

MONOPOLY POWER AS A PREREQUISITE

THE fact that price discrimination has at times been used by strong concerns to kill off weaker rivals, or at least to prevent their growth, has led to the widespread belief that discrimination is essentially a method used "to create a monopoly." To believe that price discrimination could create monopoly power where none had existed before is to overlook the fact that it is the existence of at least some degree of monopoly (in the wider sense of the word) that makes discrimination possible. Even in the simplest cases of price discrimination, the basic fact is that the seller accepts orders that leave him different net prices;[2] some prices are satisfactory to him, others

[2] A businessman selling to different places with different transport cost, in different kinds of packing, with different discounts, etc., can compare these prices

are less so or are even unsatisfactory, made perhaps only to spite a rival. A higher degree of competition would make every seller run after the good orders and refuse the bad ones—until the good ones would be less good and the bad ones better. Where this does not happen the market is "imperfectly competitive," that is, monopolistic.

A seller can of course make special prices to his friends or to poor people even if he is in a position of pure competition. But is there any use speaking of price discrimination if a farmer gives away some of his eggs or milk to poor children in the village? Acts of friendship, charity, patriotism, etc., may take the form of special pricing, but we may omit them in this discussion.

2. Classifications of Price Discrimination

NEITHER an analysis nor even an elementary description of price discrimination can do without some classification. For economic analysis a classification according to the *purposes* for which sellers practice price discrimination, another according to the *techniques* they use, and a third according to the *degree of discriminating power* are most helpful. This is, however, too much for this survey. We shall describe more than twenty types of price discrimination, grouped according to techniques employed, but distinguished also by purposes served, effects achieved, or special conditions required. The selected types are named with their suggestive catchwords to convey their character.

THREE MAIN CLASSES

THE techniques of price discrimination are grouped into three main classes: personal discrimination, group discrimination, and product discrimination.[3] Personal discrimination makes differences between individual customers the basis for extending differential treatment to them. Group discrimination differentiates not between individuals as such but between categories or classes of customers. Product discrimination selects neither individual customers nor customer groups for different treatment but allows customers to choose freely among different products (qualities) offered at discriminatory prices.

---

only by deducting the differential expenses, that is, by reducing them to a common basis. Thus he computes his "net prices."

[3] Ralph Cassady, Jr., "Techniques and Purposes of Price Discrimination," *Journal of Marketing*, Vol. 11, 1946, pp. 135-143.

PERSONAL DISCRIMINATION

WITH one important exception, personal discrimination is by its very nature an unsystematic form of discrimination. Prices may be differentiated according to the seller's appraisal of the individual customer's bargaining strength, of his eagerness to buy, of his income, or of the use he intends to make of the product and the consequent earning power it may have for him.

An extreme example of this class is the *haggle-every-time* type which appears only in a relatively unorganized market. The buyers are not regular customers with constantly recurring demand but a fluctuating group of varying composition. The seller tries to size up each buyer's ability to pay, urgency of demand, and knowledge of the market and then drives as hard a bargain as he can. This type of discrimination is interesting more for the art of personnel selection and for studies in buyer psychology than for economic analysis. It occurs chiefly in certain types of retail trade—for example in antique dealings—or at time in parts of the automobile market by way of trade-in allowances. But it may also occur in other types of trade or industry. The concessions made to a strong bargainer may be in terms of price or method of payment or in terms of extra costs (freight) assumed by the seller. The seller, while not adopting any systematic policy of discounts or freight absorption, may be influenced in his dealings with a particular customer by the terms upon which this customer claims he can buy the goods from a rival and bargaining may take place over price, terms, extra services, and delivery costs.

A similar kind of individual bargaining exists also in markets where the buyers are regular customers with constantly recurring demand. The sellers in considerable number, but none of dominant size, offer a little differentiated product in an unorganized and imperfect market in which transactions are secret and "knowledge of the market" is based chiefly on rumors—so that buyers can play one seller against the other. Each deal is separately negotiated and sellers are sometimes willing to make special concessions in competing for particular hard-to-get orders. This *give-in-if-you-must* type of discrimination is practiced chiefly in a buyers' market, where business is slack and producers have a difficult time keeping their plants busy. (The theorist who is anxious to fit the case to his given set of tools might discuss the weakness of the seller vis-à-vis

401

the hard-bargaining buyer in terms of a high elasticity of that separate portion of the demand.)

The *let-him-pay-more* type is a more systematic but not very important type of personal discrimination. Sellers who for the greater part of their business are in a fairly competitive position with little control over price may have a few customers whom they can consistently "overcharge." These may be the "nice" customers who do not take the trouble to shop around, or customers who, although they have free access to a more competitive market, are located so near the particular producer and so far from the central market that they fare better at a high discriminatory price than at the uniform market price. "Let them pay more," thinks the seller and exacts higher prices. To the seller these discriminatory sales are merely some toothsome morsels, the bulk of his business being done in a competitive market. (It would be a different type of discrimination if a larger part of the output could be sold in the discriminatory fashion.)

The *size-up-his-income* type of discrimination is often practiced by doctors and lawyers. In rendering their bills, they ask themselves how much the particular patients or clients can afford to pay for their professional services. Doctors may treat impecunious patients for much less than wealthy patients. Middle-class patients are charged "moderate" fees, not so much out of kindheartedness as in consideration of the greater elasticity of demand for medical treatment of this class of people. In charging little to the poor, the doctors may be motivated by sheer philanthropy and generosity. Their ability to make their rich patients make up for it will depend on their quasi-monopolistic position in the field, a position supported by the strict code of ethics which effectively reduces competition in the medical profession.[4]

The *measure-the-use* type of discrimination is, in contrast to the other types of personal discrimination, a very systematic way of adjusting the price approximately to the profits which the buyer makes from using the sold or leased article. The monopolistic position of the seller or lessor in these cases must be well protected, for example through patents or copyrights. Patented machines are often

[4] One of the most famous examples of the *size-up-his-income* type of price discrimination is reported in our history books dealing with the fifteenth and early sixteenth century: "indulgences for sins" and promises to remit punishment in purgatory were sold by the Church on a sliding scale of prices adjusted to the sinner's means. The grossness of the sin was another factor in determining the price.

leased to users whose rentals are fixed per unit of output produced on the machines or in percentages of sales of fabricated goods. The exhibitors of motion pictures usually pay for the copyrighted films on the basis of their actual or prospective box office success in their theaters. A newspaper usually pays for the use of syndicated columns, comic strips, and news services in rough proportion to the size of its circulation. The underlying theory of all these schemes is that the prices charged should be at least roughly in accordance with the earning power which the acquired rights provide to the buyer.

GROUP DISCRIMINATION

GROUP discrimination is in a sense semi-personal. It depends on differences between different groups of buyers and aims at taking advantage of these differences in such a way that the buyers cannot easily evade the discriminatory prices. Prices, for example,[5] may be differentiated according to the age of the customer (half fares for children, children's haircuts); the sex of the customer (reduced admission for ladies at ball games); the military status of the customer (reduced theater tickets for men in uniform); membership in certain organizations (sales to members of clubs or associations); the public nature of the buyer (transportation for the government). Discrimination between functional or occupational categories of buyers is often found in subscription rates for papers and magazines, in selling prices of books (educational rates, trade and college editions), and in advertising rates (manufacturers' advertisements in newspapers). Social welfare schemes of public authorities to assist specified groups in the community by the use of discriminatory pricing may also come into this category (the Food Stamp Plan).

Group discrimination may also be based upon the location of the customer (goods sold at uniform delivered prices in all markets or at different zone prices, or surpluses sporadically dumped in a market geographically separated from the seller's regular market); upon the patronage status of the customer (special rates for new customers, or quantity and volume discounts to large ones); and upon the use to which the product is put (fluid milk for consumption and for industrial purposes, railroad transportation for high-valued finished goods and for low-valued raw materials, or postal service for letters and for parcels).

[5] Almost all the examples are taken from Cassady's classification cited in note 3.

The most important types of group discrimination come under the headings just indicated—consumer location, patronage status of the customer, and product use—and we shall select them for more detailed discussion. We shall find, however, that the techniques involved are less significant than the purposes they are intended to serve. For example, several methods of separating different buyer groups exploit differences in the "squeezability" of the separate groups—their ability to stand higher prices. Discrimination according to the patronage status of the customer may be used to develop new clientele, reward cooperating customers and punish disobedient ones, or strengthen strong distributors or fabricators at the expense of weaker ones. Discrimination based upon the consumer's location—"locational" or "geographic" discrimination—may be used to squeeze more money out of the market, it may be part of a scheme of predatory competition, or it may not have any direct or conscious purpose but be merely an incidental by-product of a particular pricing practice.

CONSUMER LOCATION

THIS section briefly describes seven types of geographic discrimination. In some of these the discrimination lies not in price differentials, but rather in price uniformities or price similarities in the face of cost differences. Thus, only comparisons of net prices realized after deducting the costs "absorbed" by the seller can reveal the price discrimination.

The *forget-the-cost-difference* type of discrimination consists of a failure to adjust selling prices exactly to the existing cost differentials, a failure arising from an inclination "not to bother" or to "forget about it." The cost differentials may be too small in relation to the cost—clerical or other—of differentiating the prices accordingly.

For example, if a retail store charges fifteen cents for local delivery regardless of the distance, this will imply discrimination against nearby customers in favor of more distant customers. It would not pay to calculate delivery charges on the basis of miles and pounds. If goods are delivered without extra charge, the cash-and-carry customers are discriminated against. If the manufacturer of a nationally advertised article finds it desirable to have it sold at the same price everywhere all over the country, he absorbs the freight differences and thus discriminates against the buyers near his plant.[6]

---

[6] It is interesting to observe that delivered prices or "freight allowed" systems (i.e. systems under which the seller absorbs all freight costs) are often practiced

By way of digression we may note here that price discrimination through the neglect of small cost differences is not always geographic discrimination: instead of transportation costs some other expenses may be absorbed by the seller. The underlying principle is the same. For example, if charge account sales are made at the same prices as sales to cash customers the latter pay part of the cost of credit to the former.

In all these instances, the failure to take account of certain cost differentials and to have them reflected in the selling prices may be due to the desire to save the effort or cost of figuring and charging adequate price differentials or to the desire to gain and maintain customer loyalty by avoiding any "annoying" charges.[7] There are other instances, however, in which the seller has altogether differ-ent reasons for absorbing cost differences. In several "freight allowed" systems of pricing, the seller is not motivated by convenience. Instead he tries to maintain resale prices by a pricing system which discourages interzonal competition among distributors.

Under this *keep-them-in-their-zones* type of price discrimination the seller quotes his prices "f.o.b. factory, freight allowed." This means that the manufacturer will ship the product to the wholesaler's establishment and permit him to deduct the freight from the bill. What this seller calls his "f.o.b. factory price" is really a delivered price, every distributor getting the product at exactly the same price c.i.f. destination. While the manufacturer thus absorbs the freight to the distributors or to destinations within their zones, any further freights must be paid by the distributors. The distributor in Zone A pays for shipments into his zone the same delivered price that the distributor in Zone B pays for shipments into B. If the Zone A distributor tried to sell in Zone B, a territory not assigned to him, he would have to pay the freight from his zone to the other and the goods would therefore cost him more than they

---

for the nationally advertised brands while they are not practiced for the un-advertised brands of the same commodities. The greater degree of competition in the more standardized commodities makes it unprofitable to practice the geographic price discrimination which is inherent in freight absorptions. For example, unadvertised brands of tea, coffee, cocoa, canned soups, and crackers are sold f.o.b. shipping place without freight absorption. Advertised brands of the same goods are sold at uniform delivered prices or with "freight allowed." See Saul Nelson and Walter G. Keim, *Price Behavior and Business Policy*, Temporary National Economic Committee, Monograph 1, 1940, pp. 298-300.

[7] A United States Circuit Court once concluded that where freight differences were small, charging uniform prices was economical and convenient. *United States v. Corn Products Refining Co.*, 234 Fed. 994 (1916).

cost the appointed zone distributor. Distributors are thus discouraged from invading each other's territories and the manufacturer avoids what he calls "demoralization" of his market.

The motives of sellers who absorb freight under systematic freight equalization schemes are of a different nature. The *match-the-freight* type of price discrimination is practiced if a seller, in an attempt to overcome the competitive disadvantage of being located farther away from a customer than some of his competitors, offers to absorb any excess of the actual freight over the lowest freight from any competitor's plant to the destination. Thus he matches the freight charges from but not the price quoted by competing firms. Delivered prices quoted by competing sellers would be identical if all competitors not only offered to match the lowest freight charges but also to quote identical f.o.b. mill prices or use identical base prices. Freight equalization alone would not, therefore, imply identical delivered prices. Freight equalization—a system of meeting lower freight charges, but not lower prices—is discriminatory in that the seller absorbing a difference in freight costs accepts a lower mill net price; but the scheme does not exclude price competition.

Price competition is excluded under a system where sellers systematically meet the lowest quoted prices as well as freight charges. Such a scheme, ensuring equal delivered prices quoted by all firms, is not only inherently discriminatory, because the mill net prices which a seller realizes from sales to buyers in different locations ordinarily must vary considerably, but is also inherently collusive, because it involves a common course of action with regard to prices. In view of the collective or cooperative character of the pricing scheme we may speak of the *play-the-game* type of price discrimination.[8] The official name is the basing-point system.

Under a single-basing-point system, every seller quotes delivered prices by adding to the openly announced base price the calculated freight cost from the common basing point to the destination, no matter whether he is located at the basing point or elsewhere. A

[8] The catchwords "play-the-game" (or cooperative) discrimination are borrowed from Frank A. Fetter, *The Masquerade of Monopoly* (Harcourt, Brace, 1931), p. 310. We ought to distinguish: (1) price agreements which *intend* to secure a certain scheme of discriminatory prices and (2) price agreements which result *incidentally* in a scattering of discriminatory prices. The latter is the type discussed now as the play-the-game type. It results when a geographical pricing scheme is adopted by all firms in the industry and the firms "play-the-game 100 percent" in order to avoid "tearing down the price structure." These phrases were used by the U.S. Supreme Court in *Federal Trade Commission* v. *The Cement Institute*, 333 U.S. 683 (1948).

seller located at the basing point will realize the base price from all his shipments, whereas a seller at another location will realize different net prices from shipments to different destinations.

Under a multiple-basing-point system each seller quotes as his delivered price the cheapest combination of any of the announced base prices and the freight costs from basing point to destination. For each bid the seller ascertains which of the basing points is applicable for the particular destination point and adds to the relevant base price the freight from the applicable basing point to the destination. A mill located at a basing point uses it as a basis for calculating delivered prices only for destinations within what is called its own "natural market territory." For other destinations other base prices are applicable. If four basing points are established for a certain product made by twenty different mills in the country there will be in effect four territories, in each of which all delivered prices are calculated as the sum of the base price announced for the governing basing point and the railroad freight from that basing point to the destination, regardless of the actual point of shipment. A nonbase mill located closer to a certain destination than to the basing point collects unspent freight on its shipments to that point. On its shipments to destinations closer to any of the basing points than to its own location, the nonbase mill has to absorb freight, that is, it collects a mill net price lower than the relevant base price. A base mill shipping into areas governed by other basing points collects a mill net price less than its own base price.

If all mills were base mills, that is, if every production point were a basing point, this would not eliminate the discriminatory differentials in mill net prices which each mill would realize from different sales, inasmuch as each mill would serve customers at points governed by different basing points. This would not be so if each mill were to use only its own location as its basing point for all its sales—but then the industry would no longer have a basing-point system; it would be under a general f.o.b. mill price system, resulting in uniform net realizations by each firm and not in identical delivered prices quoted by different competitors. It is the very essence of the basing-point system that each seller accepts the base prices announced by his competitors as the basis for his own delivered price quotations in their territories. This may achieve two results: first, it eliminates effective price competition among the sellers and, second, it may allow the powerful firms in the industry to control the sales volumes, and thus check the potential growth, of the smaller firms. Because of these possible effects the basing-point system of pricing—which has been used not only by the steel industry but also by the cement, pulp, sugar, and lead industries among others—has been vigorously attacked as one of the worst forms of monopolistic pricing. Its discriminatory nature, however, although inherent, is not intentional but merely incidental. There is no intention of favoring some buyer groups or harming others. Since near-by buyers are discriminated against in favor of distant buyers but each buyer may be distant from some producer, it is conceivable that the discriminations practiced by all sellers will cancel out. In practice some regions will be harmed by the way the system actually works, but the discriminatory price differentials received by sellers need not reflect the effects of the discriminations upon buyers, localities, or regions.[9]

When the play-the-game type of price discrimination is used to hold down smaller firms it becomes a type of local price cutting by giant firms, similar to the *kill-the-rival* type of discrimination. This type achieved greatest notoriety and raised issues which furnished strong arguments for the early trust-busting campaigns in the United States. For the most part it is of lesser interest to the economic theorist than to the economic historian and the lawyer. The kill-the-rival or oppress-the-rival type of discrimination was made unlawful in the United States by the Clayton Act, which (in Section 2) declares it to "be unlawful . . . to discriminate in price between different purchasers of commodities of like grade and quality . . . where the effect of such discrimination may be substantially to lessen competition. . . ."

Competition was indeed lessened if, through local price cutting by the financially powerful concern, smaller competitors were killed off—either forced to close down or to sell out to their stronger opponent. Competition was also lessened when the competitors came to terms, when they stopped ambitious attempts to draw more business from the larger concern, or when they became willing to fall into line with the policies of the leader. In these latter cases the rivals were not eliminated as other sources of supply but were eliminated as factors disturbing the exercise of the stronger firm's control over price.

The best-known illustrations of the kill-the-rival type of price discrimination are the cases discussed before the courts in the suits

9 Fritz Machlup, *The Basing-Point System* (Blakiston, 1949), esp. pp. 151-156, 233-247.

leading up to the dissolution in 1911 of the Standard Oil Co. of New Jersey and the American Tobacco Co. In the records of the Standard Oil case we can read that the "defendants have pursued a system of unfair competition against their competitors, whereby the independent companies selling and marketing petroleum have either been driven out of business or their business so restricted that the Standard Oil Company has practically controlled the prices and monopolized the commerce in the products of petroleum in the United States. This system has taken the form of price cutting in particular localities while keeping up high prices, or raising them still higher, in other localities where no competition exists; of paying rebates to customers as a part of said system of·price cutting, . . ."[10]

While it is easy to describe the kill-the-rival or oppress-the-rival type of price discrimination, it is difficult to prove that a particular situation in reality is of this type. Local price cutting may be practiced for different reasons and intent can rarely be proved. Hence one will have to search for criteria by which to distinguish instances of local price discrimination that look alike but are different in purpose as well as in effect.

The sixth type of geographic discrimination to be included in this survey is sufficiently different from the others to be clearly set apart. The *dump-the-surplus* type of price discrimination is characterized by its unsystematic and sporadic nature. In order to move his surpluses without spoiling his regular market a seller may dispose of them in a different territory at lower prices. Such dumping is often highly disturbing to other sellers whose regular market becomes the occasional dumping ground for goods withheld from their usual outlets. But in spite of the numerous complaints which this type of sporadic discrimination arouses in international and interregional trade, it does not offer difficult problems for economic analysis.

Permanent dumping—charging lower net prices for exports than for domestic sales—differs from any of the six types of geographic price discrimination thus far discussed. It is not of the sporadic nature which characterizes the dump-the-surplus policy. It is not designed to stabilize existing market conditions as are the keep-them-in-their-zones and play-the-game policies. It is not used to

[10] *United States* v. *Standard Oil Co.*, 1909, *Brief for the United States*, Vol. 1, pp. 187-188.

eliminate a competitor as is the kill-the-rival policy. And it is not as incidental to the techniques of freight-cost absorption as are the forget-the-cost-difference and match-the-freight policies. Its purpose is to exploit the differences in elasticity between the demands of different regions or countries in order to squeeze more revenue out of the total market without attempting to influence the existing market conditions. Geographic price discrimination of this sort is one of the cases of discriminatory pricing to which the theoretical model of price determination for the purpose of profit maximization is most directly applicable. (The principle involved resembles closely the principle of charging-what-the-traffic-will-bear that has been employed in discussions of railroad rate setting.) We may call this seventh type of geographic price discrimination the *get-the-most-from-each-region* type of discrimination.

Examples of this type could be found in the domestic and export price policies of many large concerns—if information were available. One instance that became known from the congressional investigation of, and the court case against, the glass container industry is the geographic discrimination in the sale of milk bottles. The combination of protection under restrictive patent licenses with the geographic separability of the market allowed a manufacturer to sell his milk bottles in Texas at much higher net prices than elsewhere.[11]

Much illustrative material could probably be found in the files of various European cartels with centralized selling organizations. Probably the price differentials these cartels fixed for exports to different countries distinctly reflected the differences in the elasticities of demand resulting from national tariff policies and domestic competition within the various countries.[12]

[11] *Investigation in the Concentration of Economic Power*, Hearings before the TNEC, 1939, Part 2, pp. 611-612.

[12] The writer was at one time connected with the Austrian cardboard cartel. This cartel practiced geographic price discrimination, charging the highest prices for exports to Turkey and the lowest prices for other overseas exports. All markets except the last were protected by tariffs and by international agreements (sometimes involving concealed preferential tariffs). This case of discrimination was unusual in that the domestic market was not charged the highest price; the elasticities of demand in the Hungarian and Italian markets were lower than that in the domestic Austrian market, and they were therefore charged higher prices. Prior to the formation of the cartel as well as after its dissolution, geographic discrimination was impossible because of the sharp competition among the Austrian producers who thus received the same net prices from sales in the domestic and the various export markets.

410

CUSTOMER STATUS

WE HAVE referred to three different purposes for which group discrimination based upon the patronage status of the customer may be practiced. New customers, large customers, or cooperating customers may be the groups selected for more favorable treatment in the seller's pricing policy.

In the *promote-new-custom* type of discrimination, the existing demand that the seller can attract by discriminatory price cutting does not currently provide enough business to warrant his price policy. But the seller expects that this demand will grow—that people will develop a taste for the product or will acquire complementary appliances needed for additional consumption—and that the new demand (pictured by the economist as a new demand curve) will then provide the business and the profits for which he strives. He may then continue his low price or, more likely, he may raise it. Promotional rates or prices—promotional discrimination—will be needed only for development of the demand, not for its continued service.

On the other hand, the seller may wish to favor groups of especially important old customers. The *favor-the-big-ones* type of price discrimination is best characterized by a quantity discount in excess of the economies connected with dealing with large buyers. There are many economies involved in large-quantity business: economies in producing big lots and in selling, handling, transporting, recording and collecting large items. Quantity discounts, rebates, allowances or other forms of price differentials in favor of large buyers do not constitute price discrimination as long as, and to the extent to which, they merely reflect the savings in outlays, risk or trouble.[13] In fact, however, quantity discounts and volume discounts (the latter are allowed on a customer's total purchases over a year regardless of the size of his single orders) are often primarily devices to favor the large and handicap the small customers.

Favoritism shown to large buyers is not always desired by the seller; indeed he may feel that he is being "robbed," a victim of the violence of an important customer. The yielding seller "just could

[13] When the Goodyear Tire & Rubber Co. delivered automobile tires to Sears, Roebuck and Co. under a contract which had been effective from 1926 until 1937, the gross price discrimination as compared with sales to smaller retail sellers varied between 29 and 40 per cent. The net price discrimination after due allowance for cost differentials was computed to range from 11 to 22 per cent. See *Report on Monopolistic Practices in Industries*, Federal Trade Commission, 1939, Part 5A, pp. 2311-2312.

not afford to lose the customer." (Where the discrimination is in favor of an individual buyer, not of large buyers in general, the case is really one of the "give-in-if-you-must" type.) Legislation that prohibits price discrimination may in such cases be welcomed by the seller as a substitute for his lack of strength or backbone.

In contrast to these instances in which the discriminatory scheme in favor of large buyers is imposed upon a weak seller, there are many others in which it is a deliberate policy of a strong seller trying to improve his monopolistic position by creating a more monopolistic position for his chief customers. The degree of competition in the market in which his customers have to sell—that is, in the selling market of the distributors or processors of his product —will be reflected in the prices he can obtain in the long run. He may therefore be greatly interested in helping his customers to improve their market position by cleaning out excessive competition among them. Price discrimination against the small fry can be very effective in establishing such an increased degree of monopoly for his favored customers in their respective markets.[14] It was primarily this type of price discrimination that the Robinson-Patman Act of 1936 made unlawful when the effect was "to substantially lessen competition."

We often hear large retailers protest that a certain manufacturer would not give them the same wholesale allowance he was granting to much smaller wholesale houses. This looks like a policy of favoring the little ones; but the manufacturer undoubtedly discriminates against the large buyers, not because of their size but rather because they are retailers selling to the ultimate consumer while the favored small buyers are middlemen selling to retailers. He probably believes that the middlemen fulfill a useful function and should not be squeezed out of the market. This policy may be called the *protect-the-middleman* type of price discrimination. It is practiced by a manufacturer who regards it as "healthier" in the long run if

14 The FTC has made the following statement concerning this type of price discrimination: "The Commission considered that a manufacturer, under the Clayton Act, . . . may not make his bargains according to his own interest by discriminating as he pleases, however honest and justifiable such courses might be from the standpoint of commercial principles. Large industrial companies, through price discrimination, can control competitive business conditions among their customers to the extent of enriching some and ruining others. . . . If it were left to a manufacturer to make the price solely on account of quantity, he could easily make discounts by reason of quantity so high as to be practically open to the largest dealers only, and in that manner might hand over the whole trade in his line of commerce to a few or a single dealer." *Ibid.*, p. 2312.

he protects the middlemen by removing some of the advantages a large retailer would find in by-passing them. His concern for a healthy situation may of course have a great deal to do with his interest in resale price maintenance.

Discrimination in favor of customers who obey and against those who do not obey the seller's resale price maintenance or similar schemes may be called the *hold-them-in-line* type of price discrimination. It serves to control policies of the customers, and to enforce price maintenance and compliance with the seller's wishes by granting discounts to those who "behave" and by excluding those who do not. The procedure is either to grant the discount to all buyers except those on a black list or to grant the discount exclusively to buyers who are on a white list. The latter procedure is, from the point of view of legality, much safer and therefore more common. One way of doing this type of business is to give the discount to all buyers who are members in good standing of a certain organization or association; but, of course, there are many other ways of doing it. For example, through refunds distributed through the association of the "behaving" customers, or through free services rendered or other forms of preferential treatment accorded to the behaving customers.

PRODUCT USE

DISCRIMINATION based upon the use made of the product is the most interesting type for economic analysis because the differences in eagerness to buy and ability to pay, and the profits made through exploiting them, are the basis and *raison d'être* of the discriminatory pricing. (All but one of the types of group discrimination thus far discussed have been practiced for other reasons.) A seller's profit will surely be higher if he can squeeze each group to just the right extent, exacting high prices from groups that can stand them and conceding low prices to groups that could not afford to use much of the product at higher prices. The seller will be able to do this if the market can be divided by objective criteria and the buyer groups thus separated respond very differently to various price levels for the product. In other words, the elasticities of demand of the separate groups must be different if price discrimination is to yield increased revenues.

The classical application of this principle has been in the railroad industry. It became known there as the charge-what-the-traffic-will-bear principle of freight rate making and we shall speak therefore of the *charge-what-the-traffic-will-bear* type of price discrimination.

The phrase "charge what the traffic will bear" can easily be misunderstood. First of all, it certainly does not mean that the highest possible price is charged without consideration of its effect on sales. Secondly, if it were taken to mean nothing else but that a maximum net revenue is extracted from the business, then this principle would obviously be applicable to every type of business, not merely to discriminating monopolies. The seller in a purely competitive market will also charge what the traffic will bear—but the traffic will not bear more than the uniform market price. And, likewise, the seller with great control over the price of his product but without being able to discriminate between his customers will charge what the traffic will bear—but it will be one uniform price, rather than a set of different prices, that will bring the highest possible net revenue. We prefer, however, to use the phrase not in this all too general sense, but only in connection with the problem of discrimination. Although the phrase is often applied by way of analogy to other industries, we shall reserve it for its original and historical meaning in the discussion of railroad rates.

Traditionally three kinds of discrimination are distinguished in the field of railroad transportation: personal discrimination (which was always unlawful), local discrimination (one phase of which was prohibited by the famous long-and-short-haul clause[15]) and commodity discrimination (which was always regarded as legitimate). Commodity discrimination is applied between groups of users of the transportation service according to the commodities they ship.[16] This kind of discrimination is generally practiced by railroads and is condoned by the regulatory agencies of the government; indeed, it has been considered indispensable for railroad operation on a paying basis.

Thus, while the law—chiefly the Interstate Commerce Act—for-

[15] The long-and-short-haul clause is a provision of the Interstate Commerce Act of 1887 and of its amendment of 1910, forbidding a greater charge for a short than for a long haul over the same line if circumstances were substantially similar.

[16] On first thought one may be inclined to interpret commodity discrimination in transportation as a type of product discrimination instead of a type of group discrimination. Product discrimination, however, refers to different products or product qualities offered by a seller at discriminatory prices. Commodity discrimination in railroad transportation, on the other hand, refers to one product —transportation service which the railroad offers at discriminatory prices to different groups, namely persons using the service for different commodities.

bids rate differentials giving particular *shippers* or particular *locali-ties* an undue advantage over others, it permits differentials giving particular *industries* substantial advantages over others. Incidentally, it is often overlooked that discriminatory rates for various commodi-ties may imply discriminatory treatment of the localities or regions in which the different industries are located. The rates for trans-portation per ton-mile are much higher for expensive materials like silk than for cheap materials like coal or gravel. (Expensive and cheap refer here to value per unit of weight.) The rates for copper are higher than those for steel, the rates for fluid milk higher than those for gasoline. Since railroad rates are under gov-ernment regulation it is difficult to state whether or not the ap-proved rate structure is really all that the traffic will bear in the opinion of the railroad management. The inflexibility of court decisions and commission rules, the emphasis on the fair return theory, and perhaps the insertion of various social and political objectives, make it doubtful that both level and structure of rates conform fully to the principle of maximization of net revenues. The approved rate *levels* are possibly lower in prosperity periods and higher in depression periods than some alert managements would set them if they were entirely free to charge what the traffic could bear. The rate differentials—that is, the essentially discriminatory rate *structure*—probably tally more closely with the managements' views about the relative elasticities of different segments of the demand for transportation than the rate level tallies with their views about the combined elasticities of the total market.

The application of the charge-what-the-traffic-will-bear principle to industries other than transportation may be called the *get-the-most-from-each-group* type of price discrimination. It is often prac-ticed by public utilities (although also modified by public regula-tion of rate making). Electric current for household consumption is usually sold at much higher rates than the current for industrial use. And even these two markets are sometimes subdivided accord-ing to the amount or kind of use made of the electricity. In some communities electric current for hot-water heating or space heating in households is cheaper than for lighting; current for very large industrial users, who might find it cheaper to produce their own power, is sometimes cheaper than for small industrial users.

For several reasons we know of relatively few illustrations of the get-the-most-from-each-group type of discrimination for manu-factured products. First, discrimination in railroad and utility rates is socially approved and publicly regulated, while discrimination in industrial pricing is usually under suspicion and often in danger of being construed as unlawful. Secondly, it is difficult to divide the market into distinct groups of users, while such separations are easy in utilities and transportation. A domestic household can hardly purchase electric current in the disguise of a factory, and milk cannot very well travel in the disguise of gasoline, whereas in the case of manufactured goods the purchasers who are supposed to buy at higher prices may succeed in securing their supply at the lower price, either by "sneaking in" with the preferred group or by having someone else do the buying for them. Thirdly, it is almost impossible to discover the presence of discrimination for manufactured products where there are actual or alleged cost differentials. The extra cost of transporting bulky articles, or the differences in the cost of transporting in tank cars, box cars, and platform cars, can be much more easily proved or disproved than cost differences in the production of innumerable varieties of manufactured goods. No public commission digs into the cost accounts of manufacturing companies in order to compare costs with selling prices. Finally, an enduring system of price discrimination requires a degree of monopoly which is not so easily achieved in manufacturing industry, unless the government helps to reduce competition through special legislation, patent and copyright laws, or similar devices.

The examples we have of price discrimination practiced by manufacturing industry in the United States usually come from court cases or congressional hearings. In the glass container industry, under the protection of patents which were used for the organization of a tight cartel through licensing contracts, instances of discrimination between groups of users became notorious. Exactly the same kinds of glass container were sold at higher prices as "domestic fruit jars" than as "packers' ware."[17] The elasticity of demand for jars for household use was apparently smaller.

A case of discrimination between different groups of users that achieved much notoriety concerned a chemical product. Manufacturers of plastics, protected by patents and patent license agreements, sold a certain material for use in dentures at a price many times higher than the price they charged for the same material for industrial use.[18] In the dental use the cost of the material was only

[17] *Investigation in the Concentration of Economic Power*, as cited, pp. 572-574, 591.

[18] The price differential was further increased by markups—protected by price

a negligible fraction of the cost of the complementary highly skilled labor and, therefore, the elasticity of derived demand was so much smaller that it could stand the strikingly increased price. The manufacturers were of course anxious to prevent the material bought at low prices by industrial users from being diverted to dental use. In order to make sure that such diversion would not occur they advertised that the material sold to industrial users might contain ingredients injurious to a patient's health.[19] This slight "differentiation" of the product might make us wonder whether the case should not be discussed as one of product discrimination, rather than group discrimination, since the seller offered two different products, allowing buyers to choose between a cheap material apparently unfit for dental use and an expensive one that could be so used. The case demonstrates that the lines drawn between classes of phenomena are arbitrary and anything but watertight.[20]

Two other cases that might be classified either under product discrimination or user group discrimination may be cited. The Aluminum Corp. of America used to sell aluminum ingots at a higher price per pound than it sold aluminum in cable form.[21] Effective competition from copper cables was the obvious reason for the lower price on aluminum cables. This segment of the aluminum market would not stand the higher price that was charged for ingots, the less fabricated product. Similarly, producers of plate glass charged a much higher price per square foot for large pieces than for small pieces, although all plate glass is produced in large sheets. The differential was at times more than 100 percent of the price for small sizes. The elasticity of demand for plate glass in small pieces was high because of the heavy competition of ordinary window glass; in large pieces plate glass had no serious substitutes in its chief uses and the producers took advantage of the lower demand

---

maintenance arrangements—of the distributors. "Thus methyl methacrylate when marketed for ordinary commercial purposes sold for 85 cents per pound, but when sold for denture purposes costs the dental profession approximately $50 per pound." *Patents*, Hearings before the Senate Committee on Patents, 77th Cong., 2d Sess. (1942), Part 2, p. 719.

[19] *Ibid.*, p. 721.

[20] I chose to discuss the case as one of user group discrimination rather than product discrimination because the differentiation of the product was only a device for preventing the diversion of the substantially identical product from the favored users to those held up for the higher price.

[21] The buyers of aluminum cable had to agree not to melt it. "Report on the Aluminum Industry" (mimeographed), National Recovery Administration, 1935, p. 14.

elasticity.[22] Patent protection and patent contracts enabled them to practice this discrimination without disturbance either from insiders' defection or outsiders' invasion.

User group discrimination in the marketing of agricultural products is practiced either under governmental plans or by agricultural cooperatives aided by governments. The scheme of the Surplus Commodities Administration, distributing surplus commodities at reduced prices to relief families (the so-called Food Stamp Plan) was price discrimination with a partly social objective—and thus may not belong to the type under discussion—but conceivably a monopolistic seller of these commodities might, if he could, choose the same system in trying to get the most from each group.

A two-price and sometimes three-price system has been created in the distribution of milk, with very substantial price differentials according to the use to which it is put. The highest price is charged for milk for fluid consumption, a much lower price for milk for industrial uses (cheese and ice cream), and sometimes a medium high price for milk separated as cream. The monopolistic organizations needed for the maintenance of these price differentials were provided by producers' cooperatives and large-scale distributors, but it soon became necessary to give the scheme governmental support. Various laws and regulations prohibit competition in this field in order to secure the operation of the system which enables the producer to collect a high price for fluid milk for direct consumption and to dispose of all surplus milk at lower prices for industrial purposes.

PRODUCT DISCRIMINATION

PRODUCT discrimination does not depend upon a separation of buyers in such a way that they cannot evade the demarcation lines, but upon a differentiation of the products in such a way that the buyers will separate themselves and buy at discriminatory prices. A seller may do this by differentiating his products as to design, label, quality, time of sale, or distribution channel having a different appeal to different consumers—or by offering different products.

The *appeal-to-the-classes* type of price discrimination is based on a systematic attempt to divide the market according to the ability (or willingness) to pay of different customer groups, not by discriminating between buyers locally, personally, or through any seller-determined criterion, but merely by offering the good or

22 Myron W. Watkins, *Industrial Combinations and Public Policy* (Houghton Mifflin, 1927), p. 170.

service in slightly differentiated grades or classes among which the buyers may choose. Cases in point are Grade A and Grade B milk in New York City and many other places (with only a small difference in quality or cost); standard and deluxe models of automobiles (with price differences larger than cost differences); railroad fares in pullman parlor cars and day coaches (with a relatively small difference in the cost of the service); expensive and cheap seats in theaters and concert halls (with no difference in cost to the management); goods in fancy containers and the same goods without containers (with price differences far in excess of the cost of packing); books in deluxe binding and in ordinary or even paper binding (with price differentials greater than cost differentials); dining room service and coffee shop service in the same restaurant (with no or only a trivial difference in the cost of the service); and many other goods which come in high grades and cheaper ones (with no cost differentials accounting for the price differentials).

Most instances of the appeal-to-the-classes type of price discrimination are considered as perfectly legitimate business practices. In some of these instances the service to the buyer who pays the higher price is really superior in quality, even if its short-run marginal cost to the seller is not higher than that of the service sold at lower price. (An orchestra seat at a play is certainly *better* than a seat in the rear section of the balcony.) In other instances the inherent class implication is worth its price to the buyer (as in the case of services to people who purchase the distinction with the higher price).

This relatively unobjectionable type of price discrimination is different from the *make-them-pay-for the-label* type, where the whole differentiation lies in the brand or label of the article and is designed to deceive the buyer by making him believe he is acquiring a more durable or more hygienic or otherwise technologically superior good.

The Federal Trade Commission reported the case of a feather bed pillow manufacturing company which "marketed their products under the five brand names 'Princess,' 'Progress,' 'Washington,' 'Puritan,' and 'Ideal.' In its advertising the manufacturer represented that these products were of different grades in the order named and correspondingly different prices were charged for each. The Commission found, however, that all these five brands were of the same quality, and that the material price differential between the 'Princess' and the 'Ideal' brand reflected a difference in the label only."[23]

[23] Quoted from Nelson and Keim, *op. cit.*, p. 80. The case is Docket No. 1129 of the FTC.

The make-them-pay-for-the-label type of price discrimination is definitely obnoxious when it is combined with deceptive advertising and misrepresentation, as in the case just described. Where differences in quality are not falsely claimed but merely indirectly suggested through different names or labels, the practice is not so offensive. It has become customary for certain producers to sell the same quality of goods at higher prices under a nationally advertised name or label and at lower prices under other names or labels. Certain chemical substances, cosmetics, toothpastes, etc. are sold under nonproprietary names much more cheaply than under proprietary names.[24] The wholesale price difference for nationally advertised hosiery and the same merchandise under private label was, before 1938, up to $1.25 a dozen.[25]

A seller may also differentiate his product in the *clear-the-stock* type of price discrimination by presenting it at special times or, in the case of retail trade, in special parts of his store. In this type the seller disposes of stock on hand in order to make room for new stock. The best-known example occurs in the inventory sales of retail stores, where customers may buy regular stock at much reduced prices either at times especially advertised by the seller or in special parts (for example, the basement) of the store.

The temporal discrimination which is involved in the clear-the-stock type of price discrimination may be sporadic or periodic. In any event the seller does not want his bargain sales to encroach to any large extent on his regular sales. The less business is switched from regular prices to bargain prices, the more nearly is his objective fulfilled. There is a different type of temporal discrimination which a seller practices precisely in order to switch some of the demand for his services from busy to slack periods during the day, the week, or the year. The *switch-them-to-off-peak-times* type of price discrimination is practiced in public utility rates (rates for off-peak electricity; night-and-Sunday rates for long-distance telephone calls) in street-car fares (lower fares for travel between rush hours), in hotel rates (lower off-season rates in resorts), in theater tickets (matinee prices in theaters), and probably other instances in which the demand for services tends to be concentrated at particular time intervals, leaving capacity underutilized at other times. In some of these instances differential pricing need not be discrim-

[24] According to *ibid.*, p. 81, the saving for such purchases under nonproprietary names averaged 76 per cent in 1938.
[25] See *Knit Goods Weekly*, January 3, 1938, p. 8.

inatory pricing. For there would be differentials even if these services were supplied by pure competitors without any control over prices. Price differentials are called discriminatory only if they are "administered" and deviate from those that would have emerged under purely competitive conditions. Of course, in practice such a comparison may not be possible.

In most types of pricing described in this section the exercise of discrimination against some buyers is based upon their own decisions. The segregation of the buyers is voluntary, for it is up to each buyer whether to choose the cheaper or the more expensive product or service. In some cases, to be sure, particularly where prices are differentiated according to the time the product or service is acquired, the buyer's choice may not be entirely free. (For example, long-distance business calls can usually be made only during business hours; and certain industrial users of electricity could not possibly confine their operations to off-peak hours.) In other cases the choice may be a matter of mere convenience; again in others, a matter of comparative costs. Where quality appeal is the basis of the price differential, the buyer's belief in the higher quality of the higher-priced good or service is the reason for his preference. In other instances it may be the discrimination itself for which he deliberately pays: he may want to be in the more exclusive division, in the company of others who choose to distinguish themselves by getting the more expensive variety. (The parlor car passenger pays chiefly for the pleasure of traveling with "better-class" people; the dining room guest wants to eat in an environment more distinguished than the cheaper coffee shop.)[26]

All types of product discrimination thus far discussed referred to differentiated products, that is, to products not sufficiently dissimilar to call them different products. To be sure, no hard and fast line can be drawn between differentiated and different products. Different shapes of aluminum—ingots and cables—may with equal justification be regarded as differentiated aluminum or as different aluminum

[26] The determination of the most profitable price differentials in cases of product discrimination is an interesting problem in theory as well as in practice. It is a difficult one because the elasticities of demand for the separate varieties are interdependent. That is to say, the demand for the separate varieties is not given in the sense that it depends only on the price charged for the particular variety. It depends also on the prices charged for the other varieties. Economic theory has nice solutions for the determination of the optimum set of discriminatory prices under the assumption of independent demand curves. A solution for interdependent demand curves requires a more complicated apparatus than that traditionally employed in geometric price analysis.

products. Likewise one may look either way at different glass containers, different steel products, different plastic materials, etc. But the line of products sold by a firm may be so diversified that the various items cannot without excessive strain be called differentiated types of one product but must be regarded as different products. Yet the different products sold by one firm may have something in common: materials or parts produced by the firm, processes carried out with its equipment, hence, a productive contribution of some sort; and it will then be possible to make a calculation reducing the different products to their common components. The net prices received for the common components sold in the form of the different products can be ascertained by deducting from the selling price of each of the products all cost elements that are not related to the common components. This will reveal the extent of price discrimination practiced in the sale of the different products of the firm. We may call it the *get-the-most-for-each-product* type of discrimination.[27]

We shall not here go into the possible complications in analysis which arise from the possibility that the various products of the firm may be technologically complementary or substitutable in the sense that an increase in the output of one product may reduce or increase the cost of making the others. The most manageable case for our purpose is that of two products which up to a certain stage of production are only one product but differ in their further career toward completion. The units of output are still homogeneous at the end of a certain number of productive processes and then part company to undergo different treatment of processing, fabrication, or finishing, at costs which are separate and independent. The deduction of these costs from the prices at which the products are sold permits the comparison of the net prices of the part which they have in common. For example, a manufacturer of electric appliances may sell the same electromotor in an electric fan and in a vacuum cleaner and, if account is taken of the separate costs of each of the two products, it may perhaps be seen that the motor is sold cheaper to those who want to sit under cooler air than to those who want to sit on a cleaner couch. The manufacturer would

[27] In the case of merchandising the firm may be regarded as a seller of "merchandising service." It sells this service in conjunction with a very large number of goods; that is, the contribution of the marketing organization of the firm is the common component of all items sold. By deducting from the selling price of each item its purchase price and all separate or differential cost elements attributable to it, one can arrive at the net price at which the firm sells "merchandising service in connection with the particular item.

find it profitable to do this if at a uniform price the derived demand for electromotors were more elastic in the electric fan business than in the vacuum cleaner business, as it may well be if the former is more competitive than the latter.

3. *Essential Differences between ·Types*

A CLASSIFICATION that distinguishes between different types will be really helpful only if it also furnishes the criteria by which they can be recognized. How, for example, can we safely distinguish local price discrimination of the get-the-most-from-each-region type from local price discrimination of the kill-the-rival type? Are the differences between the two manifest enough to permit a diagnosis? And if the promote-new-custom type happens to result in local price discrimination, can it be safely kept apart from a kill-the-rival policy? How can we avoid confusion between different kinds of meeting competition, for example, between the seller who "gives in if he must" in order to capture an order and the seller who "plays the game" of quoting the same prices as his competitors? Some tentative comments on these questions will be offered here.

MAKE-THE-MOST VERSUS KILL-THE-RIVAL

LET US assume that complaints of local price cutting are received and we should decide whether it is a case of predatory or of fair competition. The similarities between situations of a kill-the-rival type and of the get-the-most-from-each-region type may easily deceive the observer. In both situations there may be a large firm charging lower prices in the localities served by a competitor than it charges elsewhere. The essential difference, unfortunately, cannot be observed: the immediate intent of the discriminating seller. In the one case his objective is to drive the competitor out of business by cutting prices to a level at which he cannot cover his costs. In the other case the seller resorts to local price cutting in order to "meet competition in good faith," that is, in more technical language, in order to raise his revenue by taking account of the greater elasticity of demand for his product where he is faced with the competing supply. A higher price, so he might reason, would surrender the bulk of the local business to the competitor, while a lower price would secure him as much of the local business as appears worth taking.

To the confusion of the observer, low prices in these more competitive markets—in the markets with greater elasticity of demand—may be below cost, just as in the case of predatory price cutting. When can local price cutting, which in both cases involves selling below cost, be identified as predatory policy, designed to kill off the rival, and when as a fair-though-tough competitive policy, designed to meet competition and to make the most of a weaker market? It is of no avail to examine who started the price cutting. And it is less than satisfactory to wait for the demise of some firms as evidence of the oppressive character of the survivor's price policy. If it was his intention to eliminate competitors, it is too bad that he could not have been stopped before he succeeded. On the other hand, the exit of less efficient competitors is by no means any evidence of the survivor's intent to kill. If they were inefficient they ought not to be able to stay in business.

Preliminary to a solution of the problem is the recognition of the fact that selling below cost can pay even where there is no hope that market conditions will change. If the particular sales add more to total revenue than to total costs, they will be lucrative and it may be bad business to miss such an opportunity of increasing one's profit, or reducing one's loss, merely because the selling prices are below average total unit cost. As long as the additional revenue derived from the sales at discriminatory low prices is not below the *additional* cost (this additional cost may, of course, be much below the *average* cost), the sales are directly remunerative and the discrimination can be explained as a part of a get-the-most-from-each-region policy. If, however, the business at cut prices is not only below average cost but does not even cover the added cost which it entails, then it is not directly remunerative and the objective must be found on another plane.

This other plane may possibly be one of extra-economic motivations. For example, the policies of the seller may rest on his desire for prestige, political ambitions, philanthropy, resentment, vengeance, etc. If the motivation is economic, his policies of discriminatory price cutting, where the additional business does not cover its additional cost, must be oriented on anticipated effects to be realized in the future. The kill-the-rival type of discrimination is a case in point, but so would be promotional price cutting. Between these types of discrimination and the get-the-most-from-each-region type of discrimination we have found an essential difference. The latter is good business under existing demand conditions and would remain good business, from the seller's point of view, even if conditions never changed and the seller had to continue forever to serve the favored market at a price below average cost.[28]

KILL-THE-RIVAL VERSUS PROMOTE-NEW-CUSTOM

IF WE find that the local price cutting and selling below cost is not a get-the-most-from-each-region policy, there may still be either the predatory kill-the-rival or the fair promote-new-custom type of competition.

Both these policies are nonremunerative under existing market conditions but look forward to a change which they are supposed to effect. The price cutter, in the kill-the-rival case, anticipates that his policy will eliminate some of the competition and that, as a result, the demand for his products will be either greater or less elastic in the future. Thus it is the expected change of the selling opportunities (i.e. demand curve) that makes economic sense of the currently unprofitable cut-rate business. The same is true of the promote-new-custom type of price discrimination. The price cutting to new customers does not provide enough business under given demand conditions to warrant the price policy. It is the expectation of new demand conditions which justifies the price cutting.

In the kill-the-rival case, the price cutter anticipates raising prices to the now favored customers when his competitor is knocked out. In the promote-new-custom case he may raise prices to the now favored customers when they have become attached to his product, or he may figure that at the eventually increased sales volume his costs will be so much reduced that he would make profit even if he kept his prices at the now unprofitably low level. If the price cutter's hopes of creating for himself a new clientele and a higher business volume should not be fulfilled, his price cutting would turn out to be bad business. But so would the predatory price cutting if it did not succeed in eliminating the competitors.

We can solve our problem by examining (a) who the injured competitors are and (b) whether the product or service offered by the seller who practices local price discrimination is essentially different or substantially the same as that offered by the injured competitors. Let us first assume that the products or services are substantially

[28] That local price discrimination of the get-the-most-from-each-region variety is regarded as good business from the producer's point of view does not necessarily imply that it is desirable for society to tolerate it. Its consequences for total output, growth, and allocation of productive resources cannot be inferred merely from the fact that the policy appears profitable to a seller with monopoly power and the power to discriminate.

alike. From where is the additional business for the price cutter to come? Is it to come from one or two particular competitors who would not be able to stand the loss of clientele, or is it to come from a larger number of competitors, each of whom would not suffer badly enough to be forced out of business?

It is interesting to reflect on the different evaluation that society puts on the two policies designed to effect changes in the demand conditions facing a seller. The "disreputable" kill-the-rival policy and the "respectable" promote-new-custom type of price discrimination have in common that they involve selling below cost (not only in the usual sense of selling below average total cost but also in the narrow sense of selling below marginal cost) and that they are used to increase the demand for the seller's product at some time in the future. Trade is to be diverted in the one case from *definite* sources of supply and in the other from *indefinite* ones. The new custom to be fostered by promotional discrimination will not seriously injure the trade of any particular rival seller; the newly promoted business will compete with a multitude of products and services supplied by a multitude of different producers. On the other hand, the trade which the predatory price cutter acquires after his rivals have succumbed to his cut-throat competition is all inherited from the particular victims of his attacks.

Thus, one may say that discriminatory pricing which diverts trade from many unknown sellers is called promotional and considered respectable; discriminatory pricing (of substantially equal products) which diverts trade from a few known sellers is regarded as predatory and obnoxious. This may sound rather arbitrary, as if based on the fact that we know the injured businessmen in the one instance and do not know them in the other. The real moral behind the different evaluation, however, derives from the consumer's interest. His interest is furthered by the increased competition and by the enlarged scope of his freedom of choice which result from promotional discrimination; but it is harmed by the eventual reduction of competition and the restricted scope of his freedom of choice which result from predatory discrimination.

The proposed criterion for distinguishing promotional from predatory discrimination—injury to unknown versus known competitors—does not, however, fit all instances of promotional discrimination. A seller may wish to promote a new type of product and know full well who will be the competitors harmed and perhaps eliminated by his competition. He may wish to introduce in a certain locality an improved kind of product or service and may feel it necessary to resort to local price discrimination in order to overcome consumer conservatism. Sellers of the "old-fashioned" product or service that will be replaced by the novel one, may be severely damaged; we and the public at large may know these sellers as well as the newcomer does; and yet his discriminatory practice may not be disapproved or regarded as predatory. The criterion which in this case distinguishes promotional from predatory price discrimination is the fact that it is a modern and better product or service which is offered to the buyers and that, if certain sellers should be forced out of business, the public will nevertheless be served better than before.

GIVE-IN-IF-YOU-MUST VERSUS PLAY-THE-GAME

To REDUCE a price quotation in order to meet a competitor's price is a practice generally accepted as fair and sound even if it is discriminatory. But price discrimination with the intention of meeting competition is not always of the give-in-if-you-must type. The seller who participates in a pricing scheme which the industry has adopted in order to reduce competition is also wont to say that he quotes the same price as his competitor because he must "meet the competition." How can we find out whether he merely "plays the game" or whether he "gives in" to the customer because he needs his order and cannot land it otherwise? How can we find out whether he meets competitors' prices to maintain a scheme of regulated competition—nonprice competition—or rather to take business away from them?

A firm is not always equally anxious to get more orders; at one time it has a backlog of orders, at other times it is in need of more business. If the firm is not a party to a pricing scheme, it will sometimes ask higher prices than the competitors, sometimes undercut them. There is no reason for quoting always the same prices as the competitors—unless this is a rule of a game that they all play.

A firm which meets a lower price quoted by a competitor, and does so because it badly needs more business and must fight for it, will not always just meet the price but will also undercut it. If the firm earnestly means to compete, it will not allow an order to go to the competitor when it can afford another slight concession that might clinch it. But to lose the order rather than do a little more than meet the competitor's price makes sense if the firm "plays the game."

427

A firm which engages in price competition and fights for business for delivery to very distant places, and does so by absorbing plenty of freight and meeting the competitors' prices, will also fight for the business of its near-by customers. But to leave this more profitable near-by business to its competitors without a fight, to let them take the most desirable orders and to make no attempt to fight back by offering a slight price concession—in other words, to compete for bad orders with high freight charges but not to compete for good orders unburdened by high freights—this makes sense only for a party to a collusive scheme.[29]

A firm which practices the give-in-if-you-must type of price discrimination acts in secrecy; a firm quoting discriminatory prices as it "plays the game" has a policy of open prices. The former engages in price competition, the latter observes price maintenance. The former reduces prices paid by consumers, the latter increases freights paid to railroads.

The discriminatory pricing of the give-in-if-you-must type is the result of individual bargaining in the course of which the seller realizes that he cannot get the order at the price he first asked and reluctantly gives in to the buyer's arguments. The discriminatory pricing of the play-the-game type is a matter of systematic list-price quoting, the seller sticking by the list and the buyer realizing that negotiations for concessions would be of no avail.

There are probably still more differences between the two types of discriminatory pricing. It should not be difficult to keep the two types apart. Any confusion that may exist about the matter arises from the attempt by counsel of formula-price quoters to explain their pricing system in terms of "meeting the price of a competitor." The attempt is understandable because, if successful, it would make a collusive practice appear as if it were one of vigorous price competition.

4. Discrimination and the Public Interest

CLASSIFICATIONS and descriptive discussions of the classified types are not sufficient preparation for appraisals. Evaluations of the effects of the various types of discrimination can be made only after careful analysis. But most people are impatient and prefer hasty generalizations and tentative conclusions now to promises of well-reasoned generalizations and judicious conclusions later. They want

[29] Machlup, op. cit., pp. 177-180.

to know now whether the Robinson-Patman Act should be given more extensive or more restricted interpretation and whether certain legal prohibitions may possibly hit socially desirable forms of competition worse than the harmful practices against which these prohibitions were primarily directed. Perhaps we can make concessions to the impatient and comment on some possible presumptions regarding particular types of price discrimination.

I should like to warn, however, that my classification, not being based on principles relevant to public policy but rather on an eclectic combination of criteria designed to include most of the discriminatory pricing practices found in business, is not the best framework for a discussion of policy. After all, the sellers' motives or techniques were given as much attention as their possible effects. But I submit that an indiscriminate catalogue of discriminatory practices has at least one advantage: the issues are less likely to be prejudged by the selection.

THE FAVORED AND THE ILL-TREATED

DISCRIMINATION is always against some buyers and in favor of others, and the former often complain. There are no accepted standards for determining whether the buyers who pay the relatively high prices are being exploited by the seller or whether the seller is being exploited by the buyers who pay the relatively low price. Both complaints may be made at the same time and there is no safe ground on which to decide the issue.

In some instances it can be shown that the less-favored buyers are not put to any real disadvantage by the more favorable treatment of others. Indeed, they may even be better off in consequence of the discriminatory policy. For example, the price they have to pay may be high relative to the price paid by others and yet, at the same time, lower than the price they would have had to pay in the absence of discrimination. This may be so because discriminatory price reductions may permit the sale and production of a larger output and resulting economies may permit this increased output to be produced at lower marginal cost. One must not assume, however, that this is a frequent case, although much is made of it even where it cannot possibly apply.

Very often buyers do not know whether they are beneficiaries or victims of price discrimination. Sometimes the discrimination is in favor of those who pay the higher price while the ones who pay less are actually discriminated against. This is the case when a cost differential would justify (and, under competitive conditions, create) a larger price differential than the seller charges. For example, he may fail to charge the full fabricating cost to the buyers of a more fabricated product because their demand is more elastic than the demand for less fabricated products. Or, a seller of season and off-season services, or peak and off-peak services, would discriminate against off-season or off-peak consumers if he did not charge them sufficiently less to account fully for the fact that a portion of the firm's fixed capacity was installed only to serve the season or peak consumers, who alone ought to be charged for its cost. The ill-treated consumers believe they are favored by a lower rate while in fact they pay part of the cost of the service to other consumers.

The buyer under the let-him-pay-more type of discrimination is also quite satisfied with the treatment that he receives. For while the price he pays is an extraordinarily good one for the seller—who therefore discriminates against this buyer—it is also a very good one for the buyer, who is getting the product more cheaply than if he had to buy it through the ordinary channels of trade.

Promotional price discrimination is probably resented by the old customers who must pay the regular price while new customers are favored by introductory offers. If the practice relates to retailed consumers goods, the old customers may easily get into the group of new buyers. But the old subscribers of journals and magazines are sometimes irritated and feel like suckers because they must pay so much more than the new subscribers. The same is true sometimes when buyers pay the regular price for merchandise which they could have bought a few days earlier or later at a stock clearing sale. But the irritation is not serious because they know that next time they may be the beneficiaries of this type of discrimination.

Sometimes the victim of discriminatory pricing will readily concede the fairness of a higher charge. For example, when a newspaper with large circulation has to pay much more for permission to print a syndicated feature, column, or comic strip than a paper with small circulation, there will be scarcely any recriminations on anybody's part. The "ability to pay" principle of taxation is carried over with all its connotations of fairness and justice into the field of exploiting intellectual property protected by copyright.

There are tricky cases of discrimination where it is hard to find out whether a buyer gains or loses by the practice. Consider the case of the buyer of a product, priced under a multiple-basing-point system, who is located in some outlying region. He pays a delivered price which of course is higher than the delivered price paid by more centrally located buyers; but, in terms of the mill-net prices received by a seller shipping from a mill far from the applicable basing point, the buyer appears to be the beneficiary of a price discrimination implied in the freight absorption by the seller; yet the operation of the system may have been responsible for a location of industry which works to the disadvantage of this same buyer in that the establishment of a mill in his region may have been prevented in consequence of this pricing practice. Thus, he pays a higher gross price, is favored by discrimination in terms of net prices, and is injured in terms of long-run supply prices under the resulting location of industry.[30]

Predatory price discrimination has several peculiar aspects. Most of the buyers who are discriminated against will not be aware of it, inasmuch as the local price cutting takes place in a different locality. The buyers whom this price cutting favors will benefit from it while it lasts, but may pay for it later if and after it removes local competition. The complaints against this kind of discrimination, however, arise not from sympathy with the consumers who may be exploited when prices are put up at some time in the future, but rather from partiality for the local competitors who lose money because of the low prices charged by the perpetrators of the discrimination.

PRIVATE VERSUS PUBLIC INTEREST

COMPLAINTS about injured interests of special groups in the economy are rarely safe guides to sound appraisal of the public interest. If society were to prohibit all instances of price discrimination against which the interested parties have protested, and were to condone those about which the interested parties have been silent or satisfied, the economic welfare of society would probably be reduced. I am not suggesting that private complaints should be overlooked. They must of course be investigated. I merely submit that injury to the public interest is not correlated with the presence or loudness of private protests.

Every instance of price discrimination implies two distinct deviations from the competitive norm. Since discrimination is based on the exercise of some degree of monopoly, it reveals the presence of monopoly and thus points to the likelihood of distortions in the allocation of resources among the various lines of production. Dis-

[30] *Ibid.*, pp. 151-156, 241-247.

431

criminatory pricing, secondly, implies distortions in the distribution of the products in question. The second distortion may either alleviate or aggravate the first. For example, while the exploitation of a monopoly position would imply a restriction in the production of a certain set of products, the application of price discrimination might, in the particular case, tend to raise production above the volume most profitably sold under nondiscriminatory pricing. However, the two effects may just as well be additive and the combined result would then be worse than that of monopoly without price discrimination.

One way of appraising instances or types of price discrimination would be to take the existence and degree of monopoly for granted and to ask whether the application of discrimination would more likely increase or further restrict the volume of monopoly output. This way of appraising, however, would be shortsighted for it would neglect the effects of discriminatory pricing upon the maintenance, fortification, or relaxation of the underlying monopoly positions. These effects may be more important, in the long run, than the direct effects upon the output of the monopolized products. Under certain circumstances price discrimination tends to induce a monopolistic seller to sell more than he would sell at a uniform price; but at the same time the practice of discrimination may be important for the maintenance of his monopoly position. If so, the fillip that discrimination might give to the current production volume would be small compensation indeed if society had to forego the expansion of the industry that might come with a gradual weakening of the monopolistic positions involved.

An examination of types of price discrimination cannot enable us to form judgments upon the output-expanding or restricting effects of the discriminatory practices. Such judgments presuppose investigations of the circumstances of each case, particularly of the elasticity estimates of the separated markets and of the cost conditions of the firms in question. It is possible, on the other hand, without studying the precise circumstances of each individual situation, to come to a tentative judgment of effects which discrimination of certain types tends to have upon the maintenance, fortification, or relaxation of the underlying monopoly position. If it is an accepted principle of public policy to combat private monopoly wherever it is found to be serious and avoidable at a reasonable social cost, and to prohibit practices the effect of which may be to

432

lessen competition, an attempt to judge discriminatory practices from this point of view is undoubtedly in order.

THE EFFECTS UPON COMPETITION

LET us then review the types of price discrimination that were included in our classification and size up the contribution they are likely to make either toward maintaining and reinforcing or toward weakening the monopolistic positions of the firms concerned. We shall distinguish four categories: (1) where the presumption is strong that the practices will aid in maintaining or strengthening monopolistic positions or in reducing competition; (2) where the presumption is strong that the practices will tend to invigorate competition; (3) where there is no strong presumption either way and the effects more likely are either neutral or harmless; and (4) where nothing can be said without a more careful analysis of the circumstances of the case.

1. *Aiding monopoly, injuring competition*: The keep-them-in-their-zones type and the hold-them-in-line type of price discrimination are devices by which a monopolistic seller may regulate or restrict competition among his distributors or fabricators, devices used in the enforcement of all sorts of monopolistic arrangements, such as division of territory and resale price maintenance. The protect-the-middleman type of discrimination, if not combined with zoning or black-list arrangements, may be a mild policy with similar purposes.

The favor-the-big-ones type of discrimination likewise can be used to reduce competition in the markets in which the distributors, processors, or fabricators sell. But this policy need not always be injurious to competition and may even invigorate it, at least in the short run. Only if the small distributors, processors, or fabricators are squeezed out of the market will the long-run effects of this practice be unfavorable to competition. This difference between short and long run must be observed also with the kill-the-rival type of discrimination, for only if the rival is eliminated will competition be injured. If the policy, though pursued with this end in mind, turns out to be unsuccessful, if competitors are merely squeezed but not squeezed out, the effects may be favorable to competition. It is very difficult, if not impossible, to legislate a prohibition of these types of discrimination in such a way that it applies only to those instances in which competition is really injured. The danger is great that legal prohibitions are too extensively interpreted and through the discouragement of competitive discrimination reduce competition more seriously than it would be reduced by any of the practices designed to get rid of weak customers and weak competitors.

The play-the-game type of price discrimination is unquestionably harmful to competition, not on account of the discrimination but rather through the collusive scheme that is involved. Nevertheless, participants of the "game" have been prosecuted for charging discriminatory prices rather than for conspiracy in restraint of trade—just as offenders of all kinds have been prosecuted for income tax evasion.

2. *Aiding competition*: Among the practices which often invigorate competition are the give-in-if-you-must type and, in some of its forms, the forget-the-cost-difference type of price discrimination. It would be too bad if these were prohibited or even discouraged. Likewise, the dump-the-surplus and clear-the-stock types of discrimination provide outlets for the competitive spirit where it may be under restraint in the ordinary business. Again, legislatures should be careful lest some sellers be kept from resorting to these methods of competing.

The promote-new-custom type of price discrimination may invigorate competition in the short run as well as in the long run.

3. *Neutral or harmless*: Among the neutral or harmless types of price discrimination are the haggle-every-time, the let-him-pay-more, and the appeal-to-the-classes types. Harmless though seriously irritating is the make-them-pay-for-the-label type.

The switch-them-to-off-peak-times type of discrimination is probably neutral in that it will hardly make the public utilities that practice it more monopolistic or the theaters or hotels less competitive—if indeed the rate differentials in question can properly be called discriminatory in view of the cost differentials that are usually involved, though visible only to the sophisticated analyst.

The match-the-freight type of price discrimination may be listed among the neutral or harmless ones, with the warning that the systematic use of pricing formulas such as those euphemistically called freight equalization systems do not belong here. Freight matching is not price matching, and its occasional use in price competition is quite different from its systematic use in nonprice competition.

4. *Require case studies*: The other types of price discrimination cannot be evaluated without case studies. There is no presumption

that their practice tends either to strengthen monopolistic positions or to invigorate competition, but neither is there a presumption of their neutrality.

To be sure, there seems to be no obvious way in which the practice of the size-up-his-income type of discrimination, or of the measure-the-use type, could contribute to either monopoly or competition. Undoubtedly they could not be practiced were it not for the protected position of the seller, but the question is whether and how this protection might be affected by its exploitation. One might perhaps say that prolonged practice results in public acceptance and this tends to strengthen the social or legal arrangements on which the protection of the seller's position rests.

The four remaining types—get-the-most-from-each-region, charge-what-the-traffic-will-bear, get-the-most-from-each-group, and get-the-most-for-each-product—are the ones for which economic theory has developed its intriguing geometric and algebraic techniques of analysis, based on the assumption of a maximum squeeze of the buyers to attain maximum profit for the seller. One might argue that the optimal exploitation of a monopolistic position will *ipso facto* help toward its maintenance and reinforcement. But an argument of such generality will hardly be accepted as a sufficient basis for public policy. If public action be proposed against these discriminatory practices, the supporting argument will have to rest on other grounds and will presuppose more specific research and analysis. And if a good case can be made against these discriminatory practices, it may still be inexpedient to outlaw them and to embark on a hopeless task of enforcement; it may be more feasible to attack them indirectly by attacking the monopolistic positions that make them possible.

COMMENT

Ronald Coase, University of Buffalo

Machlup describes with a wealth of picturesque detail the various forms which price discrimination can take and he places them within a classificatory framework. I do not propose to subject his classification or analysis to any close examination. My purpose is to indicate certain broad conclusions to which, I think, consideration of his paper should lead us.

Machlup's treatment shows that it is practically impossible to confine a serious discussion of the problem of price discrimination to the case of a single product sold at different prices in different markets. Early in his paper he refers to price discrimination as "selling (leasing) at prices disproportionate to the marginal costs of the products sold." He adds that if the "markup" over marginal cost varies from one product to another, there is discrimination.[1] Even in the simplest cases, Machlup tells us, the costs incurred in supplying different markets will not be the same and it is necessary to analyze the position in terms of "net prices." It is clear that, in most cases, a seller wishing to discriminate would differentiate his product, in part so that the consumers will sort themselves out into the various groups between which it is desired to discriminate, in part to conceal the existence of the discrimination. But this is by no means the whole story. The fact that for an undifferentiated product the elasticity of demand would not be the same for the various groups is likely to mean that the demand is not the same in other respects and that sellers will find it profitable to produce different products (or grades of product) for the various markets.

All this is recognized by Machlup. But he attempts, or so it seems to me, to handle these problems while retaining the simpler system of analysis. If I exaggerate, the reader can judge. But if it is agreed that we are in effect dealing with a multiproduct firm, it would appear to be an undue simplification not to take into account explicitly that the costs of and the demands for the various products will often be interrelated. Machlup does at one point explain that to take account of interdependent demands "requires a more complicated apparatus than that traditionally employed in geometric price analysis." But it is not so complicated as to be unmanageable, and in Machlup's case we can be sure that it was respect for tradition rather than a distaste for intellectual subtlety which led him to exclude from his analysis the problem of interrelated costs and demands.

A more serious objection to my argument might be that, if accepted, it would result in the problem of price discrimination being swallowed up in the general monopoly pricing problem. This is so. And I approve of it. If I may be allowed to speak softly so as not

[1] I would observe that if prices are to be proportional to marginal cost, it is necessary that the markup over marginal cost should vary from product to product (except in the case in which marginal cost is equal to price and the markup is zero), and consequently there would appear to be an inconsistency in Machlup's criteria for price discrimination. However, he indicates that he is not using the word "proportionate" in a precise sense and he is no doubt aware of the difficulty.

to revive the marginal cost pricing controversy, we must recognize, it seems to me, that to make prices equal to marginal cost would have undesirable results and furthermore that not to make prices equal to marginal cost would also have undesirable results. Insofar as we are concerned with public policy, the question is always one of choosing out of the practical alternatives the one which *on balance* seems to give the best results. Which probably means that it is not possible to carry the analysis very far except on an industry by industry basis.

If we are to use our analysis as a guide to public policy, it is also necessary to take into account a point which Machlup brings out very clearly in the latter part of his paper. Situations which are alike from the point of view of formal analysis may be quite different when looked at from the point of view of public policy. We would all accept the fact that lowering the price of a product in the present may increase the demand for that product in the future, and it is a comparatively simple matter to analyze price determination in these conditions. But it makes a good deal of difference for public policy whether the increase in demand is due to the fact that new consumers attracted by the low price have acquired a taste for the product, or whether it is the result of driving away competitors (Machlup's "kill-the-rival"), or whether it is due to the fact that equipment installed as a result of the lower price in the first period makes it economical to consume more in the future than would otherwise have been the case. If we are interested in public policy, it is necessary to go behind the cost and demand schedules.

A. G. PAPANDREOU, University of Minnesota

MACHLUP's paper on discrimination is essentially classificatory in character. A classificatory schema can be appraised in terms of two criteria: (1) its internal consistency; (2) its usefulness. I can find nothing lacking in the paper so far as internal consistency is concerned. Given the space limitations and the nontechnical language chosen by Machlup, the classificatory schema is both consistent and impressively inclusive. Concerning the usefulness of the classification of types of discrimination I have some serious misgivings. The usefulness of his schema can be appraised either from an analytical or from a public policy point of view. I am inclined to believe that it fails somewhat on both counts. In what follows I shall attempt to give the reasons for my dissatisfaction.

437

To begin with I do not wish to argue with the elementary categories of his schema (i.e. "let-him-pay more," "size-up-his-income," etc.). The failure of the classification lies, I believe, in the principle employed by Machlup for grouping these elementary categories into more inclusive sets. Machlup's three main classes, namely, "personal discrimination," "group discrimination," and "product discrimination," seem to have been chosen by him primarily on the grounds of expository convenience. This kind of major breakdown of discrimination types does not serve us well either in the formulation of public policy in regard to, or in the development of a unified analytical attack upon, the problems arising from discriminatory behavior. Machlup's presentation of discrimination types leads, in fact, to a rather complex jigsaw puzzle, which obstructs the emergence of a unified approach in both the analytical and the public policy dimensions of the problem. It seems to me that a somewhat more satisfactory basis for classifying types of discrimination can be founded on a threefold distinction among principles of behavior that may be adopted by firms. The three principles are: (1) the "make-the-most" or "independent maximization" principle; (2) the "play-the-game" or "collusion" principle; (3) the "kill-the-rival" or "predatory competition" principle. It does not matter for our purposes whether or not these principles are subservient to some more inclusive principle such as the maximization, the minimax, or some other over-riding principle.

Economic theorists have been primarily concerned with the discriminatory practices that arise in connection with the "make-the-most" principle. All this is too well known to require extensive discussion on my part. A few comments are in order, nevertheless. We may distinguish effectively, I believe, between cases of discrimination in which the seller is a price maker (in Scitovsky's sense) and discriminatory action arising in competitive bargaining situations. The competitive bargaining type of discrimination includes Machlup's "haggle-every-time" and "give-in-if-you-may" elementary categories. It is clear that no complex theoretical apparatus need be constructed to deal with cases of this sort. The discriminatory practices arising in cases where the seller is a price maker can be handled satisfactorily in terms of the Pigovian-Robinsonian models. A somewhat superior analytical model has been developed recently by Eli W. Clemens.[1] The Pigovian third-degree type of discrimination is

[1] Eli W. Clemens, "Price Discrimination and the Multiple-Product Firm," *Review of Economic Studies*, 1950-1951, pp. 1-11.

attacked by Clemens as a problem in *multiple-product* behavior. The other Pigovian degrees of discrimination are considered as problems in *splintering the market* in the process of maximizing profits. Clemens' analysis imparts a high degree of analytical unity to the treatment of discriminatory behavior by price makers (on the principle of "independent maximization"). The "splintering-the-market" process may be shown to include, by way of illustration, Machlup's "let-him-pay-more," "size-up-his-income," "measure-the-use," "promote-new-custom," "charge-what-the-traffic-will-bear," and "get-the-most-from-each-group" elementary categories. The "multiple-products" case may, in turn, be shown to include the "get-the-most-from-each-region," "appeal-to-the-classes," "make-them-pay-more-for-the-label," "switch-them-to-off-peak-times," "clear-the-stock," and "get-the-most-for-each-product" categories.

It is well known that public policy makers in the United States have not shown much concern over discriminatory practices that arise in the process of "making-the-most" except insofar as their effects on competitive structure and behavior may be similar to those obtaining under the "play-the-game" and "kill-the-rival" principles. In sharp contrast to the attitude of policy makers, the economists have expended substantial effort in appraising the welfare implications of discriminatory practices arising from the "make-the-most" principle. It must be stressed, nevertheless, that the economists' concern arises primarily from the fact that discrimination implies monopoly power, and it, in turn, implies a nonoptimal pattern of resource allocation.

The "play-the-game" and "kill-the-rival" principles of firm behavior lead to discriminatory practices that have been foremost in the thoughts of public policy makers. Our antitrust law comes to grip with discrimination only insofar as its effects can be anticipated on the basis of "kill-the-rival" and "play-the-game" principles of behavior. In sharp contrast to the public policy makers' interest in this type of discrimination, the economic theorists' interest has been rather mild. This is probably due to the fact that they have been unable to evolve a satisfactory approach to behavior in oligopolistic markets where the "play-the-game" and "kill-the-rival" principles are apt to be useful for purposes of prediction.

One final remark is in order in connection with Machlup's paper. His concepts have not been formulated in an operationally meaningful fashion, even though the section on "Essential Differences be-

439

tween Types" is devoted primarily to this task. Needless to say, Machlup cannot be blamed for this. Economists have been notoriously unable to develop operational definitions in this field of investigation. Without them the analytical results cannot be employed effectively either in the formulation of policy or in the tasks of prediction.

THE NATURE OF PRICE FLEXIBILITY
AND THE DETERMINANTS OF RELATIVE
PRICE CHANGES IN THE ECONOMY

RICHARD RUGGLES
YALE UNIVERSITY

DISCUSSIONS of price flexibility in the literature of economics are not all concerned with the same subject matter. Three quite different topics can be distinguished. The first two deal with the effects of price flexibility or inflexibility on the operation of the system as a whole; the third deals primarily with the nature and causes of price flexibility itself, and only secondarily with its consequences.

The first topic considers the effect of price flexibility or rigidity on the level of economic activity. Discussions in this area have frequently been concerned either with the analysis of the Keynesian and classical models[1] or with the development of certain other specific aggregative models. On the more empirical side, a great deal has been written about the effects which might have been expected to flow from greater price flexibility or greater price rigidity in specific historical instances. Much of both the theoretical and empirical work has been predominantly concerned with the flexibility of the wage rate and its repercussions on prices, output, and employment.

The second topic contemplates price flexibility from a long-run point of view. Interest in this area has been focused primarily on the efficiency of the economic system in allocating its resources— i.e. whether in the long run prices do tend to be determined by competitive forces. The literature in this area is not so extensive as that in the preceding area, perhaps because economists have, in recent years, been preoccupied more with problems of income and employment than with those of resource allocation.

The third category of price-flexibility literature is considerably less homogeneous with respect to final objectives than either of the two preceding groups. It is rather the common starting point which

[1] See, for example, R. M. Bissell, Jr., "Price and Wage Policies and the Theory of Employment," *Econometrica*, July 1940; Oscar Lange, *Price Flexibility and Employment* (Cowles Commission Monograph 8, Principia Press, 1944); Don Patinkin, "Price Flexibility and Full Employment," *American Economic Review*, September 1948, pp. 543-564.

suggests the treatment of this segment as a unified body of literature. Writers in this area usually start from a consideration of the empirical fact that during economic fluctuations there is substantial variance in the relative price changes of different products and factors of production, and they propose to investigate the causes of this variance. Branching out from this starting point are a number of different definitions of price flexibility and a number of different analyses of causal factors.

It is this third topic with which this paper will be concerned. To the extent that this literature also attempts to evaluate the significance of existing price flexibility or inflexibility, it does have some relation to the first two topics, but the following discussion will not be primarily concerned with the effects of price flexibility on either the level of activity of the economic system or the efficiency of resource allocation. Attention will be focused on (1) an examination of definitions and measures of price flexibility in the literature, (2) a restatement of the problem of price flexibility in terms of traditional value theory and a discussion of the determinants of relative price changes, (3) an empirical investigation of relative price changes and price-cost interrelationships in various sectors of the economy, and (4) the application of the foregoing analysis to certain specific problems. The paper will be divided into four parts corresponding to this general outline.

Part 1 will examine the various definitions and measurements of price flexibility which appear in the literature. These concepts differ considerably, and no attempt will be made in this section to present a comprehensive picture of the entire literature; the focal point of the discussion will be the differences among the concepts, so that where one concept has been discussed by a number of writers only one or two of such writers will be mentioned.

Part 2 will attempt to evaluate the various definitions of price flexibility discussed in Part 1 in the light of a restatement of the problem in terms of the traditional theory of the firm. This discussion will be especially concerned with developing an analysis which will be applicable to existing empirical material. The section will have two parts: it will explore the nature of price flexibility itself, and, pursuing the question somewhat further, it will consider the determinants of relative price changes in the economy.

Part 3 will apply the analysis developed in Part 2 to the observed price behavior of various sectors of the economy, in an effort to explain why the relative price changes in the various sectors differ.

Since output prices for earlier stages of production become costs for later stages of production, the sectors will be classified as far as possible according to the flow of goods through the channels of production; the price-cost interrelationships in agriculture, agricultural processing industries, mining, mineral processing industries, and the distributive trades will be considered in turn. The analysis will not be primarily statistical, although use will be made of readily available empirical material.

Part 4 will test the theory of price behavior presented in Part 3 in yet another way. The behavior of various aggregative price indexes will be examined to see whether their general movement and relative differences can be explained readily in terms of the theory. First, the actual behavior of the components of the cost-of-living index will be examined to see whether their relative differences conform to what would be expected in terms of the theory of the determinants of price behavior. Secondly, the wholesale-price index will be similarly examined, and its general movements will be contrasted with those of the cost-of-living index. The process of analyzing these two price indexes necessarily raises the question of the meaningfulness of an aggregate index, given the systematic changes in the components which will occur if the postulated theory is found to be tenable. Finally, the index of real wages will be examined in the light of this theory of price behavior. Although it will not of course be possible in this brief analysis to offer a complete statistical test of the theory, it will be studied in relation to past statistical literature.

1. Definitions and Measurements of Price Flexibility in the Literature

IN THE mid-thirties, Gardiner C. Means published a statistical study[2] of price inflexibility in the American economy which stirred up considerable interest. A number of writers had been concerned with various aspects of this subject before that time, but none of their

[2] For the original study see Gardiner C. Means, *Industrial Prices and Their Relative Inflexibility*, S. Doc. 13, 74th Cong., 1st Sess., 1935. Parts of this original study and in some cases additional supplementary material are included in the following: Gardiner C. Means, "Price Inflexibility and the Requirements of a Stabilizing Monetary Policy," *Journal of the American Statistical Association*, June 1935, pp. 401-413; Gardiner C. Means, "Notes on Inflexible Prices," *American Economic Review*, Proceedings, March Supplement, 1936. pp. 23-24; *The Structure of the American Economy*, National Resources Committee, 1939. Part I, Chap. VIII, pp. 122-152; Saul Nelson and Walter G. Keim. *Price Behavior and Business Policy*, Temporary National Economic Committee (TNEC). Monograph 1, 1940, Chap. II, pp. 11-53 and Appendix I, pp. 165-241.

publications had had the explosive effects of Means's study. Means's chief interest was in pointing out the presence in the economy of inflexible administered prices, which, he claimed, had highly disruptive effects on the functioning of the economy and were largely responsible for the failure of *laissez faire*.[3] As proof of the existence of inflexible administered prices, Means presented a chart showing the results of a tabulation of the frequency of price change for 747 of the items included in the Bureau of Labor Statistics monthly wholesale-price index over a 95-month period from 1926 through 1933. The frequency distribution of the numbers of price changes for individual items was found to be *U*-shaped. To Means, this *U*-shaped distribution indicated that prices could be divided into two quite different types. The highly flexible prices grouped at one end of the distribution (i.e. prices which changed frequently) he interpreted as those which for the most part were market determined, and around which traditional economic analysis was built. The inflexible prices at the other end of the distribution (i.e. prices which changed infrequently) he interpreted as those which were administratively established and held for appreciable periods of time. Considering the frequency of price change as a measure of price flexibility thus enabled Means to satisfy himself that two quite different pricing systems existed: flexible prices, resulting from many forces continually interacting in that part of the economy in which markets existed; and inflexible prices, set by administrative action and held constant.

One of the first comments on Means's analysis of price inflexibility was that it did not and could not show whether the economy as a whole had been shifting from market to administered prices. It was suggested that the differences in the frequency of price change found by Means might be a normal phenomenon, and that the period examined was no different in this respect from previous periods. A number of writers[4] undertook to discover whether any evidence could be found that in recent periods an increasing proportion of prices had fallen into Means's "infrequent change" classification. For this purpose, distributions of the frequency of price

[3] Means, *Industrial Prices and Their Relative Inflexibility*, as cited, p. 1.

[4] Don D. Humphrey, "The Nature and Meaning of Rigid Prices, 1890-1933," *Journal of Political Economy*, October 1937, pp. 651-666; R. S. Tucker, "The Reasons for Price Rigidity," *American Economic Review*, March 1938, pp. 41-54; E. S. Mason, "Price Inflexibility," *Review of Economic Statistics*, Vol. 20, 1938, pp. 53-64; Jules Backman, "Price Inflexibility—War and Post War," *Journal of Political Economy*, October 1948, pp. 428-437.

changes were made for periods as far back as 1837.[5] The proportion of items falling into the rigid category in different periods was not found to differ greatly and did not reveal a trend toward rigidity in the more recent periods. Furthermore, over the period 1890-1936 there was no trend in the actual changes observed in the component series for each year expressed as a percentage of the total changes which would have taken place if each series had changed each month during the year.[6] These negative results seemed to indicate that there was no adequate statistical basis for believing that the price system was becoming any more rigid than it had been in any previous period for which data were available.

The frequency of price change as a measure of relative price flexibility or inflexibility was quickly supplemented by the amplitude of price change. In his original presentation, Means had shown that the frequency of price change was highly correlated with its amplitude. However, he did not use amplitude as a measure of flexibility, but rather considered it an accompanying characteristic with further economic implications. Means demonstrated the relationship between the frequency and the amplitude of price change in two ways. First, he presented a conventional scatter diagram of the two variables, which showed the existence of a correlation. Then he separated the items in the BLS index into ten groups on the basis of their frequency of price change, and for each of these groups he drew up charts showing the distribution of amplitude of change. For those groups with relatively infrequent price changes, he found that the amplitude of change was relatively small.

This discussion of the relation of frequency of price change to amplitude of price change was continued by a number of other writers,[7] and the focus of interest quickly shifted to the amplitude of price change alone, on the ground that this element was theoretically more significant for the incidence of price distortion in the economy. But a simple distribution of the relative amplitude changes of the various items in the BLS wholesale-price index similar to that which Means had made for frequency of price change proved to be unhelpful, since the distribution usually came out unimodal[8] and so did not provide any convenient means of dis-

[5] Tucker, *op. cit.*, p. 43.

[6] Mason, *op. cit.*, p. 59.

[7] Mason, *op. cit.*; *The Structure of the American Economy*, as cited, *loc. cit.*; Nelson and Keim, *op. cit.*

[8] Mason, *op. cit.*, p. 61; *The Structure of the American Economy*, as cited, p. 128.

tinguishing between flexible and inflexible prices. With a unimodal distribution it was of course impossible to say what amplitude of price change represented true price flexibility. Therefore, although a great deal was written about price flexibility in terms of the amplitude of price change and its effect in distorting the price structure, it was not very successfully developed into a tool of analysis. In practice, the amplitude of price change was primarily used for the comparison of the relative flexibility of specific groups of commodities—that is, the flexibility of chemicals and drugs as a group compared with that of farm products as a group.[9] In this sense it was possible to speak of one group as more or less flexible than another, but Means's original concept, that of a "market" sector of the economy operating with perfectly flexible market prices, could not be explored by this method.

A third concept of price flexibility concerns the change in price per unit of a commodity relative to its change in quantity. A wealth of statistical material on the price-quantity behavior of various commodities and products has been provided by F. C. Mills[10] in his various studies of price behavior, but these actual statistical measures did not become a subject of discussion in the general price-flexibility literature. Instead, writers on this subject usually confined themselves to setting out lists of commodities or making scatter diagrams wherein the amplitude of price change and the amplitude of quantity change were shown explicitly. Means, for example, in his original study listed ten industries, for which he showed both the percentage drop in prices and the percentage drop in production.[11] As was the case in his use of the amplitude of price change, Means did not consider the price-quantity relationship to be a measure of price flexibility; rather he used it as a part of the description of the differences in the attributes of market and administered prices. Similarly, scatter diagrams of price-quantity relationships have been

[9] Mason, op. cit., p. 62; The Structure of the American Economy, as cited, p. 132; Nelson and Keim, op. cit., p. 30; Backman, op. cit., p. 432.

[10] F. C. Mills: The Behavior of Prices (National Bureau of Economic Research, 1927); Changes in Prices, Manufacturing Costs and Industrial Productivity, 1929-1934, Bulletin 53 (National Bureau of Economic Research, 1934); Prices in Recession and Recovery (National Bureau of Economic Research, 1936); "Elasticity of Physical Quantities and the Flexibility of Unit Prices in the Dimension of Time," Journal of the American Statistical Association, December 1946, pp. 439-467; Price-Quantity Interactions in Business Cycles (National Bureau of Economic Research, 1946).

[11] Means, Industrial Prices and Their Relative Inflexibility, as cited, p. 8.

446

widely used in the literature to show similarities or differences in the reaction of prices of products having different attributes, for example the pattern of price-quantity reactions of concentrated versus nonconcentrated industries, and of durable versus nondurable goods.[12] Like the study of the amplitude of price change, the study of price-quantity reactions did not yield a meaningful definition of absolute price flexibility, but rather was used to establish differences in relative price flexibility.

A quite different measure of price flexibility was introduced into the discussion by J. T. Dunlop.[13] Employing Lerner's measure of the degree of monopoly, that is, the ratio of the gap between marginal cost and price to price (price minus marginal cost divided by price),[14] Dunlop proposed the change in the degree of monopoly as a measure of price flexibility. He argued that the degree of monopoly (thus measured) was more significant analytically than other existing measures of flexibility because of its relation to the determinants of output and employment. An increase in Lerner's degree of monopoly for a given commodity during a period of falling prices would mean that the marginal cost of the producer of the commodity fell faster than the price of the final output. A decrease in Lerner's degree of monopoly in such a situation would mean that marginal cost did not fall as fast as the price of the final output. Dunlop's measure thus attempts to relate the amplitude of the change in marginal cost to the amplitude of the change in price of the final output. His analysis of price flexibility thus differed from the preceding analyses in that it attempted to take into account the price-cost relationship within an industry. Where input prices and output prices move together, the price of the final good is said to be as flexible as costs. For the industries which he studied, Dunlop concluded that the degree of monopoly increased in the depression

[12] Willard L. Thorp and Walter F. Crowder, "Concentration and Product Characteristics as Factors in Price-Quantity Behavior," *American Economic Review*, February, Supplement, 1941, pp. 390-408; Jules Backman, "Price Inflexibility and Changes in Production," *American Economic Review*, September 1939, pp. 480-486; Nelson and Keim, *op. cit.*

[13] John T. Dunlop, "Price Flexibility and the Degree of Monopoly," *Quarterly Journal of Economics*, August 1939, pp. 522-533.

[14] A. P. Lerner, "The Concept of Monopoly and the Measurement of Monopoly Power," *Review of Economic Studies*, 1933-1934, pp. 157-175. In order that the gap between marginal cost and price divided by price shall be equivalent to the inverse of the elasticity of demand, and thus measure the degree of monopoly in Lerner's sense, it is of course necessary for the firm to be at the point of maximum profits so that marginal cost will equal marginal revenue.

447

of the thirties, i.e. that the cost elements fell faster than the prices of the finished goods.

Another analysis of price flexibility in terms of price-cost relationships was made by A. C. Neal in an effort to discover the importance of industrial concentration to price flexibility.[15] On the basis of changes in costs, Neal calculated for each of a number of industries for the period 1929-1933 what the price would have been if the overhead margin had been kept a constant absolute amount per unit of output. This calculated price he called the expected price. Actual prices that matched this expected price, he reasoned, could be considered flexible. It should be noted that there is a conceptual difference between Dunlop's and Neal's measures. Dunlop's measure of flexibility depended on the equality of *percentage* changes in costs and prices, whereas Neal's measure required that *absolute* changes in costs be exactly reflected in price, so that the dollar amount of the producer's overhead margin per unit of output would remain unchanged. Neal's study covered a much larger number of industries than had Dunlop's, and the close relationship which he found between his expected prices and the actual prices led him to believe that the differential price behavior among industries could be explained for the most part by differential direct cost behavior, rather than by concentration of industry.

More recently, Sho-Chieh Tsiang[16] has made yet another analysis of price flexibility that relies on price-cost relationships. Starting from Lerner's measure of the degree of monopoly, Tsiang further develops the idea that the percentage gross profit margin (total value of product minus prime costs expressed as a percentage of the total value of product) is an expression of the inverse of the elasticity of demand. In this respect, his approach is in fact a combination of those used by Dunlop and Neal. He follows Dunlop in that he singles out Lerner's degree of monopoly as a starting point, and as a result considers the percentage margin between price and marginal cost rather than the absolute margin used by Neal. On the other hand, Tsiang follows Neal in conceiving of the problem in terms of a margin concept, which Dunlop did not do. Tsiang is concerned with the computation of the gross profit margin for the

[15] Alfred C. Neal, *Industrial Concentration and Price Inflexibility* (American Council on Public Affairs, 1942).
[16] Sho-Chieh Tsiang, *The Variations of Real Wages and Profit Margins in Relation to the Trade Cycle* (Pitman, 1947).

aggregate of all United States manufacturing for the period 1919 to 1937. This aggregative analysis is in marked contrast with the interproduct and interindustry studies of price flexibility discussed above. With the term "price flexibility" thus interpreted, Tsiang found[17] that there was some evidence for the widely held view that the price system in United States manufacturing industries was becoming less flexible. On the basis of his data, he felt that there had been a persistent tendency since 1923 for the average gross profit margin in manufacturing industries as a whole to be negatively associated with the average unit prime cost, i.e. that there had been a persistent tendency for the average value per unit of output to change less than proportionally to the changes in average prime cost.

A number of other definitions of price flexibility have appeared in the general literature, but most of them have been incapable of application as tools of empirical analysis. Mason, in his survey of price flexibility, has given an excellent summary of these concepts.[18] He points out that price flexibility is often used in a normative sense, flexible prices being said to exist where actual price behavior coincides with desirable price behavior, on some definition of desirable.[19] In this context, prices would be considered rigid not because they change infrequently or fail to respond to changes in certain economic forces, but rather because they do not behave as they should behave if economic stability or some other desirable economic objective is to be achieved. Mason also[20] considers price flexibility in terms of the rate or degree of movement of a price in response to the changes in price-determining variables. As he indicates, however, if all the factors which influence prices were included in the list of price-determining variables, actual price movements would by definition be completely explained and there would be no such thing as either flexibility or inflexibility. For a concept of price flexibility to have any meaning, therefore, the analysis can include only some of the price-determining variables. To the extent that any of these definitions depend on either perfect knowledge of all pricemaking factors or on elaborate normative judgments, they are of course not relevant to empirical analysis.

[17] *Ibid.*, p. 85.
[18] Mason, *op. cit.*
[19] *Ibid.*, p. 57.
[20] *Ibid.*, p. 56. At this point Mason takes up Gunnar Myrdal's notion of price flexibility which would "group all prices statistically according to the speed with which they change under the influence of a changing impulse."

2. The Concept of Price Flexibility and the Determinants of Relative Price Change

DESPITE the large volume of literature on the subject of price flexi-bility, there has been no very significant cumulative development, and the majority of readers may well agree with R. S. Tucker[21] that the discovery of differences in price flexibility in the system is "no more important and no less ridiculous than the discovery by Mo-lière's bourgeois gentilhomme that he had been speaking prose all of his life." If one were to take into account all of Jules Backman's factors and conditions which may affect price flexibility,[22] the sub-ject might be found to be of such a complex institutional nature that it would defy any simple theoretical model. There are, further-more, many quite serious criticisms, both theoretical and empirical, which can be made of much of the discussion in the literature. Be-fore proceeding further, it will be useful to consider some of the criticisms.

One of the most serious questions regarding Means's U-shaped distribution of the frequency of price changes in the components of the BLS wholesale-price index was raised by Tibor Scitovsky.[23] He pointed out that the U-shaped distribution may be due only to the particular form in which the data happen to be available, and that the distribution of the number of *actual* price changes need not be U-shaped at all. His argument runs as follows.

Means's frequency distribution is based upon the changes which occur in the BLS monthly series. If the price of a commodity changes many times during a month, the BLS figure, which represents one monthly observation, obviously would not show it. Therefore, al-though there is no limit to the *actual* number of times that a price could have changed during the 95-month period studied by Means, the largest number of changes that can appear in the data is 94. In other words, the 94-change class interval would include all com-modities from those which actually did change just once a month up to all those which changed daily (i.e. roughly 2,900 changes in the 95 months) or oftener. The lower frequencies of price change would be affected only slightly by shifting from a monthly to, say, a daily reporting of prices; a price with zero change throughout the period

21 Tucker, *op. cit.*, p. 54.

22 Jules Backman, "The Causes of Price Inflexibility," *Quarterly Journal of Economics*, May 1940, pp. 474-489.

23 Tibor Scitovsky, "Prices under Monopoly and Competition," *Journal of Political Economy*, October 1941, p. 681.

would have zero change regardless of the time interval between observations, and prices which changed only a few times in the 95
months would have months of zero change in which the daily
changes would also be zero. As the frequency of change increases,
however, Means's monthly observations would correspond less and
less to actual price changes, and at high frequencies it is quite apparent that price changes would be greatly understated. On a daily
observation basis, the high-frequency end of the distribution would
be extended. The cases which now occur in the high-frequency area,
say from 80 to 94 monthly changes (181 cases), would be distributed
over all the frequencies from 80 to 2,850. There seems to be no adequate reason to believe that the distribution would remain U-shaped,
although again a slight cluster might occur at the high frequencies
for the same reason—prices which changed more than once daily
would be lumped with those which changed only once daily. If, instead of daily changes, all actual price changes were recorded for
each commodity, it seems reasonable that there would be a continuously decreasing number of cases, even at the very highest frequencies of change.

By raising doubts about the validity of Means's U-shaped distribution, Scitovsky in effect destroyed much of the meaningfulness of the
dichotomy between rigid and flexible prices. Without a significant
cluster at the high end of the distribution, there is no adequate
criterion of perfect price flexibility, so that Means would be forced
back into the same position as the writers who discussed amplitude
of change: frequency of change can serve only as a relative measure,
and no judgment can be made on whether a price is or is not flexible.

There have been other criticisms of Means's basic data. A number
of them attack the assumptions in the use of the BLS wholesale-
price index. One such criticism points to the prevalence of quality
changes, with nominal price kept the same. For example, according
to the National Resources Committee,[24] during the depression a
shirt of quality and workmanship that originally sold for $1.95
could be purchased by the consumer for $1.69 or less. Yet the quoted
prices of shirts apparently remained rigid. Changes in price took
the form of changes in workmanship and style, rather than in the traditionally established wholesale price. Furthermore, Neal[25] has
pointed out that the BLS price quotations do not always include
all the discounts which sellers give their customers, so that the quoted

24 *The Structure of the American Economy*, as cited, Part 1, Appendix 1, p. 182.
25 Neal, *op. cit.*, pp. 40-42.

price may not be representative of the actual price. Thus, in the BLS quotations, salt and fertilizer prices remained stable at a time when in point of fact vigorous price competition existed in the form of exceptional discounts. In considering the validity of the BLS price data, the National Resources Committee[26] concluded that it was imperative to use caution whenever individual price series were involved. In analyses of price rigidity, they felt, it was essential that emphasis be placed upon broad and consistent relationships and that reliance upon small differences in absolute figures be avoided.

A theoretical criticism of Means's use of frequency of change as a measure of price rigidity and price flexibility was raised by D. H. Wallace.[27] He pointed out that in cases where no price-determining factor had changed, the price, by definition, should not change either, yet by Means's definition such a price would be considered rigid. Furthermore, by his definition a price might well be flexible even though it moved in the direction opposite from that which would have been indicated by normal price-determining forces. Means's measure is therefore not really relevant to an analysis of the economic forces in the system.

The use of amplitude as a measure of price flexibility is open to many of these same criticisms. It has already been pointed out that the amplitude of change of a price series gives no clue to the absolute flexibility or rigidity of the series; price flexibility in this sense is purely relative. Most of the studies of the amplitude of price fluctuation, furthermore, used the same BLS data which were used in the studies of frequency of change, and there is reason to believe that the difference between actual prices and prices quoted in the BLS index introduces a more serious distortion in amplitude than in frequency. In a period of depression, the divergence between actual and quoted price may increase cumulatively. Lloyd Reynolds[28] has shown that in a few cases there are major divergences. The drop in the price of aluminum from 1929 to 1933, for example, was reported as 5 per cent by the BLS, but according to census information it amounted in fact to 35 per cent. In the price of sulphuric acid, a zero drop reported by the BLS was a 12 per cent drop according to the Bureau of the Census. Further examples of disparities were

[26] *The Structure of the American Economy*, as cited, p. 185.

[27] D. H. Wallace, "Monopoly Prices and Depression," in *Explorations in Economics* (McGraw-Hill, 1936), p. 347.

[28] Lloyd Reynolds, "Producers' Goods Prices in Expansion and Decline," *Journal of the American Statistical Association*, March 1939, p. 33.

cited by the National Resources Committee study.[29] Although these disparities are probably the exceptions rather than the general rule, they are nevertheless serious enough to raise questions about the suitability of the BLS data for any refined analysis. Finally, with amplitude as with frequency, it does not seem valid to consider a price inflexible just because it does not change, if there has been no change in price-determining factors. The fact that prices have different actual amplitudes of change does not mean that they are differentially sensitive to specific price-determining forces, yet this is how the findings on amplitude have often been interpreted.

Mills's price-quantity ratio has never seriously been proposed as a measure of price flexibility, in the sense that this term is understood in the literature; Mills himself considered it to be a description of the general patterns of price-quantity movements. Given the demand curve, Mills's ratio is the reciprocal of the Marshallian elasticity of demand, but when both demand and supply schedules shift, the resulting coefficient is somewhat ambiguous. The more usual use of price-quantity relationships as a measure of price flexibility, as was indicated in Part 1, has been in terms of scatter diagrams for different categories of goods, and to this use many of the objections raised with respect to amplitude and frequency also apply. When the BLS wholesale-price data are used, some of the price-quantity relationships which appear will be spurious. Furthermore, the price-quantity relationships again provide only relative and not absolute measures of price flexibility, and the measure obtained is not directly relevant to the question of the correspondence of price to price-making forces.

Dunlop's measure of price flexibility, as was noted above, represents a considerable departure from the measures which had been used in other empirical studies. Unlike them, Dunlop's measure does set up an absolute criterion for a flexible price. By this criterion, prices are flexible when they move with costs. If price does not change when marginal cost is rigid, the price is stable but not necessarily inflexible. The fuller implications of this concept will be taken up later in this paper, but it will be useful at this juncture to consider some possible criticisms of the empirical side of Dunlop's work. To obtain marginal cost for an industry, Dunlop took (1) the National Industrial Conference Board index of average hourly earnings for the industry, and (2) the BLS wholesale-price index for one representative raw material for the industry, and weighted these ac-

[29] The Structure of the American Economy, as cited, p. 183.

cording to the respective importance of wages and materials in value of product in 1933, as given in the Biennial Census of Manufactures. The ratio of the change in marginal cost computed in this manner to the change in the BLS wholesale price he considered to be an approximation to Lerner's degree of monopoly, and thus a measure of the flexibility of prices. If the ratio was greater than 1 (i.e. if the change in computed marginal cost exceeded the change in the BLS price), the degree of monopoly would have increased, and prices would be inflexible. If the ratio was less than 1, the opposite would obtain. Dunlop made yearly comparisons for six industries for the period 1929 to 1935; and for eight industries (four of which were included in the first six) changes in the gap between marginal cost and price were shown through the phases of the cycle (1929-1933 and 1933-1936) rather than from year to year. Dunlop's statistical methods are thus certainly open to criticism. He used data from a variety of sources which employ different industrial classifications and have special unmatched definitions. Changes in average hourly earnings, furthermore, have been shown to be a rather poor indicator of changes in unit wage costs.[30] The use of one representative raw material for each industry (for example, the fall in the price of pig iron as an indicator of the decline in all raw-material costs in the steel industry) requires heroic assumptions. Reliance on the BLS wholesale-price data for both raw-material and finished-goods prices requires just that sort of dependence on the accuracy of individual series which the National Resources Committee advised against. And finally, in spite of Dunlop's conclusion that the gap between price and marginal cost widens in the depression, by his own analysis this was true in only four of the eight cases examined. However, Dunlop did recognize the limitations of his data, and he intended the article as a first approximation rather than a detailed statistical analysis of the problem. It is certainly true that he brought to the subject a completely new orientation, one which promised to be much more useful than previous approaches.

Neal's work bears a marked resemblance to Dunlop's. However, although Neal wrote some three years after Dunlop, there does not seem to be much evidence that he was in fact developing Dunlop's original ideas. Both Neal and Dunlop attempted to study the relationship between marginal cost and price, but Dunlop was interested

[30] Committee on Price Determination, Conference on Price Research, *Cost Behavior and Price Policy* (National Bureau of Economic Research, 1943), pp. 131-143.

in the percentage difference between marginal cost and price, while Neal was interested in the absolute difference. Statistically, Neal's study was very much the more comprehensive of the two. Neal analyzed a group of 106 industries from the Census of Manufactures data. Since he used matched data from one major source, his results probably have greater statistical significance than Dunlop's, and the census data are probably also more pertinent to the study of the effects of actual prices on producers' net receipts than are the BLS wholesale-price statistics. Neal derived an expected price for each industry by computing the price changes implicit in the direct costs of the industry and assuming a constant absolute margin over these direct costs. He then took the position that the extent to which his computed "expected" price was *correlated* with the actual price was a measure of the degree to which changes in direct cost could be used to explain changes in price. There is, however, one major objection to this procedure. Although the correlation between his expected price and the actual price was high, there was a systematic difference between the two: for the period 1929 to 1931, in 82 out of the 106 industries, Neal's expected price was higher than the actual price, and for the period 1929 to 1933 the same was true for 72 out of 84 industries. When the expected price exceeds the actual price, of course, the assumption of constant absolute margins is not in fact borne out by the data; in absolute terms margins for the majority of industries declined. But Neal was interested primarily in the subject of industrial concentration and its relation to price flexibility, so that when he had proved to his own satisfaction that the degree of industrial concentration was only a minor factor in price inflexibility he went no further. He considered only manufacturing in his study, and made no effort to see how the other parts of the economy—such as agriculture, mining, and the distributive trades—fitted into the analysis. He was thus not concerned with the question of why prices and costs actually did move differently from one another, but only with establishing that the reason was not related to concentration.

Tsiang used the same source as Neal for his statistical data; he analyzed the data on direct costs and value of product given in the Census of Manufactures. There were two major differences in his approach, however. First, Tsiang considered only four sets of data: the aggregated data for all United States manufacturing, and summary data for each of three broad industry groups—cotton textiles, paper and pulp, and iron and steel. This is in marked contrast to the 106 industries studied by Neal. Secondly, instead of deriving estimates of expected value per unit on the basis of constant absolute margins and correlating the expected values with actual value per unit as Neal did, Tsiang derived percentage margins and analyzed their changes from period to period in relation to changes in direct costs. In other words, Tsiang was interested in the behavior of percentage margins as direct costs rise and fall.

The chief weakness of Tsiang's analysis lies in its aggregative nature; this becomes especially important when it is recalled that the differences in price and cost changes among the various industries are very great indeed. Tsiang did try one test of aggregation; he examined the gross-profit margins of four different groups of industries: capital goods, consumer goods, construction materials, and producers' supplies. Because the average gross-profit margins of these industries were all about the same in 1929, Tsiang concluded that the aggregate gross-profit margin for all United States industry would not be changed by a shift in the composition of industry due to differential rates of expansion and contraction over the cycle. However, many other types of aggregation difficulties might be encountered. Within an industry, for instance, it is quite possible that producers with large margins would have a different rate of expansion or contraction than producers with small margins. Rather than attempting to prove that the process of aggregation is legitimate by making various partial tests, it would be simpler to use somewhat less aggregated data and study the behavior of gross-profit margins at more homogeneous levels. In attacking the problem on such an aggregative level, furthermore, Tsiang also neglected any explicit discussion of the differential behavior of prices and costs in different industries.

Despite these criticisms, and despite the diversity of the approaches of the various writers discussed above, certain common elements do emerge. The major concern of all these economists is with the differences in the relative amplitude of price change in the economy during periods of economic fluctuation. Price flexibility as Means conceived it became a subject of study because it was obvious from even a casual examination that during periods of economic fluctuation the price behavior of some sectors of the economy was quite different from that of other sectors. Means would not have considered differences in the frequency of change significant if in terms of amplitude all prices had moved approximately together during the period 1926-1933.

The importance of economic fluctuations as a frame of reference for this consideration of price flexibility cannot be overemphasized. The writers in this group gave very little attention to the long-run type of flexibility mentioned at the beginning of this paper, nor did they concern themselves with the question of how changes in productivity are transmitted through the system in the form of higher wage rates for labor, increased profits for the producer, or lower prices for the consumer, or with the manner in which the secular growth or decline of an industry affects factor returns and prices in that industry. Instead, they were interested in trying to see to what extent differences in the short-run cyclical price behavior of the different sectors of the economy could be explained by the method of price fixing (market or administered), the degree of fabrication of the good (raw material or finished goods), the durability of the good, and other attributes which appeared to be related to differential price behavior. Dunlop, Neal, and Tsiang, for example, were interested in the extent to which the price changes of various industries in the manufacturing sector of the economy could be explained by changes in direct cost as the single determinant. Backman, on the other hand, listed a great many possible determinants of price and implied that he felt most price changes could be explained only in terms of a variety of determinants. Thus, in the context of the literature the study of price flexibility has been the study of the short-run determinants of price behavior in different sectors of the economy during periods of economic fluctuation.

A mere review of this literature, however, still leaves much to be desired. It is clear that the next step should be some consideration of the type of price behavior that might be expected under various assumptions, and an investigation of the extent to which this expected behavior corresponded to what actually took place. The remaining portion of Part 2 will therefore be devoted to the consideration of the major determinants of price. Parts 3 and 4 will then examine price data for the various sectors of the economy to see whether or not the differences in relative price change which are in fact found can be adequately explained in terms of these major determinants of price.

It has already been pointed out in the review of Mason's discussion of the various measures of price flexibility that a definition of price flexibility that took into account *all* the determinants of price would be meaningless. Divergence between actual and expected price in such a circumstance would not be an indication of price inflexibility; rather it would simply indicate that some of the price-determining factors had inadvertently been left out of the analysis in the computation of the expected price. In other words, any concept of price flexibility, except a purely normative one, must be defined in a partial sense. A price can be called inflexible only if it does not change when an expected price computed on the basis of certain specified partial determinants changes. Before any analysis can be made, therefore, the specific determinants which are to be taken into account must be decided upon.

In traditional value theory, the major specific determinants of price are generally considered to be cost and demand. Economists have long recognized that cost and demand are not the only elements in price determination; such factors as expectations, the temperament of the producer, and even public opinion may have an effect on price, and in some instances inertia due to the difficulty of changing prices once they are set may be important. If we exclude all such factors in considering the determinants of individual prices, however, the term "price flexibility" can be given analytic meaning: to the extent that these excluded factors are in fact operative and seriously influence the actual price changes, prices can be considered inflexible or perverse. As a first approximation, therefore, prices will be considered flexible if they react as would be expected in response to changes in cost and demand conditions, inflexible if they do not change as much as would be expected, and perverse if they move in the direction opposite from that expected. As the analysis develops, certain modifications will be made in this definition.

The framework of traditional value theory can be used in developing the expected reaction of price to various types of change in cost and demand. The analysis will start by reviewing the price behavior of an individual firm or industry that is supposed to follow various types of change in costs and demand under the usual assumption of profit maximization in perfect competition and monopolistic competition; the problem of oligopoly will be considered briefly at the close of the discussion. For simplicity in studying price behavior under perfect and monopolistic competition, cost and demand changes will be considered separately. Two questions will therefore be distinguished: (1) how changes in demand would affect price, in a situation in which cost conditions do not change; and (2) how changes in cost would affect price, in a situation in which demand conditions do not change.

458

1. Under the principle of profit maximization, equilibrium price and output will occur where marginal cost equals marginal revenue, and the relation between marginal cost (which equals marginal revenue) and price (which equals average revenue) will be determined by the elasticity of demand. (This is the basis of Dunlop's use of Lerner's degree of monopoly as a measure of price flexibility.)

From this general observation it follows that if demand shifts but the *elasticity* of demand remains the same, the firm should, in order to maximize its profits, keep the same percentage markup over marginal cost and sell whatever it can at that price. With a horizontal marginal-cost curve, for example, even though demand falls drastically it would be in the interest of the firm to keep its price unchanged as long as costs do not change and the elasticity of demand remains the same. With a rising marginal-cost curve, a fall in demand without a change in elasticity would require a price drop proportional to the drop in marginal costs which would accompany the reduced level of output. Thus if the elasticity of demand does not change, a shifting level of demand would trace out a pattern of equilibrium prices above the marginal-cost curve and in fixed ratio to marginal cost at every point;[31] any change in marginal cost resulting from operation at a different level of output would be directly reflected in an equivalent percentage change in price.

If the elasticity of demand changes, the relation between price and marginal cost must also change. An increase in elasticity would narrow the range between price and marginal cost, and a decrease in elasticity would widen the range.

In a competitive industry, price is determined by the intersection of the industry demand curve and the industry marginal supply price. With a constant marginal supply price, any shift in demand would leave price unchanged. With a rising marginal supply price, a falling demand would trace out a falling pattern of equilibrium prices along the supply curve. With a falling supply curve that was compatible with competition (e.g. economies of scale external to this industry), a fall in demand would actually raise price.

In summary, then, for the individual firm faced with a sloped demand curve, a shift in demand which left elasticity unchanged would require a price change directly proportional to any change in

---

[31] If the marginal-revenue curve for the firm intersects the marginal-cost curve at a point where marginal cost is vertical (i.e. discontinuous), a fall in marginal revenue within this range with no change in the elasticity of demand would result in a fall in price and maintained output in the firm.

marginal cost resulting from movement along the marginal-cost curve. For a competitive industry, a shift in demand would move price along the marginal supply price curve. In either case, the ratio of price to marginal cost would change following a shift in demand only if the elasticity of demand also changed.

2. If demand is kept constant and cost is permitted to change, consideration of the elasticity of demand is again necessary. In the case of the individual firm faced with a sloped demand curve, a change in cost would be directly reflected in a proportional change in price if the elasticity of demand at the new point of equilibrium is the same as at the old. If with a movement along the demand curve demand becomes less elastic, and the marginal-cost curve is horizontal, an upward shift of the marginal-cost curve would result in a more than proportional price rise, and a downward shift would result in a less than proportional price fall. Any movement along the demand curve which increases elasticity would of course operate in the opposite direction.

Under competitive conditions, shifts in the marginal supply price schedule would lead to equilibrium prices which lie on the demand curve, and the equilibrium price would equal marginal supply price at every point.

Thus, when the elasticity of demand for the individual firm remains constant, and in all cases of pure competition, the equilibrium price will move directly proportionally with marginal cost. Price and marginal cost will diverge only when the elasticity of demand for the individual firm at the new point of equilibrium is different from that at the old. When demand becomes less elastic, a fall in marginal cost will not be matched by a proportional fall in price, and a rise in marginal cost will lead to a price rise which is more than proportional. The obverse would hold when demand becomes more elastic.

This analysis throws some light on the question of the relative price behavior of firms in monopoly and competition during economic fluctuations. As Scitovsky has pointed out,[32] the belief that prices are more variable under competition than under monopoly probably sprang from the fact that competitive producers tend to undercut one another's price in response to flagging demand and falling costs, while the monopolist in a similar situation *can* keep up his price. But, as Scitovsky says, the heart of the question is not whether the monopolist can maintain prices which are less variable

[32] Scitovsky, *op. cit.*, p. 663.

than those which would obtain under competitive conditions, but whether it is really in his interest to do so.[33] It has already been noted that under pure competition if the marginal supply price schedule is horizontal any change in factor costs would be directly reflected in price. For the individual firm faced with a sloped demand curve and a horizontal marginal-cost curve, price would not equal marginal cost but would move exactly with it, if the elasticity of demand did not change. The relevant question, therefore, is whether in economic fluctuations a fall in demand would be associated with an increase or a decrease in the elasticity of demand.

According to Harrod,[34] a fall in demand will make people more sensitive to price differences. In his view the imperfection of competition is due to habit, inertia, and lack of knowledge. The pressure of poverty is necessary to drive people to the trouble of avoiding waste; why, he asks, should a man in more comfortable circumstances make as much effort to find the cheapest market? "With an expanding income a man may slip by imperceptible stages into careless habits. A contraction recalls him to his senses. He is loath to relinquish enjoyments to which he has been accustomed and immediately begins to cast about for means of meeting adversity with the least inconvenience to himself. . . . He seeks to economize with the smallest possible loss in substantive utility."[35] Thus Harrod argues

[33] Tsiang, for example (*op. cit.*, pp. 23-24) observes that under imperfect competition the prices of individual products are more or less under the control of the individual producers. From this he suggests that a rise in demand need not imply a rise in market price, as is necessarily the case under perfect competition where the demand confronting each producer is horizontal. In this connection it should be noted, however, that if the elasticity of demand for the product did not change and if marginal costs were constant over the relevant range of output for the producer in imperfect competition, no change in price could be expected to occur with a rise in demand—that is, the reaction in imperfect competition would differ from the reaction in perfect competition only because of the assumed difference in cost structure.

To the extent that producers do not maximize profits in the short run, prices may move differently (more or less) from what would be expected on the basis of changes in costs and demand. In perfect competition producers may refrain from placing goods on the market or conversely may dump their stocks, thus producing prices different from what would be expected on the basis of change in current costs and demand. If producers in perfect competition feel that a drop in demand is temporary, goods may be held off the market, and prices will not drop as much as would have been expected in terms of the fall in demand and marginal costs in the individual plants.

[34] R. F. Harrod, "Imperfect Competition and the Trade Cycle," *Review of Economic Statistics*, May 1936, pp. 84-88.

[35] *Ibid.*, p. 87.

461

that demand will become more elastic in times of depression and less elastic as prosperity returns.

The validity of Harrod's argument has been questioned a number of times, and Galbraith has gone so far as to state the opposite. He says: "Where the decrease in demand is the result of depression an increase in elasticity may be considered improbable. People with decreased money incomes and increased concern for their economic security are less rather than more responsive to lower prices. Producers and consumers alike tend to postpone purchases of durable equipment."[36]

Of the two arguments, Harrod's seems the more persuasive. Galbraith has not given any reason why people who have increased concern for their economic security feel that they can afford to neglect price considerations. The fact that producers and consumers tend to postpone their purchases of durables has more to do with the level of demand than with its elasticity.

Whether or not Harrod is correct as a general rule, however, it is obvious that for different goods the elasticity of demand will be affected differently by economic fluctuations. A situation which increases people's price sensitivity between bread and potatoes may make the demand curve for train rides from New Haven to New York more inelastic by taking away from it a large portion of the rather elastic demand of those who travel for pleasure and leaving as the major element the rather inelastic demand of those who travel on business. Without much more knowledge of a great many more variables, it does not seem likely that the change in elasticity of demand to be expected in any particular instance can be predicted. It does not follow, therefore, that a monopoly would always have less variable prices during periods of economic fluctuation than would a purely competitive industry. Indeed, to the extent that Harrod's arguments are valid, in order to maximize profits the monopolist should have the more variable prices.

It is apparent from the discussion above that the determination of changes in elasticity for any individual producer might be very difficult (if not impossible). If change in the elasticity of demand is included as one of the factors determining the expected change in price, therefore, it would be impossible to compute the expected price behavior. Furthermore, under certain forms of industrial organization the change in the elasticity of demand is one of the key

[36] J. K. Galbraith, "Monopoly Power and Price Rigidities," *Quarterly Journal of Economics*, May 1936, p. 463.

factors determining the expected reaction of price to a change in cost. In assessing the flexibility of prices associated with various types of industrial organization, it is important not to include in the measure of expected prices elements which are implicitly correlated with a specific form of industrial organization, and the effect of a change in the elasticity of demand is just such an element. Under perfect competition, changes in the elasticity of demand for various products will not affect the expected price; it will remain equal to marginal cost. For the individual firm faced with a sloped demand curve, however, any shift in the elasticity of demand will cause the expected price to rise or fall faster or slower than marginal cost. The inclusion of changes in elasticity as one of the factors determining the expected change in price will therefore obscure the influence of industrial organization on price behavior.

For these reasons, the definition of price flexibility given above (page 458) will be modified so as to relegate changes in the elasticity of demand to the same category as changes in expectations, etc., discussed above on page 457. The expected change in price will be determined on the basis of the change in marginal cost only; a change in the elasticity of demand, like a change in expectations, will (if profits are maximized) result in what will be defined as price inflexibility. Perfect price flexibility will then be a situation in which price changes by the same percentage as marginal cost. If price moves less than marginal cost, the price is inflexible; if it moves more than marginal cost, it is excessively flexible; and if it moves in the opposite direction from marginal cost it is inversely flexible.[37]

Thus far, the discussion of price behavior has been couched entirely in terms of perfect and monopolistic competition, and the more complex area of oligopoly has not been considered. In an oligopolistic market, it would not necessarily be true that if profits are to be maximized the prices charged for a product will change in response to changes in the elasticity of demand and changes in marginal cost; that kinked demand curves can lead to price inflexibility has often been pointed out.[38] However, the determination of

[37] This definition corresponds to that implicit in Lerner's measure of the degree of monopoly, which both Dunlop and Tsiang used. Constancy in the percentage margin between price and marginal cost would indicate that prices and marginal costs moved by the same percentage.

[38] For a discussion of the possible role of the kinked demand curve and other oligopolistic influences, see George J. Stigler, "The Kinky Oligopoly Curve and Rigid Prices," *Journal of Political Economy*, October 1947, pp. 432-449, and Sho-Chieh Tsiang, *op. cit.*, pp. 69-74.

the effect of the exact conditions and assumptions under which an oligopolist is operating is not unlike the problem of change in the elasticity of demand in monopolistic competition. In the first place, the actual assumptions made by the different firms in an oligopolistic industry cannot be derived empirically, so that it is virtually impossible to establish any norm for expected price behavior in these instances. Furthermore, the very difference in behavior between firms in oligopoly and firms in perfect competition is an element which it would be interesting to measure. With the definition of price flexibility suggested above, the effects of oligopolistic conditions would tend to appear as price inflexibility, so that the importance of such an industrial organization in this respect could be assessed.

The following section will apply this definition of price flexibility to the various sectors of the economy. The statistics are purely illustrative. No attempt has been made to carry out a comprehensive empirical survey; such a study would absorb considerable resources and would involve extensive detailed analyses. Part 3 will only show what general indications do exist with respect to the empirical facts of price flexibility, and suggest the directions in which further work might proceed.

3. Cost, Price, and Output Behavior of Various Sectors of the American Economy, 1929-1932

THE depression of the thirties affords an opportunity for studying the reaction of different industrial sectors of the economy to a sharp and deep contraction in the level of income and demand. It is essential to confine this sort of analysis to short periods of time, in order to minimize the influence of such secular factors as technology, institutional change, and the growth and decline of industries. For this reason the empirical analysis in this section will generally be restricted to the period 1929 to 1932. For some sectors (agriculture and distributive trades) data for a few years after 1932 will be presented in order to throw some light on the relation of cycle to trend. For manufacturing, only 1929 and 1931 will be considered, since the basic source of data is the Biennial Census of Manufactures.

In the following presentation the flow of goods will be followed through the different stages of the production process, and in each stage the relationship among the changes in costs, prices, and output will be examined. The production of agricultural goods will be considered first, and then that part of manufacturing which is con-

464

cerned with the processing or fabrication of agricultural materials. A few of the major mineral products will then be examined, and from this the analysis will proceed to the manufacturing industries which utilize mineral products. Finally, finished goods will be followed through the distributive channels to the consumer. The exact form of the discussion will differ among sectors, depending on both the special problems arising in the particular sector and the nature of the available statistical material.

AGRICULTURE: FIELD CROPS

IN AGRICULTURE, any analysis of output and prices must take into account the special role played by variations in harvests. The effect of over-all economic fluctuations is overlaid on a pattern of good and bad harvests, so that an analysis of the effect of a fall in demand on price and output must take account of variations in crop size due solely to weather. No simple correction can be made to eliminate the influence of weather and predict what would have occurred under "normal" conditions. Even for years which can be considered "normal," the effect of previous abnormal years will be reflected in the level of stocks, and this in turn will influence prices. Rather than attempt a correction of agricultural price and output data, therefore, an indirect approach will be utilized. From an examination of the nature of cost conditions for various products, the reactions of farmers to economic fluctuations in terms of altered *inputs* will be predicted. Data on agricultural inputs will then be consulted to see how far the actual statistics agree with what would be expected.

In crop production, farmers generally provide much of the necessary labor themselves and receive as compensation the residual after other costs are paid. Hired labor is relatively unimportant; in 1929 it amounted to only 8.5 per cent of the gross cash income from marketings.[39] The farmer attempts to maximize his residual share, so that from the point of view of cost-output determination his own labor return becomes part of overhead, like his other fixed costs and the return on his capital. Marginal costs for the individual producer of agricultural crops involve primarily such things as seed, fertilizer, gasoline, twine, sacks, and small amounts of hired labor. Data for

[39] *Material Bearing on Parity Prices*, Dept. of Agriculture, 1941, p. 9, and *Income Parity for Agriculture*, Dept. of Agriculture, 1939, Part 11, Section 1, p. 5.

the year 1938[40] indicate that for most agricultural crops marginal costs would not be more than 15 to 20 per cent of total costs. Of course when the farmer reaches capacity, in the sense that all the land available to him is in full use, the marginal-cost curve will rise sharply, becoming discontinuous at this point. In the production of crops, therefore, the marginal-cost curve will be very low at points below full cultivation and will become vertical at the point of full cultivation. The farmer does produce at the point where marginal cost equals price: the vertically rising marginal-cost curve at full capacity will cut the horizontal demand curve at that point, so that it pays the farmer to produce as much as he can. With a fall in demand, the demand curve for the individual farmer will move downward, but it will still be horizontal, and unless demand should fall far enough so that price would be below the farmer's minimum marginal cost, it will still be in his interest to maintain capacity production. Even if the prices to the farmer of the elements going into marginal cost should change, the vertical portion of the marginal-cost curve will remain the same, so that regardless of changes in cost and demand the farmer will generally find it to his profit to cultivate his land fully.

Not only will the individual farmer maintain his output, but, in the face of a general fall in income and demand, marginal farmers will not leave the industry. Those marginal farmers who would if demand falls receive an inadequate residual return for their labor and fixed costs, should under normal conditions be attracted away from agriculture by superior opportunities elsewhere. But when there is a general fall in income and demand in the economy there are no employment opportunities elsewhere, and the farmer finds that he has little or no possibility of getting out of agriculture.

It seems reasonable to expect, therefore, that the number of acres harvested by farmers should not decline in the depression. Statistics on the total number of acres harvested by farmers and the acres of various crops harvested are given in Table 1.

The total quantity of crops harvested did not change appreciably in the sharp decline of income and demand from 1929 to 1932. Governmental restriction of production shows up in the year 1934. The statistics for individual crops show considerable variation, but it would be difficult to tell without further detailed analysis whether the variations are in fact due to changes in income and demand.

[40] *Agricultural Statistics, 1940,* Dept. of Agriculture, 1940, p. 568.

TABLE 1

Indexes of Acres Harvested of Various Crops, 1929-1939

Year	Total of 46 Crops	Corn	Wheat	Hay	Cotton	Oats	Barley	Potatoes
				Total Acres (thousands)				
1929	356,989	97,805	63,332	55,728	43,232	38,153	13,526	3,019
				Indexes (1929 = 100)				
1930	101	104	99	97	98	104	93	103
1931	100	109	91	100	90	105	83	115
1932	102	113	91	100	83	109	97	118
1933	93	108	78	100	68	96	72	113
1934	83	94	69	100	62	77	48	119
1935	94	98	81	100	64	104	91	117
1936	88	95	77	103	69	88	62	101
1937	95	96	102	98	78	93	74	105
1938	96	94	110	102	56	94	78	100
1939	91	91	85	105	55	87	93	100

Source: *Agricultural Statistics, 1940*, Dept. of Agriculture, pp. 541-542.

Some of the changes, such as the decline in cotton, are probably due to secular influences. Insofar as other crops are substituted for cotton, they too will show a secular influence. Furthermore, to the extent that farmers do react to differential price changes due to different weather conditions in various regions, the actual analysis becomes very complex. But it seems clear that the depression directly following 1929 did not cause farmers as a group to contract the total number of acres harvested.

As noted above, differences in the year-to-year yield of the various crops make it almost impossible to analyze the impact of changes in demand on price changes of agricultural goods. Nevertheless, an examination of the price indexes for the crops whose acreage is given in Table 1 can illustrate the general magnitude of the impact which the depression had upon these prices. These price indexes are shown in Table 2. It can be seen from this table that a price drop of 60 per cent was not unusual—the smallest price drop for any crop was 30 per cent, and even this was large compared with the acreage changes shown in Table 1.

AGRICULTURE: LIVESTOCK PRODUCTION

FARMERS who are primarily engaged in raising livestock may face a cost situation somewhat different from that described for the producers of field crops. To the extent that cattle are grazed on grasslands or the farmer grows his own feed, marginal cost still may be small relative to total value of product until full capacity is reached, becoming discontinuous at that point. However, if the farmer purchases his feed, marginal cost may be high relative to total value of product at all levels of output. The individual producer cannot afford to stay in business if the price of his output falls below his marginal costs, so that it might seem that price could not fall very far without causing a contraction in output. But according to the analysis of field crops presented above, the quantity of feed grown does not contract in depressions. The demand for feed is entirely derived from the demand for livestock, so that the price of feed will fall proportionally to the price of livestock. Any contraction in livestock production would immediately leave surplus feed which would drive the price of feed down until it would all be taken. Thus, taking into account the effects on the price of feed, the volume of livestock production would not be expected to contract in a depression, although of course there may be substitution among types of live-

TABLE 2

Indexes of Season Average Prices Received by Farmers, 1929-1939

(1929 = 100)

Year	Corn (1)	Wheat (2)	Hay (3)	Cotton (4)	Oats (5)	Barley (6)	Potatoes (7)
1930	75	65	104	56	77	75	70
1931	40	38	74	34	51	61	35
1932	40	37	55	39	38	41	29
1933	65	72	67	61	80	81	63
1934	102	85	115	74	115	127	34
1935	82	80	64	66	63	70	45
1936	130	99	93	73	107	145	87
1937	65	93	75	50	72	100	40
1938	63	54	59	51	57	68	42
1939	70	65	65	54	71	82	52

Source: *Agricultural Statistics, 1940*, Dept. of Agriculture: column 1, p. 55; column 2, p. 10; column 3, p. 316; column 4, p. 108; column 5, p. 62; column 6, p. 74; column 7, p. 261.

stock, or perhaps even between some field crops and livestock. Table 3 gives the production of various kinds of livestock; from these figures it does not appear that the fluctuations in production in the period 1929-1932 were any more significant in magnitude than they were in other parts of the 1929-1939 period.

Agriculture, then, because of the nature of its marginal costs, would be expected to maintain its output in the face of a fall in demand, and this expected behavior is in fact borne out by the statistics on crops and livestock. The whole impact of a contraction in demand falls on price; price will decline until the full quantity produced can be absorbed by the economy.

MANUFACTURING: AGRICULTURAL RAW MATERIALS

MANUFACTURING plants that process agricultural raw materials are of course related to agriculture, but the nature of the relationship between price and marginal cost is quite different. In order to examine whether the price behavior of agricultural processing plants corresponds to what would be expected on the basis of changes in their marginal costs, it will be necessary to give attention to (1) the nature and shape of their cost functions, (2) the price changes in the elements of cost, and (3) the changes in their output prices.

1. Exact determination of the shape of the marginal-cost curve is not feasible for each individual industry. No reliable methods are at present available for measuring the shape of marginal-cost curves from empirical data.[41] However, another attack on the problem is possible. By making a simple arbitrary assumption about the nature of marginal cost, the process as a whole can be made operational, and any results which are derived can then be reconsidered in terms of possible alternative assumptions about the shape of marginal costs. For the purpose of the preliminary analysis, therefore, it will be assumed that marginal cost was constant over the relevant range of output, and that in the periods studied the technical coefficients of the input factors were also fairly constant. In this connection user cost of plant and equipment will be neglected, both because it is impossible to measure and because its influence on marginal costs is probably very minor. These assumptions imply that within relevant production ranges each additional unit of output would require a specific fixed amount of labor and materials

[41] Hans Staehle, "The Measurement of Statistical Cost Functions: An Appraisal of Some Recent Contributions," abstracted in *American Economic Review*, November Supplement, 1942, p. 349.

TABLE 3

Indexes of Livestock and Dairy Products, 1929-1939

Year	Cattle on Farms (1)	Cattle Slaughtered (2)	Calves Slaughtered (3)	Hogs on Farms (4)	Hogs Slaughtered (5)	Chickens on Farms (6)	Eggs (7)	Milk (pounds) (8)
				Total Number (thousands)				
1929	58,877	12,038	7,406	59,042	71,012	449,006	37,921,000	98,976,000
				Indexes (1929 = 100)				
1930	104	100	104	94	95	104	103	101
1931	107	100	108	93	98	100	101	104
1932	112	99	106	100	101	97	96	105
1933	119	108	114	105	103	99	94	106
1934	126	129	135	99	97	97	91	103
1935	116	122	129	66	65	87	88	103
1936	115	134	137	72	83	89	90	104
1937	113	127	136	72	76	94	99	104
1938	112	123	123	75	83	86	98	108
1939	113	120	119	83	93	92	101	110

Source: *Agricultural Statistics, 1940*, Dept. of Agriculture: column 1, p. 344; column 2, p. 359; column 3, p. 359; column 4, p. 364; column 5, p. 375; column 6, p. 461; column 7, p. 476; column 8, p. 428.

irrespective of the output level, and the relative changes in the prices of capital, labor, and materials would not in the short run cause significant substitutions among the input elements. At the end of the analysis, these assumptions will be reviewed by considering what effect other kinds of assumptions would have on the analysis.

2. With an assumed constancy of marginal cost and fixed relations among the input factors of labor and materials for incremental changes in output, it is possible to construct a price index of the change in marginal cost from available empirical materials, as follows. Under the given assumptions, labor and materials costs would have approximately the same relative importance in both marginal costs and average direct costs.[42] Therefore, if the price change in labor cost per unit and the price change in materials cost per unit were combined according to their relative importance in direct costs, an approximation of the price change in marginal cost should be obtained.[43]

3. The changes in output prices can best be computed from the same body of statistical data that was used to derive direct costs. It is more meaningful to consider value per unit of output than quoted prices. Such factors as shifts in the composition of output, the importance of discounts, and the existence of special prices for some customers will affect total receipts and so will be reflected in value per unit of output, whereas they might well be omitted in an analysis of quoted prices. In the census statistics, furthermore, the value of product which is recorded for an industry is from the same set of plant questionnaires that furnish the data on cost of materials and

[42] In the following discussion the term "direct costs" will be used to denote the census classifications of (1) wages paid to direct labor, plus (2) cost of materials used. Changes in average direct costs can be obtained by dividing the total change by an index of output change. It is assumed that these direct costs do not contain any overhead labor or materials costs. In Tsiang's terminology, these direct costs are referred to as prime costs.

[43] This procedure is somewhat similar to Dunlop's calculation of the price changes in marginal cost by using census weights for combining price indexes of wages and raw materials. The main difference between the two approaches is that instead of utilizing Dunlop's indexes for wage rates and raw materials, the present calculation derives average labor cost per unit and average materials cost per unit from the census statistics. In contrast with Dunlop's assumptions, it is interesting to note that Neal and Tsiang make the assumption that average direct cost is equal to marginal cost, and thus use the census statistics directly for computing the change in marginal cost. The actual statistical result achieved by this process is identical with the other method. However, it should be pointed out that their assumption that average direct cost equals marginal cost is overly restrictive, since for the process to be legitimate it is only necessary that the change in average direct cost be equal to the change in marginal cost.

wages paid. The use of a matched set of data makes more reasonable the assumption that the same industrial classifications, the same time period, and the same concepts of output were used in obtaining both costs and receipts. It was on this basis that the data in the Census of Manufactures were used to obtain approximations of the changes which took place in marginal cost, price, and output for various industries in the period 1929-1931.

Table. 4 shows the percentage changes in labor cost per unit, materials cost per unit, direct cost per unit, value per unit, and out-

TABLE 4

Percentage Change in Unit Costs and in Output, Various Agricultural Processing Industries, 1929-1931

Industry	Labor Cost	Materials Cost	Direct Cost	Value	Output
	(p e r	u n i t)			
Flour	—15	—42	—41	—38	—9
Meat packing	—14	—35	—33	—33	—5
Butter	—25	—39	—39	—39	+2
Cane-sugar refining	0	—12	—11	—10	—13
Cotton goods	—13	—42	—32	—34	—22
Woolen and worsted goods	—12	—32	—27	—26	—19
Women's clothing	—24	—25	—25	—26	+3
Textile gloves	—16	—31	—27	—27	—33
Cloth hats	—18	—20	—19	—21	—40
Leather	—3	—37	—32	—30	—19
Leather boots and shoes	—13	—22	—20	—20	—16

Source: Cost and value data, *Biennial Census of Manufactures: 1933*, Bureau of the Census, pp. 42-44, 133-135, 380; output data, Solomon Fabricant, *The Output of Manufacturing Industries, 1899-1937* (National Bureau of Economic Research, 1940), pp. 385, 387, 395, 404, 427, 430, 436, 437, 457, 462, 474.

put for a number of manufacturing industries which process agricultural goods. Labor cost in this table relates to production workers only. The wage and salary payments made to administrative, sales, technical, office, and supervisory personnel (with the exception of working foremen and gang bosses) are all excluded. The output data given in Table 4 have been taken from Solomon Fabricant.[44] They may not be fully satisfactory for many industries; to the extent that the quality of a product changes while the unit in which output is measured does not change, the real output rate may be obscured. Fortunately, it is not crucial that the output indexes be truly valid. The major point of the analysis is to examine the *rela-*

[44] Solomon Fabricant, *The Output of Manufacturing Industries, 1899-1937* (National Bureau of Economic Research, 1940), Appendix B.

tive changes in labor cost, materials cost, and value per unit within each industry; the output index is used only to reduce the total figures to averages. The relationship among labor cost, materials cost, and value per unit will be the same regardless of the output index, since for any one industry the total figures are all divided by the same constant. The only reason for using an output index at all was to get some idea of similarities and differences among the different industries. Only if the output indexes possess a relatively high degree of validity will these interindustry comparisons be meaningful, and in any case very little accent should be placed on small differences among industries.

The industries shown in Table 4 were chosen because they involve the use of a number of different agricultural products, and also because they illustrate a number of different analytic points. The most outstanding findings which emerge from the table as a whole are that labor cost dropped less than materials cost in all instances, and that together these direct costs dropped by about the same percentage as price. Thus if the change in direct costs is taken to be an approximation of the change in marginal cost, price in the industries shown moved directly with marginal cost.

A more detailed examination of Table 4 brings out some additional points of interest. There is considerable variation among the industries in the extent of the drop in labor costs, and no simple explanation of the causes of such variation is apparent. Differential changes in wage rates or in the wage structure might account for some of the variation, but probably of equal importance are the differences in productivity changes among industries, the substitution of the owner's labor for hired labor in small firms (for example, the butter industry), the differential rate of contraction of firms having high labor costs compared with firms having lower labor costs, and finally the doubtful validity of the output index as an indicator of real output changes.

The variations among the industries in the changes in materials cost are somewhat more easily explained. The drop in materials cost is greatest for those industries that directly consume unprocessed farm products, and is less for those industries that utilize partly processed agricultural products. Thus, the drop in materials cost was substantial for flour, meat packing, butter, cotton goods, and leather, and somewhat less for women's clothing, textile gloves, cloth hats, and boots and shoes. The woolen and worsted industry is hard to classify because it is composed of a number of different sub-

474

industries, some of which supply various intermediate products to later processing stages, and so represents a mixture of plants at various stages of processing. Cane-sugar refining has been included to illustrate what happens in an agricultural processing industry when materials prices are less variable. Most cane sugar for refining is imported, and since this import price did not drop as much as the prices of other agricultural materials the price of refined sugar did not drop as much as the prices of the other processed agricultural goods shown.

A separate examination of the drop in labor costs and the drop in materials costs is not sufficient to account for all the variations in final goods prices in the various industries. The relative importance of labor and materials in the production process must be taken into account, in order to give an accurate appraisal of the change in direct costs. The significance of this point is well illustrated by a comparison of the butter and the cotton industries. The percentage drop in labor costs for the butter industry (25 per cent) was considerably greater than it was for the cotton industry (13 per cent). The drop in materials costs was about the same for the two industries (butter, 39 per cent; cotton, 42 per cent). Because of the greater importance of labor in the cotton industry, the output price of cotton goods dropped somewhat less (34 per cent) than it did for butter (39 per cent). Materials were so much more important than labor in the butter industry that the output price of butter changed by exactly the same percentage as did materials.

Finally, there are significant differences in the degree to which prices (value per unit) dropped in the various industries shown in Table 4; these differences can all be explained adequately in terms of (1) the changes in labor costs and materials costs and (2) the relative importance of labor and materials in the production process. The higher the degree of fabrication, the more important labor becomes in relation to materials and the more closely will price change follow the change in labor cost. The prices at which processed agricultural goods are sold to distributors, therefore, will depend in large part on how highly they are fabricated before they are ready for the consumer. The variations in relative price changes even within the agricultural processing industries are not inconsiderable. Excluding cane-sugar refining, the drop in finished-goods prices in Table 4 ranges from 20 per cent for boots and shoes to 39 per cent for butter. But, insofar as output prices shown in Table 4 do tend to move with cost, they can all be called flexible, despite the fact

475

that the amplitude of change differs considerably from industry to industry.

As noted above, the use of the change in direct cost per unit as an indicator of the change in marginal cost involves the assumptions of constant marginal costs and a lack of substitution among capital, labor, and materials in the period under study. It will be useful at this juncture, therefore, to examine the effects of different assumptions about marginal cost upon the analysis.

If the marginal-cost curve, instead of being constant, were upward sloping (i.e. marginal cost increasing with increases in output) the drop in direct costs shown in Table 4 would be an understatement of the actual drop in marginal costs. Under such circumstances, instead of the roughly equivalent movement of marginal costs and prices indicated in Table 4 by the change in direct costs and prices, marginal cost would in fact generally have fallen more than prices, so that according to the definition of price flexibility adopted above prices would be somewhat inflexible. Conversely, if marginal costs were downward sloping (i.e. marginal costs decreasing with increasing output) the fall in direct costs shown in Table 4 would overstate the actual drop in marginal costs, and prices would be overly flexible.

In assessing the suitability of the assumptions made earlier with respect to the probable shape of the marginal-cost curves for the industries shown in Table 4, the following points should be borne in mind. For a good many industries, it does not seem reasonable to expect that the amount of materials required per unit of output should vary in any manner except directly with output—especially, for example, in such industries as flour, butter, and cane-sugar refining. In these industries, too, labor costs are not a very large proportion of direct costs, so that any variation in the amount of direct labor required per unit of output as output increases would have relatively little influence on the level of marginal cost. And in certain other industries, it may be true, as Reynolds has suggested for cotton textiles,[45] that the fixed factors which are usually assumed to be indivisible are in fact highly divisible. Many plants are made up of batteries of similar machines, each of which can be operated as an independent unit. If the machines are of equal efficiency, the putting into use of successive units need not involve any increase or decrease in marginal cost. Finally, shifts in the marginal-cost func-

[45] Lloyd G. Reynolds, "Relations Between Wage Rates, Costs, and Prices," *American Economic Review*, March Supplement, 1942, pp. 275-301, esp. p. 277.

tion due to technological changes are somewhat less likely to have taken place in the downswing period under consideration (1929-1931) than in other periods. All things considered, an attempt to arrive at more realistic assumptions about the shape of the marginal-cost function (and technological change) in many of the agricultural processing industries would probably result in refinements which would be matters of detail rather than of consequence. This would not be true in every case, but it would be true in the majority of cases.

MINING

THE minerals industries present yet a different set of problems. Unfortunately, in this sector any analysis is seriously hampered by the lack of adequate data. The various types of mining, furthermore, cannot be treated as one homogeneous group in the way agricultural crop production was. Each particular branch of the mineral industry has its own peculiarities.

In coal mining, labor cost is even more important than it is in most manufacturing industries. For the year 1929, labor costs represented about 60 per cent of the value of the product in both the anthracite and bituminous industries.[46] Materials costs amount to about 15 per cent of the value of the product. It is difficult to find data showing how materials costs changed from 1929 to 1932 or what materials were used, but very probably few if any direct products of agriculture were involved. To the extent that materials used were highly processed goods, their costs should change in about the same way as labor costs. And in any case, since labor costs constitute 80 per cent of the total direct cost in coal mining, a relatively small error would be introduced by assuming that total direct costs moved about the same way as labor costs. The data in Table 5 have been drawn up on this assumption. This table shows that prices and labor costs did move together for the period 1929-1932, a period in which production of coal was cut back sharply.

The data on iron-ore production are difficult to interpret because of the vertical integration of the industry. Quoted prices of iron ore did not change at all throughout the depression, but even though these unchanging prices did nominally appear on the books of vertically integrated firms, their significance may be questioned. The separation of the accounts of the operation of iron-ore mining from

[46] *Abstract of the Fifteenth Census of the United States*, Bureau of the Census, 1933, p. 583.

the production of steel within the same firm is of necessity an arbitrary procedure, and the resulting statistics represent imputations which are irrelevant from the point of view of the total profits of the firm.

TABLE 5

Indexes of Labor Cost and Value per Unit in the Extractive Industries, 1929-1932

(1929 = 100)

Industry	1930	1931	1932
Anthracite coal:			
Labor cost per unit	102	95	82
Value per unit	98	95	84
Output	94	81	68
Bituminous coal:			
Labor cost per unit	95	86	71
Value per unit	95	87	72
Output	87	71	58
Crude petroleum:			
Labor cost per unit	97	73	56
Value per unit	94	51	68
Output	89	84	78
Metalliferous mining:			
Labor cost per unit	104	90	84
Value per unit	90	78	73
Output	75	50	26

Source: *Statistical Abstract of the United States, 1939,* Dept. of Commerce, p. 340; *Statistical Abstract of the United States, 1940,* Dept. of Commerce, pp. 784, 791, 804.

The production of petroleum and nonferrous metals differs from coal production in that the differing richness of deposits is a very important factor. No generalization can be made about cost curves in either industry. Some oil wells or mines utilize low-grade deposits and have relatively high marginal costs in the form of labor and some materials. Other wells or mines are much richer, having very low marginal costs and yielding considerable rent. With a fall in demand, high-cost producers will be forced to abandon operations completely, while the low-cost producers can continue to operate. This situation is well illustrated by the Michigan copper-mining industry. In 1929, the yield of copper per ton of ore was 24.5 pounds; in 1930, 25.4 pounds; in 1931, 33.1 pounds; and finally in 1932, 47.6 pounds.[47] Similarly, output per man-hour in the production of crude pe-

[47] *Mineral Resources of the United States, 1931,* Geological Survey, 1934, Part 1, p. 246; and *Minerals Yearbook, 1932-33,* Bureau of Mines, p. 146.

troleum was 35 per cent[48] greater in 1932 than it was in 1929, and in lead and zinc mining it was 68 per cent greater.[49] High-yield deposits thus account for a relatively larger share of the total output of the industry when demand falls. The cost curves of a high-yield producer are very much like those of a farmer. Marginal costs are relatively low, becoming discontinuous (i.e. vertical) at capacity production. With a fall in demand, a high-yield mine, in order to maximize *present* income, should continue full production; although price has fallen, price would still be equal to marginal cost.[50] In considering how price should move relative to *direct* cost actually incurred with a fall in demand, however, one would expect price to come closer to direct cost, since direct cost actually incurred lies on the portion of the curve just before the vertical rise. Thus, the fall in price would tend to be greater than that in actual direct cost. Exact prediction of the movement of price relative to direct cost would require engineering knowledge of the difference in the richness of deposits in the industry and economic knowledge of the structure of the industry. The data for petroleum and metalliferous mining in Table 5 show that, as would be expected in these industries, if the change in labor cost is again taken as an index of the change in direct costs prices fell faster than direct costs.

It will be apparent that this discussion of the mineral industries has in fact been concerned with the shape of the supply curves in the various industries. For coal mining and probably also for quarrying, the abundance of deposits of roughly similar productivity leads to supply curves for these products that are almost horizontal for a wide range below capacity production. If costs do not change, a fall in demand would probably result in a fall in output rather than in price. It is only if the supply curve shifts downward due to falling labor costs that any significant price decline can take place. In contrast, those minerals which are found in deposits of widely varying richness will have rising industry supply curves, and a fall in demand will intersect the supply curve at a lower point, thus permit-

---

[48] *Production, Employment, and Productivity in the Mineral Extractive Industries, 1880-1938*, National Research Project, Works Project Administration, p. 63.

[49] *Employment and Output per Man in the Mineral Extractive Industries*, National Research Project, Works Project Administration, 1940, Report S-2, p. 74.

[50] In some cases the owner of a very valuable natural resource might prefer shutting down operations long before price fell to the point where it equalled direct operating costs. Since minerals are exhaustible resources, mining involves a cost akin to user cost, and if the mine is very rich and the producer has high future expectations this user cost might be great.

ting a price fall as well as a contraction in output. Any downward shift in costs, of course, would increase the price drop and permit a larger output than would otherwise be possible.

MANUFACTURING: MINERAL RAW MATERIALS

THE processing of mineral materials by manufacturing industries can be examined in a manner similar to that used for the processing of agricultural materials. Table 6 presents the relevant data for a

TABLE 6

Percentage Change in Unit Costs and in Output, Various Mineral Processing Industries, 1929-1931

Industry	Labor Cost	Materials Cost	Direct Cost (p e r u n i t)	Value	Output
Lime	−18	−17	−18	−20	−22
Clay products	−14	−7	−11	−11	−52
Petroleum refining	−10	−34	−33	−36	−9
Fertilizer	−13	−15	−14	−15	−22
Tin cans	−20	−16	−17	−18	−8
Wire drawn from purchased rods	−4	−29	−24	−24	−49
Nonferrous metal products	−20	−45	−41	−38	−41
Washing machines	−24	−24	−24	−22	−21
Buttons	−14	−18	−16	−17	−12
Pens	−1	−24	−17	−16	−17
Clocks and watches	−4	−5	−5	−3	−26
Manufactured heating and illuminating gas	−12	−12	−12	−1	−8

Source: Cost and value data, *Biennial Census of Manufactures: 1933*, Bureau of the Census, pp. 308, 358, 397, 427, 428, 491, 492, 523, 631, 632; output data, Solomon Fabricant, *The Output of Manufacturing Industries, 1899-1937* (National Bureau of Economic Research, 1940), pp. 497, 517, 531, 522, 552, 553, 556, 559, 578, 593, 596.

number of different industry groups. Like the agricultural processing industries, the mineral processing industries in Table 6 show a correspondence between direct costs and prices, with one significant exception. This exception is manufactured heating and illuminating gas; in this industry direct costs dropped 12 per cent while price dropped only 1 per cent. The reason for this discrepancy is obvious: gas is a public utility and its rates are fixed. It has been included in the selection of industries in Table 6 to show how an inflexibility of prices relative to costs would show up, even in a case where costs were not particularly flexible.

The mineral processing industries are very different from the ag-

480

ricultural processing industries with respect to the magnitude and consistency of the drop in materials cost. For the agricultural processing industries it was noted that materials costs dropped considerably, and in all cases more than labor cost. In contrast, the materials costs for lime, clay products, fertilizer, tin cans, buttons, clocks and watches, and manufactured gas dropped less than for any agricultural processing industry, and in some of these cases fell less than did labor costs. The industries which exhibit this smaller drop in materials costs are either those which obtain a significant portion of their materials from those extractive industries in which the price drop would be expected to be small, or else those which use more highly fabricated materials, which already have a considerable amount of labor cost in them. Petroleum refining and nonferrous metal products behave differently from the industries just listed, in that their material costs do drop significantly. Again this is what would be expected, because of the nature of the mineral industries supplying them. The remaining industries require further explanation. Wire drawn from purchased rods uses both steel and copper. The drop in materials cost for the wire industry, therefore, should fall somewhere between those of these two raw materials. If the fall in materials cost for tin cans and the fall in price of nonferrous metal products are taken as indicators for steel and copper respectively (since nothing better is available), materials cost in the wire industry does behave as expected. For washing machines, labor cost declines more than it does for any other industry in Table 6, which is hardly to be expected. The explanation here may lie in the lack of validity of a production index which does not take into account a change in the quality of the product. If cheaper washing machines were produced in 1931, the real output would have fallen more than indicated by the production index, and the declines in both labor cost and materials cost would have been smaller than appear here.

The conclusion that is reached from an examination of these mineral processing industries, then, is in accord with that reached for agricultural processing industries. The prices of producers tend to move in accordance with their direct costs, computed as the weighted average of labor and materials costs. In some of the mineral processing industries, a fall in demand does not produce a sharp decline in materials cost; instead the decline in materials cost is about equal to the decline in labor cost so that price, materials cost, and labor cost all move together. In those cases where materials cost does

481

decline sharply, the reaction will be like that in the agricultural processing industries. The higher the degree of fabrication the more closely the change in the price of the product will approach the change in labor cost, since labor cost is relatively a more important part of the total value of the product.

Again, it should be noted that the use of the change in direct cost as an indicator of marginal cost in this analysis implies all the restrictive assumptions that were discussed above with reference to the agricultural processing industries. It is quite possible that a number of the industries listed in Table 6 did not have constant marginal costs and fixed technical coefficients among their inputs in this period. If the quantitative importance of these deviations was not overly great, however, the changes in direct costs may still reflect the approximate change in marginal costs. In some instances, it may even be true that some of the discrepancies shown in Table 6 would disappear if a better approximation to the change in marginal costs could be obtained. Thus, for instance, if the marginal-cost function in nonferrous metal products actually declined with expanding output, the drop in direct cost shown in Table 6 would overstate the actual drop in marginal cost, so that marginal cost and price might have moved more closely together than did direct cost and price.

MANUFACTURING: SUMMARY

Up to this point in the analysis, specific industries in manufacturing have been discussed to illustrate particular points, but there has been no discussion of how well manufacturing as a whole fits this pattern. It would not be meaningful to combine all of manufacturing, for reasons which have already been pointed out. The aggregation of agricultural processing industries with mineral processing industries, and materials-producing industries with those making highly fabricated goods, would, because of the relative shifts in the importance of these various groups, obscure the very relationships which were being investigated. Some disaggregation is therefore necessary. To cover all of manufacturing, and yet preserve to some extent the differences among the different major industries, the 16 major industry groups used in the census classification are presented in Table 7. For three of the industry groups, production indexes are not available.

Generally speaking, the correspondence between the drop in direct costs and the drop in prices for the various industries is quite close. In 7 of the 16 industries, the drop in price was within one percentage point of the drop in direct cost. In 5 industries prices dropped more than direct costs, and in 4 industries less. The 2 industries in which the discrepancy was greatest were chemicals and rubber; in both of these price would have been expected to fall more than it did. In forest products, iron and steel, and nonferrous metal products, price dropped somewhat more than would have been expected. There does not seem to be any single simple explanation that can account for these divergences.

TABLE 7

Percentage Change in Unit Costs and in Output,
Major Industry Groups, 1929-1931

Industry Group	Labor Cost	Materials Cost	Direct Cost	Value	Output
		(per	unit)		
Food and kindred products	—11	—30	—28	—25	—9
Textiles and their products	—18	—32	—28	—28	—13
Forest products	—13	—10	—11	—15	—45
Paper and allied products	—14	—18	—17	—16	—14
Printing, publishing, and allied industries	+1	—10	—6	—6	—16
Chemicals and allied products	—9	—23	—21	—15	—15
Products of petroleum and coal	—4	—27	—25	—25	—17
Rubber products	22	—37	—33	—21	—31
Leather and its manufactures	—12	—28	—24	—25	—18
Stone, clay, and glass products	—13	—10	—11	—11	—34
Iron and steel and their products	+2	—7	—5	—8	—50
Nonferrous metals and their products	—8	—41	—37	—33	—42
Transportation equipment	+9	+3	+5	+5	—55

	INDUSTRIES WITH NO OUTPUT INDEXES			
Industry Group	Total Labor Cost	Total Materials Cost	Total Direct Cost	Total Value
Machinery	—48	—44	—46	—18
Railroad repair shops	—68	—54	—62	—58
Miscellaneous	—61	—63	—62	—68

Source: Cost and value data, *Biennial Census of Manufactures: 1933*, Bureau of the Census, pp. 42, 133, 218, 262, 280, 307, 358, 372, 380, 397, 426, 491, 522, 593, 618, 630; output data, Solomon Fabricant, *The Output of Manufacturing Industries, 1899-1937* (National Bureau of Economic Research, 1940), pp. 410, 460, 475, 481, 485, 486, 514, 519, 535, 543, 556, 565, 592.

Aggregation like that of Table 7 has both advantages and disadvantages in drawing conclusions regarding the behavior patterns of individual firms. Since many firms are included in the aggregate, the effect of normal random variance is reduced, and the average change for the group as a whole takes on more significance. On the other hand, aggregation combines what are essentially unhomogeneous groups. Any single industry includes a variety of products, and some of these products will have wider margins between direct cost and price than others (margin in this sense equals price minus direct cost divided by price). If with a fall in demand the rates of contraction of high-margin and low-margin products are different, the aggregate would show a change in the average margin even if the margin for every individual product remained unchanged. The use of finer industry classifications in Tables 4 and 6 was in part an attempt to avoid some of these aggregation problems. Even with a single homogeneous industry, however, the aggregation problem would not be entirely overcome. Margins in large firms may differ from those in small firms, and the rate of contraction of firms in a depression may be related to size. Or, margins for plants in one part of the country may be different from margins in another part, and the contraction in output may be more severe in one section of the country than in others. For an accurate appraisal of the behavior of the relation between direct costs and prices, it would in fact be necessary to make the analysis product by product and plant by plant throughout the country. Examination of a few representative individual plants, furthermore, would not be sufficient; every plant has special conditions, and there is ample evidence that the change in margins from year to year is highly variable in individual cases. What would be required would be distribution curves of margins for all the plants and products in a given industry. Preliminary investigation along these lines has indicated that, although there is wide dispersion in the behavior of individual plants, there is a central tendency, and this central tendency normally is around the point of zero change in margins (i.e. the gap between price and direct cost is a constant percentage of price).

This discussion is not intended to imply that all the discrepancies between the changes in direct costs and the changes in price which appear in Table 7 can in fact be explained by problems of aggregation. On the contrary, some of the actual correspondence between direct cost and price change may well be the result of the fact that a number of essentially dissimilar groups have been combined, and in doing so their differences have been averaged out.

There are a number of other considerations, besides that of aggregation, which should be taken into account in appraising these statistics. First, the records upon which the statistics are based are accounting records, and for small firms especially records of labor cost and materials cost are not kept uniformly and consistently from year to year or from firm to firm; similarly, the valuation of inventories on different bases will obviously lead to difficulties in interpretation. Secondly, price would be expected to move with marginal cost only when there have been no technological changes, no significant institutional changes, and no secular growth or decline. Over a two-year period some such changes are bound to occur, and to the extent that they do margins could be expected to shift. Finally, it has been assumed that marginal cost corresponds to direct cost, with direct cost computed as average labor and materials cost per unit of output (i.e. that all production functions are linear). In actual fact, the productivity of labor in many industries is affected by the scale of output,[51] and in such cases the change in direct cost may not be a good indicator of the change in marginal cost and so should not necessarily agree with the change in price. Any adequate analysis of the discrepancies between the change in direct costs and the change in prices in manufacturing industries must take all of these factors into account.

DISTRIBUTIVE TRADES

THE products processed by the manufacturer, and some of the products coming direct from the farmer, must pass through the channels of distribution. Direct costs in the distributive trades are primarily the goods purchased for resale to other distributors or to consumers. The labor costs and other materials costs and the rent can generally be considered fixed over rather wide ranges of output, so that the purchase price of goods for resale (including transportation) is fairly closely identified with the industry's marginal cost. Here again, the analysis is hampered by the fact that very little information is available, but something can be done with the concept of gross margins. In the distributive trades the difference between the prices paid by the distributors for goods and the prices received by them for the same goods is normally expressed as a percentage of final price and is termed gross margin. This concept differs from markup in that it is calculated on the basis of actual receipts (including discounts, sales, etc.) rather than on the basis of quoted prices. Table 8 gives

[51] In this connection see the studies of the *Production, Employment, and Productivity in 59 Manufacturing Industries*, National Research Project, Works Progress Administration, 1939.

the percentage gross margins for a variety of different distributors. For almost all groups there is no significant change in gross mar-

TABLE 8

Percentage Gross Margins in the Distributive Trades, 1929-1932

Type of Establishment	Number of Stores	Percentage Gross Margin			
		1929	*1930*	*1931*	*1932*
Wholesale grocers, Ohio	17	12	11	11	10
Wholesale machinery supply	35-44	24	24	24	25
Meat markets, Chicago	34-50	22	25	28	29
Food chains	17,754-33,147	20	n.a.	22	22
Clothing stores, sales, to $100,000	n.a.	35	36	34	33
Specialty stores	70-85	34	34	33	32
Chain shoestores	661-1,361	34	n.a.	n.a.	33
Variety chains	1,579-2,188	33	n.a.	32	31
Department stores, sales, to $10 million	21-30	34	34	34	34
Department stores, sales, $4-$10 million	44-54	34	34	33	33
Department stores, sales, $1-$4 million	110-142	32	32	32	32
Department stores, sales, $500,000-$1,000,000	57-95	31	31	31	31
Department stores, sales, $250,000-$500,000	115-167	29	30	29	29

n.a. (not available).

Source: M. P. McNair, S. F. Teele, and F. G. Mulhearn, *Distribution Costs* (Harvard University Press, 1941), pp. 419, 583, 431, 387, 246, 222, 285, 288, 112, 113, 108, 109, 106, 107, 105.

gins in the period 1929-1932. The one major exception is Chicago meat markets; gross margins here rose from 22 per cent in 1929 to 29 per cent in 1932. Whether or not meat markets are a significant exception cannot really be determined on evidence at present available, but by and large it does not appear that the gross margins in the distributive trades change violently with a contraction in demand and costs. In other words, prices charged by the distributive trades tend to follow closely the prices they have to pay for the goods they sell.

SUMMARY

THIS examination of the different industrial sectors of the economy during the period 1929-1932 indicates that their actual behavior was consistent with the explanations which would be offered by a student taking his first course in value theory. At no stage in the discussion has it been necessary to consider the effect of industrial concentration to explain the relation between the fall in direct costs and the fall in price. The major determinants of price changes, according to both the theory and the empirical findings, should be (1) the relative importance of agriculture in the economy, and the extent to which demand for agricultural goods falls; (2) the nature of mineral resources and the importance of labor cost in mining, coupled with the extent to which demand for mineral goods falls; (3) the fall in the wage rate and its effect on labor cost;[52] and (4) the shape of production functions.

Generally speaking, economists are accustomed to taking as given the technological and institutional elements of the economic system. The relative magnitude of agriculture in the economy, the distribution of mineral resources, and the shape of production functions are all of this nature. The change in demand and the change in the wage rate and its relation to labor cost, however, are more properly economic problems. Income analysis in its more recent forms attempts to predict the changes in the patterns of consumption and investment in the economy; if this attempt becomes successful it should be possible by studying behavior patterns to predict changes in demand for various kinds of final goods and trace these back to the derived demands for agricultural and mineral goods.

An adequate theory of the wage rate is, however, still lacking. This lack is much more serious than might at first appear. Throughout the analysis up to this point, it has been implicitly assumed that when changes in direct costs agreed with changes in prices, it was not because the direct costs themselves were determined by prices. Should the causality run in the opposite direction, i.e. should direct costs be determined by prices instead of by other forces, the question of what determines prices would still remain open. It is probable that the price of a producer's final product does not affect the cost of his materials except through its effect on his demand for the materials, but this is not necessarily true of labor cost. If the wage rate in a plant is sensitive to the price of the final good which the plant produces rather than to the profit or loss of the plant or to the change in output, it may well be that costs will cease to

[52] To the extent that differences in the behavior of the wage rate might be explained by differences in industrial concentration, however, it is still possible that industrial concentration would in fact affect prices. For an analysis of monopoly as a possible determinant of interindustry wage structure, see Joseph W. Garbarino, "A Theory of Interindustry Wage Structure Variation," *Quarterly Journal of Economics*, May 1950, pp. 282-305.

be an explanation of prices, and that instead it will be possible to predict wage changes by changes in prices. This matter would bear further looking into, and until some adequate explanation of what wage rates do depend on can be given, the theory itself is incomplete.

As a final qualification of the empirical findings, it should be noted that the relationships observed for the period 1929-1932 may no longer be relevant.[53] If, for example, there is considerable public pressure to limit the profits of producers, it would be quite possible that producers would not operate so as to maximize profits in the short run. Furthermore, it may no longer be true that the price of agricultural materials will rise and fall more than labor cost. Industry-wide bargaining and the sensitivity of labor to changes in the cost-of-living index may render wages more highly variable, at least in the upward direction,[54] and in the downward direction agricultural price supports may prevent the normal fall in agricultural prices. Finally, governmental action in imposing rationing and price control might have a strong effect on price-cost relationships. For all these reasons today's pattern may be quite different from the pattern of twenty years ago.

The relevance of the findings in Part 3 for the topic of price flexibility as it was conceived by Means and those who came after him needs no particular elaboration. The major patterns of price behavior in the economy can be adequately explained in terms of factors other than industrial concentration. This is not to say that in some instances the consideration of the industrial organization of an industry might not be necessary, nor that in explaining wage-price relationships monopoly and monopolistic relationships need

[53] The empirical evidence for the period 1929-1932 does not throw any light on what would happen with rising income and demand. Periods of upswing are more difficult to analyze because the movement tends to be slower and because technology is more apt to change. An examination of the relatively rapid upswing of 1921-1923 has been made, however, and it appears that price behavior in this upswing was in general accord with what would be expected.

[54] In this connection the significance of guaranteed annual wages is interesting. Insofar as guaranteed annual wages remove some of the cost-of-production workers from marginal cost and make their wages a fixed cost which must be paid regardless of the level of operation, the importance of labor in marginal cost would be reduced over certain ranges of output. At points of production above the level consonant with the guaranteed wage, however, the normal relation of price to direct labor and materials cost would continue. If materials costs in the industry in question are variable, prices with guaranteed annual wages would tend to be more variable at points under "normal" output, but not different at points above "normal" output.

not be explored. What can be said, rather, is that *even if monopoly did not exist* a price system very similar to the existing one would emerge as long as wages were less flexible than agricultural prices and some mineral prices.

4. *The Theory of Price Behavior and Aggregative Price Indexes*

IN THE preceding section, the theory of price behavior has been analyzed in terms of a disaggregation of the economy. There still remains, however, the question whether this theory of price behavior is compatible with the aggregative price indexes covering the economy as a whole. For an explanation of price behavior to be completely satisfactory, it is necessary to show that it can in fact explain both micro- and macroeconomic behavior. This final section, therefore, will consider whether or not the theory of price behavior outlined in the preceding section provides a valid explanation of (1) the behavior of component prices in consumer-price indexes, (2) the behavior of the wholesale-price index, and (3) the relative movements of real and money wage rates.

THE CONSUMER-PRICE INDEX

THE major components of the consumer-price index which are available for the United States are food, apparel, rent, gas and electricity, other fuels, ice, house furnishings, and miscellaneous. The price indexes for these components are shown in Table 9 for the period 1929-1951, along with the cumulative decline from 1929 to various stages of the depression and the cumulative rise from 1933 to various stages of recovery. The price indexes for food show the greatest cumulative movement in each stage. This is of course what would be expected, since foods are agricultural products that reach the consumer without any very great degree of processing by labor. The indexes for apparel move somewhat less than those for food; again this would be expected since, although most of the materials involved come from agriculture, the goods go through more processing by labor before they reach the consumer. House furnishings are somewhat similar to apparel, but contain more non-textile components. In the first two years of the decline house furnishings did drop more than apparel, but by 1932 and 1933 the drop in apparel was very much greater. Rent presents a special problem. In the earlier stages of the depression the rent index did not drop as much as food, apparel, or house furnishings, but by 1933 it had dropped considerably more than house furnishings and

TABLE 9

Consumers-Price Index by Commodity Groups, 1929-1951,
and Cumulative Percentage Changes, 1929-1941

Year	Total	Food	Apparel	Rent	Gas and Electricity	Other Fuels	Ice	House Fur- nishings	Miscel- laneous
				INDEXES	(1935-1939 = 100)				
1929	123	133	115	141		113		112	105
1930	119	126	113	138		111		109	105
1931	109	104	103	130		109		98	104
1932	98	87	91	116		103		85	102
1933	92	84	88	100		100		84	98
1934	96	93	96	94		102		93	98
1935	98	100	97	94	103	99	n.a.	95	98
1936	99	101	98	96	191	199	n.a.	96	98
1937	103	105	103	101	99	191	n.a.	104	101
1938	101	98	102	104	99	101	n.a.	103	102
1939	99	95	101	104	99	99	100	101	101
1940	100	97	102	105	98	102	100	101	101
1941	105	106	106	106	97	108	104	107	104
1942	117	124	124	109	97	115	110	122	111
1943	124	138	130	108	96	121	114	136	116
1944	126	136	139	108	96	126	116	136	121
1945	128	139	146	108	95	128	116	146	124
1946	139	159	160	109	92	137	116	159	129
1947	159	193	186	111	92	156	126	184	140
1948	171	210	186	117	94	183	135	195	150
1949	169	202	190	121	97	188	140	189	155
1950	172	205	188	131				190	157
1951	186	228	205	136				211	165

CUMULATIVE PERCENTAGE CHANGES

Year	Total	Food	Apparel	Rent	Gas, Fuels, Ice	House Fur- nishings	Miscel- laneous
1929-1930		—5	—2	—2	—2	—3	0
1929-1931		—22	—10	—8	—4	—12	—1
1929-1932		—35	—31	—18	—9	—24	—3
1929-1933		—37	—34	—31 ⎫	—13	—25	—7
1933-1934		+11	+9	—6 ⎬ —44	+2	+11	0
1933-1935		+19	+10	—6		+13	0
1933-1936		+20	+11	—4		+14	0
1933-1937		+25	+17	+1		+24	+3
1937-1938		—7	—1	+3		—1	+1
1933-1939		+13	+14	+4		+20	+3
1933-1940		+15	+16	+5		+20	+3
1933-1941		+26	+20	+6		+27	+6

n.a. (not available).

Sources: *Statistical Abstract of the United States, 1950,* Dept. of Commerce, p. 285; *Federal Reserve Bulletin,* May 1952, p. 548.

it continued to drop in 1934, reaching a level 44 per cent below 1929—a greater drop than that shown by any other component. Rents could be expected to be somewhat sticky in their response to a decline in economic activity, because they are contracted for on a longer-term basis than most consumer prices. However, it would appear that the relatively fixed stock of housing makes rent very sensitive to demand if the period of adjustment is long enough. For gas and electricity, fuel, and ice, only a combined index is available for the period 1929-1933. It is evident from inspection of the component indexes for later years, however, that this index combines a number of different types of price behavior. Gas and electricity show very little variability, as would be expected in view of public-utility price-setting procedures. Ice uses as materials primarily electricity and water—both utilities—and these combined with some labor would determine its price behavior. As would be expected the price of ice is, next to gas and electricity, the least variable of the consumer-price components. The fuel index is based largely upon price changes in coal and fuel oil. The price of coal would be expected to be considerably less variable than that of fuel oil, since it has a much larger labor component; thus the fuel index combines a fairly invariant price index with a more variable one to yield an index of about the same variability as those of apparel and house furnishings. The index for miscellaneous items, finally, is composed of such prices as street-car and bus fares, upkeep of automobiles, medical care, newspapers, radios, motion pictures, other recreation, barber and beauty shop services, and toilet articles. These prices tend to be relatively less variable because of such factors as rate regulation and customary prices, as well as the importance of labor services and the high degree of fabrication.

The behavior of the different components of the index followed somewhat the same pattern after 1939 as before, except that the effects of price control are quite evident. Food prices did not rise as much as would have been expected in terms of the rise in apparel and house furnishings. From 1941 to 1945, in fact, the prices of both apparel and house furnishings rose by 37 per cent, whereas food rose by only 31 per cent. This is probably due to the greater ease of controlling food prices—the lower-priced lines in apparel and house furnishings tended to disappear from the market. With the end of the war and the removal of price control, the prewar relationship among the components in the consumer-price index was restored.

It is thus apparent that the relative movements of the various components of the consumer-price index do behave approximately as would be expected on the basis of the preceding analysis of the determinants of relative prices. Any detailed analysis of the exact year-to-year movements would of course have to take into account such factors as the relative sizes of the agricultural harvests, the extent of government and foreign demand for agricultural products, the various rounds of wage increases, and the secular changes in productivity in different parts of the economy. Each of these elements has a role in determining relative price movements. But the basic structure of consumers' prices and the major changes that can be expected in this structure during periods of economic fluctuation do emerge quite clearly from this relatively simple analysis.

THE WHOLESALE-PRICE INDEX

THE BLS wholesale-price index is based on some 900 price series and 1,700 price quotations.[55] Prices for the same commodity at several different stages of production are often included. For example, cotton appears in the index as raw cotton, cotton yarn, cotton gray goods, cotton piece goods, and cotton clothing. For each of these stages a representative commodity sample has been selected and priced at the primary market level of distribution. In the remaining space of this paper it would not be feasible to go through each of these series in the manner that was done for the cost-of-living index. Instead, it will be useful to give some brief attention to the general aggregative nature of the series. The wider variability of the wholesale-price index over the cost-of-living index is well known. In terms of the theory of price behavior suggested by this paper, this greater variability would be expected. As was pointed out in Part 3 above, the prices of agricultural raw materials and semifinished goods would be expected to exhibit greater variability than the prices of finished goods. This expectation is based on the observation that (1) the labor-cost element tends to be less variable than the prices of agricultural raw materials; and (2) the higher the degree of fabrication, the more important labor costs become relative to the cost of the original agricultural raw materials in the total direct cost. Since price tends to move with direct cost, the larger the influence of labor costs in direct cost, the more the variability of final output prices will tend to decline to that of labor costs. Many

55 *Handbook of Labor Statistics, 1950*, Dept. of Labor, 1951, p. 117.

492

agricultural raw materials and semifinished products are included in the wholesale-price index, whereas these same items are excluded from the consumers-price index, since only fully processed goods reach the consumer. Since the theory of price behavior outlined in Part 2 would thus produce a greater variability for the wholesale-price index, and since this greater variability is in fact found, there is no evidence from this test that there is any basic contradiction between the general nature of the wholesale-price index and the theory of price behavior.

The wholesale-price concept originated in the period when economic theory was concerned with the relation between the "price level" and the quantity of money. Economic statisticians regarded the wholesale-price index as a sampling of prices in the system, and thus in some sense a measure of the level around which prices tended to cluster. Economists tried to differentiate between situations in which relative prices in the price structure changed and those in which the general level of price itself changed. Changes in the price level were considered to involve only random changes in the price structure. But such a dichotomy is possible only if changes in the level are not systematically related to changes in the structure. According to the foregoing analysis of the determinants of price change, any price movement in the system necessarily involves relative price changes; a change in level without a change in structure is impossible. With a change in income the primary response will be in the prices of agricultural goods, and the repercussions will diminish as the goods become more and more highly fabricated. The "price level" of agricultural materials and some mineral materials is thus always in flux, being affected by such things as the level of income, foreign demand, and weather conditions. But the "price level" of highly processed goods may hardly vary at all.

As an indicator of the "level" of prices, therefore, the wholesale-price index is not a meaningful economic construct; rather it is merely a conglomeration of those price quotations which are easiest to get. Vertically unintegrated industries will provide a much greater number of price quotations, and even if these more numerous prices are weighted by value added at each stage the result will not be the same as that which would be obtained using the final-goods price of an integrated industry. Whenever a product contains materials of agricultural origin or of mineral origin with variable prices, the price variation will be dampened as the degree of fabrication increases, approaching the variation of labor cost. The variability at-

493

tributed to an industry's prices in the wholesale-price index, there-fore, will depend upon the particular stages in the fabrication process for which price quotations are included. It is probably no exaggeration to say that the wholesale-price index is no better as an indicator of inflation and deflation than freight-car loadings are of the deflated gross national product—if as good.

RELATIVE MOVEMENT OF REAL AND MONEY WAGE RATES

STATISTICAL information on the movement of an index of the real wage rate has appeared in the economic literature from time to time, but the conclusions to be drawn from this data were never very clear.[56] The analysis of the determinants of relative price changes presented in the body of this paper is related to this discussion and can throw some light on what should be expected in terms of the relation between the consumer-price index and the money wage rate.

With a fall in the money wage rate and a contraction in income, the components of the consumer-price index can be divided into groups of commodity and service prices which will (1) fall faster than the wage rate, (2) fall with the wage rate, and (3) fall less than the wage rate. Goods whose value contains an appreciable propor-tion of agricultural or variable-priced mineral materials will vary more than the money wage rate. Goods which are highly fabricated or whose value is mostly labor services will vary directly with the money wage rate. Finally, goods whose prices are administratively fixed, i.e. utilities, will change less than the money wage rate. Rent

[56] See for example John T. Dunlop, "The Movement of Real and Money Wages," Economic Journal, September 1938; J. M. Keynes, "Relative Movements of Real Wages and Output," Economic Journal, March 1939, pp. 34-51; L. Tarshis, "Changes in Real and Money Wages," Economic Journal, 1939, pp. 150-154; J. Henry Richardson, "Real Wage Movements," Economic Journal, September 1939; Richard Ruggles, "The Relative Movements of Real and Money Wage Rates," Quarterly Journal of Economics, November 1940, pp. 130-149. In his original article, Keynes stated that prices would rise faster than money wages in recovery because in perfect competition a producer would be faced with a rising marginal-cost function, and prices of output would therefore have to rise faster than the wage rate as output expanded. In attempting to generalize the problem for an economy as a whole, Dunlop used the cost-of-living index as a measure of price change, but these are in fact not the prices which are ger-mane to the theoretical discussion. Prices in this context should have been re-stricted to the selling prices of the producers who actually paid the wage rates. The cost-of-living index is a conglomeration of prices which are paid by con-sumers. It includes agricultural prices, import prices, rent, and prices of con-sumer services. However, although the cost-of-living and money-wage-rate con-troversy was not meaningful in terms of its original problem, it is still interesting to ask how real wage rates behave at different phases of economic fluctuations.

is the one element in consumers' expenditures which cannot be classified in this manner. As noted above, in the short run rent may be fairly inflexible because of contractual obligations, but in the longer run it becomes extremely flexible. The question whether a decrease in the money wage rate will cause an increase or a decrease in the real wage rate will thus depend on the importance in terms of weights and degree of variability of the prices which are more variable than the money wage rate compared with the prices which are less variable than the money wage rate. The relative variability of the different prices will depend on the magnitude of the total income decline which accompanies the decline in the money wage rate. For an exact prediction in any particular instance, it would be necessary to know how much investment, government expenditures, and the propensities of various groups to consume change, as well as changes in foreign demand for agricultural goods and the influence of changes in weather conditions. But some general conclusions can be drawn. In a mild recession or in the early phases of a major depression it would be quite possible for the real wage rate to decline, largely because of the lag in the response of rent to changes in income. In a deeper, more prolonged depression, however, it seems likely that the real wage rate would rise. Rent becomes more variable than money wage rates in the longer run, so that the only components of expenditures whose prices remain less flexible than money wage rates are a few public utilities.

An adequate empirical investigation of this problem would be particularly hard because of the difficulty of obtaining a measure of the money wage rate for an economy as a whole. In addition, retail-price quotations always involve the problem of the failure to take adequate account of the change in the quality of goods. For these reasons, the problem of the movement of real and money wage rates will probably remain in the sphere of pure theory for some time.

COMMENT

KERMIT GORDON, Williams College

THE positive content of Ruggles' paper is essentially the development of a few simple hypotheses to account for the broad patterns of price behavior in the United States in the period 1929-1931. These hypotheses may be summarized as follows:

1. The collapse in the prices of agricultural goods was attributable to the stability of agricultural output in the face of a drop in demand, which stability was in turn attributable to the shape of marginal cost curves in agriculture.

2. The prices of some minerals fell by about the same percentage as unit direct costs, while the prices of others fell more sharply than unit direct costs. By and large, price behavior of the former type occurred in minerals industries in which supply curves tended toward the horizontal, while that of the latter type characterized industries with rising supply curves.

3. The prices of manufactured goods tended to decline in the same proportion as unit direct costs; the decline in unit direct costs in turn tended to be large if agricultural raw materials or some minerals bulked large in direct costs, and to be small to the extent that labor, some minerals, and labor-intensive manufactured goods bulked large in direct costs.

4. The prices of goods sold in the distributive trades tended also to decline in the same proportion as the decline in unit direct costs.

Two significant inferences may be drawn from Ruggles' findings, one of which is implicit in the structure of his argument, while the other is explicitly set forth. First, if we assume the validity of a series of quite daring assumptions, Ruggles' findings may be interpreted as indicating that firms by and large tended to equate marginal cost and marginal revenue in approved textbook fashion. It must be emphasized, however, that the empirical validation of this proposition involves so many bold assumptions, both of a theoretical and a statistical character, that it can hardly be regarded as more than a plausible conjecture.

In the context of the present volume, the second conclusion is the more relevant—i.e. that "the major patterns of price behavior in the economy can be adequately explained in terms of factors other than industrial concentration." While Ruggles does not entirely rule out the possibility that differences in concentration ratios (or in some other index of market organization) may have some effect on differences in cyclical price behavior, he does feel, at least for the period he has studied, that the influence of these factors is at best peripheral, and that the forces emphasized in his own analysis are overwhelmingly more important. In manufacturing and distribution, Ruggles appears to feel that the correspondence between changes in unit direct costs and changes in price is so close that little remains to be explained. Thus Ruggles appears to go even farther than Neal,[1] with whose principal conclusions he is in sub-stantial agreement, for Neal went on to study the relation between concentration ratios and the sensitivity of price to changes in unit direct costs, finding that concentration "does affect the flexibility of price relative to direct cost," but "only to a minor extent."[2]

In one respect at least, Ruggles' claim is certainly too broad. He concludes his discussion of agricultural price behavior with this statement: "Agriculture, then, because of the nature of its marginal costs, would be expected to maintain its output in the face of a fall in demand. . . . The whole impact of a contraction in demand falls on price; price will decline until the full quantity produced can be absorbed by the economy."

If this statement were so, Ruggles would have succeeded in ac-counting for the broad movements of agricultural prices without introducing considerations of market organization. But the shape of the farmer's marginal cost curve does not in itself explain the fact that he will maintain output in the face of a fall in demand; a monopolistic firm might have a marginal cost curve for all the world like a wheat farmer's, but its response to a decline in demand might be quite different. Ruggles' conclusion follows only if it is also specified that the firm in agriculture is operating in a steeply rising range of its marginal cost curve, but this is so only because an unregulated agriculture, in its major branches, is purely com-petitive. Hence it appears to be logically necessary to invoke con-siderations of market organization to explain the behavior of agri-cultural prices.

A similar point relates to Ruggles' treatment of price behavior in the minerals industries. Here he finds a more complex pattern of price movements than in the other major sectors of the economy, but his explanation of price behavior in this area is somewhat ob-scure and is marred by the implicit assumption of the prevalence of pure competition—an assumption not valid in many branches of minerals production.

Some comments may be made, also, regarding Ruggles' explana-tion of the behavior of the prices of manufactured goods. His find-ings, taken together with those of Neal, establish quite conclusively that the predominant influence governing price behavior in the period studied was the behavior of unit direct costs. The link be-

[1] Alfred C. Neal, *Industrial Concentration and Price Flexibility* (American Council on Public Affairs, 1942).
[2] *Ibid.*, p. 140.

tween prices and direct costs is so strong that it must certainly be the starting point in any future analysis of cyclical price flexibility of manufactured goods.

However, the following qualifications and amplifications suggest themselves:

1. Additional calculations indicate that if Ruggles had used a broader sample for his comparisons of percentage changes in unit direct cost and unit value in various agricultural and minerals processing industries, the correspondence between the two might have been somewhat less striking. (See his Tables 4 and 6.) Industries are easy to find in which the divergence between percentage decline in unit direct cost and percentage decline in value per unit was significantly greater than in most of the industries represented in these tables. Indeed, there are some cases in which unit direct cost fell so much more sharply than unit value that the unit overhead-plus-profit margin increased.[3]

2. In industries in which unit direct cost in 1929 stood in a very high ratio to unit value, it would seem a priori unlikely that the percentage decline in these two variables could diverge widely. At one extreme, unit value is not free, except in very unusual circumstances, to fall below unit direct cost; at the other extreme, given the condition of markets in depression, few industries will be in a position to raise the unit overhead-plus-profit margin (i.e. the difference between unit direct cost and unit value) above the pre-depression level. If these two points are taken as establishing the limits of the extent to which the degrees of decline may diverge, and if the ratio of unit direct cost to unit value in a particular industry in 1929 was, say 90 per cent, then a decline in unit direct cost of, say 30 per cent is consistent with a price decline of not less than 27 per cent and not more than 37 per cent. By contrast, if an industry in 1929 had a low ratio of unit direct cost to unit value— say 50 per cent—then a 30 per cent decline in unit direct cost would be compatible on these assumptions with a decline in unit value of as much as 65 per cent and as little as 15 per cent. Hence the higher the ratio of unit direct cost to unit value, the narrower are the limits within which percentage declines in these variables are free to diverge.

An examination of the 1929 census data for the manufacturing

[3] This category would include such industries as ice cream, malt, linoleum, soap, rubber tires and tubes, asbestos products, and wall board and plaster

industries studied by Ruggles (Tables 4 and 6) indicates that these industries tended to have higher ratios of direct costs to value of products than did the broader industry groups into which they fell. Of twenty-two manufacturing industries listed in Tables 4 and 6,[4] sixteen had ratios of direct costs to value of products that were higher than the ratios for their census industry groups. An extreme case is the food and kindred products industry group. For the group as a whole, the ratio of direct costs to value of products was 79 per cent, but for the four industries in Table 4 that fell into this group, the ratios ranged from 85 to 91 per cent.

Hence there is some reason to believe that a different sample of industries, in which the ratios of direct cost to value of product were more representative of the respective industry groups, might have displayed a less perfect relationship between percentage price decline and percentage direct cost decline than did the industries studied by Ruggles.

3. Although the unit overhead-plus-profit margin is simply the difference between unit direct cost and unit value, one may not properly infer from the fact of an approximately equal percentage decline in direct cost and unit value that the unit overhead-plus-profit margin fell by about the same percentage. This seeming paradox arises because a high ratio of unit direct cost to unit value implies a low ratio of unit overhead-plus-profit to unit value; hence a relatively slight divergence in the degree of decline of unit direct cost and unit value may make possible a large divergence between these two percentages and the percentage decline in the unit overhead-plus-profit margin.

For example, Ruggles' Table 4 shows, for cane sugar refining, a decline in unit direct cost of 11 per cent as compared with a decline in unit value of 10 per cent. However, since the 1929 ratio of direct cost to value of products in this industry was 90 per cent, the narrow margin by which the decline in unit cost exceeded the decline in unit value resulted in a decline in the unit overhead-plus-profit margin of only 2 per cent.

Hence it it not permissible, from a knowledge of percentage change in unit direct cost and unit value alone, to draw any conclusion concerning the behavior of the unit overhead-plus-profit margin. This observation amplifies rather than qualifies Ruggles'

---

[4] Including all but manufactured heating and illuminating gas, which Ruggles treats as an atypical case.

analysis, but it is a point that deserves emphasis because much of the past interest in the question of cyclical price flexibility has been closely associated with an interest in the cyclical behavior of margins.

4. If one concludes that Ruggles' essay suggests a somewhat greater sensitivity of the prices of manufactured goods to direct cost changes than probably prevailed in 1929-1931, one is then led to ask whether market organization factors may have played some part in accounting for differences in degrees of sensitivity. This question was studied in a particular framework by Neal,[5] who used the well-known census concentration ratios in conjunction with an analysis of price—direct-cost behavior. Neal found, as previously noted, that concentration does affect the sensitivity of price to direct cost changes, but the relationship appears to be quite weak. Neal's evidence fully supports his conclusion.

This might well be the end of the matter, if there were not abundant reason to be dissatisfied with the census concentration data as a measure of market characteristics that may be associated with differences in the sensitivity of price to cyclical direct cost changes. The shortcomings of the census concentration ratios as measures of market power are numerous and well known. Hence it must still be considered an open question as to whether a more reliable index of degree of market power, if it were possible to devise one, might show a closer relationship between extent of market power and sensitivity of price to direct cost changes.

GEORGE H. HILDEBRAND, University of California

RUGGLES has set four principal tasks for himself in this interesting paper: (1) to summarize the present state of the literature on price flexibility; (2) to develop his own criterion of flexibility; (3) to test price behavior during 1929-1931 in various parts of the economy, using his criterion; and, rather indirectly (4) to evaluate the importance of industrial concentration as a determinant of price flexibility. His central conclusion is a strong one and deserves mention at the outset. It is that the "major patterns of price behavior in the economy can be adequately explained in terms of factors other than industrial concentration." As will become evident subsequently, his explanation squares perfectly with the traditional theory of short-

[5] Neal, *op. cit.*, Chap. VI.

period price formation. Clearly, this finding is somewhat novel for the concentration field, and in any case of high interest.

Perhaps the most important purpose of studies of concentration is to gauge its significance for short- and long-period changes in the structure of relative prices. The question is certainly appropriate. Interest in concentration was originally stimulated by the recognition that in certain industries sellers were few, which suggested the possibility that fewness could lead to unusual power over price. If so, then these prices should show some variance of behavior relative to those formed in markets involving large numbers. On this reasoning, Gardner Means some twenty years ago opened up the issue with his now famous study of the comparative flexibility of industrial and agricultural prices. Means' findings have since been severely criticized on sound technical grounds, but interest in the problems he raised remains very much alive.

Inquiry into the possible impacts of concentration upon changes in price structure takes two main forms. With the publication of Schumpeter's provocative and unorthodox views concerning concentration, large-scale enterprise, and their connection with technological change, the way was opened to investigation of changes in relative prices over very long periods. So far, this problem has received only limited attention, though its importance is recognized. By contrast, much effort has been applied to the short-period, investigation given impetus by price behavior during the great depression. These studies have been concerned with the impacts upon relative prices of marked change in aggregate demand. Ruggles' paper is an important contribution to this literature.

The fact that prices change relatively to one another when effective demand changes is only the beginning of the question. Certainly there is no a priori reason to expect all prices to change proportionally and in the same direction. Thus the inquiry cannot be limited simply to one of measurement. It must be informed by some guiding theoretical conception. In other words, the theorist requires some criterion for the comparison of "expected" with "actual" price changes in particular cases. Only then can he isolate deviant cases. Many criteria have been proposed, some normative, which proclaim how much all prices *ought* to change; others purely hypothetical, which attempt to predict how much prices *would have* changed if certain determinants were effective and others not.

Clearly, if the question of structural flexibility is to be linked to something we may vaguely call monopoly power, then what is needed is a criterion by which those cases in which that power is effective can be isolated from the universe of prices as a whole. If I interpret him correctly, Ruggles has attacked the question by adoption of the Walrasian model as a reference point (nonnormative) for the formation of relative prices. By use of a criterion derived from this model, he has then attempted to find out whether changes in relative prices during 1929-1931 did or did not conform to the predictions yielded by that model.

Conventional short-period price theory emphasizes two principal determinants, those of demand and of cost. Selling price will shift to a new equilibrium (barring the kinked-oligopoly case) with a shift in either determinant or of both together. However, if with a change of demand or a cost-invoked move along the demand schedule, the *elasticity* of demand is the same at the new point ·of equilibrium as it was at the old, then selling price will change proportionally to and in the same direction as the change in short-period marginal cost. Furthermore, this will be true whether the change in marginal cost involves a *shift in* or a *move along* the cost schedule. Thus it is a change in the elasticity of demand that makes for perverse behavior of the price-cost relationship in a given case. Alternatively, on Ruggles' criterion, prices show perfect flexibility when they move directly and proportionally with short-period marginal cost. Otherwise they are inflexible, excessively flexible, or inversely flexible.

Using this criterion of perfect price flexibility, Ruggles can isolate the effects of changes in demand elasticity without undertaking the impossible task of measuring them. He can limit the statistical problem to measurement of relative changes in prices and costs. If the results fail to conform to the criterion, then he infers that a change in demand elasticity has intervened as an additional determinant.

Changes in elasticity of demand normally can be expected when the seller has a sloped demand curve and his cost schedule shifts, or when his sloped demand curve shifts and he must find a new price-output equilibrium. Such phenomena would occur in cases of monopolistic competition or pure monopoly. Oligopoly is more difficult because competition is "co-respective" and various alternative hypotheses become possible. Still, even here if the behavior of prices under oligopoly were deviant, Ruggles' criterion would reveal it. Assuming that the data are adequate to its use, then, Ruggles can contend that his criterion is a workable method for turning up important cases of impure markets—"important" in the sense that prices there were found to be rigid, sluggish, or perverse relative to changes in marginal costs.

When it comes to the empirical utility of his approach, Ruggles displays appropriate caution and declares that his findings are "purely illustrative." They are studded with many needed reservations and qualifications. I must admit, however, that at times I found it difficult to follow the exact nature of the statistical operations employed. If I comprehend them correctly, they rest upon these principles: (1) to use average direct cost (suitably weighted for relative amounts of cost pertaining to production labor and to materials) as an approximation of short-period marginal cost; (2) to use average value product as a measure of selling "price" for the composite product; and (3) to use matched census data for the foregoing in each category examined. On this basis, Ruggles tests for flexibility for a group of rather narrowly defined and relatively homogeneous industries, and also for broader and in my opinion less reliable aggregates.

The inevitable statistical frailties and expedient assumptions turned up, and these are candidly noted and evaluated. Moreover, it is a marked advantage to use data that in the main are homogeneous as to reporting source; to use wage costs for production labor rather than that treacherous substitute, average hourly earnings; and to use value product per unit of output as a synthetic price, in place of frequently deceptive quoted prices. Yet, as Ruggles himself observes, the value product technique has its own shortcomings. Given an "industry" in the sense of a statistical box, one will usually find multiple products and multiple markets; and varying markups by product, by firm, and by plant. Value product will serve as a measure of price only when the contents of the statistical box are really homogeneous. Otherwise one will derive an artifact rather than an indicator of actual price change. For this reason more confidence may be placed in Ruggles' findings for the narrower segments of the economy.

The outcome of his inquiry led Ruggles to the conclusions mentioned earlier, that relative prices in 1929-1931 changed in a manner that could be expected from value theory, and that the patterns found could be explained without appeal to industrial concentration as a special factor. In that period, direct costs throughout the system were determined by these influences: (1) the prices of agricultural raw materials, which mainly are "demand-controlled" because the shape of the cost function leads to continuous production at capacity; (2) the prices of mineral products, which tend to move inversely with output because of varying richness of deposits; (3) the form of the production and marginal cost functions in each industry; and (4) the level of the wage rate. The forces of technological change and of secular growth or decay of industries may be ignored because the period is short.

As Ruggles views the behavior of prices during 1929-1931, deflation lowered agricultural demand, and through this the prices of farm products. This helped depress wage costs. Materials and wage costs together lowered direct costs in varying degrees in the later stages of processing and fabrication, and selling prices generally moved downward in the same proportions. Prices paid by distributive trades thus fell, and even with constant gross margins, their selling prices also dropped.

While I certainly would not dispute Ruggles' account of price formation or of the interrelations among prices in the system, I think his conclusions are likely to be misleading. His statistical inquiry is described as illustrative and necessarily limited. But his conclusions could be used as a generalization when in fact they apply only to a single empirical case, that of 1929-1931. They may also be misleading because they could be interpreted to mean that concentration, taken as a symptom of monopoly power, is of little or no importance for price behavior. Actually, all Ruggles himself suggests is that concentration was of no apparent significance for price behavior as he observed it in one case with what he himself terms a limited investigation. Fuller study might fortify this conclusion, to be sure. Yet there remain many well-known cases of rigidity, sluggishness, and perversity, as well as other exhibits in the museum of economic horrors. Ruggles himself is quite aware of them, but his conclusion might suggest otherwise. In my opinion, it is likely that his statistical scalpel was necessarily too blunt an instrument to lay them bare.

Thus it is the adequacy of the instrument that gives me concern. I have no quarrel whatever with Ruggles' technique for testing the influence of concentration upon price changes in the short-period. Quite the contrary. Further inquiry on these lines is urgently needed, as I shall argue below. Statistical tests of this type are a kind of screen for sifting out industries in need of more intensive study. The difficulty is, however, that the mesh of the screen may be made so coarse by the available data that it may be incapable of yielding definitive results.

Accordingly, alternative approaches become necessary, and here the old-fashioned technique of case study acquires renewed importance. Inquiry should begin with those prominent cases in which sellers are few, to determine the nature and vigor of competition. Within this context, several tests of competitiveness can be made. Are there technical indivisibilities that make for few producers, or are there other reasons? Is entry possible? If not, why not? Are profits relatively high because of growing demand and rapid innovation, or because of restrictive devices? Is there effective cross-product competition? What kind of price policies have the rivals followed? What has been the behavior of their price-cost relationships by products in periods of rapidly changing demand?

The value of concentration studies of Ruggles' type is great and beyond question. All that I wish to stress is that the problems of competition and monopoly call for other tests and other approaches as well, before definitive conclusions can be drawn.

I also suggest that one case, that of 1929-1931, is not enough in itself. This, of course, Ruggles acknowledges, and he has carried part of his study forward in time in order to broaden its scope. Other suggestions are possible. For instances of deflation, inquiry would be desirable and probably possible for 1920-1922, 1937-1938, and 1948-1949. Cases of inflation also deserve investigation. Certainly 1940-1942 belongs here, and at this time price and wage controls were not effective. The period 1935-1937 might also be classed in this group. More interesting would be the immediate postwar years, say 1946-1948. Wage control was a dead letter after August 1945, and price control became such within a year. It would be of great importance to see what happened to price-cost relationships, starting from the distortions invoked by direct controls and the large backlog of vastly increased cash holdings. No doubt there would be difficulties. Yet here would exist a prime case in which to test the importance of concentration for its effects upon prices in a period of rapid change.

It may well turn out that our economic system has been, and remains, far more competitive according to the standards of traditional wage and price theory than many of us have hitherto suspected. However, before we can adopt this view as a firm conclusion we shall require much more work, using a variety of tools. For this purpose, Ruggles' approach and findings are of high significance.

INDEX

Adelman, M. A., 44n, 116, 130n, 147n, 155n, 171n, 228, 239n, 253n, 279, 281n, 382n
Alexander, Sidney S., 262n, 288n
Allied Chemical and Dye Corp., 208-209
Allis Chalmers Manufacturing Co., 160n, 198
American Hide and Leather Co., 160n, 197
American Ice Co., 160
American Tobacco Co., 206-207
Andrews, P. W. S., 365n, 366n, 367, 368, 370, 371n, 375, 381, 382n, 387, 388, 389, 391
Automobile industry, *see* Motor vehicle industry

Backman, Jules, 444n, 446n, 447n, 450, 457
Bain, Joe S., 94n, 119n, 120n, 125n, 127, 128, 129, 134, 374n, 375n
Baker, Henry D., 162n
Balderston, Frederick E., 321n
Barkin, S., 187n
Basing-point systems, 406-408
Basset, William R., 155
Berger, J. G., 228
Berle, Adolf A., 57n, 200
Bissel, R. M., Jr., 441n
Blair, John M., 44n, 60n, 63n, 176, 177, 184, 185n, 220n, 224n, 227
Bollinger, Lynn L., 245n
Borden Co., 41-42
Borts, George H., 228, 229n
Boulding, Kenneth E., 124n
Bressler, Raymond G., Jr., 228
Brown, Donaldson, 361n, 365n
Brumberg, Richard, 231n
Buchanan, Norman S., 122n
Bullock, Charles J., 142n
Burns, Arthur F., 150n
Burns, Arthur R., 119n, 376n, 377n
Butters, J. Keith, 60n, 153n, 174n, 176, 177, 178n, 179, 183n, 184, 185, 186, 188n, 245n, 251n, 253n, 258n, 261n, 269n, 270n, 272n, 292n

Carnation Co., 41-42
Cary, W. L., 153n, 174n, 179, 183n, 188n, 253n, 269n, 270n, 272n
Cassady, Ralph, Jr., 400n, 403n

Chamberlin, Edward H., 119n, 122n, 125n, 133n, 362n, 386, 389
Chenery, Hollis B., 221, 222, 227
Clark, John Maurice, 119n, 352
Clemens, Eli W., 438
Coase, R. H., 282n
Collier, W. M., 154, 155n
Competition, concepts of, 119-123
Conant, Luther, Jr., 146n, 147, 148, 150, 157n, 162n
Concentration: actual data on Canada, by industry, 66-68; actual data on U.K., by industry, 74-75; actual data on U.S., by industry, 65, 74-75, 90; comparison of, in U.S. and U.K., 70-77; concepts and definitions, 5-6, 42-49, 57-63; effect of taxes on, 9-11, 179, 239-280; effect on allocation of resources, 104-106, 124, 128-129, 431-432; effect on distribution of social and political power, 103, 345-348, 351-352, 358-359; effect on efficiency of the firm, 106-108; effect on income distribution, 102-103; effect on rate of technological progress, 108-109, 113-114; and full-cost pricing, 14, 373-378; measurement of, *see* Measurement of concentration; and price behavior, 12-14, 373-379; and price discrimination, 13, 399-400, 431-432; and price flexibility, 13, 134-135, 361, 447-449, 455, 460-462, 488-489, 496, 501-505; significance of, in relation to monopoly power, 7, 44-45, 48-49, 57, 95-97, 109, 113-115, 130-136, 155-156; sources of data on, 16-17; trends in, 77-83; *see also* Conglomerate firms, Monopoly power, and Size of firm
Conglomerate firms: concepts and definitions, 331-333, 352-359; creation through mergers, 171-173, 207-209; insulation from market forces, 350-352, 358-359; manifestations of power, 337-352; sources of power, 12, 334-337, 353-357; and traditional monopoly theory, 12, 352-359; *see also* Concentration, Monopoly power, and Size of firm
Cooper, W. W., 372n
Corn Products Refining Co., 207

507

NATIONAL BUREAU OF ECONOMIC RESEARCH
PUBLICATIONS IN REPRINT

An Arno Press Series

Barger, Harold. **The Transportation Industries, 1889-1946:** A Study of Output, Employment, and Productivity. 1951

Barger, Harold and Hans H. Landsberg. **American Agriculture, 1899-1939:** A Study of Output, Employment, and Productivity. 1942

Barger, Harold and Sam H. Schurr. **The Mining Industries, 1899-1939:** A Study of Output, Employment, and Productivity. 1944

Burns, Arthur F. **The Frontiers of Economic Knowledge.** 1954

Committee of the President's Conference on Unemployment. **Business Cycles and Unemployment.** 1923

Conference of the Universities-National Bureau Committee for Economic Research. **Aspects of Labor Economics.** 1962

Conference of the Universities-National Bureau Committee for Economic Research. **Business Concentration and Price Policy.** 1955

Conference of the Universities-National Bureau Committee for Economic Research. **Capital Formation and Economic Growth.** 1955

Conference of the Universities-National Bureau Committee for Economic Research. **Policies to Combat Depression.** 1956

Conference of the Universities-National Bureau Committee for Economic Research. **The State of Monetary Economics.** [1963]

Conference of the Universities-National Bureau Committee for Economic Research and the Committee on Economic Growth of the Social Science Research Council. **The Rate and Direction of Inventive Activity:** Economic and Social Factors. 1962

Conference on Research in Income and Wealth. **Input-Output Analysis:** An Appraisal. 1955

Conference on Research in Income and Wealth. **Problems of Capital Formation:** Concepts, Measurement, and Controlling Factors. 1957

Conference on Research in Income and Wealth. **Trends in the American Economy in the Nineteenth Century.** 1960

Conference on Research in National Income and Wealth. **Studies in Income and Wealth.** 1937

Copeland, Morris A. **Trends in Government Financing.** 1961

Fabricant, Solomon. **Employment in Manufacturing, 1899-1939:** An Analysis of Its Relation to the Volume of Production. 1942

Fabricant, Solomon. **The Output of Manufacturing Industries, 1899-1937.** 1940

Goldsmith, Raymond W.   **Financial Intermediaries in the American Economy Since 1900.** 1958

Goldsmith, Raymond W.   **The National Wealth of the United States in the Postwar Period.** 1962

Kendrick, John W.   **Productivity Trends in the United States.** 1961

Kuznets, Simon.   **Capital in the American Economy:** Its Formation and Financing. 1961

Kuznets, Simon.   **Commodity Flow and Capital Formation.** Vol. One. 1938

Kuznets, Simon.   **National Income:** A Summary of Findings. 1946

Kuznets, Simon.   **National Income and Capital Formation, 1919-1935:** A Preliminary Report. 1937

Kuznets, Simon.   **National Product in Wartime.** 1945

Kuznets, Simon.   **National Product Since 1869.** 1946

Kuznets, Simon.   **Seasonal Variations in Industry and Trade.** 1933

Long, Clarence D.   **Wages and Earnings in the United States, 1860-1890.** 1960

Mendershausen, Horst.   **Changes in Income Distribution During the Great Depression.** 1946

Mills, Frederick C.   **Economic Tendencies in the United States:** Aspects of Pre-War and Post-War Changes. 1932

Mills, Frederick C.   **Price-Quantity Interactions in Business Cycles.** 1946

Mills, Frederick C.   **The Behavior of Prices.** 1927

Mitchell, Wesley C.   **Business Cycles:** The Problem and Its Setting. [1927]

Mitchell, Wesley C., et al.   **Income in the United States:** Its Amount and Distribution 1909-1919. Volume One, Summary. [1921]

Mitchell, Wesley C., editor.   **Income in the United States:** Its Amount and Distribution 1909-1919. Volume Two, Detailed Report. 1922

National Accounts Review Committee of the National Bureau of Economic Research.   **The National Economic Accounts of the United States.** 1958

Rees, Albert.   **Real Wages in Manufacturing, 1890-1914.** 1961

Stigler, George J.   **Capital and Rates of Return in Manufacturing Industries.** 1963

Wealth Inventory Planning Study, The George Washington University.   **Measuring the Nation's Wealth.** 1964

Williams, Pierce.   **The Purchase of Medical Care Through Fixed Periodic Payment.** 1932

Wolman, Leo.   **The Growth of American Trade Unions, 1880-1923.** 1924

Woolley, Herbert B.   **Measuring Transactions Between World Areas.** 1966